S0-AVM-685

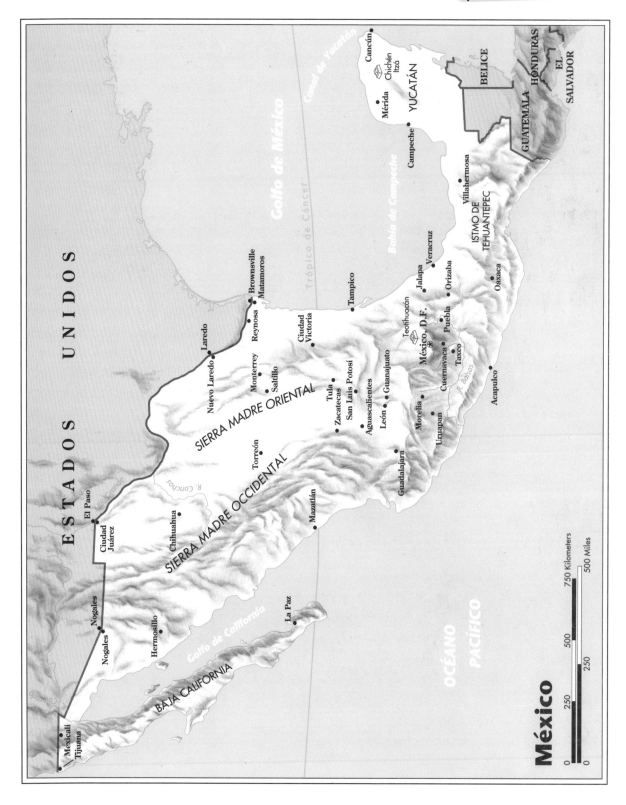

México

ESTADOS UNIDOS

Golfo de México

Canal de Yucatán

Trópico de Cáncer

Bahía de Campeche

OCÉANO PACÍFICO

Golfo de California

BAJA CALIFORNIA

SIERRA MADRE OCCIDENTAL

SIERRA MADRE ORIENTAL

ISTMO DE TEHUANTEPEC

BELICE

GUATEMALA

HONDURAS

EL SALVADOR

YUCATÁN

R. Conchos

Río Grande

R. Balsas

Tijuana
Mexicali
Nogales
Nogales
Hermosillo
La Paz
Chihuahua
Ciudad Juárez
El Paso
Mazatlán
Torreón
Laredo
Nuevo Laredo
Monterrey
Reynosa
Matamoros
Brownsville
Saltillo
Tula
Zacatecas
San Luis Potosí
Aguascalientes
León
Guanajuato
Guadalajara
Morelia
Uruapan
Cuernavaca
Taxco
Acapulco
Ciudad Victoria
Tampico
México, D.F.
Teotihuacán
Puebla
Orizaba
Jalapa
Veracruz
Oaxaca
Villahermosa
Campeche
Mérida
Chichén Itzá
Cancún

750 Kilometers
500 Miles
0   250   500
0   250   500

¿Cómo se dice...?

INSTRUCTOR'S ANNOTATED EDITION

¿Cómo se dice...?

SEVENTH EDITION

Ana C. Jarvis
Chandler-Gilbert Community College

Raquel Lebredo
California Baptist University

Francisco Mena-Ayllón
University of Redlands

Houghton Mifflin Company   Boston   New York

Director, World Languages: New Media and Modern Language Publishing: Beth Kramer
Sponsoring Editor: Amy Baron
Development Editor: Rafael Burgos-Mirabal
Senior Project Editor: Carol Newman
Senior Production/Design Coordinator: Jodi O'Rourke
Senior Manufacturing Coordinator: Priscilla Bailey
Marketing Manager: Tina Crowley Desprez

Cover Image: Forms, Symbols, and Images, 1967, José Gurvich

Copyright © 2002 by Houghton Mifflin Company. All rights reserved.

No part of this work may be reproduced or transmitted in any form or by any means, electronic or mechanical, including photocopying and recording, or by any information storage or retrieval system without the prior written permission of Houghton Mifflin Company unless such copying is expressly permitted by federal copyright law. Address inquiries to College Permissions, Houghton Mifflin Company, 222 Berkeley Street, Boston, MA 02116-3764.

Printed in the U.S.A.

Library of Congress Catalog Card Number: 2001131512

IAE ISBN: 0-618-10367-8

2 3 4 5 6 7 8 9-VH-05 04 03 02

Contents

Introduction to the Instructor's Annotated Edition

¿Cómo se dice...?, Seventh Edition, is a complete, fully integrated, introductory Spanish program for two- and four-year colleges and universities. The purpose of this Annotated Edition is to acquaint the instructor with the features of the Student's Edition and of the other program components, and to offer suggestions for implementing the program effectively. To accomplish this aim the Annotated Edition is divided into two parts. The first part describes the program and its objectives, offers teaching suggestions for implementing the various components, presents sample lesson plans, and provides an answer key to the cloze exercises in the text. The remainder of the Annotated Edition consists of the complete Student's Edition, with marginal annotations that suggest teaching strategies, supplementary cultural information, and additional activities to enhance students' oral and written communicative skills.

I. INSTRUCTOR'S GUIDE

Program Components

¿Cómo se dice...?, Seventh Edition, features a full range of fully integrated components, designed with flexibility in mind to accommodate a variety of individual teaching styles.

The complete program consists of the following items:

- Student's Edition with free Student Audio (cassette or CD)
- Instructor's Annotated Edition
- Workbook/Laboratory Manual
- Audio Program (cassettes or CDs)
- HM Testing (dual platform)
- *¿Cómo se dice...?* Video
- *¿Cómo se dice...?* Web site and Spanish Web resources
- *¿Cómo se dice...?* Multimedia CD-ROM 3.0
- *¿Cómo se dice...?* Online Course (Blackboard/WebCT ePack)
- Class Prep Instructor CD-ROM
- Instructor's Resource Kit
  Instructor's Activities Manual
  Instructor's Resource Manual (Testing Program/Audioscript/Videoscript/
    Check Your Progress Answer Key)
  ¿Cómo se dice...? Overhead Transparencies
  Situation Cards Kit
  Spanish History Booklet

New to the Seventh Edition

A recognized leader in its field, *¿Cómo se dice...?* owes its success to its emphasis on developing communicative skills, its solid grammar foundation, and the adaptability of its balanced, four-skills approach to a variety of teaching styles. Users of previous editions will instantly recognize the retention of the program's solid, proven framework, as well as the value of changes that have been made to the Seventh Edition in response to suggestions from reviewers and from users of the previous edition. The following lists highlight the major changes in the Student's Edition and in the components designed to respond to these needs.

The Student's Edition

- The student text now consists of eighteen regular lessons. Most of the material originally in the preliminary lesson is now in Lesson 1.

- The grammatical scope and sequence has been revised to suit courses that use *¿Cómo se dice...?* over two or three semesters, or over trimesters. At the end of the first semester of a two-semester course, students will be able to communicate about situations occurring in the present and in the past (Lessons 1–9). The subjunctive is studied throughout the second semester (Lessons 10–18). In a three-semester or trimester configuration, students will have covered the present by the end of the first term (Lessons 1–6), and will have studied the past tenses, the present subjunctive, and the formal commands by the end of the second term (Lessons 7–12). In addition, attention has been paid to introducing some basic formal commands as discrete vocabulary items prior to their formal introduction in Lesson 12.

- About one-third of the opening passages now include realia-like formats to provide variety in the presentation of contextualized linguistic input. In addition, the gender balance among the dialogue speakers has been improved.

- *¿Lo sabía Ud.?* culture sections now include follow-up questions in Spanish that allow students to personalize the cultural content and to approach it comparatively.

- Appearing in Lessons 10 through 18, the new *Pronunciación en contexto* section expands on the pronunciation practice provided in the *Pronunciación* sections in Lessons 1 through 9, and includes the pronunciation of certain words and sound combinations within full sentences.

- The *Estructuras* sections include more examples to illustrate certain grammar structures or usage.

- All translation exercises have been replaced with other types of activities, with the exception of the exercise targeting the preterit versus the imperfect.

- Questions in the *Entrevistas* sections have been revised to better promote collaborative learning.

- Five *¡Vamos a leer!* readings have been replaced. The new readings appear in Lessons 1, 3, 13, 15, and 17.

- The video activity sections (*Teleinforme* and *Así somos*) have been completely revised to improve accessibility and updated according to the revisions made to the *¿Cómo se dice...?* Video Program.

■ The key vocabulary for each videoclip has been reduced and has been moved to the Instructor's Activities Manual (IAM). The vocabulary lists are available as activity sheets in the IAM for instructors who may want to photocopy and distribute the lists for further viewing support.

The Components

■ The Workbook/Laboratory Manual and Audio Program for the Seventh Edition have been revised to reflect changes in the Student's Edition.

■ The contents of the Instructor's Resource Manual (the Audioscript, the Videoscript, the Answer Key to the *Check Your Progress* section and the printed Testing Program) have been revised to reflect changes in the Student's Edition, the Workbook/Laboratory Manual, and the video. Completely revised for the Seventh Edition, the Testing Program now offers midterms and final exams for both two- and three-semester course schedules, Situations for Oral Exams (for two- and three-semester course schedules), and a quiz on each *Panorama hispánico* photo essay to assess cultural competency.

■ Each activity in the Instructor's Activities Manual (IAM) is now keyed to material in the Instructor's Annotated Edition by means of special annotations. In addition, the IAM contains the considerably shortened versions of the supplementary vocabulary lists for the video modules, originally appearing in the *Así somos* and *Teleinforme* video activity sections in the previous Student's Edition.

■ The *Teleinforme* modules of the *¿Cómo se dice...?* video have been revised to improve accessibility. The voiceover has been made more accessible for beginning students and the footage has been updated.

■ The upgraded *¿Cómo se dice...?* Web site now features an instructor's component. This includes an instructor's guide, a technology integration guide, and PowerPoint slides that contain grammar charts. The student's component includes Web search activities, online self-tests, and a new flashcard feature designed to help students review terms, images, and definitions. Audio- and video-based activities are now part of the student's component.

■ The new *¿Cómo se dice...?* multimedia CD-ROM 3.0 is a state-of-the-art program that integrates video viewing, listening comprehension and interpretation activities, language practice exercises, a grammar reference, and a bilingual glossary.

■ The new Class Prep Instructor CD-ROM includes, in electronic format, all the materials in the Instructor's Resource Manual as well as PowerPoint slides of grammar explanations.

■ The new *¿Cómo se dice...?* Online Course Blackboard/WebCT provides support materials and exercises for online instruction.

All the components of *¿Cómo se dice...?*, Seventh Edition, are fully integrated with the Student's Edition and are described in greater detail on the following pages. The extent to which each will be used in any given course will vary in accordance with such factors as schedule requirements and student ability and motivation. This range of teaching resources allows instructors the flexibility they require to accommodate those factors as well as the instructional goals of their curricula.

Objectives of the Program

The balanced, four-skills approach of *¿Cómo se dice...?*, Seventh Edition, emphasizes the use of language for oral communication without neglecting the other basic language skills. Students who complete the program successfully should be able to achieve the following goals in the basic skill areas listed.

Speaking

■ Pronunciation of all of the sounds of Spanish with sufficient accuracy to be understood by a native speaker of the language

■ Effective communication in basic survival situations that require the ability to greet; ask questions; express basic needs, attitudes, and emotions; exchange information; and persuade, using the vocabulary and structure covered in the text

Listening

■ Perception of all Spanish sounds and their distinction from one another

■ Comprehension of ideas expressed within the framework of the vocabulary and grammatical structures presented

■ Ability to guess at unfamiliar vocabulary based on context

Reading

■ Understanding of simple Spanish prose on nontechnical, high-frequency topics

■ Intelligent guessing at new vocabulary items based on context

■ Ability to demonstrate comprehension by answering questions on reading passages

Writing

■ Creating in class—without a dictionary—a paragraph in Spanish on topics covered by the text with sufficient clarity to be understood without difficulty by a native speaker (major errors such as verb or adjective agreement may appear)

■ Preparing outside of class a paragraph on any topic covered by the text, without major errors and with sufficient clarity to be understood upon first reading by a native speaker

Culture

■ Elementary knowledge of important aspects of culture in the Spanish-speaking world, such as climate and geography, family life, school and university life, rural and urban life, and how they differ from U.S. culture

■ Elementary knowledge of culturally conditioned behavioral patterns such as table manners, *el abrazo*, and shades of formality; ability to demonstrate control of these behavioral patterns in interactions with others

To achieve these objectives, both the text and the ancillary components introduce and reinforce practical vocabulary in culturally authentic contexts and follow up with activities and cultural materials that emphasize communicative and cultural competency as well as mastery of key structures. By opting for a balanced, four-skills approach with a solid grammar foundation, *¿Cómo se dice...?*, Seventh Edition, takes full advantage of college students' highly developed cognitive skills as it provides communicative, task-oriented practice in using the language.

Organization of the Textbook: Features and Teaching Strategies

¿Cómo se dice...? consists of eighteen lessons, six self-tests, nine full-color *Panorama hispánico* photo essays, and a reference section. Odd-numbered lessons and the *Panoramas* conclude with video activities. Also, odd-numbered lessons feature reading activities right before the *Así somos* video activities. The reference materials at the end of the text include an appendix on pronunciation, a summary of regular and irregular verb conjugations, a glossary of grammatical terms, translation of the opening passages, an answer key to the self-tests, a glossary of professions and trades, and Spanish–English and English–Spanish end vocabularies. To assist instructors in implementing the various features of the text, strategies for their use are provided as each is described in detail.

Lessons 1–18

The following features recur in each of the eighteen lessons or at regular intervals throughout the text.

Statement of Objectives: This brief outline of the communicative and grammatical objectives of each lesson enables students to establish and verify performance goals.

Opening passages and ¡Conversemos!: To develop communicative competence, students must be exposed to language samples presented in realistic contexts. The opening passages serve this function as they introduce the vocabulary and structures that will be practiced throughout the remainder of the lesson. As the models from which subsequent practice exercises and conversational activities are developed, the opening passages also facilitate communication among students. Comprehension questions on the opening passage (*¡Conversemos!*) follow the vocabulary section to provide immediate reinforcement of the vocabulary and communicative functions presented in the opening passage.

Teaching Strategies: Especially in the early lessons, instructor modeling of each exchange followed by choral and individual repetition are appropriate techniques. Choral repetition will build students' confidence, while individual repetition allows them to demonstrate their auditory memory and control of pronunciation. Next, role-playing the dialogues can provide student interaction while allowing the instructor to observe each pair of students and help with specific pronunciation or intonation problems. Overcorrection should be avoided at this stage, however, since it may inhibit students' desire to communicate in Spanish.

Point out that the headset icon indicates that the opening passages are recorded on the Student Audio accompanying the text, as well as on the Audio Program.

Alternative methods of presenting the opening passages are (1) use of advance organizers (overhead transparencies or sketches on the board depicting the main action accompanied by questions, sentence completions, or other comprehension checks) that preview the opening passage's content before students read it; (2) personalized questions related to the topic; (3) a brief brainstorming session in which students guess from the title or the accompanying photograph where, when, and why the action takes place and who or what is involved; (4) use of realia or visuals to introduce key vocabulary; (5) a brief summary in Spanish by the instructor, followed by students' descriptions in simple sentences of the person speaking, the location of the action, and other key information; and (6) assignment of the opening passage and the questions for individual listening and rehearsal before class.

The *¡Conversemos!* questions may be used as a pre-reading or pre-listening device to give students a general idea of the opening passage's content before presenting it, assigned as written homework followed by discussion in class, or simply done on the spot as a comprehension check after presentation of the opening passage. After discussion of the questions, students may be asked to give a brief summary, orally or in writing, using their responses to the questions as a guide.

It is important to remember that the opening passages are intended to present the new concepts in context; therefore, class activities should not center around opening passage recitation, but rather around the student's creative use of new language for communicative purposes.

Translations of the Opening Passages

The translations of the opening passages in Appendix D allow students working independently to check their comprehension. The translations are equivalents of the Spanish opening passages in idiomatic American English, not word-for-word translations.

Teaching Strategies: Explain to students that the purpose of the translations is to convey an immediate sense of the meaning of the opening passage before the formal presentation of new structures, but tell them to try to guess the meaning of the new words and structures from context before consulting the appendix. Students should be told to avoid word-for-word translation and to concentrate instead on developing their ability to predict, skim, scan, and draw inferences as they read the opening passage for the first time.

Vocabulario

The *Vocabulario* sections that follow the opening passages list all new words and expressions by parts of speech or under the headings *Cognados* and *Otras palabras y expresiones*. A subsection, *Vocabulario adicional*, presents other words and phrases related to the central lesson theme in thematic groupings, many of which are illustration-based, for use in free communicative activities. Entries in this list are to be learned for active use.

Teaching Strategies: To check students' vocabulary acquisition, multiple-choice questions, open-ended completion statements, realia, and visual aids such as the

¿Cómo se dice...? Overhead Transparencies may be used. The following variation of "Bingo" is both a useful comprehension check and a welcome diversion. Have students fill in a 25-block grid with words chosen from the vocabulary list; then call out words from the list at random, telling students to mark these words with an "X" if they have them on their grids, until a student checks off all the words on his or her grid to win the game. This is also an excellent activity to check and improve comprehension of numbers.

¿Lo sabía Ud.?

These notes convey information on cultural themes or points mentioned in the opening passages and are followed by several questions that personalize the cultural points. In addition to providing insights into different cultural aspects of life in the Hispanic world, the notes also reinforce reading skills because they are written in simple Spanish.

Teaching Strategies: Since the notes are thematically related to the opening passages, they may be incorporated into the presentation. The questions following the notes may be used to invite comparisons between the target culture and the students' own cultures. Alternatively, the notes may be used as reading assignments and followed up with a brief comprehension check. This may consist of simple informational questions or true/false statements. Often, the full-color *Panorama hispánico* photo essays, the *¿Cómo se dice...?* Video, the maps from the text and from the *¿Cómo se dice...?* Overhead Transparencies, personal slides, photographs, posters, or realia may be used to illustrate these cultural notes. Spanish-language newspapers and magazines, as well as embassies or consulates, are excellent sources of authentic cultural material.

Pronunciación

Lessons 1–9 contain pronunciation and linking exercises designed to acquaint students with basic Spanish sounds, with those sounds that pose problems for English speakers, and with the ways in which Spanish words are combined in natural speech. Because these factors will strongly influence students' listening comprehension and oral abilities, it is important to spend sufficient time to ensure that all students are familiarized with the material these sections contain.

The *Pronunciación en contexto* sections in Lessons 10–18 focus on several sounds or words from the opening passage that may pose some pronunciation challenges. The target words and phrases are presented in the sentences in which they originally appear in the opening passage to provide students with focused pronunciation practice within sentence-level phonic contexts.

Teaching Strategies: These exercises may be used in class to reinforce particular sounds that cause problems due to interference from English, such as /d/, /t/, and /r/. The sentences in the instructor's annotations for Lessons 1–9 may also be dictated to check student progress. For efficient self-correction, one student may be sent to write the sentences on the chalkboard while the remainder write them at their seats, or the sentences may be displayed using an overhead projector. Students should also be referred to Appendix A for additional information on Spanish pronunciation and spelling. Point out that the headset icon indicates that both the *Pronunciación* sections and the Introduction to Spanish Sounds in

Appendix A are recorded on the Student Audio so that students can easily practice outside of class.

Estructuras

All grammar explanations are presented clearly and succinctly in English, with numerous examples of usage so that students may use these sections for independent study and reference. All grammatical terms are followed by their Spanish equivalents. When appropriate, new structures are compared and contrasted with previously learned Spanish structures or with their English equivalents. The *¡Atención!* heading signals areas of potential interference between Spanish and English and points out important exceptions to the primary grammar rules whenever necessary. The instructor's annotations offer suggestions for clarifying and illustrating each point, and frequently provide additional examples for reinforcement.

Teaching Strategies: Assigning each grammar point as outside reading the day before it will be covered in class allows the instructor to devote more time to illustrating and practicing the grammar in context through the activities provided in the textbook and in the annotations.

Práctica

Each structure introduced in the *Estructuras* sections is immediately followed by a subsection entitled *Práctica*, which reinforces the grammar points through exercises that range from controlled drills to open-ended contextualized activities. Among the many exercise formats featured are substitution drills, transformations, illustration-based activities, fill-ins, personalized questions, sentence completions, and interviews.

Teaching Strategies: Many of these exercises are designed to be done either orally or in writing at the instructor's discretion. Cloze exercises may be assigned as written homework to reinforce the new material; the more open-ended activities may be assigned as homework if advance preparation is needed or done orally in class in pairs or groups so that all students have the opportunity to communicate in Spanish. The instructor's annotations contain many suggestions for varying or expanding these activities for additional communicative practice. Grouping students with different partners each week and varying the class routine will help to accommodate students' different learning styles.

¡A ver cuánto aprendió!

Through a series of progressively more open-ended activities, students synthesize new grammar and vocabulary presented in the lesson and apply what they have learned to communicating in Spanish both orally and in writing. The following activities are included in each lesson:

¡Repase el vocabulario!

A variety of formats is used in this section to review new vocabulary presented in the lesson.

Teaching Strategies: These exercises are suitable for independent vocabulary review. Additional activities for promoting vocabulary acquisition are (1) word association games in which students must respond to a stimulus word with a related vocabulary item; (2) team generation of crossword puzzles to be solved by classmates individually or in pairs, with simple definitions, cognates, synonyms, and antonyms as cues; (3) an adaptation of the T.V. game "Jeopardy" in which teams select four or five categories and generate questions and answers for each; students on rival teams then individually pick a category, are shown the answer, and must supply the question to earn points.

Entrevista

In this personalized pair activity, students take turns interviewing each other on topics related to the lesson theme.

Teaching Strategies: Brainstorming with the class or having students take turns asking questions of the instructor before they work in pairs will help prepare them to ask and respond to questions on their own.

Situaciones

In this activity, students working in pairs or small groups must express themselves orally in Spanish to resolve a realistic situation involving the use of known vocabulary and structures.

Teaching Strategies: As the course progresses, the instructor may wish to copy situations on cards, combining them with those from previous lessons for more sustained speaking practice and added review. These cards may also be used for individual oral testing.

Para escribir

These activities are designed to develop students' ability to express themselves in writing in a variety of formats, such as notes, postcards, letters, dialogues, and compositions.

Teaching Strategies: To emphasize communication, the instructor may want to personalize the writing assignments, for example, by asking students to address the notes and letters to other members of the class, and then respond to and comment on each others' letters orally or in writing. *Para escribir* topics may also serve as the basis for an in-class journal activity in which students write in class for five to ten minutes once or twice weekly.

En la vida real

As its title suggests, this end-of-lesson activity section promotes and develops oral proficiency by involving students in realistic, communicative situations in Spanish. The activities, designed for pair or small group work, engage students in lively, meaningful, and practical tasks such as planning an event, asking for information, or solving a problem. Each of these sections also contains at least one activity based on an authentic document, such as a magazine or newspaper ad, a travel brochure, or a recipe, from which students must gather and use information.

Teaching Strategies: It is important to stress the practical nature of these highly motivating, creative activities, and to emphasize their cultural authenticity and their similarity to situations that students would encounter in Spanish-speaking countries. Especially in the early lessons, brainstorming sessions that focus on the ways in which the situations might evolve and the vocabulary needed to respond appropriately may prove beneficial, particularly to students experiencing difficulty. Assigning pairs or groups so that weaker students work with more able peers can also be helpful.

Así somos

All odd-numbered lessons conclude with this video activities section, designed for use with the candid interview segments of the *Así somos* modules of the *¿Cómo se dice...?* Video, which reinforces the lesson themes, vocabulary, and language functions. The *Preparación* (pre-viewing), *Comprensión* (post-viewing comprehension), and *Ampliación* (post-viewing expansion) activities employ true-false, sentence completion, comprehension questions, matching, multiple choice, brainstorming, and role-playing formats. A supplementary vocabulary list for each *Así somos* module may be found in the Instructor's Activities Manual as the last activity sheet for the corresponding lesson. This sheet can be photocopied and distributed to further support students' comprehension of the video material.

Teaching Strategies: Before working with the video in class, familiarize yourself with the module's content. Read the script and the activities, and watch the module at least twice. The documentary scenes at the beginning of each *Así somos* module contain valuable cultural information and serve as an advance organizer. After showing this segment, pause the video and have students identify, describe, or list the images they saw. Then ask students to make cross-cultural comparisons using this information and/or to predict the topics that will be discussed in the video. Have students complete the *Preparación* activities in pairs or in small groups and then show the video, pausing it after each interview segment or video clip so students can do the corresponding *Comprensión* activity. In some instances, students may need to view a video segment more than once before they fully comprehend it. To prepare students for the video, have them read the *Comprensión* activities beforehand. Once students have demonstrated their understanding of the video's content, the open-ended *Ampliación* activities provide an opportunity for active, creative oral communication.

The *Vocabulario* is provided for reference rather than for active use. Students can review the list after they have seen the video to pick up any words they missed or in preparation for the post-viewing activities. Throughout the course of the activities, emphasize to students that they must be active rather than passive viewers. The instructor's annotations provide numerous suggestions for emphasizing the cultural content of the video and for additional activities.

¡Vamos a leer!

These readings, which appear in all odd-numbered lessons right before the *Así somos* video activities section, are designed to develop reading comprehension while reinforcing the structures and vocabulary introduced in the preceding lessons. Five of the readings are new to this edition. The first four readings are related to the lesson themes; the final five readings consist of authentic literary selections chosen for their appeal and accessibility to students. New cultural concepts and words and phrases other than cognates are explained in marginal glosses. To develop students' reading skills, *Antes de leer*, a series of pre-reading questions, precedes each selection. Personalized, open-ended questions *(Díganos)* follow each reading and provide opportunities for students to discuss their own opinions and experiences in relation to the reading topic or theme.

Teaching Strategies: Students should be encouraged to skim, scan, and get the gist of passages rather than to comprehend all of the details of the text as they read. Using advance organizers such as pictures and the *Antes de leer* questions before students read the selection will alert them to important details and prepare them to focus on meaning rather than on translating every word. After they have read the selection, students may be asked to paraphrase it orally or in writing using the *Antes de leer* questions as an outline, to describe what they think might happen next, or to offer a brief personal assessment of the characters or the content.

Self-Tests

The Self-Tests that follow Lessons 3, 6, 9, 12, 15, and 18 contain exercises designed to review the vocabulary, structures, and cultural information introduced in the three preceding lessons. Organized by lesson and by grammatical structure, they enable students to determine quickly what material they have mastered and which concepts to target for further review. The answer key in Appendix E provides immediate verification.

Panorama hispánico and *Teleinforme*

The full-color *Panorama hispánico* photo essays follow all even-numbered lessons. Each *Panorama hispánico* provides students with key historical, geographic, cultural, and economic information on a different area of the Hispanic world. Each photo is accompanied by a caption in simple Spanish that is accessible to students and a question that invites cross-cultural comparison. Regions featured in the *Panoramas* are Hispanic culture in the United States *(Panoramas 1 and 9)*, Canada *(Panorama 1)*, Spain *(Panoramas 2 and 3)*, Mexico *(Panorama 4)*, Central America *(Panorama 5)*, the Caribbean *(Panorama 6)*, and South America *(Panoramas 7 and 8)*.

   The *Teleinforme* sections reinforce the content of the photo essays and, in conjunction with the captivating images presented through the authentic footage in the *Teleinforme* modules of the *¿Cómo se dice...?* Video, they expand upon and enhance students' cultural knowledge of the Hispanic world. These sections include a full range of pre-viewing, post-viewing, and expansion activities. Supplementary vocabulary lists for each *Teleinforme* module are found in the Instructor's Activities Manual for distribution at the instructor's discretion.

Teaching Strategies: Because the photo captions and discussion questions are written in Spanish, students should be encouraged to practice their reading strategies in this enjoyable, highly stimulating context. The photos and cultural highlights may also be used to support the information presented in the dialogues and the *¿Lo sabía Ud.?* sections and as the basis for class discussions.

To maximize students' assimilation of the information presented on specific countries or cultural topics, focus on one or two photos and the corresponding video clips together, rather than having students read the entire photo essay and then watch the video. As preparation for the experience of viewing authentic video footage, the *¿Cuánto saben Uds. ya?* previewing activity is designed to activate students' cultural knowledge through the review of relevant cultural information featured in the corresponding/preceding *Panorama hispánico*. The video clips may be viewed as many times as necessary for student comprehension, with pauses on specific images for explanations or questions. Students should demonstrate their understanding of the video clip through successful completion of the *Comprensión* exercises before moving on to the open-ended, communicative *Ampliación* activities. The instructor's annotations provide additional activities and teaching suggestions for promoting cultural awareness.

Appendixes

The six appendixes in the reference section provide a variety of useful information.

- **Appendix A:** This convenient summary of Spanish sounds and pronunciation features explanations of rhythm, intonation, the various sound-letter associations of the Spanish alphabet, syllable formation, and accentuation, with abundant examples. This appendix is recorded on the Student Audio.

- **Appendix B:** The conjugations of the highest frequency regular, stem-changing, and irregular Spanish verbs are organized in a convenient, readily accessible format for quick reference and review.

- **Appendix C:** This glossary of all grammatical terms used in the text, with examples of usage, will be an invaluable resource to students with limited knowledge of the structure of language.

- **Appendix D:** This appendix contains translations of the opening passages for students' reference.

- **Appendix E:** This answer key to all Self-Tests enables students to check their own progress quickly throughout the course.

- **Appendix F:** A list of trades and professions expands the treatment of this topic in Lesson 16 and facilitates classroom discussion.

End Vocabularies

Spanish–English and English–Spanish vocabularies are provided for students' reference. The Spanish–English vocabulary contains both active and passive vocabulary found in the student text. All active words and expressions are followed by the number of the lesson in which they are activated. No lesson reference is given for passive vocabulary entries because students are not expected to internalize them. The English–Spanish vocabulary contains only active vocabulary presented in the lesson vocabularies.

II. Supplementary Materials

Workbook/Laboratory Manual

Each lesson of the Workbook/Laboratory Manual is correlated to the corresponding lesson in the student's text and is divided into two sections. The *Workbook Activities* section offers an array of writing activities—sentence completion, sentence transformation, fill-in charts, dehydrated sentences, answering questions, crossword puzzles, and illustration-based exercises—that reinforce the structures and vocabulary presented in the textbook. Reading comprehension passages appear after each odd-numbered lesson to further skill development in that area. *Check Your Progress* sections provide a comprehensive review of key vocabulary and structures after every two lessons. The *Laboratory Activities* section includes pronunciation, structure, listening comprehension, and dictation exercises to be used in conjunction with the Audio Program. An answer key for all written exercises with discrete answers in both the Workbook and the Laboratory sections is provided for self-correction. The answer key to the *Check Your Progress* sections is included in the Instructor's Resource Manual for the convenience of instructors who wish to use those sections as extra quizzes.

Audio Program

The Audio Program for *¿Cómo se dice...?*, Seventh Edition, available in cassettes or CDs for student purchase, is fully supported by the Workbook/Laboratory Manual. The following recorded material is provided for each lesson:

Para escuchar y contestar

- The opening passages recorded once at natural speed and once with pauses for student repetition
- Questions concerning the content of the opening passages, which serve to verify comprehension
- An open-ended activity that elicits responses appropriate to given situations

Pronunciación

- Pronunciation activities that parallel the pronunciation sections in Lessons 1–9 of the textbook and provide ongoing practice in subsequent lessons

¡Vamos a practicar!

- Four to six structured, mechanical exercises that reinforce the grammar concepts

Ejercicio de comprensión

- Lively, contextualized conversations followed by comprehension questions

Para escuchar y escribir

- A listening exercise in which students write information based on what they hear in taped listening passages containing realistic simulations of radio advertisements, announcements, newscasts, and other types of authentic input
- A dictation covering the target lesson vocabulary and structures

¿Cómo se dice...? Video

The video for the Seventh Edition has been revised to allow for greater linguistic accessibility by students without compromising the video's authentic cultural content. The video provides a unique opportunity to develop listening skills and to promote cultural and linguistic awareness through multiple levels of viewing materials: unrehearsed interviews with native speakers from sixteen Spanish-speaking countries on a wide variety of topics, authentic as well as adapted footage, and candid images of everyday life. The video consists of eighteen modules that correlate to the *Así somos* and *Teleinforme* sections in the student's text. Filmed during the Semana Panamericana at the Universidad Autónoma de Guadalajara in Mexico, the nine *Así somos* modules reinforce the lesson themes, vocabulary, and language functions. They enable students to see, hear, and interact with Hispanics in authentic settings. In each module, students listen to a series of basic questions posed by María Isabel, the host, and the interviewees' responses. The segment concludes with María Isabel asking the viewers a question to which they provide a personalized response. The special *Entrevista* section, which appears at the end of Lessons 3, 7, 13, 15, and 17, features interviews with selected professionals. The nine *Teleinforme* modules present a broad cultural overview of the Hispanic world through authentic as well as adapted television footage from a number of Hispanic countries. Each *Teleinforme* includes two to four clips with a wide range of content: interviews, travelogues, festivals, and commercials. The content reinforces in a visually appealing and lively manner the cultural material of the *Panoramas hispánicos.*

¿Cómo se dice...? Multimedia CD-ROM 3.0

This new CD-ROM is an interactive multimedia program featuring short clips from the *¿Cómo se dice...?* Video with accompanying transcripts and access to a bilingual glossary. The clips are supported by a variety of comprehension and interpretation activities to help students hone their listening skills. Language practice exercises corresponding to the language points presented in *¿Cómo se dice...?* are also included on this CD-ROM. The exercises contain links to a grammar reference to help students who need additional review/reinforcement of grammatical concepts.

Instructor's Activities Manual

This component provides a wide range of supplementary material that allows instructors the flexibility to tailor their classes to meet specific needs of their students. It contains communicative and listening comprehension activities, games, and vocabulary and grammar exercises that can be photocopied and distributed to students for additional practice. In this edition, all activities included in this component have been cross-referenced to pertinent material in the Instructor's Annotated Edition by means of special annotations. The supplementary vocabulary lists of the *Así somos* and the *Teleinforme* video modules are now included in this component for the convenience of instructors who wish to photocopy and distribute as further video-viewing preparation or support.

Instructor's Resource Manual

This component contains the printed version of the Testing Program, the Audioscript, the Videoscript, and the answer key to the *Check Your Progress* sections of the Workbook. Completely revised, the Testing Program now features mid-term and final examinations for both two- and three-semester course schedules. It includes two versions (A and B) of quizzes for each of the eighteen lessons of *¿Cómo se dice...?*, quizzes for the nine *Panoramas hispánicos*, midterm examinations to be given after Lessons 4 and 13 (or Lessons 3, 9, and 15), final examinations to be given after Lessons 9 and 18 (or Lessons 6, 12, and 18), and an answer key for each quiz and each exam. The quizzes on the eighteen lessons and the exams evaluate students' mastery of target vocabulary and grammar as well as their listening comprehension and writing skills. The *Panorama hispánico* quizzes evaluate students' knowledge of the cultural information presented in the section.

HM Testing

This is a test generator that enables instructors to customize the existing Testing Program by selecting specific items, and by adding, deleting, or modifying items. It includes new grade management software and it allows instructors to administer the tests online.

Class Prep Instructor CD-ROM

For the convenience of the instructor, the materials in the Instructor's Resource Manual (the Testing Program, the Audioscript, the Videoscript, and the answer key to the *Check Your Progress* sections of the Workbook) as well as PowerPoint slides of grammar charts and explanations are made available in electronic format in this new CD-ROM.

The *¿Cómo se dice...?* Web Site and Spanish Web Resources

The new instructors' component of the textbook's Web site includes an instructor's guide, a technology integration guide, and PowerPoint slides that contain grammar charts. The upgraded student's web site features Web search activities related to the content of the lessons in the textbook. A self test for each lesson serves as an additional check for students of their progress in Spanish. This version of the *¿Cómo se dice...?* Web site also includes a new flashcard feature designed to help students review terms, images, and definitions. Audio- and video-based activities are now part of the student's component. In addition, the Spanish Web Resources page provides links to authentic Spanish sites, maps of the Spanish-speaking world, and downloadable generic transparencies. The Web sites are accessible at *http://spanish.college.hmco.com/instructors*.

¿Cómo se dice...? Online Course

This new component provides materials in online formats in Blackboard and WebCT to those instructors or institutions moving to online instruction. To aid in this transition, it includes an Integration Guide that provides suggestions on how to use media-based components in conjunction with print components.

¿Cómo se dice...? Overhead Transparencies

This supplement contains fifty-six full-color text-specific or thematic visuals and a series of maps of the Spanish-speaking world. The overhead transparencies facilitate vocabulary presentation or provide visual clues for activities that reinforce the vocabulary and structures in the textbook.

Situation Cards Kit

This set of 120 cards with its own Instructor's Guide enables instructors to monitor students' development of oral proficiency.

Spanish History Booklet

This booklet contains supplementary information on the history, politics, and cultures of Spain and Hispanic America.

Instructor's Resource Kit

This conveniently boxed supplement package assists the instructor in presenting, reviewing, expanding, and reinforcing the materials in the textbook. The Instructor's Resource Kit for *¿Cómo se dice...?*, Seventh Edition, contains the following materials:

- The Instructor's Resource Manual
- The Instructor's Activities Manual
- The *¿Cómo se dice...?* Overhead Transparencies
- The Situation Cards Kit
- The Spanish History Booklet

III. Course Planning

¿Cómo se dice...?, Seventh Edition, can easily be adapted to a variety of course plans and schedules. Careful attention has been paid to the sequencing of grammatical concepts and to the development of activities to ensure that the text may be used effectively in courses meeting on a two-semester, three-semester, or a trimester system, as follows:

■ **Two-semester System:** The first semester includes Lessons 1–9. The second semester covers Lessons 10–18.

■ **Three-semester and Trimester Systems:** The first semester/trimester includes Lessons 1–6, the second semester/trimester Lessons 7–12, and the third semester/trimester Lessons 13–18.

Lesson Plan for Lección 1

A sample lesson plan is offered here for the first three days of class, using *Lección 1*.

Day 1

Begin by greeting students with **Buenos días** or **Buenas tardes** as appropriate and encouraging them to reply. Then introduce yourself: **Me llamo... . Soy el (la) ...** (call yourself **señor, señora,** or **señorita** so that students will learn how to address you). Next, have individual students introduce themselves.

Play the recording of the greetings and introductions in *Lección 1* as students follow along in their texts. Next, have students repeat them as a group and then in pairs. Finally, ask individual students to reenact the introductions, replacing the characters' names and circumstances with their own.

Briefly go over the *Vocabulario;* explain the concept of formal versus informal address by teaching **¿Cómo te llamas?**

Introduce the alphabet by having students listen and repeat. Practice by writing short words on the board and having the group spell them out loud as a class. As a listening activity, dictate simple words and ask students to write them down. Call upon individual students to spell the words aloud. Do the *Práctica* on page 8, having students circulate and ask each other's names and how to spell them.

Introduce the numbers 1–30 by having students listen and repeat. Practice by counting forward, backward, and by two in odd and even numbers. As a listening activity, dictate simple addition and subtraction problems, asking students to write out and solve each problem. Call upon individual students to give the solution.

At some point you may wish to explain the general objectives of the course, the value of some of the techniques you plan to use, and the importance of laboratory attendance and class participation. Emphasize that class time will be devoted to using the language for communication.

Homework: Review the greetings and the introductions, vocabulary, and numbers. Read the culture note (*¿Lo sabía Ud.?*), Colors, Days of the week, and *Month and seasons of the year*. Practice the pronunciation of the Spanish **a** and **e**, and prepare to do the *Práctica* activities on page 9.

Day 2

Warm up by using the greetings introduced in *Lección 1*. Ask an additional question of each student (**¿Cómo está Ud. hoy?**) to convey a sense of natural, spontaneous communication.

Review numbers by asking **¿Cuál es su número de teléfono?** and doing the *Práctica* on page 9.

Introduce colors, asking students to listen and repeat. Reinforce them by pointing to objects in the classroom and asking, **¿De qué color es?** Have students work briefly in pairs, asking each other the colors of their clothing, notebooks, etc.

Use a calendar to introduce the days of the week. See the annotations on page 11 for suggested practice activities for this material.

Introduce months and seasons by having students listen and repeat. Ask **¿Qué fecha es hoy?** and write the date on the board. Do the *Práctica A* on page 13.

Homework: Review the colors, the days of the week, and the months and seasons of the year. Do the *Práctica* activities on pages 11 and 13. Read Subject pronouns and Present indicative of **ser.** Prepare to do the *Práctica A* activity on page 14.

Day 3

Warm up by using the greetings introduced in *Lección 1*. Ask a few questions that incorporate colors, days of the week, and months and seasons of the year.

Review colors by having students circulate to do the *Práctica A*. Alternatively, ask students to do *Práctica B* on page 10 in pairs.

Review days of the week by having pairs of students do the *Práctica B* on page 11.

Review the month and seasons of the year by having students work in pairs. On the blackboard have **¿Cuándo es tu cumpleaños?** *(When is your birthday?)*/**El** *[followed by any date].* already written. Have each student ask the question to his or her partner.

Present the subject pronouns. See the annotation on page 13 for suggestions. Do the *Práctica A* on page 14 in small groups. Then have individual students report to class.

Introduce the present indicative of **ser** using the PowerPoint slide with the **ser** conjugation chart, available in the Class Prep CD-ROM or the instructor's Web site. Alternatively, write the conjugation chart on the blackboard beforehand. Ask students to listen and repeat the subject pronouns with the corresponding form of the verb. Then provide a drill based on a subject-substitution exercise: Say a simple sentence such as **Soy norteamericano(-a)** and provide new subject pronouns to individual students so each one transforms the original sentence according to the subject given to him or her.

Have students do the activities in *¡A ver cuánto aprendió!* in pairs. See the annotations for additional suggestions. End each activity by asking random questions of the whole class to spot-check accuracy, pronunciation, and intonation.

Pair students with different partners for each of the two *En la vida real* activities. Circulate among the pairs giving individual attention. Have several pairs of students role-play their *Encuentros* dialogues for the class.

If time does not permit completion of the *En la vida real* activities, use those activities for warm up or review on Day 4.

Homework: Review subject pronouns and the present indicative of **ser.** Assign the *Práctica* exercises on pages 14–15 and on pages 16–17, and the *¡Vamos a leer!* section.

Sample Syllabi

Two-semester course

These syllabi are designed for a course that meets five class periods per week for fourteen weeks. The syllabus for each semester includes a mid-term exam, quizzes after each lesson and Panorama hispánico, and one or two review sessions.

First semester of a two-semester course

Week	Day 1	Day 2	Day 3	Day 4	Day 5
1	1	1	1	1	1
2	1	Prueba: Lección 1	2	2	2
3	2	2	2	Panorama hispánico 1 + Teleinforme	Pruebas: Lección 2 + Panorama hispánico 1
4	3	3	3	3	3
5	3	Prueba: Lección 3	4	4	4
6	4	4	4	Panorama hispánico 2 + Teleinforme	Pruebas: Lección 4 + Panorama hispánico 2
7	Repaso	Examen	5	5	5
8	5	5	5	Prueba: Lección 5	6
9	6	6	6	6	6
10	Panorama hispánico 3 + Teleinforme	Pruebas: Lección 6 + Panorama hispánico 3	7	7	7
11	7	7	7	Prueba: Lección 7	8
12	8	8	8	8	8

Week	Day 1	Day 2	Day 3	Day 4	Day 5
13	Panorama hispánico 4 + Teleinforme	Pruebas: Lección 8 + Panorama hispánico 4	9	9	9
14	9	9	9	Prueba: Lección 9	Repaso

Second semester of a two-semester course

Week	Day 1	Day 2	Day 3	Day 4	Day 5
1	10	10	10	10	10
2	10	Panorama hispánico 5 + Teleinforme	Pruebas: Lección 10 + Panorama hispánico 5	11	11
3	11	11	11	11	Prueba: Lección 11
4	12	12	12	12	12
5	12	Panorama hispánico 6 + Teleinforme	Pruebas: Lección 12 + Panorama hispánico 6	13	13
6	13	13	13	13	Prueba: Lección 13
7	Repaso	Examen parcial	14	14	14
8	14	14	14	Panorama hispánico 7 + Teleinforme	Pruebas: Lección 14 + Panorama hispánico 7
9	15	15	15	15	15
10	15	Prueba: Lección 15	16	16	16
11	16	16	16	Panorama hispánico 8 + Teleinforme	Pruebas: Lección 16 + Panorama hispánico 8
12	17	17	17	17	17

Week	Day 1	Day 2	Day 3	Day 4	Day 5
13	17	Prueba: Lección 17	18	18	18
14	18	18	18	Panorama hispánico 9 + Teleinforme	Pruebas: Lección 18 + Panorama hispánico 9

Three-semester course

These syllabi are designed for a course that meets five class periods per week for fourteen weeks. The syllabus for each semester includes a mid-term exam, quizzes after each lesson and Panorama hispánico, and one review session.

First semester of a two-semester course

Week	Day 1	Day 2	Day 3	Day 4	Day 5
1	1	1	1	1	1
2	1	1	1	1	1
3	Prueba: Lección 1	2	2	2	2
4	2	2	2	2	2
5	2	Panorama hispánico 1 + Teleinforme	Pruebas: Lección 2 + Panorama hispánico 1	3	3
6	3	3	3	3	3
7	3	3	Prueba: Lección 3	Repaso	Examen parcial
8	4	4	4	4	4
9	4	4	4	4	4
10	Panorama hispánico 2 + Teleinforme	Pruebas: Lección 4 + Panorama hispánico 2	5	5	5
11	5	5	5	5	5
12	5	5	Prueba: Lección 5	6	6

Week	Day 1	Day 2	Day 3	Day 4	Day 5
13	6	6	6	6	6
14	6	6	6	Panorama hispánico 3 + Teleinforme	Pruebas: Lección 6 + Panorama hispánico 3

Second semester of a three-semester course

Week	Day 1	Day 2	Day 3	Day 4	Day 5
1	7	7	7	7	7
2	7	7	7	7	7
3	Prueba: Lección 7	8	8	8	8
4	8	8	8	8	8
5	8	Panorama hispánico 4 + Teleinforme	Pruebas: Lección 8 + Panorama hispánico 4	9	9
6	9	9	9	9	9
7	9	9	Prueba: Lección 9	Repaso	Examen parcial
8	10	10	10	10	10
9	10	10	10	10	10
10	Panorama hispánico 5 + Teleinforme	Pruebas: Lección 10 + Panorama hispánico 5	11	11	11
11	11	11	11	11	11
12	11	11	Prueba: Lección 11	12	12
13	12	12	12	12	12
14	12	12	12	Panorama hispánico 6 + Teleinforme	Pruebas: Lección 12 + Panorama hispánico 6

Third semester of a three-semester course

Week	Day 1	Day 2	Day 3	Day 4	Day 5
1	13	13	13	13	13
2	13	13	13	13	13
3	Prueba: Lección 13	14	14	14	14
4	14	14	14	14	14
5	14	Panorama hispánico 7 + Teleinforme	Pruebas: Lección 14 + Panorama hispánico 7	15	15
6	15	15	15	15	15
7	15	15	Prueba: Lección 15	Repaso	Examen parcial
8	16	16	16	16	16
9	16	16	16	16	16
10	Panorama hispánico 8 + Teleinforme	Pruebas: Lección 16 + Panorama hispánico 8	17	17	17
11	17	17	17	17	17
12	17	17	Prueba: Lección 17	18	18
13	18	18	18	18	18
14	18	18	18	Panorama hispánico 9 + Teleinforme	Pruebas: Lección 18 + Panorama hispánico 9

Trimester system

These syllabi are designed for a course that meets five class periods per week for ten weeks. The syllabus for each trimester includes a mid-term exam, quizzes after each lesson and Panorama hispánico, and three sessions.

First trimester

Week	Day 1	Day 2	Day 3	Day 4	Day 5
1	1	1	1	1	1
2	1	Prueba: Lección 1	2	2	2
3	2	2	2	Panorama hispánico 1 + Teleinforme	Pruebas: Lección 2 + Panorama hispánico 1
4	3	3	3	3	3
5	3	Prueba: Lección 3	Repaso	Examen parcial	4
6	4	4	4	4	4
7	Panorama hispánico 2 + Teleinforme	Pruebas: Lección 4 + Panorama hispánico 2	5	5	5
8	5	5	5	Prueba: Lección 5	6
9	6	6	6	6	6
10	6	Panorama hispánico 3 + Teleinforme	Pruebas: Lección 6 + Panorama hispánico 3	Repaso	Repaso

Second trimester

Week	Day 1	Day 2	Day 3	Day 4	Day 5
1	7	7	7	7	7
2	7	Prueba: Lección 7	8	8	8
3	8	8	8	Panorama hispánico 4 + Teleinforme	Pruebas: Lección 8 + Panorama hispánico 4
4	9	9	9	9	9
5	9	Prueba: Lección 9	Repaso	Examen parcial	10
6	10	10	10	10	10
7	Panorama hispánico 5 + Teleinforme	Pruebas: Lección 10 + Panorama hispánico 5	11	11	11
8	11	11	11	Prueba: Lección 11	12
9	12	12	12	12	12
10	12	Panorama hispánico 6 + Teleinforme	Pruebas: Lección 12 + Panorama hispánico 6	Repaso	Repaso

Third trimester

Week	Day 1	Day 2	Day 3	Day 4	Day 5
1	13	13	13	13	13
2	13	Prueba: Lección 13	14	14	14
3	14	14	14	Panorama hispánico 7 + Teleinforme	Pruebas: Lección 14 + Panorama hispánico 7
4	15	15	15	15	15
5	15	Prueba: Lección 15	Repaso	Examen parcial	16
6	16	16	16	16	16
7	Panorama hispánico 8 + Teleinforme	Pruebas: Lección 16 + Panorama hispánico 8	17	17	17
8	17	17	17	Prueba: Lección 17	18
9	18	18	18	18	18
10	18	Panorama hispánico 9 + Teleinforme	Pruebas: Lección 18 + Panorama hispánico 9	Repaso	Repaso

IV. ANSWERS TO TEXT EXERCISES

Lección 1

¡Conversemos!, página 6   1. Es de California. Es estudiante.   2. Laura Estévez es de Arizona. Es maestra.   3. María Luisa es secretaria. Marcos es analista de sistemas.   4. Marisa Barrios es mexicana. Es dentista.   5. Rafael Hernández es de Tejas. Es piloto.   6. Beatriz López es puertorriqueña. Es profesora (de español).

¿Lo sabía Ud.?, página 7   *Answers will vary.*

Ejercicio A, página 8   1. efe-be-i   2. i-be-eme   3. ene-a-a-ce-pe   4. pe-te-a   5. ene-be-a   6. ene-hache-efe   7. ce-i-o   8. a-efe-ele

Ejercicio B, página 8   *Answers will vary.*

Ejercicio A, página 9   *Answers will vary.*

Ejercicio B, página 9   1. seis, ocho, diez, doce, catorce, dieciséis, dieciocho, veinte, veintidós, veinticuatro, veintiséis, veintiocho   2. siete, nueve, once, trece, quince, diecisiete, diecinueve, veintiuno, veintitrés, veinticinco, veintisiete   3. seis, nueve, doce, quince   4. ocho, doce, dieciséis, veinte, veinticuatro

Ejercicio A, página 10   *Answers will vary.*

Ejercicio B, página 10   *Answers will vary.*

Ejercicio A, página 11   1. No, hoy es martes.   2. No, hoy es sábado.   3. No, hoy es jueves.   4. No, hoy es lunes.   5. No, hoy es viernes.   6. No, hoy es miércoles.

Ejercicio B, página 11   *Answers will vary.*

Ejercicio A, página 13   1. el cuatro de julio   2. el treinta y uno de octubre   3. el primero de enero   4. el cinco de mayo   5. el doce de febrero   6. el veinticinco de diciembre   7. el veintiuno de marzo   8. el dos de abril   9. el veinte de junio   10. el nueve de septiembre   11. el trece de agosto   12. el once de noviembre

Ejercicio B, página 13   1. invierno   2. verano   3. primavera   4. invierno   5. otoño   6. verano   7. primavera   8. otoño

Ejercicio C, página 13   *Answers will vary.*

Ejercicio A, página 14   1. yo   2. tú   3. nosotros   4. nosotras   5. ellos   6. ustedes   7. él   8. ella   9. usted

Ejercicio B, página 14   1. usted   2. ustedes   3. tú   4. usted   5. tú   6. ustedes

Ejercicio C, página 15   1. ellos   2. ellas   3. nosotras   4. nosotros   5. ellos   6. ustedes

Ejercicio A, página 16   1. Teresa es de Uruguay. La capital de Uruguay es Montevideo.   2. Carlos y yo somos de Chile. La capital de Chile es Santiago.   3. Juan, Mario y José son de Perú. La capital de Perú es Lima.   4. Tú eres de Ecuador. La capital de Ecuador es Quito.   5. Ellos son de Colombia. La capital de Colombia es Bogotá.   6. Nosotras somos de Brasil. La capital de Brasil es Brasilia.   7. Ustedes son de Argentina. La capital de Argentina es Buenos Aires.   8. Julio es de Paraguay. La capital de Paraguay es Asunción.

Ejercicio B, página 17   1. Teresa es uruguaya.   2. Carlos y yo somos chilenos.   3. Juan, Mario y José son peruanos.   4. Tú eres ecuatoriana.   5. Ellos son colombianos.   6. Nosotras somos brasileñas.   7. Ustedes son argentinos.   8. Julio es paraguayo.

¡A ver cuánto aprendió!

Repase el vocabulario, página 17   1. días / están   2. llamo / llamas   3. soy   4. profesora   5. sistemas   6. norteamericano   7. nuevo   8. mexicana   9. Bien   10. Hasta   11. vemos   12. vuelo

Entrevista, página 17   *Answers will vary.*

Situaciones, página 18   1. Buenos días, profesor(-a). ¿Cómo está usted?   2. ¿Qué hay de nuevo?   3. Hola, ¿qué tal? (¿Cómo estás?)   4. Hasta mañana.   5. Adiós (Chau). Nos vemos el lunes.   6. ¿Cómo se llama usted?   7. ¿Qué día es hoy?   8. ¿Qué fecha es hoy?

Sumas y restas, página 18   1. Ocho más quince son veintitrés.   2. Dieciocho menos catorce son cuatro.   3. Treinta menos trece son diecisiete.   4. Siete más once son dieciocho.   5. Veintisiete menos doce son quince.   6. Dieciséis más nueve son veinticinco.

Por teléfono, página 18   1. tres-cinco-seis-siete-nueve-tres-dos   2. siete-cero-uno-ocho-nueve-seis-cinco   3. cuatro-siete-cinco-cero-cuatro-tres-dos   4. nueve-cinco-dos-cero-cero-tres-ocho   5. seis-ocho-seis-nueve-cinco-dos-ocho   6. cuatro-tres-uno-siete-cero-seis-ocho   7. cinco-seis-dos-cero-cuatro-tres-siete   8. nueve-uno-uno   9. cuatro-nueve-ocho-seis-cinco-tres-cero   10. nueve-ocho-siete-tres-cero-seis-cinco   11. nueve-cuatro-tres-siete-cinco-uno-cero   12. siete-nueve-dos-tres-cinco-ocho-siete   13. cuatro-ocho-dos-tres-uno-cinco-siete   14. cuatro-nueve-tres-siete-uno-nueve-seis   15. cuatro-siete-cero-nueve-dos-seis-cinco

Para escribir, página 19   *Answers will vary.*

¡Vamos a leer!

Antes de leer, página 20   1. Ellos son actores de televisión.   2. Sí, son mexicanos.   3. Es norteamericano.

4. No, es estudiante.   5. Es cubana.   6. No, es médica.
7. Es de San Juan.   8. Es piloto.

Díganos, página 20   *Answers will vary.*

Así somos

Preparación, Ejercicio A, página 21   *Answers will vary.*

Ejercicio B, página 21   *Answers will vary.*

Comprensión, Ejercicio A, página 21   1. a   2. a   3. b
4. a   5. b   6. a   7. d   8. b   9. c

Ejercicio B, página 22   1. b   2. d   3. i   4. g   5. c
6. a   7. e   8. f   9. j   10. h

Ejercicio C, página 22   1. V   2. V   3. F, calle Andalucía,
31, Santa Cruz   4. F, Ésa es la dirección de Héctor. La
dirección de Leonardo es Flores Guijón y Sotomayor.

Ejercicio D, página 22   1. a   2. e   3. d   4. c   5. b

Ampliación, Ejercicio A, página 22   1. panameña
2. español   3. puertorriqueña   4. mexicano   5. peruana
6. colombianos

Ejercicio B, página 22   *Answers will vary.*

Lección 2

¡Conversemos!, página 27   1. El gusto es mío.   2. De
nada.   3. Hay... estudiantes.   4. Se dice "por favor".
5. Quiere decir *"excuse me"*.   6. Calle Magnolia número
98.   7. Trabaja en un hospital.   8. Tomo cinco clases.
9. Habla francés.   10. Sí, habla un poco de italiano y de
portugués.

¿Lo sabía Ud.?, página 27   *Answers will vary.*

Ejercicio, página 29   1. el mapa   2. la tiza   3. el
escritorio   4. el señor   5. la doctora   6. la profesora
7. la pizarra   8. el libro   9. la mujer   10. la puerta
11. la ventana   12. la pluma   13. el hombre   14. el día
15. el secretario   16. la mano   17. el cuaderno   18. el
doctor   19. la silla   20. la señora

Ejercicio, página 29   1. mapas   2. relojes   3. tizas
4. lápices   5. ventanas   6. puertas   7. lecciones
8. escritorios   9. borradores   10. días   11. luces
12. profesores

Ejercicio A, página 30   1. la silla   2. el lápiz   3. las
estudiantes   4. el profesor   5. los mapas   6. las ventanas

Ejercicio B, página 31   1. un hombre   2. unos estudiantes
3. unas mujeres   4. unos relojes   5. un libro   6. una
pizarra

Ejercicio C, página 31   *Answers will vary.*

Ejercicio, página 32   1. Dr. José Carreras: cuatro, cero
dos, cuarenta y uno, ochenta; Dr. Francisco Rivas: ocho,
veintinueve, treinta y siete, ochenta y cinco   2. Dra.
Rosaura M. García: seis, cero, siete, cincuenta y tres,
noventa y uno; Dr. Marcelo Torres: dos, cuarenta y tres,
setenta y uno, sesenta   3. Dr. Arnaldo López: siete,
cincuenta, cuarenta y cinco, treinta y ocho; Dra. Eloísa
Ugarte: nueve, sesenta y dos, sesenta y ocho, setenta y cinco
4. Dra. Carolina Méndez: ocho, cero, seis, noventa y nueve,
cincuenta y dos; Dra. Estela Rodríguez: seis, noventa y tres,
cuarenta y nueve, treinta y uno   5. Dr. Gustavo Barrios:
tres, cuarenta y dos, setenta y ocho, cincuenta y nueve; Dra.
Cristina Martínez: cinco, sesenta y uno, sesenta y dos,
noventa y cuatro

Ejercicio A, página 34   1. Son las cinco.   2. Son las diez y
media.   3. Son las cinco menos diez.   4. Es la una menos
cuarto.   5. Son las seis y cinco.   6. Son las doce.   7. Son
las seis menos cuarto.   8. Es la una y cuarto.   9. Es la una
y veinte.   10. Es la una y media.   11. Son las seis menos
veinte.   12. Son las once menos cuarto.

Ejercicio B, página 35   *Order of questions and answers
will vary.*

Ejercicio A, página 36   1. estudian / Estudiamos
2. trabajas / trabajo   3. regresan / regreso / regresa
4. hablan / habla / habla / hablas / Hablo   5. necesitan /
Necesitamos   6. toma / tomo

Ejercicio B, página 37   1. Habla francés.   2. Habla
alemán.   3. Habla español.   4. Habla italiano.   5. Habla
inglés.   6. Habla portugués.

Ejercicio C, página 37   *Answers will vary.*

Ejercicio D, página 37   1. Nosotros hablamos inglés.
2. Yo estudio por la noche.   3. Mario habla con Roberto.
4. La Dra. Santos trabaja en el hospital.   5. Ellas necesitan
dinero.   6. Tú regresas a la clase a las doce y media.

Ejercicio A, página 39   1. No, yo no hablo francés.
2. No, yo no trabajo en un hospital.   3. No, yo no
necesito el libro de español.   4. No, yo no regreso a clase a
las cinco.   5. No, yo no estudio por la noche.   6. No, yo
no soy de Madrid.

Ejercicio B, página 39   1. ¿Estudian inglés Uds.?
(¿Estudian Uds. inglés?)   2. ¿Tú trabajas en el hospital
hoy?   3. ¿De dónde son Uds.?   4. ¿Uds. hablan alemán?
5. ¿Qué necesitan ellos?   6. ¿Dónde trabaja ella?   7. ¿A
qué hora regresa Carlos?   8. ¿Ud. es (Tú eres) enfermera?

Ejercicio A, página 40   1. el profesor de María   2. los
libros de la Srta. Martínez   3. la dirección de Elena
4. los estudiantes de la Sra. López   5. las amigas de Sergio
6. el escritorio de la profesora

Ejercicio B, página 40 1. los estudiantes de la Srta. Vera 2. los mapas de Carmen 3. el reloj de Jorge 4. los cuadernos de Marta 5. las amigas de Amanda 6. la silla de Javier 7. la clase de la Sra. Valle 8. el número de teléfono de la señorita

Ejercicio C, página 41 *Answers will vary.*

¡A ver cuánto aprendió!

¡Repase el vocabulario!, Ejercicio A, página 41 1. el reloj 2. la ventana 3. el profesor 4. la estudiante 5. los libros 6. el escritorio 7. la pared 8. el borrador 9. el cuaderno 10. el pupitre 11. la pluma 12. el bolígrafo 13. la silla 14. el estudiante 15. la pizarra 16. la luz 17. el mapa 18. la tiza 19. la puerta 20. el lápiz 21. el papel

Ejercicio B, página 41 1. hora 2. dice / inglés 3. asiento 4. toma / semestre 5. hay 6. quiere 7. Calle / número 8. hora 9. día 10. solamente 11. poco 12. avenida

Entrevista, página 42 *Answers will vary.*

Situaciones, página 42 *Answers will vary. Possibilities:* 1. Profesor(-a), ¿cómo se dice *"you're welcome"* en español? 2. ¿Cuál es tu dirección? 3. ¿A qué hora es la clase de español? 4. Profesor(-a), el doctor Cortés. 5. Pase y tome asiento. 6. Perdón, ¿qué hora es?

Para escribir, página 43 1. ¿Cómo te llamas? / ¿De dónde eres? / ¿Cuál es tu número de teléfono? / ¿Cuál es tu dirección? 2. Me llamo Roberto Soto. / El gusto es mío. / Hoy es viernes. / Se dice "treinta y cinco". / Quiere decir "hasta la vista". / Hasta luego. 3. Muchas gracias, profesora. / Hasta luego. (Adiós.)

En la vida real

Presentaciones, página 43 *Answers will vary.*

Horario de clases, página 44 *Order of responses will vary.*

Mi horario, página 44 *Answers will vary.*

Un inventario de la clase, página 44 *Answers will vary.*

Teleinforme

Preparación, página 49 1. treinta 2. Nuevo México, Tejas, California, Nueva York, Nueva Jersey, la Florida 3. educación 4. periódicos y revistas 5. Miami, la Florida

Comprensión, Ejercicio A, página 49 1. f 2. a 3. d 4. b 5. e 6. c

Ejercicio B, página 49 1. todos los años 2. Miami 3. Muchas 4. a la reina 5. la calle Ocho

Ampliación, Ejercicio A, página 50 *Answers will vary.*

Ejercicio B, página 50 *Answers will vary.*

Lección 3

¡Conversemos!, página 55 1. Desea ser abogados. 2. Desea hablar con Pedro. 2. Regresa a las nueve de la noche. 4. Habla con Marisa. 5. No, no comen en la cafetería. 6. Tiene que leer varios artículos. 7. Tiene que estudiar para un examen. 8. Es un amigo de Raquel. 9. Necesita dinero. 10. Necesita dinero también. 11. Estudia en la biblioteca. 12. Sí, Pedro tiene novia.

¿Lo sabía Ud.?, página 56 *Answers will vary.*

Ejercicio A, página 58 1. la pared 2. la mesa 3. el turismo 4. el hospital 5. los problemas 6. la ciudad 7. la sociedad 8. el borrador 9. la mano 10. la lumbre 11. la libertad 12. los idiomas 13. la organización 14. el día 15. la solución 16. la conversación 17. la universidad 18. la muchedumbre

Ejercicio B, página 58 *Answers will vary.*

Ejercicio A, página 59 1. de Uds. / Nuestra 2. tu / Mi 3. sus / mis 4. de él / de ella 5. de Uds. / Nuestro 6. sus

Ejercicio B, página 60 1. No, no es su novia. 2. No, no necesito mi libro. 3. No, nuestra profesora no es de México. 4. No, no son mis amigos. 5. No, no son nuestros profesores. 6. No, no necesito tus cuadernos. 7. No, no necesito su dirección. 8. No, no son sus amigas.

Ejercicio A, página 60 1. cuatrocientos, quinientos, seiscientos, setecientos, ochocientos, novecientos 2. cuarenta mil, cincuenta mil, sesenta mil, setenta mil, ochenta mil, noventa mil 3. cuatrocientos cuarenta, quinientos cincuenta, seiscientos sesenta, setecientos setenta, ochocientos ochenta, novecientos noventa

Ejercicio B, página 61 *Order of responses will vary.* El mapa cuesta ciento sesenta y cinco dólares. / La silla cuesta ciento ochenta dólares. / El teléfono cuesta ciento cinco dólares. / El escritorio cuesta cuatrocientos noventa y ocho dólares. / El sofá cuesta mil quinientos dólares. / El reloj cuesta ciento setenta y ocho dólares. / La pizarra cuesta doscientos quince dólares. / Los libros cuestan trescientos cuarenta y seis dólares. / La mesa y las sillas cuestan dos mil novecientos setenta y cuatro dólares. / La casa cuesta trescientos mil setecientos ochenta dólares.

Ejercicio A, página 63 1. No, es moreno. 2. No, son delgadas. 3. No, son altos. 4. No, es simpática. 5. No, es bonita. 6. No, soy pesimista. 7. No, es gordo. 8. No, son rubias.

Ejercicio B, página 63 *Answers will vary.*

Ejercicio A, página 64 1. comen / Comemos 2. vives / Vivo 3. reciben / recibo / recibe 4. leen / Leen 5. venden / creo / abren 6. beben / bebemos / bebe 7. debo / debe 8. escriben / escribimos

Ejercicio B, página 64 1. Yo bebo café. 2. Nosotros aprendemos español. 3. Uds. leen el *Times*. 4. Carlos y Rosa escriben con una pluma roja. 5. Tú abres la puerta. 6. Las chicas viven en un apartamento. 7. Ud. come tacos. 8. Nosotros debemos estudiar hoy. 9. Susana decide tomar portugués.

Ejercicio C, página 64 *Answers will vary.*

Ejercicio D, página 65 *Answers will vary.*

Ejercicio A, página 66 *Answers will vary.*

Ejercicio B, página 66 1. Sí, (No, no) tengo tu número de teléfono. 2. Sí, (No, no) tengo tu dirección. 3. Sí, (No, no) tiene mi número de teléfono. 4. Venimos a la universidad por la noche (por la mañana). 5. Venimos a la clase de español a la(s)... 6. Sí, (No, no) vengo a la clase con mis amigos. 7. Sí, (No, no) vengo a clase los sábados. 8. Sí, (No, no) vienen a clase los domingos.

Ejercicio C, página 66 *Answers will vary. Possibilities*: 1. Silvia tiene que estudiar. 2. John tiene que hablar español. 3. Nosotros tenemos que trabajar. 4. Tengo que escribir con lápiz. 6. Tengo que llamar más tarde.

Ejercicio D, página 66 *Answers will vary.*

¡A ver cuánto aprendió!
¡Repase el vocabulario!, página 67 1. informe 2. biblioteca 3. comemos 4. debe / tiene 5. sentimentales / dinero 6. Llamo 7. morena / pelirroja 8. ella 9. realista 10. universitarios 11. varios 12. vives

Entrevista, página 67 *Answers will vary.*

Situaciones, página 67 *Answers will vary.*

Para escribir, página 68 *Answers will vary.*

En la vida real
¡Por teléfono!, página 68 *Answers will vary.*

Un mensaje telefónico, página 68 1. Carlos Vega 2. hospital El Samaritano 3. Jorge Ibarra 4. Hotel Plaza 5. 386–4127 6. Desea hablar con Ud. 7. diez y media / mañana / miércoles 8. las reservaciones del hotel para la convención

¡Vamos a leer!
Antes de leer, página 70 1. Javier es su novio. 2. Es muy inteligente y muy guapo. 3. Es baja, morena y muy linda. 4. Son estudiantes universitarios. 5. Viven en Phoenix. 6. Trabaja en la biblioteca. 7. No, solamente estudia.

8. Comen en la cafetería los lunes y miércoles. 9. Estudian en la casa de Aurora. 10. Porque mañana tienen un examen.

Díganos, página 70 *Answers will vary.*

Así somos
Preparación, Ejercicio A, página 71 *Answers will vary.*

Ejercicio B, página 71 *Answers will vary.*

Comprensión, Ejercicio A, página 71 1. b 2. e 3. d 4. a 5. c

Ejercicio B, página 71 1. F Yolanda es casada. 2. V 3. F Orlando no es casado.

Ejercicio C, página 71 1. alegre y sincero 2. serio y trabajador 3. guapa y alta

Ejercicio D, página 72 1. V 2. F Carolina tiene dos hermanos. 3. V 4. Tiene ojos marrones *(brown)* y pelo negro y largo.

Ejercicio E, página 72 1. Yurida Guzmán Robles 2. trabajo 3. vive 4. 813-04-37 5. Universidad Autónoma de Guadalajara

Ampliación, Ejercicio A, página 72 *Answers will vary.*

Ejercicio B, página 72 *Answers may vary, but should include:* ¿Cómo te llamas? ¿De dónde eres? ¿Qué estudias? ¿Tienes hermanos?; ¿cómo son? *or* ¿Cómo es tu familia? ¿Cuál es tu número de teléfono?

Lección 4 X diezpocho

¡Conversemos!, página 83 1. Va a dar una fiesta de fin de año. 2. Adela vive en la calle 18 de Julio. Vive en Montevideo. 3. La fiesta comienza a las 21 horas (a las nueve de la noche). 4. Muchos de sus compañeros de la universidad van a venir a la fiesta. 5. Humberto va a traer unos discos compactos y las empanadas. 6. La mamá de Humberto va a preparar las empanadas. 7. Adela y su familia van a preparar pollo, entremeses y ensalada de papas. Todo va a estar delicioso. 8. Humberto quiere comer un sándwich. Quiere beber un vaso de agua. 9. Julio y Teresa piensan ir al club con Humberto y Adela. 10. Teresa cumple veinte años. 11. Lo pasan muy bien. 12. Porque está un poco cansada y tiene mucho calor. 13. Quiere brindar con champán. 14. Comen doce uvas.

Ejercicio A, página 86 1. — / — 2. a / a / a 3. a / a 4. — 5. — / — 6. —

Ejercicio B, página 87 *Answers will vary.*

Ejercicio A, página 87 1. del / del 2. a las / A las 3. del / de la 4. al / a la 5. a los / A la / del

Ejercicio B, página 88   1. Los libros son del profesor.
2. El escritorio es de la Srta. Paz.   3. Llevo a los chicos.
4. Invitamos al Sr. Vega   5. Llaman a las muchachas.
6. Llevan a las muchachas al club.   7. Venimos del club.
8. No, los libros son de las muchachas.

Ejercicio A, página 89   1. Jorge tiene miedo.   2. Yo tengo
hambre.   3. Tú tienes sueño.   4. La profesora tiene prisa.
5. Ud. tiene frío.   6. Felipe tiene calor y tiene sed.
7. Marisa y Elena tienen calor.   8. Ella tiene cuatro años.

Ejercicio B, página 90   *Answers will vary.*

Ejercicio C, página 90   1. Tengo mucho calor (y tengo
sed).   2. Tengo miedo.   3. Tengo prisa.   4. Tengo mucho
frío.   5. Tengo mucha hambre.   6. Tengo mucho sueño.
7. Tengo mucho calor (y tengo sed).   8. Tengo treinta
años.

Ejercicio A, página 91   vas / da / voy / vas / dan / estoy /
estás / van / están / Están

Ejercicio B, página 91   *Answers will vary.*

Ejercicio C, página 91   *Answers will vary. Verbs:*
1. estamos   2. das   3. voy   4. están   5. da   6. vamos
7. está

Ejercicio D, página 92   *Answers will vary.*

Ejercicio A, página 92   *Answers will vary. Possibilities:*
1. Yo voy a leer en mi casa por la noche.   2. Los
estudiantes van a estar en la clase por la mañana.
3. Nosotros vamos a bailar en el club por la noche.
4. Tú vas a comer en la cafetería a las doce.   5. El profesor
va a enseñar en la universidad por la tarde.   6. Julio y
Teresa van a conversar en la terraza a las diez de la noche.
7. Susana va a estudiar en su casa por la mañana.   8. Uds.
van a pasarlo bien en la fiesta por la noche.

Ejercicio B, página 93   1. —¿Qué va a beber Roberto?
—Va a beber champán.   2. —¿A quién va a llamar Elisa?
—Va a llamar a Gustavo.   3. —¿Qué van a beber Julio y
Estrella? —Van a beber ponche.   4. —¿Qué va a celebrar
Daniel? —Va a celebrar su cumpleaños.   5. —¿Qué va a
traer Eduardo? —Va a traer cintas.   6. —¿Qué va a comer
Graciela? —Va a comer pollo.

Ejercicio C, página 94   *Answers will vary.*

Ejercicio A, página 95   1. prefieren / Preferimos
2. quieren / quiere / queremos   3. piensan / Pensamos
4. cierran / cierran   5. pierden / perdemos   6. empiezan /
empezamos / empieza

Ejercicio B, página 95   *Answers will vary.*

Ejercicio C, página 95   *Answers will vary.*

Ejercicio D, página 95   *Answers will vary.*

¡A ver cuánto aprendió!

Repase el vocabulario, página 96   1. De quién   2. fin /
uvas / medianoche   3. magnífica   4. canta   5. Adónde
6. nuevo   7. contenta   8. sed   9. cintas   10. cansado(-a)
11. Cuánto   12. árbol / pequeño   13. brindis
14. cumpleaños   15. ocupado(-a)   16. estereofónico

Entrevista, página 96   *Answers will vary.*

Situaciones, página 96   *Answers will vary.*

Para escribir, página 97   *Answers will vary.*

En la vida real
Una visita, página 97   *Answers will vary.*

Un espectáculo, página 98   1. El espectáculo se llama
"Holiday on Ice".   2. Presentan el espectáculo en el
Palacio de Deportes de Madrid.   3. Va a estar en Madrid
solamente hasta el 2 de agosto.   4. Va a Valladolid y
Bilbao.   5. Hay setenta artistas en el grupo.   5. No, son
de diversas nacionalidades.   7. Dedican el espectáculo a
México y a Rusia.   8. Es a las nueve y media de la noche.
8. Desde 500 a 1.400 pesetas por entrada.   10. Está en la
avenida Felipe II.

¡Damos una fiesta!, página 99   *Answers will vary.*

Teleinforme
Preparación, página 104   1. Madrid   2. Cervantes
3. arquitecto   4. Barcelona   5. setecientos   6. Córdoba,
Granada, Sevilla   7. Cervantes   8. islas   9. palacio,
árabes (moros)

Comprensión, Ejercicio A, página 104   1. F. Está en el
centro del país.   2. V   3. F. Hay un monumento a la diosa
romana Cibeles.   4. V   5. V

Ejercicio B, página 104   1. nuevo   2. apartamentos
3. mosaicos de vivos colores   4. ambiciosa   5. la Sagrada
Familia

Ejercicio C, página 104   1. sur   2. fortaleza militar
3. complicados   4. doce

Ampliación, Ejercicio A, página 105   *Answers will vary.*

Ejercicio B, página 105   *Answers will vary.*

Lección 5

¡Conversemos!, página 110   1. Es de los Estados Unidos y
ahora vive en Salamanca, España.   2. Estudia en la
Universidad de Salamanca.   3. Ahora está en un café al
aire libre y está hablando con dos amigos españoles.   4. Es
rubio, delgado y de estatura mediana.   5. Va a viajar a
México con su esposa y sus dos hijas.   6. Empiezan a
asistir a la escuela el quince de septiembre.   7. Porque es

tan cómodo como el coche, no cuesta mucho y no tienen que conducir (manejar). 8. Están en el Museo del Prado. 9. Comen en Casa Botín. 10. No, si llueve no va a ir. 11. Vuelven el sábado por la noche o el domingo. 12. La fiesta de Marisol es en su casa y es mañana.

¿Lo sabía Ud.?, página 110 *Answers will vary.*

Ejercicio A, página 113 1. más gordo que / mucho más delgado(-a) 2. menos inteligente 3. menos de cincuenta / más de setenta 4. tanto dinero como 5. tantos discos compactos como 6. tan alta como 7. tan bien como 8. tantas chicas (muchachas) como

Ejercicio B, página 114 1. más baja (más gorda) que 2. más alta (más delgada) que 3. más alto que 4. más alto que 5. más bajo (más delgado) que 6. más delgado (más bajo) que 7. más bajo 8. más alto

Ejercicio C, página 114 1. Michael Jordan es más alto que Danny de Vito. 2. Cuba es más pequeña que Canadá. 3. La clase de alemán es más difícil que la clase de español. 4. El coche es más (menos) cómodo que el ómnibus. 5. Argentina es más grande que Puerto Rico. 6. Antonio Banderas es más guapo que (tan guapo como) Jim Carrey.

Ejercicio A, página 115 1. Su sobrina es mayor. Su sobrino es menor. 2. Su tía es menor. Su tío es mayor. 3. El profesor (La profesora) habla mejor el español. 4. José es el peor estudiante. Pedro es el mejor estudiante.

Ejercicio B, página 115 *Answers will vary.*

Ejercicio C, página 115 *Answers will vary.*

Ejercicio A, página 116 *Answers will vary.*

Ejercicio B, página 116 MARITÉ: encuentro / puedo / almuerzo / cuestan / recuerdo / recuerdas / vuela / llueve / vuelvo TERESA: puedo MARITÉ: duermes

Ejercicio C, página 117 1. ¿Cuánto cuesta su (tu) equipo estereofónico? 2. ¿Dónde almuerzan Uds.? 3. ¿A qué hora vuelven Uds. a (su) casa? 4. ¿Duerme(s) mucho? 5. ¿Recuerda Ud. (Recuerdas) el número de teléfono de Ana? 6. ¿Cuándo vuela(s) a Los Ángeles? 7. ¿Puede(s) ir a mi casa esta noche?

Ejercicio D, página 117 *Answers will vary.*

Ejercicio A, página 118 1. Tú estás comiendo. 2. Yo estoy escribiendo. 3. Raúl y Sara están bailando. 4. Eva está sirviendo café. 5. La profesora está leyendo un libro. 6. Nosotros estamos hablando por teléfono y el chico está durmiendo.

Ejercicio B, página 119 1. estás comiendo / estoy comiendo 2. están leyendo / Estamos leyendo 3. están sirviendo / estoy sirviendo / está sirviendo 4. está diciendo / está diciendo 5. está estudiando / está durmiendo

Ejercicio C, página 119 *Answers will vary.*

Ejercicio, página 120 *Answers will vary.*

Ejercicio A, página 120 *Answers will vary.*

Ejercicio B, página 121 1. es / Es / está / es / es 2. es / es / es / Es / Es / está / Está 3. es / Son / es / es / estoy 4. estás / Estoy / Está / está 5. es / es / Es / es 6. es / es

Ejercicio C, página 122 *Answers will vary.*

Ejercicio A, página 122 1. conmigo / contigo con ella 2. Para él / para ella / para mí / Para ti / para Uds. / para ellas

Ejercicio B, página 123 *Answers will vary.*

¡A ver cuánto aprendió!

¡Repase el vocabulario!, página 123 1. j 2. d 3. m 4. h 5. n 6. o 7. k 8. b 9. f 10. l 11. c 12. e 13. i 14. g 15. a

Entrevista, página 123 *Answers will vary.*

Situaciones, página 124 *Answers will vary.*

Para escribir, página 124 *Answers will vary.*

En la vida real

Objetivos, página 125 *Answers will vary.*

Árbol geneológico, página 125 *Answers will vary.*

¿Quieres ver mis fotos?, página 125 *Answers will vary.*

¿A qué museo vamos?, página 126 1. Está en la avenida de Herrera Oria. 2. No, no podemos ir al Museo de Arte Contemporáneo el lunes porque está cerrado. 3. Cuesta 450 pesetas. 4. Los estudiantes no pagan nada. 5. Debemos tomar el metro Atocha. 6. Sí, podemos ir en el autobús número 27. 7. El Museo del Prado es antiguo. 8. La entrada al Museo de Arte Contemporáneo es más barata. 9. No, encontramos pinturas de las escuelas italianas, flamencas y holandesas, entre otras. 10. No es necesario pagar los sábados en el Museo del Prado.

¡Vamos a leer!

Antes de leer, página 126 1. El apellido de Ana María es Estévez. 2. Ella es de Chile. 3. Su familia está en Miami. 4. Está estudiando matemáticas, historia del arte, inglés y sociología. 5. Porque no habla muy bien el inglés. 6. Sí, trabaja en el laboratorio de lenguas. 7. Sí, creo que va mucho a la playa porque le gusta mucho. 8. Piensa ir con unos amigos cubanos. 9. Va a estar en Miami unos cuatro años. 10. Algún día. Porque echa mucho de menos a su familia.

Díganos, página 127 *Answers will vary.*

Así somos

Preparación, Ejercicio A, página 128   *Answers will vary.*

Ejercicio B, página 128   *Answers will vary.*

Comprensión, Ejercicio A, página 128   1. V   2. V   3. V
4. V   5. F, Tamara tiene dos hermanas.

Ejercicio B, página 129   1. a comer   2. de vez en cuando
3. su familia   4. sus niños

Ejercicio C, página 129   1. e   2. d   3. c   4. g   5. a, b
6. f   7. e, f

Ampliación, Ejercicio A, página 129   *Answers will vary.*

Ejercicio B, página 129   *Answers will vary.*

Lección 6

¡Conversemos!, página 134   1. Las ruinas de Machu
Picchu   2. Muestra su pasaporte y pasa por la aduana.
3. Compra algunos objetos de oro y plata para su familia.
4. Va para conseguir información.   5. Lee un anuncio del
Hotel Bolívar.   6. Está situado en el centro de la ciudad.
7. Tienen baño privado, aire acondicionado y televisor.
8. Aceptan tarjetas de crédito y cheques de viajero.
9. Pide una habitación sencilla.   10. Prefiere el cuarto
interior porque es más barato.   11. La sirven hasta las
once.   12. Decide ir a la piscina porque hace calor.

¿Lo sabía Ud.?, página 135   *Answers will vary.*

Ejercicio A, página 137   *Answers will vary.*

Ejercicio B, página 138   1. dices / digo / dice   2. sirven /
Servimos / sirves / sirvo   3. piden / pido / pide
4. consigo / consigues

Ejercicio C, página 138   *Answers will vary.*

Ejercicio A, página 139   1. Raquel nunca viaja en el
verano.   2. Ana no va con Raquel y Jorge no va con ella
tampoco.   3. Nunca piden habitaciones dobles.   4. Nunca
compran nada cuando viajan.   5. Nunca compran ningún
objeto de oro.   6. No cenan ni en la pensión ni en una
cafetería.   7. Nunca hay nadie en su casa.   8. El esposo
de Luisa siempre habla con alguien.   9. Carlos siempre
averigua algo.   10. Elsa nunca pide información.

Ejercicio B, página 140   1. No quiero viajar ni a Bolivia ni
a Perú.   2. No tengo ningún amigo en Perú.   3. No hablo
portugués tampoco.   4. Nunca viajo en invierno.
5. Nunca viajo con nadie.   6. No compro nada cuando
voy de vacaciones.

Ejercicio C, página 140   *Answers will vary.*

Ejercicio A, página 141   *Answers will vary.*

Ejercicio B, página 141   Yo salgo para Bolivia esta noche.
Voy con mi amiga Susana. Conduzco al banco para
comprar cheques de viajero, regreso a mi casa, pongo todos
los documentos en mi bolso de mano y después hago las
maletas. Como sé que hay mucho tráfico, salgo de mi casa
temprano para ir al aeropuerto. Cuando llego al
aeropuerto, veo que Susana está allí.

Ejercicio A, página 141   1. conozco / sabes / sé
2. conoces / sé   3. conoces / sé   4. Sabes   5. sabe

Ejercicio B, página 142   *Answers will vary.*

Ejercicio A, página 143   te / la / la / la / los / nos / los / las

Ejercicio B, página 144   1. Yo los llamo.   2. Yo las
compro.   3. Yo los voy a traer (voy a traerlos).   4. Yo lo
consigo.   5. Yo la traigo.   6. Yo los preparo.   7. Yo lo
voy a traer (voy a traerlo).   8. Yo las llevo.

Ejercicio C, página 144   1. Sí, (No, no) me van a llamar
esta noche. / Sí, (No, no) van a llamarme esta noche.   2. Sí
(No, no) las tenemos.   3. Sí, (No, no) los voy a comprar. /
Sí, (No, no) voy a comprarlos.   4. Sí, (No, no) la tengo.
5. Sí, (No, no) la llevo.   6. Sí, (No, no) las vamos a
visitar. / Sí, (No, no) vamos a visitarlas.   7. *(Nombre)* nos
va a llevar. / *(Nombre)* va a llevarnos.   8. Sí, (No, no) te
llevamos.

Ejercicio A, página 145   1. llueve   2. no hace frío (hace
calor)   3. llovizna   4. no hace frío (hace calor)   5. hace
sol   6. hace mucho frío   7. nieva   8. paraguas /
impermeable

Ejercicio B, página 146   1. Hace frío. Llueve (Nieva).
2. Hace mucho frío. Nieva.   3. Hace mucho calor. Hace
sol.   4. Hace frío. Hay niebla.   5. Hace mucho viento.

Ejercicio C, página 146   *Answers will vary.*

Ejercicio D, página 146   *Answers will vary.*

¡A ver cuánto aprendió!

¡Repase el vocabulario!, página 146   1. c   2. b   3. b
4. c   5. a   6. c   7. b   8. c   9. a   10. c   11. b
12. a   13. b   14. c   15. b   16. b

Entrevista, página 147   *Answers will vary.*

Situaciones, página 148   *Answers will vary.*

¿Qué pasa aquí?, página 148   *Answers will vary.*

Para escribir, página 149   *Answers will vary.*

En la vida real

Discusión, página 149   *Answers will vary.*

¿Dónde hospedarse?, página 150   1. La familia Salcedo se
va a hospedar en el Hotel Aloha Puerto Sol porque son
muchas personas y tienen poco dinero.   2. Gustavo y

Carolina se van a hospedar en el Hotel Atlanterra Sol porque tienen mucho dinero y ahí hay espectáculos y una discoteca donde pueden bailar. 3. Teresa, Raquel y Rebeca se van a hospedar en el Hotel Atlanterra Sol porque hay una discoteca y una cancha de tenis.

De viaje, página 150 *Answers will vary.*

Teleinforme

Preparación, página 162 1. El fútbol, el ciclismo y el baloncesto 2. Son pequeñas porciones de diferentes comidas; se sirven en los bares por la tarde. 3. La Semana Santa 4. La paella 5. El flamenco 6. La corrida de toros

Comprensión, Ejercicio A, página 162 1. V 2. F, Está en Segovia 3. V 4. V 5. F, Está cerca de Madrid

Ejercicio B, página 162 1. Andalucía 2. La Giralda 3. La Torre del Oro 4. El Alcázar 5. La Exposición Iberoamericana 6. los gitanos

Ampliación, Ejercicio A, página 163 *Answers will vary.*

Ejercicio B, página 163 *Answers will vary.*

Lección 7

¡Conversemos!, página 167 1. No, hace media hora que hablan por teléfono. 2. Le está contando de su viaje a Perú. 3. Le gustó más Machu Picchu. 4. Le prestó una maleta y un bolso de mano. 5. Sí, pagó exceso de equipaje porque llevó tres maletas. 6. Le costó 3.500 pesos. 7. Viajó a Cuzco en avión. 8. Salió con dos horas de retraso. 9. Son magníficas. 10. Van a viajar en tren. 11. Teresa va al cine con Cecilia y Silvia. 12. Silvia ya almorzó.

¿Lo sabía Ud.?, página 168 *Answers will vary.*

Ejercicio A, página 171 1. estas / este / estos 2. esa / esos / esas 3. aquel / aquellas / aquellos

Ejercicio B, página 171 1. aquél 2. ésos 3. aquélla 4. ésas 5. éstas 6. éste

Ejercicio C, página 171 *Answers will vary.*

Ejercicio A, página 173 1. Nos 2. Les 3. Le 4. Le 5. Les 6. Le 7. Te 8. Le 9. Les 10. Me

Ejercicio B, página 173 1. Le / me / te 2. Les / les 3. le / le 4. nos / Les / le

Ejercicio C, página 173 *Answers will vary.*

Ejercicio D, página 174 1. Sí, les estoy escribiendo. 2. Les estoy diciendo que... 3. Les voy a llevar... 4. Sí, (No, no) me va a dar su cámara. 5. Sí, (No, no) les voy a escribir... 6. Sí, (No, no) te voy a dejar la llave de mi casa. 7. Les voy a traer... 8. Te voy a traer...

Ejercicio E, página 174 *Answers will vary.*

Ejercicio A, página 175 1. A mí me gustan más las ciudades grandes. 2. ¿A ti te gusta más el bolso de mano azul? 3. A nosotros nos gusta más viajar en barco. 4. A Marcelo le gustan más los hoteles pequeños. 5. A ellos les gusta más pasar las vacaciones en México. 6. ¿A usted le gusta más viajar en tren o en avión? 7. A Adela le gustan más los asientos de ventanilla. 8. A ustedes les gusta más la comida italiana.

Ejercicio B, página 176 *Answers will vary.*

Ejercicio C, página 176 *Answers will vary.*

Ejercicio D, página 176 *Answers will vary.*

Ejercicio E, página 176 *Answers will vary.*

Ejercicio A, página 177 1. Hace veinte minutos que Alfredo y Marta bailan. 2. Hace tres años que Eva vive en la calle Lima. 3. Hace una hora que Ana, Luis y Paco conversan. 4. Hace dos horas que José estudia. 5. Hace siete horas que Jorge duerme. 6. Hace quince días que Pablo está en el hospital.

Ejercicio B, página 177 *Answers will vary.*

Ejercicio C, página 178 *Answers will vary.*

Ejercicio A, página 179 1. hablaste / hablé / llamé / charlamos 2. volvieron / volví / volvió / volviste 3. Recibiste / mandé / recibí 4. llegó / Llegué / comencé 5. Cerraron / cerramos / abrimos

Ejercicio B, página 179 *Answers will vary.*

Ejercicio C, página 180 *Answers will vary.*

¡A ver cuánto aprendió!

¡Repase el vocabulario!, página 180 1. sección 2. salida 3. devolver 4. asiento 5. embarque / auxiliar 6. avión (vuelo) 7. juntas / todo 8. tal / poco 9. retraso (atraso) 10. loco 11. buen 12. vuelta 13. tarjeta 14. equipaje 15. presentar

Entrevista, página 180 *Answers will vary.*

Situaciones, página 181 *Answers will vary.*

Para escribir, página 181 *Answers will vary.*

En la vida real

En una agencia de viajes, página 182 *Answers will vary.*

Planes para un viaje, página 182 1. Van a viajar a la República Dominicana. 2. Viajan en clase turista.

3. Van a estar en el Hotel Bávaro Casino.   4. Tienen que pagar 137.500 pesetas. Por dos semanas, tienen que pagar 165.000 pesetas.   5. Sí, lo incluye.   6. Salen de Madrid. 7. Salen todos los jueves y viernes.

¿Adónde vamos?, página 183   *Answers will vary.*

¡Vamos a leer!

Antes de leer, página 183   1. Sí, son buenas amigas. Lo sé porque Teresa siempre piensa en Ángela.   2. No, ya está de vuelta de su viaje a Perú.   3. Dice que le gustaron mucho y que son muy interesantes.   4. No le mandó tarjetas postales a nadie.   5. Se llama José Luis Vera Vierci. Es de Buenos Aires.   6. Conversaron de todo tema imaginable. 7. Dice que son encantadores.   8. La llevaron a muchos lugares, especialmente al teatro, al cine y a restaurantes. 9. Le recomienda una visita a Perú.   10. Va a ir a cenar con sus padres, porque hoy es el cumpleaños de su papá.

Díganos, página 184   *Answers will vary.*

Así somos

Preparación, Ejercicio A, página 184   *Answers will vary.*

Ejercicio B, página 185   *Answers will vary.*

Comprensión, Ejercicio A, página 185   1. V   2. F, Juan piensa que viajar es muy interesante.   3. V   4. F, A Gustavo le gusta mucho viajar.   5. F, A Ángela le gusta viajar bastante.

Ejercicio B, página 185   1. Europa   2. Estados Unidos 3. conoce   4. no conoce

Ejercicio C, página 185   1. d   2. b   3. c   4. a

Ejercicio D, página 185   1. V   2. V   3. F, Su casa está en Caracas.   4. F, Pasó sus vacaciones con su familia.

Ejercicio E, página 185   1. piloto (aviador profesional) 2. mexicano   3. viajar mucho   4. Estados Unidos, México, Costa Rica, Cuba   5. sí   6. no

Ampliación, Ejercicio A, página 186   *Answers will vary.*

Ejercicio B, página 186   *Answers will vary.*

Lección 8

¡Conversemos!, página 191   1. Es el primero de diciembre. 2. Lidia dice que es muy elegante y Jorge dice que es excelente.   3. La especialidad de la casa es lechón asado y arroz con frijoles negros.   4. Lidia pide sopa, camarones y arroz y Jorge pide lechón asado y arroz con frijoles negros. 5. Beben primero un vermut y después media botella de vino tinto.   6. Fueron a la fiesta que dio Eva. 7. Compraron una pulsera.   8. Se la enseñaron anteayer. 9. Sí, la consiguieron a muy buen precio.   10. Deja una buena propina.   11. Dicen—Feliz aniversario.   12. Porque llueve a cántaros y el teatro queda lejos.

¿Lo sabía Ud.?, página 192   *Answers will vary.*

Ejercicio A, página 195   1. se la   2. te las   3. me lo 4. se la   5. se los   6. -nosla

Ejercicio B, página 195   1. Mi amigo me las compra. 2. Mi amigo te los trae.   3. Mi amigo nos las sirve. 4. Mi amigo se lo presta.   5. Mi amigo se lo da.   6. Mi amigo se las trae.   7. Mi amigo se la envía.   8. Mi amigo me los da.

Ejercicio C, página 195   1. No, no puedo traértelas. 2. No, no puedo dárselo.   3. No, no puedo comprárselo. 4. No, no puedo prestártelos.   5. No, no puedo traérselo. 5. No, no puedo dárselas.

Ejercicio D, página 195   1. No, no te las puedo traer. 2. No, no se lo puedo dar.   3. No, no se lo puedo comprar. 4. No, no te los puedo prestar.   5. No, no se lo puedo traer.   6. No, no se las puedo dar.

Ejercicio E, página 196   *Answers will vary.*

Ejercicio A, página 196   1. fuiste / Fui / di   2. Fueron / fuimos / dimos   3. fueron / fue / fuimos   4. diste / di 5. fueron / Fuimos / dieron

Ejercicio B, página 197   *Answers will vary.*

Ejercicio A, página 198   1. fui / pedí   2. Conseguí 3. Salí / mentí   4. fuimos / pedí / pidió   5. volví / dormí 6. invitaron / preferí   7. di / serví

Ejercicio B, página 198   *Answers will vary.*

Ejercicio, página 199   *Answers will vary.*

Ejercicio A, página 200   1. por tren   2. por la ventana 3. para Ana   4. por dos meses   5. treinta y cinco dólares por   6. por la mañana

Ejercicio B, página 200   *Answers will vary.*

Ejercicio C, página 200   para / por / para / por / por / por / por / por / por / para / para / por / por

Ejercicio D, página 201   *Answers will vary.*

Ejercicio A, página 201   1. cuarto   2. décimo 3. primero   4. séptimo   5. segundo   6. octavo 7. tercero   8. noveno   9. quinto   10. sexto

Ejercicio B, página 201   *Answers will vary.*

¡A ver cuánto aprendió!

¡Repase el vocabulario!, página 202   1. n   2. i   3. d
4. p   5. a   6. k   7. c   8. o   9. m   10. e   11. b
12. h   13. f   14. j   15. l   16. g

Entrevista, página 202   *Answers will vary.*

Situaciones, página 203   *Answers will vary.*

Para escribir, página 203   *Answers will vary.*

En la vida real

¿Qué les servimos?, página 203   *Answers will vary.*

¡Vamos a cenar!, página 204   *Answers will vary.*

¡Buen provecho!, página 204   1. Podemos ir a Las Redes.
2. Debemos llamar al 825–2607.   3. La especialidad es
"Langosta Florida a Las Redes".   4. Es famoso por el
bistec cubano con papas fritas.   5. Hay música los fines de
semana.   6. Cuesta desde $3.95.   7. Sirven bistec
carretero con mojo criollo, lechón asado con yuca, costillas
BBQ con su salsa especial y masitas de puerco con frijoles o
moros.   8. Debemos ir a El Bodegón Castilla.   9. Está en
la calle 8 y la avenida 25.   10. Sirven comida española.

Teleinforme

Preparación, página 211   1. La Ciudad de México   2. La
Ciudad de México (México-Tenochtitlán)   3. 23
4. Cancún, Acapulco, Puerto Vallarta, Ixtapa y Mazatlán
5. De Jalisco   6. Es española colonial y moderna.   7. El
primero y el dos de noviembre.   8. Las personas llevan
comida a las tumbas de sus familiares y se quedan allí toda
la noche.

Comprensión, Ejercicio A, página 211   1. V   2. F, Sí, hay
metro.   3. V   4. F, Es distinto por el cambio de altitud.
5. V

Ejercicio B, página 211   1. 1542   2. menor   3. Jalisco
4. torres

Ejercicio C, página 211   1. maya   2. la península de
Yucatán   3. ciudad   4. la ingeniería

Ampliación, Ejercicio A, página 212   *Answers will vary.*

Ejercicio B, página 212   *Answers will vary.*

Lección 9

¡Conversemos!, página 216   1. Se levantaron temprano
para terminar de limpiar el apartamento.   2. Van a ir a un
concierto.   3. Mirta le va a pasar la aspiradora a la
alfombra.   4. Va a planchar su vestido rojo para ponérselo
esta noche.   5. Eva celebra su cumpleaños mañana.
6. No, no sabe qué ponerse.   7. No se pone el vestido azul

porque no le queda bien.   8. Tiene que bañar al perro,
ducharse y vestirse.   9. No quiere una permanente porque,
cuando ella quiere rizos, usa el rizador.   10. Dejó la
cartera en el mostrador.   11. Le pregunta si la cartera es
suya.   12. Es mejor ir por la mañana porque hay menos
gente.

¿Lo sabía Ud.?, página 217   *Answers will vary.*

Ejercicio A, página 221   1. se despierta   2. me levanto
3. se afeita   4. nos bañamos   5. se lava   6. se visten
7. me desvisto / me acuesto   8. se preocupa

Ejercicio B, página 222   1. duerme   2. se duermen
3. quita   4. se quita   5. levanto / mano   6. me levanto
7. pone / plato / mesa   8. se pone / vestido   9. llama
10. se llama / Paz

Ejercicio C, página 223   *Answers will vary.*

Ejercicio D, página 224   *Answers will vary. Possibilities:*
1. me levanto   2. se lava la cabeza   3. vistes   4. se lo
prueba   5. nos ponemos un abrigo   6. se peina   7. se
afeita   8. se preocupan   9. se duermen   10. se acuestan

Ejercicio A, página 225   *Answers will vary.*

Ejercicio B, página 225   1. la señorita / la señora / el
vestido   2. las manos / me las lavé   3. Las mujeres / los
hombres / Las mujeres   4. la escuela / la cárcel   5. la
doctora / la educación

Ejercicio A, página 227   1. suya (de él)   2. nuestras
3. tuyo   4. suyas (de ella)   5. mías   6. suyo (de Ud.)
7. suyos (de ellas)   8. suya (de él)

Ejercicio B, página 227   1. las tuyas / Las mías / las suyas
2. las suyas / las mías / las tuyas   3. los suyos / Los míos

Ejercicio C, página 227   *Answers will vary.*   1. Los míos
son de...   2. El mío tiene...   3. Los míos viven...   4. El
mío es en...   5. Las mías son...   6. La mía es...   7. El mío
es...   8. Las mías son...

Ejercicio A, página 229   estuviste / Viniste / dije / Estuve /
Tuve / pude / pudiste / quisiste / pusiste / traduje / trajiste /
trajeron / vinieron / dijeron

Ejercicio B, página 229   *Answers will vary.*

Ejercicio C, página 229   *Answers will vary.*   1. Ayer yo
estuve...   2. Ayer tú viniste...   3. Ayer Paquito hizo...
4. Ayer Julio tuvo... etc.

Ejercicio D, página 229   *Answers will vary.*

Ejercicio A, página 230   1. fácilmente   2. felizmente
3. claramente   4. raramente   5. necesariamente
6. frecuentemente   7. tristemente   8. trágicamente
9. alegremente   10. desgraciadamente

Ejercicio B, página 230   *Answers will vary.*

Ejercicio C, página 230   *Answers will vary.*

Ejercicio D, página 230   *Answers will vary.*

¡A ver cuánto aprendió!

¡Repase el vocabulario!, página 231   1. ilógico   2. ilógica
3. lógica   4. lógica   5. ilógica   6. ilógica   7. ilógica
8. lógica   9. lógica   10. ilógica   11. ilógica   12. lógica
13. lógica   14. ilógica   15. lógica

Entrevista, página 231   *Answers will vary.*

Situaciones, página 231   *Answers will vary.*

Para escribir, página 232   *Answers will vary.*

En la vida real

¡Vamos a la peluquería!, página 232   1. Es treinta y cinco
dólares.   2. Puedo ir al salón de belleza La Época.
3. No, porque la peluquería Anabel no es para hombres.
4. Puede ir al salón de belleza La Época, porque tiene
barberos.   5. Es importante tenerlo para recibir un diez
por ciento de descuento.   6. Hay que pagar $23.
7. Debe ir el martes porque hay precios especiales para
mayores de 50 años.   8. Debe llamar al 287–2308.   9. La
especialidad es permanentes.   10. La dirección es avenida
Paz, número 28.

Una visita importante, página 233   *Answers will vary.*

¿Qué es?, página 233   *Answers will vary.*

¡Vamos a leer!

Antes de leer, Ejercicio A, página 234   *Answers will vary.*

Ejercicio B, página 234   1. La liebre se burla de la tortuga
porque la tortuga es muy lenta.   2. La desafía a tener una
carrera.   3. La liebre dice que la tortuga no puede ganar la
carrera.   4. Nombran juez al zorro.   5. Durante la
carrera, la liebre tomó una siesta mientras la tortuga sigue
caminando lentamente.   6. La tortuga gana la carrera.
7. La moraleja es, *Con perseverancia se gana a veces la
carrera.*

Díganos, página 235   *Answers will vary.*

Así somos

Preparación, Ejercicio A, página 235   *Answers will vary.*

Ejercicio B, página 235   *Answers will vary.*

Comprensión, Ejercicio A, página 236   1. V   2. F, Pedro
come en casa con su familia.   3. V   4. F, Se levanta
temprano, a las seis o a las siete de la mañana.   5. F, Tiene
clases desde las siete hasta las cuatro.   6. V   7. V   8. V
9. F, Sale antes de cenar.   10. F, Tiene hijos.   11. V
12. F, Llega a las ocho y diez.

Ejercicio B, página 236   1. c   2. e   3. a   4. b   5. d

Ampliación, Ejercicio A, página 236   *Answers will vary.*

Ejercicio B, página 236   *Answers will vary.*

Lección 10

¡Conversemos!, página 247   1. Silvia fue de vacaciones
con sus padres. Sí, se está divirtiendo mucho.   2. Hace una
semana que llegaron.   3. Fueron a acampar junto al río de
los Sauces.   4. El papá y el hermano de Silvia armaron las
tiendas de campaña. Todos durmieron en sus bolsas (sacos)
de dormir. Durmieron profundamente.   5. Fue de pesca
con Miguel Ángel. No, no pescó nada.   6. Fue a la fiesta
porque su papá la convenció.   7. Allí conoció a Gustavo,
un muchacho de Santiago.   8. Silvia bailó toda la noche
con Gustavo.   9. Los hoteles en Buenos Aires son caros.
Silvia dice que cuestan un ojo de la cara.   10. Planea ir a
Bariloche con su familia.   11. Iban a Bariloche.   12. Su
mamá le dijo que Gustavo la estaba esperando.   13. Silvia
y Gustavo van a planear otra fiesta.   14. Silvia aprendió a
apreciar la naturaleza, el campo y a los muchachos
chilenos.

¿Lo sabía Ud.?, página 248   *Answers will vary.*

Ejercicio A, página 250   1. Hace tres horas que armamos
la tienda de campaña. (Armamos la tienda de campaña
hace tres horas.)   2. Hace cuatro meses que ellos fueron a
esquiar. (Ellos fueron a esquiar hace cuatro meses.)
3. Hace cuatro días que tú montaste a caballo. (Tú
montaste a caballo hace cuatro días.)   4. Hace quince
minutos que empecé a nadar. (Empecé a nadar hace quince
minutos.)   5. Hace quince días que yo alquilé la cabaña.
(Yo alquilé la cabaña hace quince días.)   6. Hace ___ años
que Carlos compró el saco de dormir. (Carlos compró el
saco de dormir hace ___ años.)

Ejercicio B, página 250   *Answers will vary.*

Ejercicio A, página 251   Mi familia y yo vivíamos en
Buenos Aires. Mi padre trabajaba para la compañía
Sandoval y mi madre enseñaba en la universidad. Era una
profesora excelente. Mis hermanos y yo asistíamos a la
escuela. Generalmente pasábamos las vacaciones en Mar
del Plata. Allí nadábamos, pescábamos y tomábamos el sol.
Como a mi padre le gustaba ir a las montañas para esquiar,
en invierno íbamos a Bariloche. Mis abuelos vivían en
Rosario y no los veíamos mucho, pero siempre les
escribíamos.

Ejercicio B, página 252   *Answers will vary.*

Ejercicio C, página 252   *Answers will vary.*

Ejercicio D, página 252   *Answers will vary.*

Ejercicio A, página 254 *(Preterit)* 1. Yo fui al lago el año pasado. 2. Yo estuve enfermo(-a) todo el día. *(Imperfect)* 1. Yo iba al lago cuando vi a Mary. 2. Yo siempre estaba enfermo(-a). 3. Yo tenía frío. Ellos estaban muy contentos aquí. 4. Él dijo que quería una bolsa (un saco) de dormir. 5. Eran las seis de la mañana. 6. Mi sobrina tenía cinco años. 7. Mi novio era alto y guapo.

Ejercicio B, página 254 1. tenías / viniste / Tenía 2. dijo / dijo / necesitaba 3. hacía / salieron / Hacía / nevaba 4. iban / eran / íbamos / decidieron / fueron 5. era / llegaste / Eran / Fuiste / fui / íbamos / vimos / Murió / murió

Ejercicio C, página 254 ¿Dónde naciste? / ¿Cuántos años tenías cuando ustedes fueron a vivir a Madrid? / ¿Cómo eras tú cuando eras niña? / ¿Tenías un perro? / ¿Qué te gustaba hacer cuando eras niña? / ¿Dónde estudiaste? / ¿En qué año empezaste a trabajar en televisión? / ¿En qué año viniste a Buenos Aires? / ¿Estuviste en París el año pasado? / ¿Cuánto tiempo estuviste en París? / ¿Piensas volver a España?

Ejercicio D, página 255 *Answers will vary.*

Ejercicio E, página 255 *Answers will vary.*

Ejercicio A, página 256 *Answers will vary.*

Ejercicio B, página 257 sabías / supe / quisieron / conoció / quería / conocía

¡A ver cuánto aprendió!

¡Repase el vocabulario!, página 257 1. Ilógico. El señor se hospedó en el hotel. 2. Lógico. 3. Lógico. 4. Ilógico. Es muy caro; cuesta un ojo de la cara. 5. Ilógico. Alquilé una cabaña. 6. Ilógico. Van a escalar la montaña. 7. Lógico. 8. Ilógico. Jugamos al tenis en el club. 9. Lógico. 10. Ilógico. Está en la playa tomando el sol. 11. Ilógico. Viven en Nueva York porque les gusta el este de los Estados Unidos. 12. Ilógico. Voy a comprar una bicicleta para montar en bicicleta. 13. Lógico. 14. Ilógico. Voy a poner los sándwiches en la mochila. 15. Ilógico. Durmió muy bien; durmió profundamente toda la noche. 16. Lógico.

Entrevista, página 257 *Answers will vary.*

Situaciones, página 258 *Answers will vary.*

¿Qué pasa aquí?, página 258 *Answers will vary.*

Para escribir, página 258 *Answers will vary.*

En la vida real

Nuestras vacaciones, página 259 *Answers will vary.*

Viajes a México, página 259 1. Son fabulosas. 2. Son para viajeros sofisticados y exigentes, amantes del sol, el mar y la buena vida. 3. Salieron el jueves y estuvieron tres noches en Ixtapa. 4. Pagaron $16.300.00 cada una. 5. Recibieron membrecía por un año en el Club Mediterranée y seguro de vida contra accidentes por $1.000.000.00 durante el transporte aéreo. 6. Les costó $25.800.00 cada uno.

El viaje de fin de curso, página 260 *Answers will vary.*

Teleinforme

Preparación, página 265 1. El canal de Panamá 2. Costa Rica tiene el más alto nivel de educación de Centroamérica. 3. "La Suiza de América" por su tradición pacifista. 4. En Panamá, Costa Rica, El Salvador, Honduras, Nicaragua y Guatemala 5. la naturaleza y la ecología

Comprensión, Ejercicio A, página 265 1. V 2. V 3. F, Está en la costa del Pacífico. 4. F, Sí, es moderna. 5. V 6. V

Ejercicio B, página 265 1. fincas 2. madera 3. ruedas 4. muchos

Ejercicio C, página 265 1. una flor 2. 800 3. 150 4. inglés 5. la Universidad 6. la naturaleza

Ampliación, Ejercicio A, página 266 *Answers will vary.*

Ejercicio B, página 266 *Answers will vary.*

Lección II

¡Conversemos!, página 270 1. Quiere quedarse en la cama hasta tarde porque está muy cansado. 2. Sergio tiene que levantarse. 3. Tiene que hacer varias diligencias. 4. Estaban en la tintorería. 5. Originalmente eran blancos. Ahora son rosados. 6. Va al departamento de fotografía. 7. Son en colores. 8. No puede sacar doscientos dólares de su cuenta de ahorros porque no tiene suficiente dinero. 9. Es veinte dólares. 10. Porque alguien le robó la motocicleta. 11. Sergio no tiene hermanos. Dice que es hijo único. 12. Piensa que el próximo martes trece no sale de casa.

¿Lo sabía Ud.?, página 271 *Answers will vary.*

Ejercicio, página 273 1. solicite / reciba / traiga / diga / camine / coma / vea 2. escribas / cobres / decidas / regreses / vengas / barras / aparques 3. grite / haga / mande / salga / anote / espere 4. cocinemos / depositemos / leamos / pongamos / paguemos 5. caminen / deban / roben / conozcan / vendan / salgan / empiecen

Ejercicio, página 274 1. duerma / mienta / recomiende / dé / piense / vaya 2. vuelvas / estés / seas / prefieras / recuerdes / mueras / veas / pidas 3. cierre / sepa / pierda / pruebe / dé / sirva / siga 4. sintamos / vayamos / demos / durmamos / perdamos / cerremos / sepamos / seamos 5. estén / sean / recuerden / sepan / encuentren / repitan

Ejercicio A, página 276   1. Yo les sugiero que compren un coche.   2. Yo te sugiero que te pruebes el vestido en tu cuarto.   3. Yo le sugiero que abra una cuenta de ahorros.   4. Yo les sugiero que vayan mañana.   5. Yo le sugiero que dé una fiesta el sábado.   6. Yo le sugiero que sea profesor de inglés.   7. Yo les sugiero que vengan el lunes.   8. Yo les sugiero que vayan en auto.   9. Yo le sugiero que pague la cuenta el mes próximo.   10. Yo les sugiero que hagan ensalada.

Ejercicio B, página 277   1. La abuelita de Tito quiere que él lleve los pantalones a la tintorería.   2. El papá de Julia quiere que ella deposite $300.   3. La tía de Beto quiere que él vaya al banco.   4. El profesor quiere que los estudiantes estén en clase a la una.   5. La mamá de Hugo quiere que él se acueste temprano.

Ejercicio C, página 278   *Answers will vary.*

Ejercicio D, página 278   *Answers will vary. The sentences expressing volition:* 1. Yo quiero que tú lleves los pantalones a la tintorería.   2. Yo quiero que tú lleves a revelar el rollo de película.   3. Yo quiero que tú deposites el cheque en el banco.   4. Yo quiero que tú lleves la motocicleta al taller de mecánica.   5. Yo quiero que tú compres las bebidas para la fiesta.   6. Yo quiero que tú lleves los discos compactos a casa de Ana.   7. Yo quiero que tú alquiles un video.   8. Yo quiero que tú compres los billetes para la excursión.   9. Yo quiero que tú recojas las entradas para el concierto.   10. Yo quiero que tú le pidas prestada la grabadora a Rosita.   11. Yo quiero que tú vayas a la oficina de turismo para pedir la lista de hoteles.   12. Yo quiero que tú compres el regalo para Eva.   13. Yo quiero que tú le devuelvas las maletas a Luis.

Ejercicio E, página 279   *Answers will vary.*

Ejercicio F, página 279   *Answers will vary.*

Ejercicio A, página 280   1. Siento que tengas que quedarte en casa.   2. Siento que tu hermano y tú no se sientan bien.   3. Me alegro de que tu mamá esté mejor.   4. Me alegro de que tu hijo sea muy inteligente.   5. Me alegro de que tu hermana sepa cocinar muy bien.   6. Siento que no haya suficiente dinero en tu cuenta corriente.   7. Me alegro de que tus padres vayan a Buenos Aires.   8. Siento que tus profesores te den muchos problemas.

Ejercicio B, página 281   *Answers will vary.*

Ejercicio C, página 281   *Answers will vary.*

¡A ver cuánto aprendió!
¡Repase el vocabulario!, página 281   1. ropa   2. cobran / revelar   3. sacar / depositar   4. comprobante   5. Pobre   6. modo   7. rato   8. hacia   9. contado   10. talonario / efectivo   11. ahorrar   12. ahorros   13. cajero   14. despertador   15. parecen   16. libre

Entrevista, página 282   *Answers will vary.*

Situaciones, página 282   *Answers will vary.*

Para escribir, página 282   *Answers will vary.*

En la vida real
Mis diligencias, página 283   *Answers will vary.*

¿Qué dice tu horóscopo?, página 283   *Answers will vary.*

Tenemos algunas quejas..., página 284   *Answers will vary.*

¡Vamos a leer!
Antes de leer, Ejercicio A, página 285   *Answers will vary.*

Ejercicio B, página 285   1. Va al mercado.   2. Lleva un cántaro en la cabeza.   3. Va pensando en el dinero que va a ganar con la venta de la leche.   4. Primero va a comprar un canasto de huevos.   5. Se van a convertir en pollitos.   6. Va a comprar un cochino.   7. Le va a pedir que lleve el cochino al mercado y que lo venda.   8. Va a comprar una vaca y un ternero.   9. El cántaro se le cae de la cabeza y se rompe.   10. Por estar haciendo castillos en el aire.   11. No anheles impaciente el bien futuro porque ni el presente está seguro.

Díganos, página 286   *Answers will vary.*

Así somos
Preparación, Ejercicio A, página 287   *Answers will vary.*

Ejercicio B, página 287   *Answers will vary.*

Comprensión, Ejercicio A, página 287   1. El papá   2. Olga   3. Ricardo   4. todos

Ejercicio B, página 287   1. Va a hacer depósitos de ahorros.   2. No, no va con mucha frecuencia.   3. Cambiar algún cheque, depositar dinero en su cuenta de ahorros.   4. Una vez por mes.

Ejercicio C, página 288   1. a   2. c   3. a   4. b

Ejercicio D, página 288   1. F, Sí, cuando es una compra grande.   2. V   3. V   4. F, Son seguras.   5. V   6. V   7. V   8. F, No tiene ninguna.   9. F, Dice que no son difíciles de obtener.

Ampliación, Ejercicio A, página 288   *Answers will vary.*

Ejercicio B, página 288   *Answers will vary.*

Lección 12
¡Conversemos!, página 293   1. Hace una semana que está en Madrid.   2. Visitó el Parque del Retiro, el Palacio Real y las ciudades de Segovia, Ávila y Toledo.   3. Se lo pregunta a un señor que está parado en la esquina. / Se lo

pregunta al Sr. Gómez.   4. Debe doblar a la derecha.
5. Es antiguo y está frente a la estación del metro.   6. No
puede recogerlo porque no tiene documento de identidad
(identificación). / Porque dejó su pasaporte en el hotel.
7. Puede comprar sellos en la ventanilla número dos.
8. Va a enviarlas por vía aérea.   9. Sale por la puerta
principal y cruza la Plaza de La Cibeles.   10. Va a El Corte
Inglés y allí se encuentra con su amiga, Pilar.   11. Dice que
no siempre llegan tarde y que a veces son puntuales.   12.
Está en el tercer piso.

¿Lo sabía Ud.?, página 294   *Answers will vary.*

Ejercicio A, página 296   1. Vengan a clase temprano. /
Abran el libro. / Vayan a la pizarra. / Hagan los ejercicios. /
Cierren el libro. / Hablen solamente español. / No hablen
inglés en la clase.   2. Esté en la oficina a las ocho. / Traiga
las cartas. / Traduzca los documentos. / Lleve las cartas al
correo. / Compre estampillas. / Llame por teléfono al Sr.
Paz. / Consiga la dirección del Banco de Ponce. / No vuelva
hasta las tres.

Ejercicio B, página 297   1. Vaya por la calle Carretas
hasta la Puerta del Sol, doble a la derecha en la Carrera de
San Gerónimo y a la derecha en el Paseo del Prado.
2. Vaya por el Paseo del Prado, doble a la izquierda en la
Carrera de San Gerónimo y tome la calle Postas.   3. Vaya
por la calle Mayor hasta llegar a la calle de Bailén, y están
a la izquierda.   4. Vaya por la calle de Bailén y doble a la
derecha en la cuesta San Vicente.   5. Tome la Gran Vía,
pase la Plaza del Callao y tome la calle del Carmen.
6. Vaya por la calle de Alcalá hasta la Plaza de la Cibeles, y
está a la derecha.

Ejercicio A, página 298   1. Levántense a las siete, báñense
y vístanse.   2. Hagan unos sándwiches y pónganlos en el
refrigerador.   3. Escríbanle una carta a la abuela y échenla
al correo.   4. Mándenle un paquete a Teresa.   5. Llamen
a la Dra. Peña, pero no la llamen antes de las tres.
6. Cómprenle el regalo a mamá, pero no se lo den hoy.
7. Díganle a Marta que la fiesta es mañana, pero no se lo
digan a Raúl.   8. No se acuesten muy tarde.

Ejercicio B, página 298   1. Sí, tráigamela, por favor. (No,
no me la traiga.)   2. Sí, sírvamela primero, por favor.
(No, no me la sirva primero.)   3. Sí, póngasela, por favor.
(No, no se la ponga.)   4. Sí, ábrala, por favor. (No, no la
abra ahora.)   5. Sí, tráigamela, por favor. (No, no me la
traiga.)   6. Sí, sírvamelo ahora, por favor. (No, no me lo
sirva ahora.)   7. Sí, tráigamela, por favor. (No, no me la
traiga ahora.)

Ejercicio C, página 299   *Answers will vary. Possible
commands:* 1. Recójanlo. (Envíenlo.)   2. Cómprenlo.
(Envíenlo.)   3. Escríbanlos. (Envíenlos.)   4. Escríbanlas.
(Envíenlas.)   5. Cómprenlo. (Denlo./Envíenlo.)
6. Pruébenselos. (Cómprenlos.)   7. Ábranla. (Ciérrenla.)
8. Fírmenlo. (Tráiganlo.)

Ejercicio D, página 299   *Answers will vary.*

Ejercicio A, página 300   1. que / quien   2. que
3. quienes / que   4. quien   5. que / quien

Ejercicio B, página 300   *Answers will vary.*

Ejercicio A, página 302   1. Sí, es verdad que Texas es más
grande que Maine.   2. No es verdad que haga más calor
en Alaska que en Arizona. Hace más calor en Arizona.
3. No es verdad que Buenos Aires sea la capital de Chile; es
la capital de Argentina.   4. No es verdad que México esté
al norte de los Estados Unidos; está al sur de los Estados
Unidos.   5. No es verdad que celebremos la independencia
de nuestro país el 25 de diciembre; la celebramos el cuatro
de julio.   6. No es verdad que el presidente del país pueda
ser extranjero; debe ser norteamericano.   7. No, no es
verdad que necesitemos un documento de identidad para
comprar estampillas; necesitamos dinero.   8. No, no es
verdad que revelen rollos de película en el correo; los
revelan en el departamento de fotografía.   9. Sí, es verdad
que echamos las cartas en el buzón.   10. Sí, es verdad que
podemos comprar un giro postal en el correo.

Ejercicio B, página 302   *Answers will vary.*

Ejercicio C, página 302   *Answers will vary.*

¡A ver cuánto aprendió!

¡Repase el vocabulario!, página 303   1. arriba / abajo
2. parados   3. Parque / Palacio   4. estación   5. giro
6. montón   7. casillero   8. aérea / certificado
9. mismo / cruzar   10. semáforo   11. encontrarme
12. cada   13. subir   14. oficina   15. doblar

Entrevista, página 303   *Answers will vary.*

Situaciones, página 303   *Answers will vary.*

Para escribir, página 304   *Answers will vary.*

En la vida real

¿Cómo voy...?, página 304   *Answers will vary.*

Señales de tráfico, página 305   1. c   2. d   3. e   4. a
5. b

Nuestra casa es su casa, página 305   *Answers will vary.*

Teleinforme

Preparación, página 315   1. Van para visitar las playas.
2. La construyeron los españoles para defender la isla de los
piratas.   3. La Habana   4. La Habana Vieja   5. La
Universidad de La Habana es la más antigua y tiene dos
sedes.   6. La Española   7. el béisbol   8. la Catedral de
Santa María la Menor en Santo Domingo

Comprensión, Ejercicio A, página 315   1. norte   2. los
españoles   3. fortalezas   4. calles   5. vólibol, el "surfing"

Ejercicio B, página 315   1. Golfo de México   2. la Perla   3. quinta   4. La Habana Vieja   5. españoles   6. Muchos

Ejercicio C, página 315   1. V   2. V   3. F, el hijo   4. F, Cada doce de octubre   5. V

Ampliación, Ejercicio A, página 316   *Answers will vary.*

Ejercicio B, página 316   *Answers will vary.*

Lección 13

¡Conversemos!, página 321   1. No, no estudian en su país. 2. Quieren mudarse porque necesitan un apartamento que esté cerca de la universidad.   3. No, no van a tener que comprar muebles porque el apartamento es amueblado. 4. Dicen que tiene dos recámaras, sala, comedor, cocina y cuarto de baño.   5. Lucía quiere que llame para ver el apartamento.   6. Sí, porque necesitan un apartamento que tenga garaje.   7. Van a ver el apartamento.   8. Sí, le encanta.   9. Le dice que está loca porque nadie puede trabajar tiempo completo y estudiar en la universidad. 10. La cocina del apartamento tiene refrigerador, microondas, lavaplatos, una cocina nueva y un fregadero grande.   11. Le dice que no van a encontrar ningún apartamento que sea tan bueno como ése.   12. No quiere alquilar el apartamento porque con el salario que ganan no pueden pagar el alquiler.   13. David le dice que no diga tonterías.   14. No, Lucía se casó con un hombre pobre.

¿Lo sabía Ud.?, página 322   *Answers will vary.*

Ejercicio A, página 324   1. Levántate temprano. 2. Estudia y no hables por teléfono con tus amigos. 3. Haz la tarea y no mires televisión.   4. Escríbele una carta a la abuela.   5. Baña al perro.   6. Ve al mercado y compra frutas.   7. Recoge la ropa de la tintorería. 8. Llama por teléfono a Carlos y dile que traiga los discos compactos.   9. Lava el mantel y las servilletas, pero no laves las sábanas.   10. Limpia tu cuarto.   11. Pon la mesa.   12. Barre la cocina pero no le pases la aspiradora a la alfombra.

Ejercicio B, página 324   1. Ve al cine.   2. Sal con Mauricio.   3. Ve de compras.   4. Compra un traje de baño.   5. Regálale una cámara fotográfica.   6. Cómprale un vestido.   7. Haz sopa y pollo.   8. Dile que te lleve al baile.   9. Ponlo en el Banco de América.   10. Córtatelo.

Ejercicio C, página 325   *Answers will vary.*

Ejercicio D, página 325   *Answers will vary.*

Ejercicio E, página 325   1. Irene, pon las sábanas en la cómoda.   2. David, lleva el ventilador al salón de estar. 3. Carolina, haz la cama.   4. Magda, pásale la aspiradora a la alfombra.   5. Alejandro, pon la lámpara en la mesa. 6. Felipe, limpia la ventana.

Ejercicio A, página 326   1. ¿Cuál es su (tu) apellido? / ¿Cuál es su (tu) dirección? / ¿Cuál es su (tu) número de teléfono?   2. ¿Qué es una sangría? / ¿Qué es una paella?

Ejercicio B, página 326   *Answers will vary.*

Ejercicio A, página 327   1. En mi clase no hay nadie que sea de Paraguay.   2. En mi clase no hay nadie que conduzca un Mercedes Benz.   3. En mi clase no hay nadie que hable francés.   4. En mi clase no hay nadie que tenga solamente quince años.   5. En mi clase no hay nadie que sepa tocar el violín.   6. En mi clase no hay nadie que dé fiestas todos los sábados.   7. En mi clase no hay nadie que vaya a Europa todos los veranos.   8. En mi clase no hay nadie que venga a la universidad los domingos.   9. En mi clase no hay nadie que siempre esté ocupado.   10. En mi clase no hay nadie que salga de su casa a las cinco de la mañana.

Ejercicio B, página 328   1. Busco (Quiero, Necesito) una casa que tenga tres dormitorios. / En mi barrio hay una casa que tiene tres dormitorios.   2. Necesito (Busco, Quiero) una casa que esté cerca de la universidad. / En mi barrio hay una casa que está cerca de la universidad. 3. Quiero (Busco) una casa que no cueste un ojo de la cara. / En mi barrio hay una casa que no cuesta un ojo de la cara. 4. Quiero (Busco, Necesito) un coche que tenga aire acondicionado. / Todos los coches tienen aire acondicionado.   5. Busco (Quiero) muebles que sean baratos. / Hay muchos muebles que son baratos. 6. Necesito (Busco, Quiero) un empleo que pague bien. / Hay un empleo que paga bien.   7. Busco (Necesito) a alguien que me ayude a mudarme. / En mi barrio hay alguien que puede ayudarte a mudarte.   8. Busco (Quiero) un restaurante que sirva hamburguesas. / En mi barrio hay un restaurante que sirve hamburguesas.

Ejercicio C, página 328   *Answers will vary.*

Ejercicio D, página 328   *Answers will vary.*

Ejercicio E, página 328   *Answers will vary.*

¡A ver cuánto aprendió!

¡Repase el vocabulario!, página 329   1. c   2. b   3. a   4. b   5. a   6. b   7. c   8. c   9. a   10. c   11. a   12. b

Entrevista, página 330   *Answers will vary.*

Situaciones, página 330   *Answers will vary.*

Para escribir, página 331   *Answers will vary.*

En la vida real

Mi pareja ideal, página 332   *Answers will vary.*

Casas y apartamentos, página 332   *Answers will vary.*

En busca de apartamento, página 333   1. El Conjunto Residencial de Tiana está a ocho kilómetros de Barcelona.

Cada apartamento tiene cuatro dormitorios. El conjunto tiene piscina. El número de teléfono es 321–32–36.   2. Sí, hay apartamentos que están a cinco minutos de la playa. Los apartamentos están en la calle Muralla, número 3. Son más bien pequeños. Tienen plazas de parking.   3. Sí, hay apartamentos cerca del parque Guinardo. Se pueden ver de 5:30 a 8:30 de la tarde. El más barato cuesta siete millones de pesetas.   4. En los apartamentos de Torredembarra se puede poner una lavadora. Se puede pagar la hipoteca en 15 años. Se pueden ver cualquier día excepto lunes y martes. Cuestan cuatro millones de pesetas.

¡Vamos a leer!

Antes de leer, Ejercicio A, página 334   *Answers will vary.*

Ejercicio B, página 334   1. Juan Echerry le escribe al segundo comandante del batallón Gerona, Domingo Echizarraga.   2. Don Pedro Uriondo es un capitán español. Es muy simpático.   3. Tiene la manía de proponer apuestas por todo y sobre todo. Siempre las gana.   4. Le aconseja que no le acepte ninguna apuesta al capitán Uriondo y que les advierta lo mismo a sus amigos.   5. Dice que vale en oro lo que pesa y que ya es el favorito de la oficialidad.   6. Sale de regreso mañana. Lleva cartas del general Valdés para el Virrey.   7. Se debía a un lunar que el comandante tenía en la pierna izquierda.   8. Le apostó a que podía convencerlo de la existencia del lunar.   9. Le apostó seis onzas.   10. El comandante ganó la apuesta porque no tenía ningún lunar.   11. La apuesta era que el capitán Uriondo le iba a hacer enseñar la pantorrilla al comandante el día de los Inocentes.   12. Habían apostado treinta onzas.

Díganos, página 336   *Answers will vary.*

Así somos

Preparación, Ejercicio A, página 336   *Answers will vary.*

Ejercicio B, página 336   *Answers will vary.*

Comprensión, Ejercicio A, página 337   1. D   2. C   3. C   4. D   5. C   6. D   7. C

Ejercicio B, página 337   1. d   2. e   3. a   4. f   5. b   6. c

Ejercicio C, página 337   1. optimista y realista   2. Ve lo positivo.   3. muy tranquilo   4. alegre   5. muy tímido   6. optimista   7. con buena cara

Ejercicio D, página 338   1. V   2. V   3. V   4. F, Con españoles, alemanes, americanos, canadienses, centroamericanos y mexicanos.   5. V   6. F, Son las más caras.   7. F, Son grandes: tienen sala, comedor, cocina, 3 recámaras y estudio.

Ampliación, Ejercicio A, página 338   *Answers will vary.*

Ejercicio B, página 338   *Answers will vary.*

Lección 14

¡Conversemos!, página 343   1. Tienen una cita con dos amigas venezolanas.   2. Está leyendo la guía de espectáculos para ver qué película ponen.   3. Hoy ponen *Amor prohibido*.   4. Dice que está nominada como la mejor película del año.   5. Le pregunta si tiene ganas de ver una buena película.   6. Quiere ir a la cafetería Versailles.   7. Se abre a las siete.   8. Necesitan comprar mantequilla, leche una docena de huevos, pan y azúcar.   9. Compran dos latas de frijoles.   10. Necesitan manzanas, uvas, naranjas, melón, toronjas y peras.   11. Porque las compras les van a costar una fortuna.   12. Porque tienen que limpiar el apartamento y preparar la cena antes de que lleguen las chicas.

¿Lo sabía Ud.?, página 344   *Answers will vary.*

Ejercicio A, página 346   antes de que llegue / en caso de que tenga / para que pueda / a menos que (tú me) des / con tal de que (tú me lo) devuelvas / sin que (me) vea

Ejercicio B, página 346   1. Mañana, en cuanto llegue a casa, voy a llamar a mi amiga.   2. El próximo viernes, vamos a esperar al profesor hasta que llegue.   3. El mes próximo, tan pronto como recibamos el sueldo, vamos a depositarlo en el banco.   4. La semana próxima, cuando Uds. vayan a verla, le van a llevar un regalo.   5. Dígaselo a ellos cuando los vea.

Ejercicio C, página 347   1. tan pronto como (en cuanto) ellos lleguen / para que podamos comer   2. cuando lo veo   3. sin que los niños nos vean / a menos que salgamos   4. antes de que lleguen mis amigos / hasta que yo vuelva / con tal (de) que estés aquí

Ejercicio A, página 348   *Answers will vary.*

Ejercicio B, página 348   *Answers will vary.*

Ejercicio A, página 349   1. Se prohíbe estacionar (aparcar, parquear)   2. Se sale por la izquierda   3. Aquí se habla español   4. Se prohíbe tirar basura   5. Se prohíbe cruzar   6. Se prohíbe nadar   7. Se venden coches

Ejercicio B, página 349   *Answers will vary.*

¡A ver cuánto aprendió!

¡Repase el vocabulario!, página 350   1. c   2. b   3. b   4. c   5. b   6. c   7. b   8. b   9. b   10. a   11. b   12. c

Entrevista, página 351   *Answers will vary.*

Situaciones, página 351   *Answers will vary.*

Para escribir, página 352   *Answers will vary.*

En la vida real

Discusión, página 352   *Answers will vary.*

De la cocina a la mesa, página 353   *Answers will vary.*

Teleinforme

Preparación, página 359   1. Está en Perú, Ecuador, Colombia, Brasil y Venezuela   2. Quito, Caracas 3. Sucre y La Paz   4. El Salto Ángel, que está en Venezuela   5. Fue héroe nacional y libertador de Perú, Argentina y Chile.

Comprensión, Ejercicio A, página 359   1. de la capital 2. colonial   3. lo moderno   4. miles   5. el cerro

Ejercicio B, página 359   1. V   2. F, Queda a tres horas por avión.   3. V   4. F, Atrae a muchos turistas.   5. V

Ejercicio C, página 359   1. variada   2. volcanes 3. colonial   4. inca   5. monumento   6. mercado

Ampliación, Ejercicio A, página 360   *Answers will vary.*

Ejercicio B, página 360   *Answers will vary.*

Lección 15

¡Conversemos!, página 366   1. Van a ir de compras porque necesitan ropa.   2. Tienen una gran liquidación. 3. Va a estar abierta 12 horas.   4. Para mujer, aparecen blusas y faldas. Para hombre aparecen camisas y trajes. 5. La ropa de Hugo es vieja y pasada de moda.   6. Van a El Corte Inglés, que está en el centro de Madrid.   7. Se queda en la planta baja y se encuentra con Tere.   8. Se prueba una blusa y una falda en el probador.   9. Porque le queda grande.   10. Hugo compró dos camisetas y un chaleco, y después fue a la zapatería a cambiar unas botas. 11. Van a comer porque están muertos de hambre. 12. Hugo quiere que Anita le regale un traje.

¿Lo sabía Ud.?, página 367   *Answers will vary.*

Ejercicio, página 369   1. tenido   2. traído   3. cerrado 4. dicho   5. aprovechado   6. apretado   7. cortado 8. vuelto   9. roto   10. cubierto   11. cambiado 12. sentido   13. entrado   14. salido   15. hecho 16. puesto   17. abierto   18. escrito   19. visto 20. aceptado   21. devuelto   22. leído   23. dado 24. sacado

Ejercicio A, página 370   1. Sí, ya está cerrada.   2. Sí, ya están abiertas.   3. Sí, ya está hecha.   4. Sí, ya está envuelto.   5. Sí, ya están escritas.   6. Sí, ya está pagada. 7. Sí, ya están cubiertos.   8. Sí, ya está lavada.

Ejercicio B, página 370   1. hechas   2. abierta / cerradas 3. puesta / servida   4. usada / usado   5. escritos / traducidos   6. envueltos

Ejercicio A, página 372   1. Tú has envuelto los regalos. 2. Tú y yo hemos cubierto el sofá.   3. Los chicos han roto la ventana.   4. Yo he puesto la mesa.   5. Mi mamá ha planchado la falda.   6. Uds. han visto la película.

Ejercicio B, página 373   *Specific answers will vary. Questions and sample answers:* 1. —¿Has comprado ropa últimamente? —Sí, he comprado ropa. —¿Qué compraste? 2. —¿Has visto alguna película últimamente? —Sí, he visto una película. —¿Cuál viste?   3. —¿Has dado alguna fiesta últimamente? —Sí, he dado una fiesta. —¿Dónde diste la fiesta?   4. —¿Has mandado algún mensaje electrónico últimamente? —Si, he mandado un mensaje electrónico. —¿A quién le mandaste el mensaje?   5. —¿Has tomado algún examen últimamente? —Sí, he tomado un examen. —¿En qué clase?   6. —¿Has visitado algún lugar interesante últimamente? —Sí, he visitado un lugar interesante. —¿Cuál?   7. —¿Has escrito alguna carta últimamente? —Sí, he escrito una carta. —¿A quién le escribiste?   8. —¿Has puesto dinero en el banco últimamente? —Sí, he puesto dinero en el banco. —¿En cual?   9. —¿Has leído algún libro últimamente? —Sí, he leído un libro. —¿Cuál leíste?   10. —¿Has recibido algún regalo últimamente? —Sí, he recibido un regalo. —¿De quién?

Ejercicio C, página 373   *Answers will vary.*

Ejercicio A, página 374   1. Cuando él llegó, yo ya había barrido la cocina.   2. Cuando él llegó, los chicos ya le habían pasado la aspiradora a la alfombra.   3. Cuando él llegó, Roberto y yo ya habíamos hecho la comida. 4. Cuando él llegó, Elsa ya había planchado la ropa. 5. Cuando él llegó, tú ya habías limpiado el refrigerador. 6. Cuando él llegó, Carmen y Elena ya habían bañado al perro.   7. Cuando él llegó, Anita ya había puesto la mesa. 8. Cuando él llegó, Raúl y Carlos ya habían comprado las bebidas.   9. Cuando él llegó, Mirta ya había lavado las sábanas.   10. Cuando él llegó, Raúl y yo ya habíamos envuelto los regalos.

Ejercicio B, página 375   *Answers will vary.*

Ejercicio C, página 375   *Answers will vary.*

¡A ver cuánto aprendió!

¡Repase el vocabulario!, página 375   1. el chaleco 2. hace juego   3. Me quedan grandes.   4. calcetines 5. liquidación   6. me gustan mucho   7. la chaqueta 8. moda   9. usa   10. la corbata   11. la billetera 12. ponerme   13. mediana   14. planta baja   15. de lunares

Entrevista, página 376   *Answers will vary.*

Situaciones, página 376   *Answers will vary.*

Para escribir, página 376   *Answers will vary.*

En la vida real

Haciendo las maletas, página 376   *Answers will vary.*

¡De compras!, página 377   1. Son en agosto.   2. Puede comprarle camisetas lisas y estampadas y playeros en distintos colores.   3. Venden mocasines en piel de búfalo, con piso de suela por 150 euros.   4. Puede comprarse vestidos lisos y estampados y pareos estampados en distintos dibujos y colores.   5. Puede comprar bañadores, bikinis, playeros y pareos.   6. *Answers will vary.*   7. Son para seis personas.   8. El sillón cuesta 525 euros.

La última moda, página 378   *Answers will vary.*

¡Vamos a leer!

Antes de leer, Ejercicio A, página 378   *Answers will vary.*

Ejercicio B, página 378   1. Porque es demasiado vago. 2. No. Almuerza de una a dos y a veces a las tres.   3. Va a estar de siete a ocho.   4. Que el amigo no viene.   5. Que la puntualidad es algo completamente absurdo.   6. Porque uno ahorra mucho tiempo para hacer otras cosas.

Díganos, página 380   *Answers will vary.*

Así somos

Preparación, Ejercicio A, página 380   *Answers will vary.*

Ejercicio B, página 381   *Answers will vary.*

Comprensión, Ejercicio A, página 381   1. jeans 2. camisetas   3. informal   4. ropa casual   5. jeans 6. ropa informal

Ejercicio B, página 381   1. d   2. d   3. f   4. e   5. a 6. b   7. c

Ejercicio C, página 381   1. V   2. V   3. F, ropa informal 4. V   5. V   6. F, hace mucho calor

Ejercicio D, página 382   1. no   2. en las boutiques   3. en un almacén   4. muchos   5. muy buena   6. en un almacén 7. en una boutique   8. sí

Ejercicio E, página 382   1. F, También venden camisas. 2. F, Venden diferentes marcas.   3. V   4. F, Le gusta. 5. V   6. V

Ampliación, Ejercicio A, página 382   *Answers will vary.*

Ejercicio B, página 382   *Answers will vary.*

Lección 16

¡Conversemos!, página 394   1. Sí, estará ocupado. Tendrá que matricularse para las clases de otoño.   2. Piensa tomar administración de empresas, psicología y sociología.   3. Le ha sugerido que tome una clase de química o de física. Daniel no quiere seguir su consejo porque nunca le han gustado las ciencias.   4. Le gustaría ir a Buenos Aires. No podrá ir porque tiene exámenes finales hasta el veinte. 5. Debe mantener un promedio de "A" porque tiene una

beca.   6. Se habrá graduado para el año 2004.   7. Habría ahorrado dinero para el pasaje.   8. Creen que sus clases son lo único que debería importarles a los estudiantes. 9. Dice que será una periodista magnífica.   10. Irá a los Estados Unidos. Va a tomar unos cursos especiales. 11. Habría estudiado medicina.   12. Van a ir a un partido de fútbol.

¿Lo sabía Ud.?, página 395   *Answers will vary.*

Ejercicio A, página 397   1. Jorge irá de vacaciones a México.   2. Marta y yo saldremos para Colombia en julio. 3. Mis padres vendrán a visitarme en agosto.   4. Ana tendrá que trabajar en el verano.   5. Yo tomaré una clase de francés.   6. Ustedes pondrán alfombra nueva en su casa.   7. Tú viajarás por Latinoamérica.   8. Usted pasará dos semanas en Sevilla.

Ejercicio B, página 398   *Answers will vary. Conjugations:* 1. Iremos a...   2. Saldremos el...   3. Viajaremos en... 4. Estaremos estudiando...   5. Sí, podremos (No, no podremos) visitar muchas ciudades.   6. Visitaremos... 7. Sí, les enviaremos (No, no les enviaremos) tarjetas postales a nuestros amigos.   8. Necesitaremos...   9. Sí, se lo pediremos (No, no se lo pediremos) a nuestros padres. 10. Volveremos...

Ejercicio C, página 398   *Answers will vary.*

Ejercicio D, página 398   *Answers will vary.*

Ejercicio E, página 398   *Answers will vary.*

Ejercicio A, página 400   1. Uds. se levantarían a las... 2. Ana y Luis estudiarían...   3. Nosotros vendríamos a la universidad en...   4. Yo tomaría clases de...   5. Elsa se bañaría...   6. Usted se acostaría a la(s)...   7. Ellos irían a...   8. Tú saldrías con...

Ejercicio B, página 400   *Answers will vary.*

Ejercicio C, página 401   *Answers will vary.*

Ejercicio D, página 401   *Answers will vary.*

Ejercicio A, página 402   1. se habrá acostado / habrá salido   2. habrán vuelto / habremos vuelto   3. habrás terminado / habré terminado   4. habrán limpiado 5. habrán cenado

Ejercicio B, página 402   *Answers will vary.*

Ejercicio A, página 403   1. Nosotros habríamos ido a... 2. Nosotros habríamos viajado en...   3. Yo me habría sentado en...   4. Mi mamá habría preparado...   5. Mi amigo y yo habríamos bebido...   6. Mi amigo se habría quedado en...   7. Nosotros nos habríamos quedado en... 8. Mis padres habrían ido a...   9. Yo habría ido a... 10. Nosotros habríamos visitado...   11. Mi amigo habría visitado...   12. Nosotros habríamos estado en... por...

Ejercicio B, página 404   *Answers will vary.*

¡A ver cuánto aprendió!

¡Repase el vocabulario!, página 404   1. suspendido
2. empresas   3. tratar   4. Derecho   5. informe
6. vendedor   7. consejero(-a)   8. fútbol   9. mantener
10. único   11. periodista   12. ingeniero(-a)
13. especialización   14. mitad   15. negocios
16. cocinero

Entrevista, página 405   *Answers will vary.*

Situaciones, página 405   *Answers will vary.*

¿Qué pasa aquí?, página 406   *Answers will vary.*

Para escribir, página 406   *Answers will vary.*

En la vida real

El primer empleo, página 406   *Answers will vary.*

Necesitamos trabajo, página 407   1. Optim necesita
secretario(-a).   2. Necesitas hablar alemán.   3. El
laboratorio farmacéutico está en Barcelona.   4. Debes
tener tres años en el servicio de extranjero.   5. Necesitas
mandar una foto para solicitar el puesto de la empresa
financiera.   6. Debes tener entre 35 y 45 años de edad.
7. Debes enviar el *curriculum vitae*.

Teleinforme

Preparación, página 412   1. Buenos Aires, Santiago
2. diez millones   3. el Obelisco   4. Brasil y Paraguay
5. El Iguazú y el Paraná   6. "Agua grande"

Comprensión, Ejercicio A, página 412   1. París
2. franceses/alemanes/italianos   3. anchas   4. italianos
5. el tango

Ejercicio B, página 412   1. V   2. F, Es Asunción   3. V
4. F, En dos regiones   5. F, Tiene una salida al mar, el río
Paraná   6. V   7. V

Ejercicio C, página 412   1. una región   2. sur   3. 6.600
4. Argentina   5. ciudad

Ampliación, Ejercicio A, página 413   *Answers will vary.*

Ejercicio B, página 413   *Answers will vary.*

Lección 17

¡Conversemos!, página 417   1. Se encuentran en un
restaurante para almorzar.   2. Mirta tiene fiebre y le duele
mucho la cabeza.   3. Espera que ya haya llamado al
doctor Valdivia.   4. Teresa le sugirió a Mirta que viera a la
doctora Vargas.   5. No le receta penicilina a Mirta porque
ella es alérgica a la penicilina.   6. Tiene que tomar las
pastillas cuatro veces al día.   7. Tuvo un accidente y ahora

está en la sala de emergencia.   8. A Oscar lo atropelló un
coche.   9. El médico le dijo que le desinfectara y le
vendara la herida a Oscar.   10. No, no le va a poner una
inyección porque sólo hace dos años que le pusieron una a
Oscar.   11. Lo lleva a la sala de rayos X para hacerle una
radiografía.   12. Le enyesa la pierna porque la tiene rota.

¿Lo sabía Ud.?, página 418   *Answers will vary.*

Ejercicio, página 420   1. ganara, volviera, pidiera, dijera,
recibiera   2. fueras, durmieras, quisieras, dieras, conocieras
3. fuera, estuviera, pusiera, condujera, sirviera
4. supiéramos, pudiéramos, regresáramos, consiguiéramos,
hiciéramos   5. tuvieran, recetaran, comenzaran, siguieran,
mintieran

Ejercicio A, página 420   1. fuera / hiciera / viera
2. llevara / pudiera / llamaras   3. tomara / hablara
4. supiera / estudiara   5. pudieras / llamara / dijera /
vinieras

Ejercicio B, página 421   1. les escribiera todas las
semanas   2. los llamara por teléfono los domingos
3. tomara varias clases el primer semestre   4. estudiara
mucho   5. abriera una cuenta corriente en el banco
6. hiciera la tarea todos los días   7. me levantara
temprano   8. los visitara en las vacaciones

1. viviera lejos de la universidad   2. fuera a muchas
fiestas   3. comiera hamburguesas todos los días
4. gastara mucho   5. les pidiera dinero extra todos los
meses   6. condujera muy rápido   7. me olvidara de tomar
la medicina   8. me acostara muy tarde

Ejercicio C, página 421   *Answers will vary.*

Ejercicio A, página 422   1. Te acordaste de / me olvidé de
2. insistió en   3. aprendió a / enseñaron a   4. se enamoró
de / se fijó en / se casó con   5. Me alegro de / invitarte a /
asistir a

Ejercicio B, página 423   *Answers will vary. Possibilities:*
1. ¿Con quién se casa Marisa? / Marisa se casa con Daniel.
2. ¿Con quién se compromete Raúl? / Raúl se compromete
con Mirta.   3. ¿De qué no se acuerda Graciela? / Graciela
no se acuerda del número de teléfono de Pepe.   4. ¿Por
qué se alegra Marisol? / Marisol se alegra de ver a Tito.
5. ¿En qué insiste Pedro? / Pedro insiste en ir con Alina.
6. ¿Con qué sueña Carmen? / Sueña con ir a París.

Ejercicio C, página 423   *Answers will vary.*

Ejercicio A, página 424   1. haya puesto / haya ido
2. haya tenido   3. haya muerto   4. haya dicho   5. hayan
llevado   6. hayamos tomado

Ejercicio B, página 425   *Answers will vary.*

Ejercicio C, página 425   *Answers will vary.*

¡A ver cuánto aprendió!

¡Repase el vocabulario!, Ejercicio A, página 425 1. No 2. Sí 3. No 4. Sí 5. Sí 6. Sí 7. No 8. No 9. Sí 10. No 11. No 12. No 13. Sí 14. No 15. Sí 16. Sí 17. No 18. No

Ejercicio B, página 426 1. el pelo 2. la cabeza 3. la cara 4. el pecho 5. la mano 6. el estómago 7. las rodillas 8. los dedos 9. los tobillos 10. los pies 11. la espalda 12. el cuello 13. los ojos 14. la nariz 15. los dientes 16. la boca 17. la oreja 18. el oído

Entrevista, página 426 *Answers will vary.*

Situaciones, página 427 *Answers will vary.*

Para escribir, página 427 *Answers will vary.*

En la vida real

Llenando una hoja clínica, página 427 *Answers will vary.*

Buenos consejos, página 428 1. No debe consumir mucho alcohol. 2. Debe hacer ejercicio. 3. No debe consumir mucha azúcar. Debe consumir menos calorías. 4. Debe aprender a relajarse. No debe trabajar en exceso. 5. Debe dormir lo suficiente. 6. Debe aprender a relajarse, evitar la tensión y pensar positivamente. 7. No debe comer mucha grasa. Debe comer más vegetales y frutas y tener una dieta balanceada. 8. Debe visitar al médico periódicamente. 9. Debe consumir menos calorías y controlar su peso. 10. Debe controlar su peso y consumir menos calorías. 11. Debe comer más vegetales y frutas y tener una dieta balanceada. 12. No debe fumar.

¡Vamos a leer!

Antes de leer, Ejercicio A, página 429 *Answers will vary.*

Ejercicio B, página 429 1. Nació en 1853. 2. Murió en Cuba, en el campo de batalla en 1895. 3. Los temas principales de su poesía son: la libertad, la justicia, la independencia de su patria y la defensa de los pobres y de los oprimidos. 4. Viene de todas partes y va hacia todas partes. 5. Se describe como arte entre las artes y monte entre los montes. 6. Para el poeta la amistad es más importante que el amor. 7. Lo compara con la joya mejor. 8. Dice que antes que luz fue carbón. 9. Porque su patria no es libre. 10. Dice que quiere salir por la puerta natural. 11. Dice que mueren en lo oscuro. 12. Dice que él morirá de cara al sol porque él es bueno.

Díganos, página 430 *Answers will vary.*

Así somos

Preparación, Ejercicio A, página 431 *Answers will vary.*

Ejercicio B, página 431 *Answers will vary.*

Comprensión, Ejercicio A, página 431 1. ejercicio 2. carnes rojas 3. consume drogas 4. caminar 7. las reglas universales

Ejercicio B, página 432 1. b 2. d 3. a 4. c

Ejercicio C, página 432 1. F, Sí, la reciben. 2. V 3. F, Sí, incluye las medicinas. 4. F, Es para todo el mundo.

Ejercicio D, página 432 1. buenos 2. asistencia médica 3. buena 4. medicinas

Ejercicio E, página 432 1. veintiún 2. cardiología 3. gabinete de rayos X *(X-ray)* 4. ultrasonido

Ampliación, Ejercicio A, página 432 *Answers will vary.*

Ejercicio B, página 432 *Answers will vary.*

Lección 18

¡Conversemos!, página 436 1. Gloria y Julio están en la carretera y van a San José. 2. Es de noventa kilómetros por hora. 3. Si un policía lo ve, le va a poner una multa. 4. Están a cuarenta kilómetros de San José. 5. Necesitan ir a una gasolinera porque el tanque de su coche está casi vacío. 6. No, el tanque está casi vacío. 7. Llena el tanque y revisa el aceite y las llantas. 8. Tuvo un pinchazo y el mecánico le dijo que necesitaba neumáticos nuevos. 9. Sí, está de acuerdo con él. 10. Necesita un acumulador nuevo y una bomba de agua nueva. Además, tienen que arreglar los frenos. 11. Sí, ella cree que va a costar una fortuna. 12. Si pudiera, compraría un coche nuevo ahora mismo.

¿Lo sabía Ud.?, página 437 *Answers will vary.*

Ejercicio A, página 439 1. ...yo hubiera hecho la comida. 2. ...Quique hubiera lavado el coche. 3. ...nosotros hubiéramos llevado a Raulito a la escuela. 4. ...tú le hubieras escrito a tío Carlos. 5. ...Uds. hubieran devuelto los libros a la biblioteca. 6. ...Eva y Luis hubieran comprado la batería. 7. ...Irma hubiera puesto la mesa. 8. ...Eva y yo le hubiéramos pasado la aspiradora a la alfombra. 9. ...Daniel hubiera llevado el coche al taller. 10. ...Jorge y yo hubiéramos cambiado las llantas.

Ejercicio B, página 439 1. Yo dudaba que Pepe hubiera arreglado los frenos. 2. Yo dudaba que tú hubieras salido de viaje. 3. Yo dudaba que mis amigos hubieran podido cambiar el filtro. 4. Yo dudaba que el policía les hubiera puesto una multa. 5. Yo dudaba que nosotros hubiéramos tenido la culpa. 6. Yo dudaba que el mecánico hubiera conseguido las piezas de repuesto. 7. Yo dudaba que Uds. hubieran venido ayer. 8. Yo dudaba que Irma hubiera comprado un coche con bolsas de aire.

Ejercicio C, página 439   *Answers will vary. Conjugations:*
1. ...los recién casados se hubieran ido a Costa Rica.
2. ...el mecánico hubiera revisado el coche.   3. ...ella hubiera conducido el coche a cien millas por hora.
4. ...Carlos hubiera tenido que llamar una grúa.
5. ...nosotros hubiéramos decidido no arreglar el coche.
6. ...el policía le hubiera puesto una multa a mi hermano.
7. ...ellos hubieran llevado el coche al taller de mecánica.
8. ...tú hubieras cambiado la llanta.

Ejercicio A, página 441   *Answers will vary.*

Ejercicio B, página 441   *Answers will vary. Possibilities:*
1. Si yo hubiera estudiado más el semestre pasado, mi promedio no habría sido de "C".   2. Si Teresa tuviera tiempo, iría al cine.   3. Si tenemos suficiente dinero, vamos a comprar un coche nuevo.   4. Si yo supiera la dirección de Pedro, se la daría a Juan.   5. Si me hubieran gustado las matemáticas, habría sido contador.   6. Si tus padres te regalan una computadora, puedes estudiar para programador(-a).   7. Si yo no hubiera tenido que trabajar, habría llevado a Marta al estadio.   8. Si el profesor hubiera estado en la universidad, nosotros habríamos hablado con él.

Ejercicio C, página 441   *Answers will vary.*

Ejercicio A, página 442   1. llegues / estudiar / lleve / valga / podamos / poder / quiere / quieres / pudiera

Ejercicio B, página 443   *Answers will vary.*

Ejercicio C, página 443   *Answers will vary.*

¡A ver cuánto aprendió!

¡Repase el vocabulario!, página 443   1. el neumático
2. descompuesto   3. vacío   4. manejando muy rápido
5. los frenos no funcionaban   6. camino   7. una grúa
8. casados   9. ese letrero   10. portaguantes   11. arreglo
12. pena   13. culpa   14. acuerdo   15. el capó
16. bolsas

Entrevista, página 444   *Answers will vary.*

Situaciones, página 444   *Answers will vary.*

¿Qué pasa aquí?, página 445   *Answers will vary.*

Para escribir, página 445   *Answers will vary.*

En la vida real

¡Nos vamos!, página 445   *Answers will vary.*

Comprando coche, página 446   1. ¿Está el automóvil en perfectas condiciones? / ¿Le dejarán probar el automóvil antes de entregárselo?   2. ¿Qué garantía tiene el automóvil?   3. Si el automóvil se descompone, ¿quién va a componerlo? / Si el automóvil necesita ser reparado, ¿quién pagará la reparación?   4. ¿El automóvil será aprobado en la inspección del Estado?   5. ¿Qué precio de reventa tendrá el automóvil cuando Ud. quiera venderlo?

En la agencia de seguros, página 446   *Answers will vary.*

Teleinforme

Preparación, página 457   1. En Tejas, Colorado, Nuevo México, Arizona y California   2. Son de Puerto Rico, la República Dominicana, Centroamérica y Cuba   3. En Miami, Florida   4. En Los Ángeles, California   5. Se ven piñatas, mariachis y puestos de artesanía mexicana   6. El edificio Ávila

Comprensión, Ejercicio A, página 457   1. antiguas
2. mercancías   3. celebración   4. *Answers will vary, but may include:* tamales, arepas, frijoles, tortillas, pollo, carnitas, among others.   5. fiestas, música

Ejercicio B, página 457   1. F, Fue creada en Nueva York
2. F, Ondeó en 1952   3. V   4. V   5. F, Muchas personas asisten   6. V

Ampliación, Ejercicio A, página 457   *Answers will vary.*

Ejercicio B, página 457   *Answers will vary.*

¿Cómo se dice...?

¿Cómo se dice...?

SEVENTH EDITION

Ana C. Jarvis
Chandler-Gilbert Community College

Raquel Lebredo
California Baptist University

Francisco Mena-Ayllón
University of Redlands

Houghton Mifflin Company   **Boston**   **New York**

Director, World Languages: New Media and Modern Language Publishing: Beth Kramer
Sponsoring Editor: Amy Baron
Development Editor: Rafael Burgos-Mirabal
Senior Project Editor: Carol Newman
Senior Production/Design Coordinator: Jodi O'Rourke
Senior Manufacturing Coordinator: Priscilla Bailey
Marketing Manager: Tina Crowley Desprez

Cover Image: Forms, Symbols, and Images, 1967, José Gurvich.

Copyright © 2002 by Houghton Mifflin Company. All rights reserved.

No part of this work may be reproduced or transmitted in any form or by any means, electronic or mechanical, including photocopying and recording, or by any information storage or retrieval system without the prior written permission of Houghton Mifflin Company unless such copying is expressly permitted by federal copyright law. Address inquiries to College Permissions, Houghton Mifflin Company, 222 Berkeley Street, Boston, MA 02116-3764.

Printed in the U.S.A.

Library of Congress Catalog Card Number: 2001131512

Student Text ISBN: 0-618-10366-X

23456789-VH-05 04 03 02

CONTENTS

Planes para un fin de semana   106

Comunicación: Family relationships and personal characteristics
Pronunciación: The Spanish **p, t, c,** and **q**   111
Estructuras

Un viaje a Perú   130

Comunicación: Foreign travel
Pronunciación: The Spanish **j, g** (before **e** or **i**), and **h**   136
Estructuras

Hablando de las vacaciones   164

Comunicación: Travel experiences
Pronunciación: The Spanish **ll** and **ñ**   168

Lección 8

Lección 9

Las vacaciones de Silvia   243

Lección **10**

Comunicación: Leisure activities

Pronunciación en contexto   249

Estructuras

¡A ver cuánto aprendió!   257

En la vida real   259

Teleinforme   265

Haciendo diligencias   267

Lección **11**

Comunicación: Daily occurrences, running errands

Pronunciación en contexto   272

Estructuras

¡A ver cuánto aprendió!   281

En la vida real   283

Así somos   286

Pidiendo información   289

Lección **12**

Comunicación: Asking for directions, postal services

Pronunciación en contexto   295

Lección 15

De compras   361

Comunicación: Clothing, shopping

Pronunciación en contexto   368

Estructuras

1. The past participle   368
2. The present perfect   370
3. The past perfect (pluperfect)   374

¡A ver cuánto aprendió!   375

En la vida real   376

¡VAMOS A LEER!: *El tiempo y el espacio*   378

Así somos   380

SELF-TEST Lecciones 13–15   383

Lección 16

Las carreras   389

Comunicación: College activities, careers

Pronunciación en contexto   396

Estructuras

1. The future   396
2. The conditional   399
3. The future perfect and the conditional perfect   401

¡A ver cuánto aprendió!   404

En la vida real   406

■ **Panorama hispánico 8:** América del Sur (II)   408

Teleinforme   412

Lección 17

Problemas médicos   414

Comunicación: Medical care

Pronunciación en contexto   418

Estructuras

1. The imperfect subjunctive   419
2. Uses of some prepositions after certain verbs   421
3. The present perfect subjunctive   424

¡A ver cuánto aprendió!   425

En la vida real   427

An Overview of Your Textbook's Main Features

● **Provides focus for learning.** The **Lesson Opener** presents the thematic topic and an outline of the lesson's communicative goals and grammatical structures.

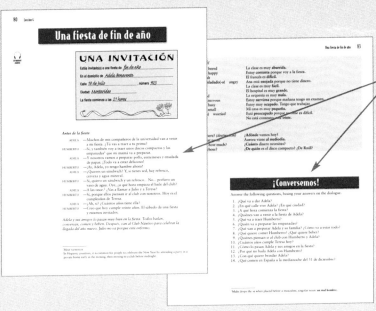

● **Offers a natural setting for introducing language.** The **Opening Passage** serves as a lively, realistic context in which to learn the lesson's vocabulary and structures. The *¡Conversemos!* comprehension questions provide immediate reinforcement. Translations appear in Appendix D.

● **Leads to an understanding of the cultures of the Spanish-speaking world.** Written in simple Spanish, the *¿Lo sabía Ud.?* culture notes convey information on cultural themes or points mentioned in the lesson's opening passage.

Provides a solid foundation for building communication skills.

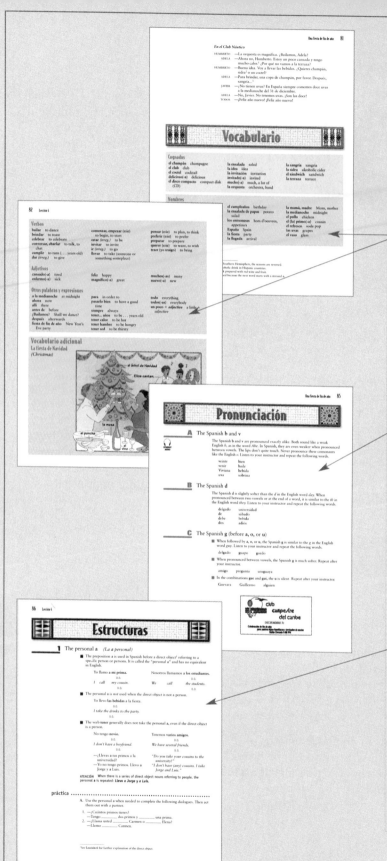

● The *Vocabulario* section lists all active vocabulary, new words, and expressions introduced in the opening passage, as well as *Vocabulario adicional*, or words and phrases related to the lesson theme.

● Now appearing in Lecciones 1–18, the *Pronunciación* section contains pronunciation and linking exercises designed to acquaint you with the basic Spanish sounds; with sounds, words, and expressions that are challenging for English speakers; and with natural speech.

● The *Estructuras* section presents an average of four or five clear and succinct grammar points in English with more examples of practical use that can be consulted for independent study and reference. Each structure is immediately followed by *Práctica* exercises that range from controlled drills to open-ended activities, including illustration-based activities.

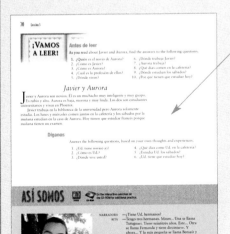

● **Presents opportunities to actively use the language in the classroom.** The *¡A ver cuánto aprendió!* review section consists of a series of progressively more open-ended activities, including personalized pair activities, activities for vocabulary review, and pair and small group activities. The section ends with a writing activity on a topic related to the thematic goals of the lesson.

● **Reinforces learning while strengthening communication skills.** Often based on authentic material, the activities in *En la vida real* ask you to synthesize what you've learned in order to communicate in real-life situations.

● **Promotes the development of reading skills.** Appearing at the end of each odd-numbered lesson, the *¡Vamos a leer!* sections develop reading comprehension while reinforcing the structures and vocabulary introduced in the preceding lessons. Pre-reading questions focus your attention on detail, and open-ended post-reading questions allow you to personalize topics related to the reading.

New! There are new readings in Lecciones 1, 3, 13, 15, and 17!

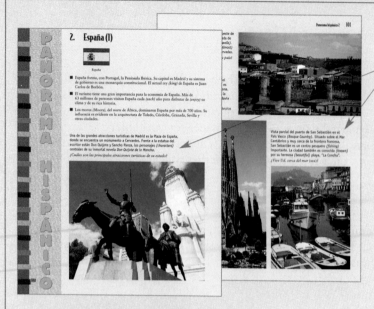

● **Expands your knowledge of geography, history, and culture.** After every two lessons, the *Panorama hispánico* photo essays explore the culture, geography, economy, and history of the Hispanic world. Regions featured include South America, the Caribbean, the United States, Canada, Central America, Mexico, and Spain.

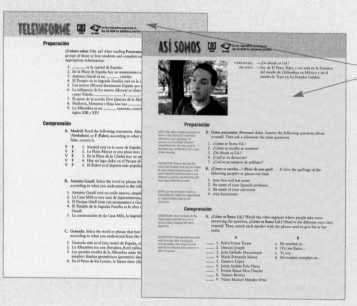

● **Broadens exposure to native speech and the cultures of the Spanish-speaking world.** Through a series of previewing, viewing comprehension, and expansion activities, the *Teleinforme* sections (after even-numbered lessons) and the *Así somos* sections (after odd-numbered lessons) support viewing of authentic as well as adapted footage. Each *Teleinforme* features footage from the region covered in the preceding *Panorama hispánico* photo essay. The *Así somos* footage consists of unrehearsed interviews with native Spanish speakers on topics related to the lesson theme.

● **Encourages self-assessment of learning objectives.** Following Lecciones 3, 6, 9, 12, 15, and 18, the **Self-Tests** contain exercises designed to review the vocabulary and structures of the three preceding lessons.

Preface

¿Cómo se dice...?, Seventh Edition, is a complete, flexible program designed to present the fundamentals of Spanish to two- and four-year college and university students. This edition continues to feature the balanced, eclectic approach to language instruction that has made *¿Cómo se dice...?* one of the most widely used programs of its kind. To achieve its goal of helping attain linguistic proficiency, *¿Cómo se dice...?*, Seventh Edition, systematically involves you in activities requiring the communicative use of all four language skills: listening, speaking, reading, and writing. Because cultural awareness is as important to successful communication as linguistic competence, special care has been devoted in the Seventh Edition to providing up-to-date, practical insights into the cultural diversity of the Spanish-speaking world. Since it is essential to understand the underlying philosophy and organization of the program to use it to greatest advantage, the student's text and other components are described in detail below.

The Student's Text

The organization of this central component of the *¿Cómo se dice...?*, Seventh Edition, program reflects its emphasis on the active use of Spanish for practical communication in context. The student's text is organized in eighteen lessons. Each lesson focuses on a high-frequency communicative situation and contains the features listed below.

Objectives: Each lesson begins with a list of grammatical and communicative objectives.

Opening passages and ¡*Conversemos!*: New vocabulary and structures are first presented in the context of a conversation in idiomatic Spanish dealing with the high-frequency situation that is the lesson's central theme. An English translation of the opening passages is provided in Appendix D for you to verify meaning deduced from context. A headset icon indicates that the opening passages are recorded on the Student Audio. Comprehension questions on the opening passages (¡*Conversemos!*) follow the vocabulary section to provide immediate reinforcement of the vocabulary and communicative functions presented in the opening passage.

Vocabulario: All new words and expressions introduced in the opening passages are listed by parts of speech or under the headings *Cognados* and *Otras palabras y expresiones*. The *Vocabulario adicional* section offers thematic groupings of other words and phrases related to the lesson theme; many are presented through illustrations to help you assimilate them more readily. Entries in these lists are to be learned for active use.

¿Lo sabía Ud.?: These notes expand on cultural information and themes introduced in the opening passages in simple, easy-to-read Spanish. Follow-up questions invite cross-cultural comparisons.

Pronunciación: Lessons 1–9 *(Pronunciación)* present and practice the sounds of the Spanish language with special attention to features that pose difficulty for English speakers. Lessons 10–18 *(Pronunciación en contexto)* focus on several sounds or words from the lesson opening passage that may pose pronunciation challenges. The target words and phrases are presented as part of sentences from the opening passage in which they originally appear to address these pronunciation issues in context. A headset icon indicates that the pronunciation sections are recorded on the Student Audio.

Estructuras and ***Práctica:***   Each new grammatical structure featured in the opening passage is explained clearly and concisely in English so that the explanations may be used independently as an out-of-class reference. All explanations are followed by numerous examples of their practical use in natural Spanish. The *¡Atención!* head signals exceptions to the grammar rules presented or instances where knowledge of an English structure may interfere with learning the equivalent Spanish structure. After each explanation, the *Práctica* activities offer immediate reinforcement of new concepts through a variety of structured and communicative activities.

¡A ver cuánto aprendió!:   This series of progressively less structured activities allows you to synthesize the lesson's new vocabulary and structures. *¡Repase el vocabulario!* uses a variety of proven activity formats to review new vocabulary presented in the lesson. *Entrevista* has you interview a classmate on topics related to the main lesson theme. *Situaciones* involves pairs or small groups of learners in using new structures and vocabulary in brief conversational exchanges. *Para escribir* guides you to express yourself in writing in a variety of formats, such as notes, postcards, letters, dialogues, and compositions.

En la vida real: This section develops oral proficiency by using authentic documents and role-plays to involve you in more complex and extended communicative tasks, such as planning an event, asking for information, or solving a problem. Each lesson includes an activity that involves reading and using information gained from an authentic text, for example, a newspaper ad or a travel brochure. Most of the activities are designed for work in pairs or small groups, and all of them require spontaneous use of Spanish in practical, meaningful, communicative tasks intended to motivate and to underscore the usefulness of language study.

In addition, the following features appear at regular intervals throughout the student's text:

Así somos: All odd-numbered lessons end with a series of activities designed for use with the candid interview segments of the *Así somos* modules of the *¿Cómo se dice...?* video, which reinforce the lesson themes. The previewing, post-viewing, and expansion activities use a variety of formats, including true/false, sentence completion, questions, matching, and multiple choice.

¡Vamos a leer!:   Right before the *Así somos* video activities section, every odd-numbered lesson features a reading section that reinforces the structures and vocabulary presented in the text. Five readings are new to the Seventh Edition. The first four readings are related to the lesson themes; the final five readings consist of authentic literary selections that provide an appealing introduction to reading literature in Spanish. To develop reading skills, *Antes de leer*, a series of pre-reading questions, precedes each selection. Personalized, open-ended questions *(Díganos)* follow each reading and provide opportunities to discuss your own opinions and experiences in relation to the reading topic or theme.

Self-Tests: The Self-Tests, which appear after Lessons 3, 6, 9, 12, 15, and 18, enable you to review the structures, vocabulary, and cultural information of the three preceding lessons. Organized by lesson and by grammatical structure, the Self-Tests help you to determine quickly what material you have mastered and which concepts to target for further review. An answer key is provided in Appendix E for immediate verification.

***Panorama hispánico* and *Teleinforme*:** These sections, which appear after each even-numbered lesson, focus on the life-style, culture, geography, economy, and history of specific regions of the Spanish-speaking world. The full-color *Panorama hispánico* photo essays feature captions in simple Spanish; each caption ends with a question that invites cross-cultural comparison. The *Teleinforme* sections, which reinforce the content of the photo essays, include previewing, post-viewing, and expansion activities designed to enhance comprehension of the authentic footage featured in the *Teleinforme* modules of the *¿Cómo se dice...?* video.

Reference Materials: The following sections provide useful reference tools throughout the course:

- *Maps:* Colorful, up-to-date maps of the Hispanic world appear on the inside front and back covers of the textbook for quick reference.

- *Appendixes:* Appendix A summarizes the sounds and key pronunciation features of the Spanish language, with abundant examples; this section is also recorded on the Student Audio so you can hear and practice proper pronunciation of the Spanish sounds outside of the classroom. Conjugations of high-frequency regular, stem-changing, and irregular Spanish verbs constitute Appendix B. Appendix C is a glossary of all grammatical terms used in the text, with examples. Appendix D provides English translations of the opening passages. Appendix E is the answer key to the Self-Tests. Appendix F provides a list of the Spanish names of more than 100 professions and occupations to facilitate personalized classroom discussion.

- *Vocabularies:* Spanish-English and English-Spanish glossaries list all active, core vocabulary introduced in the *Vocabulario* lists that follow the opening passages and in the *Estructuras* sections. Active vocabulary is identified by the number of the lesson in which the word or phrase first appears. The Spanish-English vocabulary also lists passive vocabulary, which consists of those words glossed by an English equivalent in the text.

Supplementary Materials

Student Audio: A free ninety-minute audio (in cassette or CD) containing recordings of the opening passages, the pronunciation sections, and the introduction to Spanish sounds from Appendix A is packaged with each copy of the student's text. This cassette is designed to maximize exposure to the sounds of natural spoken Spanish and improve your pronunciation.

Workbook/Laboratory Manual: Each lesson of the Workbook/Laboratory Manual is correlated to the corresponding lesson in the student's text and is divided into two sections. The *Workbook Activities* section offers an array of writing activities—sentence completion, sentence transformation, fill-in charts, dehydrated sentences, answering questions, crossword puzzles, and illustration-based exercises—that reinforce the structures and vocabulary presented in the textbook. Reading comprehension passages appear after each odd-numbered lesson to further skill development in that area. *Check Your Progress* sections provide a comprehensive review of key vocabulary and structures after every two lessons. The *Laboratory Activities* section includes pronunciation, structure, listening comprehension, and dictation exercises to be used in conjunction with the Audio Program. An answer key for all written exercises with discrete answers in both the Workbook and the Laboratory sections is provided for self-correction.

Audio Program: The complete Audio Program to accompany the *¿Cómo se dice...?* Workbook/Laboratory Manual, Seventh Edition, is available for purchase. The textbook opening passages are included as listening and pronunciation exercises in each lesson; they are dramatized once at natural speed, then reread with pauses for repetition. They are followed by comprehension questions, an open-ended activity that elicits responses appropriate to given situations, structured grammar exercises, a listening comprehension activity, and a dictation. A comprehensive review section of questions follows Lessons 9 and 18. Answers to all exercises, except for those that require a written response, are provided on the audio.

¿Cómo se dice...? Multimedia CD-ROM 3.0:   This new CD-ROM is an interactive multimedia program featuring short clips from the *¿Cómo se dice...?* Video with accompanying transcripts and access to a bilingual glossary. The clips are supported by a variety of comprehension and interpretation activities to help hone your listening skills. Language practice exercises corresponding to the language points presented in *¿Cómo se dice...?* are also included on this CD-ROM. The exercises contain links to a grammar reference that provides additional review of grammatical concepts.

¿Cómo se dice...? Video: This revised video program provides a unique opportunity to develop listening skills and cultural awareness through multiple levels of viewing materials: unrehearsed interviews with native speakers from sixteen Spanish-speaking countries on a wide variety of topics, authentic as well as adapted footage, and images of everyday life. The video consists of eighteen modules that correlate to the *Así somos* and *Teleinforme* sections in the student's text. Filmed during the Semana Panamericana at the Universidad Autónoma de Guadalajara in Mexico, the nine *Así somos* modules reinforce the lesson themes, vocabulary, and language functions. They enable you to see, hear, and interact with Hispanics in authentic settings. In each module, students listen to a series of basic questions posed by María Isabel, the host, and the interviewees' responses. The segment concludes with María Isabel asking the viewers a question to which they provide a personalized response. The special *Entrevista* section, which appears at the end of Lessons 3, 7, 13, 15, and 17, features interviews with selected professionals. The nine *Teleinforme* modules present a broad cultural overview of the Hispanic world through authentic as well as adapted television footage from a number of Hispanic countries. Each *Teleinforme* includes two to four clips with a wide range of content: interviews, travelogues, festivals, and commercials. The content reinforces in a visually appealing and lively manner the material presented in the *Panoramas hispánicos*.

The *¿Cómo se dice...?* Web Site and Spanish Web Resources: The upgraded student's web site features web search activities related to the content of the lessons in the textbook. A self test for each lesson serves as an additional check of your progress in Spanish. This version of the *¿Cómo se dice...?* Web Site also includes a new flashcard feature designed to help review terms, images, and definitions. Audio- and video-based activities are now part of the web site. In addition, the Spanish Web Resources page provides links to authentic Spanish sites, maps of the Spanish-speaking world, and downloadable generic transparencies. The web site is accessible at *http://spanish.college.hmco.com/students*.

***¿Cómo se dice...?* Blackboard/WebCT ePack:**   This new component provides materials in online formats to those institutions moving to online instruction.

Acknowledgments

We wish to express appreciation to the following colleagues for the many valuable suggestions they offered in their reviews of the Seventh Edition.

Richard Auletta, LIU, Brookville, NY
Ann Baker, University of Evansville
Joanne de la Parra, Queen's University
Roxana Levin, St. Petersburg Junior College
Li McCleod, University of Saskatchewan
Kathy McConnell, Point Loma Nazarene University
Matthew Tornatore, Truman State University

We also extend our sincere appreciation to the Modern Languages Staff of Houghton Mifflin Company, College Division: Beth Kramer, Director; Amy Baron, Sponsoring Editor; Rafael Burgos-Mirabal, Development Editor; Carol Newman, Senior Project Editor; Jodi O'Rourke, Production/Design Coordinator; Priscilla Bailey, Senior Manufacturing Coordinator; and Henry Rachlin, Senior Designer.

Ana C. Jarvis
Raquel Lebredo
Francisco Mena-Ayllón

We would like to hear your comments on and reactions to *¿Cómo se dice...?*, Seventh Edition. Reports on your experiences using this program would be of great interest and value to us. Please write us care of Houghton Mifflin Company, College Division, 222 Berkeley Street, Boston, MA 02116–3764 or e-mail us at college_mod_lang@hmco.com.

About the Authors

Ana C. Jarvis, a native of Paraguay, was born in Asunción and attended school in Buenos Aires, Argentina. She received her Ph.D. in Spanish from the University of California, Riverside, in 1973. Presently an instructor of Spanish at Chandler-Gilbert Community College in Chandler, Arizona, Dr. Jarvis previously taught at Mesa Community College, the University of California, Riverside, San Bernardino Valley College, Brigham Young University, and Riverside City College. In addition to authoring numerous Spanish textbooks, she has published several short stories in Spanish and is presently at work on a novel. In 1988 she was chosen "Faculty Member of the Year" at Chandler-Gilbert Community College.

Raquel Lebredo was born in Camagüey, Cuba. She attended school in Havana and later enrolled at the University of Havana, where she received a Ph.D. in Education in 1950. She was subsequently employed as an elementary school principal, and taught literature and language at a preparatory school in Havana. After living in Spain for a period of time, she moved in 1968 to the United States. Dr. Lebredo was awarded a Ph.D. in Spanish from the University of California, Riverside, in 1973. Since then she has taught Spanish at Claremont Graduate School, Crafton Hills College, the University of Redlands, and California Baptist University, and has authored several Spanish textbooks. In 1985 she was chosen "Faculty Member of the Year" by the student body at California Baptist University, and in 1991 she received a YWCA "Women of Achievement" award.

Francisco Mena-Ayllón, a native of Madrid, Spain, received his Ph.D. in Spanish from the University of California, Riverside, in 1973. He has taught Spanish language and literature courses at the University of California, Riverside, Oberlin College, California State University, Chico, the University of Redlands, and Crafton Hills College. In addition to authoring numerous Spanish textbooks in the United States, he has published a book about Federico García Lorca and several volumes of his own poetry. His poetry has been published in Spain, Latin America, and the United States. His work has also been included in several anthologies of contemporary Spanish poets, and he is listed in *Quién es quién en las letras españo-las, 1978* (Who's Who in Spanish Letters), as an important contributor to contemporary Spanish literature.

¿Cómo se dice...?

¡Mucho gusto!

Lección 1

OBJECTIVES

Pronunciation

The Spanish **a** and **e**

Structure

The alphabet • Cardinal numbers 0–30 • Colors • Days of the week • Months and seasons of the year • Subject pronouns • Present indicative of **ser**

Communication

You will learn some greetings and farewells, how to introduce yourself and say where you are from and what your profession is, how to get people's phone numbers, and how to talk about days of the week and dates.

¡Mucho gusto!

STUDENT
AUDIO

¡Buenos días! Me llamo Juan Carlos Mirabal y soy de California. Soy estudiante de la Universidad de California. ¿Y tú? ¿De dónde eres?

¡Buenas tardes! Me llamo Laura Estévez y soy de Arizona. ¿Cómo te llamas tú? ¿Eres estudiante? Yo soy maestra.

¡Hola! Me llamo María Luisa Vargas Peña y soy de Nuevo México. Soy secretaria. Y yo me llamo Marcos Fuentes y soy de Tejas. Soy analista de sistemas. ¿Ustedes son estudiantes?

¿Qué tal? Me llamo Marisa Barrios y soy mexicana. Soy dentista. ¿Ustedes son norteamericanos?

¡Buenas noches! Me llamo Rafael Hernández y soy de Tejas. Soy piloto. ¿Cómo están ustedes? ¿Bien?

Me llamo Beatriz López y soy de Puerto Rico. Soy profesora de español. ¿Cómo estás? ¿Qué hay de nuevo?

—¡Hasta luego!
—¡Hasta mañana!
—¡Nos vemos el lunes!
—¡Adiós!
—¡Chau!

Vocabulario

Cognados (Cognates)[1]

el (la) dentista[2] dentist	el (la) piloto pilot	el (la) secretario(-a) secretary
el (la) estudiante student	el (la) profesor(-a) professor	la universidad university
mexicano(-a)[3] Mexican		

Nombres (Nouns)

el (la) analista de sistemas[4] systems analyst	el lunes Monday	el (la) profesor(-a) de español[4] Spanish teacher
el español[5] Spanish (language)	el (la) maestro(-a) teacher (at elementary school level)	

Verbo (Verb)

ser   to be

Adjetivo (Adjective)

norteamericano(-a)[3]   North
American

NOTE: Explain that **buenas noches** may be used both for greeting and for taking leave. The shortened form, **buenas**, and **muy buenas** may also be used. Also discuss the appropriate time of day for each greeting.

Saludos y despedidas (Greetings and farewells)

adiós good-bye	buenos días good morning	hola hello
buenas noches good evening, good night	chau[6] bye	Nos vemos. See you.
buenas tardes good afternoon	hasta luego see you later	
	hasta mañana see you tomorrow	

SUGGESTION: Encourage students to use these greetings as they enter the classroom each day.

Otras palabras y expresiones (Other words and expressions)

¿cómo? how	Mucho gusto. How do you do? Nice to meet you.	usted (Ud.) you (formal)
de from		y and
dónde where	tú you (familiar)	

Note: Vocabulario = Vocabulary

[1]words that are very similar in both languages

[2]Nouns ending in -**ista** are used for both feminine and masculine.

[3]When modifying a feminine pronoun or noun, the adjective will end in -**a**. Notice also that adjectives of nationality are not capitalized.

[4]English uses a noun with the function of an adjective. Spanish uses the **de** phrase: **analista de sistemas; profesora de español.**

[5]Names of languages are not capitalized in Spanish.

[6]from the Italian "ciao"

Preguntas y respuestas útiles *(Useful questions and answers)*

¿Cómo te llamas tú?[1] What is your name?

Me llamo... My name is . . .

¿Cómo está usted? How are you? *(formal)*

¿Cómo estás? How are you? *(familiar)*

¿Cómo están ustedes? How are you? (when speaking to more than one person)

¿Qué tal? How is it going? *(familiar)*

¿Qué hay de nuevo?[2] What's new?

bien fine, well

muy bien very well

no no, not

no muy bien not very well

SUGGESTION: Prepare name tags for students to wear until everyone knows everyone else's name. You may want to include the Spanish equivalent of each name. Students may then introduce themselves using **Me llamo...**, and refer to themselves and each other by name.

RELATED VOCABULARY: Other informal expressions are **¿Cómo te va?, ¿Qué hay?, Hasta la vista**, and **Hasta pronto.** Present several mini-dialogues in which you incorporate some of the expressions. Then have students practice these informal exchanges in small groups.

Vocabulario adicional *(Additional vocabulary)*

Otras profesiones *(Other professions)*

el (la) auxiliar de vuelo
flight attendant

el (la) enfermero(-a)
nurse

el (la) médico(-a)
doctor (medical)

el (la) programador(-a)
programmer

el (la) recepcionista
receptionist

---

[1]**¿Cómo se llama usted?** is used in a formal situation.
[2]Possible answers: **No mucho.** *(Not much.)* or **Nada.** *(Nothing.)*

Títulos *(Titles)*

doctor (Dr.)   doctor[1] *(masculine)*
doctora (Dra.)   doctor *(feminine)*
profesor   professor, teacher,
   instructor *(masculine)*

profesora   professor, teacher,
   instructor *(feminine)*
señor (Sr.)   Mr., sir, gentleman

señora (Sra.)   Mrs., madam, lady
señorita (Srta.)   Miss, young lady

¡Conversemos!

Team up with a classmate and respond appropriately to the following questions.

1. ¿Juan Carlos Mirabal es de California o de Arizona? ¿Es estudiante o profesor?
2. ¿De dónde es Laura Estévez? ¿Es estudiante o maestra?
3. ¿María Luisa es recepcionista o secretaria? ¿Cuál es la profesión de Marcos?
4. ¿Marisa Barrios es norteamericana o mexicana? ¿Es enfermera o dentista?
5. ¿De dónde es Rafael Hernández? ¿Es auxiliar de vuelo o piloto?
6. ¿Beatriz López es puertorriqueña o mexicana? ¿Es médica o profesora?

Note: ¡Conversemos! = Let's talk!
[1]In most Spanish-speaking countries, lawyers and members of many other professions who hold the equivalent of a Ph.D. are addressed as **doctor** or **doctora**.

¿Lo sabía Ud.?

■ María es un nombre *(name)* muy popular en España *(Spain)* y en Latinoamérica. Frecuentemente se usa con otros *(with other)* nombres: **Ana María, María Isabel, María Teresa, María Luisa,** etc. Se usa también como segundo nombre *(middle name)* para hombres *(men)*: **José María, Luis María,** etc.

■ En los países *(countries)* hispánicos las personas generalmente usan dos apellidos *(last names)*: el apellido del padre *(father's)* y el apellido de la madre *(mother's)*. Por ejemplo *(For example)*, los hijos de María **Rivas** y Juan **Pérez** usan los apellidos **Pérez Rivas.**

■ En una guía telefónica *(phone book)* en español, alfabetizan *(they alphabetize)* los nombres según *(according to)* los dos apellidos; por ejemplo:

Peña Aguilar, Rosa
Peña Aguilar, Sara Luisa
Peña Gómez, Raúl
Quesada Álvarez, Javier
Quesada Álvarez, Octavio
Quesada Benítez, Ana María

UNIVERSIDAD NACIONAL	
Nombre	Ana Luisa Méndez Díaz
Número de identidad	80259956
Fecha de expedición	Válido hasta
20 julio 01	31 diciembre 2006
Firma	*Ana Luisa Méndez Díaz*

• ¿Cuál *(What)* es un nombre muy popular en inglés *(English)*?

• ¿Cuáles son sus *(your)* dos apellidos?

See the *¿Cómo se dice...?* Web site for activities on authentic cultural material: http://spanish.college.hmco.com/students

INTERNET

Note: ¿Lo sabía Ud.? = Did you know?

Pronunciación

STUDENT AUDIO

A The Spanish a

The Spanish **a** is pronounced like the *a* in the English word *father*. Listen to your teacher and repeat the following words.

Ana	Ágata
Marta	sábado
llamas	mayo
analista	hasta mañana

SUGGESTION: Model each word and have the class repeat the sounds and words chorally and individually. Then have students repeat the following sentences for additional pronunciation practice using words in context.

B   The Spanish e

The Spanish e is pronounced like the *e* in the English word *eight*. Listen to your teacher and repeat the following words.

a: Ada llama a la dama. Las
   naranjas van a Granada.

e: Teresa y Elena beben el café de
   René. Él lee el papel de Pepe.

qué	usted
enero	Pepe
Ester	teléfono
secretaria	Teresa

Estructuras

1   The alphabet   *(El alfabeto)*

NOTE: Mention that Spanish speakers often pronounce acronyms as if they were words (examples: CIA, UCLA).

Letter	Name	Letter	Name	Letter	Name
a	a	k	ka	s	ese
b	be	l	ele	t	te
c	ce	m	eme	u	u
d	de	n	ene	v	ve
e	e	ñ	eñe	w	doble ve
f	efe	o	o	x	equis
g	ge	p	pe	y	i griega
h	hache	q	cu	z	zeta
i	i	r	ere		
j	jota	rr	erre		

práctica ....

A. Spell these well-known acronyms in Spanish.

1. FBI   5. NBA
2. IBM   6. NHF
3. NAACP   7. CIO
4. PTA   8. AFL

B. A Spanish-speaking person may not know how to spell your name. If that person wants to write it, he or she might ask, **¿Cómo se escribe?** *(How do you spell it?)*. Learn how to spell your name in Spanish and ask other members of the class how to spell theirs.

2 Cardinal numbers 0–30 *(Números cardinales 0–30)*

SUGGESTION: Have students practice numbers from zero to thirty by counting forwards, backwards, and by twos in odd and even numbers.

0 cero	7 siete	14 catorce	21 veintiuno
1 uno	8 ocho	15 quince	30 treinta
2 dos	9 nueve	16 dieciséis[1]	
3 tres	10 diez	17 diecisiete	
4 cuatro	11 once	18 dieciocho	
5 cinco	12 doce	19 diecinueve	
6 seis	13 trece	20 veinte	

ATENCIÓN   **Uno** changes to **un** before a masculine singular noun: **un profesor** *(one professor)*. **Uno** changes to **una** before a feminine singular noun: **una profesora** *(one professor)*.

práctica ••

ACTIVITY SUGGESTION: See the *IAM (Instructor's Activities Manual)* for an additional in-class activity: **Bingo.**

A. To ask someone for his or her phone number, say, "**¿Cuál es tu[2] número de teléfono?**" *(What is your phone number?).* Ask several members of the class for their phone numbers.

B. Complete the following series of numbers.

1. dos, cuatro,... treinta
2. uno, tres, cinco,... veintinueve
3. cero, tres,... dieciocho
4. cero, cuatro,... veintiocho

3 Colors *(Colores)*

SUGGESTION: Use the overhead transparency to introduce the colors.

RELATED VOCABULARY: Point out that the adjectives **claro** *(light)* and **oscuro** *(dark)* are frequently used with some colors.

EXPANSION: Name a color and then have students point to an object in the classroom or to items in the text photographs of that color. Also have students say how **verde, rosado, anaranjado, morado,** and **gris** can be obtained by mixing other colors.

I—Azul y amarillo.
S—Verde.

■ You will see different colors in the classroom. Learn how to say them in Spanish.

amarillo   anaranjado   azul   blanco   gris   marrón (café)

morado   negro   rojo   rosado   verde

---

[1]The numbers 16 to 29 may also be spelled as separate words: **diez y seis..., veinte y uno...,** and so on.
[2]**tu** = *your* (when addressing a friend or a very young person). Say, "**¿Cuál es su número de teléfono?**" when addressing someone as **usted.**

práctica ••

A. To ask someone whether he or she likes something, you say, "**¿Te gusta...?**"[1] To say that you like something, say, "**Me gusta...**" Conduct a survey of your classmates to find out which color is the most popular in class, following the model.

> MODELO: —¿Qué color te gusta?
> —*Me gusta el color rojo.*

B. *A splash of color!* This is an open-air market in Guatemala. With a partner, takes turns naming the colors that you see here in Spanish. You will need to include:

claro   *light*
oscuro   *dark*
(i.e., **azul oscuro** = *dark blue*)

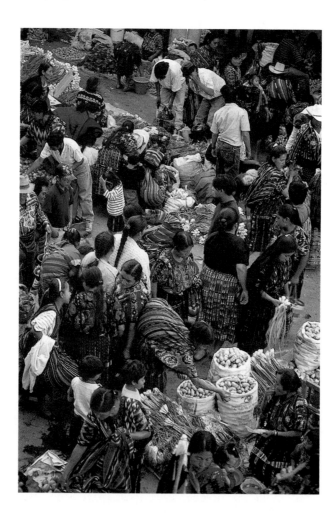

---

[1]When addressing someone as **usted**, use **¿Le gusta...?**

4 Days of the week *(Los días de la semana)*

SEPTIEMBRE

LUNES	MARTES	MIÉRCOLES	JUEVES	VIERNES	SÁBADO	DOMINGO
		1	2	3	4	5
6	7	8	9	10	11	12
13	14	15	16	17	18	19
20	21	22	23	24	25	26
27	28	29	30			

—¿Qué día es hoy? ¿**Jueves?**   *"What day is today? Thursday?"*
—No, hoy es **viernes.**   *"No, today is Friday."*

- In Spanish-speaking countries, the week starts on Monday.
- Note that the days of the week are not capitalized in Spanish.
- The days of the week are masculine in Spanish. The masculine definite articles **el** and **los** are often used with them to express *on*.

práctica ....

SUGGESTION: Give a day of the week. Have individual students say the day before and after the day given.

EXPANSION: Personalize the calendar by asking students to give days of familiar events.

¿Cuál es tu día favorito?
¿Qué día es el programa *60 Minutos* en televisión?
¿Qué día es tu clase de... (inglés, historia, psicología, antropología, ciencias políticas, etc.)?

A. The person asking these questions is always a day ahead. Respond, following the model.

> MODELO: —¿Hoy es lunes?
> —*No, hoy es domingo.*

1. ¿Hoy es miércoles?
2. ¿Hoy es domingo?
3. ¿Hoy es viernes?
4. ¿Hoy es martes?
5. ¿Hoy es sábado?
6. ¿Hoy es jueves?

B. Using the calendar sheet on this page, students take turns asking a classmate what day a certain date falls on.

> MODELO: —¿Qué día es el 18 de septiembre?
> —*Es sábado.*

5 Months and seasons of the year   *(Los meses y las estaciones del año)*

SUGGESTION: Ask students to identify the seasons based on the visual clues given on Transparency 11.

El invierno

La primavera

El verano

El otoño

■ To ask for the date, say:

    —¿Qué fecha es hoy?   *"What's the date today?"*

■ When giving the date, always begin with the phrase **"hoy es el..."**

    —Hoy es el veinte de mayo.   *"Today is May twentieth."*

■ Begin with the number, followed by the preposition **de** *(of)*, and then the month.

el quince de agosto	*August fifteenth*
el diez de septiembre	*September tenth*
—¿Qué fecha es hoy? ¿**El primero de mayo?**	*"What's the date today? May first?"*
—No, hoy es **el treinta de abril.**	*"No, today is April thirtieth."*

ATENCIÓN   **Primero** *(First)* is the only ordinal number used with dates. Also, the months are not capitalized in Spanish.

práctica ••

EXPANSION A: Write the following holidays on the board or on the overhead. Explain the cultural significance of some of these dates and the ways in which holidays are celebrated in different Hispanic countries.

El Año Nuevo–el 1 de enero
La Navidad–el 25 de diciembre
El Día de Reyes–el 6 de enero
El Día de la Independencia de los EEUU–el 4 de julio
El Día de los Muertos–el 2 de noviembre
El cumpleaños de Lincoln–el 12 de febrero
El cumpleaños de Washington–el 22 de febrero

A. Give the Spanish equivalent of the following dates.

1. July fourth
2. October thirty-first
3. January first
4. May fifth
5. February twelfth
6. December twenty-fifth
7. March twenty-first
8. April second
9. June twentieth
10. September ninth
11. August thirteenth
12. November eleventh

B. Indicate in which season the following months fall in the Northern Hemisphere.

1. febrero
2. agosto
3. mayo
4. enero
5. octubre
6. julio
7. abril
8. noviembre

C. Conduct a survey of your classmates to find out which season is the most popular, following the model. Which one is the least popular?

MODELO: —¿Qué estación te gusta?
—Me gusta el (la) _____.

6 Subject pronouns *(Pronombres personales usados como sujetos)*

SUGGESTION: Write the subject pronouns on the chalkboard, then pronounce them while pointing to yourself and to one or more students. You may also draw stick figures on the board or on flash cards to practice the subject pronouns with students in groups or individually.

Singular	Plural
yo *I*	**nosotros** *we* (masc.) / **nosotras** *we* (fem.)
tú *you* (familiar)	**vosotros** *you* (masc., familiar) / **vosotras** *you* (fem., familiar)
usted *you* (formal) / **él** *he* / **ella** *she*	**ustedes** *you* (formal) / **ellos** *they* (masc.) / **ellas** *they* (fem.)

■ The **tú** form is used as the equivalent of *you* to address a friend, a coworker, a relative, or a child. The **usted** form is used in general to express deference or respect. In most Spanish-speaking countries today, young people tend to call each other **tú** even if they have just met. If in doubt, use **usted.**

■ The plural form of **tú** is **vosotros(-as),** which is used only in Spain. In Latin America, the plural form **ustedes** (abbreviated **Uds.**) is used as the plural form of both **usted** (abbreviated **Ud.**) and **tú.**

■ The masculine plural forms can refer to the masculine gender alone or to both genders together.

Ellos (Luis y Carlos) son de Panamá.
They (Luis and Carlos) are from Panama.
Ellos (María, Marta y Raúl) son de España.
They (María, Marta, and Raúl) are from Spain.
Nosotros (Ana María, Carlos y yo) somos estudiantes.
We (Ana María, Carlos, and I) are students.

práctica ···

A. Identify the personal pronoun that corresponds to each picture below.

1. _____

2. _____

3. _____

4. _____

5. _____

6. _____

7. _____

8. _____

9. _____

SUGGESTION A: Tell students that in some Hispanic families children use **Ud.** with parents and/or grandparents.

B. Say whether you would use **tú, usted,** or **ustedes** to address the following people.

1. the president of the university
2. two strangers
3. a new classmate
4. your instructor
5. your best friend
6. your neighbor's children

C. What pronouns would be used to refer to the following persons?

1. Teresa y José
2. María y Verónica
3. Victoria y yo *(fem.)*
4. Enrique y yo
5. Carlos y Roberto
6. usted y Patricia

7 Present indicative of **ser** *(Presente de indicativo del verbo ser)*

ser	*to be*	
Singular		
yo	**soy**	*I am*
tú	**eres**	*you are* (fam.)
Ud.		*you are* (form.)
él	**es**	*he is*
ella		*she is*
Plural		
nosotros(-as)	**somos**	*we are*
vosotros(-as)	**sois**	*you are* (fam.)
Uds.		*you are* (form.)
ellos	**son**	*they are* (masc.)
ellas		*they are* (fem.)

■ The verb **ser,** *to be,* is irregular. Its forms, like the forms of other irregular verbs, must be memorized.

SUGGESTION: Bring, or have students bring, photos of famous people (historical figures, actors, scientists, etc.) to class. Have students take turns asking questions about the photos: **¿Quién es? ¿De dónde es?**

■ The verb **ser** is commonly used to express identity, place of origin, occupation, and nationality.

—¿Ud. **es** profesor?[1]   *"Are you a teacher?"*
—No, **soy** estudiante.   *"No, I'm a student."*

—¿Carlos Paz **es** mexicano?[1]   *"Is Carlos Paz Mexican?"*
—Sí, **es** de Guadalajara.   *"Yes, he's from Guadalajara."*

—¿Quién **es** él?   *"Who is he?"*
—**Es** Héctor Díaz.   *"He is Héctor Díaz."*

—¿De dónde **es**?   *"Where is he from?"*
—**Es** de Ecuador.   *"He is from Ecuador."*

---

[1]The indefinite article is not used after the verb **ser** when describing profession, nationality, religion, or party affiliation unless an adjective follows the noun: **Ella es católica. Ana es una profesora excelente.**

práctica ....

A. Say where these people are from, using the information found in the illustrations. Also, say the capital of each country.

MODELO: yo
Yo soy de Venezuela. La capital de Venezuela es Caracas.

EXPANSION A: Use Transparency 9–10, which shows the United States. Move tokens that represent people around the map while asking students questions such as, **"¿De dónde es Juan?"** You may also present basic geographical terms (**norte, sur, oeste, este, río, montaña, lago, estado,** etc.), and ask students questions based on the map (e.g., **¿Cuál es la capital de...?).** Stress the fact that many cities and states in the United States have names of Spanish origin.

NOTE A: A definite article is sometimes used with certain countries, e.g., **el Perú.** Since these articles are appearing less frequently in both written and spoken Spanish, they are not used in **¿Cómo se dice...?**

SUGGESTION A: Point out that Bolivia has two official capitals, La Paz and Sucre.

1. Teresa
2. Carlos y yo
3. Juan, Mario y José
4. tú
5. ellos
6. nosotras
7. Uds.
8. Julio

B. Say what nationality everyone is, using the list below. Follow the order used in Exercise A.

> MODELO: yo
> *Yo soy venezolana.*

argentino(-a)	chileno(-a)	uruguayo(-a)
boliviano(-a)	ecuatoriano(-a)	venezolano(-a)
brasileño(-a)	paraguayo(-a)	
colombiano(-a)	peruano(-a)	

¡A ver cuánto aprendió!

INTERNET

See the *¿Cómo se dice...?* Web site for additional grammar and vocabulary practice: http://spanish.college. hmco.com/students

¡Repase el vocabulario!

Complete the following sentences using vocabulary learned in **Lección 1.**

1. Buenos _____. ¿Cómo _____ ustedes?
2. Me _____ Carlos Sandoval. ¿Cómo te _____ tú?
3. Yo _____ de Guadalajara.
4. Ella es _____ de español.
5. Julio es analista de _____.
6. David es _____; es de California.
7. Hola, ¿qué hay de _____?
8. Lupe es _____; es de Acapulco.
9. ¿Cómo estás? ¿_____?
10. _____ luego, Antonio.
11. Nos _____ el lunes.
12. Eduardo es auxiliar de _____.

ACTIVITY SUGGESTION: Do **¡Escucha!**, the in-class listening comprehension activity that reviews vocabulary and grammar structures introduced in the lesson. It appears in the answer key of the *IAM*.

ACTIVITY SUGGESTION: See the *IAM* for an additional in-class activity: **Palabras escondidas.**

Entrevista

ACTIVITY SUGGESTION: See the *IAM* for an additional in-class activity: **¿Cómo respondes?**

With a partner, interview each other by asking the following questions.

1. ¿Cómo te llamas?
2. ¿Cómo estás?
3. ¿Tú eres norteamericano(-a)?
4. ¿De dónde eres?
5. ¿Tú eres profesor(-a) o estudiante?
6. ¿Cuál es tu número de teléfono?
7. ¿Qué día es hoy?
8. ¿Qué color te gusta?

Note: ¡A ver cuánto aprendió! = Let's see how much you learned!

Situaciones

What would you say in the following situations? What might the other person say? Act out the scenes with a partner. Take turns playing each role.

1. You encounter your instructor in the morning and ask how he or she is.
2. At the mall, you run into a friend you haven't seen for a while.
3. You meet a friend's twelve-year-old daughter and ask how she is.
4. You leave your instructor's office. You have an appointment with him or her tomorrow.
5. You say good-bye to a friend and add that you will see him or her on Monday.
6. You meet an older person and want to know what his or her name is.
7. You want to know what day today is.
8. You ask someone what today's date is.

Sumas y restas *(Additions and subtractions)*

Solve these arithmetic problems, using the following mathematical terms.

+ más   − menos   = son

1. 8 + 15 =
2. 18 − 14 =
3. 30 − 13 =
4. 7 + 11 =
5. 27 − 12 =
6. 16 + 9 =

Por teléfono *(By phone)*

Imagine that you and a classmate are in Madrid, Spain. Take turns reading the telephone numbers you must call according to the following needs.

1. You are having car trouble.
2. You need to cash a check.
3. You need some medicine.
4. You want to send roses to a friend.
5. You want to see a play.
6. You have to travel by plane.
7. You need to have your picture taken.
8. You want to report an accident.

Estación de Policía 911

Banco Nacional 701-8965

Farmacia "La Gran Vía" 475-0432

Aerolíneas Mexicanas 943-7510

Aeropuerto de Barajas 431-7068

Fotografía "Marín" 562-0437

Museo de Arte 792-3587

Teatro Madrid 686-9528

Hospital Municipal 482-3157

Apartamentos de lujo 987-3065

Dr. Manuel Vega Dentista 470-9265

Florería "Carrón" 952-0038

Estación de Ómnibus 493-7196

Taller de Mecánica "San Carlos" 356-7932

Servicio de Ambulancia 498-6530

9. A friend needs to go to the emergency room.
10. You need a place to live.
11. You want to buy a plane ticket to Mexico.
12. You want to see Picasso's paintings.
13. One of your friends has been hospitalized.
14. You want to travel to a nearby city.
15. You have a toothache.

 Para escribir (*To write*)

Following the style of the introductions on pages 2 and 3, write your own.

En la vida real

CD-ROM

Do the interactive exercises on the CD-ROM for additional practice.

FOLLOW-UP: Have students act out the dialogue so that they meet you or another teacher. Remind them to use the appropriate formal forms.

Encuentros (*Encounters*)

Imagine that you and a classmate meet outside of class. How would you greet each other in Spanish? How would you find out each other's complete name and phone number? How would you say good-bye? Act out this situation with a partner. You may want to include these additional phrases:

¿Cómo te va?	*How is it going (for you)?*
Hasta la vista.	*Until I see you again.*

Presentaciones

The class will be divided into groups of four. Each student will say who he or she is and where he or she is from. One member of the group will introduce his or her partners to the rest of the class.

Note: En la vida real = In real life.

Antes de leer *(Before reading)*

As you read the information below, find the answers to the following questions:

1. ¿Cuál es la profesión de José María Estévez y de Esmeralda Olmos?
2. ¿Son mexicanos?
3. ¿David Smith es norteamericano o mexicano?
4. ¿Es profesor?
5. ¿Rosalba Rojas es mexicana o cubana?
6. ¿Es enfermera?
7. ¿De dónde es Rafael Burgos?
8. ¿Cuál es la profesión de Rafael Burgos?

Mis compañeros°

My classmates

José María Estévez y Esmeralda Olmos son dos actores de televisión. Son de Guadalajara.
David Smith es de Tejas. Es estudiante.
Rosalba Rojas es de La Habana. Es médica.
Rafael Burgos es de San Juan. Es piloto.

Díganos... *(Tell us . . .)*

1. ¿Cómo se llama usted?
2. ¿Es usted norteamericano(-a)?
3. ¿De dónde es?
4. ¿Es usted estudiante o profesor(-a)?

Note: ¡Vamos a leer! = Let's read!

ASÍ SOMOS

VIDEO   CD-ROM

Do the interactive exercises on
the CD-ROM for additional practice.

NARRADORA —¿De dónde es Ud.?

ORLANDO —Soy de El Paso, Tejas, y eso está en la frontera
del estado de Chihuahua en México y en el
estado de Tejas en los Estados Unidos.

Preparación

NOTE: The video-related vocabulary is listed in the *Instructor's Activities Manual* for your reference. Its purpose is to facilitate students' comprehension. You may want to distribute the vocabulary to the class before viewing.

A. Datos personales (*Personal data*). Answer the following questions about yourself. Then ask a classmate the same questions.

1. ¿Cómo se llama Ud.?
2. ¿Cómo se escribe su nombre?
3. ¿De dónde es Ud.?
4. ¿Cuál es su dirección?
5. ¿Cuál es su número de teléfono?

SUGGESTION: Before showing the video, tell students that they are about to hear unrehearsed interviews with native Spanish speakers from many different countries and that they will hear many different accents.

B. ¿Cómo se escribe...? (*How do you spell . . . ?*) Give the spellings of the following people's or places out loud.

1. your first and last name
2. the name of your Spanish professor
3. the name of your university
4. your hometown

NOTE: See the Instructor's Edition frontmatter for additional suggestions on implementing video in the classroom.

Comprensión

SUGGESTION: Have students do the *Preparación* activities in pairs or groups before viewing the video segments.

A. ¿Cómo se llama Ud.? Watch the video segment where people take turns answering the question, **¿Cómo se llama Ud.?** Observe the different ways they respond. Then, match each speaker with the phrase used to give his or her name.

SUGGESTION: Have students complete each exercise after viewing the corresponding video segment and have them compare their answers in pairs or groups.

A	B
_____ 1. Pedro Urista Torres	a. Mi nombre es...
_____ 2. Otmara Joseph	b. (Yo) me llamo...
_____ 3. Juan Galindo Mascaraque	c. Yo soy...
_____ 4. María Fernanda Matos	d. Mi nombre completo es...
_____ 5. Gustavo López	
_____ 6. Jaime Andrés Polo Nieto	
_____ 7. Ivonne Iliana Silva Orneles	
_____ 8. Tamara Berríos	
_____ 9. Víctor Manuel Méndez Ortiz	

FOLLOW-UP B: Have students locate the capitals of the countries listed on the maps on the inside front and back cover of their textbooks.

B. Soy de... Match each person's name with his or her country of origin.

	A		B
_____	1. Jaime	a.	Puerto Rico
_____	2. Pedro	b.	Colombia
_____	3. Víctor Manuel	c.	España
_____	4. Leonardo	d.	El Salvador
_____	5. Juan	e.	Paraguay
_____	6. Héctor	f.	Bolivia
_____	7. Gustavo	g.	Ecuador
_____	8. Milka	h.	Estados Unidos
_____	9. Otmara	i.	México
_____	10. Orlando	j.	Panamá

C. ¿Verdadero (True) o falso? Read the following statements. Circle **V** (**Verdadero**) or **F** (**Falso**) according to what you understood from the video. If a statement is false, correct it.

V F   1. La dirección de Carolina es avenida El Cortijo 230 en Monte Rico, Lima.

V F   2. La dirección de Sofía es Andama 130, Interior 1.

V F   3. La dirección de Milka es calle Santa Cruz, 31.

V F   4. La dirección de Leonardo es Las Delicias, calle 14 en Ponce, Puerto Rico.

D. Números de teléfono. Match each statement with the name of the person who said it.

SUGGESTION: Have students answer orally or in writing the questions posed by the **narradora** at the end of the video: **Y tú, ¿cómo te llamas y de dónde eres?**

	A		B
_____	1. 4-35-17-09	a.	Carolina
_____	2. 33-22-51	b.	Zaida
_____	3. Mi teléfono es el 6-32-96-22.	c.	Juan
_____	4. Es el 6-38-68-36.	d.	Milka
_____	5. Mi teléfono en Caracas es 241-32-01.	e.	Gustavo

Ampliación

FOLLOW-UP: In groups, have students make a list of the university situations and activities they saw at the beginning of the video. Ask them how life on campus compares with their own experience. Ask them to describe the gestures people use to greet each other.

A. Las nacionalidades. Complete the following sentences with the nationality that matches the native country of each person.

1. Otmara es de Panamá; es _____.
2. Juan es de España; es _____.
3. Tamara es de Puerto Rico; es _____.
4. Víctor es de México; es _____.
5. Carolina es de Perú; es _____.
6. Jaime y Ángela son de Colombia; son _____.

B. ¿Cuál es la dirección de...? Take turns interviewing a classmate to find out the addresses of the following locations.

1. su restaurante favorito
2. su casa
3. la casa de sus padres
4. la casa de su mejor amigo(-a)

El primer día de clases

OBJECTIVES

Pronunciation

The Spanish **i, o,** and **u**

Structure

Gender and number • Definite and indefinite articles • Cardinal numbers 31–100 •
Telling time • Present indicative of regular **-ar** verbs • Negative and interrogative sentences •
Possession with **de**

Communication

You will learn vocabulary related to the classroom, useful questions and answers, and some
polite expressions.

El primer día de clases

SRTA. ALBA	—*(En la puerta)* Con permiso. Buenos días, profesor.
PROFESOR	—Buenos días. Pase y tome asiento, por favor.
SRTA. ALBA	—Muchas gracias.
PROFESOR	—Señorita Alba, el[1] doctor Díaz.
SRTA. ALBA	—Mucho gusto, doctor Díaz.
DR. DÍAZ	—El gusto es mío, señorita Alba.
SRTA. ALBA	—¡Perdón!, profesor, ¿qué hora es?
PROFESOR	—Son las once y media.
SRTA. ALBA	—¿A qué hora es la clase hoy?
PROFESOR	—Es a las tres de la tarde.

LUISA	—¿Cuál es tu dirección, Mario?
MARIO	—Calle Magnolia, número 98.
LUISA	—Ah, también necesito la dirección de Pedro. Él es amigo de Rocío, ¿no?
MARIO	—Sí. La dirección es avenida Olmos, número 175.
RAÚL	—Mario, ¿cuántos estudiantes hay en la clase?
MARIO	—Hay cuarenta estudiantes.

SUGGESTION: Have students practice this dialogue in groups of three. They may greet and introduce each other using their own names with the appropriate titles of **señor, señora,** or **señorita.**

ESTUDIANTE	—Profesor, ¿cómo se dice "de nada" en inglés?
PROFESOR	—Se dice *"you're welcome."*
ESTUDIANTE	—¿Qué quiere decir *"to return"*?
PROFESOR	—Quiere decir "regresar."

SUGGESTION: While role-playing this dialogue, students should review vocabulary from **Lección 1** by asking each other the meanings of words and phrases.

---

[1]When you are speaking about a third person (indirect address) and use a title with the name, the definite article is required.

LAURA   —¿Tú trabajas, Daniel?
DANIEL   —Sí, yo trabajo en un hospital. ¿Y tú?
LAURA   —Yo no trabajo; solamente estudio.
DANIEL   —¿Cuántas clases tomas?
LAURA   —Tomo cinco clases. Oye, ¿tú tomas francés este semestre?
DANIEL   —No, porque yo ya hablo francés. Tomo una clase de alemán con el Dr. Smith.
LAURA   —Yo no hablo francés, pero hablo un poco de italiano y de portugués.

 SUGGESTION: Use Transparency 14 to practice the pronunciation of the names of countries and languages.
 I—¿Qué idioma hablan en Berlín?
S1—Hablan alemán.
 I—¿Dónde hablan francés?
S2—En París.

Vocabulario

Cognados

la clase class	**el hospital** hospital
el italiano Italian *(language)*	**el portugués** Portuguese *(language)*

Nombres

el alemán   German *(language)*
el (la) amigo(-a)   friend
la avenida   avenue
la calle   street
la clase de alemán   German class
el día   day

la dirección, el domicilio   address
el francés   French *(language)*
el inglés   English *(language)*
el número   number
la puerta   door
la tarde   afternoon

 EXPANSION: Use Transparency 1–2 to present the different languages and dialects of Spain and surrounding countries, using the same question/response format.

Portugal	portugués
España	español
Galicia	gallego
País Vasco	vascuence
Cataluña	catalán
Valencia	valenciano
Francia	francés
Islas Baleares	mallorquín

Verbos

estudiar to study	**necesitar** to need	**tomar** to take
hablar to talk	**regresar** to return	**trabajar** to work

Otras palabras y expresiones

ah   oh
con   with
¿cuál?   what?, which?
¿Cuántos(-as)?   How many?
de la tarde   P.M.
el primer día de clases   the first day of classes

en   in, at
en inglés   in English
este semestre   this semester
hay   there is, there are
hoy   today
oye   listen

porque   because
sí   yes
solamente   only
también   too, also
un poco de   a little
ya   already

Preguntas y respuestas útiles

¿A qué hora...? At what time . . . ?

A la (las)... At . . . *(when referring to time of day)*

¿Cómo se dice...? How do you say . . . ?

Se dice... You say . . . , One says . . .

¿Cuál es tu dirección?[1] What's your address?

Mi dirección es... My address is . . .

¿Qué hora es? What time is it?

Son las... It's . . . *(when referring to time of day)*

¿Qué quiere decir...? What does . . . mean?

Quiere decir... It means . . .

Expresiones de cortesía

Point out that **perdón** is used to apologize for bumping into someone, for example.
Con permiso fits better in situations such as trying to get through a crowd.

Mucho gusto. Pleased to meet you.

El gusto es mío. The pleasure is mine.

Con permiso. Excuse me.

Perdón. Pardon me.

Pase. Come in.

Tome asiento. Have a seat.

Por favor. Please.

Muchas gracias. Thank you very much.

De nada. You're welcome.

Vocabulario adicional

En la clase *(In the class)*

RELATED VOCABULARY: An additional phrase to get someone's attention or request permission to pass by is **permiso.**

RELATED VOCABULARY: **el sacapuntas** *(pencil sharpener);* **el cesto de papeles** *(wastebasket);* **la regla** *(ruler);* **la mochila** *(backpack);* **el maletín** *(briefcase);* **el tablero de anuncios** *(bulletin board);* **la hoja de papel** *(sheet of paper);* **la calculadora** *(calculator);* **el marcador** *(felt-tip marker);* **la goma de borrar** *(eraser).*

NOTE: Point out these variations of vocabulary items: **pluma** or **pluma estilográfica** *(fountain pen);* **alumno(-a)** *(student);* **maestro(-a)** *(elementary teacher).*

ACTIVITY SUGGESTION: See the *IAM* for an additional in-class activity: **Encuentre las respuestas.**

---

[1]When addressing someone as **Ud.**, say, **¿Cuál es su dirección?**
[2]Also "watch"
[3]Ballpoint pen

¡Conversemos!

SUGGESTION: Have students switch roles to practice initiating as well as responding to statements.

Team up with a classmate and respond appropriately to the following questions or statements.

1. Mucho gusto, señor (señora, señorita).
2. Muchas gracias.
3. ¿Cuántos estudiantes hay en la clase?
4. ¿Cómo se dice "*please*" en español *(Spanish)*?
5. ¿Qué quiere decir "con permiso"?
6. ¿Cuál es la dirección de Mario?
7. ¿Dónde trabaja Daniel?
8. ¿Cuántas clases toma Laura este semestre?
9. ¿Daniel habla francés o portugués?
10. ¿Laura habla italiano?

¿Lo sabía Ud.?

■ Para los horarios *(schedules)* de aviones *(planes)*, trenes, ómnibus, teatros, televisión y algunas *(some)* invitaciones, se usa el sistema de veinticuatro horas. Por ejemplo, las cuatro de la tarde son las dieciséis horas.

■ En España y en Latinoamérica, muchas personas estudian inglés en la escuela secundaria *(high school)* y en la universidad.

• ¿Se usa el sistema de 24 horas en los Estados Unidos *(United States)*?

• ¿Qué idioma *(language)* toma la mayoría de los estudiantes norteamericanos en la escuela secundaria?

INTERNET

See the *¿Cómo se dice...?* Web site for activities on authentic cultural material: http://spanish.college.hmco.com/students

Pronunciación

A The Spanish i

STUDENT AUDIO

The Spanish **i** is pronounced like the double *e* in the English word *see*. Listen to your teacher and repeat the following words.

sí	dirección
dice	domicilio
inglés	necesitar
días	hospital
cinco	

SUGGESTION: Model each word and have the class repeat the sounds and words chorally and individually. Then have students work with the following sentences for additional pronunciation practice using words in context.

B The Spanish o

The Spanish **o** is a short, pure vowel. It corresponds to the *o* in the English word *no*, but without the glide. Listen to your teacher and repeat the following words.

luego	número
no	noche
como	ocho
doctor	teléfono

i: Isabel y Ricardo viven en Miami, El pillín tira el balín.
o: Todo el oro es de Rodolfo. El señor Moreno toma Coca-Cola.
u: Usted estuvo en el museo en Perú. Las uvas de mi huerta son buenas.

C The Spanish u

The Spanish **u** is shorter in length than the English *u*. It corresponds to the *ue* sound in the English word *Sue*. Listen to your teacher and repeat the following words.

estudiar	Susana
usted	puerta
mucho	universidad
luz	gusto

1 Gender and number   *(Género y número)*

A. Gender, Part I

■ In Spanish, all nouns—including those denoting non-living things—are either masculine or feminine.

Masculine		Feminine	
el hombre	el lápiz	la mujer	la ventana
el profesor	el estudiante	la profesora	la estudiante
el cuaderno	el secretario	la tiza	la secretaria

■ Most nouns that end in **-o** or denote males are masculine: **cuaderno** *(notebook)*; **hombre** *(man)*.

■ Most nouns that end in **-a** or denote females are feminine: **mes***a* *(table)*; **profesor***a* *(female professor)*; **mujer** *(woman)*.

ATENCIÓN   Some common exceptions include the words **el día** *(day)* and **el mapa** *(map)*, which end in **-a** but are masculine, and the word **la mano** *(hand)*, which ends in **-o** but is feminine.

SUGGESTION: Point to various objects in the classroom and have students name each object, telling whether it is masculine or feminine in Spanish.

EXPANSION: Tell students to close their books. Pick nouns from the vocabulary lists in random order. Say each word and ask students to provide the definite article plus the noun.

I—tiza   S1—la tiza
I—día   S2—el día

Divide the class into groups of three or four and appoint a leader for each group. This person should refer to the vocabulary lists and ask the other members of the group to identify nouns by asking, "**¿Cómo se dice** *the chalkboard*?" Students should take turns giving a complete response. "**Se dice** *la pizarra.*" The group leader should check each response for accuracy and comment, "**correcto**" or "**incorrecto.**"

- Here are some helpful rules to remember about gender:
- Some masculine nouns ending in -o have a corresponding feminine form ending in -a: **el secretario/la secretaria**.
- When a masculine noun ends in a consonant, the corresponding feminine noun is often formed by adding -a: **el profesor/la profesora**.
- Many nouns that refer to people use the same form for both genders: **el estudiante/la estudiante**. In such cases, gender is indicated by the article **el** (masculine) or **la** (feminine).

práctica

Place **el**[1] or **la**[1] before each noun.

1. mapa	6. profesora	11. ventana	16. mano
2. tiza	7. pizarra	12. pluma	17. cuaderno
3. escritorio	8. libro	13. hombre	18. doctor
4. señor	9. mujer	14. día	19. silla
5. doctora	10. puerta	15. secretario	20. señora

B. Plural forms

- The plural of nouns is formed by adding -s to words ending in a vowel and -es to words ending in a consonant.

señora → señoras   reloj → relojes
silla → sillas   borrador → borradores
libro → libros   lección → lecciones

ATENCIÓN   Note that the plural form of **lección** does not have a written accent. See Appendix A.

- When a noun ends in -z, change the -z to c and add -es.

lápiz → lápices   luz *(light)* → luces

- When the plural is used to refer to two or more nouns of different genders, the masculine form is used.

dos secretarias y un secretario → tres secretarios

práctica

Give the plural of the following nouns.

1. mapa	5. ventana	9. borrador
2. reloj	6. puerta	10. día
3. tiza	7. lección	11. luz
4. lápiz	8. escritorio	12. profesor

SUGGESTION: Write nouns in the plural on the chalkboard, using colored chalk to emphasize plural endings. Then have students explain to you the rules for plural formation.

FOLLOW-UP: Play the game **¿Qué ves?** Introduce the first- and second-person singular of the verb **ver** by writing the question **¿Qué ves?** and the answer **Veo...** on the chalkboard. Ask a student to tell what he or she sees in the classroom. Then ask the next student, **"Y tú, ¿qué ves?"** He or she must repeat the original phrase and add one more item.

I—¿Qué ves?
S1—Veo los libros.
I—Y tú, ¿qué ves?
S2—Veo los libros y la pizarra.

You may want to have students play the game in groups of five or six.

2 Definite and indefinite articles *(Artículos determinados e indeterminados)*

A. The definite article

EXPANSION: Have students close their books and practice changing the nouns from the vocabulary lists from singular to plural or vice versa, identifying the appropriate articles.

I—profesor
S1—el profesor, un profesor
S2—los profesores, unos profesores

■ Spanish has four forms that are equivalent to the English definite article *the*.

	Masculine	Feminine	English
Singular	el	la	*the*
Plural	los	las	

el profesor	**los** profesores
la profesora	**las** profesoras
el lápiz	**los** lápices

ATENCIÓN It is a good idea to learn new nouns with their corresponding definite articles—this will help you to remember their gender.

B. The indefinite article

■ The Spanish equivalents of *a (an)* and *some* are as follows.

	Masculine	Feminine	English
Singular	un	una	*a (an)*
Plural	unos	unas	*some*

un libro	**unos** libros
una silla	**unas** sillas
un profesor	**unos** profesores

práctica ....

EXPANSION: In pairs, have students ask each other how many objects or people there are in each drawing. Point out that the interrogative **¿Cuántos(-as)?** must agree with the noun it modifies.

S1—¿Cuántas sillas hay?
S2—Hay una silla.

A. Identify the following objects or people using the appropriate definite article.

1.

2.

3.

4.

5.

6.

ACTIVITY SUGGESTION: See the *IAM* for an additional in-class activity: **En la clase.**

B. Identify the following objects or people using the appropriate indefinite article.

1.   2.   3.

4.   5.   6.

C. With a partner, take turns saying what you need. Use the appropriate indefinite article.

MODELO: Yo necesito un lápiz.

---

3 Cardinal numbers 31–100   *(Números cardinales 31–100)*

31	**treinta y uno**
32	**treinta y dos** (and so on)
40	**cuarenta**
41	**cuarenta y uno** (and so on)
50	**cincuenta**
53	**cincuenta y tres**
60	**sesenta**
68	**sesenta y ocho**
70	**setenta**
77	**setenta y siete**
80	**ochenta**
84	**ochenta y cuatro**
90	**noventa**
95	**noventa y cinco**
100	**cien (ciento)**

■ Note that **y** appears only in numbers between 16 and 99.

práctica ••

When saying phone numbers, people in many Spanish-speaking countries tend to say the first number alone and the rest of the numbers in pairs. Using this system, give the names and phone numbers of the specialists the following people would call for each situation.

1. Your nephew has a bad case of acne.
2. Your best friend thinks she is pregnant.
3. Your grandmother has blurred vision.
4. Your friend's child is sick.
5. Your neighbor has frequent chest pains.

ACTIVITY SUGGESTION: See the *IAM* for an additional in-class activity: **Bingo.**

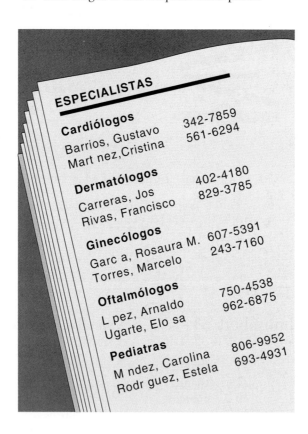

ESPECIALISTAS

Cardiólogos
Barrios, Gustavo   342-7859
Mart nez,Cristina   561-6294

Dermatólogos
Carreras, Jos   402-4180
Rivas, Francisco   829-3785

Ginecólogos
Garc a, Rosaura M.   607-5391
Torres, Marcelo   243-7160

Oftalmólogos
L pez, Arnaldo   750-4538
Ugarte, Elo sa   962-6875

Pediatras
M ndez, Carolina   806-9952
Rodr guez, Estela   693-4931

4 Telling time   *(La hora)*

SUGGESTION: Bring in a clock, make one out of a paper plate, or draw clock faces on the board to illustrate the time.

■ To ask what time it is, say, "**¿Qué hora es?**" To tell the time in Spanish, the following word order is used:

Es la or Son las	+	*hour*	+	y or menos	+	*minutes*

■ **Es** is used with **una.**

  Es la una.

■ **Son** is used with all the other hours.

Son las cuatro.

■ The feminine definite article is always used before the hour, since it refers to *la* **hora.**

Es **la** una y media.

Son **las** diez y cuarto.

■ The hour is given first, then the minutes.

Son las **once** menos **veinte.**

■ The equivalent of *past* or *after* is **y.**

Es la una **y** veinticinco.

■ The equivalent of *to* or *till* is **menos.** It is used with fractions of time up to a half hour.

Son las ocho **menos** cinco.

SUGGESTION: Emphasize the
difference between *it's* (**es, son**) and
at (**a la, a las**).

ATENCIÓN   The equivalent of *at* + *time* is **a** + **la(s)** + *time.*

—¿Qué hora es?	*"What time is it?"*
—Son las cinco menos diez.[1]	*"It's ten to five."*
—¿A qué hora es la clase?	*"At what time is the class?"*
—La clase es a las cinco.	*"The class is at five o'clock."*

■ To specify whether the time is A.M. or P.M., use **de la mañana** or **de la tarde,** respectively.

—¿La clase es a las 7 de la mañana?	*"Is the class at 7 A.M.?"*
—No, ¡es a las 7 de la tarde!	*"No, it's at 7 P.M.!"*

■ To indicate that an activity takes place at an undefined time in the morning or in the afternoon, use **por la mañana** or **por la tarde,** respectively.

—¿Estudiamos por la mañana?	*"Shall we study in the morning?"*
—No, por la tarde.	*"No, in the afternoon."*

---

[1]It is becoming increasingly popular to substitute **y quince** for **y cuarto, y treinta** for **y media,** and **y treinta y cinco, y cuarenta,** etc., for **menos veinticinco, menos veinte,** and so on.

práctica ···

A. With a partner, take turns giving the time indicated on the clocks in the illustration. Start with clock number one.

FOLLOW-UP A: Using a map of the world, ask students to tell time in the different time zones. Introduce the expressions **...de la mañana, ...de la tarde,** and **...de la noche.**

I—Son las dos de la tarde en Chicago.
  ¿Qué hora es en Madrid?
  ¿Y en Japón?

Have students take turns asking each other the different times in other cities and countries.

Desde Montevideo, Uruguay...
MÚSICA Y NOTICIAS DEL PARAGUAY
Dirección Periodística:
Carlos Caballero

Sábados y Domingos 13.30 horas

CX 14 El Espectador 810 AM

B. With a partner, take turns asking each other what time the programs in the listing are on and what programs are on at different times.

Modelos: —¿A qué hora es "Telediario"?
—*Es a las seis.*

—¿Qué hay a las seis?
—*"Telediario."*

Programación del Canal 36

Viernes ───────────────────────────

6:00	Telediario	**9:00**	Noticiero Televisa
6:50	Noticias Internacionales	**9:30**	Música
7:00	Religión	**10:00**	Fútbol
7:30	Música Latina	**11:00**	Noticias de última hora
8:00	"María" (Telenovela)		

---

5 Present indicative of regular -ar verbs *(Presente de indicativo de los verbos regulares terminados en -ar)*

■ Spanish verbs are classified in three main patterns of conjugation, according to the infinitive ending. The three infinitive endings are **-ar, -er,** and **-ir.**

hablar	to speak		
Singular			
yo	hablo	Yo **hablo** español.	*I speak Spanish.*
tú	hablas	Tú **hablas** francés.	*You (inf.) speak French.*
Ud.	habla	Ud. **habla** alemán.	*You (form.) speak German.*
él	habla	Él **habla** italiano.	*He speaks Italian.*
ella	habla	Ella **habla** portugués.	*She speaks Portuguese.*
Plural			
nosotros(-as)	hablamos	Nosotros **hablamos** español.	*We speak Spanish.*
vosotros(-as)	habláis	Vosotros **habláis** francés.	*You (inf.) speak French.*
Uds.	hablan	Uds. **hablan** alemán.	*You (form.) speak German.*
ellos	hablan	Ellos **hablan** italiano.	*They (masc.) speak Italian.*
ellas	hablan	Ellas **hablan** portugués.	*They (fem.) speak Portuguese.*

SUGGESTION: Be sure students know what verb conjugation means. Have them conjugate the verb *to be* orally in English.

—¿Qué idioma **hablas?**   *"What language do you speak?"*
—Yo **hablo** español.   *"I speak Spanish."*
—¿Y Pierre?   *"And Pierre?"*
—Él **habla** francés.   *"He speaks French."*

SUGGESTION: Write verb endings on the board:

-o   -amos
-as   -áis
-a   -an

SUGGESTION: Review subject pronouns by pointing to students or stick figures on the board or on index cards. Write the infinitive form of the verb on the board with additional choices to complete a simple sentence.

Yo / Tú / Él, Ella / Ud. (etc.)

hablar

español / francés / italiano (etc.)

Then have students form complete sentences by giving the correct pronoun you elicit and a choice from the list.

SUGGESTION: Ask students simple, personalized questions about themselves and their friends. Illustrate vocabulary words and write cognates on the board.

¿Qué necesitas, dinero o amor?
¿Dónde trabajas, en (city) o en (city)?
¿Qué lenguas hablas/estudias, español o inglés?
¿A qué hora regresas de clase?
¿Deseas estudiar o hablar por teléfono?

SUGGESTION: Drill students on the following verb forms and encourage them to use the forms in sentences.

1. *yo:* trabajar, hablar, necesitar, regresar
2. *tú:* necesitar, estudiar, hablar, desear
3. *Luis:* trabajar, hablar, regresar, desear
4. *Ud.:* trabajar, hablar, necesitar, estudiar
5. *nosotros:* necesitar, estudiar, trabajar
6. *ellas:* trabajar, hablar, regresar, desear

■ Regular verbs ending in -ar are all conjugated as **hablar** in the chart on page 35. Some other common -ar verbs are:

desear	*to want, wish*	**necesitar**	*to need*
estudiar	*to study*	**regresar**	*to return*
llamar	*to call*	**trabajar**	*to work*

—¿Uds. **estudian** por la noche?	*"Do you study in the evening?"*
—No, nosotros **estudiamos** por la tarde.	*"No, we study in the afternoon."*
—¿Qué **necesitas** tú?	*"What do you need?"*
—Yo **necesito** un libro.	*"I need a book."*

ATENCIÓN   Notice that the verb forms for **Ud., él,** and **ella** are the same. In addition, **Uds., ellos,** and **ellas** share common verb forms. This is true for all verbs in all tenses.

■ The infinitive of Spanish verbs consists of a stem (such as **habl-**) and an ending (such as **-ar**).

■ The stem **habl-** does not change. The endings change with the subject.

■ The Spanish present tense is equivalent to three English forms:

Yo **hablo** inglés.
$\begin{cases} \textit{I speak English.} \\ \textit{I do speak English.} \\ \textit{I am speaking English.} \end{cases}$

■ Because the verb endings indicate who is performing the action, the subject pronouns are frequently omitted.

Necesito un lápiz.	*I need a pencil.*
Estudiamos inglés.	*We study English.*
Hoy **trabajo.**	*I work today.*

■ Subject pronouns can, however, be used for emphasis or clarification.

—¿**Ellos** hablan inglés?	*"Do they speak English?"*
—**Ella** habla inglés y **él** habla alemán.	*"She speaks English, and he speaks German."*

■ In Spanish, as in English, when two verbs are used together, the second verb remains in the infinitive.

—¿Con quién **necesita hablar** Ud.?	*"With whom do you need to speak?"*
—**Necesito hablar** con Roberto.	*"I need to speak with Roberto."*

práctica ••

A. Complete the following dialogues, using the present indicative of the verbs given. Then act them out with a partner.

1. estudiar   —¿Qué _____ Uds.?
             —_____ alemán.

2. trabajar   —¿Tú _____ en el hospital por la noche?
             —No, _____ por la tarde.

3. regresar   —¿Cuándo *(When)* _____ Uds.?
             —Yo _____ el lunes y Jorge _____ el miércoles.

EXPANSION A:

1. Have students work in groups of three or four and take turns asking each other how to say verb phrases.

   ¿Cómo se dice _"we speak"_?

   The other members of the group should correct any errors.

2. Ask students to give the corresponding subject pronoun as you or another student gives a list of verb forms.

I—estudias	S—tú estudias
I—deseamos	S—nosotros deseamos

3. Write a short sentence builder on the board and ask students to combine the elements to form five original sentences.

   Yo / Ud. / Tú / Ellas / Paco

   trabajar / necesitar / estudiar

   a las seis / en la clase / cuadernos

EXPANSION D: Have students work in pairs to quickly sketch three scenes that would elicit sentences using the verbs and structures they have studied. The scenes should differ from the ones presented here. At the end of five minutes, each pair should select their best illustration and quickly draw it on the board. The other members of the class must then give one or two sentences to describe the sketch.

4. hablar   —¿Qué idioma _(language)_ _____ ellos?
—Carlos _____ español y Michele _____ francés.
—¿Cuántos idiomas _____ tú?
—_____ tres: español, italiano y portugués.

5. necesitar —¿Qué _____ Uds.?
—_____ unas tizas.

6. tomar   —¿Cuántas clases _____ Ud.?
—Yo _____ cinco clases.

B. What language do these people speak?

1. Pierre
2. Hans
3. Carlos
4. Vittorio y Pietro
5. John
6. un señor de Portugal

C. Interview a classmate, using the following questions. When you have finished, switch roles.

1. ¿Dónde trabajas? _(name of city)_
2. ¿Qué idiomas hablas?
3. ¿Qué idioma estudias?
4. ¿Estudias por la mañana, por la tarde o por la noche?
5. ¿Qué necesitas?
6. ¿A qué hora regresas a casa _(home)_?

D. Talk about what is going on in these drawings, using the subject pronouns given and the verbs **trabajar, hablar, necesitar, regresar, llamar, estudiar,** and **desear.**

6 Negative and interrogative sentences   *(Oraciones negativas e interrogativas)*

SUGGESTION: Write a short sentence builder similar to EXPANSION A (page 40). Ask students to make as many negative statements as possible in three to five minutes.

A. Negative sentences

■ To make a sentence negative, simply place the word **no** in front of the verb.

Yo trabajo en el hospital.	*I work at the hospital.*
Yo **no** trabajo en el hospital.	*I don't work at the hospital.*
Ella habla inglés.	*She speaks English.*
Ella **no** habla inglés.	*She doesn't speak English.*

■ If the answer to a question is negative, the word **no** will appear twice: at the beginning of the sentence, as in English, and in front of the verb.

—¿Habla Ud. español?	*"Do you speak Spanish?"*
—**No,** yo **no** hablo español.	*"No, I don't speak Spanish."*

The subject pronoun may be omitted.

—No, no hablo español.	*"No, I don't speak Spanish."*

B. Interrogative sentences

■ In Spanish, there are several ways of asking a question to elicit a *yes* or *no* answer.

¿**Ud.** habla español?	
¿Habla **Ud.** español?	**Sí,** yo hablo español.
¿Habla español **Ud.?**	

■ These three questions ask for the same information and have the same meaning. The subject may be placed at the beginning of the sentence, after the verb, or at the end of the sentence.

NOTE: Point out that Spanish uses an inverted exclamation mark at the beginning of exclamations.

■ Note that written questions in Spanish begin with an inverted question mark.

■ Another common way to ask a question in Spanish is to add tag questions such as **¿no?** and **¿verdad?** at the end of a statement.

Ud. habla español, **¿verdad?**	*You speak Spanish, don't you?*

■ Questions that ask for information begin with an interrogative word, and the verb, not the subject, is placed after the interrogative word.

¿Dónde **trabajas** tú?	*Where do you work?*
¿Cuándo **regresan** ellos?	*When do they return?*
¿Qué **necesita** Ud.?	*What do you need?*
¿Quién **es** el profesor?	*Who is the professor?*

ATENCIÓN   Spanish does not use an auxiliary verb, such as *do* or *does,* in negative or interrogative sentences.

práctica ••

A. With a partner, take turns answering the following questions in the negative.

1. ¿Tú hablas francés?
2. ¿Tú trabajas en un hospital?
3. ¿Tú necesitas el libro de español?
4. ¿Tú regresas a la clase a las cinco?
5. ¿Tú estudias por la noche?
6. ¿Tú eres de Madrid?

SUGGESTION: Have students work in pairs and take turns asking and answering their questions.

B. Write the questions that will elicit each of the following answers.

1. —_____
   —Sí, nosotros estudiamos inglés.
2. —_____
   —No, yo no trabajo en el hospital hoy.
3. —_____
   —Somos de Colombia.
4. —_____
   —No, nosotros no hablamos alemán.
5. —_____
   —Ellos necesitan los bolígrafos.
6. —_____
   —Ella trabaja en la universidad.
7. —_____
   —Carlos regresa a las ocho de la noche.
8. —_____
   —No, no soy enfermera.

7 Possession with **de** *(El caso posesivo)*

■ The **de** + *noun* construction is used to express possession or relationship. Spanish does *not* use the apostrophe.

SUGGESTION: You may want to point out that **de** can also be used with a noun or verb as an adjective: **la profesora de español, el papel de escribir.**

SUGGESTION: Emphasize that in Spanish the apostrophe is not used to show possession. Point out the parallelism between the English construction *noun phrase* + of + *noun phrase* and the Spanish construction *noun phrase* + **de** + *noun phrase: the son of John* vs. **el hijo de John.**

NOTE: The contraction **de** + **el** = **del** is fully discussed in **Lección 3.** You may want to include a brief explanation at this point to give students more practice with the structures.

SUGGESTION: Walk around the room, holding up objects belonging to students (a pen, a book, etc.) while asking, "**¿Es la pluma de Samantha?**" Then collect the objects, place them on your desk, and hold up each one individually while asking the class, "**¿De quién es...?**"

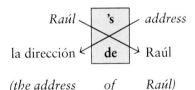

(the address   of   Raúl)

la clase **de la Dra. Peña**   *Dr. Peña's class*
el libro **de Dora**   *Dora's book*

ATENCIÓN Note the use of the definite article before the words **dirección, clase,** and **libro.**

—¿Quién es Francisco Acosta?   *"Who is Francisco Acosta?"*
—Es **el profesor de Carmen.**   *"He is Carmen's professor."*

—¿Cuál es **la dirección de Irene?**   *"What is Irene's address?"*
—Calle Magdalena, número seis.   *"Six Magdalena Street."*

práctica ....

A. Express possession or relationship as it is shown in each drawing (e.g., the Spanish equivalent of María's professor.)

EXPANSION A: Bring in pictures of items from the vocabulary lists or close cognates. Hold up each picture and ask a student:

I—¿Deseas comprar el auto?
S1—Sí, deseo comprar el auto. *(Give the photo to the student.)*
I—¿De quién es el auto?
S2—El auto es de *(name of student who made the "purchase").*

1.

2.

3.

4.

5.

6.

SUGGESTION B: Have students do this exercise on the board; then have the class check the responses together.

EXPANSION B: Have students work in pairs and take turns pointing to objects in the classroom.

S1—¿Qué es?
S2—Es el cuaderno de Leo.

B. Give the following phrases in Spanish.

1. Miss Vera's students
2. Carmen's maps
3. Jorge's clock
4. Marta's notebooks
5. Amanda's friends
6. Javier's chair
7. Mrs. Valle's class
8. the young lady's phone number

C. The students will take turns asking other members of the class if they need certain items.

> MODELO: —David, ¿tú necesitas el libro de John?
> —*Sí, yo necesito el libro de John.*
> *(No, yo no necesito el libro de John.)*

¡A ver cuánto aprendió!

See the *¿Cómo se dice...?* Web site for additional grammar and vocabulary practice: http://spanish.college. hmco.com/students

ACTIVITY SUGGESTION: Do **¡Escucha!**, the in-class listening comprehension activity that reviews vocabulary and grammar structures introduced in the lesson. It appears in the answer key of the *IAM*.

ACTIVITY SUGGESTION: See the *IAM* for an additional in-class activity: **Palabras escondidas.**

¡Repase el vocabulario!

A. Review the words referring to people and objects you see in the classroom, then name the numbered items below, using the definite article.

B. Supply the missing words and read aloud.

1. ¿Qué _____ es? ¿Las nueve?
2. ¿Cómo se _____ "puerta" en _____?
3. Tome _____, por favor.
4. ¿Qué clases _____ Sergio este _____?
5. ¿Cuántos estudiantes _____ en la clase?

6. ¿Qué _____ decir *"the pleasure is mine"*?
7. ¿Dirección? _____ Martí, _____ treinta.
8. ¿A qué _____ es la clase?
9. Hoy es el primer _____ de clases.
10. Rosa no trabaja; _____ estudia.
11. Yo hablo un _____ de portugués.
12. ¿Es una calle o una _____?

Entrevista

ACTIVITY SUGGESTION: See the *IAM* for additional in-class activities: **Para conocernos mejor** and **Una encuesta.**

With a partner, interview each other by asking the following questions.

1. ¿Tú trabajas los sábados?
2. ¿Tú trabajas o solamente estudias?
3. ¿Tú estudias por la mañana, por la tarde o por la noche?
4. ¿Tú tomas una clase de historia este semestre?
5. ¿Cuántas clases tomas este semestre?
6. ¿Tú hablas italiano? (¿portugués?)
7. ¿Cómo se dice *"door"* en español?
8. ¿Qué quiere decir "domicilio"?
9. ¿Necesitas un lápiz? (¿una pluma?)
10. ¿Qué hora es?
11. ¿A qué hora regresas a casa *(home)*?
12. ¿Cuál es tu dirección?

Situaciones

What would you say in the following situations? What might the other person say? Act out the scenes with a partner. Take turns playing each role.

1. In class, you're not sure how to say "you're welcome" in Spanish.
2. You need to know a classmate's address.
3. You can't remember what time your Spanish class meets. Your roommate is also in the class.
4. You are with Dr. Cortés and your teacher, who have never met before.
5. Your elderly neighbor stops by to say hello. You invite him to sit down.
6. You don't know what time it is. The person next to you on the bus is wearing a watch.

Para escribir   *(To write)*

Complete the following dialogues.

EXPANSION: After completing the dialogues, students should work in pairs and act out each situation. Remind them to change names and other information to reflect their own personal situations.

1. *Julia talks with a classmate.*

JULIA   —_____
ELENA   —Me llamo Elena Martínez.
JULIA   —_____
ELENA   —Soy de Madrid.
JULIA   —_____
ELENA   —486-3497.
JULIA   —_____
ELENA   —Calle Roma, número veintiocho.

2. *Professor Mena and Mr. Roberto Soto are in the classroom. Today is Friday.*

PROF. MENA   —¿Cómo se llama usted, señor?
ROBERTO   —_____
PROF. MENA   —Mucho gusto, señor Soto.
ROBERTO   —_____
PROF. MENA   —¿Qué día es hoy?
ROBERTO   —_____
PROF. MENA   —¿Cómo se dice *"thirty-five"* en español?
ROBERTO   —_____
PROF. MENA   —¿Qué quiere decir *"Until I see you again"*?
ROBERTO   —_____
PROF. MENA   —Muy bien. Hasta luego, señor Soto.
ROBERTO   —_____

3. *A student thanks her teacher.*

MARISA   —_____
PROFESORA   —De nada, señorita García. Hasta luego.
MARISA   —_____

Presentaciones   *(Introductions)*

CD-ROM

Do the interactive exercises on the CD-ROM for additional practice.

Form groups of three. After one person introduces the other two, make small talk: find out everybody's address, how many classes everybody is taking, and talk about what day it is and what time it is. You might want to include the following words or phrases:

A sus órdenes.   *At your service.*
Encantado. (If you are male) }
Encantada. (If you are female) }   *Charmed (It's a pleasure).*

Horario de clases

SUGGESTION: Write a list of popular courses on the chalkboard. In order to encourage real communication, you may want to introduce the following questions and statements:

S1—¿Qué estudias?
S2—Estudio...
S1—¿Cuándo es la clase?
S2—Los martes y jueves.
S1—¿A qué hora es la clase de...?
S2—Es a la(s)...
S1—¿Cómo se llama el (la) profesor(-a)?
S2—Se llama...

After completing the schedule, students should check their partner's notes to see if each has the correct information.

This is María Elena's schedule. With a classmate, try to figure out when her classes are.

MODELO: —¿Cuándo es la clase de tenis?
—*La clase de tenis es los sábados.*
—¿A qué hora?
—*A las nueve.*

HORA	LUNES	MARTES	MIÉRCOLES	JUEVES	VIERNES	SÁBADO
8:00-9:00	Psicología		Psicología		Psicología	
9:00-10:00	Biología		Biología		Biología	Tenis
10:00-11:30		Historia		Historia		
12:15-1:00			ALMUERZO[1]			
1:00-2:00	Literatura		Literatura		Literatura	Laboratorio de Biología
5:00-6:30		Educación Física		Educación Física		
7:00-8:30	Arte		Arte			

Mi horario

With the help of a dictionary and/or your instructor, work with a classmate to make up each other's schedules.

Un inventario de la clase

With a classmate, conduct an inventory of everything in your classroom, using **hay.**

MODELO: Hay una pizarra en el salón de clases.

---

[1]lunch

1. El español en los Estados Unidos y en Canadá

Estados Unidos   Canadá

- Más de *(More than)* 30 millones de hispanos viven *(live)* en los Estados Unidos. Los hispanos son el grupo minoritario de mayor crecimiento *(growth)* en la nación. Los estados con la mayor concentración de hispanos son Nuevo México, Tejas, California, Nueva York, New Jersey y la Florida.

- Los nombres de muchas ciudades, estados y zonas geográficas de los Estados Unidos vienen del español: Arizona, California, Los Ángeles, El Paso, Sierra Nevada y Río Grande, por ejemplo. En Canadá, la gran península al este del país tiene un nombre de origen hispano: Labrador *(Farmer)*.

- El español es el idioma extranjero *(foreign)* más popular en las escuelas y universidades de los Estados Unidos. Más de 650.000 estudiantes universitarios estudian español cada año *(each year)*.

- En Canadá hay más de 200.000 habitantes de habla hispana; la mayoría de ellos son de España, Chile, El Salvador y México. La mayor parte vive en Toronto, Montreal y Vancouver.

Durante la época colonial, las órdenes religiosas españolas establecieron misiones en el suroeste de los Estados Unidos, y muchas aún *(still)* existen. La Misión de San Francisco de Asís es la más famosa de Nuevo México.

¿Cuáles son otras atracciones turísticas en el suroeste?

En muchas partes de los Estados Unidos hay servicios bilingües de tipo social, educativo y legal para los residentes hispanos.

¿Hay muchas personas de habla hispana en su ciudad?

Los programas de educación bilingüe ayudan *(help)* a muchos niños hispanos en sus estudios primarios.

¿La educación bilingüe es una buena idea?

En muchas ciudades norteamericanas hay periódicos *(newspapers)* y revistas *(magazines)* en español. Muchos hispanos los leen *(read them)* porque tienen más información sobre *(about)* la comunidad latina. (Los Ángeles, California)

¿Qué periódicos lee Ud.?

Las emisoras de televisión hispanas son una fuente *(source)* de información importante en ciudades como Nueva York, donde vive *(live)* más de un millón de puertorriqueños, más que en San Juan, la capital de Puerto Rico. En la foto, un grupo musical anima la carroza *(float)* de una estación de televisión hispana de Nueva York.

¿Qué canales de televisión mira Ud.?

En "La Pequeña Habana", un barrio *(neighborhood)* hispano de la ciudad de Miami, las tiendas, los cafés, los restaurantes y los mercados tienen nombres en español, y el español es el idioma más hablado *(spoken)*.

¿Cómo se llama el barrio de Ud.?

La comida *(food)* mexicana es tan *(so)* popular en los Estados Unidos que para muchos norteamericanos la primera clase de español es en un restaurante.

¿Le gusta la comida mexicana? ¿Cuál es su plato favorito?

En muchas de las grandes ciudades de Canadá hay fiestas y actos interculturales en los que se nota *(one notes)* la influencia hispana. La música hispana, especialmente la mexicana, la salsa, el merengue y el tango, son muy populares. En varias ciudades también se celebra el "Cinco de Mayo".

¿Celebran fiestas hispanas en su ciudad? ¿Cuáles?

TELEINFORME

 VIDEO   CD-ROM Do the interactive exercises on the CD-ROM for additional practice.

Preparación

NOTE: The video-related vocabulary is listed in the *Instructor's Activities Manual* for your reference. Its purpose is to facilitate students' comprehension.

SUGGESTION: Before showing the video, tell students that they are about to hear Spanish narrations from native speakers. They should not worry about understanding every word, but just try to get the gist of what the people are saying. Also, remind students that the video provides many visual clues to help them comprehend each segment.

¿Cuánto saben Uds. ya? After reading **Panorama hispánico 1**, get together in groups of three or four students and complete each statement with the appropriate information.

1. Hay más de _____ millones de hispanos en los Estados Unidos.
2. Muchos hispanos viven en los estados de _____, _____, _____, _____, _____ y _____.
3. En muchas ciudades de los Estados Unidos existen programas de _____ bilingüe para los niños hispanos.
4. Hay _____ y _____ en español en muchas grandes ciudades norteamericanas.
5. La Pequeña Habana está en la ciudad de _____, en el estado de _____.

Comprensión

NOTE: See the Instructor's Edition frontmatter for additional suggestions on implementing video in the classroom.

SUGGESTION: Have students read the *Panorama hispánico* segment of the textbook and do the *Preparación* activities in small groups before viewing the video segments.

SUGGESTION: The *Comprensión* sections are organized by individual video clip to provide greater flexibility in lesson planning. Have students complete each exercise after viewing the corresponding video clip and have them compare their answers in pairs or groups.

A. **Anuncios.** Read the following slogans in Spanish. Match the slogan with the name of the company in the second column according to what you understood in the video.

A	B
1. Su dinero vale mucho *(is worth a lot)* y muchas cosas más.	a. AT&T
2. La mejor decisión *(the best decision)*.	b. Kodak
3. De familia en familia.	c. Maybelline
4. Colores vivos *(bright)* y reales.	d. Ford
5. ¡Qué momento! ¡Qué sabor...!	e. McDonald's
6. Los cosméticos que le ayudan a embellecerse *(help to make you beautiful)*.	f. Sears

B. **El Festival de la calle Ocho.** Select the word or phrase that best completes each statement according to what you understood in the video.

1. El Festival de la calle Ocho de la Pequeña Habana se celebra (todos los años, cada semana).
2. La Pequeña Habana está en (Miami, Los Ángeles).
3. (Muchas, Pocas) personas disfrutan del festival.
4. De noche coronan (a la reina, al rey) en un concurso de belleza *(beauty pageant)*.
5. Hay una carrera *(road race)* a lo largo *(along)* de (Miami, la calle Ocho).

49

Ampliación

A. **Publicidad.** In groups of three or four, try to guess the meaning of the following words. Then brainstorm a list of companies that might advertise their products in Spanish to the Spanish-speaking communities in the U.S. Choose one company and write an original Spanish slogan for a particular product.

1. cosméticos
2. perfumes
3. champú
4. aspirinas
5. automóviles
6. televisores
7. computadoras
8. servicios telefónicos

B. **Un festival típico.** In pairs or small groups, describe a typical festival or celebration in your town, state, or country. Use the following questions as a guide. Then compare your celebrations to the one you see in the video.

1. ¿Cómo se celebra el festival?
2. ¿Dónde se celebra?
3. ¿Cuándo se celebra?
4. ¿Cuáles son las actividades más importantes?
5. ¿Qué hacen *(do)* de día?
6. ¿Qué hacen de noche?

OBJECTIVES

Pronunciation
Linking

Structure
Gender, Part II • Possessive adjectives • Cardinal numbers 101–1,000 • Descriptive adjectives: Forms, position, and agreement with articles and nouns • Present indicative of regular -er and -ir verbs • Present indicative of the irregular verbs **tener** and **venir**

Communication
You will learn vocabulary used to make and to receive phone calls.

Por teléfono

STUDENT
AUDIO

Raquel, Pedro, Marisa, y Carmen son estudiantes universitarios que viven en Los Ángeles, y son muy buenos amigos. Raquel desea ser médica, Pedro desea ser abogado, y Marisa y Carmen desean ser maestras. Pedro es moreno, alto y muy simpático. Las chicas son inteligentes y bonitas.

Raquel desea hablar con Pedro.

MARISA	—¿Sí?
RAQUEL	—Hola. ¿Está Pedro?
MARISA	—No, no está. Lo siento.
RAQUEL	—¿A qué hora regresa?
MARISA	—A las nueve de la noche.
RAQUEL	—Entonces llamo[1] más tarde.
MARISA	—Muy bien. Adiós.

Carmen habla con su amiga Marisa.

MARISA	—Bueno.
CARMEN	—Hola. ¿Está Marisa?
MARISA	—Sí, con ella habla… ¿Carmen?
CARMEN	—Sí. ¿Qué tal, Marisa?
MARISA	—Muy bien, gracias. ¿Qué hay de nuevo?
CARMEN	—Nada. ¡Oye! ¿Dónde comemos[1] mañana? ¿En la cafetería?
MARISA	—No, mañana tengo que escribir un informe y debo leer varios artículos en la biblioteca.
CARMEN	—Yo también tengo que estudiar para un examen.
MARISA	—Entonces nos vemos[1] el martes.

Pedro habla con Raquel.

ROSA	—Dígame.
PEDRO	—Hola. ¿Está Raquel?
ROSA	—Sí. ¿Quién habla?
PEDRO	—Pedro Morales.
ROSA	—Un momento por favor.
RAQUEL	—*(A Rosa)* ¿Quién es?
ROSA	—Es tu amigo Pedro.
RAQUEL	—Hola, Pedro. ¿Qué tal?
PEDRO	—Bien, ¿y tú?
RAQUEL	—Más o menos.
PEDRO	—¿Por qué? ¿Problemas sentimentales?
RAQUEL	—No, problemas económicos. ¡Necesito dinero!

---

[1]The present indicative is often used in Spanish to express a near future.

SUGGESTION: Have students work in pairs and pretend they are phoning different classmates, using the dialogue as a guide. For added realism, have the pairs sit back-to-back during their brief conversations. Encourage students to expand upon the conversations when possible. See **¿Lo sabía Ud.?** on page 56 for additional ways to answer the telephone.

ACTIVITY SUGGESTION: See the *IAM* for an additional in-class activity: **¿Cómo respondes?**

PEDRO	—¡Yo también! Oye, ¿tú tienes que trabajar en el hospital esta noche?
RAQUEL	—No, hoy no trabajo por la noche. Los lunes mi novio y yo estudiamos en la biblioteca.
PEDRO	—¿Tú vienes a mi casa mañana?
RAQUEL	—No, porque mañana tengo que ir a otro hospital a solicitar trabajo.
PEDRO	—Entonces, adiós.
ROSA	—*(A Raquel)* Oye, ¿cómo es tu amigo Pedro? ¿Es guapo?
RAQUEL	—Es guapo y muy inteligente, pero… tiene novia.

Vocabulario

Cognados

el artículo   article
la cafetería   cafeteria

el examen   exam
inteligente   intelligent

Nombres

el (la) abogado(-a)   lawyer
la biblioteca   library
la casa   house, home
la chica, muchacha   girl, young woman

el chico, muchacho   boy, young man
el dinero   money
el informe   report
la noche   evening, night

la novia   girlfriend, fiancée, bride
el novio   boyfriend, fiancé, groom
el trabajo, el empleo   job, work

Verbos

comer   to eat
deber   must, have to, should
escribir   to write

leer   to read
solicitar   to apply
tener   to have

venir   to come
vivir   to live

Adjetivos

alto(-a)   tall
bonito(-a), lindo(-a)   pretty
bueno(-a)[1]   good

moreno(-a)[2]   dark, brunet
otro(-a)   another, other
simpático(-a)   charming, nice

universitario(-a)   related to university
varios(-as)   several

---

[1]**Bueno** becomes **buen** when used before a masculine singular noun.
[2]**Castaño** is used as the equivalent of *brown* when describing hair or eye color.

Otras palabras y expresiones

a   at, to, in order to
bueno, dígame   hello *(answering the phone)*
¿Cómo es...?   What is . . . like?
con ella habla   this is she *(speaking)*
de   of
en   on, in, at
entonces   then, in that case
¿Está... + *(name)?*   Is . . . *(name)* there?
esta noche   tonight
lo siento   I'm sorry
mañana   tomorrow
más o menos   so-so, more or less
más tarde   later
nada   nothing
no está   he or she is not here
o   or
para   for
pero   but
¿por qué?   why?
por teléfono   on the phone
problemas económicos   financial problems
problemas sentimentales   love problems
que   who, that
¿quién?   who?
¿quién es?   who is it?
¿Quién habla? ¿De parte de quién?   Who is speaking?
su   his, her, its, your *(formal)*, their
tener que + *infinitive*   to have to + infinitive *(do something)*
tengo que ir   I have to go
un momento   one moment

Vocabulario adicional
Características

antipático(-a) unpleasant	Antonio no es **antipático;** es muy simpático.
bajo(-a) short	Marco es **bajo;** no es alto.
delgado(-a) thin, slender	Roberto es alto y **delgado.**
feo(-a) ugly	Paco no es **feo;** es guapo.
gordo(-a) fat	¿María es delgada o **gorda?**
guapo(-a) handsome	Mario es muy **guapo.**
optimista[1] optimist	Yo soy muy **optimista.**
pelirrojo(-a) red-headed	Teresa es **pelirroja.**
pesimista[1] pessimist	Pedro es muy **pesimista.**
realista[1] realist	Debemos ser **realistas.**
rubio(-a) blond	Sergio es **rubio.**

---

[1]The ending of this kind of adjective (**-ista**) does not change, regardless of gender: **el profesor optimista, la profesora optimista.**

Datos personales *(Personal data)*

lugar donde trabaja place of employment

nombre del esposo (de la esposa) husband's (wife's) name

nombre y edad de los hijos children's names and ages

número de la licencia de conducir driver's license number

número de seguro social social security number

ocupación occupation

profesión profession

SOLICITUD DE TRABAJO *(Job Application)*

Apellidos y nombre *García López, Susana*
(Surnames and first name)

Fecha de nacimiento
(Date of birth)

Día *7*   Mes *12*   Año *80*
(Day)   *(Month)*   *(Year)*

Número de identidad *86407423*
(Identification number)

Edad *22 años*
(Age)

Dirección *Calle 6, 258*   Ciudad *Caracas*   Zona postal *70-824*
(City)   *(Zip Code)*

Teléfono *862-4221*

Nacionalidad *Venezolana*   Lugar de nacimiento *Caracas*
(Place of birth)

Estado civil: ☒ Soltero(-a)   ☐ Casado(-a)   ☐ Divorciado(-a)   ☐ Viudo(-a)
(Marital status)   *(Single)*   *(Married)*   *(Divorced)*   *(Widowed)*

Sexo *(Sex)*   ☐ Masculino   ☒ Femenino

Educación
Institución   Años
Universidad de Caracas   *1997-2001*
Instituto San Pedro   *1993-1997*

Experiencia
Compañía   Años
Farmacia Bernardino   *2001 (6 meses)*

SUGGESTION: Use Transparency 16 to present this vocabulary. Complete the application with your own personal data or that of a student.

¡Conversemos!

Answer the following questions, basing your answers on the dialogue.

1. ¿Pedro desea ser abogado o maestro?
2. ¿Raquel desea hablar con Marisa o con Pedro?
3. ¿Pedro regresa a las nueve de la mañana o de la noche?
4. ¿Carmen habla con Marisa o con Raquel?
5. ¿Carmen y Marisa comen o no comen en la cafetería?

6. ¿Marisa tiene que leer o escribir varios artículos?
7. ¿Carmen tiene que estudiar para una clase o para un examen?
8. ¿Pedro es el novio o un amigo de Raquel?
9. ¿Raquel necesita libros o dinero?
10. ¿Pedro necesita un reloj o necesita dinero también?
11. ¿Raquel trabaja o estudia en la biblioteca esta noche?
12. ¿Raquel tiene que solicitar trabajo en un hospital o en una universidad?

¿Lo sabía Ud.?

■ Contestando el teléfono *(Answering the phone):*
En España *(Spain):* "Diga", "Dígame", "¿Sí?"
En Cuba y en otras regiones del Caribe: "Oigo"
En México: "Bueno"
En Argentina: "¿Sí?", "Hable", "Hola", "¿Aló?"

■ En Latinoamérica y en España los estudiantes frecuentemente estudian juntos *(together).*

■ "Español" y "castellano" son *(are)* equivalentes.

■ "El español es el idioma nativo de unos *(about)* 400.000.000[1] de personas.

● ¿Cómo contestan el teléfono en los Estados Unidos?

● ¿En los Estados Unidos los estudiantes estudian juntos?

● ¿Hay muchas *(many)* personas en los Estados Unidos que hablan español?

Estudiantes de la Universidad Iberoamericana, Ciudad de México, haciendo investigación en la biblioteca.

[1]Note that in Spanish numbers, a period is used instead of a comma to indicate thousands.

INTERNET

See the *¿Cómo se dice...?* Web site for activities on authentic cultural material: http://spanish.college.hmco.com/students

Pronunciación

Linking

STUDENT AUDIO

SUGGESTION: Model each phrase and have the class repeat it chorally and individually. The following sentences provide additional pronunciation practice using words in context.

En Honduras hay un hospital muy grande. Nadie habla nunca con mis simpáticas sobrinas. Pepe está aquí y Ernesto está allá. Esta orquesta es fantástica.

■ In Spanish, a final consonant is always linked with the next initial vowel sound.

  el͜ amigo   los͜ hospitales[1]   problemas͜ económicos

■ When two identical consonants are together, they are pronounced as one.

  es͜ simpática   Voy con͜ Norma.

■ When two identical vowels are together, they are pronounced as one long vowel.

  Rodolfo͜ Ochoa   Habla͜ Ana.

■ The final vowel of one word is linked with the initial vowel of the following word to form one syllable.

  la͜ amiga de͜ Olga   trabaja͜ esta noche   hablo͜ español

Estructuras

1 Gender, Part II *(Género, Parte II)*

SUGGESTION: Write the noun endings on the board in the following manner:

-a
-ción (-sión)
-tad   } femenino
-dad
-umbre

-o   } masculino
-ma *(Greek origin)*

NOTE: Explain that recognizing cognates is very useful in developing language skills. Also ask students to guess the meaning of cognates they have never seen before (**corporación, medicina,** etc.).

In **Lección 2** you learned that words that end in **-o** in Spanish are generally masculine, and those that end in **-a** are generally feminine. Here are other useful rules to help you determine the gender of nouns that do not end in **-o** or **-a**.

■ Nouns ending in **-sión, -ción, -tad, -dad,** and **-umbre** are feminine.

la televi**sión**	*television*	**la** ciu**dad**	*city*
la conversa**ción**	*conversation*	**la** universi**dad**	*university*
la liber**tad**	*liberty, freedom*	**la** certid**umbre**	*certainty*

■ Many words that end in **-ma** are masculine.[2]

el poe**ma**	*poem*	**el** cli**ma**	*climate*
el telegra**ma**	*telegram*	**el** idio**ma**	*language*
el progra**ma**	*program*	**el** proble**ma**	*problem*
el siste**ma**	*system*	**el** te**ma**	*subject, theme*

---

[1]In Spanish the letter **h** is silent.
[2]Some feminine words end in **-ma,** such as **la cama** *(bed)* and **la rama** *(branch).*

■ You must learn the gender of nouns that have other endings and that do not refer to male or female beings. Remember that it is helpful to memorize each noun with its corresponding article.

la pared   el reloj
el lápiz   la luz
el borrador

práctica ••

EXPANSION: Have students close their books and practice changing the nouns from singular to plural, adding the appropriate definite and indefinite articles. Go quickly around the room.

I—pared
S1—la pared
S2—las paredes
S3—una pared
S4—unas paredes

A. Read the following words, adding the corresponding definite article (**el, la, los,** or **las**).

1. pared
2. mesa
3. turismo
4. hospital
5. problemas
6. ciudad
7. sociedad
8. borrador
9. mano
10. lumbre *(fire)*
11. libertad
12. idiomas
13. organización
14. día
15. solución
16. conversación
17. universidad
18. muchedumbre *(crowd)*

B. With a partner, take turns asking each other whether or not you need certain items in your classroom.

MODELO: —¿Necesitas un borrador?
          —*Sí, necesito un borrador.*
          —*No, necesito una tiza.*

2 Possessive adjectives   *(Los adjetivos posesivos)*

SUGGESTION: Before you begin class, ask five or six students to place an object they own on a table in front of the room. Students should then try to find out what belongs to whom. They may direct questions to you or to other members of the class in order to try to identify the owner of each article. Encourage them to take notes (similar to the tally sheet in the board game *Clue*) to facilitate the search for the owner.

S1—*(to instructor)* ¿Es el libro de Silvia?
  I—No, no es su libro.
S2—*(to student)* ¿Es tu libro?
S3—No, no es mi libro.

Forms of the Possessive Adjectives

Singular	Plural	
mi	mis	*my*
tu	tus	*your* (fam.)
su	sus	*your* (form.) / *his* / *her* / *its* / *their*
nuestro(-a)	nuestros(-as)	*our*
vuestro(-a)	vuestros(-as)	*your* (fam.)

—¿**Tu** novio es de Buenos Aires?   *"Is your boyfriend from Buenos Aires?"*

—No, **mi** novio es de Asunción.   *"No, my boyfriend is from Asunción."*

■ Possessive adjectives always precede the nouns they introduce. They agree in number with the nouns they modify.

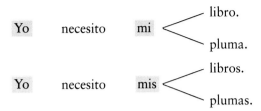

■ **Nuestro** and **vuestro** are the only possessive adjectives that have the feminine endings **-a** and **-as.** The others take the same endings for both genders.

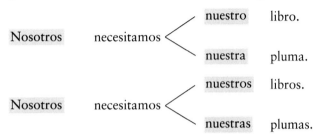

■ Possessive adjectives agree in gender with the thing possessed and *not* with the possessor. For example, two male students referring to their female professor will say *nuestra* profeso*ra.*

■ Because **su** and **sus** each have several possible meanings, the form **de él** (or **de ella, de ellos, de ellas, de Ud.,** or **de Uds.**) can be substituted to avoid confusion. The "formula" is: *article + noun + de + pronoun.*

    sus plumas   las plumas **de él** (**ella, Ud.,** etc.)

    su libro   el libro **de él** (**ella, Ud.,** etc.)

práctica •••

A. Complete the following dialogues, using the Spanish equivalent of the words in parentheses. Then act them out with a partner.

1. —¿A qué hora es la clase _____? *(your)*
   —_____ clase es a las ocho. *(Our)*
2. —¿Cuál es _____ dirección, Anita? *(your)*
   —_____ dirección es calle Lima, 230. *(My)*
3. —¿Necesita Ud. _____ libros, señora? *(your)*
   —No, necesito _____ cuadernos. *(my)*
4. —¿Es la casa _____? *(his)*
   —No, es la casa _____. *(her)*
5. —¿De dónde es el profesor _____? *(your)*
   —_____ profesor es de Montreal. *(Our)*
6. —¿Con quiénes hablan Teresa y Victoria?
   —Hablan con _____ amigas. *(their)*

B. Answer the following questions in the negative, using possessive adjectives.

ACTIVITY SUGGESTION: See the *IAM* for an additional in-class activity: **Conversaciones breves.**

1. ¿Estela es la novia de Alberto?
2. ¿Necesitas tu libro de español?
3. ¿La profesora de Uds. es de México?
4. ¿Carlos y Daniel son tus amigos?
5. ¿El doctor Paz y la doctora Ruiz son los profesores de Uds.?
6. ¿Tú necesitas mis cuadernos?
7. ¿Tú necesitas la dirección de los chicos?
8. ¿Marisa y Olga son las amigas de Claudia?

3 Cardinal numbers 101–1,000 *(Números cardinales 101–1.000)*

SUGGESTION: Dictating numbers at random is a good exercise. A game of bingo in Spanish may also be popular with students (see the Introduction for instructions).

NOTE: Remind students that when counting objects, plural hundreds should agree in gender and number with the noun they modify.

trescientos	trescientas
libros	sillas
quinientos	quinientas
pesos	pesetas

101	**ciento uno** (and so on)	600	**seiscientos**
200	**doscientos**	700	**setecientos**
300	**trescientos**	800	**ochocientos**
400	**cuatrocientos**	900	**novecientos**
500	**quinientos**	1.000	**mil**

■ To ask how much a single item costs, say, "**¿Cuánto cuesta?**" For multiple items, use "**¿Cuánto cuestan?**"

—¿Cuánto cuesta el escritorio?　　*"How much does the desk cost?"*
—Cuesta ciento cincuenta dólares.　*"It costs a hundred and fifty dollars."*

—¿Cuánto cuestan las ventanas?　　*"How much do the windows cost?"*
—Cuestan mil cien dólares.　　　　*"They cost eleven hundred dollars."*

■ When counting beyond 100 (101 to 199), **ciento** is used.

■ **Y** appears only in numbers between 16 and 99. It is not used to separate thousands, hundreds, and tens from each other: **mil quinientos ochenta y seis.**

■ In Spanish, one does not count in hundreds beyond 1,000; thus, 1,100 is expressed as **mil cien**. After 1,000, thousands are counted **dos mil, tres mil,** and so on. Note that Spanish uses a period rather than a comma to indicate thousands.

■ When modifying a feminine noun, the feminine form is used: **doscientas sillas.**

práctica •••

A. Complete the following series of numbers.

1. cien, doscientos, trescientos,… mil
2. diez mil, veinte mil, treinta mil,… cien mil
3. ciento diez, doscientos veinte, trescientos treinta,… mil cien

B. With a partner, look at the illustration at the top of the next page and ask each other how much everything costs.

> **Modelo:** —¿Cuánto cuesta la silla?
> —*La silla cuesta ciento ochenta dólares.*

EXPANSION A:

1. Write a list of complex numbers on the board. Have students read them as a class or individually.
2. Practice dates by asking students when specific events occurred. You may want to write a list of eight to ten events and dates on the board or overhead to facilitate recall; for example:
    La guerra de Independencia de los EEUU (1776)
    Cristóbal Colón descubre América (1492)
    Primera guerra mundial (1914–18)
    Segunda guerra mundial (1939–45)
    Guerra civil de los EEUU (1861–65)
    El primer hombre en la luna (1969)
    Bell inventa el teléfono (1875)

FOLLOW-UP A: Have students name important dates in their own family history: births, marriages, graduations, etc.

EXPANSION B: Bring in a target language newspaper or photocopy ads that include the product name and price. Have students work in pairs and take turns asking, **"¿Cuánto cuesta?"** You may also want to discuss currency values in different countries. *The Wall Street Journal* gives the daily exchange rate, and students may practice changing dollars into target language currency.

SUGGESTION: Use Transparency 17 to present descriptive adjectives.

4   Descriptive adjectives: Forms, position, and agreement with articles and nouns   *(Adjetivos calificativos: Formas, posición y concordancia con artículos y nombres)*

A. Forms of adjectives

■ Descriptive adjectives identify characteristics or qualities such as color, size, and personality. In Spanish, these adjectives agree in gender and number with the nouns they modify. Adjectives ending in **-o** are made feminine by changing the **-o** to **-a.**

el muchach**o** mexican**o**	la muchach**a** mexican**a**
el chico rubi**o**	la chica rubi**a**
el lápiz roj**o**	la pluma roj**a**

■ Adjectives ending in **-e** or in a consonant have the same form for the masculine and the feminine.

el chico inteligent**e**	la chica inteligent**e**
el esposo feli**z** *(happy)*	la esposa feli**z**
el libro fáci**l** *(easy)*	la clase fáci**l**

SUGGESTION: Write the following list of descriptive adjectives on the board to complement the list in the basic vocabulary. Then have students describe their ideal friend, parent, boy/girlfriend, etc., as completely as possible.

paciente – impaciente	tolerante – intolerante
responsable – irresponsable	feliz – infeliz
rico – pobre	pesimista – optimista
independiente	interesante
popular	importante

■ Adjectives of nationality that end in a consonant add an **-a** in the feminine.

el muchacho español	la muchacha español**a**
el señor inglés	la señora ingles**a**

■ Adjectives ending in **-or, -án, -ón,** or **-ín** add an **-a** in the feminine.

el alumno trabajad**or**
la alumna trabajad**ora** } *the hard-working student*

ATENCIÓN   Adjectives that have an accent in the last syllable of the masculine form drop it in the feminine: **inglés → inglesa.**[1]

■ To form the plural, adjectives follow the same rules as nouns. Adjectives ending in a vowel add **-s**; adjectives ending in a consonant add **-es**; adjectives ending in **-z** change the **-z** to **c** and add **-es**.

norteamericana	norteamericana**s**
español	español**es**
feliz	feli**ces**

B. Position of adjectives

■ Descriptive adjectives generally follow the noun.

Miguel es un chico **inteligente.**	*Miguel is an intelligent boy.*
Necesito dos plumas **rojas.**	*I need two red pens.*

■ Adjectives denoting nationality always follow the noun.

El profesor **mexicano** trabaja en la universidad.

C. Agreement of articles, nouns, and adjectives

■ In Spanish, the article, noun, and adjective agree in gender and number.

un muchacho alto	**una** muchacha alta
los muchachos altos	**las** muchachas altas

■ When an adjective modifies two or more nouns, the plural form is used.

la silla y la mesa **rojas**

■ If two nouns described together are of different genders, the masculine plural form of the adjective is used.

la chica mexicana
el chico mexicano } la chica y el chico mexicanos

[1]For rules on accent marks, see Appendix A.

práctica ••

A. With a partner, take turns asking the following questions. In your answers, contradict what is stated.

> MODELO: —¿Rosaura es alta?
> —No, *es baja.*

1. ¿El novio de Adriana es rubio?
2. ¿Las mujeres son gordas?
3. ¿Los muchachos son bajos?
4. ¿Tu profesora es antipática?
5. ¿La novia de Daniel es fea?
6. ¿Tú eres optimista?
7. ¿El hermano de Olga es delgado?
8. ¿Ellas son morenas?

FOLLOW-UP B: Have students select a photograph from a magazine and write a description. Remind them to review the uses of **ser** in **Lección 1.** Tape selected pictures on the board and number them 1, 2, 3, etc. After students read the descriptions, the class must decide which photograph is being described. Photos from the textbook could also be used.

B. Describe the following people, places, or things, using as many descriptive adjectives as possible.

1. Julia Roberts
2. Ricky Martin
3. Roseanne
4. Nueva York
5. su mejor *(best)* amigo
6. las chicas de la clase
7. los chicos de la clase
8. el presidente de los Estados Unidos

5 Present indicative of regular -er and -ir verbs *(Presente de indicativo de los verbos regulares que terminan en -er y en -ir)*

SUGGESTION: Present this material as you presented **-ar** verbs. Emphasize that the endings for **-er** and **-ir** verbs are the same except for the **nosotros(-as)** and **vosotros(-as)** forms.

comer *to eat*		**vivir** *to live*	
yo	como	yo	vivo
tú	comes	tú	vives
Ud. él ella	come	Ud. él ella	vive
nosotros(-as)	comemos	nosotros(-as)	vivimos
vosotros(-as)	coméis	vosotros(-as)	vivís
Uds. ellos ellas	comen	Uds. ellos ellas	viven

■ Other verbs conjugated like **comer:**

aprender	*to learn*	**beber**	*to drink*
creer	*to believe, to think*	**vender**	*to sell*
leer	*to read*	**deber**	*must, should, ought to*

—¿Dónde **comen** Uds.?
—Nosotros **comemos** en la cafetería y Elsa **come** en su casa.

"Where do you eat?"
"We eat in the cafeteria and Elsa eats at her house."

—¿Qué **lees** tú?
—**Leo** mi libro de español.

"What are you reading?"
"I'm reading my Spanish book."

■ Other verbs conjugated like **vivir:**

abrir	*to open*	**escribir**	*to write*
recibir	*to receive*	**decidir**	*to decide*

—¿Dónde **viven** Uds.? *"Where do you live?"*
—**Vivimos** en la calle Magnolia. *"We live on Magnolia Street."*

—¿Tú **escribes** con lápiz o con pluma? *"Do you write with a pencil or with a pen?"*
—**Escribo** con bolígrafo. *"I write with a (ballpoint) pen."*

práctica

SUGGESTION A: Drill students on the following verb forms and encourage them to use the forms in sentences.

1. *yo:* vivir, deber, creer, escribir
2. *tú:* aprender, abrir, comer, decidir
3. *ella:* leer, vivir, creer, recibir
4. *tú y yo:* vender, decidir, beber, vivir
5. *Luis y Rosa:* vivir, deber, creer, escribir
6. *Uds.:* recibir, beber, deber, escribir

EXPANSION A: Write a short sentence builder on the board and ask students to combine the elements to form as many sentences as possible in five minutes. Encourage them to write interrogative as well as affirmative and negative statements.

Yo / Ella / Tú / Ellas / Tú y yo / Uds.

comer / recibir / aprender / leer / beber / vender / abrir / vivir

las cartas / los tacos, burritos / el español, francés, alemán / el champán, café, té, refresco / la puerta, ventana / el libro / la solicitud, tarea / en un apartamento

A. Complete the following dialogues, using the present indicative of the verbs given. Then act them out with a partner.

1. comer — ¿Dónde _____ Uds.?
—_____ en la cafetería.

2. vivir — ¿Dónde _____ tú?
—_____ en la calle Montalvo.

3. recibir — ¿Cuánto dinero _____ Uds.?
—Yo _____ quinientos dólares y él _____ cuatrocientos.

4. leer — ¿Qué periódico *(newspaper)* _____ ellos?
—_____ el *Times*.

5. vender / creer / abrir — ¿Dónde _____ (ellos) sándwiches?
—En la cafetería, pero yo _____ que (ellos) no _____ la cafetería hasta *(until)* las siete.

6. beber — ¿Qué _____ Uds.?
—Nosotros _____ Coca-Cola y Ana _____ 7-Up.

7. deber — ¿Qué _____ estudiar (yo)?
—Ud. _____ estudiar alemán.

8. escribir — ¿Uds. _____ en inglés?
—No, _____ en español.

B. Describe what these people do, must do, or decide to do, using **-er** or **-ir** verbs.

1. Yo / café
2. Nosotros / español
3. Uds. / el *Times*
4. Carlos y Rosa / con una pluma roja
5. Tú / la puerta
6. Las chicas / en un apartamento
7. Ud. / tacos
8. Nosotros / estudiar hoy
9. Susana / tomar portugués

EXPANSION C: Ask these or similar questions of individual students; then include alternative questions as a follow-up.

I—¿Comes en la cafetería?
S1—Sí, como en la cafetería.
I—¿Cómo son los sándwiches allí?
S1—Son deliciosos.

C. Interview a classmate, using the following questions and two questions of your own. When you have finished, switch roles.

1. ¿Dónde vives?
2. ¿Dónde comes?
3. ¿Comen sándwiches tú y tus amigos?

4. ¿Bebes Sprite o Coca-Cola?
5. ¿Aprendes mucho en la clase de español?
6. En la clase, ¿leen Uds. en español?
7. ¿Lees bien el español?[1]
8. ¿Escribes en español o en inglés?
9. ¿Vendes tus libros?
10. ¿Qué periódico lees tú?
11. ¿Debes trabajar mañana?
12. ¿Reciben mucho dinero tus amigos?

D. Take turns asking the instructor the questions in the preceding activity. Make sure to use the **Ud.** form.

6 Present indicative of the irregular verbs **tener** and **venir**
*(Presente de indicativo de los verbos irregulares **tener** y **venir**)*

SUGGESTION: Emphasize the similarities between **tener** and **venir**.

SUGGESTION: Practice the verb **venir** by asking students where they were before class.

I—¿De dónde vienes tú?
S1—Yo vengo de mi clase de historia.

tener *to have*		**venir** *to come*	
yo	tengo	yo	vengo
tú	tienes	tú	vienes
Ud. } él } ella }	tiene	Ud. } él } ella }	viene
nosotros(-as)	tenemos	nosotros(-as)	venimos
vosotros(-as)	tenéis	vosotros(-as)	venís
Uds. } ellos } ellas }	tienen	Uds. } ellos } ellas }	vienen

SUGGESTION: Have students ask five or six classmates where they have come from and then report their findings to the rest of the class.

S1—Pablo y Ramón vienen de la residencia, Susana viene de la cafetería y Simón viene de su casa.

—¿Cuántas clases **tienen** Uds.?   *"How many classes do you have?"*
—**Tenemos** dos. ¿Cuántas **tienes** tú?   *"We have two. How many do you have?"*
—Yo **tengo** cuatro.   *"I have four."*

ATENCIÓN   **Tener que** means *to have to,* and it is followed by an infinitive. Olga **tiene que trabajar** hoy. *Olga has to work today.*

---

[1]The definite article is used with names of languages except after the prepositions **en** and **de,** or after the verbs **hablar** and usually **estudiar.**

SUGGESTION: Using colored chalk to emphasize the word **que**, write the following on the board.

I	have		to work.
Yo	**tengo**	**que**	**trabajar.**

SUGGESTION: Practice the structure **tener que** + *infinitive* by asking students what they or their friends must do after class, in the evening, tomorrow, etc.

—¿A qué hora **vienen** Uds.? *"What time are you coming?"*
—Sergio y yo **venimos** a las dos, y Olga **viene** a la una. *"Sergio and I are coming at two and Olga is coming at one."*
—¿Tú **tienes que** venir a la universidad mañana? *"Do you have to come to the university tomorrow?"*
—No. *"No."*

práctica ....

ACTIVITY SUGGESTION: See the *IAM* for an additional in-class activity: **¿Qué hacemos?**

SUGGESTION A: Have students change the verbs, according to the new subjects.

1. *Yo* **tengo** dinero. (Él, Uds., Ud. y yo, Su esposo, Ellas)
2. *Él* **viene** con Roberto. (Tú, Juana y él, Juan, Uds., Yo, Ud.)

EXPANSION B: Practice the verb **tener** by asking students, "Who has what?"

I—¿Quién tiene muchos exámenes?
S1—Nosotros tenemos muchos exámenes.

Other suggested phrases: **mi número de teléfono, un auto rojo, un periódico, mucho dinero, un amigo guapo, una amiga casada, una licencia de conducir, un sándwich de jamón, un profesor antipático, una clase de filosofía, problemas sentimentales.**

SUGGESTION C: Have students change the verbs, according to the new subjects.

1. *Yo* **tengo que trabajar.** (Tú, Nosotros, Él, Ellos, Uds.)
2. *Él* **tiene que estudiar.** (María, Uds., Tú, Ellos, Nosotros, Yo)

SUGGESTION D: Have students use the cues below to say what the following people must do, using **tener que** + *infinitive*.

1. Uds. / venir a clase mañana
2. Tú / venir a las ocho
3. Juan / trabajar mucho
4. María y Carmen / estudiar la Lección 3
5. Uds. / hablar español en clase
6. Él / vender los libros

A. Give each of the following sentences a logical ending.

1. Yo tengo un examen de español y ella…
2. Uds. vienen los sábados y nosotros…
3. Ella tiene veinte dólares y nosotros…
4. Ana viene con Roberto y tú…
5. Ellos vienen a las seis y yo…
6. Nosotros tenemos dos mapas y ellos…

B. Interview a classmate, using the following questions.

1. ¿Tienes mi número de teléfono?
2. ¿Tienes mi dirección?
3. ¿Tiene la profesora tu número de teléfono?
4. ¿Vienen Uds. a la universidad por la noche o por la mañana?
5. ¿Tienes que solicitar otro trabajo?
6. ¿A qué hora vienen Uds. a la clase de español?
7. ¿Vienes a la clase con tus amigos?
8. ¿Vienes a clase los sábados?
9. ¿Vienen los estudiantes a clase los domingos?

C. Say what the following people have to do, using **tener que** + *infinitive*.

1. Silvia tiene un examen mañana.
2. John tiene una amiga de Madrid que no habla inglés.
3. Nosotros necesitamos dinero.
4. Necesito escribir y no tengo pluma.
5. Necesito hablar por teléfono con Marta, y ella no está.

D. Make a list of tasks or errands for the week; then, with one or two classmates, take turns asking each other what you have to do (**¿Qué tienes que hacer?**) each day.

> **MODELO:** el lunes: leer un libro
> —¿Qué tienes que hacer el lunes?
> —*Tengo que leer un libro.*

¡A ver cuánto aprendió!

INTERNET

See the *¿Cómo se dice...?* Web site for additional grammar and vocabulary practice: http://spanish.college. hmco.com/students

¡Repase el vocabulario!

Complete the following sentences using vocabulary learned in **Lección 3**; then read them aloud.

1. Tengo que escribir un _____ para mi clase de francés.
2. ¿Las chicas estudian en la _____ o en su casa?
3. Nosotros _____ sándwiches en la cafetería.
4. Teresa _____ estudiar porque mañana _____ un examen.
5. ¿Tienes problemas _____ o económicos? ¿Necesitas _____?
6. ¿No está? _____ más tarde.
7. ¿Ella es rubia, _____ o _____?
8. —¿Está Rosaura? —Con _____ habla.
9. ¿Eres optimista o pesimista? ¿O eres _____?
10. Nosotros somos estudiantes _____.
11. Tengo que leer _____ artículos.
12. ¿En qué calle _____ tú?

ACTIVITY SUGGESTION: Do **¡Escucha!**, the in-class listening comprehension activity that reviews vocabulary and grammar structures introduced in the lesson. It appears in the answer key of the *IAM*.

ACTIVITY SUGGESTION: See the *IAM* for an additional in-class activity: **Palabras escondidas.**

Entrevista

With a partner, interview each other by asking the following questions.

1. ¿Tú trabajas esta noche?
2. ¿Tienes que trabajar mañana?
3. ¿Qué tienes que estudiar hoy?
4. ¿Tú debes estudiar más *(more)*?
5. ¿Tú aprendes mucho en la clase de español?
6. ¿Cuántos idiomas hablas tú?
7. ¿Tú vienes a la universidad los sábados?
8. ¿Hablas por teléfono con tus amigos?
9. ¿Cómo es tu mejor amigo?
10. ¿Qué periódico *(newspaper)* lees?
11. Yo necesito 500 dólares. ¿Cuánto dinero necesitas tú?
12. ¿Tú comes comida *(food)* italiana? ¿Mexicana?

ACTIVITY SUGGESTION: See the *IAM* for additional in-class activities: **Para conocernos mejor** and **Una encuesta.**

FOLLOW-UP: After completion of the **Entrevista,** have each student write a brief description of his or her partner. You may want to suggest other questions to increase the amount of information exchanged.

¿Qué estudias en la universidad?
¿Dónde deseas trabajar?
¿De dónde eres?
¿Qué deseas ser? (profesor, piloto, etc.)
¿Qué necesitas? (dinero, amigos[-as], etc.)

The following day, collect the descriptions and read several to the class. Students should try to guess **¿Quién es?**

Situaciones

EXPANSION: Have students work in pairs to write mini-dialogues based on the situations given. Remind them to be creative. Have students present the dialogue of their choice at the beginning of the next class.

You are talking on the telephone. What would you say in the following situations? What might the other person say? Act out the scenes with a partner. Take turns playing each role.

1. You want to know whether your friend Carlos is at home.
2. Someone calls and asks for your sister, who is at home.
3. Someone asks to speak to you.

4. You tell someone you'll call later.
5. Someone has asked to talk to you, and you want to know who it is.
6. You are telling someone what you have to do tomorrow.

Para escribir

Describe your parents. Give as many details as you can.

Mi mamá…   Mi papá…

En la vida real

¡Por teléfono!

CD-ROM

Do the interactive exercises on the CD-ROM for additional practice.

With a classmate, act out the following phone conversations in Spanish.

1. Call your classmate's home. His or her roommate or a member of his or her family answers (your classmate is not home). Find out when he or she will be back.
2. You and a friend are planning to have dinner together on Saturday. Ask each other whether you eat different types of food (**comida**). You might want to include: **china** (Chinese) and **japonesa** (Japanese).

Un mensaje telefónico

Based on the information provided in the phone message, complete the statements next to it.

Hospital El Samaritano

MENSAJE PERSONAL

Para *Carlos Vega*

De parte de *Jorge Ibarra*

De la compañía *Hotel Plaza*

Teléfono *386-4127*

Llamó por teléfono a la(s) *10:30*

☑ de la mañana ☐ de la tarde ☐ de la noche

MENSAJE
   Desea hablar con usted.

ASUNTO
   Problemas con las reservaciones del hotel para la convención.

Día *Miércoles*

1. El mensaje es para _____.
2. El Sr. Vega trabaja en el _____.
3. El mensaje es de parte de _____.
4. El Sr. Ibarra trabaja para el _____.
5. El número de teléfono del hotel es _____.
6. El mensaje es _____.
7. El Sr. Ibarra llamó *(called)* a las _____ de la _____ del día _____.
8. En el hotel hay problemas con _____.

La solicitud

EXPANSION: Have students work in pairs as employer and job applicant. The employer should ask for the spelling of the future employee's name, his or her address, and other information on the application. Write words and phrases on the board that might be used in completing a job application; for example:

¿Cómo se escribe su apellido? (mayúscula, minúscula, con acento)
¿Cuál es su dirección?
Repita, por favor. Hable más despacio.

At the end of the "interview," students should exchange papers and check the information to make sure it is correct and complete.

Imagine that you are applying for a job. Fill out the application with your own personal data.

SOLICITUD DE TRABAJO

Apellidos y nombre

_____

| Fecha de nacimiento |
| Día   Mes   Año |

Número de identidad

_____

Edad

Dirección   Ciudad   Zona postal

_____

Teléfono

_____

Nacionalidad   Lugar de nacimiento

_____

Estado civil: ❏ Soltero(-a)   ❏ Casado(-a)   ❏ Divorciado(-a)   ❏ Viudo(-a)

Sexo ❏ Masculino   ❏ Femenino

Educación
Institución   Años

_____

_____

Experiencia
Compañía   Años

_____

_____

¡VAMOS A LEER!

Antes de leer

As you read about Javier and Aurora, find the answers to the following questions.

1. ¿Quién es el novio de Aurora?
2. ¿Cómo es Javier?
3. ¿Cómo es Aurora?
4. ¿Cuál es la profesión de ellos?
5. ¿Dónde viven?
6. ¿Dónde trabaja Javier?
7. ¿Aurora trabaja?
8. ¿Qué días comen en la cafetería?
9. ¿Dónde estudian los sábados?
10. ¿Por qué tienen que estudiar hoy?

Javier y Aurora

Javier y Aurora son novios. Él es un muchacho muy inteligente y muy guapo. Es rubio y alto. Aurora es baja, morena y muy linda. Los dos son estudiantes universitarios y viven en Phoenix.

Javier trabaja en la biblioteca de la universidad pero Aurora solamente estudia. Los lunes y miércoles comen juntos en la cafetería y los sábados por la mañana estudian en la casa de Aurora. Hoy tienen que estudiar francés porque mañana tienen un examen.

Díganos

Answer the following questions, based on your own thoughts and experiences.

1. ¿Ud. tiene novio(-a)?
2. ¿Cómo es Ud.?
3. ¿Dónde vive usted?
4. ¿Qué días come Ud. en la cafetería?
5. ¿Estudia Ud. los sábados?
6. ¿Ud. tiene que estudiar hoy?

NOTE: The video-related vocabulary is listed in the *Instructor's Activities Manual* for your reference. Its purpose is to facilitate students' comprehension. You may want to distribute the vocabulary to the class before viewing.

 ASÍ SOMOS

 VIDEO CD-ROM **Do the interactive exercises on the CD-ROM for additional practice.**

NOTE: See the Instructor's Edition frontmatter for additional suggestions on implementing video in the classroom.

NARRADORA —¿Tiene Ud. hermanos?

RITA —Tengo tres hermanas. Mmm... Una se llama Tutuguari. Tiene veintitrés años. Este... Otra se llama Fernanda y tiene diecinueve. Y ahora... Y la más pequeña se llama Bensaír y también tiene diecinueve años.

NARRADORA —¿Cómo es su mejor amiga?

RITA —Es una persona muy dinámica. Baila ballet. Toma clases de equitación. Habla inglés, francés y es muy alegre.

Preparación

SUGGESTION: In groups, have students make a list of the activities they see people doing at the beginning of the video.

A. Descripciones. With a partner, answer the following questions based on your own information. You will hear answers to these same questions when you watch the video. After viewing the video, compare your answers with those you hear.

1. ¿Cuál es su profesión u ocupación?
2. ¿Es Ud. casado(-a)?
3. ¿Cómo es su novio(-a)?
4. ¿Tiene Ud. hermanos?
5. ¿Cómo es su mejor amigo(-a)?

B. En una entrevista. Make a list of the questions you might expect to hear during a job interview. Share your questions with the class.

Comprensión

SUGGESTION: Pause the video after each interview segment so students have time to complete the corresponding comprehension activity.

A. Profesiones. Match each person's name with his or her profession or occupation.

A	B
_____ 1. Manuel	a. Es gerente *(manager)* de la Librería de Cuba.
_____ 2. Ricardo	b. Es piloto.
_____ 3. José	c. Es estudiante.
_____ 4. Rosalía	d. Es médico cirujano *(surgeon)*.
_____ 5. Héctor	e. Es ingeniero *(engineer)*.

B. ¿Verdadero o falso? Read the following statements. Circle **V (Verdadero)** or **F (Falso)** according to what you understood from the video. If a statement is false, correct it.

V   F   1. Yolanda no es casada.
V   F   2. Carolina no tiene novio.
V   F   3. Orlando es casado.

C. ¿Cómo es? Complete the following statements with the appropriate adjective from the list below.

alegre *(happy)*
sincero(-a)
serio(-a)
trabajador(-a) *(hard-working)*
alto(-a)
guapo(-a)

1. El novio de Paola es _____ y _____.
2. El novio de Milka es _____ y _____.
3. La novia de Juan es _____ y _____.

NOTE: Exercise D includes two
interview segments.

D. ¿Verdadero o falso? Read the following statements. Circle **V** (**Verdadero**) or **F** (**Falso**) according to what you understood from the video. If a statement is false, correct it.

V F   1. Ivonne tiene dos hermanos y dos hermanas.
V F   2. Carolina tiene tres hermanos.
V F   3. La mejor amiga de Carolina es delgada y estudia periodismo.
V F   4. La mejor amiga de Milka tiene ojos azules y pelo rubio.

E. Entrevista (*Interview*). Watch the video segment called *Entrevista* at the end of Lesson 3. Select the word or phrase that best completes each statement, according to what you understood from the interview.

1. El nombre completo de Yurida, la persona entrevistada *(the interviewee)*, es (Guzmán Robles, Yurida Guzmán Robles, Vanesa Rinconada).
2. Yurida busca *(is looking for)* un nuevo (trabajo, teléfono, apartamento).
3. Rinconada Buganvillas, 3597 es donde (vive, trabaja, estudia) Yurida.
4. El teléfono de Yurida es (813-08-37, 803-04-36, 813-04-37).
5. Estudió *(She studied)* en la (Universidad Autónoma de México, Universidad Autónoma de Guadalajara).

Ampliación

A. Mi novio(-a) ideal. Interview a classmate about his or her ideal boyfriend or girlfriend. First, make a list of the questions you would ask him or her. Then make a list of the adjectives to describe this ideal person. Compare the answers with the rest of the class.

EXPANSION: You may want to have
students role-play the situation in
Ampliación B.

B. Un(-a) nuevo(-a) compañero(-a) de cuarto. You are doing a telephone interview of a potential roommate in your university apartment. What questions would you ask to elicit the following responses?

SUGGESTION: Have the class write a
list on the board of the adjectives they
use to describe people.

TÚ   —_____
ESTUDIANTE   —Me llamo Miguel Andrés Martínez.
TÚ   —_____
ESTUDIANTE   —Soy de San Juan, Puerto Rico.
TÚ   —_____
ESTUDIANTE   —Estudio administración de empresas.
TÚ   —_____
ESTUDIANTE   —Tengo un hermano y una hermana. Mi hermano es mayor y es casado, con un hijo. Mi hermana es menor y también estudia en la universidad.
TÚ   —_____
ESTUDIANTE   —Es 781-54-58.

Take this test. When you have finished, check your answers in the answer key provided in Appendix E. Then use a red pen to correct any mistakes you may have made. Are you ready?

Lección 1

A. The alphabet

Spell the following last names in Spanish.

1. Barrios
2. Acosta
3. Díaz
4. Ferreyra
5. Guevara
6. Henao
7. Jiménez
8. Leyva

B. Cardinal numbers (0–30)

Write these numbers in Spanish.

1. 11
2. 17
3. 30
4. 20
5. 15
6. 13
7. 28
8. 19
9. 12
10. 14

C. Colors

What colors come to mind when you think of the following?

1. a leaf
2. an orange
3. a banana
4. rosy cheeks
5. coal
6. a plum
7. coffee
8. the American flag

D. Days of the week

Give the days of the week that come *before* the ones mentioned here.

1. lunes
2. jueves
3. sábado
4. miércoles
5. domingo
6. viernes

E. Months and seasons of the year

Give the months and seasons that come before the ones mentioned here.

1. diciembre
2. abril
3. agosto
4. febrero
5. junio
6. octubre
7. invierno
8. verano

73

F. Subject pronouns and the present indicative of the verb *ser*

Complete the following dialogue, using the present indicative of the verb **ser.**

—¿De dónde _____ ustedes?
—Nosotros _____ de California. ¿De dónde _____ tú?
—Yo _____ de Tejas.
—Y Carlos y María?
—Carlos _____ de Arizona y María _____ de Nuevo México.
—¿De dónde _____ los profesores?
—De Nueva Jersey.

G. Just words . . .

Match each question in column A with the best response in column B.

A	B
1. ¿Cómo están ustedes?	a. No, médica.
2. ¿Cómo te llamas?	b. No, martes.
3. ¿Qué hay de nuevo?	c. Soy analista de sistemas.
4. ¿Ud. es enfermera?	d. Cuatro-dos-seis-veintidós-treinta.
5. ¿Cuál es su profesión?	e. De Buenos Aires.
6. ¿Ella es la secretaria?	f. No, él es auxiliar de vuelo.
7. ¿De dónde eres tú?	g. Bien, gracias.
8. ¿Qué día es hoy?	h. No, estudiantes.
9. ¿Hoy es lunes?	i. No, la recepcionista.
10. ¿Cuál es tu número de teléfono?	j. Ana María Belgrano.
11. ¿Uds. son profesores?	k. Miércoles.
12. ¿Carlos es piloto?	l. Nada.

H. Culture

Answer the following questions based on the **¿Lo sabía Ud.?** section.

1. ¿Cuál es un nombre muy popular en España y en Latinoamérica?
2. ¿Se usa también para hombres? Dé *(Give)* un ejemplo.

Lección 2

A. Gender and number and definite articles

Place **el, la, los,** or **las** before each noun.

1. _____ pizarra
2. _____ luz
3. _____ lápices
4. _____ día
5. _____ libros
6. _____ relojes
7. _____ mapa
8. _____ plumas
9. _____ pared
10. _____ pupitre

B. Gender and number and indefinite articles

Place **un, una, unos,** or **unas** before each noun.

1. _____ tizas
2. _____ borradores
3. _____ mano
4. _____ hombres
5. _____ mujer
6. _____ secretario
7. _____ profesores
8. _____ papel

C. Cardinal numbers (31–100)

Write the following numbers in Spanish.

1. 38
2. 100
3. 91
4. 85
5. 72
6. 57
7. 46
8. 63

D. Telling time

Use the clues given to say at what time the following classes are.

1. la clase de español / 10:30 A.M.
2. la clase de inglés / 1:15 P.M.
3. la clase de literatura / 8:40 P.M.

E. Present indicative of -ar verbs and negative and interrogative sentences

Complete the following dialogues, using the Spanish equivalent of the words in parentheses.

1. —¿Dónde _____ tú?
   —Yo _____ en la universidad.
   —¿A qué hora _____ a tu casa?
   —A las cuatro.
   (work / work / return)

2. —¿Uds. _____ por la mañana?
   —No, nosotros _____ por la mañana.
   —¿Cuántas clases _____ ustedes?
   —Cinco.
   (study / don't study / take)

3. —¿Qué _____ Carlos y Aurora?
   —Carlos _____ lápices y Aurora _____ bolígrafos.
   (need / needs / needs)

4. —¿ _____ llamar más tarde, Anita?
   —Sí, yo _____ más tarde.
   (Do you wish / will call)

5. —¿ _____ inglés en la clase?
   —No, nosotros _____ inglés en la clase.
   (Do you speak / don't speak)

F. Possession with *de*

Give the Spanish equivalent of each phrase.

1. Miss Vega's students
2. Amanda's professor *(masc.)*
3. Paco's friends

G. Just words . . .

Complete the following sentences using vocabulary from **Lección 2.**

1. No es una calle; es una _____.
2. Mi _____ es: calle Olmos, número 124.
3. ¿Cómo se _____ *"door"* en español?
4. ¿Qué _____ decir "borrador"?
5. Tome _____, por favor.
6. En Berlín hablan _____ y en París hablan _____.
7. ¿_____ estudiantes hay en la clase? ¿Treinta?
8. Con _____. Buenos días, profesora.
9. Elsa no trabaja; _____ estudia.
10. Pedro habla un _____ de portugués.

H. Culture

Answer the following questions based on the **¿Lo sabía Ud.?** section.

1. Si usamos el sistema de 24 horas, ¿qué hora es cuando decimos *(when we say)* "las 18 horas"?
2. En España y en Latinoamérica, ¿qué idioma extranjero *(foreign language)* estudian muchos estudiantes en la escuela secundaria?

Lección 3

A. Gender, Part II

Place **el, la, los,** or **las** before each noun.

1. _____ desilusión
2. _____ libertad
3. _____ programas
4. _____ universidad
5. _____ muchedumbre *(crowd)*
6. _____ ciudades
7. _____ sistema
8. _____ lecciones
9. _____ problemas
10. _____ conversación

B. Possessive adjectives

Give the Spanish equivalent of the words in parentheses.

1. Necesito _____ y _____. *(my ballpoint pen / my books)*
2. _____ es muy grande, pero _____ es pequeña. *(His house / her house)*
3. _____ es de Colombia. Es una mujer muy inteligente. *(Our professor)*
4. _____ son de Buenos Aires. *(Our friends)*
5. ¿Tú necesitas _____, Anita? *(your pencils)*
6. _____ habla español. ¿Qué idioma habla _____? *(Their professor / your (pl.) professor)*

C. Cardinal numbers (101–1,000)

Write the following numbers in Spanish.

1. 195
2. 286
3. 371
4. 460
5. 553
6. 644
7. 732
8. 827
9. 918
10. 1.513

D. Descriptive adjectives

Change the articles and the adjectives according to the nouns in parentheses.

1. El chico es alto. (chica)
2. La pizarra es pequeña. (escritorio)
3. Los chicos son norteamericanos. (chicas)
4. Es un hombre muy simpático. (mujer)
5. Necesito los lápices rojos. (plumas)

E. Present indicative of regular *-er* and *-ir* verbs

Complete the following sentences using the Spanish equivalent of the verbs in parentheses.

1. Nosotros _____ mucho en la clase de español. *(learn)*
2. ¿Tú _____ en la cafetería? *(eat)*
3. Yo _____ que Elena habla alemán. *(think)*
4. ¿Ustedes _____ muchos libros? *(read)*
5. Carlos _____ champán. *(drinks)*
6. Usted _____ estudiar. *(must)*
7. Ellos _____ sus libros. *(sell)*
8. Yo _____ las ventanas. *(open)*
9. Ellos _____ muchas cartas *(letters)*. *(receive)*
10. Nosotros _____ en inglés. *(write)*

F. Just words . . .

Match each question in column A with the best response in column B.

<table>
<tr><td colspan="2" align="center">A</td><td colspan="2" align="center">B</td></tr>
<tr><td>1.</td><td>¿Ana es tu novia?</td><td>a.</td><td>No, soy realista.</td></tr>
<tr><td>2.</td><td>¿Dónde estudian?</td><td>b.</td><td>Sí, ¡y muy simpática!</td></tr>
<tr><td>3.</td><td>¿Estudian esta noche?</td><td>c.</td><td>Menéndez.</td></tr>
<tr><td>4.</td><td>¿Cómo estás?</td><td>d.</td><td>No, es muy guapo.</td></tr>
<tr><td>5.</td><td>¿Es bonita?</td><td>e.</td><td>Enfermera.</td></tr>
<tr><td>6.</td><td>¿Está Jorge?</td><td>f.</td><td>En la biblioteca.</td></tr>
<tr><td>7.</td><td>¿Eres pesimista?</td><td>g.</td><td>No, es rubia.</td></tr>
<tr><td>8.</td><td>¿Es feo?</td><td>h.</td><td>No, es muy antipática.</td></tr>
<tr><td>9.</td><td>¿Es simpática?</td><td>i.</td><td>No, mañana.</td></tr>
<tr><td>10.</td><td>¿Cuál es su apellido?</td><td>j.</td><td>De Mauricio Díaz.</td></tr>
<tr><td>11.</td><td>¿Estado civil?</td><td>k.</td><td>Más o menos.</td></tr>
<tr><td>12.</td><td>¿Ocupación?</td><td>l.</td><td>No, es bajo.</td></tr>
<tr><td>13.</td><td>¿Es morena?</td><td>m.</td><td>No, es una amiga.</td></tr>
<tr><td>14.</td><td>¿Es alto?</td><td>n.</td><td>Soltero.</td></tr>
<tr><td>15.</td><td>¿De parte de quién?</td><td>o.</td><td>Con él habla.</td></tr>
</table>

G. Culture

Answer the following questions based on the **¿Lo sabía Ud.?** section.

1. ¿Cómo contestan el teléfono en México?
2. "Español" y "castellano", ¿son equivalentes?

Una fiesta de fin de año

Lección
4

OBJECTIVES

Pronunciation

The Spanish **b, v, d,** and **g** (before **a, o,** or **u**)

Structure

The personal **a** • Contractions • Expressions with **tener** • Present indicative of the irregular
verbs **ir, dar,** and **estar** • **Ir a** + *infinitive* • Present indicative of **e:ie** stem-changing verbs

Communication

You will learn vocabulary related to party activities, foods, and beverages.

Una fiesta de fin de año

STUDENT
AUDIO

SUGGESTION: Before presenting the dialogue, introduce the new vocabulary on page 81 by asking students to categorize words they think are appropriate to describe **"una fiesta de fin de año."** Suggested categories are: **comida, bebida, entremeses, actividades, lugares,** and **invitados.** Remind them to refer to previous vocabulary lists for other words. Write their suggestions on the board, and then have the class describe their ideal New Year's Eve party. Their plans should include: **los invitados, la hora, la comida/la bebida,** and **el entretenimiento (baile, música,** etc.).

SUGGESTION: Refer students to **Panorama hispánico 8** for more information about Uruguay.

SUGGESTION: Have students act out the dialogues in groups.

UNA INVITACIÓN

Estás invitado(a) a una fiesta de _fin de año_

En el domicilio de _Adela Benavente_

Calle _18 de Julio_ , número _923_

Ciudad: _Montevideo_

La fiesta comienza a las _21 horas_

Antes de la fiesta

ADELA —Muchos de mis compañeros de la universidad van a venir a mi fiesta. ¿Tú vas a traer a tu prima?

HUMBERTO —Sí, y también voy a traer unos discos compactos y las empanadas[1] que mi mamá va a preparar.

ADELA —Y nosotros vamos a preparar pollo, entremeses y ensalada de papas. ¡Todo va a estar delicioso!

HUMBERTO —¡Ay, Adela, yo tengo hambre ahora!

ADELA —¿Quieres un sándwich? Y, si tienes sed, hay refresco, cerveza y agua mineral.

HUMBERTO —Sí, quiero un sándwich y un refresco... No... prefiero un vaso de agua. Oye, ¿a qué hora empieza el baile del club?

ADELA —A las once.[2] ¿Vas a llamar a Julio y a Teresa?

HUMBERTO —Sí, porque ellos piensan ir al club con nosotros. Hoy es el cumpleaños de Teresa.

ADELA —¿Ah, sí? ¿Cuántos años tiene ella?

HUMBERTO —Creo que hoy cumple veinte años. El sábado da una fiesta y estamos invitados.

Adela y sus amigos lo pasan muy bien en la fiesta. Todos bailan, conversan, comen y beben. Después, van al Club Náutico para celebrar la llegada del año nuevo. Julio no va porque está enfermo.

---

[1]Meat turnovers

[2]In Hispanic countries, it is common for people to celebrate the New Year by attending a party in a private home early in the evening, then moving to a club before midnight.

En el Club Náutico

HUMBERTO	—La orquesta es magnífica. ¿Bailamos, Adela?
ADELA	—Ahora no, Humberto. Estoy un poco cansada y tengo mucho calor.[1] ¿Por qué no vamos a la terraza?
HUMBERTO	—Buena idea. Voy a llevar las bebidas. ¿Quieres champán, sidra[2] o un coctel?
ADELA	—Para brindar, una copa de champán, por favor. Después, sangría...[3]
JAVIER	—¿No tienen uvas? En España siempre comemos doce uvas a la medianoche del 31 de diciembre. *treinta y uno*
ADELA	—No, Javier. No tenemos uvas. ¡Son las doce!
TODOS	—¡Feliz año nuevo! ¡Feliz año nuevo!

Vocabulario

Cognados

el champán champagne
el club club
el coctel cocktail
delicioso(-a) delicious
el disco compacto compact disk (CD)

la ensalada salad
la idea idea
la invitación invitation
invitado(-a) invited
mucho(-a) much, a lot of
la orquesta orchestra, band

la sangría sangria
la sidra alcoholic cider
el sándwich sandwich
la terraza terrace

Nombres

el agua[4] water *(fem.)*
el agua mineral mineral water
el baile dance
la bebida drink, beverage
la cerveza beer
el (la) compañero(-a) de clase classmate
la copa glass, goblet

el cumpleaños birthday
la ensalada de papas potato salad
los entremeses hors d'oeuvres, appetizers
España Spain
la fiesta party
la llegada arrival

la mamá, madre Mom, mother
la medianoche midnight
el pollo chicken
el (la) primo(-a) cousin
el refresco soda pop
las uvas grapes
el vaso glass

---

[1]In the Southern Hemisphere, the seasons are reversed.
[2]An alcoholic drink in Hispanic countries.
[3]A drink prepared with red wine and fruit.
[4]**El** is used because the next word starts with a stressed **a**.

Verbos

bailar to dance
brindar to toast
celebrar to celebrate
conversar, charlar to talk, to
  chat
cumplir to turn (. . . years old)
dar *(irreg.)* to give

comenzar, empezar (e:ie)
  to begin, to start
estar *(irreg.)* to be
invitar to invite
ir *(irreg.)* to go
llevar to take (someone or
  something someplace)

pensar (e:ie) to plan, to think
preferir (e:ie) to prefer
preparar to prepare
querer (e:ie) to want, to wish
traer (yo traigo) to bring

Adjetivos

cansado(-a) tired
enfermo(-a) sick

feliz happy
magnífico(-a) great

muchos(-as) many
nuevo(-a) new

Otras palabras y expresiones

a la medianoche at midnight
ahora now
allí there
antes de before
¿Bailamos? Shall we dance?
después afterwards
fiesta de fin de año New Year's
  Eve party

para in order to
pasarlo bien to have a good
  time
siempre always
tener... años to be . . . years old
tener calor to be hot
tener hambre to be hungry
tener sed to be thirsty

todo everything
todos(-as) everybody
un poco + *adjective* a little +
  adjective

Vocabulario adicional
La fiesta de Navidad
(Christmas)

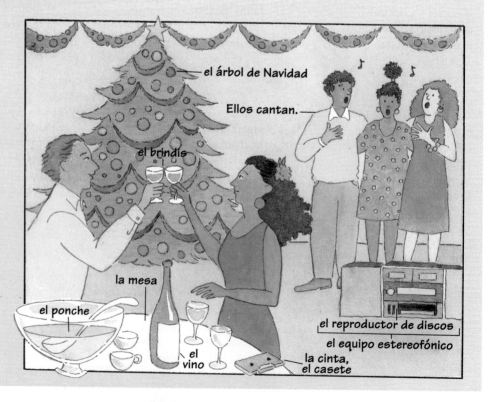

el árbol de Navidad

Ellos cantan.

el brindis

la mesa

el ponche

el vino

el reproductor de discos

el equipo estereofónico

la cinta,
el casete

Para describir

aburrido(-a)	bored	La clase es muy **aburrida**.
contento(-a)	happy	Estoy **contenta** porque voy a la fiesta.
difícil	difficult	El francés es **difícil**.
enojado(-a), enfadado(-a)	angry	Ana está **enojada** porque no tiene dinero.
fácil	easy	La clase es muy **fácil**.
grande	big	El hospital es muy **grande**.
malo(-a)[1]	bad	La orquesta es muy **mala**.
nervioso(-a)	nervous	Estoy **nerviosa** porque mañana tengo un examen.
ocupado(-a)	busy	Estoy muy **ocupado**. Tengo que trabajar.
pequeño(-a)	small	Mi casa es muy **pequeña**.
preocupado(-a)	worried	Está **preocupado** porque su clase es difícil.
triste	sad	No está contento; está **triste**.

Para aclarar

¿adónde?	where? *(destination)*	**¿Adónde** vamos hoy?
al mediodía	at noon	Aurora viene **al mediodía**.
¿cuánto(-a)?	how much?	**¿Cuánto** dinero necesitas?
¿de quién?	whose?	**¿De quién** es el disco compacto? ¿De Raúl?

ACTIVITY SUGGESTION: See the *IAM* for an additional in-class activity: **¿Cómo respondes?**

¡Conversemos!

Answer the following questions, basing your answers on the dialogue.

1. ¿Qué va a dar Adela?
2. ¿En qué calle vive Adela? ¿En qué ciudad?
3. ¿A qué hora comienza la fiesta?
4. ¿Quiénes van a venir a la fiesta de Adela?
5. ¿Qué va a traer Humberto?
6. ¿Quién va a preparar las empanadas?
7. ¿Qué van a preparar Adela y su familia? ¿Cómo va a estar todo?
8. ¿Qué quiere comer Humberto? ¿Qué quiere beber?
9. ¿Quiénes piensan ir al club con Humberto y Adela?
10. ¿Cuántos años cumple Teresa hoy?
11. ¿Cómo lo pasan Adela y sus amigos en la fiesta?
12. ¿Por qué no baila Adela con Humberto?
13. ¿Con qué quiere brindar Adela?
14. ¿Qué comen en España a la medianoche del 31 de diciembre?

---

[1]**Malo** drops the -o when placed before a masculine, singular noun: **un mal hombre**.

¿Lo sabía Ud.?

■ En España y en Latinoamérica, no existe tanta *(as much)* separación entre *(among)* generaciones como en los Estados Unidos. Los niños, los padres y los abuelos frecuentemente van juntos a fiestas y a celebraciones.

■ En los países *(countries)* hispanos, las chicas y los muchachos generalmente van en grupos a fiestas, al teatro y a conciertos.

■ Los hispanos generalmente celebran el cumpleaños y también el día de su "santo", que corresponde al santo de su nombre en el calendario católico. Por ejemplo, si un niño nace *(is born)* en junio y sus padres lo llaman Miguel, celebra su cumpleaños en junio y celebra el día de su "santo" el 29 de septiembre, que es el día de San Miguel. veinte y nueve

■ En algunos *(some)* países hispanos no existe una edad mínima para comprar *(buy)* o tomar bebidas alcohólicas.

■ En español se dice "¡Salud!" *(Cheers!)* al brindar. En España, también dicen "Salud, amor y pesetas" *(Health, love, and pesetas)*.

1. En este país *(country)*, ¿los chicos prefieren salir en grupos o en parejas *(couples)*?

2. En este país, ¿las personas celebran el día de su santo?

3. ¿Cuál es la edad mínima para comprar o tomar bebidas alcohólicas en este país?

INTERNET See the *¿Cómo se dice...?* Web site for activities on authentic cultural material: http://spanish.college.hmco.com/students

Una familia argentina celebrando un cumpleaños.

Pronunciación

A The Spanish b and v

STUDENT AUDIO

The Spanish **b** and **v** are pronounced exactly alike. Both sound like a weak English *b*, as in the word *Abe*. In Spanish, they are even weaker when pronounced between vowels. The lips don't quite touch. Never pronounce these consonants like the English *v*. Listen to your instructor and repeat the following words.

veinte	bien
venir	baile
Viviana	bebida
uva	sobrina

SUGGESTION: Model each word and have the class repeat the sounds and words chorally and individually. The following sentences provide additional pronunciation practice using words in context.

b/v: Basilio y Víctor venden bebidas baratas.
Benito y Bárbara van a viajar a Bolivia.

B The Spanish d

d: Déme dos docenas de dátiles.
Doña Dolores desea bailar con don Diego.

The Spanish **d** is slightly softer than the *d* in the English word *day*. When pronounced between two vowels or at the end of a word, it is similar to the *th* in the English word *they*. Listen to your instructor and repeat the following words.

delgado	universidad
de	sábado
debe	bebida
dos	adiós

C The Spanish g (before a, o, or u)

g: Los enemigos de mis enemigos son mis amigos.
Un lago es más grande que una laguna.

■ When followed by **a**, **o**, or **u**, the Spanish **g** is similar to the *g* in the English word *guy*. Listen to your instructor and repeat the following words.

delgado	guapo	gordo

■ When pronounced between vowels, the Spanish **g** is much softer. Repeat after your instructor.

amigo	pregunta	uruguaya

■ In the combinations **gue** and **gui**, the **u** is silent. Repeat after your instructor.

Guevara	Guillermo	alguien

club
campestre
del caribe
DICIEMBRE 31
Celebración de fin de año
para padres-hijos-familiares e invitados de socios
Salón Dorado 9:00 PM

Estructuras

1 The personal a *(La a personal)*

SUGGESTION: Use an inductive presentation for personal **a.** Write paired sentences on the overhead projector or board to illustrate the use and omission of the personal **a.**

1. Miro a Tomás.
   Miro el libro de Tomás.
2. Busco a Pablo.
   Busco el examen de Pablo.
3. Llevo a tres personas en mi auto.
   Llevo la comida en mi auto.
4. Escucho a los estudiantes.
   Escucho la radio.
5. Visito a mi novio.
   Visito el pueblo de mi novio.

Ask students to compare and contrast the sentences and have them explain to you the rules for use of the personal **a.**

NOTE: Mention that the personal **a** may also be used with a personified noun, such as a pet.

Llevo a mi perro al veterinario.

■ The preposition **a** is used in Spanish before a direct object[1] referring to a specific person or persons. It is called the "personal **a**" and has no equivalent in English.

Yo llamo **a mi prima.**
              D.O.
I call   my cousin.
            D.O.

Nosotros llamamos **a los estudiantes.**
                     D.O.
We   call   the students.
                   D.O.

■ The personal **a** is *not* used when the direct object is not a person.

Yo llevo **las bebidas** a la fiesta.
           D.O.
I take the drinks to the party.
        D.O.

■ The verb **tener** generally does not take the personal **a,** even if the direct object is a person.

No tengo **novio.**
           D.O.
I don't have a boyfriend.
            D.O.

Tenemos **varios amigos.**
           D.O.
We have several friends.
           D.O.

—¿Llevas **a** tus primos a la universidad?
—Yo no tengo primos. Llevo **a** Jorge y **a** Luis.

"Do you take your cousins to the university?"
"I don't have (any) cousins. I take Jorge and Luis."

ATENCIÓN   When there is a series of direct object nouns referring to people, the personal **a** is repeated: **Llevo *a Jorge* y *a Luis.***

práctica ●●

A. Use the personal **a** when needed to complete the following dialogues. Then act them out with a partner.

1. —¿Cuántos primos tienes?
   —Tengo _____ dos primos y _____ una prima.
2. —¿Llama usted _____ Carmen o _____ Elena?
   —Llamo _____ Carmen.

---

[1]See **Lección 6** for further explanation of the direct object.

3. —¿Tu amigo lleva _____ Rosa a la biblioteca?
   —No, lleva _____ su novia.
4. —¿Adónde lleva usted _____ los libros?
   —A la clase.
5. —¿Tienes _____ muchos amigos?
   —Sí, tengo _____ muchos amigos.
6. —¿Qué lees?
   —Leo _____ el libro de español.

B. With a partner, decide which members of the class you'll call, take, or invite to a party. Give reasons for your choices.

2 Contractions *(Contracciones)*

SUGGESTION: Review *"possession with de"* in **Lección 2.** See the SUGGESTION on pages 39–40. Include questions such as **¿Es el libro de la señorita Smith o del señor Jones? ¿Es el bolígrafo del estudiante o de la profesora? ¿De quién es el cuaderno?** Remind students that when referring to someone with a title [**señor(-a), señorita, doctor(-a),** etc.], the definite article is used.

■ There are only two contractions in Spanish: **al** and **del.** Both the preposition **a** *(to, toward)* and the personal **a** followed by the article **el** contract to **al.**

| Llevo | **a** | + | **el** | profesor. |
| Llevo | **al** | | | profesor. |

■ The preposition **de** *(of, from)* followed by the article **el** contracts to **del.**

| Tiene los libros | **de** | + | **el** | profesor. |
| Tiene los libros | **del** | | | profesor. |

—¿Llevas **al** amigo de Ana?   *"Are you taking Ana's friend?"*
—No, llevo **a las** primas de Eva.   *"No, I'm taking Eva's cousins."*

—¿La casa es **de la** Sra. Vega?   *"Is it Mrs. Vega's house?"*
—No, es **del** Sr. Parra.   *"No, it's Mr. Parra's."*

ATENCIÓN   **A** + **el** and **de** + **el** must always be contracted to **al** and **del.** None of the other combinations (**de la, de las, de los, a la, a las, a los**) is contracted: **Llaman *a los* hijos *de los* profesores.**

práctica ···

SUGGESTION: Emphasize to students that the **a** in **al** may be a personal **a** with no equivalent in English and the **de** in **del** may be equivalent to the *'s* form in English.

A. Complete the following dialogues, using **de la, de las, del, de los, a la, a las, al,** or **a los.** Then act them out with a partner.

1. —¿De dónde vienes?
   —Vengo _____ club. ¿Y tú?
   —Yo vengo _____ hospital.
2. —¿A qué hora llamas _____ chicas?
   —_____ dos.
3. —¿Los mapas son _____ Sr. Vega?
   —No, son _____ Srta. Ruiz.
4. —¿Tienes que ir _____ club?
   —No, tengo que ir _____ biblioteca.
5. —¿Adónde llevas _____ chicos?
   —_____ clase _____ Sr. Peña.

B. With a partner, take turns asking and answering the following questions, using the cues provided.

1. ¿De quién son los libros?   (profesor)
2. ¿De quién es el escritorio?   (Srta. Paz)
3. ¿A quiénes llevas a la universidad?   (chicos)
4. ¿A quién invitan ustedes?   (Sr. Vega)
5. ¿A quiénes llaman los chicos?   (muchachas)
6. ¿Adónde llevan a las muchachas?   (club)
7. ¿De dónde vienen ustedes?   (club)
8. ¿Los libros son de los muchachos?   (no, muchachas)

3 Expressions with **tener**   *(Expresiones con **tener**)*

■ Many useful idiomatic expressions that use *to be + adjective* in English are formed with **tener** + *noun* in Spanish.

tener (mucho) frío	*to be (very) cold*
tener (mucha) sed	*to be (very) thirsty*
tener (mucha) hambre	*to be (very) hungry*
tener (mucho) calor	*to be (very) hot*
tener (mucho) sueño	*to be (very) sleepy*
tener (mucha) prisa	*to be in a (great) hurry*
tener (mucho) miedo	*to be (quite) afraid, scared*
tener cuidado	*to be careful*
tener razón	*to be right*
no tener razón[1]	*to be wrong*
tener... años de edad	*to be . . . years old*

—¿Tienes calor?   "*Are you hot?*"
—Sí, y también **tengo** mucha **sed**.   "*Yes, and I'm also very thirsty.*"

—¿Deseas comer pollo?   "*Do you want to eat chicken?*"
—No, gracias, no **tengo hambre**.   "*No, thank you, I'm not hungry.*"

—¿Cuántos **años tienes**?   "*How old are you?*"
—**Tengo** diecinueve **años**.   "*I'm nineteen years old.*"

ATENCIÓN   Note that Spanish uses **mucho(-a)** *(adjective)* + noun (as in **mucha hambre**) the way English uses *very + adjective* (as in *very hungry*).

SUGGESTION: Review the verb **tener** before presenting these expressions. Emphasize that the idioms should not be translated literally, but should be learned as a whole. Point out that not every English construction of this kind has a Spanish counterpart with **tener**: e.g., *I am tired* translates as **Estoy cansado(-a)**.

SUGGESTION: Use Transparency 19 to introduce these idiomatic expressions. Ask students as a class and individually to describe each sketch by supplying the correct expression. You may also refer to the Instructor's Resource Manual (IRM) that accompanies the transparencies for additional activities and exercises related to **tener** expressions.

ADDITIONAL EXPRESSIONS: **tener suerte** *(to be lucky)*, **tener éxito** *(to be successful)*, **tener ganas de** *(to feel like)*.

SUGGESTION: Introduce **tener... años de edad** by showing photos of famous people or by listing their names and professions on the board. Have students identify them and give their approximate ages. You may want to introduce **aproximadamente** at this time.
GLORIA ESTEFAN—Es una cantante cubana. Tiene aproximadamente **cuarenta** años.
RICKY MARTIN—Es un cantante puertorriqueño. Tiene unos **treinta** años.

[1]Incorrectness is also conveyed by the expression **estar equivocado(-a)**.

práctica ....

A. ¿Qué tienen?

1. Jorge

2. Yo

3. Tú

4. La profesora

5. Ud.

6. Felipe

7. Marisa y Elena

8. Ella

B. Interview a classmate, using the following questions. When you have finished, switch roles.

1. ¿Qué bebes cuando tienes sed? ¿Y cuando tienes frío?
2. ¿Qué comes cuando tienes hambre?
3. ¿Cuántos años tienes?
4. ¿Cuántos años tiene tu mamá? ¿Y tu papá *(Dad)*?
5. En tu familia, ¿quién tiene razón siempre? ¿Y en la clase?
6. ¿Tienes miedo a veces *(sometimes)*?

C. Which expression with **tener** would you use in each of the following situations?

1. You are in the Sahara desert in the middle of summer.
2. A big dog is chasing you.
3. You have only a minute to get to your next class.
4. You are in Alaska in the middle of winter.
5. You haven't eaten for an entire day.
6. You got up at four A.M. and it is now midnight.
7. You just ran for two hours in the sun.
8. You are blowing out thirty candles on your birthday cake.

4 Present indicative of the irregular verbs **ir, dar,** and **estar**
(Presente de indicativo de los verbos irregulares ir, dar y estar)

SUGGESTION: After introducing the verb **ir**, write the following list of places on the board.

cafetería	oficina del
biblioteca	(de la)
banco	profesor(-a)
club	residencia
clase de...	fiesta
	trabajo
	librería

Referring to the list, students should work in groups of four and ask each other where they plan to go after class, in the afternoon/evening, and at midnight.

S1—¿Adónde vas después de la clase (esta tarde/noche, a medianoche)?
S2—Voy a la cafetería.

SUGGESTION: Use Transparency 20 to practice the verb **estar.** Students should use the prepositions **en, lejos de,** and **cerca de** in their responses.

I—¿Dónde está el hospital?
S—Está en la avenida Presidente.
I—¿Dónde está el parque?
S—Está cerca/lejos del hospital.

Afterward, have students work in pairs and ask each other about the location of various places on campus.

	ir *to go*	**dar** *to give*	**estar** *to be*
yo	voy	doy	estoy
tú	vas	das	estás
Ud. él ella	va	da	está
nosotros(-as)	vamos	damos	estamos
vosotros(-as)	vais	dais	estáis
Uds. ellos ellas	van	dan	están

—Susana **da** una fiesta hoy. ¿Tú **vas?**
—No, no **voy** porque **estoy** muy cansada.
—Entonces invito a tu hermana. ¿Dónde **está?**
—**Está** en la universidad. Viene a las tres.

"Susana is giving a party today. Are you going?"
"No, I'm not going because I am very tired."
"Then I'm inviting your sister. Where is she?"
"She is at the university. She is coming at three o'clock."

■ The verb **estar,** *to be,* is used here to indicate current condition (**Estoy muy cansada.**) and location (**Está en la universidad.**). **Ser,** another equivalent of the

English verb *to be*, has been used up to now to refer to origin (**Él es de Chile.**), nationality (**Ellas son mexicanas.**), characteristics (**Jorge es rubio.**), profession (**Elsa es profesora.**), and time (**Son las doce.**).

■ Other frequent uses of **dar** are **dar un examen, dar una conferencia** *(lecture)*, and **dar una orden** *(order)*.

ACTIVITY SUGGESTION: See the *IAM* for an additional in-class activity: **En una fiesta.**

práctica ••

SUGGESTION A: Write the following adjectives on the board with one model sentence. Then have students take turns describing how they feel and why.

cansado(-a)	sorprendido(-a)
deprimido(-a)	triste
aburrido(-a)	contento(-a)
furioso(-a)	enojado(-a)
nervioso(-a)	enfermo(-a)
desilusionado(-a)	tranquilo(-a)
preocupado(-a)	ocupado(-a)

I—¿Cuándo estás nervioso?
S1—Estoy nervioso cuando tengo examen.
I—¿Cuándo estás contenta?
S2—Estoy contenta cuando recibo una buena nota.

A. Complete the following conversation, using the appropriate forms of the verbs **ir, dar,** and **estar.** Then act out the dialogue with a partner.

JOSÉ   —Rosa, ¿tú _____ a la fiesta que _____ Estrella el sábado?

ROSA   —Sí, _____ con Inés. ¿Tú _____ también?

JOSÉ   —Sí. Oye, ¿estudiamos esta noche? El Dr. Vargas y la Dra. Soto _____ exámenes mañana.

ROSA   —Ay, José, _____ muy cansada.

JOSÉ   —Pero, Rosa, ¡tú siempre _____ cansada!

ROSA   —No siempre. ¿Por qué no estudias con Jorge y Raúl? Ellos no _____ al club esta noche.

JOSÉ   —Buena idea. ¿Dónde _____ ellos ahora?

ROSA   —_____ en la universidad.

EXPANSION B: Encourage students to give expanded responses for each question.

S1—¿Estás cansado hoy?
S2—Sí, estoy cansado. Tengo mucho sueño y deseo ir a casa.

For homework, have students write a brief paragraph based on the information their partners have given.

B. Interview a classmate, using the following questions. When you have finished, switch roles.

1. ¿Cómo estás?
2. ¿Estás contento(-a) o triste hoy?
3. ¿Quién no está en clase hoy?
4. ¿Está muy ocupado(-a) el profesor (la profesora)?
5. ¿El profesor (la profesora) da exámenes fáciles o difíciles?
6. ¿Adónde vas los sábados por la noche con tus amigos?
7. ¿Van Uds. a un club? (¿A cuál?)
8. ¿Con quién vas a las fiestas?
9. ¿Das muchas fiestas en tu casa?
10. ¿Das una fiesta de fin de año? ¿De Navidad?
11. ¿Adónde van Uds. mañana? ¿Por qué?
12. ¿Dónde están tus amigos ahora?

SUGGESTION C: Have students do this exercise on the board; then have the class compare and check the responses. Use some of the students' sentences in a dictation exercise the following day as a quick review.

C. Complete the following sentences in a logical manner.

1. Roberto está allí y nosotros...
2. Yo doy una fiesta esta noche y tú...
3. Tú vas a la universidad y yo...
4. Yo estoy muy enojado(-a) y ellos...
5. Nosotros damos una fiesta de Navidad y él...
6. Ellos van hoy y nosotros...
7. Ella está nerviosa y su novio...

D. Here is a list of places that people go to:

la playa *(beach)*   el concierto *(concert)*
la piscina *(swimming pool)* del club   el museo *(museum)*
el teatro *(theatre)*   el parque *(park)*
el cine *(movies)*   la tienda *(store)*

Imagining that you or you and one classmate are walking around town, walk around the class. You will bump into several of your classmates. Ask them where they are going now.

> MODELO: —¡Hola! ¿Adónde vas?
> —Voy al cine. ¿Y tú?
> —Yo voy a la tienda.

After everyone sits down, the instructor will ask where everyone is going.

5 Ir a + *infinitive* (Ir a + *infinitivo*)

■ Ir a + *infinitive* is used to express future action. It is equivalent to the English expression *to be going (to)* + *infinitive*. The "formula" is as follows:

ir *(conjugated)*	+ a +	infinitive
Voy	a	**trabajar.**
I am going		*to work.*

—¿En qué universidad **van a estudiar** Uds.? "*At what university are you going to study?*"
—**Vamos a estudiar** en la Universidad de Costa Rica. "*We're going to study at the University of Costa Rica.*"

—¿Ud. **va a dar** una conferencia? "*Are you going to give a lecture?*"
—Sí, **voy a dar** una conferencia el viernes. "*Yes, I'm going to give a lecture on Friday.*"

—¿Tú **vas a cantar**? "*Are you going to sing?*"
—No, **voy a bailar**. "*No, I'm going to dance.*"

práctica ·······················

SUGGESTION A: Ask two or three students to read the sentences aloud. The class should listen to each sentence and correct the responses if necessary.

A. What do you think these people are going to do? Consider where they are and what time of day it is.

> MODELO: —José / en el hospital / por la tarde
> —José va a trabajar en el hospital por la tarde.

1. Yo / en mi casa / por la noche
2. Los estudiantes / en la clase / por la mañana
3. Nosotros / en el club / por la noche

4. Tú / en la cafetería / a las doce
5. El profesor / en la universidad / por la tarde
6. Julio y Teresa / en la terraza / a las diez de la noche
7. Susana / en su casa / por la mañana
8. Uds. / en la fiesta / por la noche

B. What are these people going to do? With a partner, take turns asking and answering questions, using the information in the illustrations.

MODELO: —¿Con quién va a bailar Marisol?
—*Va a bailar con Tito.*

Marisol

1. Roberto

2. Elisa

3. Julio y Estrella

4. Daniel

5. Eduardo

6. Graciela

FOLLOW-UP C: Ask students additional personalized questions; then have them ask one another about their future plans in groups of three or four.

¿Qué vas a hacer hoy? ¿mañana? ¿este verano?

¿Dónde vas a pasar tus vacaciones?

¿Cuándo vas a terminar tus estudios?

¿Cuándo vas a regresar a casa?

For homework, have students write responses to the questions in a short paragraph describing what they and their partners are going to do tomorrow.

C. Interview a classmate, using the following questions. When you have finished, switch roles.

1. ¿Dónde vas a comer hoy?
2. ¿Con quién vas a comer?
3. ¿A qué hora van a comer Uds.?
4. ¿Qué van a comer?
5. ¿Qué van a tomar Uds.?
6. ¿Qué vas a hacer (to do) mañana por la tarde?
7. ¿Qué van a estudiar tú y tus amigos?
8. ¿Qué van a hacer Uds. por la noche?
9. ¿Dónde vas a trabajar mañana?
10. ¿Tu amigo(-a) va a trabajar también?

6 Present indicative of e:ie stem-changing verbs (Presente de indicativo de los verbos que cambian en la raíz e:ie)

■ Some Spanish verbs undergo a stem change in the present indicative. For these verbs, when e is the last stem vowel and it is stressed, it changes to ie as follows.

preferir	*to prefer*		
yo	prefiero	nosotros(-as)	preferimos
tú	prefieres	vosotros(-as)	preferís
Ud. / él / ella	prefiere	Uds. / ellos / ellas	prefieren

—¿A qué hora **piensas** ir a la fiesta?
"What time are you planning to go to the party?"
—**Prefiero** ir a las diez. ¿Y tú?
"I prefer to go at ten. And you?"
—Yo **no quiero** ir. Estoy cansado.
"I don't want to go. I'm tired."

—¿A qué hora **empiezan** a[1] estudiar Uds.?
"What time do you start to study?"
—**Empezamos** a las tres.
"We start at three."

■ Note that the stem vowel is not stressed in the verb forms used with **nosotros(-as)** and **vosotros(-as)**; therefore, the e does not change to ie.

■ Stem-changing verbs have the same endings as regular -ar, -er, and -ir verbs.

SUGGESTION: Ask students personalized questions based on the verbs and phrases used in the suggested sentence builder.

1. ¿Cuándo empieza tu clase de...?
2. ¿Quieres ir a un concierto?
3. ¿Prefieres la clase de... o la clase de...?
4. ¿Dónde prefieres vivir?
5. ¿Qué/Dónde prefieres comer?
6. ¿Adónde quieres ir mañana (el sábado, etc.)?
7. ¿Dónde quieres tomar un refresco?
8. ¿Qué idiomas entiendes?

[1]The preposition **a** is used after **empezar** and **comenzar** when they are followed by an infinitive.

■ Some verbs that undergo this change:

cerrar   *to close*
comenzar   *to begin, to start*
empezar   *to begin, to start*
entender   *to understand*
pensar   *to think*

pensar *(+ infinitive)*   *to plan*
    (to do something)
perder   *to lose*
querer   *to want, to wish, to*
    love

práctica ....

SUGGESTION A: Drill students on the following verb forms and encourage them to use the forms in sentences.

1. *Yo* quiero ir con ellas. (Tu hermana y yo, Tú, Ellos, Él, Nosotras)
2. *Yo* empiezo las clases. (Tú, Yo y ella, Ellos, Nosotros, Mi amigo)
3. ¿*Tú* cierras la puerta? (Ud., Yo, Ella, Nosotros, Uds.)

SUGGESTION B; Write a short sentence builder on the board and ask students to combine the elements to form ten original sentences.

Yo / Tú / Él / Ella / Nosotros(-as) / Usted(es) / La clase / El banco / Las tiendas

cerrar / entender / perder / querer / empezar / comenzar / pensar / preferir

traer a su amigo / un refresco / ir a la fiesta / el inglés / las puertas y las ventanas / a estudiar en febrero / las cintas del laboratorio / tomar unas vacaciones a... / la Lección trece / celebrar el año nuevo / todo su dinero en Las Vegas / ir juntos al concierto / vivir en...

SUGGESTION C: Encourage students to substitute items in the original questions to create alternative choices.

A. Complete the following dialogues, using the verbs given. Then act them out with a partner, expanding each dialogue by adding one or two sentences.

1. preferir —¿Dónde _____ comer Uds.? ¿En la cafetería o en su casa?
   —_____ comer en nuestra casa.

2. querer —¿Qué _____ comer Uds.?
   —Rosa _____ comer pollo y Oscar y yo _____ comer entremeses.

3. pensar —¿Adónde _____ ir Uds. el domingo?
   —_____ ir al club.

4. cerrar —¿No _____ (ellos) la cafetería los sábados?
   —No, creo que no _____ la cafetería los sábados.

5. perder —Cuando Uds. van a Las Vegas, ¿_____ mucho dinero?
   —Sí, _____ mucho.

6. empezar —¿A qué hora _____ Uds. a trabajar?
   —Nosotros _____ a las ocho y Luis _____ a las nueve.

B. You have just enrolled at a new university, and some current students are helping to orient you. Compare their routines and preferences with your own.

1. Comenzamos las clases a las nueve.
2. No entendemos inglés.
3. Pensamos trabajar mañana.
4. Queremos ir al club.
5. Preferimos beber refrescos.
6. No cerramos las ventanas por la noche.

C. Interview a classmate, using the following questions. When you have finished, switch roles.

1. ¿Entienden tú y tus amigos inglés?
2. ¿Entiendes una conversación en español?
3. ¿Entiendes la lección?
4. ¿Quieres tomar un refresco?
5. ¿Prefieres Coca-Cola o Sprite?
6. ¿Quieren Uds. comer en su casa o en la cafetería?
7. ¿Piensas ir a un baile el sábado?
8. Para bailar, ¿prefieres una orquesta o discos compactos?

D. With a classmate, prepare four questions to ask your instructor, using stem-changing verbs.

¡A ver cuánto aprendió!

INTERNET

See the *¿Cómo se dice...?* Web site for additional grammar and vocabulary practice: http://spanish.college. hmco.com/students

ACTIVITY SUGGESTION: Do **¡Escucha!**, the in-class listening comprehension activity that reviews vocabulary and grammar structures introduced in the lesson. It appears in the answer key of the *IAM*.

ACTIVITY SUGGESTION: See the *IAM* for an additional in-class activity: **Palabras escondidas.**

¡Repase el vocabulario!

Complete the following sentences with the appropriate words; then read them aloud.

1. ¿__De Quien__ son los discos compactos? ¿De Rosa?
2. En las fiestas de __fin__ de año en España, comen doce __uvas__ a la __media noche__
3. La orquesta es muy, muy buena. ¡Es __magnifica__!
4. Enrique Iglesias __canta__ muy bien.
5. ¿__Adonde__ vas? ¿Al club?
6. ¡Feliz año __nuevo__!
7. Marta está __contenta__ porque va al baile del club.
8. ¿Tienes refrescos? Tengo mucha __sed__.
9. No tengo __cines__, pero tengo discos compactos.
10. No quiero bailar ahora porque estoy muy __cansada__
11. ¿__Cuanto__ dinero tiene Ud.? ¿Mil pesos?
12. ¿Quién va a traer el __árbol__ de Navidad? ¿Es grande o __pequeno__?
13. Un __brindis__. Vamos a brindar con sidra.
14. Hoy vamos a celebrar el __cumpleaños__ de Julio.
15. ¿Estudiamos esta noche o vas a estar __ocupada__?
16. Tengo un equipo __estereofonico__, pero es muy malo.

Entrevista

ACTIVITY SUGGESTION: See the *IAM* for additional in-class activities: **Para conocernos mejor** and **Una encuesta.**

SUGGESTION: Write the situations on individual index cards. Give one card to each pair of students and instruct them to initiate a conversation based on the information given on the card. Students should answer the question as completely as possible. Based on that reply, their partners should offer an appropriate response.

With a partner, interview each other by asking the following questions.

1. ¿Cuántos años tienes? ¿Cuándo es tu cumpleaños?
2. ¿Celebras tu cumpleaños con una fiesta?
3. ¿Das muchas fiestas en tu casa? ¿Cuándo vas a dar una fiesta?
4. ¿Estás invitado(-a) a una fiesta el sábado?
5. ¿Bailas bien? ¿Lo pasas bien cuando vas a un baile?
6. ¿Dónde vas a comer mañana? ¿A qué hora vas a comer? ¿Con quién?
7. ¿Tienes hambre? ¿Qué quieres comer? ¿Vas a preparar algo *(something)*?
8. ¿Prefieres beber vino, cerveza, refrescos o agua mineral?
9. ¿Tienes cintas o discos compactos?
10. ¿Adónde vas esta noche?
11. ¿Vas a estar ocupado(-a) mañana? ¿Piensas estudiar?
12. ¿Qué tienes que hacer *(to do)* mañana por la tarde?

Situaciones

What would you say in the following situations? What might the other person say? Act out the scenes with a partner. Take turns playing each role.

1. You want to ask someone to dance with you.
2. You are having a party. Offer one of your guests a selection of beverages.

After three minutes have students exchange cards with another pair and repeat the activity using the new situation. You may want to use the situations as a class activity to elicit responses.

3. Your friend is hungry. You have plenty of food in the house.
4. You call a friend to say that you are going to bring the drinks for a party.
5. It's 12:00 A.M. on January 1.
6. It's your best friend's birthday.
7. You tell a friend how old you're going to be (turn) in . . . (the month of your birthday).

Para escribir

ACTIVITY SUGGESTION: See the *IAM* for an additional in-class activity: **¡Adivinen!**

Look at the photo and make up a story about the people you see. Give their names, describe them, and say how they are related. Say who is giving the party, the occasion for the party, what they are doing, and so on.

En la vida real

Una visita

CD-ROM

Do the interactive exercises on the CD-ROM for additional practice.

With a classmate, plan activities you would have in your hometown to entertain a visitor from a Spanish-speaking country. Give your visitor a name and decide which country he or she is from. In your plans include a party, visits to places of interest, and outdoor activities. Decide who is going to do what, and include food and drinks you are going to offer your visitor.

FOLLOW-UP: After students have completed this activity in pairs, divide the class into "hosts" and "visitors." The host pair should write a short letter to a visiting pair of students telling them about their entertainment plans. When they receive the letter, the visiting pair should write a brief note of response. This activity may also be used to send letters from one class to another.

Some additional words or phrases you may want to include are:

la hamburguesa	*hamburger*	**la montaña**	*mountain*
el perro caliente	*hot dog*	**el picnic**	*picnic*
el pollo frito	*fried chicken*	**la playa**	*beach*
el cine	*movie theater*		
la discoteca	*disco*		
el museo	*museum*		
el teatro	*theater*		

el partido *(game)* **de** { béisbol / básquetbol / fútbol *(soccer)* / fútbol americano }

Un espectáculo

FOLLOW-UP: Instruct students to bring in an ad from the entertainment section of their local newspaper, or you may bring in ads from a target language newspaper. Divide the class into pairs and instruct them that one student is planning to take the other, a Spanish exchange student, to see the event described in the ad. Each should role-play the situation in which they decide where to go through questions and responses based on the ad. Instruct them to use the questions below as a guide.

¿Cómo se llama el espectáculo?
¿Dónde se presenta? ¿Qué día/fecha?
¿Cuántos artistas/actores hay? ¿Quiénes son? ¿Cómo son?
¿A qué hora empieza?
¿Cuánto dinero necesitamos para comprar las entradas?
¿Adónde vamos después?

In Spain, you and a classmate come across this ad about a show and decide to go see it. What information can you get from the ad? After reading the ad, take turns answering the questions that follow.

MADRID ABIERTO

«Holiday on Ice», en el Palacio de Deportes

✶✶✶✶✶✶

Música y acrobacias en una fiesta sobre hielo

Setenta artistas del patinaje, de diversas nacionalidades, participan en el espectáculo musical «Holiday on Ice», que se presenta en Madrid solamente hasta el 2 de agosto, antes de continuar hacia Valladolid y Bilbao.

El «show» ofrece dos horas de números musicales, bailes y acrobacias dedicadas a México y a Rusia. La «danza de los platillos» y las acrobacias de los hermanos Ribelli son lo mejor.

El espectáculo se presenta a las 21,30 horas. Hay entradas desde 500 a 1.400 pesetas, con precios especiales para los niños menores de doce años. Venta anticipada por las tardes, de 18 a 21 horas, en el **Palacio de Deportes de la Comunidad** (avenida Felipe II, 19).

Zdenek Pazdirek, doble campeón checoslovaco.

1. ¿Cómo se llama el espectáculo?
2. ¿Dónde presentan el espectáculo?
3. ¿Hasta *(Until)* cuándo va a estar en Madrid el grupo?
4. De Madrid, ¿adónde va el grupo?

5. ¿Cuántos artistas hay en el grupo?
6. ¿Son todos mexicanos?
7. ¿A qué países dedican los artistas el espectáculo?
8. ¿El espectáculo es a las nueve y media de la mañana o de la noche?
9. En España no usan dólares; usan pesetas. ¿Cuánto dinero necesitan Uds. para comprar las entradas *(buy the tickets)*?
10. ¿En qué calle está el Palacio de Deportes de la Comunidad?

¡Damos una fiesta!

Get together with two or three students and plan a party. Discuss the following:

1. how much money you have
2. when you are going to have the party
3. where you are going to have the party
4. whom you are going to invite
5. what you are going to eat and who is going to bring the food
6. what you are going to drink and who is going to bring the drinks
7. what you are going to do
8. who is going to bring the CDs and tapes
9. what kinds of music you want

2. España (1)

España

- España forma, con Portugal, la Península Ibérica. Su capital es Madrid y su sistema de gobierno es una monarquía constitucional. El actual rey *(king)* de España es Juan Carlos de Borbón.

- El turismo tiene una gran importancia para la economía de España. Más de 63 millones de personas visitan España cada *(each)* año para disfrutar de *(enjoy)* su clima y de su rica historia.

- Los moros *(Moors)*, del norte de África, dominaron España por más de 700 años. Su influencia es evidente en la arquitectura de Toledo, Córdoba, Granada, Sevilla y otras ciudades.

Una de las grandes atracciones turísticas de Madrid es la Plaza de España, donde se encuentra un monumento a Cervantes. Frente a la estatua del escritor están Don Quijote y Sancho Panza, los personajes *(characters)* centrales de su inmortal novela *Don Quijote de la Mancha*.

¿Cuáles son las principales atracciones turísticas de su estado?

La ciudad de Ávila, situada al noroeste de Madrid, está completamente rodeada de murallas románicas *(Romanesque walls)*. Aunque las murallas tienen casi *(almost)* 1.000 años, están muy bien conservadas.

¿Hay ciudades como Ávila en su país?

El Templo de la Sagrada Familia, del arquitecto catalán Antonio Gaudí, es un símbolo de la ciudad de Barcelona. Gaudí murió en 1926 sin terminar la construcción de la iglesia, que todavía no está acabada *(finished)*.

¿Cómo se llaman algunos arquitectos norteamericanos famosos?

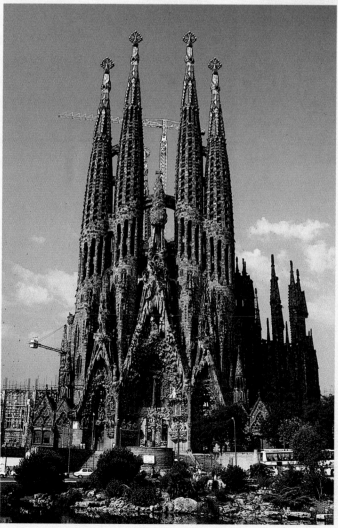

Vista parcial del puerto de San Sebastián en el País Vasco *(Basque Country)*. Situado sobre el Mar Cantábrico y muy cerca de la frontera francesa, San Sebastián es un centro pesquero *(fishing)* importante. La ciudad también es conocida *(known)* por su hermosa *(beautiful)* playa, "La Concha".

¿Vive Ud. cerca del mar (sea)*?*

El pueblo de Alcázar de San Juan, en la región de La Mancha. Esta región, una extensa llanura *(plain)*, y sus molinos de viento *(windmills)* son famosos en todo el mundo gracias a la novela *Don Quijote de la Mancha*, de Miguel de Cervantes.

¿Qué sabe Ud. de Don Quijote?

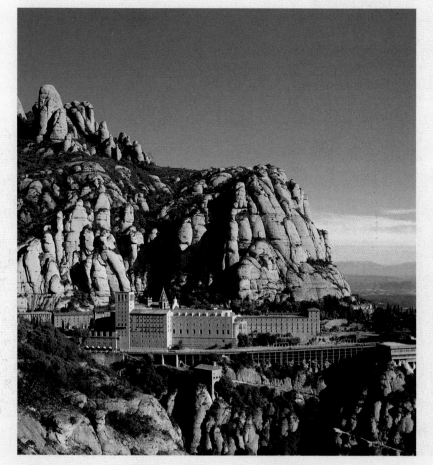

El Monasterio de Montserrat, situado en la montaña del mismo *(same)* nombre, cerca de Barcelona, es famoso por la estatua de la Virgen María y el Niño. La Virgen de Montserrat, a la que los catalanes llaman "la Moreneta", por su color negro, es la patrona de Cataluña. En el monasterio hay varios museos y una de las bibliotecas más importantes de España.

¿Hay algún museo importante en su ciudad? ¿Cuál?

Las ferias *(fairs)* son muy populares en toda España. La feria de abril de Sevilla, que se celebra después de la Semana Santa *(Holy Week)*, es una de las más famosas del país.

¿Dónde hay ferias en su país?

El Patio de los Leones de la Alhambra de Granada. La Alhambra es un palacio inmenso, construido por los árabes en los siglos XIII y XIV. Los salones y jardines del palacio forman una especie *(sort)* de laberinto.

¿Dónde está su edificio favorito?

Mallorca, Menorca e Ibiza, las Islas Baleares, están situadas en el Mar Mediterráneo y pertenecen a España. Más de cinco millones de turistas visitan estas islas todos los años. Sin embargo, las islas aún conservan muchas de sus típicas aldeas *(small towns)* de pescadores, como la que vemos en la foto.

¿Qué islas pertenecen a los Estados Unidos?

TELEINFORME

 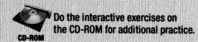 Do the interactive exercises on the CD-ROM for additional practice.

VIDEO   CD-ROM

Preparación

NOTE: The video-related vocabulary is listed in the *Instructor's Activities Manual* for your reference. Its purpose is to facilitate students' comprehension.

NOTE: See the Instructor's Edition frontmatter for additional suggestions on implementing video in the classroom.

SUGGESTION: Have students read the *Panorama hispánico* segment of the textbook and do the *Preparación* activities in small groups before viewing the video segments.

¿Cuánto saben Uds. ya? After reading **Panorama hispánico 2**, get together in groups of three or four students and complete each statement with the appropriate information.

1. _____ es la capital de España.
2. En la Plaza de España hay un monumento a _____.
3. Antonio Gaudí es un _____ catalán.
4. El Templo de la Sagrada Familia está en la ciudad de _____.
5. Los moros *(Moors)* dominaron España por más de _____ años.
6. La influencia de los moros *(Moors)* se observa en la arquitectura de ciudades como Toledo, _____, _____ y _____.
7. El autor de la novela *Don Quijote de la Mancha* es _____.
8. Mallorca, Menorca e Ibiza son tres _____ en el mar Mediterráneo.
9. La Alhambra es un _____ inmenso, construido por los _____ en los siglos XIII y XIV.

Comprensión

SUGGESTION: The *Comprensión* sections are organized by individual video clip to provide greater flexibility in lesson planning. Have students complete each exercise after viewing the corresponding video clip and have them compare their answers in pairs or groups.

SUGGESTION: Have students locate Madrid, Barcelona, Granada, and the Sierra Nevada on the map on the inside front cover of their textbook.

A. Madrid. Read the following statements. After watching the video, circle **V** (**Verdadero**) or **F** (**Falso**), according to what you understood. If the statement is false, correct it.

V F   1. Madrid está en la costa de España.
V F   2. La Plaza Mayor es una plaza muy grande.
V F   3. En la Plaza de la Cibeles hay un monumento a Cervantes.
V F   4. Hay un lago *(lake)* en el Parque del Buen Retiro.
V F   5. El fútbol es el deporte más popular entre los madrileños.

B. Antonio Gaudí. Select the word or phrase that best completes each statement according to what you understood in the video.

1. Antonio Gaudí creó un estilo (nuevo, simple) de arquitectura.
2. La Casa Milá es una casa de (apartamentos, edificios).
3. El Parque Güell tiene (un monumento a Gaudí, mosaicos de vivos colores).
4. El Templo de la Sagrada Familia es la obra más (ambiciosa, insignificante) de Gaudí.
5. La construcción de (la Casa Milá, la Sagrada Familia) continúa hasta hoy día.

C. Granada. Select the word or phrase that best completes each statement according to what you understood from the video.

1. Granada está en el (sur, norte) de España, cerca de la sierra Nevada.
2. La Alhambra era una (fortaleza *[fort]* militar, fuente *[fountain]*).
3. Las paredes *(walls)* de la Alhambra están decoradas con (complicados, simples) diseños geométricos *(geometric designs)*.
4. En el Patio de los Leones, la fuente tiene (diez, doce) leones.

Ampliación

A. Dos culturas. With a partner, make a list of counterparts you can find in your local area, city, state, or country for each of the following items.

1. Madrid
2. el monumento de la Cibeles, Madrid
3. la Plaza Mayor, Madrid
4. el Parque del Buen Retiro, Madrid
5. el Templo de la Sagrada Familia, Barcelona
6. la Casa Milá, Barcelona
7. el Generalife, Granada

B. Quiero visitar... Interview a partner to determine which of the Spanish cities in the video segment he/she would like to visit. Use the following questions as a guide. Share your observations with the rest of the class.

1. ¿Te gusta Madrid? ¿Barcelona? ¿Granada?
2. ¿Qué lugares *(places)* quieres visitar? ¿Por qué?
3. ¿Cuáles son algunos de los monumentos que quieres ir a ver?

OBJECTIVES

Pronunciation
The Spanish **p**, **t**, **c**, and **q**

Structure
Comparative forms • Irregular comparative forms • Present indicative of **o:ue** stem-changing verbs • Present progressive • Uses of **ser** and **estar** • Pronouns as objects of prepositions

Communication
You will learn vocabulary related to family relationships and personal characteristics.

Planes para un fin de semana

STUDENT
AUDIO

Carol, una estudiante de los Estados Unidos, está en España. Asiste a la Universidad de Salamanca y vive en una pensión cerca de la Plaza Mayor. Quiere aprender a[1] hablar español perfectamente y por eso nunca pierde la oportunidad de practicar el idioma. Ahora está hablando con dos amigos españoles en un café al aire libre. Están comiendo sándwiches y bebiendo café.

LUIS —Oye, Carol, ¿puedes ir con nosotros a Madrid este fin de semana?

CAROL —No, no puedo... Tengo que escribir muchas cartas: a mi abuela, a mi tío, a mi hermano...

LUIS —Tú echas de menos a tu familia, ¿no?

CAROL —Sí, ...especialmente a mi hermano mayor.

CARMEN —¿Cómo es tu hermano? ¿Rubio? ¿Moreno?

CAROL —Es rubio, delgado y de estatura mediana. Estudia medicina.

CARMEN —¡Muy interesante! ¿Cuándo viene a España? ¿En el verano?

CAROL —No, va a viajar a México con su esposa y sus dos hijas.

CARMEN —¡Bah! Es casado... ¡Qué lástima! ¿No tienes otro hermano?

CAROL —No, lo siento. Aquí tengo una fotografía de mis sobrinas.

CARMEN —*(Mira la foto)* ¿Éstas son tus sobrinas? ¡Son muy bonitas!

CAROL —Empiezan a[1] asistir a la escuela el quince de septiembre.

LUIS —¡Oye! ¿Por qué no vas a Madrid con nosotros? Es más interesante que escribir cartas...

CAROL —¿Van en coche?

LUIS —No, preferimos ir en autobús. Es tan cómodo como el coche, no cuesta mucho y no tenemos que conducir.

CAROL —¡Buena idea! Yo nunca manejo en Madrid. ¿Y adónde piensan ir?

CARMEN —Al Museo del Prado. Allí están algunos de los cuadros más famosos del mundo.

LUIS —¡Es muy interesante! ¡Y Madrid tiene unos restaurantes muy buenos! Nosotros siempre almorzamos en Casa Botín que, para mí, es el mejor de todos.

CAROL —Vale. ¡Vamos a Madrid!... ¡Si no llueve! Porque si llueve no voy.

CARMEN —No, hija[2], no va a llover.

CAROL —¿Cuándo volvemos?

LUIS —El sábado por la noche o el domingo.

CARMEN —Ah, Luis, la fiesta de Marisol es mañana. ¿Dónde es?

LUIS —Es en su casa. ¿Quieren ir conmigo?

CARMEN —Sí, vamos contigo.

LUIS —¡Magnífico! Estén listas a las nueve.

NOTE: Point out that **manejar** is used primarily in Latin America and **conducir** is used in Spain.

SUGGESTION: Refer students to **Panorama hispánico 2** and **Panorama hispánico 3** and their corresponding video segments for more information about Spain.

---

[1]The preposition **a** is used after **aprender** and **empezar** when they are followed by a verb in the infinitive.

[2]In this context, "hija" is the equivalent of "child" or "dear."

Vocabulario

Cognados

¡Bah! Bah!
especialmente especially
la familia family
famoso(-a) famous
la fotografía, la foto
   photograph, photo
interesante interesting

la medicina medicine
el museo museum
la oportunidad opportunity
perfectamente perfectly
el plan plan
el restaurante restaurant

Nombres

la abuela grandmother
el autobús, el ómnibus bus
el café coffee
el café al aire libre sidewalk cafe
la carta letter
el coche, el carro, el automóvil, el
   auto car, automobile

el cuadro, la pintura painting,
   picture
la escuela school
la esposa wife
los Estados Unidos United States
el fin de semana weekend
el hermano brother

la hija daughter
el mundo world
la pensión boarding house
la plaza town square
la sobrina niece
el tío uncle

Verbos

almorzar (o:ue) to have lunch
asistir(a) to attend
conducir (yo conduzco), manejar
   to drive
costar (o:ue) to cost

echar de menos, extrañar to miss
   (feel homesick for)
llover (o:ue) to rain
mirar to look at
poder (o:ue) to be able to, can

practicar to practice
viajar to travel
volver (o:ue) to return

Adjetivos

casado(-a) married
cómodo(-a)[1] comfortable

este this (m.)
mayor older, bigger

mejor better, best

Otras palabras y expresiones

algunos(-as) some
aquí here
cerca (de) close (to), near
cuando when
de estatura mediana of medium
   height

éstas these
estén listas be ready
más more
nunca never
por eso that is why
¡qué lástima! what a pity!

si if
tan... como as . . . as
vale okay (Spain)
vamos let's go

RELATED VOCABULARY: ¡qué pena! (what a pity);
de acuerdo (okay/I agree).

---

[1]incómodo(-a) uncomfortable

Vocabulario adicional
La familia

RELATED VOCABULARY: **bisabuela** *(great-grandmother)*; **bisabuelo** *(great-grandfather)*.

SUGGESTION: Use Transparency 21 to introduce vocabulary items related to the family. Ask students to identify the individuals in the drawing, or divide the class into groups of three or four and have them practice similar questions.

¿Cómo se llama la madre de Víctor Fernández Herrera?
¿Quiénes son los hijos de Víctor y Ana?
¿Cómo se llama la cuñada de Ana Teresa?
¿Quiénes son los nietos de María y Ramón?

abuela (grandmother) / suegra (mother-in-law)

abuelo (grandfather) / suegro (father-in-law)

padres (parents)

cuñado (brother-in-law) / yerno (son-in-law)

hija (daughter) / tía (aunt) / hermana (sister) / madre (mother) / mamá (mom)

hijo (son) / padre (father) / papá (dad) / hermano (brother) / tío (uncle)

cuñada (sister-in-law) / nuera (daughter-in-law)

sobrina (niece)

sobrino (nephew) / nieto (grandson)

prima (cousin)

primo (cousin)

nieta (granddaughter)

ACTIVITY SUGGESTION: See the *IAM* for an additional in-class activity: **Árbol genealógico.**

Otros miembros de la familia

la **hermanastra**   stepsister
el **hermanastro**   stepbrother
la **hijastra**   stepdaughter
el **hijastro**   stepson
la **madrastra**   stepmother
la **media hermana**   half sister
el **medio hermano**   half brother
el **padrastro**   stepfather

Elsa no es mi hermana; es mi **hermanastra.**
Oscar es mi **hermanastro.**
Elena es mi **hijastra.**
Julio es el **hijastro** de María.
Mi **madrastra** se llama Dolores.
Yo tengo dos **medias hermanas.**
Pedro es mi **medio hermano.**
No es mi padre; es mi **padrastro.**

ACTIVITY SUGGESTION: See the *IAM* for an additional in-class activity: **Palabras y más palabras.**

EXPANSION: Have students work in pairs and take turns role-playing a "friend" describing Carol, her family, her vacation plans, etc., to another acquaintance. The "acquaintance" should ask questions about why Carol is in Spain, how she feels about her family, etc. Remind students to use the discussion questions and dialogue as a guide for their conversation.

NOTE: To illustrate the information about Spain presented here, show slides or pictures of Salamanca, Madrid, and the Museo del Prado. Ask students to describe the scenes you have chosen.

¡Conversemos!

Answer the following questions, basing your answers on the dialogue.

1. ¿De dónde es Carol y dónde vive ahora?
2. ¿Dónde estudia?
3. ¿Dónde está ahora y con quiénes está hablando?
4. ¿Cómo es el hermano de Carol?
5. ¿Con quién va a viajar a México?
6. ¿Cuándo empiezan a asistir a la escuela las sobrinas de Carol?
7. ¿Por qué cree Luis que es mejor viajar en autobús?
8. ¿Dónde están algunos de los cuadros más famosos del mundo?
9. En Madrid, ¿dónde comen Luis y Carmen?
10. Si llueve, ¿va a ir Carol a Madrid?
11. ¿Cuándo vuelven los chicos a Salamanca?
12. ¿Dónde y cuándo es la fiesta de Marisol?

¿Lo sabía Ud.?

■ La Universidad de Salamanca es una de las universidades más antiguas y famosas del mundo. Además de los cursos regulares para españoles, ofrece muchas clases para estudiantes extranjeros (foreign).

■ El Museo del Prado es uno de los museos más importantes del mundo. Tiene una colección de más de 2.000 cuadros y más de 300 esculturas. Allí están representados los grandes pintores españoles—Goya, Murillo, Velázquez, El Greco y otros. También hay cuadros de otros pintores europeos famosos.

■ En la mayoría de los países hispánicos, las universidades no tienen residencias universitarias (dorms). Los estudiantes viven con su familia o en pensiones, donde el precio incluye el cuarto y la comida (room and board).

■ El café al aire libre es una parte importante de la cultura hispánica, donde la gente (people) conversa mientras come y toma algo (something).

■ En los países de habla hispana, la fecha (date) se escribe con el día antes del mes: 2-5-01 equivale al dos de mayo del 2001.

• ¿Puede Ud. nombrar (name) dos universidades norteamericanas muy famosas?

La Universidad de Salamanca, la más antigua de España.

• ¿En qué ciudad está el famoso Museo Metropolitano de Arte?

• ¿En qué ciudades de este país hay cafés al aire libre?

INTERNET

See the ¿Cómo se dice...? Web site for activities on authentic cultural material: http://spanish.college.hmco.com/students

Pronunciación

A The Spanish p

STUDENT AUDIO

The Spanish **p** is pronounced like the English *p* as in the word *sparks,* but with no expulsion of air. Listen to your instructor and repeat the following words.

perfectamente	tiempo	oportunidad
pintura	papá	septiembre
pensión	primo	poder

p: ¿Por qué pones un pez en la piscina?
  El padre de Pablo es profesor de portugués en Potosí.

B The Spanish t

t: Hay tanto trabajo que no tengo tiempo para terminar.
  Tomás tiene su tarjeta de turista en el maletín.

The Spanish **t** is pronounced by placing the tongue against the upper teeth, as in the English word *stop.* Listen to your instructor and repeat the following words.

nieta	restaurante	practicar
tío	carta	auto
otro	este	foto

C The Spanish c

c: Clara y Camilo no comen carne nunca.
  Carmen toma una copa de coñac con el café.

The Spanish sound for the letter **c** in the combinations **ca, co,** and **cu** is /k/, pronounced as in the English word *scar,* but with no expulsion of air. Listen to your instructor and repeat the following words.

café	coche	cuñado
nunca	cómodo	cuánto
calle	simpático	cuándo

caye

D The Spanish q

q: ¿De quién es el equipaje que está aquí?
  Quedan quince cheques en mi cartera.

SUGGESTION: Model each word and have the class repeat the sounds and words chorally and individually. Then have students work with the sentences above for additional pronunciation practice.

The Spanish **q** is always followed by a **u**; it is pronounced like the *c* in the English word *come,* but without any expulsion of air. Listen to your instructor and repeat the following words.

Quintana	Roque	quien
que	quiere	orquesta *orcuesta*
aquí	queso	Quevedo

Cueso   *C*

Dodge TIENE QUE SER DODGE.

Estructuras

1 Comparative forms   (Formas comparativas)

SUGGESTION: Use Transparency 17 to present comparative forms.

SUGGESTION: Write the following sample sentence and list of adjectives on the board or on the overhead projector.

Yo soy más/menos... que...

feliz	inteligente
serio(-a)	alto(-a)
simpático(-a)	rico(-a)
independiente	pobre
interesante	paciente
trabajador(-a)	bajo(-a)

Have students compare themselves to other classmates, friends, or family members. Have them do the activity either orally or in writing.

SUGGESTION: Using the adjectives learned by students in **Lecciones 1–4**, ask personalized questions that require students to compare themselves to other classmates, friends, and family members.

I—¿Eres tan alto como (José)?
S1—Sí, soy tan alto como él.
I—¿Tienes tanto dinero como tu hermana?
S2—No, no tengo tanto dinero como ella.
I—¿Hablas tan rápido como yo?
S3—No, no hablo tan rápido como Ud.

Have students work in pairs and ask each other similar questions.

A. Comparisons of inequality

■ In Spanish, the comparative of inequality of most adjectives, adverbs, and nouns is formed by placing **más** *(more)* or **menos** *(less)* before the adjective, the adverb, or the noun and **que** *(than)* after it.

más *(more)*		*adjective*	
	+	or *adverb*	+ **que** *(than)*
menos *(less)*		or *noun*	

—¿Tú eres **más alta que** Ana?   *"Are you taller than Ana?"*
—Sí, ella es mucho **más baja que**   *"Yes, she is much shorter than I."*
yo.

ATENCIÓN   **De** is used instead of **que** before a numerical expression of quantity or amount.

Luis tiene **más de** treinta años.   *Luis is over thirty years old.*
Hay **menos de** veinte estudiantes   *There are fewer than twenty students*
aquí.   *here.*

B. Comparisons of equality

■ To form comparisons of equality with adjectives, adverbs, and nouns in Spanish, use the adjectives **tanto, -a, -os, -as**, or the adverb **tan... como**.

When comparing adjectives or adverbs:	When comparing nouns:
tan *(as)* < bonita / tarde + como	**tanto** *(as much)* dinero **tanta** plata *(money)* **tantos** *(as many)* libros + como **tantas** plumas

—¿Vas en autobús?   *"Are you going by bus?"*
—Sí, es **tan** cómodo **como** el   *"Yes, it's as comfortable as the*
coche.   *car."*

—Tengo mucho trabajo.   *"I have a lot of work."*
—Yo tengo **tanto** trabajo **como**   *"I have as much work as you*
    tú.   *(do)."*

C. The superlative

■ The superlative construction is similar to the comparative. It is formed by placing the definite article before the person or thing being compared.

		más			
definite article	+ *(noun)* +	or	+ *adjective*	+ **de**
		menos			

—¿Quieres ir al Museo del Prado?   *"Do you want to go to the Prado Museum?"*

—Sí, allí están **los cuadros más famosos de** España.   *"Yes, the most famous paintings in Spain are there."*

—Juan no es muy inteligente.   *"Juan is not very intelligent."*

—No, es el[1] **menos inteligente de** la familia.   *"No, he is the least intelligent (one) in the family."*

ATENCIÓN   Note that the Spanish **de** translates to the English *in* after a superlative.

Son los cuadros más famosos **de** España.   *They are the most famous paintings in Spain.*

Es la chica más bonita **de** la clase.   *She is the prettiest girl in the class.*

práctica ···

A. Complete the following sentences, using the Spanish equivalent of the words in parentheses.

1. Tu primo es _____ tú. *(fatter than)*
   Tú eres _____ que él. *(much thinner)*
2. Mi cuñado es _____ que ella, pero estudia mucho. *(less intelligent)*
3. Mi suegra tiene _____ años, pero mi suegro tiene _____. *(less than fifty / more than seventy)*
4. Mi abuela tiene _____ mis padres. *(as much money as)*
5. Carlos tiene _____ yo. *(as many CDs as)*
6. Mi sobrina es _____ su mamá. *(as tall as)*
7. Tu tía habla español _____ mi padre. *(as well as)*
8. Aquí hay _____ allí. *(as many girls as)*

----

[1]As in English, the noun may be omitted.

SUGGESTION: Review basic interrogative expressions. After presenting the superlative construction, ask students factual questions that begin with ¿Quién?, ¿Qué?, ¿Cuál?, ¿Dónde?, and ¿Quiénes?

¿Quién es el actor más rico de los EEUU?
¿Quién es la actriz más guapa?
¿Dónde está la montaña más alta del mundo?
¿Cuál es la ciudad más grande de España?
¿Qué coche es el más caro/barato?

EXPANSION B: Play a game of "telephone" by dividing the class into groups of five or six. Player A describes the player on his or her right to the player on his or her left. That player then describes A to the player on his or her left and repeats what A said about the player to A's right. The "phone call" should be done in a whisper. The person to A's right is the last player and reiterates aloud all he or she has heard. Each person is responsible for correcting any errors in his or her contribution to the chain.

EXPANSION C: Have students work in pairs to write five to ten "controversial" statements such as those that follow.

Los hombres son menos pacientes que las mujeres.
El español es más difícil de aprender que el chino.
El fútbol norteamericano es más violento que el boxeo.

Collect the papers and write the most interesting statements on the board, overhead projector, or a ditto to be distributed in class the next day. In groups of three or four, students must agree or disagree with the statements. Encourage students to state why they disagree or to change the original statement to one that is more acceptable.

B. Compare the people in the picture below with each other.

1. María es _____ Rosa.
2. Rosa es _____ María.
3. Carlos es _____ Rosa y que María.
4. Carlos es _____ Juan.
5. Juan es _____ Carlos.
6. Juan es _____ María.
7. Juan es el _____ de todos.
8. Carlos es el _____ de todos.

C. Establish comparisons between the following people and things, using the adjectives provided and adding any necessary words.

1. Michael Jordan / Danny De Vito (alto)
2. Cuba / Canadá (pequeño)
3. la clase de español / la clase de alemán (difícil)
4. coche / ómnibus (cómodo)
5. Puerto Rico / Argentina (grande)
6. Jim Carrey / Antonio Banderas (guapo)

Now find a partner. Take turns comparing more people and things.

2   Irregular comparative forms   *(Formas comparativas irregulares)*

■ The following adjectives and adverbs have irregular comparative and superlative forms in Spanish.

Adjective	Adverb	Comparative	Superlative
bueno	bien	mejor	el (la) mejor
malo	mal	peor	el (la) peor
grande		mayor	el (la) mayor
pequeño		menor	el (la) menor

—El restaurante El Dorado es muy **malo**.	*"The El Dorado Restaurant is very bad."*
—Sí, pero la cafetería de la universidad es **peor**.	*"Yes, but the university's cafeteria is worse."*
—Eva es una **buena** estudiante.	*"Eva is a good student."*
—Sí, es **la mejor** de la clase.	*"Yes, she's the best in the class."*

■ When the adjectives **grande** and **pequeño** refer to size, the regular forms are generally used.

Tu casa es **más grande** que la de Carolina.	*Your house is bigger than Carolina's.*

■ When these adjectives refer to age, the irregular forms are used.

Ella es **mucho mayor** que yo.	*She is much older than I.*
Teresa es **menor** que Carlos.	*Teresa is younger than Carlos.*
Ella es **la menor** de todos.	*She is the youngest of all.*

práctica ●

ACTIVITY SUGGESTION: See the *IAM* for an additional in-class activity: **Vamos a comparar.**

A. Answer the following questions with complete sentences.

1. Mi sobrina tiene siete años y mi sobrino tiene cinco. ¿Quién es mayor? ¿Quién es menor?
2. Mi tío tiene cuarenta años y mi tía tiene treinta y ocho. ¿Quién es menor? ¿Quién es mayor?
3. ¿Quién habla mejor el español, tú o el profesor (la profesora)?
4. Pedro tiene una "B" en inglés; Antonio tiene una "C"; y José tiene una "F". ¿Quién es el peor estudiante? ¿Quién es el mejor estudiante?

Now write three original comparative situations, using the ones you have just completed as models. When you have finished, take turns giving and responding to situations with a partner.

FOLLOW-UP B: Copy several pages from a *Consumer Reports* magazine and distribute the copies to students. Working in pairs, they should select products to compare and give a brief report to the class. Encourage students to tell why the products are good, better, and best, or bad, worse, and worst.

La computadora *Apple* es buena porque tiene muchos programas. La *IBM* es mejor porque...

B. Interview a classmate, using the following questions. When you have finished, switch roles.

1. ¿Tú eres mayor o menor que tu mejor amigo(-a)?
2. ¿Tu mamá es menor que tu papá?
3. ¿Quién cocina *(cooks)* mejor, tú o tu mamá?
4. ¿Quién crees tú que es el (la) mejor estudiante de la clase?
5. ¿Cuál crees que es la mejor universidad de los Estados Unidos?
6. ¿Cuál crees tú que es la mejor película *(film)* del año? ¿Y la peor?
7. De los restaurantes que tú conoces, ¿cuál es el mejor? ¿Y el peor?
8. ¿Quiénes crees tú que conducen mejor: los hombres o las mujeres?

C. With a partner, take turns comparing yourselves to members of your families, friends, and other members of the class.

3 Present indicative of o:ue stem-changing verbs
(Presente de indicativo de los verbos que cambian en la raíz o:ue)

poder	to be able
puedo	podemos
puedes	podéis
puede	pueden

■ Some verbs undergo a stem change in the present indicative. For these verbs, when **o** is the last stem vowel and it is stressed, it changes to **ue**.

—¿A qué hora **vuelven** Uds.? "At what time are you returning?"

—**Volvemos** a las doce. "We'll return at twelve o'clock."

—Entonces comemos a las doce y media. "Then we'll have lunch (eat) at twelve-thirty."

■ Note that the stem vowel is not stressed in the verb forms used with **nosotros(-as)** and **vosotros(-as)**; therefore, the **o** does not change to **ue**.

■ Other verbs that undergo this change:[1]

almorzar	to have lunch	**llover** (impersonal)	to rain
contar	to tell, to count	**morir**	to die
costar	to cost	**recordar**	to remember
dormir	to sleep	**volar**	to fly
encontrar	to find	**volver**	to return

práctica •

SUGGESTION A: Drill students on the following verb forms and encourage them to use the forms in sentences.

1. *Yo puedo llevar los discos compactos.* (Uds., Ella, Tú, Nosotros, Jorge)
2. *Ella no encuentra las cartas.* (Nosotros, Uds., Yo, Ellos, Tú)
3. *Mi nieto cuenta de uno a cien.* (Yo, Ellos, Uds., Tú, Nosotros)

EXPANSION B: Personalize the exercise by asking individual students questions based on the vocabulary and structures.

¿A qué hora duermes? ¿almuerzas? ¿vuelves a casa?
¿Cuánto cuesta el libro de español (ciencias políticas, antropología, etc.)?
¿Recuerdas el número de teléfono de tu mejor amigo(-a) (novio[-a])?

A. Interview a classmate, using the following questions. When you have finished, switch roles.

1. ¿Almuerzas en la cafetería o en tu casa?
2. ¿Cuánto cuestan los sándwiches en la cafetería?
3. ¿Cuántas horas duermes?
4. ¿Cuentas ovejas (sheep) para dormir?
5. ¿Hasta (Up to) qué número puedes contar en español?
6. ¿Encuentras difícil o fácil la clase de español?
7. ¿Cuándo vuelves a tu casa?
8. ¿Llueve mucho en tu ciudad?

B. Marité is talking to her roommate, who is sound asleep. Complete the story, supplying the missing (**o:ue**) verbs. Then read it aloud.

MARITÉ —¡Teresa, me voy! No _____ mis libros. ¿Dónde están? No _____ ir a mi clase sin (without) mis libros. ¡Oye! Hoy

---

[1]For a complete list of stem-changing verbs, see Appendix B.

_____ con Pedro en la cafetería; no tengo dinero y los sándwiches en la cafetería _____ tres dólares. ¡Ay, Teresa!, hoy tengo que llamar a Marta y no _____ su número de teléfono. ¡Teresa!, ¿tú _____ el número de Marta? ¡Oye! ¿Roberto _____ a San Francisco hoy? ¿Vas al aeropuerto con él? *(Mira por la ventana.)* ¡Ay, cómo _____! Necesito tu impermeable *(raincoat)*. ¡Ah!, hoy _____ a casa a las cinco. *(Abre la puerta de Teresa.)* ¡Teresa! ¡Teresa! ¿Por qué no contestas *(answer)*?

TERESA —*(Mmm...)* Nunca _____ dormir cuando tú estás en casa.

MARITÉ —Tú _____ mucho. No necesitas dormir más. Me voy. Nos vemos.

C. Arnaldo is very nosy and is always asking questions. Here are the answers. What are his questions?

1. ¿_____? Mi equipo estereofónico cuesta $1.000.
2. ¿_____? Nosotros almorzamos en el restaurante.
3. ¿_____? Volvemos a casa a las cinco.
4. ¿_____? No, yo no duermo mucho.
5. ¿_____? No, no recuerdo el número de teléfono de Ana.
6. ¿_____? Vuelo a Los Ángeles los domingos.
7. ¿_____? No, no puedo ir a tu casa esta noche.

D. With a classmate, prepare four or five questions to ask your instructor, using stem-changing (**o:ue**) verbs.

4   Present progressive   *(Estar + gerundio)*

22

SUGGESTION: Use colored chalk to write the endings for the following present participles on the board.

hablar: habl   *speaking*
  -ando
comer: com   *eating*
  -iendo
abrir: abr   *opening*
  -iendo

Emphasize that only **estar** is used in the present progressive. Act out a situation and ask students, "**¿Qué estoy haciendo?**" You may also point to the different people in Transparency 22 and ask students what activities are depicted.

■ The present progressive describes an action that is in progress. It is formed with the present tense of **estar** and the **gerundio**, which is equivalent to the English present participle (the *-ing* form of the verb).

Gerundio		
hablar	**comer**	**escribir**
habl **-ando**	com **-iendo**	escrib **-iendo**
speaking	*eating*	*writing*

Yo estoy comiendo.
I am eating.

—¿Estás estudiando?   *"Are you studying?"*
—No, **estoy escribiendo** una   *"No, I am writing a letter."*
carta.

—¿Qué **estás tomando**?   *"What are you drinking?"*
—**Estoy tomando** café.   *"I'm drinking coffee."*

■ The following forms are irregular:

pedir: **pidiendo**   dormir: **durmiendo**
decir: **diciendo**   traer: **trayendo**
servir: **sirviendo**   leer: **leyendo**

—¿Daniel **está leyendo**?   *"Is Daniel reading?"*
—No, **está durmiendo**.   *"No, he's sleeping."*

■ Note that as shown with **traer** and **leer**, the i of -**iendo** becomes **y** between vowels.

ATENCIÓN   In Spanish, the present progressive is *never* used to indicate a future action. The present tense is used in future expressions that would require the present progressive in English.

Trabajo mañana.   I'm working tomorrow.

■ Some verbs, such as **ser, estar, ir,** and **venir,** are rarely used in the progressive construction.

práctica ....

SUGGESTION A: Drill students on the following verb forms and encourage them to use the forms in sentences.

1. *Él* está estudiando. (Tú, Julia y Pedro, Yo, Nosotras)
2. *Yo* estoy leyendo un libro. (Tú y yo, Ella, Tú, Uds.)
3. *Tú* no estás pidiendo la llave. (Ud., Nosotros, Ellas, Yo)

A. With a partner, take turns asking each other what the following people are doing (**haciendo**).

1. Tú...   2. Yo...   3. Raúl y Sara

4. Eva...   5. La profesora...   6. Nosotros... y el chico...

SUGGESTION B: Remind students to expand upon the dialogues whenever possible.

FOLLOW-UP B: Remind students that since the present progressive is used to describe an action in progress, it is frequently used when making excuses. In pairs, students should practice inviting their partners to an event. The partner should refuse by offering an excuse that he or she is busy at that moment. Tell students to be as specific as possible in the invitation, as well as in the excuse.

S1—¿Quieres ir al cine conmigo? Hay una buena película de misterio.

S2—No, lo siento. Estoy estudiando en este momento.

B. Complete the following dialogues, using the present progressive of the verbs given. Then act them out with a partner, adding a sentence or two to each dialogue.

1. comer   —¿Qué _____ tú?
                —Yo _____ ensalada.

2. leer   —¿Qué libro _____ Uds.?
                —_____ *Don Quijote.*

3. servir   —¿Qué _____ Uds.?
                —Yo _____ refrescos y Luisa _____ vino.

4. decir   —¿Qué _____ Juan Carlos?
                —No _____ nada.

5. estudiar   —¿José _____?
    dormir   —No, _____.

C. With a partner, discuss what you think these people are doing. Give two or three possibilities for each situation.

1. la secretaria / en la oficina
2. los estudiantes / en la clase
3. los chicos / en la cafetería
4. el profesor / en la universidad
5. los muchachos y las muchachas / en la fiesta
6. el Sr. Vega / en su cuarto
7. el camarero *(waiter)* / en el restaurante
8. la Srta. Barrios / en un café al aire libre

FOLLOW-UP C: Use Transparency 22 to elicit descriptions using the present progressive. Have students describe the actions that are depicted in the drawing. Students may brainstorm as a class and write as many infinitive phrases as they can before breaking into groups.

5 Uses of **ser** and **estar**   (*Usos de ser y estar*)

The English verb *to be* has two Spanish equivalents, **ser** and **estar**. As a general rule, **ser** expresses *who* or *what* the subject is *essentially*, and **estar** indicates *state* or *condition*. **Ser** and **estar** are *not* interchangeable.

A. Uses of *ser*

Ser expresses a fundamental quality and identifies the essence of a person or thing.

SUGGESTION: Review the uses of **ser** presented in the previous lessons: origin, occupation, nationality (page 15); description (page 61); possession (pages 39 and 58); days (page 11); and time (page 32). Then review these uses by asking personalized questions.

1. ¿De dónde eres?
2. ¿Qué eres, profesor(-a) o estudiante?
3. ¿Cuál es tu nacionalidad?
4. ¿Cómo eres, alto(-a) o bajo(-a)?
5. ¿De quién es ese libro?
6. ¿Qué día es hoy? ¿Qué hora es?

◼ It describes the basic nature or character of a person or thing. It is also used with expressions of age that do not refer to a specific number of years.

> La orquesta **es** buena.
> Yo **soy** joven *(young).*

◼ It describes the material that things are made of.

> Las mesas **son** de metal.

◼ It is used to denote nationality, origin, and profession or trade.

> Sandra **es** norteamericana.
> Yo **soy** de Caracas.
> Mi mamá **es** profesora.

■ It is used with expressions of time and with dates.

> Hoy **es** miércoles, cuatro de abril.
> **Son** las cuatro y cuarto de la tarde.

■ It is used with events as the equivalent of *taking place*.

> La fiesta **es** en el club Los Violines.

■ It is used to indicate possession or relationship.

> Los discos compactos **son** de Julia.
> Antonio **es** el hermano de Raúl.

práctica ....

EXPANSION: Have students write two or more personalized questions that illustrate each use of **ser.** They should then interview each other using their questions. As a homework assignment have each student write a brief description of his or her partner, based on the information received from both sets of questions. Have several pairs share their descriptions at the next class meeting as a review.

Interview a classmate, using the following questions and two of your own. When you have finished, switch roles.

1. ¿Eres norteamericano(-a)? ¿De dónde eres?
2. ¿De qué ciudad eres?
3. ¿Cómo es tu mamá?
4. ¿Quién es tu mejor amigo(-a)?
5. ¿Es alto(-a) o bajo(-a)?
6. ¿Eres feliz?
7. ¿Dónde son tus clases?
8. ¿Qué día es hoy?
9. ¿Qué fecha es hoy?
10. ¿Qué hora es?

B. Uses of estar

Estar is used to express more transitory qualities and often implies the possibility of change.

■ It indicates place or location.

> Mi prima no **está** aquí. ¿Dónde **está**?

■ It is used to indicate condition.

> Mis amigos **están** muy cansados.
> Sara **está** enferma.

■ With personal reactions, it describes what is perceived through the senses—that is, how a person or thing seems, looks, tastes, or feels.

> El ponche **está** delicioso.

■ It is used in the present progressive tense.

> Yo **estoy** estudiando y Ana **está** leyendo.

práctica ....

A. Imagine that you and a friend are at a party at the Club Náutico, and answer the following questions.

1. ¿En qué calle está el club?
2. ¿Los amigos de Uds. están en el club?
3. ¿Sus amigos están contentos o tristes?

4. ¿Cómo están los entremeses? ¿Deliciosos?
5. ¿Quiénes están en la terraza?
6. ¿Tu mamá está en la fiesta?

B. Complete the following dialogues, using the appropriate forms of **ser** or **estar**. Then act them out with a partner.

1. —¿De dónde _____ tu mamá? ¿_____ mexicana?
   —Sí, pero ahora _____ en California.
   —¿Tu mamá _____ profesora?
   —No, _____ médica.
2. —¿Olga _____ tu prima?
   —No, _____ mi hermana.
   —¿Cómo _____ ella?
   —_____ alta, morena y delgada. _____ muy bonita.
   —¿Dónde _____ ella ahora?
   —_____ en su casa.
3. —¿Qué hora _____?
   —_____ las siete.
   —¿Dónde _____ la fiesta de Navidad?
   —_____ en el Club Náutico. ¿Tú vas a ir?
   —No, _____ muy cansada.
4. —¿Qué _____ comiendo tú?
   —_____ comiendo arroz con pollo.
   —¿_____ rico *(tasty)*?
   —Sí, _____ delicioso.
5. —¿Ése *(That)* _____ tu escritorio?
   —Sí, _____ mi escritorio.
   —¿_____ de metal?
   —No, _____ de madera *(wood)*.
6. —¡Oye! ¿Qué día _____ hoy?
   —Hoy _____ jueves.

REAL BALLET
NACIONAL DE ESPAÑA

C. With two or three other students, prepare a description of a famous person. Include as much information as possible (nationality, profession, physical characteristics, etc.). Read your description to the rest of the class and see who can identify your subject.

6 Pronouns as objects of prepositions *(Pronombres usados como objetos de preposición)*

SUGGESTION: Ask students to recall the prepositions they have used in previous lessons and to write a list on the board.

de   con
por   en
para   a

SUGGESTION: Walk around the room and pick up items belonging to students (e.g., books, pencils, etc.) and ask the class, "¿Es (son) para mí?" Students should answer, "No, no son para Ud. Son para él (ella, ellos, etc.)."

■ The object of a preposition is the noun or pronoun that immediately follows it: **La fiesta es *para María (ella)*. Ellos van *con nosotros*.**

Singular		Plural	
mí	*me*	nosotros(-as)	*us*
ti	*you* (fam.)	vosotros(-as)	*you* (fam.)
Ud.	*you* (form.)	Uds.	*you* (form.)
él	*him*	ellos	*them* (masc.)
ella	*her*	ellas	*them* (fem.)

—¿Hablan de **mí**? — "*Are you talking about me?*"
—No, no hablamos de **ti**; hablamos de **ella.** — "*No, we are not talking about you; we're talking about her.*"

—¿Vas **conmigo** o con Carlos? — "*Are you going with me or with Carlos?*"
—No voy **contigo**; voy **con él.** — "*I'm not going with you; I'm going with him.*"

■ Only the first- and second-person singular, **mí** and **ti,** are different from regular subject pronouns.

■ **Mí** and **ti** combine with **con** to become **conmigo** *(with me)* and **contigo** *(with you)*, respectively.

práctica

EXPANSION A: Based on the structures presented in this exercise, ask students personalized questions. Remind them to respond using the appropriate preposition and pronoun.

I—¿Vienes al café conmigo?
S1—Sí, voy contigo.
I—¿Los libros son de Anita y de Paula?
S2—No, no son de ellas.

A. Complete the following dialogues, using the Spanish equivalent of the words in parentheses. Then act them out with a partner, adding a sentence or two to each dialogue.

1. —¿Carlos va _____? *(with me)*
   —No, no va _____; va _____. *(with you / with her)*
2. —¿Para quién son los discos compactos, Paquito?
   ¿_____ o _____? *(For him / for her)*
   —Son _____. *(for me)*
   —¿_____? *(For you)*
   —Sí, señor.
   —¿Los cuadros son _____? *(for you, pl.)*
   —No, son _____. *(for them, fem.)*

B. Interview a classmate, using the following questions and two questions of your own. When you have finished, switch roles. Use the appropriate prepositions and pronouns in your responses.

1. ¿Hablas con tus amigos en la clase?
2. ¿Puedes estudiar español conmigo?
3. ¿Trabajas para tus padres?
4. ¿Vives cerca de tus abuelos?   *Sarca*
5. ¿Hablas mucho con tus amigos por teléfono?
6. ¿Puedo ir contigo a la biblioteca?

7.

8.

¡A ver cuánto aprendió!

¡Repase el vocabulario!

INTERNET

See the *¿Cómo se dice...?* Web site for additional grammar and vocabulary practice: http://spanish.college. hmco.com/students

EXPANSION: Ask students personalized questions based on the vocabulary and structures presented in this activity.

¿Dónde está tu familia en este momento?
¿Qué estudias por la tarde?
¿Dónde vive tu primo(-a) favorito(-a)?
¿Dónde vive tu tío(-a) favorito(-a)?

ACTIVITY SUGGESTION: Do **Escucha!**, the in-class listening comprehension activity that reviews vocabulary and grammar structures introduced in the lesson. It appears in the answer key of the *IAM*.

Match each question in column A with the best response in column B; then read them aloud.

A

1. ¿Dónde está tu familia?
2. ¿Qué estudias?
3. ¿Estás incómoda?
4. ¿Vamos al museo mañana?
5. ¿Practicas el español?
6. ¿Pedro es menor que Juan?
7. ¿No tienen dinero para ir a un hotel?
8. ¿Es la hermana de tu esposo?
9. ¿Es tu prima?
10. ¿Van en ómnibus?
11. ¿Cuándo es tu cumpleaños?
12. ¿Qué planes tienes para el fin de semana?
13. ¿Es tu nieto?
14. ¿Van a perder la oportunidad de ir a México?
15. ¿Es alta?

B

a. No, es de estatura mediana.
b. Sí, es mi cuñada.
c. El 3 de septiembre.
d. Medicina.
e. Pienso ir a Salamanca.
f. No, es mi sobrina.
g. Sí, ¡qué lástima!
h. ¡Vale!
i. Sí, es el hijo de mi hija.
j. En Canadá.
k. No, por eso van a una pensión.
l. No, vamos en coche.
m. Sí, mi silla es muy pequeña.
n. Sí, nunca pierdo la oportunidad.
o. No, es mayor.

ACTIVITY SUGGESTION: See the *IAM* for an additional in-class activity: **Palabras escondidas.**

Entrevista

ACTIVITY SUGGESTION: See the *IAM* for additional in-class activities: **Para conocernos mejor** and **Una encuesta.**

With a partner, interview each other by asking the following questions.

1. ¿Tú eres más alto(-a) o más bajo(-a) que tu papá?
2. ¿Tu mamá es alta, baja o de estatura mediana?
3. ¿Tu mamá es mayor o menor que tu papá?

4. ¿Cuál es tu clase más interesante?
5. ¿Tú quieres aprender a hablar español perfectamente?
6. ¿Dónde almuerzas generalmente?
7. ¿Cuál es el mejor restaurante de la ciudad donde tú vives?
8. Generalmente, ¿a qué hora vuelves a tu casa?
9. ¿Adónde piensas ir este fin de semana y qué piensas hacer?
10. Este verano, ¿vas a viajar o vas a asistir a la universidad?
11. ¿Cuál crees tú que es la ciudad más bonita del mundo?
12. ¿Tú tienes tanto dinero como tus padres?

Situaciones

SUGGESTION: See SUGGESTION (page 96). Distribute the situations from **Lección 4** as well as the new situations to pairs of students. For homework have students write a mini-dialogue based on the situation of their choice from **Lección 5**.

What would you say in the following situations? What might the other person say? Act out the scenes with a partner. Take turns playing each role.

1. A Spanish exchange student is visiting your home, and you don't want to miss the opportunity to speak Spanish.
2. Someone asks about your weekend plans.
3. You are with a friend who has never seen pictures of your family, and you just happen to have some in your wallet.
4. You are trying to get a reluctant friend to go with you somewhere.

Para escribir

Write a composition describing two members of your family. Include the following information for each person:

color of hair and eyes (**pelo y ojos**)
age
current residence
place of employment or study
marital status and number of children
other personal characteristics (Establish comparisons between the other members of your family and yourself.)

En calidad y economía lo tiene todo.

En la vida real

Objetivos

CD-ROM

Do the interactive exercises on the CD-ROM for additional practice.

You and a classmate have a goal: to someday speak Spanish like native speakers and to learn as much as possible about the culture of Spanish-speaking countries. Come up with a list of things you are going to do to reach that goal.

Here are some additional words and phrases you may want to include:

escuchar *(to listen to)* { **canciones** *(songs)*
las cintas del laboratorio de lenguas
programas de radio

gente   *people*
películas españolas y latinoamericanas   *Spanish and Latin American movies*
revistas   *magazines*
tener correspondencia   *to correspond*
visitar países de habla hispana   *to visit Spanish-speaking countries*

Árbol genealógico   *(Family tree)*

Prepare your family tree, following the model on page 109. Call it **"Mi árbol genealógico."** Be sure to include each family member's relationship to you.

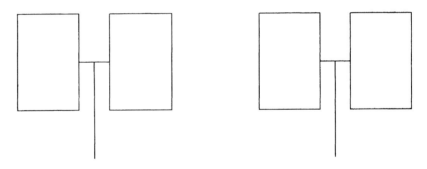

Abuelos maternos   Abuelos paternos

¿Quieres ver mis fotos?

Bring pictures of your relatives to class and tell a classmate who they are, giving information about each one. Ask each other any pertinent questions.

¿A qué museo vamos?

You and a friend want to go to a museum. Read the following ads and answer the questions.

Museo de Arte Contemporáneo

Avda. de Herrera Oria, s/n.
Metro Moncloa. Autobús 62

Teléfono 449-5071

Abierto: de 10:00 a 18:00
Cerrado los lunes.

■

Pintura y escultura española
y extranjera de los últimos años:

*Chillida, Botero, Miró, Stella,
Warhol, Gris, Dalí.*

■

Precio: 450 pesetas.
Con carné de estudiante entrada libre.

Museo del Prado

Paseo del Prado, s/n.
Metro Atocha. Autobús 27
Abierto: de 10:00 a 17:00

Instalado en un edificio del siglo XVIII.

■ Muestra de los grandes pintores españoles de los siglos XII al XVIII: Goya, Zurbarán, Velázquez, El Greco, Murillo

■ Pinturas de las escuelas italianas, flamencas, holandesa, etc.: Rafael, Rembrandt, Rubens, etc.

Precio: 600 pesetas.
Con carné de estudiante entrada gratuita.
Sábados entrada libre.

1. ¿En qué calle está el Museo de Arte Contemporáneo?
2. ¿Pueden Uds. ir al Museo de Arte Contemporáneo el lunes? ¿Por qué?
3. ¿Cuánto cuesta la entrada *(ticket)* al Museo de Arte Contemporáneo?
4. ¿Cuánto pagan *(pay)* los estudiantes para visitar el Museo de Arte Contemporáneo?
5. ¿Qué metro *(subway)* deben Uds. tomar para ir al Museo del Prado?
6. ¿Pueden ir en autobús también? ¿En cuál?
7. El Museo del Prado, ¿es antiguo *(old)* o moderno?
8. ¿En cuál de los dos museos es más barata *(cheap)* la entrada?
9. En el Museo del Prado, ¿encuentran Uds. solamente cuadros de pintores españoles?
10. ¿En qué museo no es necesario pagar los sábados?

¡VAMOS A LEER!

Antes de leer

As you read the following dialogue, find the answers to these questions.

1. ¿Cuál es el apellido de Ana María?
2. ¿De dónde es?
3. ¿Dónde está su familia?

4. ¿Qué está estudiando Ana María en la universidad?
5. ¿Por qué no son fáciles las clases para ella?
6. ¿La muchacha trabaja? ¿Dónde?
7. ¿Ud. cree que Ana María va mucho a la playa?
8. ¿Con quiénes piensa ir a Disney World?
9. ¿Cuánto tiempo va a estar ella en Miami?
10. ¿Cuándo piensa regresar a Chile? ¿Por qué?

Una entrevista°

interview

Ana María Estévez estudia en la Universidad Internacional de la Florida. Ella es de Chile, pero ahora su familia y ella viven en Miami. Hoy la entrevistamos° para el periódico de la universidad.

la... we are interviewing her

PERIODISTA	—¿Qué clases estás tomando en la universidad, Ana María?
ANA MARÍA	—Matemáticas, historia del arte, inglés y sociología. Las clases son muy difíciles para mí porque no hablo muy bien el inglés.
PERIODISTA	—¿Trabajas también?
ANA MARÍA	—Sí, trabajo en el laboratorio de lenguas.°

languages

PERIODISTA	—¿Te gusta Miami?
ANA MARÍA	—Sí, especialmente la playa.°

beach

PERIODISTA	—¿Piensas ir a Disney World?
ANA MARÍA	—Sí, pienso ir con unos amigos cubanos. Son unos chicos muy simpáticos y divertidos.°

entertaining

PERIODISTA	—¿Cuánto tiempo° vas a estar en Miami?

¿Cuánto...? How long

ANA MARÍA	—Unos cuatro años.
PERIODISTA	—¿Piensas regresar a Chile?
ANA MARÍA	—Algún° día, porque la verdad° es que echo mucho de menos a mi familia.

Some / truth

Díganos

Answer the following questions, based on your own thoughts and experiences.

1. ¿Cuál es su apellido?
2. ¿Dónde vive y estudia Ud.?
3. ¿Dónde vive su familia?
4. ¿Cuántas clases toma Ud.? ¿Son fáciles o difíciles?
5. ¿Va Ud. a la playa? ¿Con quién?
6. ¿Son divertidos sus amigos?
7. ¿A quiénes echa Ud. de menos?

ASÍ SOMOS

VIDEO   CD-ROM   Do the interactive exercises on the CD-ROM for additional practice.

NARRADORA   —¿Cómo es su familia?
TAMARA   —Mi papá se llama Carlos y trabaja en administración. Mi mamá se llama Neri; trabaja eh... como psicóloga. Tengo dos hermanas que son menores que yo. Yo soy la hija mayor y que está actualmente estudiando. Estamos todos estudiando.

Preparación

NOTE: The video-related vocabulary is listed in the *Instructor's Activities Manual* for your reference. Its purpose is to facilitate students' comprehension. You may want to distribute the vocabulary to the class before viewing.

NOTE: See the Instructor's Edition frontmatter for additional suggestions on implementing video in the classroom.

SUGGESTION: Have students make a list of the words or phrases used to describe their families and their weekend plans.

A. ¿Cómo es su familia? Answer the following questions about your family.

1. ¿Cuántos hermanos(-as) tiene?
2. ¿Cómo se llaman sus hermanos?
3. ¿Cuántos años tienen?
4. ¿Cómo se llama su tío(-a) favorito(-a)?
5. ¿En qué ciudad vive su tío(-a) favorito(-a)?
6. ¿Cuál es su profesión?

B. ¿Cómo te diviertes? Interview a classmate about his or her favorite leisure activities using the following questions.

1. ¿Qué haces los fines de semana?
2. ¿Prefieres ir al cine o al teatro?
3. ¿Vas a los museos?
4. ¿Vas a las discotecas a bailar?
5. Este fin de semana, ¿piensas ir al parque?
6. ¿Practicas algún deporte?

Comprensión

A. ¿Verdadero o falso? Read the following statements. Circle **V** (**Verdadero**) or **F** (**Falso**) according to what you understood from the video. If a statement is false, correct it.

V F   1. Carolina tiene un hermano que tiene 24 años y una hermana que tiene 17 años.
V F   2. La abuela de Juan vive con su familia.
V F   3. El padre y la madre de Jaime trabajan.
V F   4. Tamara es la menor de su familia.
V F   5. Tamara tiene cuatro hermanas.

B. **Planes de familia.** Select the word or phrase that best completes each statement, according to what you understood from the video.

1. Por lo general, Yolanda sale (a pasear, a comer) con su esposo los domingos.
2. En la familia de Rita, (siempre, de vez en cuando [*sometimes*]) comen todos juntos los domingos.
3. Héctor está con (su familia, sus amigos) durante el fin de semana.
4. Los domingos Olga está con (sus niños, sus amigas).

C. **¿Qué piensan hacer este fin de semana?** Read the statements below and match each weekend activity with the name of the person who said it in the video. More than one activity may correspond with one person.

A	B
_____ 1. Rita	a. salir a comer
_____ 2. Ivonne	b. ir a bailar a discotecas
_____ 3. Pedro	c. ir a la playa
_____ 4. Carolina	d. salir a algún lugar o estar en mi casa
_____ 5. Tamara	e. salir con mis amigos
_____ 6. Héctor	f. estudiar
_____ 7. Milka	g. ir a la fiesta de los latinoamericanos

Ampliación

FOLLOW-UP A: Have students share the family trees they investigated with the class.

EXPANSION: Have students make a list of questions they would ask a person from the video.

A. **Un árbol genealógico.** Make a list of the questions you may need to ask someone about their family. Then, interview a classmate about his or her family and create their family tree based on what you learn. Be sure to include information on names, ages, and relationships *(el parentesco)* of the various family members.

B. **Durante el fin de semana.** Work with two or three other students to make a list in Spanish of all the activities that you might do on a typical weekend. Then, divide the activities into two categories: *Actividades con mis amigos* and *Actividades con mi familia.* Share your observations with the class.

OBJECTIVES

Pronunciation

The Spanish **j**, **g** (before **e** or **i**), and **h**

Structure

Present indicative of **e:i** stem-changing verbs • Affirmative and negative expressions • Verbs with irregular first-person forms • **Saber** vs. **conocer** • Direct object pronouns • Weather expressions

Communication

You will learn vocabulary related to travel: obtaining information about accommodations, asking about transportation, and checking in at a hotel.

Un viaje a Perú

STUDENT AUDIO

Teresa, una profesora mexicana, va a pasar sus vacaciones en Perú. Ella acaba de llegar a Lima, donde piensa pasar unos días antes de ir a Machu Picchu para conocer las famosas ruinas de los incas. Teresa muestra su pasaporte y luego pasa por la aduana. En el aeropuerto Teresa ve objetos de oro y de plata, y compra algunos para su familia.

Teresa va a la oficina de turismo para conseguir información.

TERESA —Buenos días, señor. ¿Tiene Ud. una lista de hoteles y pensiones? Yo no conozco Lima.

EMPLEADO —Sí, señorita. Aquí la tiene.

Teresa lee un anuncio sobre el hotel Bolívar.

HOTEL BOLÍVAR

El mejor hotel de Lima, situado en el centro de la ciudad y cerca de muchos lugares de interés, es el favorito de miles de turistas que visitan nuestra hermosa capital. Tenemos amplios cuartos con vista a la calle o interiores. Todas las habitaciones tienen baño privado, aire acondicionado y televisor.

El hotel tiene dos restaurantes que ofrecen comida internacional y servicio de habitación. Aceptamos tarjetas de crédito y cheques de viajero. Para hacer reservaciones, llame al teléfono 285-3946

TERESA —Quiero ir al hotel Bolívar. ¿Dónde puedo tomar un taxi?

EMPLEADO —Vaya a la segunda puerta a la derecha. También hay un ómnibus que la lleva al centro.

En el hotel Bolívar, Teresa pide una habitación.

TERESA —Necesito una habitación sencilla con baño privado, por favor.

EMPLEADO —Tenemos una con vista a la calle que cuesta 208 soles[1] por día. También hay otra interior en el segundo piso por 130 soles.

TERESA —Son un poco caras. ¿No tiene alguna más barata?

EMPLEADO —No, no hay ninguna. Ahora hay pocos cuartos libres.

TERESA —Prefiero el cuarto interior. ¿A cómo está el cambio de moneda?

EMPLEADO —No sé... Voy a averiguarlo. Por favor firme aquí.

---

[1]Peruvian currency

SUGGESTION: Refer students to **Panorama hispánico 7** and the corresponding video segment for more information about Peru.

SUGGESTION: After students read the dialogues, have them role-play each section. Encourage them to use each dialogue as a guide and personalize it to reflect their own situation.

RELATED VOCABULARY: In public places the following terms are frequently used to identify restrooms: **los servicios, damas/caballeros o señores, W.C.**

RELATED VOCABULARY: **alojamiento** (accommodation), **cancelación**, **consulado** (consulate), **excursión** (tour), **pagar por adelantado** (to pay in advance).

Teresa firma el registro.

TERESA —Quiero cenar en mi habitación. ¿Hasta qué hora sirven la
cena?

EMPLEADO —La sirven hasta las once.

TERESA —¿Puede alguien llevar mis <u>maletas</u> al cuarto, por favor?

EMPLEADO —Sí, en seguida viene el botones a <u>llevarlas</u>. Aquí tiene la
llave.

Como hace calor, Teresa decide ir a la piscina.

 # Vocabulario

Cognados

el aeropuerto airport
amplio(-a) ample
la capital capital
favorito(-a) favorite
el hotel hotel
la información information
el interés interest
internacional international
interior interior

la lista list
el objeto object
la oficina office
el pasaporte passport
privado(-a) private
el registro register
la reservación, la reserva
   reservation
las ruinas ruins

el taxi taxi
el turismo tourism
el, la turista tourist
las vacaciones[1] vacation

Nombres

la aduana customs
el aire acondicionado air
   conditioning
el anuncio ad
el baño, el cuarto de baño
   bathroom
el botones bellhop
la cena dinner, supper
el centro downtown (area)

el cheque de viajero traveler's
   check
la comida food
el cuarto, la habitación room
el (la) empleado(-a) clerk
la llave key
el lugar place
la maleta, la valija suitcase
el oro gold

la piscina swimming pool
el piso floor
la plata silver
el servicio de habitación (cuarto)
   room service
la tarjeta de crédito credit card
el televisor T.V. set
el viaje trip, journey

---

[1]**vacaciones** is always used in the plural in Spanish.

Verbos

aceptar   to accept
averiguar   to find out
cenar   to have dinner, supper
comprar   to buy
conocer (yo conozco)   to know, to be acquainted
conseguir (e:i)   to get, to obtain

firmar   to sign
hacer (yo hago)   to make, to do
llegar   to arrive
mostrar (o:ue), enseñar   to show
ofrecer (yo ofrezco)   to offer
pasar   to spend (time), to pass
pasar (por)   to go through, by

pedir (e:i)   to ask for, to request
saber (yo sé)   to know
servir (e:i)   to serve
ver (yo veo)   to see
visitar   to visit

Adjetivos

alguno(-a)   some, any
barato(-a)   inexpensive, cheap
caro(-a)   expensive
hermoso(-a)   beautiful

libre   vacant
pocos(-as)   few
segundo(-a)   second
sencillo(-a)   single, simple

situado(-a)   located
unos(-as)   a few

Otras palabras y expresiones

¿A cómo está el cambio de moneda?   What is the exchange rate?
a la derecha[1]   to the right
acabar de + *infinitive*   to have just + *past participle*
alguien   someone, somebody
Aquí las tiene.   Here they are. (Here you have them.)

con vista a   overlooking
en seguida   right away
Firme aquí.   Sign here.
hace calor   it's hot
hasta   until
llame   call
luego   then, afterwards
ninguno(-a)   none, not any
por   per, for

que   which
sobre   about
vaya a   go to

Más que una Tarjeta   EUROP ASSISTANCE

---

[1]a la izquierda: to the left

Vocabulario adicional
En el hotel

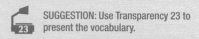
SUGGESTION: Use Transparency 23 to present the vocabulary.

la toalla
la ducha
la habitación doble
el jabón
el lavabo
la bañadera (la bañera)
el inodoro
el almuerzo
el desayuno
la escalera
el ascensor (el elevador)
la recepción

Para el turismo

la cámara de video video camera	¿Tiene Ud. una **cámara de video**?	
la cámara fotográfica camera	Voy a llevar mi **cámara fotográfica**.	
cancelar to cancel	Voy a **cancelar** la reservación.	
confirmar to confirm	Deseo **confirmar** la reservación.	
la embajada embassy	¿Dónde queda la **embajada** norteamericana?	
la lista de espera waiting list	Estoy en la **lista de espera**.	
la tarjeta de turista tourist card	Los norteamericanos necesitan una **tarjeta de turista** para visitar México.	

ACTIVITY SUGGESTION: See the *IAM* for an additional in-class activity: **Palabras y más palabras.**

EXPANSION: Based on the responses given in **¡Conversemos!,** have students practice retelling the dialogues to each other in third-person form. Encourage them to include as much information as possible, but not to refer to their books or notes. Write incomplete sentences on the board or overhead projector to facilitate this recall task.

Teresa llega a...
Ella pasa por...
En el aeropuerto, Teresa...

¡Conversemos!

Answer the following questions, basing your answers on the dialogue.

1. ¿Qué ruinas famosas hay en Perú?
2. ¿Qué muestra Teresa y por dónde pasa?

3. ¿Qué compra Teresa en el aeropuerto?
4. ¿Para qué va Teresa a la oficina de turismo?
5. ¿Qué lee Teresa?
6. ¿Dónde está situado el hotel Bolívar?
7. ¿Qué tienen todos los cuartos del hotel?
8. ¿Qué aceptan en el hotel Bolívar?
9. ¿Teresa pide una habitación sencilla o una doble?
10. ¿Qué cuarto prefiere Teresa? ¿Por qué?
11. ¿Hasta qué hora sirven la cena?
12. ¿Qué decide hacer Teresa? ¿Por qué?

¿Lo sabía Ud.?

Fachada de uno de los edificios que rodean la Plaza de San Martín en Lima, Perú.

■ Lima, la capital de Perú, es una ciudad de contrastes. Junto a *(Next to)* edificios *(buildings)* muy modernos hay otros de arquitectura colonial. El 25% de la población es de origen indígena.

■ La moneda *(currency)* que utilizan con más frecuencia los latinoamericanos cuando viajan fuera de su país es el dólar norteamericano. Esto se debe a que *(is due to the fact that)* es fácil cambiar dólares en la mayoría de los principales bancos de los países hispanoamericanos.

● ¿En qué ciudades de su país hay edificios de arquitectura colonial?

● ¿Se puede cambiar dinero de otros países en los bancos de los Estados Unidos?

INTERNET

See the *¿Cómo se dice...?* Web site for activities on authentic cultural material: http://spanish.college.hmco.com/students

Pronunciación

A The Spanish j

STUDENT AUDIO

SUGGESTION: Model each word and have the class repeat the sounds and words chorally and individually. Then have students work with the following sentences for additional pronunciation practice using words in context.

The Spanish **j** sounds somewhat like the *h* in the English word *hit*. It is never pronounced like the English *j* in *John* or *James*. Listen to your instructor and repeat the following words.

Julia	dejar	embajada
pasaje	jabón	viajero
tarjeta	objeto	jueves

j: Javier pone el trabajo del juez en el cajón.
La hija de Gerónimo jamás juega en el jardín.

B The Spanish g (before e or i)

g: El gitano compró el giro para Gerardo.
El general Gil de Gerona es inteligente.

When followed by **e** or **i**, the Spanish **g** sounds like the Spanish **j** mentioned above. Listen to your instructor and repeat the following words.

Gerardo	inteligente	agente
agencia	general	Genaro
registro	Argentina	ingeniero

C The Spanish h

h: El herrero tiene herraduras en la herrería.
Helena y Hernando van a Honduras con Horacio.

The Spanish **h** is always silent. Listen to your instructor and repeat the following words.

hay	Hilda	habitación
Honduras	hermano	hasta
ahora	hotel	hija

HORAS XXI

Todos los Martes de 21 a 23 horas
RADIO CARITAS en el 680 del dial

1 Present indicative of **e:i** stem-changing verbs *(Presente de indicativo de los verbos que cambian en la raíz e:i)*

SUGGESTION: When explaining this structure, follow the same procedure as with other stem-changing verbs. Use the boot-shaped illustration and emphasize the vowel changes by writing them in colored chalk.
Point out the chart summarizing the stem-changing verbs they have studied thus far (p. 138) and encourage students to add to this list each time they learn a new stem-changing verb.

EXPANSION A: After students have completed the original sentence builder, have them expand each sentence by adding one more bit of information that explains why, where, when, etc.

Mis padres dicen que necesitamos cheques de viajero cuando viajamos.

servir *to serve*	
sirvo	servimos
sirves	servís
sirve	sirven

■ Some **-ir** verbs undergo a special stem change in the present indicative. For these verbs, when **e** is the last stem vowel and it is stressed, it changes to **i**.

—¿Qué **sirven** Uds. en sus fiestas?   *"What do you serve at your parties?"*

—**Servimos** champán.   *"We serve champagne."*

■ Note that the stem vowel is not stressed in the **nosotros(-as)** and **vosotros(-as)** verb forms; therefore, the **e** does not change to **i**.

■ Other verbs that undergo this change:[1]

conseguir	*to get, to obtain*	**pedir**	*to ask for, to request, to order*
decir	*to say, to tell*	**seguir**	*to follow, to continue*

■ The verb **decir** undergoes the same change, but in addition it has an irregular first-person singular form: **yo digo.**

■ Note that in the present tense **seguir** and **conseguir** drop the **u** before **a** or **o**: **yo sigo, yo consigo.**

práctica •

FOLLOW-UP A: Write these or similar questions on the board. Have students ask each other personalized questions about themselves, their friends, etc.

1. ¿Qué pides para comer cuando vas a un restaurante español (italiano, francés, chino)?
2. ¿Dónde sirven comida española (francesa, italiana) en tu ciudad?
3. ¿Qué pides para beber?
4. ¿A qué hora sirven el desayuno/el almuerzo/la cena en tu casa (o residencia)?
5. ¿En qué banco consigues cheques de viajero?
6. En general, ¿sigues la moda (fashion)?
7. ¿Dónde consigues libros en español?
8. ¿Tú dices siempre la verdad (truth)?

A. Form complete sentences by combining the words in the three columns in sequence, starting with A. Use each subject and each verb at least once.

A	B	C
yo	decir	la comida
nosotros	servir	habitaciones
Ana y Eva	pedir	que necesitamos cheques de viajero
mis padres	conseguir	jabón y toalla
tú	seguir	al botones
el empleado		un cuarto con baño privado
		la llave del cuarto
		la cena

---

[1]For a complete list of stem-changing verbs, see Appendix B.

B. Complete the following dialogues, using the verbs given. Then act them out with a partner, adding a sentence or two to each dialogue.

1. decir
   —¿Tú _____ que el hotel es caro?
   —Sí, yo _____ que es caro, pero Carmen _____ que es barato.

2. servir
   —¿Qué _____ Uds. en sus fiestas?
   —_____ entremeses y refrescos. ¿Qué _____ tú?
   —Yo _____ sándwiches y cerveza.

3. pedir
   —¿Qué _____ Uds. cuando van a un restaurante mexicano?
   —Yo _____ tacos y Ernesto _____ enchiladas.

4. conseguir
   —Yo no _____ trabajo.
   —Tú no _____ trabajo porque no hablas dos idiomas.

C. With a partner, take turns asking each other two things: what you order when you go to ethnic restaurants and what you serve to eat and drink at your parties.

SUMMARY OF THE PRESENT INDICATIVE OF STEM-CHANGING VERBS

e:ie	o:ue		e:i
cerrar	almorzar	morir	conseguir
comenzar	contar	mostrar	decir
empezar	costar	poder	pedir
entender	dormir	recordar	seguir
pensar	encontrar	volar	servir
perder	llover	volver	
preferir			
querer			

Add to this list as you learn other stem-changing verbs.

2 Affirmative and negative expressions (Expresiones afirmativas y negativas)

Affirmative		Negative	
algo	something, anything	nada	nothing, not anything
alguien	someone, somebody, anyone	nadie	nobody, no one, not anyone
alguno(-a), algún	any, some	ninguno(-a), ningún	no, none, not any
siempre	always	nunca, jamás	never
también	also, too	tampoco	neither, not either
o... o	either . . . or	ni... ni	neither . . . nor

—¿Necesita Ud. **algo** más?   *"Do you need anything else?"*
—No, no necesito **nada** más.   *"No, I don't need anything else."*

—¿Tienes **algunos** amigos peruanos?   *"Do you have any Peruvian friends?"*
—No, no tengo **ningún** amigo peruano.   *"No, I don't have any Peruvian friends."*

—¿Hay **alguien** en tu cuarto?   *"Is there anybody in your room?"*
—No, no hay **nadie**.   *"No, there's no one."*

—¿Quieres café **o** Coca-Cola?   *"Do you want coffee or Coke?"*
—Yo no bebo **ni** café **ni** Coca-Cola.   *"I don't drink either coffee or Coke."*

ATENCIÓN   Note that **alguno(-a)** may be used in the plural forms, but **ninguno(-a)** is not pluralized.

ATENCIÓN   **No** is never used as an adjective, as it sometimes is in English *(No person could do all that.)*.

■ Alguno and ninguno drop the -o before a masculine singular noun: *algún* niño, *ningún* niño; but *alguna* niña, *ninguna* niña.

■ Spanish sentences frequently use a double negative form to express a degree of negation: the adverb **no** is placed before the verb and the second negative word either follows the verb or appears at the end of the sentence. If, however, the negative word precedes the verb, **no** is never used.

> No hablo español **nunca**.
> *or:* **Nunca** hablo español.   *I never speak Spanish.*

> No compro **nada nunca**.
> *or:* **Nunca** compro **nada**.   *I never buy anything.*

■ Note that Spanish often uses several negatives in one sentence.

> —Yo **no** quiero **nada tampoco**.   *I don't want anything either.*

SUGGESTION: Ask students to make a list of five things they always do and five things they never do. Then ask each student to write one sentence in each category on the board and have the class compare student *dos* and *don'ts*.

práctica ●

A. Your friend Oscar always gets the facts wrong when he talks about other people. Set him straight!

MODELO: Ana necesita algo.
Ana no necesita nada.

1. Raquel siempre viaja en el verano.
2. Ana va con Raquel, y Jorge va con ella también.
3. Siempre piden habitaciones dobles.
4. Siempre compran algo cuando viajan.
5. Siempre compran algunos objetos de oro.
6. Cenan en la pensión o en una cafetería.
7. Siempre hay alguien en su casa.

8. El esposo de Luisa nunca habla con nadie.
9. Carlos nunca averigua nada.
10. Elsa siempre pide información.

B. Answer these personal questions negatively, using the expressions you have just learned.

1. ¿Quiere Ud. viajar a Bolivia o a Perú?
2. ¿Tiene Ud. algunos amigos en Perú?
3. Yo no hablo portugués. ¿Y Ud.?
4. ¿Siempre viaja Ud. en invierno?
5. ¿Siempre viaja Ud. con alguien?
6. ¿Compra Ud. algo cuando va de vacaciones?

C. With a partner, write a list of complaints frequently heard on campus. Use the expressions you have just learned.

MODELO: *Nunca podemos comer nada en la cafetería.*

3 Verbs with irregular first-person forms   *(Verbos irregulares en la primera persona)*

SUGGESTION: To help students learn these forms, give infinitives at random, point to different students, and ask each to give you the first-person form. Do this at a very fast pace. You might also review the regular forms of these verbs by giving pronouns and nouns in order and having the class give you the corresponding verb form.

I—yo – saber
S1—yo sé
I—Teresa – ver
S2—Teresa ve

■ The following verbs are irregular in the first-person singular of the present tense.

Verb	*yo form*	*Regular forms*
salir *(to go out)*	**salgo**	sales, sale, salimos, salís, salen
hacer *(to do, make)*	**hago**	haces, hace, hacemos, hacéis, hacen
poner *(to put, place)*	**pongo**	pones, pone, ponemos, ponéis, ponen
traer *(to bring)*	**traigo**	traes, trae, traemos, traéis, traen
conducir *(to drive; to conduct)*	**conduzco**	conduces, conduce, conducimos, conducís, conducen
traducir *(to translate)*	**traduzco**	traduces, traduce, traducimos, traducís, traducen
conocer *(to know)*	**conozco**	conoces, conoce, conocemos, conocéis, conocen
caber *(to fit)*	**quepo**	cabes, cabe, cabemos, cabéis, caben
ver *(to see)*	**veo**	ves, ve, vemos, veis, ven
saber *(to know)*	**sé**	sabes, sabe, sabemos, sabéis, saben

práctica ●●●

FOLLOW-UP A: As a homework assignment, have students write two original questions for each irregular verb on the chart. As a quick review, have students work in pairs the next day to answer their partners' questions.

SUGGESTION B: Have students complete the following sentences.

1. El empleado sale del trabajo por la mañana y yo...
2. Él cabe aquí pero yo...
3. Ella ve objetos de oro y yo...
4. Él sabe japonés y yo...
5. Yo traduzco al italiano y ellos...
6. María conduce un Ford y yo...
7. Oscar trae las uvas y yo...
8. Yo pongo los platos en la mesa y mis hermanas...

A. Your classmate is traveling to Peru. Here is a list of questions you want to ask in order to help him or her prepare for the trip.

1. ¿Conoces Perú? ¿Sabes a qué distancia está de los Estados Unidos?
2. ¿Sabes a cómo está el cambio de moneda?
3. ¿Haces la reservación del hotel antes de salir de viaje?
4. ¿Dónde pones el pasaporte?
5. El día del viaje, ¿sales de casa con tiempo? ¿Conduces tu coche para ir al aeropuerto?
6. ¿Traes muchas cosas para tu familia?

B. Read this paragraph about Anabel's preparations for her trip to Bolivia and then rewrite it as if you were Anabel, starting with **Yo...** .

Anabel sale para Bolivia esta noche. Va con su amiga Susana. Conduce al banco para comprar cheques de viajero, regresa a su casa, pone todos los documentos en su bolso de mano y después hace las maletas *(packs)*. Como sabe que hay mucho tráfico, sale de su casa temprano para ir al aeropuerto. Cuando llega al aeropuerto, ve que Susana está allí.

4 Saber vs. conocer

Spanish has two verbs that mean *to know*, **saber** and **conocer**.

SUGGESTION: Teach the difference between **llevar** and **tomar** at this point.

SUGGESTION: Point out that **como** is not required to say that someone knows how to speak a language.

■ When *to know* means *to know something by heart, to know how to do something,* or *to know a fact,* **saber** is used.

No sé dónde está la piscina.	*I don't know where the pool is.*
Juan **sabe** hablar ruso.	*Juan knows how to speak Russian.*
Ellos **saben** que ella es profesora.	*They know that she's a professor.*

■ When *to know* means *to be familiar with* or *to be acquainted with a person, a thing,* or *a place,* it is translated as **conocer**.

Nosotros **conocemos** al empleado.	*We know the clerk.*
Elisa **conoce** las novelas de García Márquez.	*Elisa knows (is acquainted with) García Márquez's novels.*
¿**Conoces** Canadá?	*Do you know (have you been to) Canada?*

práctica ●●●

FOLLOW-UP A: Write the following phrase on the board. Have students describe each other, their friends, or their family members by completing the phrase.

Conozco a... Sé que...
Conozco a la profesora de español. Sé que conduce un Ford.

A. Complete the following dialogues, using **saber** or **conocer** as appropriate. Then act them out with a partner.

1. —Yo _____ al abuelo de Olga.
   —¿Tú _____ dónde vive?
   —No, pero _____ su número de teléfono.
2. —Tú _____ Brasil, ¿no?
   —Sí, pero no _____ hablar portugués.

3. —¿Tú _____ los poemas de Bécquer?
   —Sí, _____ muchos de memoria *(by heart)*.
4. —¿_____ tú qué hora es?
   —Sí, son las ocho.
5. —Jorge conduce muy mal.
   —Sí, no _____ conducir muy bien.

B. Interview a classmate, using the following questions. When you have finished, switch roles.

1. ¿Cuántos idiomas sabes hablar? ¿Cuáles son?
2. ¿Conoces a los padres de tu mejor amigo(-a)?
3. ¿Sabes dónde viven?
4. ¿Qué sabes hacer?
5. ¿Sabes tocar *(play)* el piano? ¿la guitarra? ¿el violín?
6. ¿Sabes preparar sangría?
7. ¿Conoces un buen restaurante? ¿Dónde está?
8. ¿Conoces a un actor famoso? ¿Quién es? ¿Cómo es?

5 Direct object pronouns *(Pronombres usados como complemento directo)*

SUGGESTION: Write the subject pronouns on the board and ask students to provide the corresponding direct object pronouns.
  Write English sentences on the board and give their Spanish equivalents, showing the difference in position.

They   call   us.
Ellos   nos   ↙   llaman.

  Remind students of the use of the personal **a.**

A. The direct object

■ In addition to a subject, most sentences have an object that directly receives the action of the verb.

> Ellos compran el libro.
> S.   V.   D.O.

In the preceding sentence, the subject (**Ellos**) performs the action, while **el libro,** the direct object, directly receives the action of the verb. The direct object of a sentence may be either a person or a thing.

■ The direct object can be easily identified as the answer to the questions *whom?* and *what?* about what the subject is doing.

> Ellos compran **el libro.**   What are they buying?
> Pepe visita **a su primo.**   Whom is Pepe visiting?

■ Direct object pronouns may be used in place of the direct object.

B. Forms of the direct object pronouns

	Singular		Plural	
me	*me*		**nos**	*us*
te	*you* (fam.)		**os**	*you* (fam.)
lo	*you* (form., masc.) / *him, it* (masc.)		**los**	*you* (form., masc.) / *them* (masc.)
la	*you* (form., fem.) / *her, it* (fem.)		**las**	*you* (form., fem.) / *them* (fem.)

SUGGESTION: Present the direct object pronouns by using Transparency 24. Point to specific figures and ask students questions about the actions depicted. Students should then agree or disagree with the response by repeating the sentence using the direct object pronoun.

I—Los estudiantes beben el café, ¿verdad?
S1—Sí, lo beben.
I—El chico escucha los discos, ¿no?
S2—No, no los escucha. Escucha la radio.

You may also use this transparency to review placement of the direct object pronouns with the present progressive.

1. **El chico está escuchando la radio.**
   La está escuchando. / Está escuchándola.
2. **El camarero mira el partido de fútbol.**
   Lo está mirando. / Está mirándolo.

—¿Tiene **la llave?**			*"Do you have the key?"*
—Sí,	**la**	tengo.	*"Yes, I have it."*
—¿Compra Ud. **los pasajes?**			*"Are you buying the tickets?"*
—Sí,	**los**	compro.	*"Yes, I'm buying them."*

C. Position of direct object pronouns

■ In Spanish, object pronouns are normally placed before a conjugated verb.

	D.O.		
Ellos sirven	**la cena.**		*They serve dinner.*
Ellos	**la**	sirven.	*They serve it.*

■ In negative sentences, the **no** must precede the object pronoun.

	D.O.		
Ellos sirven	**la cena.**		*They serve dinner.*
Ellos	**la**	sirven.	*They serve it.*
Ellos **no**	**la**	sirven.	*They don't serve it.*

■ When an infinitive is used with a conjugated verb, the direct object pronoun may either be attached to the infinitive or be placed before the conjugated verb. The same principle applies with the present participle in progressive constructions.

Puedo firmar**lo.**
Lo puedo firmar. } *I can sign it.*

Estoy leyéndo**lo.**
Lo estoy leyendo. } *I am reading it.*

ATENCIÓN   When a direct object pronoun is attached to a present participle (**leyéndolo, firmándola**), an accent mark is added to maintain the correct stress.

práctica ●

ACTIVITY SUGGESTION: See the *IAM* for additional in-class activities: **¿Quién lo tiene?** and **Preguntas del viajero.**

A. Complete the following dialogue, using the appropriate direct object pronouns. Then act it out with a partner.

JULIO   —¿Tú me puedes llevar a casa hoy?
DELIA   —Sí, puedo llevar _____ a las tres.
JULIO   —¡Ah! Necesito la maleta de mamá. ¿Tú _____ tienes?
DELIA   —Sí, yo _____ tengo. ¿Tú quieres llevar _____ a México?
JULIO   —Sí. También necesito comprar cheques de viajero...
DELIA   —Podemos comprar _____ esta tarde.
JULIO   —Rosa y yo tenemos que estar en el aeropuerto a las ocho de la noche. ¿Tú _____ puedes llevar?
DELIA   —Sí, yo _____ puedo llevar...
JULIO   —¡Ah! Las sobrinas de Rosa quieren ir al aeropuerto con nosotros. ¿Tú _____ puedes traer a mi casa a las siete?
DELIA   —¡No! ¡Yo no tengo un servicio de taxi!

SUGGESTION B: Have students work in pairs to complete this exercise.

FOLLOW-UP B: Use Transparency 19 to elicit responses that require the use of the direct object pronoun. Ask students to provide names for the various characters in the scene and to write the names on the transparency with a water-soluble marker. They should then respond in complete sentences to the following questions, using the correct object pronouns in their responses.

1. **¿Quién desea beber el refresco?**
2. **...llevar el suéter?**
3. **...comer pollo?**
4. **...beber la limonada?**
5. **¿Quiénes miran la película de terror?**
6. **...practican las matemáticas?**
7. **...ganan un trofeo?**
8. **...no quieren leer el libro?**
9. **...desean tomar el autobús?**
10. **...leen el periódico?**

SUGGESTION C: Have students work in pairs to complete this exercise.

B. You and your friends are planning a party. Volunteer to do the following tasks yourself.

> MODELO: ¿Quién invita a las chicas?
> *Yo las invito.*

1. ¿Quién llama a los muchachos?
2. ¿Quién compra las bebidas?
3. ¿Quién va a traer los discos compactos?
4. ¿Quién consigue el equipo estereofónico?
5. ¿Quién trae a mi compañera?
6. ¿Quién prepara *(is preparing)* los entremeses?
7. ¿Quién va a traer a Luis?
8. ¿Quién lleva a las chicas a su casa?

C. You and some friends will be traveling in Mexico shortly. Answer another friend's questions about your arrangements. Use direct object pronouns in your answers.

1. ¿Tus amigos te van a llamar esta noche?
2. ¿Tienen Uds. reservaciones para el hotel?
3. ¿Vas a comprar cheques de viajero?
4. ¿Tienes tu tarjeta de crédito?
5. ¿Llevas tu cámara fotográfica?
6. ¿Van a visitar Uds. las ruinas de Teotihuacán?
7. ¿Quién los va a llevar a Uds.[1] al aeropuerto?
8. ¿Me llevan con Uds. a México?

6 Weather expressions *(Expresiones para describir el tiempo)*

SUGGESTION: Use Transparency 25 to introduce or to practice weather expressions and to review seasons of the year.

SUGGESTION: Select color photographs from magazines. Assign one photograph to each pair of students. Students should imagine that they are visiting that country and write a postcard to a friend or relative at home describing where they are, the weather, and what they plan to do that day. Have several students read their cards to the class the next day.

■ In the following expressions, Spanish uses the verb **hacer,** *to make,* followed by a noun.

Hace (mucho) frío.	*It is (very) cold.*
Hace (mucho) calor.	*It is (very) hot.*
Hace (mucho) viento.	*It is (very) windy.*
Hace sol.	*It is sunny.*

■ To ask about the weather, say, **"¿Qué tiempo hace?"** *(What's the weather like?).*

> —¿Qué tiempo hace hoy?   *"What's the weather like today?"*
> —Hace buen (mal) tiempo.   *"The weather is good (bad)."*

---

[1]A **Uds.** is needed for clarification because **los** could also be *them.*

■ The following words used to describe the weather do not combine with **hacer;** they are impersonal verbs used only in the infinitive, present participle, past participle, and third-person singular forms of all tenses.

llover (o:ue) *to rain*	**Llueve.** *It is raining (It rains).*
lloviznar *to drizzle*	**Llovizna.** *It is drizzling (It drizzles).*
nevar (e:ie) *to snow*	**Nieva.** *It is snowing (It snows).*

■ Other weather-related words are **lluvia** *(rain)* and **niebla** *(fog).*

—¿**Hace** mucho **frío** en Buenos Aires?   *"Is it very cold in Buenos Aires?"*
—Sí, pero nunca **nieva.**   *"Yes, but it never snows."*

—¿Vas a volar hoy a San Francisco?   *"Are you going to fly to San Francisco today?"*
—No, porque **hay niebla.**   *"No, because it's foggy.[1]"*

práctica •

ACTIVITY SUGGESTION: See the *IAM* for an additional in-class activity: **¿Qué tiempo hace?**

A. Study the words in the following list, then complete the dialogues.

el paraguas   *umbrella*
el impermeable   *raincoat*
el sombrero   *hat*
el abrigo   *coat*
el suéter   *sweater*

1. —¿Necesitas un paraguas?
   —Sí, porque en Oregón _____ mucho.
2. —¿No necesitas un abrigo?
   —No, porque _____.
3. —¿Quieres un impermeable?
   —No, gracias, apenas *(hardly)* _____.
4. —¿Por qué no quieres llevar el suéter?
   —¡Porque _____!
5. —¿Vas a llevar el sombrero?
   —Sí, porque _____.
6. —¿Necesitas un suéter y un abrigo?
   —Sí, porque _____.
7. —¿Un impermeable? ¿Por qué? ¿Llueve? ¿Llovizna?
   —No, pero _____.
8. —¡Qué lluvia! Necesito un _____ y un _____.

---

[1]**hay niebla** = *it's foggy*

9 & 10

SUGGESTION: Use Transparencies 9–10. Provide students with colored water-soluble markers and instruct them to mark the map while describing the weather in the different regions of the U.S.

B. Say what the weather will be like in different locations at different times of the year.

1. Portland, Oregón—el 2 de enero
2. Anchorage, Alaska—el 25 de diciembre
3. Phoenix, Arizona—el 13 de agosto
4. Londres (London)—el 5 de febrero
5. Chicago—el 6 de marzo

C. A visiting professor from Panama is planning a weekend visit to your hometown. What questions is he or she likely to ask about the weather there and what clothes to bring? How will you respond? Act out the scene with a partner. Say at least five lines each.

D. You and a classmate are in charge of preparing the weather report for a local T.V. station. Discuss the weather in your area today.

| Sol | Nublado | Cubierto | Posibilidad de lluvia | Lluvia | Tormenta | Nieve |

¡A ver cuánto aprendió!

INTERNET

See the *¿Cómo se dice...?* Web site for additional grammar and vocabulary practice: http://spanish.college.hmco.com/students

ACTIVITY SUGGESTION: Do **¡Escucha!**, the in-class listening comprehension activity that reviews vocabulary and grammar structures introduced in the lesson. It appears in the answer key of the *IAM*.

ACTIVITY SUGGESTION: See the *IAM* for an additional in-class activity: **Palabras escondidas.**

¡Repase el vocabulario!

Choose the word or phrase that best completes each sentence.

1. En el aeropuerto debo mostrar...
   a. el registro.   b. el baño.   c. el pasaporte.

2. Quiero una habitación...
   a. en la oficina de turismo.   b. con vista a la calle.   c. en el taxi.

3. Ellos leen...
   a. la piscina.   b. el anuncio.   c. el piso.

4. Debes pasar por la aduana...
   a. con el restaurante.   b. con el piso.   c. con las maletas.

5. Voy a comprar algo para...
   a. mis padres.   b. la aduana.   c. la capital.

6. El botones va a llevar...
   a. el interés.   b. la plata.   c. las maletas.

7. ¿Dónde puedo tomar...
   a. el aire acondicionado?   b. el ascensor?   c. la tarjeta de turista?

8. Sirven la cena...
   a. a las nueve de la mañana.   b. a las tres de la tarde.
   c. a las nueve de la noche.

9. En el verano hay pocos cuartos...
   a. libres.   b. favoritos.   c. situados.

10. En el Hilton una habitación con vista a la calle cuesta ciento cincuenta dólares...
    a. por año.   b. por mes.   c. por día.

11. No tengo reservación, pero estoy en...
    a. el centro.   b. la lista de espera.   c. el cuarto.

12. La habitación no es barata; es...
    a. cara.   b. libre.   c. sencilla.

13. Ada dice que el hotel tiene...
    a. lugares de interés.   b. servicio de habitación.   c. embajada.

14. El baño tiene ducha y...
    a. elevador.   b. escalera.   c. bañadera.

15. En el baño no hay...
    a. inodoro.   b. jabón.   c. lavabo.

16. El empleado acaba de...
    a. ofrecer.   b. llegar.   c. ser.

Entrevista

ACTIVITY SUGGESTION: See the *IAM* for an additional in-class activity: **Para conocernos mejor.**

With a partner, interview each other by asking the following questions.

1. ¿Cuántas maletas llevas cuando viajas?
2. ¿Llevas cheques de viajero cuando viajas?
3. ¿Siempre llevas tu cámara fotográfica cuando viajas?
4. ¿Qué lugares de interés hay en la ciudad donde vives?
5. ¿A qué hora sirven el desayuno en la cafetería de la universidad?
6. ¿Quieres llevarme a almorzar?
7. ¿Quieres comprar una cámara de video?
8. ¿Prefieres objetos de oro o de plata?
9. ¿Hay alguien en tu cuarto ahora?
10. ¿Tu cuarto tiene baño privado?
11. ¿Usas impermeable cuando llueve?
12. ¿Sabes qué tiempo va a hacer mañana?

SUGGESTION: After students have completed their interviews, have them write a short paragraph based on their partners' responses. They should also try to include several other bits of information that are related to the topic but not included in the exercise.

VIASA
LA LINEA AEREA DE VENEZUELA

Situaciones

SUGGESTION: Suggest that students select one situation and develop a mini-dialogue. Encourage them to include as much related material as possible. Select several pairs to act out their dialogues in front of the class the next day.

What would you say in the following situations? What might the other person say? Act out the scenes with a partner. Take turns playing each role.

1. You have just checked into a hotel. You want to know what time they serve breakfast and whether they have room service.
2. Your friend is going to Alaska in February. Tell him or her what kind of weather to expect.
3. You are talking to the clerk at a tourist office. You need a list of hotels and boarding houses and a list of places of interest right away.
4. You work at an airport tourist office. Some tourists want to get downtown, and you know that they can take either a taxi or a bus.
5. You are a hotel clerk. Someone calls to reserve a single room with a private bathroom, but it is July, and you don't have any. Tell the person you can put his or her name on the waiting list.

¿Qué pasa aquí?   *(What is happening here?)*

In groups of three or four, look at the illustration and make up a story about the people you see. Give them names and say where they are coming from and where they are going. Where are they going to stay? What places of interest are they going to visit?

Para escribir

Complete the following dialogues.

1. *Carlos va a Tijuana.*

CARLOS   —¿Dónde está tu pasaporte?

ROBERTO   —_____

CARLOS   —¡Sí, lo necesitas! ¿No vas a ir a México?

ROBERTO   —_____

CARLOS   —¿Tijuana? ¿Y para eso *(that)* necesitas todas esas maletas?

ROBERTO   —_____

CARLOS   —¡No! ¡No puedo llevarlas al coche!

2. *En el hotel*

TURISTA   —¿Tienen habitaciones?

EMPLEADO   —_____

TURISTA   —No, interior.

EMPLEADO   —_____

TURISTA   —¡Cien dólares por día! ¿Aceptan cheques de viajero?

EMPLEADO   —_____

En la vida real

CD-ROM

Do the interactive exercises on the CD-ROM for additional practice.

Discusión

Four or five students (or more, according to class size) will pretend to own hotels and will make up signs describing accommodations and prices. The rest of the class will discuss the similarities and differences and will decide in pairs or individually where they would like to stay. At the end of this activity each student will explain his or her choice.

A follow-up activity: After staying at the hotel people will have encountered one or more of the following problems:

(no) hay
- **agua caliente**   *hot water*
- **cucarachas**   *cockroaches*
- **frazadas, cobijas**   *blankets*
- **sábanas limpias**   *clean sheets*

no funciona
(it's not working)
- **el aire acondicionado**   *air conditioning*
- **el ascensor, el elevador**   *elevator*
- **la calefacción**   *heater*

FOLLOW-UP: Give each student one "complaint" card from the "suggestion box." The student must respond to the complaint, offering a solution to the problem. Discuss the complaints and solutions in class the next day.

Prepare a list of complaints on a card and drop it in the "suggestion box" (the instructor's desk).

¿Dónde hospedarse?   *(Where shall we stay?)*

Imagine it's the month of August. Say whether these people are going to stay at the **Aloha Puerto Sol** hotel or at the **Atlanterra Sol** hotel. Give reasons for your choice, according to the information provided in the following ads. You should also indicate how much each group will have to pay. Start out by saying, **"Se van a hospedar en... porque..."**

1. La familia Salcedo: el papá, la mamá y dos niños. Jorgito tiene diez años y Alicia tiene ocho. No tienen mucho dinero.
2. Gustavo y Carolina, que son recién casados *(newlyweds)*. Desean ver un espectáculo y bailar. Tienen mucho dinero.
3. Teresa, Raquel y Rebeca, tres muchachas españolas que están viajando juntas. Les gusta jugar *(They like to play)* al tenis y bailar.

ESTANCIAS EN EL HOTEL ALOHA PUERTO SOL****

LE OFRECEMOS:
- Alojamiento en régimen de habitación y desayuno.
- Todas las habitaciones son mini-suites.
- Mini-bar.
- Cesta de fruta en la habitación.
- Botella de vino en la habitación.
- Entrada al Aquapark con 50% de descuento.
- Entrada gratis al Zoo de Fuengirola.
- Programa completo de deportes y animación para adultos y niños (Mini-Club).
- Espectáculos - actuaciones.

ALOHA PUERTO SOL H.D.

Precio por persona y día en habitación doble-habitación y desayuno			SUPL. M.P.	SUPL. P.C SOBRE M.P.	SUPL. INDIV.	DESCUENT 3ª PERSON
01/05 - 15/07 01/10 - 31.10	01 /09 - 30/09	16/07 - 31/06				
3.165	4.060	4.455	1.340	610	1.310	15%
Código 048			IVA NO INCLUIDO			

ESTANCIAS EN EL HOTEL ATLANTERRA SOL****

LE OFRECEMOS:
- Régimen de habitación y desayuno. Habitación doble.
- Cesta de fruta en la habitación.
- Botella de vino en la habitación.
- 1 hora de tenis gratis.
- 1 copa gratis en la discoteca.
- Programa completo de deportes y animación para niños (Mini-Club) y adultos.
- Espectáculos - actuaciones.
- Salida de la habitación a las 14 horas.
- Condiciones especiales en nuestro restaurante grill «Oasis»
- Oferta novios 10%.

ATLANTERRA SOL H.D.

Precio por persona y día en habitación doble-habitación y desayuno			SUPL. M.P.	SUPL. PC. SOBRE M/P.	SUPL. INDIV.	DESCUENT 3ª PERSON
	01/10 - 31/10	16/07 al 30/09				
	4.970	6.495	1.490	1.320	2.295	15%
Desc. niños 2 - 15 años	1° 50% 2° 35%	1° 35% 2° 35%	IVA NO INCLUIDO			
Código 054						

De viaje   *(Traveling)*

FOLLOW-UP: Have students write a travel itinerary for their prospective trip. Instruct them to organize the required information on one page or less and to make one copy for each member of the class. Students should then decide who has planned the most interesting trip, the most expensive, the cheapest, the most relaxing, etc.

Get together with a couple of your classmates and plan a trip to a Spanish-speaking country. Visit a travel agency to obtain brochures of the country you are going to visit. Find out about hotels, rates of exchange, places of interest, and so on. Discuss how and when you will be leaving, how much spending money you'll bring, what cities and special sites you intend to visit, and what you will need to take with you.

Take this test. When you have finished, check your answers in the answer key provided in Appendix E. Then use a red pen to correct any mistakes you may have made. Are you ready?

Lección 4

A. The personal *a*

Form sentences, using the elements provided. Include the personal **a** when necessary.

1. yo / llevar / prima / a / la universidad
2. nosotros / llevar / los refrescos / a / la fiesta
3. ellos / invitar / Julio / y / su novia
4. nosotros / tener / cuatro primos

B. Contractions

Complete the following sentences, using the Spanish equivalent of the words in parentheses.

1. Necesito llamar _____. *(Mr. Estrada)*
2. Yo vengo _____. *(from the club)*
3. ¿Tú vienes _____? *(from the terrace)*
4. Eduardo lleva _____ a la fiesta. *(the girls)*
5. El vaso es _____. *(Mr. Soto's)*

C. Expressions with *tener*

Write the following sentences in Spanish.

1. My classmates are in a hurry.
2. I'm not hungry, but I'm very thirsty.
3. Are you hot? I'm cold!
4. My friends are sleepy.
5. We are not scared.
6. You are right, Miss Peña. Mary is thirty years old.

D. Present indicative of the irregular verbs *ir, dar,* and *estar*

Complete the following sentences, using the present indicative of **ir, dar,** or **estar,** as appropriate.

1. Yo no _____ al baile con mis compañeros.
2. Nosotros _____ una fiesta aquí esta noche.
3. Mi hermana _____ en su casa.
4. ¿Dónde _____ el champán?
5. Las chicas _____ a la fiesta con sus amigos.
6. Tus primos no _____ mucho dinero.
7. Yo _____ cansado.
8. ¿Adónde _____ tus primos?
9. ¿Dónde _____ tú?
10. Yo no _____ mi número de teléfono.

E. *Ir a* + infinitive

Form sentences that tell what *is* or *is not* going to happen. Use the given elements.

> MODELO: mi prima / dar / fiesta / el domingo
> *Mi prima va a dar una fiesta el domingo.*

1. yo / no hablar / con mi mamá / hoy
2. mis hijos / estudiar / en España
3. mi amiga / leer / el libro
4. Uds. / traer / los discos compactos
5. tú / bailar / en la fiesta
6. nosotros / brindar / con sidra

F. Present indicative of *e:ie* stem-changing verbs

Complete the following sentences, using the present indicative of the verbs in the list, as necessary.

entender	cerrar	empezar	preferir
pensar	querer	perder	comenzar

1. Mi primo no _____ beber café.
2. Nosotros no _____ la Lección 2.
3. Ella siempre _____ mucho dinero en Las Vegas.
4. ¿_____ tú la ventana?
5. Las clases _____ hoy.
6. Nosotros _____ a bailar ahora.
7. Yo no _____ trabajar el domingo.
8. Luis y yo _____ beber refrescos.

G. Just words . . .

Choose the word or phrase in parentheses that best completes each sentence.

1. (Invitamos, Brindamos, Bailamos) a nuestros compañeros a la fiesta.
2. Siempre (comemos, empezamos, estamos) doce uvas a la medianoche el día de fin de año.
3. Aquí no beben (sidra, entremeses, pollo).
4. Esta orquesta es muy buena. ¡Es (magnífica, cansada, feliz)!
5. ¡Feliz año (simpático, nuevo, guapo)!
6. No bebo (cocteles, refresco, Coca-Cola) porque yo no tomo bebidas alcohólicas.
7. Aquí todos (bailamos, brindamos, estamos) con champán.
8. Tengo todos los (primos, pollos, discos compactos) de Ricky Martin.

H. Culture

Circle the correct answer, based on the **¿Lo sabía Ud.?** section.

1. En España y en Latinoamérica (existe, no existe) mucha separación entre las generaciones.
2. Además del cumpleaños muchos hispanos celebran su (baile, santo).
3. En algunos países hispanos (existe, no existe) edad mínima para comprar bebidas.
4. En español se dice ("¡Salud!", "¡Santo!") al brindar.

Lección 5

A. Comparative forms

Form sentences, using the elements provided. Use the comparative or the superlative, as necessary.

1. Alfredo / estudiante / más / inteligente / clase
2. la Lección 2 / menos / interesante / la Lección 7
3. mi novia / más / bonita / tu novia
4. Roberto / más / guapo / familia
5. el profesor / tener / menos / veinte estudiantes
6. Ana / tan / alta / Roberto

B. Irregular comparative forms

Complete the following sentences, using regular or irregular comparative forms, as necessary.

1. California es _____ que Maine.
2. El profesor de español habla español _____ que los estudiantes.
3. Eva tiene "A" en español, Roberto tiene "B" y Marisa tiene "F". Eva es la _____ estudiante. Marisa es la _____ estudiante.
4. Yo tengo veinte años y Raquel tiene catorce años. Yo soy _____ que Raquel.
5. Rhode Island es _____ que California.

C. Present indicative of *o:ue* stem-changing verbs

Complete the following sentences, using the present indicative of the verbs in the list, as necessary.

recordar   almorzar   costar
contar   volver   poder

1. ¿Cuánto _____ el libro?
2. Ellos no _____ ir hoy.
3. ¿_____ Ud. cuál es su número de teléfono?
4. Yo _____ de uno a veinte en español.
5. Tengo hambre. ¿A qué hora _____ (nosotros)?
6. ¿Cuándo _____ tú a España?

D. Present progressive

Complete the following sentences, using the present progressive of the verbs in the list, as necessary.

pedir   comer   hablar
leer   decir   dormir

1. Ella _____ que nosotros necesitamos más dinero.
2. Yo _____ con mi abuela.
3. Nosotros _____ un libro.
4. ¿Qué _____ tú? ¿Entremeses?
5. Luis _____ en su cuarto *(room)*.
6. ¿Uds. _____ dinero?

E. Uses of *ser* and *estar*

Form sentences, using the elements provided and the appropriate forms of **ser** or **estar**. Add the necessary connectors.

1. Elsa / mamá / Marta
2. Club Náutico / calle Siete
3. ¡Mmmm! / el pollo / delicioso
4. Roberto / de México / ahora / en California
5. cerveza / fría *(cold)*
6. escritorio / metal
7. hoy / lunes / mañana / martes
8. Elvira / médica
9. fiesta / casa / Alicia
10. orquesta / magnífica
11. ellos / cansados
12. Laura / mexicana

F. Pronouns as objects of prepositions

Complete the following sentences, using the Spanish equivalent of the words in parentheses.

1. La carta es para _____. *(me)*
2. Eduardo está hablando de _____. *(you, fam.)*
3. Hay dos libros para _____. *(them)*
4. Las fotografías son para _____. *(us)*
5. ¿Quieres almorzar _____? *(with me)*
6. Voy a dejar *(to leave)* el cuadro _____. *(with you, fam.)*

G. Just words . . .

Choose the word or phrase in parentheses that best completes each sentence.

1. El hijo de mi hija es mi (yerno, nieto, cuñado).
2. Vamos a ver (los cumpleaños, las pinturas, a la abuela) de Picasso en el museo.
3. Tengo que escribir muchas (medicinas, cartas, pensiones) este fin de semana.
4. ¿Quieres (extrañar, llover, almorzar) con él hoy?
5. ¿Tú (asistes, echas de menos, viajas) mucho a tu familia?
6. ¿No vamos a tener oportunidad de practicar el español? (¡Qué famoso!, ¡Qué lástima!, ¡Qué pequeño!)
7. Ellos quieren viajar en ómnibus; nunca (conducen su auto, comen en este restaurante, hablan francés) en Madrid.
8. ¿Quieres ver algunas (bebidas, fotos, cintas) de mi novia? ¡Es la chica más bonita del mundo!
9. Elba va a (mirar, asistir, viajar) a Madrid.
10. No es alto. Es de estatura (mayor, interesante, mediana).

H. Culture

Read the following statements and circle **V** (Verdadero) or **F** (Falso), based on the
¿Lo sabía Ud.? section.

V   F   1. La Universidad de Salamanca es una de las más famosas del mundo.
V   F   2. Sólo *(Only)* los españoles pueden estudiar en la Universidad de
            Salamanca.
V   F   3. En el Museo del Prado sólo hay cuadros de pintores españoles.
V   F   4. La mayoría de las universidades de los países hispanos no tienen
            residencias universitarias.
V   F   5. En los países hispanos la fecha se escribe con el día antes del mes.

Lección 6

A. Present indicative of *e:i* stem-changing verbs

Give the Spanish equivalent of the following sentences.

1. At the Mexico Restaurant they serve dinner at nine.
2. She requests a room overlooking the street.
3. We follow the bellboy to the room.
4. Are you *(pl.)* getting reservations in December?
5. I'm saying (I say) that he must sign the register now.

B. Affirmative and negative expressions

Change the following sentences to the affirmative.

1. Ellos no van a querer nada.
2. No hay nadie en el baño.
3. No tengo ningún objeto de oro y plata.
4. Ellos nunca pasan por la aduana.
5. Yo tampoco ceno a las nueve.
6. Jamás tiene las listas de los hoteles.
7. No puedes ir ni a la derecha ni a la izquierda.
8. Ellos nunca quieren nada tampoco.

C. Verbs with irregular first-person forms

Complete the following sentences with the present indicative of the verbs in the
list, as needed.

traducir	hacer	conocer	saber	salir
poner	caber	ver	traer	conducir

1. Yo _____ un Ford modelo 1998.
2. Yo no _____ dónde está el hotel.
3. Yo no _____ en este taxi. ¡Hay ocho personas!
4. Yo siempre _____ de la oficina a las cinco de la tarde.
5. Yo _____ las lecciones del inglés al portugués.
6. Yo no _____ los pasaportes. ¿Dónde están?

7. Yo no _____ nada los domingos.
8. Yo no _____ las llaves allí.
9. Yo no _____ Lima.
10. Yo _____ a mi amigo al aeropuerto.

D. *Saber* vs. *conocer*

Complete the following sentences with **saber** or **conocer.**

1. Yo _____ que él no quiere ir.
2. Ester no _____ a mi sobrina, pero ella _____ dónde vive.
3. Peter _____ España, pero él no _____ hablar español.
4. Ellos no _____ los poemas de memoria *(by heart).*

E. Direct object pronouns

Complete the following sentences with the Spanish equivalent of the words in parentheses.

1. ¿El libro? No quiero _____. Es muy caro.   *(to buy it)*
2. Yo _____ más tarde, Anita.   *(call you)*
3. ¿La cena? Ellos _____ a las siete.   *(serve it)*
4. ¿Los pasaportes? Rita _____.   *(has them)*
5. Mamá no _____ al baile.   *(take me)*
6. ¿Las toallas? Yo no _____.   *(need them)*
7. Yo tengo cheques de viajero, pero ellos no _____.   *(accept them)*
8. Yo no puedo _____, Sr. Vega.   *(to take you)*
9. Ellos quieren las cámaras fotográficas pero yo no _____.   *(have them)*
10. Nosotros no podemos _____, Srta. Roca.   *(to call you)*

F. Weather expressions

Complete the following sentences appropriately.

1. Necesito un paraguas. _____ mucho.
2. ¿No te vas a poner el abrigo? ¡Brrr! ¡_____!
3. ¡No necesito abrigo! ¡Hace _____!
4. En Alaska _____ mucho en el invierno.
5. Necesitas el sombrero. Hoy _____.
6. No quiero vivir en Oregón porque allí llueve mucho, y no me gusta la _____.

G. Just words . . .

Choose the correct response to each question or statement.

1. ¿Son caras las habitaciones en los hoteles del centro?
   a. No, son de oro y de plata.   b. No, son baratas.
   c. No, están en el segundo piso.

2. ¿Dónde vas a conseguir la lista de hoteles?
   a. En la oficina de turismo.   b. En el baño.   c. En un restaurante.

3. ¿Qué documentos debo mostrar?
   a. Veinte dólares.   b. El pasaporte.   c. El ascensor.

4. ¿A cómo está el cambio de moneda?
   a. No sé; voy a comprarlo.   b. No sé; voy a visitarlo.
   c. No sé; voy a averiguarlo.

5. ¿El baño tiene ducha?
   a. Sí, y desayuno.   b. Sí, y bañadera.   c. Sí, y elevador.

6. Necesitamos una habitación doble y dos habitaciones sencillas.
   a. No tenemos ningún cuarto libre.
   b. Hay pocas habitaciones modernas.   c. No hay piscina.

7. ¿Dónde trabaja el botones?
   a. En el autobús.   b. En la aduana.   c. En el hotel.

8. El cuarto con vista a la calle es muy caro.
   a. ¿Quiere una habitación interior?
   b. El ascensor está a la izquierda.
   c. No hay muchas oficinas de turismo por aquí.

9. ¿Qué desea, señorita?
   a. Una habitación sencilla con baño privado.
   b. El ómnibus está a la derecha.   c. No hay objetos de oro.

10. ¿No puedes ir a México?
    a. No, voy a confirmar la información.
    b. No, voy a cancelar las reservaciones.
    c. No soy de México; soy de Guatemala.

11. ¿Tienen jabón?
    a. Están en la embajada norteamericana.
    b. Sí, tenemos uno con vista a la calle.
    c. Sí, pero no tenemos toallas.

12. ¿Están Uds. en la lista de espera?
    a. Tengo una lista de los lugares de interés.
    b. El botones tiene la lista.
    c. No, nosotros tenemos reservaciones.

H. Culture

Circle the correct answer, based on the **¿Lo sabía Ud.?** section.

1. Lima, la capital de (Chile, Perú), es una ciudad de contrastes.
2. El (35%, 25%) de la población de Lima es de origen indígena.
3. La moneda más usada por los latinoamericanos cuando viajan es el (dólar, peso).
4. Es (fácil, difícil) cambiar dólares en los bancos hispanoamericanos.

3. España (II)

España

- España es un país que se distingue en la pintura y en la música. Algunos de los pintores más famosos del mundo son españoles: el Greco, Velázquez, Picasso, Miró y Dalí. En la música Andrés Segovia y Pablo Casals, entre otros, tienen fama internacional.

- Entre los deportes *(sports)* más populares de España están el fútbol, el ciclismo, el baloncesto *(basketball)* y, en el País Vasco, el jai alai.

- El día siete de julio se celebra en Pamplona la fiesta de San Fermín. Ese día sueltan los toros *(turn the bulls loose)* y la gente corre delante de *(in front of)* ellos hasta llegar a la plaza de toros para la corrida.

Saboreando *(tasting)* unas tapas en un bar de Málaga.
Las tapas son pequeñas porciones de diferentes comidas
típicas de España. Generalmente las tapas se sirven en los
bares por la tarde.
¿Cuáles son algunas comidas típicas de su país?

Juan Carlos I de Borbón, rey *(king)* de España, aparece aquí con la Reina Sofía y con el primer ministro de gobierno, el líder José María Aznar.

¿Quién es el presidente (o primer ministro) de su país?

La Fundación Joan Miró está en el Parque de Montjuïc de Barcelona, junto a un edificio diseñado por el arquitecto catalán Josep Lluís Sert. Aquí está el Centro de Estudio de Artes Contemporáneas, establecido por Miró. La fundación contiene muchas de las pinturas y esculturas del gran artista.

¿Quiénes son sus pintores favoritos?

La procesión de la Semana Santa, en Sevilla, es la más famosa de las procesiones religiosas en España. Todos los años, mientras miles de españoles caminan por las calles detrás de la imagen de Jesucristo, turistas de todo el mundo contemplan el espectáculo.

¿Qué fiestas religiosas se celebran en su país?

Enrique Iglesias es uno de los cantantes españoles más famosos del mundo. Iglesias ha vendido *(has sold)* más de cien millones de discos, y ha recibido el premio Grammy como el mejor cantante de música popular en español.

¿Conoce Ud. alguna canción en español? ¿Cuál es?

Una pareja come paella, un plato típico de España, preparado con arroz *(rice)* y mariscos *(shellfish)* y otras carnes. La preparación de la paella varía de región a región, pero la más famosa es la paella valenciana.

¿Cuáles son sus platos favoritos?

El Ballet Real aparece aquí en los jardines del Generalife, en Granada. El repertorio del Ballet Real incluye bailes clásicos y folklóricos. Aquí vemos una representación del baile flamenco, típico del sur de España.

¿Qué tipo de baile prefiere Ud.: clásico, moderno o folklórico?

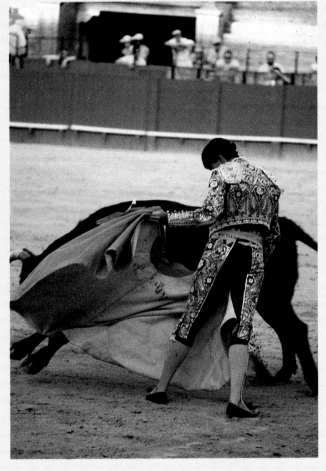

La corrida de toros tiene orígenes antiquísimos y es uno de los espectáculos más populares de España. Las corridas generalmente tienen lugar *(take place)* los domingos por la tarde en estadios especiales llamados plazas de toros, de las cuales hay más de 400 en España.

¿Quiere Ud. ver una corrida de toros algún día?

TELEINFORME

VIDEO

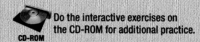
CD-ROM

Do the interactive exercises on
the CD-ROM for additional practice.

Preparación

NOTE: The video-related vocabulary is listed in the *Instructor's Activities Manual* for your reference. Its purpose is to facilitate students' comprehension.

NOTE: See the Instructor's Edition frontmatter for additional suggestions on implementing video in the classroom.

SUGGESTION: Have students read the *Panorama hispánico* segment of the textbook and do the *Preparación* activities in small groups before viewing the video segments.

¿Cuánto saben Uds. ya? After reading **Panorama hispánico 3,** get together in groups of three or four students and answer the following questions with the appropriate information.

1. ¿Cuáles son los deportes más populares de España?
2. ¿Qué son las tapas y cuándo se comen?
3. Durante la primavera, ¿qué fiesta religiosa se celebra en España con procesiones?
4. ¿Cuál es un plato típico de España?
5. ¿Qué baile es típico del sur de España?
6. ¿Cuál es uno de los espectáculos más populares de España?

SUGGESTION: Ask students what they might already know about Spain and share it with the class.

Comprensión

SUGGESTION: The *Comprensión* sections are organized by individual video clip to provide greater flexibility in lesson planning. Have students complete each exercise after viewing the corresponding video clip and have them compare their answers in pairs or groups.

SUGGESTION: Have students locate the provinces of Spain mentioned in the video on the map on the inside front cover of their textbook. Also have them locate Madrid, Sevilla, and Córdoba.

SUGGESTION: Point out that *musulmán, moro, islámico,* and *árabe* all refer to the Arab or Moorish influences on Spain.

A. España: País de contrastes. Read the following statements. After watching the video, circle **V** (**Verdadero**) or **F** (**Falso**), according to what you understood. If the statement is false, correct it.

V F 1. España forma parte de la Península Ibérica.
V F 2. El acueducto, un símbolo de la presencia romana en España, está en Sevilla.
V F 3. La invasión de los musulmanes fue decisiva en la historia de España.
V F 4. En Sevilla, Córdoba y Granada hay muchos ejemplos del arte islámico.
V F 5. El Monasterio del Escorial está cerca de Ávila.

B. Sevilla. Select the word or phrase that best completes each statement according to what you understood in the video.

1. Sevilla es la principal ciudad de (España, Andalucía).
2. (La Giralda, La Torre del Oro) es parte de una mezquita *(mosque)* demolida.
3. (La Torre del Oro, La Catedral de Sevilla) es un edificio de la época musulmana.
4. (La Giralda, El Alcázar) representa la fusión de las civilizaciones musulmana y cristiana.
5. La Plaza de España fue construida para (las Olimpiadas, Exposición Iberoamericana).
6. Se cree que el flamenco fue traído *(was brought)* por (los gitanos, los musulmanes).

Ampliación

A. **Madrid y Sevilla.** Review the video segment about Madrid *(Panorama hispánico 2)* and compare it to the segment on Sevilla *(Panorama hispánico 3).* Work in groups of three or four students to make a list of comparisons and contrasts between what you have learned about these two Spanish cities. Share your observations with the rest of the class.

B. **Dos culturas.** With a partner, describe a typical dance or custom from your area, town, state, or country that might compare to *el flamenco de Andalucía.* Try to research the custom's origin and its importance to the region's culture. Share your observations with the rest of the class.

Hablando de las vacaciones

OBJECTIVES

Pronunciation
The Spanish **ll** and **ñ**

Structure
Demonstrative adjectives and pronouns • Indirect object pronouns • Constructions with **gustar** • Time expressions with **hacer** • Preterit of regular verbs

Communication
You will learn vocabulary related to travel.

Hablando de las vacaciones

**STUDENT
AUDIO**

SUGGESTION: Before presenting the
dialogue, encourage students to read
the title and the introduction, and then
to brainstorm to generate topics that
they think Teresa might include in her
discussion of her vacation in Peru. List
their suggestions on the board.

**Transportación, Lugares visita-
dos, Descripción de Perú,** etc.

SUGGESTION: Refer students to
Panorama hispánico 7 and the
corresponding Video Segment for
more information about Peru.

*Teresa llegó ayer de su viaje a Perú y ahora está hablando por teléfono
con su amiga Silvia. Hace media hora que las chicas están charlando y
Teresa le está contando de su viaje.*

TERESA —Me gustó mucho la capital, pero me gustó más Machu
Picchu.

SILVIA —¡Y no me mandaste una tarjeta postal!

TERESA —Te compré dos, pero no las mandé. Oye, tengo que devolverte
la maleta y el bolso de mano que me prestaste.

SILVIA —No hay apuro. ¿Llevaste mucho equipaje?

TERESA —Sí, llevé tres maletas. Pagué exceso de equipaje.

SILVIA —¿Cuánto te costó el pasaje? ¿Viajaste en primera clase?

TERESA —¿Estás loca? Viajé en clase turista. ¡Y me costó tres mil
quinientos pesos![1] Ida y vuelta, claro…

SILVIA —¿Qué tal el vuelo?

TERESA —Un poco largo… Y como el avión salió con dos horas de
retraso, llegamos muy tarde.

SILVIA —¿Te pasó algo interesante en Lima?

TERESA —Bueno… en la agencia de viajes donde compré el pasaje para
Machu Picchu, conocí a un muchacho[2] muy simpático.

SILVIA —¿Viajó contigo? Tienes que contarme todo lo que pasó.

TERESA —Sí, viajé con él en avión a Cuzco, donde almorzamos juntos.
Después, conversamos durante todo el viaje en tren a Machu
Picchu.

SILVIA —No sé por qué tus vacaciones siempre son magníficas y mis
vacaciones son tan aburridas.

TERESA —Pues la próxima vez tenemos que viajar juntas.

SILVIA —Bueno, pero sólo si vamos en tren o en barco. A mí no me
gusta viajar en avión.

TERESA —Bueno, viajamos en tren. Oye, este sábado voy al cine con
Cecilia, ¿quieres ir con nosotras?

SILVIA —¿Quién es Cecilia?

TERESA —Es la chica que te presenté en la biblioteca el mes pasado.

SILVIA —Ah, ésa… ya recuerdo. Sí, vamos juntas.

TERESA —¿Quieres ir a almorzar conmigo ahora?

SILVIA —No, gracias, ya almorcé.

TERESA —Bueno, entonces nos vemos mañana.

---

[1]Mexican currency.
[2]Note that **muchacho(-a)** can be used familiarly to refer to men and women under thirty.

Vocabulario

Nombres

la agencia de viajes travel agency
el avión plane
el barco boat, ship
el bolso de mano carry-on bag
el cine movie theater, movies
la clase turista tourist class
el equipaje luggage

la hora hour
el pasaje, el billete *(Spain)* ticket (for plane, train, or bus)
　_____ **de ida** one-way ticket
　_____ **de ida y vuelta** round-trip ticket
　_____ **de primera clase** first-class ticket

el retraso, atraso delay
la tarjeta card
　_____ **postal** postcard
el tren train
la vez time (occasion)
el vuelo flight

SUGGESTION: Use Transparencies 26 and 27 to review modes of transportation and present the vocabulary.

Verbos

conocer to meet (for the first time)
contar (o:ue) to tell
devolver (o:ue) to return (something)

gustar to like, to be pleasing to
mandar, enviar to send
pagar to pay
pasar to happen

presentar to introduce
prestar to lend

Adjetivos

juntos(-as) together
largo(-a) long
loco(-a) crazy

pasado(-a) last
próximo(-a) next

Otras palabras y expresiones

ayer yesterday
bueno, bien okay, fine
claro, por supuesto of course
como since
de about
después then
durante during
ése(-a) that one
el mes pasado last month

exceso de equipaje excess baggage
la próxima vez next time
llegar tarde[1] to be late
media hora half an hour
No hay apuro., No hay prisa. There's no hurry.
primera clase first class
pues then

¿Qué tal...? How was (is) . . . ?
sólo only
tarde late
todo all
todo el viaje the whole trip
todo lo que pasó everything that happened
ya now

---

[1]**llegar temprano** to be early

Vocabulario adicional
En el aeropuerto

la puerta de salida
la tarjeta de embarque
el turista
la viajera

la sección de fumar
la sección de no fumar
el asiento de ventanilla
el asiento de pasillo
el auxiliar de vuelo
la azafata

De viaje *(traveling)*

el (la) **agente de viajes** travel agent	El **agente de viajes** me vendió los pasajes.
¡Buen viaje! Have a nice trip!	¡Adiós, Marisa! **¡Buen viaje!**
la **entrada** entrance	¿Dónde está la **entrada** al aeropuerto?
la **salida** exit	Aquella puerta no es la entrada; es la **salida**.
tener… de retraso (atraso) to be . . . behind schedule	El avión **tiene dos horas de retraso**.

ACTIVITY SUGGESTION: See the *IAM* for an additional in-class activity: **Encuentra las respuestas.**

EXPANSION: As a homework assignment, after students have read and discussed the dialogue, have them write what Teresa would have written if she had sent a postcard to Silvia.

¡Conversemos!

Answer the following questions, basing your answers on the dialogue.

1. ¿Hace una hora que Teresa y Silvia hablan por teléfono?
2. ¿De qué le está contando Teresa a su amiga?
3. ¿Qué le gustó más a Teresa, Machu Picchu o Lima?
4. ¿Qué le prestó Silvia a Teresa para el viaje?
5. ¿Pagó Teresa exceso de equipaje? ¿Por qué?
6. ¿Cuánto le costó a Teresa el pasaje?
7. ¿Viajó Teresa a Cuzco en avión o en tren?

8. ¿Con cuántas horas de retraso salió el avión?
9. ¿Las vacaciones de Teresa son magníficas o aburridas?
10. ¿Cómo van a viajar Teresa y Silvia la próxima vez?
11. ¿Adónde va Teresa este sábado? ¿Con quiénes va?
12. ¿Cuál de las chicas ya almorzó?

¿Lo sabía Ud.?

Cuzco, situado a más de diez mil pies de altura en los Andes peruanos, es la antigua capital del imperio de los incas. Hoy día, la ciudad es un gran centro turístico y artístico.

Machu Picchu, conocida también como "la ciudad perdida de los incas", está situada en la cordillera de los Andes a unos ciento diez kilómetros al noroeste *(northwest)* de Cuzco. El imperio de los incas se extendió desde el sur *(south)* de Colombia hasta el norte de Chile y Argentina.

• ¿Qué lugares turísticos hay en su ciudad?

• ¿Qué cordillera de este país es una continuación de la Cordillera de los Andes?

• ¿Qué civilizaciones indígenas existieron en este país?

Mercado de artesanías cerca de Cuzco, Perú.

See the *¿Cómo se dice...?* Web site for activities on authentic cultural material: http://spanish.college.hmco.com/students
INTERNET

Pronunciación

A The Spanish ll

STUDENT AUDIO

SUGGESTION: Model each word and have the class repeat the sounds and words chorally and individually. Then have students repeat the following sentences for additional pronunciation practice using words in context.

In most countries, the Spanish ll has a sound similar to the *y* in the English word *yes*. Listen to your instructor and repeat the following words.

calle	cuchillo	llave	botella
llevar	llegar	pollo	platillo

B The Spanish ñ

ll: El gallego llega a la ventanilla.
Allí se llaman sellos o
estampillas.
ñ: La señora Peña come piña por
la mañana.
Enrique va a estudiar español
en España.

The Spanish **ñ** is similar to the *ny* in the English word *canyon*. Listen to your instructor and repeat the following words.

español	niño	mañana	España
señor	señorita	otoño	año

Estructuras

1 Demonstrative adjectives and pronouns *(Los adjetivos y los pronombres demostrativos)*

SUGGESTION: Draw figures on the board to demonstrate the uses of **este, ese,** and **aquel.** Point out the differences between the demonstrative adjectives by using arrows or dotted lines.

SUGGESTION: Use Transparency 24 and ask students to describe what the people are doing, using the appropriate demonstrative adjectives and pronouns.

S1—Este chico está cantando.
S2—Ese estudiante está jugando a las cartas.

A. Demonstrative adjectives

■ Demonstrative adjectives point out persons or things. Like all other adjectives, they agree in gender and number with the nouns they modify. The forms of the demonstrative adjectives are as follows.

Masculine		Feminine		
Singular	Plural	Singular	Plural	
este	estos	esta	estas	*this, these*
ese	esos	esa	esas	*that, those*
aquel	aquellos	aquella	aquellas	*that, those* (at a distance in space or time)

—¿Qué necesitas?
—Necesito **esta** pluma, **ese** cuaderno y **aquellos** libros.

"*What do you need?*"
"*I need this pen, that notebook, and those books* (over there)."

B. Demonstrative pronouns

■ The forms of the demonstrative pronouns are as follows.

Masculine		Feminine		Neuter	
Singular	Plural	Singular	Plural		
éste	éstos	ésta	éstas	esto	*this* (one), *these*
ése	ésos	ésa	ésas	eso	*that* (one), *those*
aquél	aquéllos	aquélla	aquéllas	aquello	*that* (one), *those* (at a distance)

—¿Quieres este jabón o **ése**?

"*Do you want this soap or that one?*"

—No quiero ni **éste** ni **ése**; quiero **aquél.**

"*I don't want this one or that one; I want that one over there.*"

SUGGESTION: Emphasize that the plural of **este** is **estos,** and that **estos** is not the plural of **esto.**

■ The masculine and feminine demonstrative pronouns are the same as the demonstrative adjectives, except that they have a written accent.

■ Each demonstrative pronoun has a neuter form. They are **esto, eso,** and **aquello.** The neuter forms, which do not change in number or gender, are used to refer to situations, ideas, and nonspecific objects or things, equivalent to the English *this, that matter; this, that business;* and *this, that stuff.*

—¿Entiendes **eso**?
—No, no lo entiendo.

"*Do you understand that?*"
"*No, I don't understand it.*"

—¿Qué es **esto**?
—No sé...

"*What's this?*"
"*I don't know . . .*"

práctica ●●●

FOLLOW-UP A: Have students work in pairs and discuss classroom objects using the appropriate demonstrative adjectives and pronouns. Encourage them to review the use of comparatives and superlatives in **Lección 5.**

S1—Este libro es más interesante que ése pero aquél es el más interesante.

A. Change the demonstrative adjectives according to the gender and number of the nouns, to talk about what is needed.

1. Yo necesito *esta* lista, _____ mesas, _____ reloj y _____ cuadros.
2. Eva necesita *ese* escritorio, _____ silla, _____ libros y _____ llaves.
3. Nosotros necesitamos *aquella* maleta, _____ billete, _____ toallas y _____ bolsos de mano.

FOLLOW-UP B: Use Transparency 28 for additional practice of demonstrative adjectives.

B. Complete the following sentences according to the cue given.

1. Firmo este registro y _____ *(that one over there)*.
2. Quiero estos lápices y _____ *(those)*.
3. Necesito esta llave y _____ *(that one over there)*.
4. Voy a comprar esta toalla y _____ *(those)*.
5. No quiero esas maletas; quiero _____ *(these)*.
6. No voy a comer en ese restaurante. Voy a comer en _____ *(this one)*.

FOLLOW-UP C: Have students request items from their classmates seated on the other side of the room. The classmates should be encouraged to ask questions in order to be sure that the item requested is the item they have received.

S1—Quiero ese libro.
S2—¿Quieres este libro azul o el rojo?
S1—Quiero el rojo.

C. With a partner, use demonstrative adjectives to describe people or objects that are at varying distances from you.

1. sus cuadernos
2. la pizarra
3. las ventanas
4. la puerta

5. los coches en la calle
6. las chicas que están en la cafetería
7. los libros del profesor
8. su pluma (o lápiz)

---

2 Indirect object pronouns   *(Pronombres usados como complemento indirecto)*

■ In addition to a subject and a direct object, a sentence may have an indirect object.

Él **te** da **el libro.**   *He gives you the book.*
 I.O.   D.O.   I.O.   D.O.

■ An indirect object describes *to whom* or *for whom* an action is done. An indirect object pronoun can be used in place of an indirect object. In Spanish, the indirect object pronoun includes the meaning *to* or *for*: **Yo *les* mando los libros (a los estudiantes).**

■ The forms of the indirect object pronouns are as follows. Notice that the indirect object pronouns are the same as the direct object pronouns, except in the third person.

SUGGESTION: Review the forms of the direct object pronouns. Make sure students know the difference between a direct object and an indirect object by using the following example.

Él la llama "Anita".   [direct]
He calls her "Anita."
Él le escribe una   [indirect]
carta a Anita. *He writes a letter to Anita.*

	Singular		Plural
me	*(to, for) me*	**nos**	*(to, for) us*
te	*(to, for) you* (fam.)	**os**	*(to, for) you* (fam.)
le	*(to, for) you* (form.) *(to, for) him* *(to, for) her*	**les**	*(to, for) you* (form.) *(to, for) them* (masc., fem.)

■ Indirect object pronouns are usually placed in front of the conjugated verb.

—¿Qué **te** dice tu papá en la
    tarjeta?   *"What does your Dad say to you
                                        in the postcard?"*
—**Me** dice que viene por unos   *"He tells me (says to me) that he
    días.   is coming for a few days."*

—En qué idioma **les** hablan sus   *"In what language do your parents
    padres a ustedes?   speak to you?"*
—Ellos **nos** hablan en español.   *"They speak to us in Spanish."*

NOTE: Avoid using constructions that present direct and indirect object pronouns in the same sentence. This concept will be presented in **Lección 8.**

■ In sentences with a conjugated verb followed by an infinitive, the indirect object pronoun may either be placed in front of the conjugated verb or be attached to the infinitive.

Le quiero dar dinero.   }
    Quiero dar**le** dinero.   }   *I want to give him money.*

■ When used in sentences with the present progressive, an indirect object pronoun may either be placed in front of the conjugated verb or be attached to the present participle.

Nos está diciendo   que viene hoy.   }   *He is telling us that*
    Está diciéndo**nos**[1] que viene hoy.   }   *he is coming today.*

SUGGESTION: Have students practice the indirect object construction by giving objects to other members of the class while making a brief statement about the object given and the person who is to receive it. Remind them that they should use the preposition **a** and the student's name.

S1—Yo le doy el libro a Tomás.
S2—Yo les doy los papeles a Paul y a Ana.
S3—Yo te doy el lápiz a ti.

ATENCIÓN   The indirect object pronouns **le** and **les** sometimes require clarification when the person to whom they refer is not specified. Spanish provides clarification (or emphasis) by using the preposition **a** + *personal pronoun or noun.*

Le doy el pasaje.   *I am giving the ticket . . .*
                                        (to him? to her? to you?)
but: **Le** doy el pasaje **a ella.**   *I am giving the ticket to her.*

Note, however, that the prepositional phrase is optional, while the indirect object pronoun must always be used.

Le traigo un libro **a Roberto.**   *I am bringing a book to Roberto.*
¿**Les** vas a dar el dinero **a ellas?** *Are you going to give the money to them?*

---

[1]When an indirect object pronoun is attached to a present participle, an accent mark is added to maintain the correct stress.

práctica •

A. You are in an airport waiting for a friend to arrive and you overhear some people making the following comments. Complete their sentences with the appropriate indirect object pronoun.

1. _____ dan los billetes. (a nosotros)
2. _____ doy el bolso de mano. (a ellos)
3. _____ doy la maleta. (a él)
4. _____ doy los cheques de viajero. (a ella)
5. _____ traigo la tarjeta de embarque. (a Uds.)
6. _____ piden el pasaporte. (a ella)
7. _____ traigo el equipaje. (a ti)
8. _____ traen el periódico. (a él)
9. _____ decimos "gracias". (a ellos)
10. _____ dan las bebidas. (a mí)

B. Add the appropriate indirect object pronouns to the following dialogues, and then act them out with a partner.

1. —¿ _____ vas a prestar tus maletas a David?
   —No, porque él nunca _____ devuelve nada.
   —Pero él _____ presta sus libros a ti...
2. —¿ _____ vas a escribir una carta a tus padres, Rosita?
   —No, voy a mandar _____ una tarjeta postal.
3. —¿Su hermana _____ va a traer los cheques de viajero esta tarde, señorita Paz?
   —Sí, y yo _____ voy a dar mil dólares a ella.
4. —¿Qué _____ vas a traer a Sergio y a mí, tía Isabel?
   —_____ voy a traer dos cámaras fotográficas.
   —¿Y a Elsa?
   —A ella voy a traer _____ una cámara de video.

C. The following people are going on a trip and need certain items. Say who is going to give, bring, or buy the things they need.

> **MODELO:** Oscar necesita un mapa.
> *El papá de Oscar le va a traer (comprar, dar) el mapa.*

tu mamá ✓	el amigo de... ✓	mi hermano ✓
nuestros amigos ✓	el papá de... ✓	la abuela de... ✓
los chicos	el novio de... ✓	su esposo(-a)

1. Yo necesito las maletas.
2. Teresa necesita cheques de viajero.
3. Tú necesitas un bolso de mano.
4. Ana y yo necesitamos una tarjeta de crédito.
5. Carlos necesita una cámara de video.
6. Los chicos necesitan una cámara fotográfica.
7. Olga y Pedro necesitan dinero.
8. Ud. necesita una tarjeta postal.

D. You are going on a trip to Miami to visit your aunt and uncle. Discuss with a classmate what you are doing now and what you are going to do once you get there.

1. ¿Les estás escribiendo a tus tíos de la Florida?
2. ¿Qué les estás diciendo?
3. ¿Qué les vas a llevar a tus tíos?
4. ¿Tu papá te va a dar su cámara fotográfica?
5. ¿Nos vas a escribir desde *(from)* Miami?
6. ¿Me vas a dejar la llave de tu casa?
7. ¿Qué les vas a traer a tus padres?
8. ¿Qué me vas a traer a mí?

E. You are going on a trip. Say what you are going to bring the following people as souvenirs.

1. a tu mamá
2. a tus hermanos
3. a mí *(use tú form)*
4. a tu mejor amigo(-a)
5. a Carlos y a mí

3 Constructions with **gustar**   *(Construcciones con gustar)*

■ The verb **gustar** means *to like* (literally, *to be pleasing to*). **Gustar** is always used with an indirect object pronoun (**me** in the following example).

Me gusta tu casa.	*I like your house.*
I.O. V. S.	S. V. D.O.
	Your house is pleasing to me.
	S. V. I.O.

SUGGESTION: Write a short sentence builder on the board and have students make up sentences that describe what they, their friends, and their families like and don't like. Remind them to include things that are not on the list.

A mí / A ti / A mi madre, padre / A mis amigos(-as) / A (Tomás) / A los estudiantes / A nosotros

me / te / le(s) / nos

gusta(n)

estudiar / los discos de... / viajar a... / las vacaciones / hablar por teléfono con... / el champán / los exámenes

■ The two most commonly used forms of **gustar** are the third-person singular form, **gusta**, used if the subject is singular or if **gustar** is followed by one or more infinitives; and the third-person plural form, **gustan**, used if the subject is plural.

Indirect object pronouns

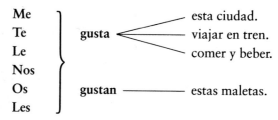

SUGGESTION: Introduce **encantar, interesar, molestar, quedar,** and **faltar** at this point. Explain that these verbs follow the same sentence pattern as **gustar,** and write several sample sentences on the board.

Me interesa mucho la política.
Te molesta tomar exámenes largos.
Le falta un año para terminar.
Nos encanta el pollo.
Les quedan dos meses de vacaciones.

Then ask students the following personalized questions or write them on the board and have students interview each other.

1. **¿Te interesa mucho la política?**
2. **¿Te molesta tomar exámenes largos?**
3. **¿Qué te encanta de la universidad?**
4. **¿Qué te molesta?**
5. **¿Cuántos años te faltan para terminar tus estudios?**
6. **¿Te interesa tomar más cursos de español? ¿Cuántos?**
7. **¿Cuántos minutos de clase nos quedan?**

■ Note that the verb **gustar** agrees with the *subject* of the sentence—that is, with the person or thing being liked.

Me gust**a Lima.**	*I like Lima.*
No me gust**an los vuelos** largos.	*I don't like long flights.*

ATENCIÓN   When what is liked is an activity, **gustar** is followed by the infinitive.

Me gust**a hablar** por teléfono.	*I like to talk (talking) on the phone.*

■ The person who does the liking is the indirect object.

Me gustan los cuadros de Picasso.
I.O.

—¿**Te** gusta San Diego?	*"Do you like San Diego?"*
—Sí, **me** gusta mucho San Diego, pero **me** gusta más San Francisco.	*"Yes, I like San Diego very much, but I like San Francisco better."*
—**A Eva le** gusta Santa Bárbara y **a nosotros nos** gusta Reno.	*"Eva likes Santa Barbara and we like Reno."*

ATENCIÓN   Note that the words **mucho** and **más** (better) immediately follow **gustar**.

■ The preposition **a** + *noun or pronoun* may be used to emphasize or specify the name of the person referred to by the indirect object pronoun.

A Eva (**A ella**) le gusta el pollo y **a mí** me gusta la ensalada.	*Eva (She) likes chicken and I like salad.*

práctica •

A. Rewrite the following sentences, using constructions with **gustar**.

> **MODELO:** Yo prefiero San Diego.
> *A mí me gusta más San Diego.*

1. Yo prefiero las ciudades grandes.
2. ¿Tú prefieres el bolso de mano azul?
3. Nosotros preferimos viajar en barco.
4. Marcelo prefiere los hoteles pequeños.
5. Ellos prefieren pasar las vacaciones en México.
6. ¿Ud. prefiere viajar en tren o en avión?
7. Adela prefiere los asientos de ventanilla.
8. ¿Uds. prefieren la comida italiana?

ESPAÑA ESPECTACULAR
10 DIAS/9 NOCHES
DESDE
$1,198⁰⁰
POR PERSONA EN HAB. DOBLE
FECHA DE SALIDA
22 de julio y 7 de octubre
VISITA:
MADRID, CORDOBA, TORREMOLINOS, SEVILLA, GRANADA, TOLEDO.

24

FOLLOW-UP B: Have students describe what the various people depicted in Transparency 24 enjoy doing. Encourage them to use **gustar** + *noun* as well as **gustar** + *verb* constructions in their descriptions.

A la mujer le gusta viajar.
Al chico le gusta la música.
A la niña le gustan las novelas de aventuras.

B. Interview a classmate to find out what the following members of his or her family like and don't like to do on weekends. When you have finished, switch roles.

> MODELO: —A tu hermana, ¿qué le gusta hacer? ¿Qué no le gusta hacer?
> —*A mi hermana le gusta ir a bailar. No le gusta trabajar.*

1. A ti
2. A tus hermanos
3. A tu padre
4. A Uds.
5. A tus primos

C. Interview a classmate, using the following questions. When you have finished, switch roles.

1. ¿Dónde te gusta pasar tus vacaciones?
2. ¿Te gustan más las ciudades grandes o las ciudades pequeñas?
3. ¿Te gusta más viajar en tren o en avión?
4. ¿Qué les gusta hacer a tus amigos los fines de semana?
5. ¿A Uds. les gusta bailar? ¿cantar?
6. ¿A tu mejor amiga le gustan las canciones de Enrique Iglesias?
7. ¿Qué estación del año te gusta más?
8. ¿Qué te gusta hacer cuando llueve?

D. With a classmate, prepare four questions to ask your instructor about his or her likes and dislikes.

E. Compare your likes and dislikes with those of two classmates. Consider your tastes in food, music, weekend activities, classes, and travel.

4   Time expressions with **hacer**   *(Expresiones de tiempo con el verbo hacer)*

SUGGESTION: Write the following sentences on the board and instruct students to complete them orally or in writing.

1. **Hace un año que yo...**
2. **Hace dos días que yo...**
3. **Hace cinco años que yo...**
4. **Hace siete meses que yo...**

■ English uses the present perfect progressive or the present perfect tense to express how long something has been going on.

> *I have been living here for twenty years.*

■ Spanish uses the following construction.

> **Hace** + *length of time* + **que** + *verb* (in the present tense)
> Hace   veinte años   que   vivo aquí.

—¿**Cuánto tiempo hace que** Ud. estudia español?	*"How long have you been studying Spanish?"*
—**Hace** tres meses **que** estudio español.	*"I have been studying Spanish for three months."*
—¿Tienes mucha hambre?	*"Are you very hungry?"*
—¡Sí! **Hace** ocho horas **que** no como.	*"Yes! I haven't eaten for eight hours."*

ATENCIÓN   To ask how long something has been going on, use the expression ¿**Cuánto tiempo hace que...?**

práctica ....

A. Tell how long each action depicted below has been going on. Use **hace... que** and the length of time specified.

1. veinte minutos

2. tres años

3. una hora

4. dos horas

5. siete horas

6. quince días

EXPANSION B: Have students interview three other members of the class and write down their responses. As a follow-up activity, have them report their findings orally or in a short paragraph.

B. Interview a classmate, using the following questions and two questions of your own. When you have finished, switch roles.

1. ¿Cuánto tiempo hace que vives en la misma *(same)* casa?
2. ¿Cuánto tiempo hace que estudias aquí?

3. ¿Cuánto tiempo hace que trabajas en esta ciudad?
4. ¿Cuánto tiempo hace que hablas español?
5. ¿Cuánto tiempo hace que no comes?
6. ¿Cuánto tiempo hace que no ves a tus padres?
7. ¿Cuánto tiempo hace que conoces a tu mejor amigo(-a)?
8. ¿Cuánto tiempo hace que no tienes vacaciones?

FOLLOW-UP C: Have groups take turns asking you one question until all of each group's questions have been asked.

C. In groups of three, prepare six questions to ask your instructor, using time expressions with **hacer.** You may want to use the verb **enseñar** *(to teach)* in your questions.

5 Preterit of regular verbs   *(Pretérito de verbos regulares)*

SUGGESTION: Write the following sentence builder on the board and ask students to form at least ten original sentences.

Ayer / La semana pasada / El año pasado / Anoche / Esta mañana / El viernes pasado

yo / tú / él / ella / nosotros / Ud. / el profesor / mi amigo(-a)

escribirle una tarjeta postal a... / beber... / viajar a... / llegar a clase a la(s)... / leer... / empezar a estudiar a la(s)... / charlar con... / trabajar en... / estudiar en... / salir con... / vender...

You should also give students practice in interrogative and negative sentences to stress the absence of any structural equivalent to the English auxiliary *did.* Ask them the following personalized questions or have students interview each other in pairs.

1. ¿Quién te escribió la semana pasada?
2. ¿Dónde pasaste tus vacaciones el año pasado?
3. ¿Cuánto costó tu libro de español?
4. ¿A quién le pediste dinero?
5. ¿Qué celebraste el mes pasado?
6. ¿Comiste en un restaurante la semana pasada?
7. ¿A quién llamaste por teléfono?
8. ¿Con quién saliste el sábado pasado?
9. ¿A qué hora cerraron la biblioteca anoche?

■ Spanish has two simple past tenses: the preterit and the imperfect. (The imperfect tense will be studied in **Lección 10.**) The preterit tense is used to refer to actions or states that the speaker views as completed in the past.

■ The preterit of regular verbs is formed as follows. Note that the endings for the **-er** and **-ir** verbs are the same.

-ar *verbs*	-er *verbs*	-ir *verbs*
tomar *to take*	**comer** *to eat*	**escribir** *to write*
tomé	comí	escribí
tomaste	comiste	escribiste
tomó	comió	escribió
tomamos	comimos	escribimos
tomasteis	comisteis	escribisteis
tomaron	comieron	escribieron

—¿**Hablaste** con Silvia ayer?
—Sí, **comimos** juntas en la cafetería.
—¿Le **escribió** Roberto?
—Sí, **recibió** una tarjeta de él ayer.

"*Did you speak with Silvia yesterday?*"
"*Yes, we ate together in the cafeteria.*"
"*Did Roberto write to her?*"
"*Yes, she received a card from him yesterday.*"

■ The first-person plural of **-ar** and **-ir** verbs is identical to the present tense forms.

—¿A qué hora **salieron** Uds.?
—**Salimos** de casa a las seis y no **llegamos** hasta las siete.

"*What time did you leave?*"
"*We left home at six, and we didn't arrive until seven.*"

■ Verbs ending in **-gar, -car,** and **-zar** change **g** to **gu, c** to **qu,** and **z** to **c** before **-é** in the first-person singular of the preterit: **pagar → pagué; buscar** *(to look for)* **→ busqué; empezar → empecé.**

—¿A qué hora **llegaste** al hospital?
—**Llegué** a las ocho y **empecé** a trabajar.

"*What time did you arrive at the hospital?*"
"*I arrived at eight and I started to work.*"

■ Certain -er and -ir verbs with the stem ending in a vowel change i to y in the third-person singular and plural endings: **leer → leyó, leyeron; creer → creyó, creyeron.**

> Él lo **leyó** en el periódico, pero no lo **creyó.**

■ Verbs of the -ar and -er groups that are stem-changing in the present indicative are regular in the preterit.

> Rosa **volvió** a las seis y **cerró** las puertas.   *Rosa returned at six o'clock and closed the doors.*

■ Spanish has no equivalent for the English word *did* used as an auxiliary verb in questions and negative sentences.

> —¿Encontraste el billete?   *"Did you find the ticket?"*
> —No lo busqué.   *"I didn't look for it."*

práctica ●●●

FOLLOW-UP A: Have students describe what the people in Transparency 29 did yesterday.

ACTIVITY SUGGESTION: See the *IAM* for an additional in-class activity: **De compras.**

A. Complete the following dialogues, using the verbs given. Then act them out with a partner.

1. hablar / hablar / llamar / charlar
   —¿Tú _____ por teléfono con tus suegros ayer?
   —Sí, _____ con ellos. Los _____ por la mañana y _____ hasta las once.

2. volver / volver / volver / volver
   —¿A qué hora _____ Uds.?
   —Yo _____ a las cuatro y Mario _____ a las seis. ¿A qué hora _____ tú?
   —A las siete.

3. recibir / mandar / recibir
   —¿_____ (tú) las tarjetas que yo te _____?
   —No, no las _____.

4. llegar / llegar / comenzar
   —¿A qué hora _____ Ud., señorita?
   —_____ a las nueve y _____ a trabajar a las nueve y media.

5. cerrar / cerrar / abrir
   —¿_____ Uds. las puertas?
   —Sí, _____ las puertas y _____ las ventanas.

B. Say what you and your friends did yesterday.

1. ¿Qué comió Ud. ayer?
2. ¿Qué bebió Ud.?
3. ¿Estudiaron Uds. español anoche *(last night)*?
4. ¿A qué hora salió Ud. de su casa?
5. ¿A qué hora llegó Ud. a su primera clase?
6. ¿Trabajaron ayer sus amigos?
7. ¿Dónde almorzó su mejor amigo(-a)?
8. ¿A qué hora volvió Ud. a su casa?
9. ¿Leyó el periódico?
10. ¿A qué hora cenó Ud.?

C. With a partner, use the verbs listed to ask each other what you did yesterday and last night (**anoche**).

> MODELO: —¿Dónde almorzaste ayer?
> —*Almorcé en la cafetería.*

almorzar	leer	practicar
cenar	llegar	salir
cerrar	mandar	trabajar
conversar	mirar	ver
devolver	pagar	buscar
escribir		

ACTIVITY SUGGESTION: See the *IAM* for an additional in-class activity: **De viaje.**

¡A ver cuánto aprendió!

INTERNET

See the *¿Cómo se dice...?* Web site for additional grammar and vocabulary practice: http://spanish.college. hmco.com/students

¡Repase el vocabulario!

Complete the following sentences with words from the lesson vocabulary.

1. No me gusta viajar en la _____ de fumar.
2. No es la entrada; es la _____.
3. Le voy a _____ a Teresa las maletas que me prestó.
4. ¿Quiere un _____ de ventanilla o de pasillo?
5. Le tengo que dar la tarjeta de _____ a la _____ de vuelo.
6. Si vas a tomar el _____ a las ocho, tienes que estar en el aeropuerto a las siete.
7. Como Ana y Elsa viajan _____, conversan durante _____ el viaje.
8. —¿Qué _____ el vuelo?
   —Un _____ largo.
9. Los viajeros llegaron tarde; llegaron con dos horas de _____.
10. —Roberto, ¿le vas a prestar mil dólares para ir a Las Vegas?
    —¡¿Estás _____?!
11. Yo les deseé _____ viaje a los turistas.
12. Compré un pasaje de ida y _____.
13. Le voy a enviar una _____ postal.
14. ¿Tienes seis maletas? ¡Vas a pagar exceso de _____!
15. Elsa, te quiero _____ a mi amigo Roberto Fuentes.

ACTIVITY SUGGESTION: Do **¡Escucha!**, the in-class listening comprehension activity that reviews vocabulary and grammar structures introduced in the lesson. It appears in the answer key of the *IAM*.

ACTIVITY SUGGESTION: See the *IAM* for an additional in-class activity: **Palabras escondidas.**

Entrevista

With a partner, interview each other, using the following questions.

1. ¿Adónde te gusta ir cuando tienes vacaciones?
2. ¿Te gusta más viajar en avión o en tren? ¿Por qué?
3. ¿Viajas en primera clase o en clase turista?
4. Cuando viajas, ¿les mandas tarjetas postales a tus amigos?

ACTIVITY SUGGESTION: See the *IAM* for additional in-class activities: **Para conocernos mejor** and **Una encuesta.**

5. ¿Llevas mucho equipaje cuando viajas?
6. ¿Conociste a alguien interesante en tus vacaciones? (¿A quién?)
7. ¿Tus vacaciones son magníficas o aburridas?
8. ¿Adónde vas a ir de vacaciones la próxima vez? ¿Vas a ir con tu familia?
9. Cuando viajas, ¿les traes algo a tus amigos?
10. ¿Viajaste el verano pasado? ¿Adónde?

Situaciones

SUGGESTION: Select several students to present their dialogues to the class the next day.

What would you say in the following situations? What might the other person say? Act out the scenes with a partner. Take turns playing each role.

1. You are checking in for a flight at the airport. The airline representative wants to know how many suitcases you have. You are not sure whether you can take your carry-on bag on the plane.
2. You are seeing a friend off at the airport.
3. A friend has borrowed your suitcase. You want to know when he or she plans to return it to you, because you are going on a trip. Arrange to see your friend tomorrow at noon.
4. You are in a travel agency. You want to buy a round-trip ticket to Bogotá. Ask for a seat assignment.

Para escribir

Write a short composition about the people in the photo. Tell who they are, what their relationship to each other is, where they went last summer, what they did, and also what they plan to do next summer.

En la vida real

CD-ROM

Do the interactive exercises on the CD-ROM for additional practice.

En una agencia de viajes

You and a classmate will play the roles of a travel agent and a tourist. Discuss the following.

- ticket prices according to destination and different kinds of transportation
- prices for first class or tourist class, one-way or round-trip
- flight schedules
- seat reservations
- how much luggage can be taken

Planes para un viaje

You are helping some friends plan a trip. With a classmate, study the ad and answer your friends' questions.

Caribe   Asómese al paraíso . . .   República Dominicana

SALIDAS EN AVION LINEA REGULAR DE IBERIA, DIRECTO A SANTO DOMINGO, TODOS LOS JUEVES Y VIERNES

PRECIOS POR PERSONA EN HABITACION DOBLE Y REGIMEN DE MEDIA PENSION

TEMPORADAS	7 NOCHES	14 NOCHES
Mayo y 1 al 21 de Junio	114.900	137.800
22 al 30 de Junio	125.900	148.800
Julio y Septiembre	137.500	165.000
Agosto	142.900	176.400
Octubre	131.500	159.000
Noviembre y Diciembre (1 al 12)	132.900	161.800

Suplemento Habitación Individual: Consultar al efectuar la reserva.
LOS PRECIOS INCLUYEN: Avión línea regular clase turista ida y vuelta. Traslados aeropuerto/hotel/aeropuerto. Estancia en habitación doble en régimen de Media Pensión (Hotel Bávaro Casino).

OFERTA VALIDA PARA SALIDAS Y REGRESOS DESDE MADRID.

1. ¿A qué país vamos a viajar?
2. ¿En qué clase viajamos?
3. ¿En qué hotel vamos a estar?
4. Queremos viajar en julio. ¿Cuánto tenemos que pagar (en pesetas) por una semana? ¿Y por dos semanas?
5. ¿El precio incluye el traslado *(transportation)* del aeropuerto al hotel y del hotel al aeropuerto?

6. ¿De qué ciudad salen los vuelos?
7. ¿Qué días de la semana salen los vuelos?

¿Adónde vamos?

You and a friend have won a radio contest. The prize is $5,000 to spend on a dream vacation. With a classmate, decide where you will go, how long you will be away, where you will stay, and what you will need to take with you.

¡VAMOS A LEER!

Antes de leer

As you read Teresa's letter, find the answers to the following questions.

1. ¿Son buenas amigas Teresa y Ángela? ¿Cómo lo sabe Ud.?
2. ¿Teresa está de vacaciones todavía?
3. ¿Qué dice Teresa de las ruinas de Machu Picchu?
4. ¿A quién le mandó Teresa tarjetas postales?
5. ¿Cómo se llama el muchacho a quien Teresa conoció en Lima? ¿De dónde es?
6. ¿De qué conversaron Teresa y el muchacho?
7. ¿Qué dice Teresa de los peruanos?
8. ¿Adónde la llevaron los amigos de su padre?
9. ¿Qué le recomienda Teresa a Ángela?
10. ¿Adónde va a ir Teresa? ¿Por qué?

Una carta de Teresa

12 de septiembre de 2002

Querida Ángela:

Hace mucho tiempo que no te escribo, pero siempre pienso en ti. Ya estoy de vuelta° de mi viaje a Perú. Me gustó todo, pero especialmente Machu Picchu, las famosas ruinas de los incas, que son muy interesantes. Ya sé que no te mandé tarjetas postales, pero tampoco le mandé ninguna a nadie.

    En Lima conocí a un muchacho argentino muy simpático y muy educado. Se llama José Luis Vera Vierci. Conversamos mucho, de todo tema° imaginable. Me mandó una tarjeta desde Buenos Aires, donde él vive.

    Los peruanos son encantadores.° Me trataron° muy bien. Los amigos de mi padre me llevaron a muchos lugares, especialmente al teatro, al cine y... ¡a restaurantes! La comida es muy buena, tan buena que aumenté° dos kilos.

    Bueno, para tus próximas vacaciones, te recomiendo una visita a Perú. Y ahora te dejo porque voy a ir a cenar con mis padres. Hoy es el cumpleaños de papá.

    Te extraño mucho. Saludos a Sandra y a Marcelo.

Un abrazo,

Teresa

estoy... *I'm back*

topic

charming / they treated

I gained

Díganos

Answer the following questions, based on your own thoughts and feelings.

1. ¿Cuánto tiempo hace que Ud. no le escribe a su mejor amigo(-a)?
2. ¿A quién le manda Ud. tarjetas postales cuando va de vacaciones?
3. ¿Qué lugares interesantes visitó Ud. el verano pasado?
4. ¿Conoció Ud. a alguien simpático(-a) durante sus vacaciones?
5. Cuando Ud. conversa con sus amigos, ¿de qué temas hablan Uds.?
6. Cuando Ud. visita a sus amigos, ¿adónde lo (la) llevan?
7. ¿Qué me recomienda Ud. para mis próximas vacaciones?
8. ¿Cuándo es el cumpleaños de su papá? ¿Y de su mamá?

ASÍ SOMOS

  VIDEO   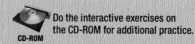 CD-ROM   Do the interactive exercises on the CD-ROM for additional practice.

NARRADORA	—¿Qué países conoce Ud.?
ÁNGELA	—Conozco Estados Unidos,... Perú, Venezuela, Ecuador,... México. Em... Conozco Europa, pues conozco Francia, Italia, España, Canadá.

SUGGESTION: In groups, have students make a list of the activities they see people doing at the beginning of the video.

Preparación

NOTE: The video-related vocabulary is listed in the *Instructor's Activities Manual* for your reference. Its purpose is to facilitate students' comprehension. You may want to distribute the vocabulary to the class before viewing.

NOTE: See the Instructor's Edition frontmatter for additional suggestions on implementing video in the classroom.

A. **Vamos a viajar.** With a partner, answer the following questions based on your own information. You will hear answers to these same questions when you watch the video. After viewing the video, compare your answers with those you hear.

1. ¿A Ud. le gusta viajar?
2. ¿Qué países conoce Ud.?
3. ¿Qué lugar le gustó más?
4. ¿Cómo pasó Ud. las vacaciones este año?

SUGGESTION: Have students locate on a map all the countries and cities mentioned on the video. Have them try to guess these countries: **Grecia, Suiza, Irlanda,** and **Turquia.**

B. Durante las vacaciones. List the different activities you might do while on a summer vacation and while on a winter vacation. Share the lists with the rest of the class.

Comprensión

A. ¿Verdadero o falso? Read the following statements. Circle **V** (**Verdadero**) or **F** (**Falso**) according to what you understood from the video. If a statement is false, correct it.

V F   1. A Tamara le encanta viajar.
V F   2. Pablo piensa que viajar es muy interesante.
V F   3. A Pablo y a Juan les gusta viajar.
V F   4. A Ángela le gusta mucho viajar.
V F   5. A Gustavo le gusta viajar bastante.

EXPANSION: Have students list the countries (or cities, states) they have visited. Have students list any Spanish-speaking places they have visited.

B. ¿Qué países conocen estas personas? Select the word or phrase that best completes each statement, according to what you understood from the video.

1. Ángela conoce (Europa, Asia).
2. Gustavo vivió en (Brasil, Estados Unidos).
3. Leonardo (conoce, no conoce) algunos países de Europa.
4. Tamara (conoce, no conoce) muchos países.

C. ¿Quién lo dijo? Match each statement with the name of the person who said it.

A	B
_____ 1. Buenos Aires es una ciudad increíble.	a. Pablo
_____ 2. Me fascinó el Medio Oriente.	b. Leonardo
_____ 3. Me gustaron los Estados Unidos y Canadá.	c. Ángela
_____ 4. De todos los países, me gusta el mío, España.	d. Gustavo

D. ¿Verdadero o falso? Read the following statements. Circle **V** (**Verdadero**) or **F** (**Falso**) according to what you understood from the video. If a statement is false, correct it.

V F   1. Tamara pasó *(spent)* sus vacaciones en Puerto Rico.
V F   2. John visitó a sus parientes *(relatives)* en los Estados Unidos.
V F   3. La casa de Zaida está en Bogotá, Colombia.
V F   4. Pablo pasó sus vacaciones con sus amigos.

FOLLOW-UP: After viewing the *Entrevista* segment, have students discuss the advantages and disadvantages of being an airline pilot.

E. Entrevista *(Interview)*. Watch the video segment called *Entrevista* at the end of Lesson 7. Answer the following questions according to what you understood from the interview.

1. ¿Qué profesión tiene Manuel Ticó?
2. ¿Cuál es su nacionalidad?
3. ¿Qué oportunidades tiene él en su trabajo?
4. ¿Cuáles son los países que conoce Manuel?
5. ¿A Manuel le gusta su trabajo?
6. ¿Tiene él una rutina en su trabajo?

Ampliación

EXPANSION: Do a class survey to find out what countries students most want to visit.

A. ¿Adónde quiere viajar? With a partner, make a list of the countries you have visited and the countries you would like to visit. Share the list with the rest of the class and determine which countries have been visited the most and which countries students would most like to visit.

EXPANSION: Have students work in pairs or small groups to plan a vacation of their dreams.

B. De vacaciones. Interview a classmate about a memorable vacation he or she has had. Include information about where you went, what activities you enjoyed, and what you learned on this vacation. Then exchange roles.

En un restaurante cubano

OBJECTIVES

Pronunciation
The Spanish **l, r, rr,** and **z**

Structure
Direct and indirect object pronouns used together • Preterit of **ser, ir,** and **dar** • Preterit of **e:i** and **o:u** stem-changing verbs • Uses of **por** and **para** • Ordinal numbers

Communication
You will learn vocabulary related to restaurant menus, ordering meals at a restaurant, and paying the bill.

En un restaurante cubano

STUDENT
AUDIO

Hoy es el primero de diciembre. Es el aniversario de bodas de Lidia y Jorge Torres y para celebrarlo van a cenar a uno de los mejores restaurantes de Miami. Ahora llegan al restaurante El Caribe.

LIDIA —¡Qué sorpresa! ¡Éste es un restaurante muy elegante!

JORGE —Y la comida es excelente.

MOZO —Por aquí, por favor. Aquí está el menú.

LIDIA —Gracias. *(Lee el menú.)*

PARA LA CENA

(Todos los platos de la lista se sirven con la sopa del día y ensalada.)

Pescados y mariscos

Langosta	$18.00	Trucha	$11.50
Salmón	$14.50	Camarones	$11.00

Carne

Albóndigas	$ 6.00	Pavo relleno	$10.00
Bistec	$12.00	Pollo frito	$ 8.50
Cordero	$13.00	Arroz con pollo	$ 6.00
Lechón asado	$17.00		

SUGGESTION: Have students act out the dialogue in groups of three.

SUGGESTION: Have students work in groups of three to familiarize themselves with the vocabulary by role-playing a waiter and customers in a restaurant. Have them use the menu on page 190 to practice ordering a complete meal. Encourage students to ask for recommendations or suggestions. You may write specific phrases on the board to aid in communication.

¿Qué desean comer? or **¿En qué puedo servirles?**
Para comer (para beber, de postre) deseamos…
¿Qué recomienda Ud.?

SUGGESTION: Refer students to **Panorama hispánico 1** and the corresponding video segment for information about Miami.

JORGE —¿Por qué no pides un filete? Aquí preparan unos filetes muy ricos. ¿O langosta?

LIDIA —No, anoche fui a la cena de los Ruiz y sirvieron langosta.

MOZO —Les recomiendo la especialidad de la casa: lechón asado y arroz con frijoles negros. De postre, helado, flan o torta helada.

JORGE —Yo quiero lechón asado y arroz con frijoles negros. ¿Y tú?

LIDIA —Yo quiero sopa, camarones y arroz.

JORGE —Para tomar tráiganos un vermut y después media botella de vino tinto.

MOZO —Muy bien, señor. *(Anota el pedido.)*

Antes de cenar, Lidia y Jorge toman vermut y conversan.

LIDIA —¿Tus padres fueron a la fiesta que dio Eva ayer?

JORGE —Sí, fue en el club Los Violines.

LIDIA —¿Le dieron el regalo que compraron para ella en México?

JORGE —¿La pulsera? Sí, se la dieron. Le encantó.

LIDIA —¿Te la enseñaron antes de dársela?

JORGE —Sí, me la enseñaron cuando fui por ellos anteayer por la tarde.

LIDIA —La consiguieron a muy buen precio en una tienda muy elegante.

Después de comer, Lidia y Jorge beben café. Jorge pide la cuenta, la paga, le deja una buena propina al mozo y salen. Tienen entradas para ir a ver una comedia y, como llueve a cántaros y el teatro queda lejos, toman un taxi.

JORGE —Feliz aniversario, mi amor. *(Le da un beso.)*

LIDIA —*(Lo abraza.)* Feliz aniversario, querido.

Vocabulario

Cognados

el **aniversario** anniversary
la **comedia** comedy
cubano(-a) Cuban
elegante elegant

la **especialidad** specialty
excelente excellent
la **lista** list, menu
el **menú** menu

el **salmón** salmon
la **sorpresa** surprise
el **teatro** theater
el **vermut** vermouth

Nombres

las **albóndigas** meatballs
el **amor** love
el **arroz** rice
el **arroz con pollo** chicken and rice
el **beso** kiss
el **bistec** steak
la **botella** bottle
los **camarones** shrimp
la **carne** meat
la **comida** food, meal
el **cordero** lamb

la **cuenta** bill
la **entrada, el boleto** ticket (i.e., for a show)
el **filete** tenderloin steak
el **flan** caramel custard
los **frijoles** beans
el **helado** ice cream[1]
la **langosta** lobster
el **lechón** pork
los **mariscos** shellfish
el **mozo, camarero**[2] waiter
el **pavo** turkey

el **pedido** order
el **pescado** fish
el **plato** dish
el **postre** dessert
el **precio** price
la **propina** tip
la **pulsera** bracelet
el **regalo** present, gift
la **sopa** soup[1]
la **tienda** store
la **torta helada** ice cream cake
la **trucha** trout

RELATED VOCABULARY: **la carta** *(menu);* **las gambas** *(shrimp/Spain);* **el mantecado** *(ice cream/Mexico, Puerto Rico)*

Verbos

abrazar to hug
anotar to write down
dejar to leave (behind)

encantar[3] to love, to like very much
pedir (e:i) to order

quedar to be located
recomendar (e:ie) to recommend
tomar to drink

Adjetivos

asado(-a) roasted
frito(-a) fried
helado(-a) iced, ice cold

medio(-a) half
relleno(-a) stuffed

rico(-a), sabroso(-a) tasty, delicious
tinto red (wine)

Otras palabras y expresiones

aniversario de bodas wedding anniversary
anoche last night
anteayer the day before yesterday
de postre for dessert

después de after
lejos far
llover (o:ue) a cántaros to rain cats and dogs, to pour down raining
mi amor my love, my darling

por aquí this way
¡Qué sorpresa! What a surprise!
querido(-a) dear, darling
se sirven are served
tráiganos bring us

---

[1]In Spanish, the verb **tomar** is used often with **helado** and **sopa.**
[2]**La camarera** means waitress.
[3]**Encantar** uses the same structure as **gustar:** Le **encantó** la pulsera.

Vocabulario adicional

SUGGESTION: Bring sample menus from other Hispanic countries to class and compare the types of dishes offered. Another good source for menus might be restaurants serving Hispanic food in your local area.

ACTIVITY SUGGESTION: See the *IAM* for an additional in-class activity: **Preferencias.**

RESTAURANTE EL CARIBE
ESPECIALIDAD EN CARNES Y MARISCOS

Menú

PARA EL ALMUERZO

Sándwich de pollo	$3.50	Papas fritas (French fries)	$1.00
Sándwich de jamón y queso (ham and cheese)	$2.50	Tortilla a la española (Omelette)	$2.50
Sándwich de huevo (egg)	$1.50	Tortilla mexicana	$ .50
Sopa del día	$2.00	Frijoles	$1.75
Ensalada	$3.50	Arroz	$1.80
Hamburguesa[1]	$2.50	Arroz con frijoles negros	$2.00

PARA LA CENA
(Todos los platos de la lista se sirven con la sopa del día y ensalada.)

Pescados y mariscos

Langosta	$18.00	Trucha	$11.50
Salmón	$14.50	Camarones	$11.00

Carne

Albóndigas	$ 6.00	Pavo relleno	$10.00
Bistec	$12.00	Pollo frito	$ 8.50
Cordero	$13.00	Arroz con pollo	$ 6.00
Lechón asado	$17.00		

POSTRES

Arroz con leche (Rice pudding)	$2.00	Helado	$1.50
		Frutas[1]	$1.25
Torta de chocolate[1]	$2.50	Queso	$3.00
Flan con crema	$2.50		

BEBIDAS

Agua mineral	$1.00	Café	$ .80
Cerveza	$3.00	Té[1]	$ .80
Champán	$6.00	Chocolate caliente (Hot chocolate)	$1.20
Vino blanco	$3.50		
Vino tinto	$3.50	Jugo de frutas (Fruit juice)	$1.50
Vermut	$3.50		
		Leche fría (Cold milk)	$1.20

---

[1]All these words are cognates, so you can guess what they mean.

Para poner la mesa *(To set the table)*

SUGGESTION: Use Transparency 31 to present the new vocabulary. Have students describe what they see in the illustration.

SUGGESTION: Bring in a place setting and have students tell you or another student how to set the table. Write a list of useful prepositions on the board as a review before beginning this activity. Hold up each item and ask the class where it should be placed.

▮—¿Dónde debo poner el tenedor?
S1—Ud. debe poner el tenedor al lado del plato.
▮—¿Qué hago con la servilleta?
S2—La servilleta va al lado del tenedor.

el vaso
el plato
las copas
la taza
la pimienta
el platillo
la sal
la servilleta
la cuchara
el tenedor
el cuchillo
la cucharita
el mantel
los cubiertos

ACTIVITY SUGGESTION: See the *IAM* for an additional in-class activity: **Vamos a poner la mesa.**

¡Conversemos!

EXPANSION: In pairs, have students simulate a telephone conversation in which a friend of Lidia and Jorge describes the anniversary celebration to another friend. Remind students that in order to simulate a real conversation, they should expand upon the information given and ask questions to clarify what they don't understand.

Answer the following questions, basing your answers on the dialogue.

1. ¿Cuándo es el aniversario de bodas de Lidia y Jorge?
2. ¿Qué dice Lidia del restaurante? ¿Y qué dice Jorge de la comida?
3. ¿Cuál es la especialidad de la casa?
4. ¿Qué pide Lidia? ¿Qué pide Jorge?
5. ¿Qué beben Lidia y Jorge?
6. ¿Adónde fueron los padres de Jorge ayer?
7. ¿Qué regalo compraron para Eva?
8. ¿Cuándo le enseñaron la pulsera a Jorge?
9. ¿La consiguieron a buen precio?
10. ¿Qué deja Jorge para el mozo?
11. ¿Qué dicen Jorge y Lidia al salir del restaurante?
12. ¿Por qué tienen que tomar un taxi para ir al teatro?

Lila's Restaurant

El Restaurant de la Familia

**EL BISTEC
CON PAPITAS FRITAS
MAS DELICIOSO DE MIAMI**

¿Lo sabía Ud.?

La ciudad de Miami en el estado de la Florida es uno de los centros turísticos más importantes del mundo. Cientos de miles de turistas latinoamericanos la visitan todos los años. Más de un millón de hispanos viven en Miami, en su mayoría cubanos. El español se usa tanto en Miami que en muchos lugares hay letreros *(signs)* que dicen *"English spoken here."*

En los países de habla hispana, el café se sirve después del postre, nunca durante la comida. Generalmente es café tipo expreso, y se sirve en tazas muy pequeñas.

Después de comer, los hispanos generalmente se quedan sentados *(remain seated)* alrededor de la mesa y conversan. A esto se le llama "hacer la sobremesa."

En los países de habla hispana, la propina que generalmente se ofrece en los restaurantes es del 10%, pero hay variación según el país y el tipo de restaurante. Con frecuencia la propina está incluida en la cuenta.

• ¿En qué otras ciudades de los Estados Unidos hay muchas personas de origen latinoamericano?

Cubanos en un café de la Pequeña Habana en Miami, Florida.

• ¿Se bebe mucho café en este país? ¿Qué tipo de café es muy popular ahora?

• Generalmente, ¿cuánto se deja de propina en este país?

 INTERNET See the *¿Cómo se dice...?* Web site for activities on authentic cultural material: http://spanish.college.hmco.com/students

Pronunciación

A The Spanish l

 STUDENT AUDIO

l: El ladrón está en la cárcel de Lima.
La luz de la luna alumbra el lago.

The Spanish l is pronounced like the *l* in the English word *lean*. The tip of the tongue must touch the palate. Listen to your instructor and repeat the following words.

langosta	Silvia	sólo
loco	helado	filete
capital	él	plato

SUGGESTION: Model each word and have the class repeat the sounds and words chorally and individually. Then have students repeat the following sentences for additional pronunciation practice using words in context.

B The Spanish r

r: Lo barato es caro y lo caro es barato.
Aurora estudia historia y literatura en Argentina.

The Spanish **r** sounds something like the *dd* in the English word *ladder*. Listen to your instructor and repeat the following words.

teatro	hora	tarde
dejar	Teresa	cordero
frijoles	primero	postre

C The Spanish rr (spelled r at the beginning of words and rr between vowels)

rr: Julia Reyes quiere recoger un paquete en el correo.
El muchacho rubio fuma cigarrillos rusos.

The Spanish **rr** is a strong trill. Listen to your instructor and pronounce the following words.

aburrido	Rosa	Reyes
rico	arroz	Roberto
recomendar	Raúl	relleno

D The Spanish z

z: La azucena simboliza la pureza.
Zulema tiene un lápiz azul.

In Latin America the Spanish **z** is pronounced like the *ss* in the English word *pressing*. In Spain it is pronounced like the *th* in the English word *think*. Avoid using the buzzing sound of the English *z* in the words *zoo* and *zebra*. Listen to your instructor and repeat the following words.

pizarra	vez	Pérez
Zulema	zoológico	taza
lápiz	mozo	azul

Estructuras

1 Direct and indirect object pronouns used together   *(Pronombres de complemento directo e indirecto usados juntos)*

SUGGESTION: Review the direct and indirect objects presented in **Lecciones 6** and **7.** Write the following on the board.

He gives it to me. (**el libro**)
Él me lo da.

Emphasize the possible combinations:

me
te
nos
se
} + lo, la
los, las

■ When an indirect object pronoun and a direct object pronoun are used together, the indirect object pronoun always comes first.

D.O.

Ana me da la maleta.   Ana me la da.

I.O.

■ With an infinitive, the pronouns can either be placed before the conjugated verb or be attached to the infinitive.

I.O. D.O.
Ana me la va a dar.

Ana   va a dármela.¹

SUGGESTION: Ask several students to exchange personal articles. Then ask each student, "¿**Quién te prestó el libro (la mochila, el lápiz,** etc.)?" The student should reply using the correct direct and indirect object pronouns. Then ask another student who loaned what to whom.

I—*(to María)* ¿Quién te prestó el libro?
S1—José me lo prestó.
I—¿Quién le prestó el libro a María?
S2—José se lo prestó.

■ With the present progressive, the pronouns can either be placed before the conjugated verb or be attached to the gerund.

I.O. D.O.
Ella te lo   está diciendo.

Ella   está diciéndotelo.¹

■ If both pronouns begin with **l**, the indirect object pronoun (**le** or **les**) is changed to **se**.

D.O.

Ana le da la cuenta.   Ana se la da.

I.O.

For clarification, it is sometimes necessary to add **a él, a ella, a Ud., a Uds., a ellos,** or **a ellas.**

—¿A quién le da la cuenta Ana?
—**Se la** da **a él.**

¹Note the use of the written accent, which follows the rules for accentuation. See Appendix A.

práctica ....

A. Complete the following dialogues, using direct and indirect object pronouns. Then act them out with a partner, adding a sentence or two to each dialogue.

1. —¿*Le* dejaste *la propina* al mozo?
   —Sí, ___*se*___ _____ dejé en la mesa.
2. —¿*Me* compraste *las entradas* para el teatro?
   —No, no ___*te*___ _____ compré. Lo siento.
3. —¿El mozo *te* sirvió *el café?*
   —Sí, ___*me*___ _____ sirvió.
4. —¿*Le* vas a dar *la pulsera* a tu madre?
   —Sí, ___*se*___ _____ voy a dar mañana.
5. —¿*Nos* va a traer *los postres* ahora?
   —Sí, ___*se*___ _____ voy a traer ahora.
6. —¿El mozo *les* va a traer a Uds. *la cuenta?*
   —Sí, va a traér ___*nos*___ en seguida.

EXPANSION B: Ask students to make a list of ten things they need or want. Using the verbs in this exercise, the other members of the class will tell them who will buy, lend, give, bring, or send them the items requested. You may want to review the **ir** + **a** + *infinitive* structure before you begin this activity.

S1—Yo necesito una maleta.
S2—Tu padre te la va a traer.
S3—Yo quiero un lápiz.
S4—Yo te lo voy a prestar.

B. You have a friend who is always willing to help others. Explain how, using the information provided.

> MODELO: Yo necesito *una maleta.* (comprar)
> *Mi amigo **me la** compra.*

1. *Yo* necesito *dos tarjetas postales.*   (comprar)
2. *Tú* necesitas *los discos compactos.*   (traer)
3. *Nosotros* queremos *frutas.*   (servir)
4. *Elsa* necesita *un bolso de mano.*   (prestar)
5. *Mis hermanos* necesitan *dinero.*   (dar)
6. *Mi prima* necesita *las maletas.*   (traer)
7. *Ud.* necesita *la cinta.*   (enviar)
8. *Yo* quiero *los libros.*   (dar)

EXPANSION C1: Have students do this activity in groups of three. Each student should answer two questions as a cranky person.

S1—¿Vas a mandarme el dinero?
S2—No, no voy a mandártelo.

EXPANSION C2: As an expansion activity for more advanced students, have students respond to the initial question and then have them say how to obtain the item requested.

S1—¿Vas a mandarme el dinero?
S2—No, no voy a mandártelo. Puedes pedírselo a tu padre.
S3—¿Puedes darle los discos a (Student 1)?
S4—No, no puedo dárselos. Puede pedírselos a su amigo.

C. You are in a bad mood, and people keep asking you to do things you don't want to do. Tell them you can't do the favors they are requesting.

> MODELO: —¿Puedes traer*me el menú?*
> —No, *no puedo traér**telo**.*

1. —¿Puedes traer*me las servilletas?*
2. —¿Puedes dar*le el mantel* a Julio?
3. —¿Puedes comprar*le el regalo* a mamá?
4. —¿Puedes prestar*me los cubiertos?*
5. —¿Puedes traer*nos el helado?*
6. —¿Puedes dar*le las cucharas* a Luisa?

D. Now repeat Exercise C, following the model below.

> MODELO: —¿Puedes traer*me el menú?*
> —No, *no **te lo** puedo traer.*

SUGGESTION E: Have students do this activity in pairs. Encourage them to make three other requests not mentioned in the exercise.

ACTIVITY SUGGESTION: See the *IAM* for an additional in-class activity: **¿Qué quieren?**

E. Interview a classmate, using the following questions and two questions of your own. When you have finished, switch roles.

1. Cuando tú necesitas dinero, ¿a quién se lo pides?
2. Cuando tú les pides dinero a tus padres, ¿te lo dan?
3. Si yo necesito tu libro de español, ¿me lo prestas?
4. Si Uds. no entienden algo, ¿se lo preguntan a su profesor(-a)?
5. Si tú y yo somos amigos(-as) y yo necesito tu coche, ¿tú me lo prestas?
6. Necesito tu pluma. ¿Puedes prestármela?
7. Necesito cheques de viajero. ¿Tú me los puedes conseguir?
8. Yo no tengo el número de teléfono del profesor (de la profesora). ¿Tú se lo puedes pedir?

2 Preterit of **ser, ir,** and **dar**   *(Pretérito de los verbos **ser, ir y dar**)*

SUGGESTION: Write a short sentence builder on the board, and have students write as many sentences as possible in three minutes.

Yo / Tú / El profesor (La profesora) / Mi(s) amigo(-a)(s) / Usted(-es) / Nosotros(-as)

ser / ir / dar

a la tienda / a la casa de… / un regalo a… / una buena nota a… / el último en llegar a la fiesta / a España / el primero en llegar a clase

■ The preterit forms of **ser, ir,** and **dar** are irregular.

ser *to be*	**ir** *to go*	**dar** *to give*
fui	fui	di
fuiste	fuiste	diste
fue	fue	dio
fuimos	fuimos	dimos
fuisteis	fuisteis	disteis
fueron	fueron	dieron

■ Note that **ser** and **ir** have identical forms in the preterit.

—Ayer **fue** el cumpleaños de Lucía, ¿no?

—Sí, Ana y yo **fuimos** a su casa y le **dimos** los regalos.

—¿**Fuiste** a la fiesta que **dio** Sara?

—Sí, **fui. Fue** la mejor fiesta del año.

"*Yesterday was Lucía's birthday, right?*"

"*Yes, Ana and I went to her house and gave her the presents.*"

"*Did you go to the party that Sara gave?*"

"*Yes, I went. It was the best party of the year.*"

práctica ●●

A. Complete the following dialogues, using the preterit of **ser, ir,** or **dar** as appropriate. Then act them out with a partner, adding a sentence or two to each dialogue.

1. —¿Adónde _____ tú ayer?
   — _____ a la tienda. Compré una pulsera de oro y se la _____ a mi esposa.
2. —¿ _____ Uds. a casa de tía Eva ayer?
   —Sí, _____ y le _____ el libro que tú mandaste para ella.
3. —¿Uds. _____ estudiantes del Dr. Paz?
   —Carlos _____ su estudiante, pero Raquel y yo _____ estudiantes de la Dra. Guerra.

4. —¿A quién le _____ (tú) la botella de vino tinto?
   —Se la _____ a Jorge.
5. —¿Adónde _____ Uds. anoche?
   — _____ al teatro. Los padres de Dora nos _____ las entradas.

B. Interview a classmate, using the following questions. When you have finished, switch roles.

1. ¿Quién fue tu profesor(-a) favorito(-a) el año pasado?
2. ¿Fuiste a la cafetería ayer? ¿A qué hora?
3. ¿Adónde fuiste el sábado pasado? ¿Con quién fuiste?
4. ¿Tus amigos fueron a visitarte?
5. ¿Dieron tus amigos una fiesta para celebrar tu cumpleaños?
6. ¿Diste una fiesta el viernes pasado? ¿Alguien dio una fiesta el sábado?

3 Preterit of **e:i** and **o:u** stem-changing verbs   *(Pretérito de los verbos que cambian en la raíz: e:i y o:u)*

SUGGESTION: Group verbs on the board in the following manner:

e:ie	e:i	o:ue
mentir	servir	dormir
preferir	pedir	morir

Practice the use of the third person of these verbs by telling one student something you did and having him or her repeat the information to the rest of the class.

I—Yo pedí café en la cafetería esta mañana.
S1—El/La profesor(-a) pidió café.

SUGGESTION: Ask the class the following personalized questions or write them on the board and have students use them to interview each other.

1. ¿Quién te mintió recientemente?
2. ¿Dónde durmió tu compañero(-a) de cuarto anoche?
3. ¿Quién te sirvió la cena anoche?
4. ¿Qué te pidió tu amigo(-a) (hermano[-a]) para su cumpleaños?
5. ¿Dónde consiguió tu padre (madre) / hermano(-a) / amigo(-a) las entradas?

■ Verbs of the -**ir** conjugation that have a stem change in the present tense change **e** to **i** and **o** to **u** in the third-person singular and plural of the preterit.[1]

preferir	*to prefer*	**dormir**	*to sleep*
preferí	preferimos	dormí	dormimos
preferiste	preferisteis	dormiste	dormisteis
prefirió	prefirieron	durmió	durmieron

■ Other verbs that follow the same pattern:

pedir	seguir
mentir *(to lie)*	conseguir
servir	morir
repetir *(to repeat)*	

—¿Cómo **durmieron** Uds. anoche?   *"How did you sleep last night?"*
—Nosotros **dormimos** bien, pero Paco no **durmió** muy bien.   *"We slept well, but Paco didn't sleep very well."*

—¿Qué **pidieron** ellos?   *"What did they order?"*
—Raúl **pidió** camarones y Rosa **pidió** langosta.   *"Raúl ordered shrimp and Rosa ordered lobster."*

—Beba dice que Ada salió con tu novio.   *"Beba says that Ada went out with your boyfriend."*
—Te **mintió**.   *"She lied to you."*

---

[1]Remember that the -**ar** and -**er** stem-changing verbs are regular in the preterit: **él cerró, ellos volvieron.** Exceptions are **poder** and **querer,** which are explained in **Lección 9.**

práctica ···

A. Find out what Andrés did yesterday by adding the correct form of the missing verbs.

1. Yo _____ (ir) a visitar a mi padre y le _____ (pedir) dinero.
2. _____ (Conseguir) entradas para el teatro.
3. _____ (Salir) con otra chica y le _____ (mentir) a mi novia.
4. Nosotros _____ (ir) a un restaurante y yo _____ (pedir) cordero asado; ella _____ (pedir) langosta.
5. Yo _____ (volver) a mi casa y _____ (dormir) dos horas.
6. Mis padres me _____ (invitar) a una fiesta pero yo _____ (preferir) no ir.
7. Por la noche, yo _____ (dar) una fiesta y _____ (servir) ponche.

B. Now, using the information above, prepare questions to ask your classmates about what Andrés did.

4 Uses of **por** and **para**   *(Usos de por y para)*

SUGGESTION: Write a summary of the uses of **por** on the board and have students give examples of each use. Write one or two of their sentences under each category.

SUGGESTION: Write the following phrases on the board, on an overhead transparency, or on a ditto sheet and have students complete each sentence. Students may also work in groups of three or four and compare their responses.

1. Camino a clase paso por…
2. A veces llego tarde por…
3. Me gusta viajar por…
4. Mi ciudad es famosa por…
5. Pagué cincuenta / cien dólares por…

A. Uses of *por*

The preposition **por** is used to express the following concepts.

■ motion or approximate location *(through, around, along, by)*

Luis salió **por** la ventana.	*Luis went out through the window.*
Enrique va **por** la calle Juárez.	*Enrique is going down Juárez Street.*
Gustavo pasó **por** el hotel.	*Gustavo went by the hotel.*

■ cause or motive of an action *(because of, on account of, on behalf of)*

Llegamos tarde **por** la lluvia.	*We were late because of the rain.*
Lo hago **por** ellos.	*I do it on their behalf.*

■ means, manner, unit of measure *(by, for, per)*

Siempre viajamos **por** tren.	*We always travel by train.*
Van a 100 kilómetros **por** hora.	*They're going 100 kilometers per hour.*

■ *in exchange for*

Te doy 50 dólares **por** esa cámara.	*I'll give you 50 dollars for that camera.*

■ period of time during which an action takes place *(during, in, for)*

Ella trabaja **por** la mañana.	*She works in the morning.*
Va a estar aquí **por** dos meses.	*He's going to be here for two months.*

■ *in search of, for*

Voy a venir **por** ti a las siete.	*I'll come by for you at seven.*

práctica ....

EXPANSION: Ask students personalized questions that reinforce the structures presented in this activity.

1. **¿Cuánto pagaste por el libro de...?**
2. **¿Pasaste por la biblioteca / cafetería / librería esta mañana?**
3. **Cuando fuiste de vacaciones, ¿cómo viajaste?**

Interview a classmate, using the following questions. When you have finished, switch roles.

1. ¿Tienes una clase por la mañana? ¿Y por la noche?
2. Antes de ir a clase, ¿vas por tus amigos? ¿Alguien viene por ti?
3. ¿Cuánto pagaste por tu libro de español?
4. ¿Pasaste por mi casa anoche?
5. Si tú pierdes la llave de tu casa, ¿entras por la ventana?
6. ¿Tus padres hacen mucho por ti?
7. ¿Tú les escribes a tus padres o prefieres llamarlos por teléfono?
8. ¿Prefieres viajar por tren o por avión? ¿Por qué?

B. Uses of *para*

The preposition **para** is used to express the following concepts.

SUGGESTION: Write the following phrases on the board, on an overhead transparency, or on a ditto sheet and have students complete each sentence by supplying correct information. Students may also work in groups of three or four and compare their responses.

1. **Voy a salir para... en junio / diciembre.**
2. **Necesito mil dólares para...**
3. **Yo quiero estudiar para...**
4. **Tengo que comprar regalos para...**
5. **Trabajo para...**

■ destination

Quiero un pasaje **para** Montevideo.	*I want a ticket for Montevideo.*
¿A qué hora hay vuelos **para** Buenos Aires?	*What time are the flights to Buenos Aires?*

■ goal for a point in the future (*by* or *for* a certain time)

Quiero el dinero **para** el sábado.	*I want the money for Saturday.*
Debo estar allí **para** el mes de noviembre.	*I must be there by the month of November.*

■ whom or what something is for

Compré una mesa **para** mi cuarto.	*I bought a table for my room.*
Compramos los libros **para** Fernando.	*We bought the books for Fernando.*

■ *in order to*

Necesito mil dólares **para** pagar el viaje.	*I need a thousand dollars in order to pay for the trip.*
Vamos al teatro **para** celebrar nuestro aniversario de bodas.	*We are going to the theater (in order) to celebrate our wedding anniversary.*

■ objective or goal

Mi novio estudia **para** médico.	*My boyfriend is studying to be a doctor.*

 Florería San Francisco

 SI USTED NECESITA ¡¡CREDITO!! Gustosamente se lo damos! Flores, Arreglos, Regalos

práctica ••

A. Look at the illustrations and describe what is happening, using **por** or **para.**

1. Fuimos _____ a Miami.

2. Daniel salió _____.

3. La torta es _____.

4. Luisa va a estar en Orlando _____.

5. Jorge pagó _____ el vino.

6. Eva sale mañana _____.

SUGGESTION B: Have students do this activity in pairs. If the question requires a yes or no response, tell students to include another statement that elaborates or explains their answer.

S1—¿Vas a pedirles dinero a tus padres para el viaje?
S2—Sí, voy a pedirles quinientos dólares porque quiero comprar muchas cosas.

FOLLOW-UP B: Based on their plans, have students write brief letters to their parents or friends describing the trip, requesting money, etc.

ACTIVITY SUGGESTION: See the *IAM* for an additional in-class activity: **¿Qué decimos...?**

B. Imagine that you and your partner are planning a trip to Spain. Take turns answering the following questions.

1. ¿Cuánto dinero necesitan Uds. para pagar el viaje?
2. ¿Van a pedirles dinero a sus padres para el viaje?
3. ¿Para qué día quieren los pasajes?
4. ¿A qué hora sale el avión para Madrid?
5. ¿Por cuánto tiempo piensan estar en Madrid?
6. ¿Van a traer regalos para su familia?
7. ¿Van Uds. a España para practicar el español?
8. John estudia para profesor de español y quiere visitar Madrid. ¿Puede ir con Uds.?

C. Complete the following description of a trip to Paraguay, using **por** or **para.**

Robert y yo salimos _____ Asunción la semana próxima. Vamos a viajar _____ avión. Tenemos pasajes _____ el sábado _____ la mañana. Pagamos tres mil dólares _____ los billetes, pero como pensamos pasar _____ Caracas y _____ Lima, donde vamos a estar _____ unos días, no es muy caro. Mañana _____ la tarde vamos a Bloomingdale's _____ comprar algunos regalos _____ nuestros amigos paraguayos. Desde Lima, vamos a llamar _____ teléfono a nuestros amigos en Asunción, y ellos van a ir al aeropuerto _____ nosotros.

D. Plan a trip to a Hispanic country with a classmate. Using the paragraph in Exercise C as a model, describe your travel plans.

5 Ordinal numbers   *(Números ordinales)*

primero(-a)[1]	*first*	**sexto(-a)**	*sixth*
segundo(-a)[1]	*second*	**séptimo(-a)**	*seventh*
terccro(-a)[1]	*third*	**octavo(-a)**	*eighth*
cuarto(-a)	*fourth*	**noveno(-a)**	*ninth*
quinto(-a)	*fifth*	**décimo(-a)**	*tenth*

■ Ordinal numbers agree in gender and number with the nouns they modify.

el segundo **chico**   la segunda **chica**
los primeros **días**   las primeras **semanas**

■ Ordinal numbers are seldom used after **décimo** *(tenth).*

ATENCIÓN   The ordinal numbers **primero** and **tercero** drop the final **-o** before masculine singular nouns.

el **primer**[2] día   el **tercer**[3] año

práctica ....

EXPANSION: In order to practice the ordinal numbers in context, ask students to identify each other by the row and seat in which they are seated. Introduce the words **asiento** and **fila** before you begin this activity.

¿Quién está en el quinto asiento de la primera fila?

A. Supply the ordinal numbers that correspond to the following cardinal numbers.

1. cuatro   6. ocho
2. diez   7. tres
3. uno   8. nueve
4. siete   9. cinco
5. dos   10. seis

B. Imagine that the whole class is staying at a hotel in Miami. Your classmates were assigned rooms on different floors. With a partner, take turns saying who is on what floor.

---
[1]abbreviated 1°, 2°, 3°, and so on
[2]abbreviated 1er
[3]abbreviated 3er

¡A ver cuánto aprendió!

¡Repase el vocabulario!

INTERNET

See the *¿Cómo se dice...?*
Web site for additional
grammar and vocabulary
practice: http://spanish.college.
hmco.com/students

SUGGESTION: After completion of the
matching exercise, personalize the
activity by modifying the questions in
column A as in the examples below.

¿Qué celebramos la semana (el
    mes) que viene?
¿Te gusta el bistec?
¿Qué bebidas prefieres?
Por lo general, ¿cuánto dejas de
    propina?
¿Vas con frecuencia a
    McDonald's?
¿Pides café después de la cena?

ACTIVITY SUGGESTION: Do ¡Escucha!,
the in-class listening comprehension
activity that reviews vocabulary and
grammar structures introduced in the
lesson. It appears in the answer key of
the *IAM*.

ACTIVITY SUGGESTION: See the *IAM*
for an additional in-class activity:
Palabras escondidas.

Match each question in column A with the answers in column B, and then read
them aloud.

A	B
1. ¿Qué celebran hoy?	a. Flan con helado.
2. ¿Está rico el pavo relleno?	b. Sí, quiero pedirlos, pero son muy caros.
3. ¿Cuál es la especialidad de la casa?	c. El pedido.
4. ¿Qué bebidas prefieres?	d. Lechón asado con arroz y frijoles negros.
5. ¿Qué quieres de postre?	e. Sí, a cántaros.
6. ¿Vas a pedir agua mineral?	f. Hamburguesas.
7. ¿Qué está anotando el mozo?	g. Sí, me encanta.
8. ¿Quieres bistec?	h. Ocho dólares.
9. ¿Adónde vamos esta noche?	i. Sí, está muy sabroso.
10. ¿Está lloviendo?	j. Ana.
11. ¿No quieres camarones?	k. Sí, una botella.
12. ¿Cuánto vas a dejar de propina?	l. No, prefiero té.
13. ¿Qué venden en McDonald's?	m. Al teatro.
14. ¿Quién paga la cuenta?	n. Su aniversario de bodas.
15. ¿Quieres café?	o. Sí, quiero comer carne.
16. ¿Te gusta la pulsera?	p. Vermut o vino tinto.

Entrevista

ACTIVITY SUGGESTION: See the *IAM*
for additional in-class activities:
Para conocernos mejor and **Una
encuesta.**

You and a classmate are at the El Caribe Restaurant. Look at the menu on page
190 and ask each other the following questions.

1. ¿Qué vas a pedir?
2. ¿Prefieres carne o pescado?
3. ¿Qué me recomiendas para comer?
4. ¿Qué prefieres tomar: vino blanco, champán o agua mineral?
5. ¿Qué quieres de postre: arroz con leche, torta o flan con crema?
6. ¿Cuánto es la cuenta?
7. ¿Cuánto vas a dejar de propina?
8. ¿Qué vas a hacer después de cenar?

Situaciones

What would you say in the following situations? What might the other person say? Act out the scenes with a partner. Take turns playing each role.

1. You are at a restaurant, and you are very hungry. Ask to see the menu; order a first and second course and something to drink while you wait for your food. Then tell the waiter what you want for dessert.
2. You are a waiter or waitress. Recommend two or three main dishes and a dessert to your customers. Ask them if they want coffee or tea.
3. You are cooking a gourmet dinner. Ask your roommate to set the table. Name the utensils and other items you want.
4. You are hosting a party at your home. Some of your guests have brought children. Offer a selection of beverages.

Para escribir

Write a dialogue between a waiter or waitress and a customer. Include the following exchanges.

- asking for a menu
- ordering the food, drink(s), and dessert
- asking for the check

En la vida real

CD-ROM

Do the interactive exercises on the CD-ROM for additional practice.

EXPANSION: Suggest that half of the class prepare menus on a very limited budget and that the other half prepare menus with unlimited funds that might include a catering service, imported foods, etc. Then have students compare several of the "menus."

¿Qué les servimos?

You and a classmate are hosting a special weekend for some foreign students. Discuss the breakfast, lunch, and dinner menus you will be preparing, taking into account your guests' different preferences.

- María Inés Soto is a vegetarian.
- Juan Carlos Reyes loves meat and dairy products.
- Isabel Peña is on a diet.
- Francisco Rojas is extremely thin and wants to gain weight.
- Raquel Arias loves seafood.

Some additional words and phrases that you might include:

el chorizo	*sausage* ⎫ **con huevos**	el pan	*bread*
el tocino	*bacon* ⎬ *with eggs*	el panqueque	*pancake*
el cereal	*cereal*	el yogur	*yogurt*
la mantequilla	*butter*	las zanahorias	*carrots*
la mermelada	*jam*		

¡Vamos a cenar!

SUGGESTION: Have students role-play this situation in groups of three, based on the dialogue and other activities studied in this lesson.

You and a classmate have received a $40.00 gift coupon to eat dinner at the El Caribe Restaurant. Select what you are going to have, including drinks and dessert. And don't forget to leave a tip!

¡Buen provecho!

You and a friend have decided to go out to dinner tonight. Read the following ads for Hispanic restaurants in Miami, and answer the questions on the next page.

1. Ud. y un amigo quieren comer pescado. ¿A qué restaurante pueden ir?
2. Si quieren hacer reservaciones en ese restaurante, ¿a qué número deben llamar?
3. ¿Cuál es la especialidad del restaurante Las Redes?
4. ¿Por qué es famoso el restaurante Segovia?
5. ¿Cuándo hay música en el restaurante Segovia?
6. ¿Cuánto cuesta el almuerzo allí?
7. ¿Qué comidas típicas cubanas sirven en el restaurante La Carreta?
8. Si quieren dar un banquete, ¿a qué restaurante deben ir?
9. ¿En qué calle está El Bodegón Castilla?
10. ¿Cree Ud. que en El Bodegón Castilla sirven comida cubana o española?

4. México

México

- Con más de veintitrés millones de habitantes en el área metropolitana, la Ciudad de México es el centro urbano más grande del mundo. Fundada por los aztecas en el año 1325, es también la capital más antigua de América.

- El turismo es una de las principales fuentes de ingreso *(sources of income)* de la economía mexicana. Cancún, Acapulco, Puerto Vallarta, Ixtapa, Mazatlán y otros centros turísticos reciben millones de visitantes todos los años, principalmente de los Estados Unidos.

- La comida mexicana es muy conocida *(well known)* en los Estados Unidos. Muchos de los alimentos típicos mexicanos, como los frijoles y las tortillas de maíz, son de origen indígena. Los platos más populares son las enchiladas, el guacamole, los tamales y los tacos.

- Antes de la conquista de México por parte de los españoles, existían allí numerosas culturas indígenas, las de los aztecas, los mayas, los toltecas y los mixtecas, entre otras. Aún hoy existen grandes concentraciones de indígenas en las regiones de Yucatán, Chiapas y Oaxaca.

En muchos lugares de México es posible visitar ruinas muy bien conservadas, como por ejemplo las pirámides, que son un elemento muy importante de la arquitectura prehispánica. Ésta es la Pirámide del Mago en Uxmal, una antigua ciudad maya en la península de Yucatán. Está formada por cinco templos construidos uno encima *(on top)* del otro.

¿Qué culturas indígenas existen en su país?

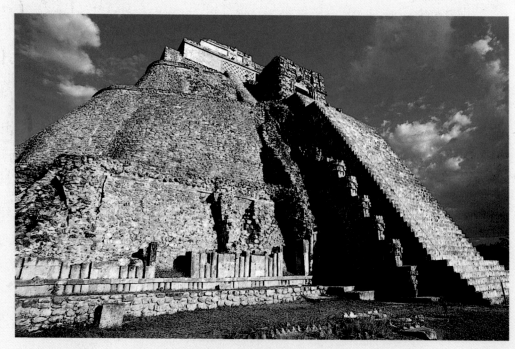

La península de Yucatán es famosa no sólo por sus ruinas mayas sino *(but)* también por sus playas *(beaches)* de aguas cálidas *(warm)* y cristalinas. A cien kilómetros de Cancún está Akumal, un centro turístico de belleza *(beauty)* inigualable.

¿Qué centros turísticos hay en el estado donde Ud. vive?

El mercado del pueblo de Tlacolula, en el estado de Oaxaca, es uno de los más famosos de México. Allí los indígenas de la región venden productos agrícolas y también objetos de artesanía, como vasijas de barro *(clay pots)* y sarapes. Lo más popular de la artesanía de Oaxaca es la cerámica negra.

¿Le gustan a Ud. los objetos de artesanía?

Este mural del famoso artista mexicano Diego Rivera presenta la historia y las costumbres de la civilización totoneca. El mural está en el Palacio Nacional, construido en el lugar donde antes estaba el palacio del emperador azteca Moctezuma. Otros murales famosos de Rivera están en el Ministerio de Educación y en la Universidad Nacional Autónoma de México, ambos *(both)* en la Ciudad de México.

¿Conoce Ud. otros pintores mexicanos? ¿Cuáles?

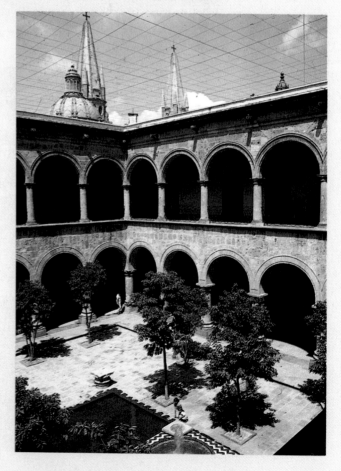

Guadalajara, capital del estado de Jalisco, con más de cinco millones de habitantes, es la segunda ciudad de México en población. La ciudad tiene una rica tradición cultural. En ella se mezclan magníficos ejemplos de la arquitectura y el arte español coloniales con modernas avenidas y edificios contemporáneos. Aquí vemos el patio del Museo del Estado, famoso por sus magníficas pinturas de José Clemente Orozco.

¿Cuál es la capital del estado donde Ud. vive?

El Ballet Folklórico de México le ofrece al público espectáculos llenos *(full)* de arte y color. El ballet actúa *(performs)* los miércoles y los domingos en el Palacio de Bellas Artes de la Ciudad de México. Sus danzas y trajes típicos son de una gran belleza *(beauty)*.

¿A Ud. le gusta bailar? ¿Por qué o por qué no?

El primero y el dos de noviembre se celebra en México el Día de los Muertos *(Dead)*. En la foto, una mujer reza *(prays)* en el Cementerio de Patzcuaro, en el estado de Michoacán. Los habitantes del pueblo llevan comida a las tumbas de sus familiares y se quedan *(they stay)* allí toda la noche. Miles de velas *(candles)* y flores de papel adornan el cementerio, creando un espectáculo inolvidable.

¿Existe un equivalente al Día de los Muertos en su país?

Estatua de Cuauhtémoc, último emperador azteca, que fue vencido *(defeated)* por Hernán Cortés en 1521. Cuauhtémoc simboliza el orgullo *(pride)* del pueblo *(people, nation)* mexicano.

¿Qué estatuas importantes hay en su ciudad?

El Paseo de la Reforma en la Ciudad de México. En este paseo hay numerosos monumentos impresionantes, entre ellos la estatua del rey Carlos IV de España, el espléndido monumento a Cristóbal Colón *(Christopher Columbus)* y el del Ángel de la Independencia, que vemos en la foto.

¿Qué monumentos históricos hay en la ciudad de Washington, D.C.?

TELEINFORME

 VIDEO

 CD-ROM   Do the interactive exercises on
the CD-ROM for additional practice.

Preparación

NOTE: The video-related vocabulary is listed in the *Instructor's Activities Manual* for your reference. Its purpose is to facilitate students' comprehension.

NOTE: See the Instructor's Edition frontmatter for additional suggestions on implementing video in the classroom.

SUGGESTION: Have students read the *Panorama hispánico* segment of the textbook and do the *Preparación* activities in small groups before viewing the video segments.

¿Cuánto saben Uds. ya? After reading **Panorama hispánico 4,** get together in groups of three or four students and answer the following questions.

1. ¿Cuál es el centro urbano más grande del mundo?
2. ¿Cuál es la capital más antigua de América?
3. ¿Cuántos millones de habitantes viven en la Ciudad de México?
4. ¿Cuáles son algunos de los centros turísticos de México?
5. ¿De qué estado mexicano es Guadalajara la capital?
6. ¿Cómo es la arquitectura de Guadalajara?
7. ¿Cuándo se celebra el Día de los Muertos?
8. ¿Cómo se celebra el Día de los Muertos en México?

Comprensión

SUGGESTION: Ask students what they might already know about Mexico and share it with the class.

SUGGESTION: The *Comprensión* sections are organized by individual video clip to provide greater flexibility in lesson planning. Have students complete each exercise after viewing the corresponding video clip and have them compare their answers in pairs or groups.

SUGGESTION: Have students locate Mexico City, Teotihuacán, Guadalajara, Cancún, and the Yucatán Peninsula on the map on the inside front cover of the textbook.

A. La Ciudad de México, Cuernavaca y Teotihuacán. Read the following statements. After watching the video, circle **V** (**Verdadero**) or **F** (**Falso**), according to what you understood. If the statement is false, correct it.

V F   1. Otro nombre para la Ciudad de México es "el D.F.".
V F   2. No hay metro en la Ciudad de México.
V F   3. La Catedral Metropolitana fue construida *(was built)* sobre templos aztecas.
V F   4. El clima de Cuernavaca es como el de la Ciudad de México.
V F   5. Teotihuacán fue una gran ciudad precolombina.

B. Guadalajara. Select the word or phrase that best completes each statement according to what you understood in the video.

1. Guadalajara fue fundada en (1542, 1452).
2. La población de Guadalajara es (menor, mayor) que la población de la Ciudad de México.
3. Guadalajara es la capital de (la República Mexicana, Jalisco).
4. La Catedral de Guadalajara tiene dos (plazas, torres) doradas *(golden)*.

C. Yucatán. Select the word or phrase that best completes each statement according to what you understood from the video.

1. La península de Yucatán fue el centro de la civilización (maya, azteca).
2. Cancún está en (Jalisco, la península de Yucatán).
3. Chichén Itzá es una (ciudad, civilización) antigua.
4. Los mayas realizaron descubrimientos importantes en (la ingeniería, la geografía).

Ampliación

FOLLOW-UP: Have groups write lists of the places they want to see and things they want to do in Mexico.

A. Dos culturas. With a partner, make a list of counterparts you can find in your local area, city, state, or country for each of the following items.

1. México, D.F.
2. Guadalajara
3. Cancún
4. Teotihuacán
5. Chichén Itzá

B. Quiero visitar... Interview a partner to determine which of the Mexican cities in the video segment he/she would like to visit. Use the following questions as a guide.

1. ¿Te gusta la Ciudad de México? ¿Guadalajara? ¿Cancún?
2. ¿Qué lugares quieres visitar? ¿Por qué?
3. ¿Cuáles son algunos de los monumentos que quieres ir a ver?
4. ¿Qué actividades te interesan?

OBJECTIVES

Pronunciation
La entonación

Structure
Reflexive constructions • Some uses of the definite article • Possessive pronouns • Irregular preterits • Formation of adverbs

Communication
You will learn vocabulary related to household chores and the hairdresser.

Un día muy ocupado

STUDENT
AUDIO

SUGGESTION: Have students make a
list of the chores Mirta and Isabel are
planning to do. Encourage students to
use the infinitive forms of the verbs.

MIRTA
barrer la cocina
pasar la aspiradora

ISABEL
limpiar el baño
cocinar
planchar
bañar al perro

Aunque hoy es sábado, Mirta e Isabel se levantaron temprano para terminar de limpiar el apartamento. Esta noche, las dos chicas están invitadas a un concierto en la Casa de Cultura Paraguaya. Isabel está un poco cansada porque anoche se acostó tarde.

MIRTA —¿Por qué viniste tan tarde anoche? ¿Dónde estuviste?

ISABEL —En la tienda. Tuve que comprar un regalo para Eva porque mañana es su cumpleaños. Bueno, ¿empezamos a limpiar?

MIRTA —Sí, yo voy a barrer la cocina y le voy a pasar la aspiradora a la alfombra.

ISABEL —Entonces yo voy a limpiar el baño. Después voy a cocinar y a planchar mi vestido rojo. Me lo voy a poner esta noche.

MIRTA —Yo no sé qué ponerme.

ISABEL —¿Por qué no te pones el vestido azul? Es muy bonito.

MIRTA —No, me lo probé ayer y no me queda bien. ¡Ah! ¿Dónde está la palita?

ISABEL —En la terraza. ¡Ay! Necesito bañar al perro, ducharme y vestirme… ¡y tengo turno en la peluquería a las tres!

MIRTA —Yo quiero lavarme la cabeza y no me acordé de comprar champú. ¿Puedo usar el tuyo?

ISABEL —Sí, está en el botiquín.

MIRTA —Gracias. Yo no pude ir a la farmacia ayer.

Cuando llegó a la peluquería, Isabel le pidió una revista al peluquero y se sentó a esperar su turno.

ISABEL —*(Al peluquero)* Quiero corte, lavado y peinado.

PELUQUERO —Tiene el pelo muy lacio. ¿No quiere una permanente?

ISABEL —No, cuando quiero rizos, uso el rizador. ¡Ay, tengo el pelo muy largo!

PELUQUERO —Últimamente está de moda el pelo corto. *(Le corta el pelo y, cuando termina, Isabel se mira en el espejo.)*

ISABEL —¡Muy bien! Ahora quiero pedir turno para mi amiga para la semana próxima.

PELUQUERO —¿El miércoles, primero de febrero, a las nueve y media? Generalmente hay menos gente por la mañana.

ISABEL —Está bien. Mi amiga se llama Mirta Ortega.

Isabel deja la cartera en el mostrador. El peluquero la llama.

PELUQUERO —¡Señorita! ¿Esta cartera es suya?

ISABEL —Sí, es mía. Gracias.

Vocabulario

Cognados

el apartamento   apartment
el champú   shampoo
el concierto   concert
la cultura   culture

la farmacia   pharmacy, drugstore
generalmente   generally
paraguayo(-a)   Paraguayan

el permanente[1]   permanent
(wave)
el turno   turn

Nombres

la alfombra   rug, carpet
la aspiradora   vacuum cleaner
el botiquín   medicine cabinet
la cartera, el bolso, la bolsa
purse, handbag
la cocina   kitchen
el corte   haircut, cut
el espejo   mirror
la gente[2]   people

el lavado   shampoo, wash
el mostrador   counter
la palita, el recogedor   dustpan
el peinado   hairdo, hairstyle
el pelo   hair
la peluquería, el salón de belleza
salon, beauty parlor
el (la) peluquero(-a)   hairdresser,
beautician

el perro   dog
la revista   magazine
el rizador   curling iron
el rizo   curl
la semana   week
el turno, la cita   appointment
el vestido   dress

RELATED VOCABULARY: In some
countries, the term **el (la) estilista**
(stylist) is used instead of **el (la)
peluquero(-a)**.

Verbos

acordarse (o:ue)[3]   to remember
acostarse (o:ue)   to go to bed
bañar(se)   to bathe (oneself)
barrer   to sweep
cocinar   to cook
cortar(se)   to cut (oneself)
ducharse   to take a shower

esperar   to wait (for)
lavar(se)   to wash (oneself)
levantarse   to get up
limpiar(se)   to clean (oneself)
llamarse   to be called
planchar   to iron
ponerse   to put on

probarse (o:ue)   to try on
quedar   to fit
sentarse (e:ie)   to sit down
terminar   to finish
usar   to use, to wear
vestirse (e:i)   to get dressed

Adjetivos

corto(-a)   short
lacio   straight (hair)

Otras palabras y expresiones

aunque   although
bueno   well, okay
cortarse el pelo   to get a haircut
estar de moda   to be in style
estar invitado(-a)   to be invited

lavarse la cabeza   to wash one's
hair
pasar la aspiradora   to vacuum
pedir (e:i) turno, cita   to make an
appointment

temprano   early
últimamente   lately

---

[1]In many countries, *la* **permanente** is used.
[2]**Gente** is used in the singular in Spanish.
[3]**Acordarse** is always used with a reflexive pronoun.

Vocabulario adicional
En la barbería

el barbero
el peine
la escoba
el cepillo
el secador
la crema de afeitar
la máquina de afeitar

SUGGESTION: Use Transparency 32 to present or to practice the vocabulary.

Verbos útiles

ensuciar(se)	to get (oneself) dirty	El niño **se ensució** las manos.
olvidarse (de)	to forget	**Me olvidé de** pedir turno en la peluquería.
peinar(se)	to comb or style one's hair	**Me voy a peinar** antes de salir.
regalar	to give (as a gift)	María me **regaló** un vestido verde.

ACTIVITY SUGGESTION: See the *IAM* for an additional in-class activity: **¿Cómo respondes?**

¡Conversemos!

Answer the following questions, basing your answers on the dialogues.

1. ¿Para qué se levantaron temprano hoy Mirta e Isabel?
2. ¿Qué van a hacer las chicas esta noche?
3. ¿Quién le va a pasar la aspiradora a la alfombra?
4. ¿Qué va a planchar Isabel? ¿Para qué?
5. ¿Quién celebra su cumpleaños mañana?

6. ¿Sabe Mirta qué ponerse esta noche?
7. ¿Por qué no se pone Mirta el vestido azul?
8. ¿Qué tiene que hacer Isabel antes de ir a la peluquería?
9. ¿Por qué no quiere Isabel una permanente?
10. ¿Dónde dejó Isabel la cartera?
11. ¿Qué le pregunta el peluquero a Isabel?
12. ¿Por qué es mejor ir a la peluquería por la mañana?

¿Lo sabía Ud.?

■ **Asunción** es la capital de Paraguay. La ciudad fue fundada en el año 1537. Allí se ve un contraste muy grande entre los edificios muy modernos y las casas coloniales. No muchos turistas visitan esta encantadora *(charming)* ciudad, pero los que lo hacen hablan muy bien de la hospitalidad de los paraguayos.

■ **Paraguay** tiene más o menos el tamaño *(size)* de California. Su moneda es el **guaraní,** que es de valor bastante estable. El idioma oficial es el español, pero los paraguayos hablan también el guaraní, un idioma indígena que aún se conserva y que se enseña en las escuelas. Alrededor *(Around)* del ochenta y uno por ciento de la población sabe leer y escribir.

● ¿Sabe Ud. cuándo fue fundada la ciudad donde Ud. vive?

● ¿El dólar es de valor estable o no?

● ¿Qué idiomas indígenas se hablan en este país?

● ¿Qué por ciento de la población de este país sabe leer y escribir?

Edificios modernos junto a casas viejas en Asunción, Paraguay.

INTERNET

See the *¿Cómo se dice...?* Web site for activities on authentic cultural material: http://spanish.college.hmco.com/students

Pronunciación

La entonación

STUDENT AUDIO

SUGGESTION: Read the following sentences in random order and have students indicate which intonation pattern is used. You may also copy the sentences onto the board or an overhead transparency for additional practice in pronunciation.

1. ¿Dónde vive tu hermano? ¿Cuál es la puerta de salida para el vuelo a Caracas? ¿Qué hicieron tus amigos anoche?
2. ¿Tus padres hacen mucho por ti? ¿Van Uds. a casa de tía Eva?
3. ¡Por suerte gané la lotería! ¡Ah, sí! ¡Caramba! ¡Ya es tarde!

Intonation refers to the variations in the pitch of your voice when you are talking. Intonation patterns in Spanish are different from those in English. Note the following regarding Spanish intonation.

1. For normal statements, the pitch generally rises on the first stressed syllable.

Yo compré el regalo para Elena.

2. For questions eliciting information, the pitch is highest on the stressed syllable of the interrogative pronoun.

¿Cómo está tu mamá?

3. For questions that can be answered with **sí** or **no,** the pitch is generally highest on the last stressed syllable.

¿Fuiste al mercado ayer?

4. In exclamations, the pitch is highest on the first stressed syllable.

¡Qué bonita es esa alfombra!

Listen to your instructor and repeat the following sentences, imitating closely your instructor's intonation.

1. Marta no trabajó anoche.
2. ¿Dónde vive tu hermano?
3. ¿Le diste el dinero a Ramona?
4. ¡Qué delgado es ese muchacho!
5. ¿Vas a ir a la peluquería?
6. ¿Quién puede llevarte?

1 Reflexive constructions *(Construcciones reflexivas)*

SUGGESTION: Conjugate a reflexive verb on the board, using colored chalk for the reflexive pronouns. Point out that in reflexive constructions, all persons agree.

(1st p. sing.)	(1st p. sing.)	(1st p. sing.)
Yo	me	visto.

A. Reflexive pronouns

Subjects		Reflexive pronouns
yo	me	*myself, to (for) myself*
tú	te	*yourself, to (for) yourself* (**tú** form)
nosotros(-as)	nos	*ourselves, to (for) ourselves*
vosotros(-as)	os	*yourselves, to (for) yourselves* (**vosotros** form)
Ud.		*yourself, to (for) yourself* (**Ud.** form)
Uds.		*yourselves, to (for) yourselves* (**Uds.** form)
él	se	*himself, to (for) himself*
ella		*herself, to (for) herself*
		itself, to (for) itself
ellos, ellas		*themselves, to (for) themselves*

■ Reflexive pronouns are used whenever the direct or indirect object is the same as the subject of the sentence.

■ Note that except for **se,** the reflexive pronouns have the same forms as the direct and indirect object pronouns.

■ The third-person singular and plural **se** is invariable.

■ Reflexive pronouns are positioned in the sentence in the same manner as object pronouns. They are placed in front of a conjugated verb: **Yo** *me* **levanto;** or they may be attached to an infinitive or to a present participle: **Yo voy a levantar*me*. Yo estoy levantándo*me*.**

B. Reflexive verbs

■ Many verbs can be made reflexive in Spanish, that is, they can be made to act upon the subject, by the use of a reflexive pronoun.

lavarse	to wash oneself
Yo **me lavo**	*I wash (myself)*
Tú **te lavas**	*You wash (yourself)* (**tú** form)
Ud. **se lava**	*You wash (yourself)* (**Ud.** form)
Él **se lava**	*He washes (himself)*
Ella **se lava**	*She washes (herself)*
Nosotros(-as) **nos lavamos**	*We wash (ourselves)*
Vosotros(-as) **os laváis**	*You wash (yourselves)* (**vosotros** form)
Uds. **se lavan**	*You wash (yourselves)* (**Uds.** form)
Ellos **se lavan**	*They* (masc.) *wash (themselves)*
Ellas **se lavan**	*They* (fem.) *wash (themselves)*

SUGGESTION: Ask students personalized questions that use reflexive and non-reflexive verbs.

1. **¿Cuántas horas duermes generalmente?**
2. **¿Qué haces cuando no puedes dormirte?**
3. **¿Cómo se llama tu novio(-a)?**
4. **¿Lo (La) llamas frecuentemente por teléfono?**
5. **¿Te gusta levantar pesas** *(weights)*?
6. **¿Te gusta levantarte temprano por la mañana?**
7. **Cuando estás en casa con tu familia, ¿quién te despierta?**
8. **¿Tu compañero(-a) de cuarto te despierta por la mañana?**
9. **¿A qué hora te despiertas los fines de semana?**
10. **¿Generalmente te bañas por la mañana o por la noche?**
11. **¿Te gusta bañar a tu perro/gato?**
12. **¿Qué te pones cuando hace frío?**
13. **¿Quién pone la mesa en tu casa?**

Julia baña al perro.

Julia se baña.

Elsa acuesta a su hijo a las siete.

Elsa se acuesta a las diez.

33

SUGGESTION: Use Transparency 33. Present the first two or three frames to students using the following structure.

A las nueve, Paco y Rosa se divierten mucho.
A las once y media, se despiden.
A las doce, Paco se desviste.

Then ask students to refer to the list of reflexive verbs and describe Paco's actions.

■ In addition to the verbs included in the vocabulary list, the following verbs are commonly used in reflexive constructions.

afeitarse   *to shave*
despertarse (e:ie)   *to wake up*
desvestirse (e:i)   *to get undressed*
preocuparse (por)   *to worry (about)*
sentirse (e:ie)   *to feel* (mood or physical condition)

—¿A qué hora **se acuestan** Uds.?   *"What time do you go to bed?"*
—Yo **me acuesto** a las diez y Ana **se**   *"I go to bed at ten and Ana goes to*
   acuesta a las doce.   *bed at twelve."*

—¿Cómo te sientes?   *"How do you feel?"*
—Me siento bien, gracias.   *"I feel fine, thank you."*

ATENCIÓN   The Spanish reflexives are seldom translated using the reflexive pronouns in English: **Yo me acuesto** = *I go to bed.*

33

FOLLOW-UP: Using the activities depicted in Transparency 33, have students describe a typical day in their lives using at least five reflexive verbs.

■ The following verbs have different meanings when they are used with reflexive pronouns.

acostar (o:ue) *to put to bed*	**acostarse** *to go to bed*
dormir (o:ue) *to sleep*	**dormirse** *to fall asleep*
ir *to go*	**irse** *to go away, leave*
levantar *to raise, lift*	**levantarse** *to get up*
llamar *to call*	**llamarse** *to be called*
poner *to put, place*	**ponerse** *to put on*
probar (o:ue) *to try; to taste*	**probarse** *to try on*
quitar *to take away*	**quitarse** *to take off*

—¿Te vas a **acostar**?   *"Are you going to go to bed?"*
—Sí, pero primero voy a   *"Yes, but first, I'm going*
   acostar a los niños.   *to put the children to bed."*

práctica •••

EXPANSION A: After students complete Exercise A, encourage them to say what each individual does afterwards. Remind them to use another reflexive verb if possible.

1. **Mi tía siempre se despierta tarde; después, tiene que bañarse rápidamente para ir al trabajo.**

A. Say what you and your relatives normally do by adding the correct form of the missing verbs.

1. Mi tía siempre _____ (despertarse) tarde.
2. Yo _____ (levantarse) muy temprano.
3. Mi padre _____ (afeitarse) en el baño.
4. Nosotros _____ (bañarse) por la mañana.
5. Mi hermana _____ (lavarse) la cabeza todos los días.
6. Mis primos _____ (vestirse) en diez minutos.
7. Yo _____ (desvestirse) y _____ (acostarse).
8. Mi mamá _____ (preocuparse) mucho cuando yo llego tarde.

SUGGESTION B: After students describe the illustrations, have them say or write questions that would elicit the responses they have given.

María duerme bien.
¿Cómo duerme María?

B. Say what these people are doing.

1. María _____ bien.

2. Los estudiantes _____ en la clase.

3. Juan le _____ el dinero al niño.

4. Pepito _____ el suéter.

5. Yo _____ la _____ en la clase.

6. Yo _____ a las seis.

7. Rosa _____ el _____
   en la _____ .

8. Rosa _____ el _____ .

ACTIVITY SUGGESTION: See the *IAM*
for an additional in-class activity:
¡Charadas!

9. Sergio _____ a Eva.

10. El muchacho _____
    Sergio _____ .

C. Interview a classmate, using the following questions and two questions of your
   own. When you have finished, switch roles.

1. ¿A qué hora te levantas tú generalmente? ¿y los sábados?
2. ¿A qué hora te levantaste hoy?
3. ¿A qué hora te acuestas?
4. ¿A qué hora te acostaste anoche?
5. ¿Puedes bañarte y vestirte en diez minutos?
6. ¿Te lavas la cabeza cuando te bañas?
7. ¿Te miras en el espejo para peinarte?
8. ¿Te acordaste de traer el libro de español?
9. ¿Cómo se llama tu mejor amigo(-a)?
10. ¿Se preocupan tus padres por ti?

D. With a partner, take turns saying what these people do according to the time and the circumstances.

1. A las seis de la mañana, yo _____.
2. En el baño, Carlos _____ con champú.
3. Antes de salir, tú te bañas y te _____.
4. En la tienda, antes de comprar un vestido, Rocío _____.
5. Cuando hace mucho frío, nosotros _____.
6. Frente al espejo, mi hermana _____.
7. Mi papá _____ con una máquina de afeitar.
8. Cuando yo vuelvo a mi casa muy tarde, mis padres _____.
9. En la clase, cuando están aburridos, los estudiantes _____.
10. A las once de la noche, Uds. _____.

Summary of Personal Pronouns

Subject	Direct object	Indirect object	Reflexive	Object of prepositions
yo	me	me	me	mí
tú	te	te	te	ti
usted (fem.)	la			usted
usted (masc.)	lo	le	se	usted
él	lo			él
ella	la			ella
nosotros(-as)	nos	nos	nos	nosotros(-as)
vosotros(-as)	os	os	os	vosotros(-as)
ustedes (fem.)	las			ustedes
ustedes (masc.)	los	les	se	ustedes
ellos	los			ellos
ellas	las			ellas

2 Some uses of the definite article *(Algunos usos del artículo definido)*

SUGGESTION: As a homework assignment, have students write two sentences that describe an action for each different use of the definite article. The next day divide the class into groups of three or four and have students take turns reading sentences for each rule. The other students should make corrections. Remind students that they may use the present and the past tenses.

1. *Parts of the body*
   Me lavé las manos antes de comer.
2. *Articles of clothing*
   Me quité la chaqueta en la clase.

The definite article has the following uses in Spanish.

■ The possessive adjective is often replaced by the definite article. An indirect object pronoun or a reflexive pronoun (if the subject performs the action upon himself or herself) usually indicates who the possessor is. Note the use of the definite article in Spanish in the following specific situations indicating possession.

■ With parts of the body

Voy a cortar**le el pelo.**   *I'm going to cut his hair.*
Me lavé **las manos.**   *I washed my hands.*

■ With articles of clothing and personal belongings

¿**Te** quitaste **el vestido?**   *Did you take off your dress?*
Ellos **se** quitaron **el suéter.**   *They took off their sweaters.*

ATENCIÓN   The number of the subject and verb generally does not affect the number of the thing possessed. Spanish uses the singular to indicate that each person has only one of any particular object.

Ellas se quitaron **el vestido.** (Each one has one dress.)	*They took off their dresses.*
but: Ellas se quitaron **los zapatos.** (Each one has two shoes.)	*They took off their shoes.*

◼ The definite article is used with abstract and generic nouns.

Me gusta **el té,** pero prefiero **el café.**	*I like tea, but I prefer coffee.*
Las madres siempre se preocupan por sus hijos.	*Mothers always worry about their children.*
La educación es muy importante.	*Education is very important.*

◼ The definite article is used with certain nouns, including **cárcel** *(jail)*, **iglesia** *(church)*, and **escuela** when they are preceded by a preposition.

—¿Vas a **la iglesia** los viernes?	*"Do you go to church on Fridays?"*
—No, voy a **la escuela.**	*"No, I go to school."*

◼ Remember that the definite article is also used with days of the week, when indicating titles in indirect address, and when telling time.

El Sr. Vega viene **el sábado** a **las tres** de la tarde.	*Mr. Vega is coming on Saturday at three o'clock in the afternoon.*

práctica ....

A. Interview a classmate, using the following questions. When you have finished, switch roles.

1. ¿Qué te gusta más, el pavo relleno o el arroz con pollo?
2. ¿Qué les gusta más a tus padres, el café o el té?
3. ¿Te gustan los rizos o prefieres el pelo lacio?
4. ¿Quién te corta el pelo?
5. ¿Con qué champú te lavas la cabeza?
6. ¿Te quitas los zapatos cuando llegas a tu casa?
7. ¿Te gustan los idiomas extranjeros *(foreign)?*
8. ¿Te gusta más el francés o el español?
9. ¿Vas a la iglesia los domingos?
10. ¿Qué es más importante para ti, el amor o el dinero?

SUGGESTION B: Have students complete this activity in pairs. Select students to act out each dialogue while the class listens. Encourage students to make corrections at the end of each presentation.

B. Supply the Spanish equivalent of the words in parentheses. Then act out the dialogues with a partner.

1. —¿Qué están haciendo _____ Paz y _____ Díaz?   *(Miss / Mrs.)*
   —Se están poniendo _____.   *(their dresses)*
2. —¿Te ensuciaste _____, Paquito?   *(your hands)*
   —Sí, pero _____.   *(I washed them)*

3. — _____ son más inteligentes que _____.   *(Women / men)*
   — _____ siempre dicen eso.   *(Women)*
4. —¿Él está en _____?   *(school)*
   —Sí, pero su hermano está en _____.   *(jail)*
5. —¿Qué dice _____ Peña?   *(Dr.)*
   —Ella dice que _____ es muy importante.   *(education)*

3 Possessive pronouns *(Pronombres posesivos)*

Singular		Plural		
Masculine	**Feminine**	**Masculine**	**Feminine**	
el mío	la mía	los míos	las mías	*mine*
el tuyo	la tuya	los tuyos	las tuyas	*yours* (fam.)
el suyo	la suya	los suyos	las suyas	{ *yours* (form.) *his* *hers*
el nuestro	la nuestra	los nuestros	las nuestras	*ours*
el vuestro	la vuestra	los vuestros	las vuestras	*yours* (fam.)
el suyo	la suya	los suyos	las suyas	{ *yours* (form.) *theirs*

■ In Spanish, possessive pronouns agree in gender and number with the thing possessed. They are generally used with the definite article.

—Aquí están **mis maletas.** ¿Dónde están **las tuyas?**   *"Here are my suitcases. Where are yours?"*
—**Las mías** están en mi cuarto.   *"Mine are in my room."*

—**Nuestro profesor** es de Colombia.   *"Our professor is from Colombia."*
—**El nuestro** es de Venezuela.   *"Ours is from Venezuela."*

—**Mi apartamento** está en la calle Palma.   *"My apartment is on Palma Street."*
—**El mío** está en la calle Estrella.   *"Mine is on Estrella Street."*

ATENCIÓN   After the verb **ser,** the definite article is frequently omitted.

—¿Estos billetes son **suyos,** señor?   *"Are these tickets yours, sir?"*
—No, no son **míos.**   *"No, they're not mine."*

■ Because the third-person forms of the possessive pronouns (**el suyo, la suya, los suyos, las suyas**) can be ambiguous, they can be replaced by the pronouns on the next page for clarification.

el de	⎧ Ud. ⎪ él ⎨ ella ⎪ Uds. ⎩ ellos ellas	el [libro] de él
la de		el **de él**
los de		
las de		**Es suyo.** *(unclarified)*
		Es el de él. *(clarified)*

—Estas maletas son de Eva y de Jorge, ¿no?	*"These suitcases are Eva's and Jorge's, aren't they?"*
—Bueno, la maleta azul es **de ella** y la maleta marrón es **de él.**	*"Well, the blue suitcase is hers, and the brown suitcase is his."*
—¿El espejo es **de Uds.?**	*"Is the mirror yours?"*
—No, es **de ellos.**	*"No, it's theirs."*

práctica ....

A. Provide the correct possessive pronoun for each subject.

> **MODELO:** Yo tengo una tarjeta postal. Es…
> *Yo tengo una tarjeta postal. Es mía.*

1. Mario tiene una revista. Es…
2. Nosotros tenemos dos entradas. Son…
3. Tú tienes un espejo. Es…
4. Inés tiene dos pinturas. Son…
5. Yo tengo dos casas. Son…
6. Ud. tiene un perro. Es…
7. Ellas tienen los vestidos. Son…
8. Paco tiene una botella de vino. Es…

B. Complete the following dialogue using the correct possessive pronoun.

1. —Mis entradas están aquí. ¿Dónde están _____, Anita? *(yours)*
   — _____ están en mi cuarto, pero Pedro no tiene _____. *(Mine / his)*
2. —Yo no tengo maletas, pero Ana me va a prestar una de _____. *(hers)*
   —O yo puedo prestarte una de _____. *(mine)*
   —¡Pero tú vas a necesitar todas _____! *(yours)*
   —Yo tengo tres maletas…
3. —Mis hijos están en Lima. ¿Dónde están _____, señor Fuentes? *(yours)*
   — _____ están en Arequipa. *(Mine)*

ACTIVITY SUGGESTION: See the *IAM*
for an additional in-class activity:
Razones.

C. With a partner, make comparisons between the objects and people described and those in your own experience. Use appropriate possessive pronouns when asking each other questions.

> **MODELO:** —El hermano de Teresa tiene quince años. ¿Y el tuyo?
> —*El mío tiene dieciocho.*

1. Los mejores amigos de Rosa son de Cuba.
2. El apartamento de Ana tiene cuatro cuartos.

3. Los padres de Ramiro viven en San Diego.
4. El cumpleaños de Jorge es en septiembre.
5. Las maletas de Alina son verdes.
6. La hermana de Rafael es muy bonita.
7. El idioma de Hans es alemán.
8. Las primas de Enrique son uruguayas.

Now, with your partner, compare other aspects of your lives, such as your room or apartment, relatives, classes, car, tapes, jobs, and so on.

4   Irregular preterits   *(Pretéritos irregulares)*

SUGGESTION: To help students learn the irregularities of these verbs, write the following groupings on the board.

uv   tener/estar
u   poder/poner/saber
i   hacer/venir/querer
j   decir/traer/conducir/traducir

SUGGESTION: Write the following phrases on the board or on an overhead transparency. In pairs, have students take turns asking each other **¿Cuándo fue la última vez que...?**

tener un examen
estar enfermo(-a)
poder ir a la peluquería (barbería)
ponerse ropa elegante
saber *(found out)* **algo interesante**
venir tarde a clase
querer comprar algo caro
decir una mentira *(lie)*
conducir más de 500 millas en un día
traducir unas frases al español
haber una fiesta en tu casa/apartamento/residencia

■ The following Spanish verbs are irregular in the preterit.

tener:	tuve, tuviste, tuvo, tuvimos, tuvisteis, tuvieron
estar:	estuve, estuviste, estuvo, estuvimos, estuvisteis, estuvieron
poder:	pude, pudiste, pudo, pudimos, pudisteis, pudieron
poner:	puse, pusiste, puso, pusimos, pusisteis, pusieron
saber:	supe, supiste, supo, supimos, supisteis, supieron
hacer:	hice, hiciste, hizo,[1] hicimos, hicisteis, hicieron
venir:	vine, viniste, vino, vinimos, vinisteis, vinieron
querer:	quise, quisiste, quiso, quisimos, quisisteis, quisieron
decir:	dije, dijiste, dijo, dijimos, dijisteis, dijeron[2]
traer:	traje, trajiste, trajo, trajimos, trajisteis, trajeron[2]
conducir:	conduje, condujiste, condujo, condujimos, condujisteis, condujeron[2]
traducir:	traduje, tradujiste, tradujo, tradujimos, tradujisteis, tradujeron[2]

—¿Por qué no **viniste** anoche?   *"Why didn't you come last night?"*
—No **pude; tuve** que trabajar.   *"I wasn't able to; I had to*
   Y tú, ¿qué **hiciste**?   *work. And you, what did you*
                                       do?"

—Yo **estuve** en casa toda la   *"I was home all night."*
   noche.

—¿Qué me **trajeron** Uds.?   *"What did you bring me?"*
—Te **trajimos** una cartera.   *"We brought you a purse."*
—¿Dónde la **pusieron**?   *"Where did you put it?"*
—La **pusimos** en tu cuarto.   *"We put it in your room."*

ATENCIÓN   The preterit of **hay** (impersonal form of **haber**) is **hubo** *(there was, there were)*.

Anoche **hubo** un concierto.   *Last night there was a concert.*

---

[1] Note that in the third-person singular form, **c** changes to **z** in order to maintain the soft sound.
[2] Note that in the third-person plural ending of these verbs, the **i** is omitted.

práctica ....

A. Elsa and David are arguing. Complete their dialogue, using the preterit of the verbs given. Then act it out with a partner.

ELSA —¿Dónde _____ (estar) (tú) anoche?
¡ _____ (Venir) muy tarde!

DAVID —¡Te lo _____ (decir)! _____ (Estar) en casa de mamá.
_____ (Tener) que hablar con papá. No te llamé porque no
_____ (poder).

ELSA —¿No _____ (poder) o no _____ (querer)?

DAVID —Bueno. ¿Dónde _____ (poner) tú las cartas que yo
_____ (traducir) ayer en la oficina?

ELSA —¡Tú no _____ (traer) ninguna carta!

DAVID —No… los empleados las _____ (traer) cuando _____
(venir) ayer.

ELSA —Ellos no me _____ (decir) nada. ¡Son unos idiotas!

SUGGESTION B: Have students make up sentences contrasting what they always do with what they didn't do on one occasion. Write the following words and phrases on the board and encourage students to use as many as possible.

normalmente   ayer
usualmente   esta mañana
siempre   anoche
frecuentemente   el año pasado
generalmente   la semana
                     pasada
                   el mes pasado

B. Answer the following questions about yourself and your friends.

1. ¿Qué tuvo que hacer ayer?
2. ¿Qué hicieron sus amigos ayer?
3. ¿Dónde estuvieron Uds. anoche?
4. ¿Hubo una fiesta en su casa ayer?
5. ¿Uds. tuvieron que limpiar la casa?
6. ¿Vino a clase la semana pasada?
7. ¿Pudo venir Ud. temprano a la universidad ayer?
8. ¿Condujo su coche ayer?

C. Read what the following people typically do. Then, using your imagination, say what everyone did differently yesterday.

1. Yo estoy en mi casa por la mañana.
2. Tú vienes a la universidad a las diez de la mañana.
3. Paquito hace la tarea por la tarde.
4. Julio tiene que trabajar en el hospital.
5. Nosotros traemos a nuestros hijos a la escuela.
6. Ellos traducen las lecciones al inglés.
7. María se pone el vestido azul.
8. Yo conduzco mi coche.

D. In groups of three, prepare some questions for your instructor about what he or she did yesterday, last night, or last week. Use irregular preterit forms in your questions.

5 Formation of adverbs *(La formación de los adverbios)*

■ Most Spanish adverbs are formed by adding **-mente** (the equivalent of the English *-ly*) to the adjective.

especial	*special*		especial**mente**	*especially*
reciente	*recent*		reciente**mente**	*recently*
general	*general*		general**mente**	*generally*

■ Adjectives ending in **-o** change the **-o** to **-a** before adding **-mente**.

lento	*slow*		lent**amente**	*slowly*
rápido	*rapid*		rápid**amente**	*rapidly*
desafortunado	*unfortunate*		desafortunad**amente**	
				unfortunately

■ If two or more adverbs are used together, both change the **-o** to **-a**, but only the last adverb takes the **-mente** ending.

—Habló clara y **lentamente.**   *He spoke clearly and slowly.*

■ If the adjective has an accent, the adverb retains it.

fácil   **fácilmente**

práctica ···

SUGGESTION A: In groups of three, have students write a list of things they commonly do (10–15 phrases). They should then take turns asking each other how well, poorly, and frequently they do the listed activities.

S1—¿Hablas bien el español?
S2—Sí, lo hablo perfectamente.

For additional practice, you may want to list other adjectives that can be changed to adverbs on the board. For example:

tranquilo(-a)	paciente
silencioso(-a)	conciso(-a)
incoherente	brillante
preciso(-a)	nervioso(-a)
cuidadoso(-a)	pensativo(-a)
elocuente	puntual

A. Change the following adjectives to adverbs.

1. fácil
2. feliz
3. claro *(clear)*
4. raro *(rare)*
5. necesario
6. frecuente *(frequent)*
7. triste
8. trágico *(tragic)*
9. alegre *(merry)*
10. desgraciado

B. Complete the following sentences with appropriate adverbs.

1. Ellos hablaron _____ y _____.
2. Mis padres vienen a verme _____.
3. Jaime llegó _____.
4. El muchacho me habló _____.
5. _____ me levanto a las siete.
6. Los muchachos cantan _____.
7. _____ no tengo dinero.
8. Compré esa máquina de afeitar _____ para ti.
9. _____ no pude ir a México con ellos.

C. Interview a classmate, using the following questions and two of your own. Include adverbs in your responses. When you have finished, switch roles.

1. ¿A qué hora te levantas tú?
2. ¿Tú y tu familia van de compras juntos?
3. ¿Tú ves a tus abuelos a menudo *(often)*?
4. ¿Vas al teatro a menudo?
5. ¿Tú tienes mucho dinero?

D. With a partner, discuss what you frequently do, rarely do, and what, unfortunately, you can't do.

¡A ver cuánto aprendió!

INTERNET

See the *¿Cómo se dice…?*
Web site for additional
grammar and vocabulary
practice: http://spanish.college.
hmco.com/students

ACTIVITY SUGGESTION: Do **¡Escucha!**,
the in-class listening comprehension
activity that reviews vocabulary and
grammar structures introduced in the
lesson. It appears in the answer key of
the *IAM*.

ACTIVITY SUGGESTION: See the *IAM*
for an additional in-class activity:
Palabras escondidas.

ACTIVITY SUGGESTION:
See the *IAM* for an
additional vocabulary
activity (Lecciones 1–9): **Familias de
palabras.**

ACTIVITY SUGGESTION: See the *IAM*
for additional in-class activities:
Para conocernos mejor and **Una
encuesta.**

¡Repase el vocabulario!

Say whether the following statements are logical or not. If they're not logical, give
a statement that is.

1. El perro limpió el apartamento.
2. No puedo afeitarme porque no tengo escoba.
3. Elvira lee una revista en la peluquería.
4. Tengo el pelo muy lacio. Necesito un rizador.
5. Generalmente pongo el recogedor en el botiquín.
6. Tengo que ir a la tienda porque necesito corte, lavado y peinado.
7. No estoy haciendo nada. Estoy muy ocupado.
8. Ahora podemos comer porque yo ya cociné. Preparé cordero y arroz.
9. No quiero una permanente porque no me gustan los rizos.
10. Una semana tiene diez días.
11. Me voy. El peluquero no terminó de cortarme el pelo.
12. Nunca me olvido de nada. Siempre me acuerdo de todo.
13. El peluquero me cortó el pelo.
14. Necesito el secador para planchar mi vestido.
15. Generalmente hay menos gente en la peluquería por la mañana.

Entrevista

With a partner, interview each other by asking the following questions.

1. ¿Te gusta el pelo corto o el pelo largo?
2. ¿Vas a pedir turno en la peluquería? ¿Para cuándo?
3. ¿Te lavas la cabeza todos los días?
4. ¿Crees que está de moda el pelo corto o el pelo largo?
5. ¿Estás invitado(-a) a alguna fiesta el sábado?
6. ¿Tienes algo que ponerte para ir a una fiesta?
7. ¿Qué le vas a regalar a tu mejor amigo(-a) para su cumpleaños?
8. ¿Barres la cocina o le pasas la aspiradora?
9. ¿Sabes cocinar?
10. ¿Siempre limpias la cocina cuando la ensucias?
11. ¿Por quién te preocupas tú a veces *(sometimes)*?
12. Generalmente ¿a qué hora te acuestas?

Situaciones

What would you say in the following situations? What might the other person
say?

1. You are at home. Ask your younger brother if he bathed and combed his hair.
   Also ask if he cleaned his room. Tell him he has to sweep the kitchen.
2. Someone asks about your schedule. Tell him or her what time you generally
   go to bed and get up. Also say how long it takes you to bathe and get dressed.

3. You are at the beauty parlor (barbershop). Tell the hairdresser (barber) what you want done. Then make an appointment for next month.

 Para escribir

Write a composition about your daily routine. Say what you do from the time you wake up until the time you go to bed.

En la vida real

CD-ROM

Do the interactive exercises on the CD-ROM for additional practice.

¡Vamos a la peluquería!

Carefully read the following ads for two hair salons, and then answer the questions that follow.

PELUQUERÍA ANABEL

Especiales de esta semana
Permanentes de . . . .$35 a $50
Tinte $15
Manicura $7
Corte $8
Corte, lavado y peinado $20

Abierto de martes a sábado
Martes a viernes de 9 a 5
Sábados de 8 a 6

Avenida Paz #28 Teléfono 287–3574

Si presenta este anuncio Ud. recibe un 10% de descuento.

Salón de belleza La Época

- Expertos peluqueros y barberos
- Especialidad en permanentes
- Tenemos los mejores equipos y los precios más bajos para hombres y mujeres.

Abierto de lunes a sábado de 9 a 5
Calle Bolívar No. 439

Para pedir su turno llame al teléfono 287–2308

Martes precios especiales para mayores de 50 años.

1. En la peluquería Anabel, ¿cuál es el precio mínimo de una permanente?
2. Si Ud. quiere cortarse el pelo el lunes, ¿a qué peluquería puede ir?
3. Su hermano desea afeitarse y cortarse el pelo. ¿Puede ir a la peluquería Anabel? ¿Por qué sí o por qué no?
4. ¿Adónde puede ir? ¿Por qué?
5. ¿Por qué es importante tener el anuncio de la peluquería Anabel?
6. ¿Cuánto hay que pagar por un tinte y por un corte de pelo?
7. Mi abuela tiene 58 años. ¿Por qué debe ir a la peluquería La Época y qué día debe ir?
8. ¿A qué teléfono debe llamar ella para pedir turno?
9. ¿Cuál es la especialidad del salón de belleza La Época?
10. ¿Cuál es la dirección de la peluquería Anabel?

Una visita importante

SUGGESTION: Before starting this activity, encourage students to write a list of ten things they would do to prepare for an important visitor.

With a classmate, act out a scene involving two roommates who are expecting a visitor. Discuss what you have to do in order to get the house (apartment) and yourselves ready for your guest, and divide up the chores that must be done.

¿Qué es?

FOLLOW-UP: Have students name three of their favorite products and tell why they think their choices are better than "Brand X." Suggest that they include some comparisons (**Lección 5**) of quality and price.

The class will be divided into two teams. Your instructor will give each student an item from the vocabulary list in this lesson to draw on the board. The other members of the team must try to guess what is being drawn. If they guess within one minute, they get a point.

¡VAMOS A LEER!

Antes de leer

A. Before you read the fable of the hare and the tortoise (**la liebre y la tortuga**), think about things you already know that may be useful to you as you read. For example, what characteristics are typically associated with hares and tortoises? What is the purpose of a fable? With the answers to these questions in mind, make a brief list of vocabulary you might expect to encounter in the reading.

B. As you read the fable, find the answers to the following questions.

1. ¿Por qué se burla continuamente la liebre de la tortuga?
2. ¿Qué le hace la tortuga a la liebre en presencia de los otros animales?
3. ¿Cómo responde la liebre?
4. ¿A quién nombran *(name)* juez de la carrera?
5. Durante la carrera, ¿qué hace la liebre? ¿Y la tortuga?
6. ¿Cómo termina la carrera?
7. ¿Cuál es la moraleja *(moral)* de la fábula?

La liebre y la tortuga

(FÁBULA DE ESOPO°)

Aesop

Una liebre° se burla° continuamente de una tortuga,° porque la pobre tortuga es muy lenta.   *hare / makes fun / tortoise*

La tortuga no quiere hacer caso de° las burlas de la liebre, pero un día, harta° de oírlas, decide desafiar° a la liebre, en presencia de los otros animales, a tener una carrera.°   **hacer...** *to pay attention to* / *fed up* / *to challenge* / *race*

—¡Qué idea! —dice la liebre—. Tú sabes muy bien que las tortugas no pueden ganar° ninguna carrera...   *win*

—¡Ésa es tu opinión! ¿Estás lista° para comenzar?   *ready*

Los animales nombran juez° al zorro° y empieza la carrera. En dos segundos, la liebre desaparece. La tortuga empieza a caminar° con su lentitud de siempre.   *judge / fox* / *to walk*

Al rato, la liebre se detiene° para esperar a la tortuga. Espera y espera hasta que empieza a tener sueño.   *stops*

—Puedo dormir una siesta° y continuar la carrera más tarde —piensa la liebre. Y se duerme, tranquila y feliz, en la verde hierba.°   *nap* / *grass*

Mientras tanto,° la tortuga sigue caminando lentamente pero sin parar° y pasa a la liebre, que continúa durmiendo.   **Mientras...** *Meanwhile /* **sin...** *without stopping*

Lenta y paciente, la tortuga gana la carrera. La liebre, avergonzada,° se queda donde está sin mirar a los animales que aclaman° a la tortuga victoriosa.   *ashamed* / *are applauding*

Moraleja: *Con perseverancia se gana a veces° la carrera.*   **a...** *sometimes*

Díganos

Answer the following questions, based on your own thoughts and experiences.

1. ¿Ud. se burla de alguien a veces? ¿Por qué?
2. ¿De qué o de quién está harto(-a) Ud.?
3. ¿Ud. se identifica con la liebre o con la tortuga? ¿Por qué?

NOTE: The video-related vocabulary is listed in the *Instructor's Activities Manual* for your reference. Its purpose is to facilitate students' comprehension. You may want to distribute the vocabulary to the class before viewing.

ASÍ SOMOS

VIDEO   CD-ROM   Do the interactive exercises on the CD-ROM for additional practice.

NARRADORA	—¿Cómo es su rutina diaria?
ZAIDA	—Mi rutina diaria comienza entre seis y siete de la mañana de acuerdo a la hora en que tenga clase. Eh... me levanto a las seis y media, tomo una ducha *(I take a shower)*, me visto para ir a la universidad. Tengo clase de siete a cuatro de la tarde todos los días. Y almuerzo a las once de la mañana...

NOTE: See the Instructor's Edition frontmatter for additional suggestions on implementing video in the classroom.

SUGGESTION: In groups, have students make a list of the activities they see people doing at the beginning of the video.

Preparación

SUGGESTION: Have students brainstorm other words and phrases used to discuss daily routines and household chores.

A. Su rutina diaria. Answer the following questions based on your own information. You will hear answers to some of these questions when you watch the video. After viewing the video, compare your answers with those you hear.

1. ¿Cómo es su rutina diaria?
2. ¿A qué hora se levanta?
3. ¿A qué hora desayuna? ¿A qué hora almuerza? ¿A qué hora cena?
4. ¿A qué hora se acuesta?
5. ¿Quién hace los trabajos de la casa? ¿Qué día los hace?

B. Mis quehaceres favoritos. Make a list of the household chores you know in Spanish. Then rate them in order of your preference, from your favorite chore to your least favorite chore. Share your list with the class.

Comprensión

SUGGESTION: Pause the video after each interview segment so students have time to complete the corresponding comprehension activity.

A. **¿Verdadero o falso?** Read the following statements. Circle **V** (**Verdadero**) or **F** (**Falso**) according to what you understood from the video. If a statement is false, correct it.

V F   1. Por lo regular *(As a rule)* Pedro hace ejercicio por la mañana.

V F   2. Pedro come con sus amigos en la universidad.

V F   3. Pedro y sus amigos juegan futbolito *(soccer)* o billar *(billiards)* por la tarde.

V F   4. Zaida se levanta muy tarde.

V F   5. Zaida tiene clase sólo por la mañana.

V F   6. Zaida va al gimnasio por la tarde.

V F   7. Juan se levanta temprano.

V F   8. Juan duerme una siestecita *(little nap)* por la tarde.

V F   9. Juan sale con su novia o con sus amigos después de cenar *(after having dinner)*.

V F   10. Anselmo no tiene hijos.

V F   11. Anselmo sale de casa a las siete y media.

V F   12. Anselmo llega a la oficina a las nueve.

B. **¿Quién lo dijo?** Match each statement with the name of the person who said it.

A	**B**
_____ 1. Una vez a la semana hacemos la limpieza general de toda la casa.	a. Zaida
_____ 2. Una señora y mi madre hacen los trabajos de la casa.	b. Gustavo
_____ 3. Mis compañeras y yo nos turnamos *(take turns)* para limpiar la casa.	c. Otmara
_____ 4. Tengo una señora que nos limpia la casa.	d. Ángela
_____ 5. Todos ayudamos y cooperamos en la casa.	e. Juan

Ampliación

EXPANSION: Have students choose a person from the video and compare their daily routine with their own routine. How are they similar? How are they different?

FOLLOW-UP: Do a class survey to find out which are the most favorite chores and the least favorite chores of the class.

A. **La rutina diaria.** With a partner, compare your daily routine on a school day with your daily routine on a weekend day. Share your observations with the class.

B. **Los quehaceres de la casa.** Make a list of all the household chores you know in Spanish. Then, make a schedule for when each chore needs to be done and assign a person to do them. Share your schedule with the class.

Take this test. When you have finished, check your answers in the answer key provided in Appendix E. Then use a red pen to correct any mistakes you may have made. Are you ready?

Lección 7

A. Demonstrative adjectives and pronouns

Give the Spanish equivalent of the following.

1. these postcards and those (over there)
2. that suitcase and this one
3. these travel agencies and those (over there)
4. this plane and that one (over there)
5. this boat and that one
6. these letters and those

B. Indirect object pronouns

Rewrite the following sentences, using indirect object pronouns to replace the words in italics.

1. Ella trae la lista *para ellos.*
2. Yo voy a preparar un sándwich *para ti.*
3. Él trae el equipaje *para Ud.*
4. Ana va a comprar las tarjetas postales *para mí.*
5. El agente de viajes trae los pasajes *para nosotros.*
6. Traen los cheques de viajeros *para ellas.*

C. Constructions with *gustar*

Write the following sentences in Spanish.

1. I don't like that travel agency.
2. He likes the aisle seat.
3. Do you like this carry-on bag?
4. We don't like to travel by plane.
5. Do they like their hotel?

D. Time expressions with *hacer*

Form sentences with the elements provided, using the expression **hace... que** to report how long an event has been going on. Follow the model.

> MODELO: una hora / nosotros / trabajar
> *Hace una hora que nosotros trabajamos.*

1. dos días / yo / no dormir
2. un mes / tú / no llamarme
3. media hora / nosotros / estar aquí
4. un año / ellos / vivir / España
5. doce horas / mi hija / no comer

E. Preterit of regular verbs

Rewrite the following sentences so that instead of describing things that *are going to happen*, they describe things that *already happened*.

1. Mañana Luisa y yo vamos a comprar los billetes. (ayer)
2. La semana próxima yo voy a viajar. (la semana pasada)
3. Hoy ella va a presentarme a sus padres. (ayer)
4. ¿No van a pagar Uds. los pasajes hoy? (ayer)
5. Esta tarde ellos van a abrir las ventanas. (al mediodía)
6. Nosotros vamos a comer en la cafetería. (el lunes)
7. ¿Vas a empezar a estudiar mañana? (esta mañana)
8. Yo voy a prestarle las maletas. (ayer)

F. Just words . . .

Complete the following sentences, using appropriate words or phrases from the vocabulary list in Lección 7.

1. Voy a la agencia de _____ para comprar el pasaje.
2. ¿Uds. van a volar a México mañana? ¡_____!
3. No puedo comprar un pasaje de primera clase. Tengo que viajar en clase _____.
4. Voy a Buenos Aires, pero no vuelvo. Quiero un pasaje de _____.
5. ¡Son las cuatro! El avión tiene tres horas de _____.
6. Mañana te voy a _____ el bolso de mano que me prestaste.
7. La _____ vez tenemos que viajar juntas.
8. Aquí está la entrada y ahí está la _____.
9. No tengo valijas; sólo un bolso de _____.
10. A Eva y a Luisa les gusta viajar _____.
11. Llevé cinco maletas y pagué _____ de equipaje.
12. Puedo ir de California a Arizona en avión, en coche, en tren o en ómnibus, pero no en _____.

G. Culture

Answer the following questions, based on the **¿Lo sabía Ud.?** section.

1. ¿A qué altura está situada Cuzco?
2. ¿De qué civilización es Cuzco la antigua capital?
3. ¿Qué es la ciudad de Cuzco hoy día?
4. ¿Cómo se conoce a Machu Picchu?
5. ¿Cuánto se extendió el imperio de los incas?

Lección 8

A. Direct and indirect object pronouns used together

Answer the following questions, using the cues provided, substituting direct object pronouns for the italicized words, and making any necessary changes.

1. ¿Cuándo le van a mandar *el pasaje* a Jorge? (mañana)
2. ¿Quién te va a comprar *las entradas*? (Elsa)

3. ¿Quién les va a traducir *las cartas* a Uds.? (Luis)
4. ¿Cuándo me vas a traer *el lechón*? (esta tarde)
5. ¿Quién le va a dar *la pulsera* a Ud.? (la profesora)

B. Preterit of *ir, ser,* and *dar*

Change the following sentences according to the new subjects.

1. Yo fui al restaurante y comí pavo asado. (Nosotros)
2. Ud. no fue mi profesor el año pasado. (Él)
3. ¿Ud. le dio la botella, señora? (Tú, querido)
4. ¿Quién pidió el bistec? ¿Fuiste tú, Tere? (Ud., señorita)
5. Ella no le dio el flan a Pedro. (Nosotras)
6. Ellos fueron al teatro. (Yo)
7. Nosotros no le dimos la cuenta. (Yo)
8. ¿Fueron ellos al restaurante anoche? (tú)
9. Carlos y yo fuimos a la fiesta la semana pasada. (Ellos)
10. ¿Fueron Uds. sus estudiantes el año pasado? (Raúl y Eva)
11. Nosotros te dimos la propina. (Yo)
12. Ella nos dio una torta helada. (Ellos)

C. Preterit of *e:i* and *o:u* stem-changing verbs

Complete the following sentences, using the preterit tense of the verbs listed below, as needed.

mentir	pedir	dormir	repetir
seguir	morir	conseguir	servir

1. ¿_____ ellos en el hotel el jueves?
2. Los chicos _____ a sus padres a la tienda.
3. Nosotros _____ sándwiches de jamón y queso.
4. Ella me _____. No tiene veinte años; tiene diez y siete.
5. ¿No _____ Ud. el dinero para ir de vacaciones?
6. ¿Qué le _____ los niños a Santa Claus?
7. El hombre _____ en un accidente.
8. Ella me _____ la pregunta *(question)*.

D. Uses of *por* and *para*

Complete the following sentences with **por** or **para,** as needed.

Ayer fui a la agencia de viajes _____ comprar un pasaje _____ Madrid. Pagué setecientos dólares _____ el pasaje, pero eso no es demasido caro. Quería *(I wanted)* el pasaje _____ el sábado, pero no pude conseguirlo. El avión sale el domingo _____ la mañana. _____ la tarde fui otra vez al centro _____ comprar un regalo _____ mi hermano, porque mañana es su aniversario de bodas. Llamé a mi padre _____ teléfono _____ decirle que no podía *(I wasn't able)* ir _____ él hasta las siete. Caminé *(I walked)* _____ el centro y pasé _____ la casa de Julia, que estudia _____ dentista. Julia me deseó buen viaje.

E. Ordinal numbers

Complete the following sentences.

1. Marzo es el _____ mes del año.
2. Mayo es el _____ mes del año.
3. Abril es el _____ mes del año.
4. El _____ mes del año es octubre.
5. Agosto es el _____ mes del año.
6. Enero es el _____ mes del año.

F. Just words . . .

Match each question in column A with the best response in column B. Use each response once.

A	B
1. ¿Qué quieres de postre?	a. No, prefiero cordero.
2. ¿Quieres café?	b. Sí, con champán.
3. ¿Quieres albóndigas?	c. No, agua mineral.
4. ¿Cuánto vas a dejar de propina?	d. Los frijoles son muy buenos aquí.
5. ¿Qué vas a pedir?	e. Es una sorpresa…
6. ¿Cómo está la comida?	f. No, prefiero jugo de frutas. Hace mucho calor.
7. ¿Qué vas a anotar?	g. No, no me gusta el pescado.
8. ¿Qué me recomiendas?	h. No sé. ¿Quieres ver el menú?
9. ¿Quieres salmón?	i. Sí, con crema, por favor.
10. ¿Qué sirven en este restaurante?	j. No, la pimienta.
11. ¿Vas a beber cerveza?	k. Sí, traigan las copas.
12. ¿Quieres chocolate caliente?	l. Sí, ¿dónde están las tazas, los platitos y las cucharitas?
13. ¿Vamos a celebrar nuestro aniversario?	m. Cinco dólares.
14. ¿Van al teatro?	n. Creo que es pescado y mariscos.
15. ¿Qué me vas a traer?	o. El pedido.
16. ¿Vamos a tomar vermut?	p. Sí, porque voy a poner la mesa.
17. ¿Cuál es la especialidad de la casa?	q. La cuenta.
18. ¿Quieres la sal?	r. No, al cine.
19. ¿No vas a servir el té?	s. Arroz con leche o flan.
20. ¿Necesitas el mantel y las servilletas?	t. Está rica.

G. Culture

Circle the correct answer, based on the **¿Lo sabía Ud.?** section.

1. Cientos de miles de turistas (franceses, latinoamericanos, españoles) visitan Miami todos los años.
2. Más de un millón de hispanos viven en Miami, en su mayoría (cubanos, mexicanos, uruguayos).
3. En los países de habla hispana, el café se sirve (después del, antes del, durante el) postre.

4. Después de comer, los hispanos generalmente "hacen la (comida, cena, sobremesa)".

5. En los restaurantes hispanos, la propina es del (10%, 25%, 15%).

Lección 9

A. Reflexive constructions

Rewrite each sentence according to the new cue. Follow the model.

> Modelo: Yo *me despierto* a las nueve. (levantarse)
> *Yo me levanto a las nueve.*

1. *La gente* se viste muy bien. (Tú)
2. Ellos *se bañan* todos los días. (afeitarse)
3. *Nosotros* nos acostamos a las once. (Ellos)
4. ¿*Tú* no te preocupas por tus hijos? (Ud.)
5. Yo *me pruebo* el vestido. (ponerse)
6. *Nosotros* nos sentamos aquí. (Juan)
7. *Ella* se lava la cabeza todos los días. (Tú)
8. Yo no *me peiné*. (cortarse el pelo)
9. *Ellos* no se acordaron de eso. (Yo)
10. Yo me fui. (Uds.)
11. ¿Cómo se llama *ella*? (tú)
12. *Los niños* no se despertaron hasta las diez. (Daniel)

B. Some uses of the definite article

Form sentences with the elements given, adding the necessary connectors. Use verbs in the present tense. Follow the model.

> Modelo: yo / ponerse / vestido
> *Yo me pongo el vestido.*

1. ¿ / tú / quitarse / suéter / ?
2. el barbero / cortarme / pelo
3. la peluquera / lavarme / cabeza
4. Uds. / no lavarse / manos
5. nosotros / preferir / té
6. madres / preocuparse / por / sus hijos
7. comunicación / ser / lo más importante

C. Possessive pronouns

Give the Spanish equivalent of the pronouns in parentheses.

1. El espejo de Nora está en la mesa. _____ está en mi cuarto. *(Mine)*
2. Mis revistas están aquí. ¿Dónde están _____, Sr. Vega? *(yours)*
3. Ellos van a enviar sus cartas hoy. ¿Cuándo vamos a enviar _____? *(ours)*
4. No tengo maletas. ¿Puedes prestarme _____, Anita? *(yours)*
5. Aquí están los regalos de Jorge. ¿Dónde están _____? *(ours)*
6. Enrique necesita tu cuaderno, Eva. _____ está en la universidad. *(His)*

D. Irregular preterits

Give the Spanish equivalent of the verbs in parentheses.

1. Ellos _____ que ir al teatro. *(had)*
2. ¿Dónde _____ Uds. anoche? *(were)*
3. Yo lo _____ al italiano. *(translated)*
4. Yo no _____ ir a la peluquería. *(was able)*
5. ¿Dónde _____ tú la aspiradora? *(put)*
6. Anoche _____ una fiesta. *(there was)*
7. Él no _____ las maletas. *(packed)*
8. Mi abuelo no _____ ayer. *(came)*
9. Ellos _____ nada. *(didn't say)*
10. Ella me _____ un secador. *(brought)*

E. Formation of adverbs

Give the Spanish equivalent of the adverbs in parentheses.

1. Me gustan esas alfombras, _____ la azul. *(especially)*
2. Yo _____ voy a conciertos. *(frequently)*
3. El profesor habló _____ y _____. *(slowly and clearly)*
4. Vino a verme _____. *(recently)*
5. _____ voy a la peluquería los sábados. *(Generally)*
6. _____ no voy al teatro. *(Unfortunately)*

F. Just words . . .

Complete the following sentences, using the appropriate words and phrases from the vocabulary list in **Lección 9.**

1. Necesito la _____ para barrer la cocina.
2. Voy a pedir turno en la peluquería para corte, _____ y _____.
3. Prefiero el pelo largo porque el pelo corto no está de _____.
4. ¿Por qué no le pasas la _____ a la alfombra?
5. Siempre como en restaurantes porque no me gusta _____.
6. Tengo que comprar _____ para lavarme la cabeza.
7. No tiene rizos; tiene el pelo muy _____.
8. No le di el dinero para comprar la _____ *Time.*
9. No puedo peinarme porque no tengo _____.
10. Voy a afeitarme. ¿Dónde está la _____ de _____?
11. Es el cumpleaños de Jorge. Tengo que comprarle un _____.

G. Culture

Read the following statements and circle **V** (**Verdadero**) or **F** (**Falso**), based on the **¿Lo sabía Ud.?** section.

V F   1. Montevideo es la capital de Paraguay.
V F   2. Paraguay es más o menos del tamaño *(size)* de California.
V F   3. Muchos turistas visitan Paraguay.
V F   4. En Paraguay hablan dos idiomas: el español y el italiano.
V F   5. La mayoría de los paraguayos saben leer y escribir.

OBJECTIVES

Pronunciation
Pronunciation in context

Structure
Hace meaning *ago* • The imperfect • The preterit contrasted with the imperfect • Verbs that change meaning in the preterit

Communication
You will learn vocabulary related to leisure activities.

Las vacaciones de Silvia

STUDENT
AUDIO

SUGGESTION: Before presenting Silvia's letter to Victoria, introduce some of the vocabulary related to outdoor activities on page 245 by asking students to categorize words they think are necessary to design or describe a vacation. Suggested categories are: **lugares, qué cosas traer, otros preparativos, actividades, comidas,** etc. Remind them to refer to previous vocabulary lists for other words.

SUGGESTION: Point out that February is a summer month in the southern countries of the southern hemisphere. Have students guess months of the year when Silvia's family will go to Bariloche.

SUGGESTION: Refer students to **Panorama hispánico 8** for more information about Argentina, Chile, and Uruguay. Also see the corresponding video segment on Argentina.

Córdoba, Argentina
12 de febrero del 2002

Querida Victoria:

¡Estaba equivocada! Creí que no me iba a gustar ir de vacaciones con mis padres y que me iba a aburrir y, sin embargo, me estoy divirtiendo mucho.

Llegamos a Córdoba hace una semana. Al día siguiente de llegar fuimos a acampar junto al Río de los Sauces. Papá y mi hermano armaron las tiendas de campaña y todos dormimos profundamente en nuestras bolsas de dormir. ¡Hice de todo! Nadé, fui de pesca con Miguel Ángel (no pesqué nada, a pesar de que tenía una caña de pescar nueva), monté a caballo y en bicicleta.

Anoche unos amigos chilenos dieron una fiesta. Yo no quería ir, pero papá me convenció y fui. Allí conocí a Gustavo, un muchacho de Santiago. ¡Bailé toda la noche con él!

¿Y a ti cómo te fue en Buenos Aires? ¿Fuiste de compras? ¿Te quedaste en casa de tus tíos? Espero que sí, porque los hoteles en Buenos Aires cuestan un ojo de la cara. Yo me hospedé en uno hace tres meses y me costó una fortuna...

El próximo año tienes que venir con nosotros. ¡En serio! Pensamos ir a Bariloche y alquilar una cabaña. Miguel Ángel dice que te va a enseñar a esquiar (cuando éramos niños íbamos a Bariloche todos los años y él aprendió a esquiar muy bien).

Bueno, me voy porque mamá me dijo que Gustavo me estaba esperando. ¡Vamos a planear otra fiesta!

Un abrazo,

Silvia

P.D. En este viaje aprendí a apreciar la naturaleza, el campo y..., ¡a los muchachos chilenos!

Vocabulario

Cognados

la bicicleta   bicycle
chileno(-a)   Chilean
la fortuna   fortune

Nombres

el abrazo   hug
el caballo   horse
la cabaña   cabin
el campo   country
la caña de pescar   fishing rod

la naturaleza   nature
el (la) niño(-a)   child
el río   river
el saco (la bolsa) de dormir
   sleeping bag

el sauce   (weeping) willow
la tienda de campaña   tent

Verbos

aburrirse   to be bored
acampar   to camp
alquilar   to rent
apreciar   to appreciate
armar   to pitch (a tent)
convencer   to convince

divertirse (e:ie)   to have a good
   time, to enjoy oneself
enseñar[1]   to teach
esquiar   to ski
hospedarse (en)   to stay (at a
   hotel)

nadar   to swim
pescar   to fish, to catch a fish
planear   to plan
quedarse   to stay, to remain

Otras palabras y expresiones

a pesar de (que)   in spite of,
   despite
al día siguiente   the next day
¿Cómo te fue?   How did it go for
   you?
costar un ojo de la cara   to cost
   an arm and a leg
de todo   everything
en serio   seriously

Espero que sí.   I hope so.
estar equivocado(-a)   to be
   wrong
ir de compras   to go shopping
ir de pesca   to go fishing
ir de vacaciones   to go on
   vacation
junto a   near, next to
montar a caballo   to ride a horse

montar en bicicleta   to ride a
   bicycle
profundamente   soundly
sin embargo   however,
   nevertheless
toda la noche   all night long

---

[1]Enseñar takes the preposition a when followed by an infinitive: Me enseñó a esquiar.

Vocabulario adicional
Actividades al aire libre (Outdoor activities)

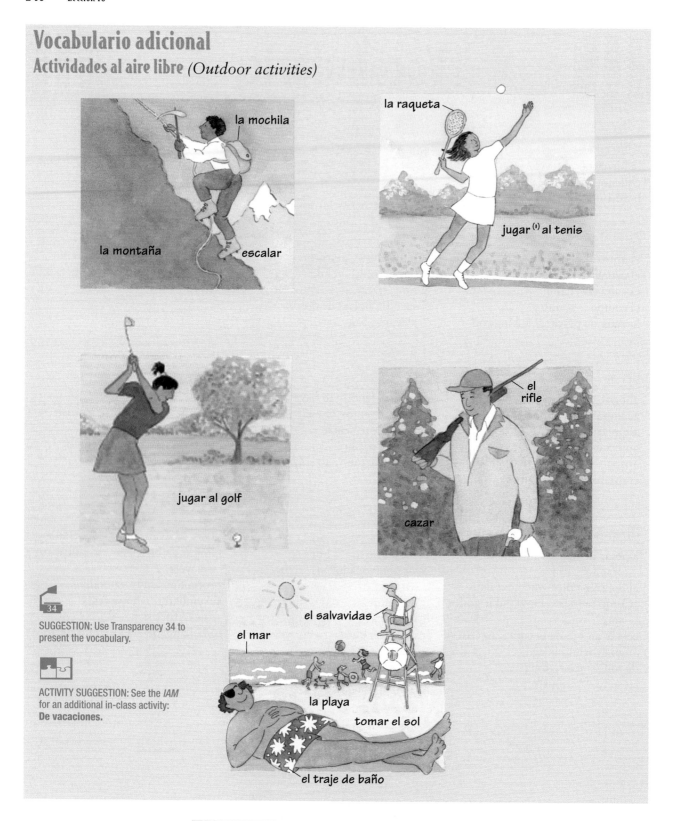

la mochila

la montaña   escalar

la raqueta   jugar[1] al tenis

jugar al golf

el rifle

cazar

34

SUGGESTION: Use Transparency 34 to present the vocabulary.

ACTIVITY SUGGESTION: See the *IAM* for an additional in-class activity: **De vacaciones.**

el salvavidas

el mar   la playa   tomar el sol

el traje de baño

[1]Present tense: **juego, juegas, juega, jugamos, jugáis, juegan**

Términos geográficos

el desierto

la nieve

el lago

Océano
Pacífico   Chile   Argentina

Océano
Atlántico

el país

Norte

Oeste   Este

Sur

ACTIVITY SUGGESTION: See the *IAM*
for an additional in-class activity:
Encuentre las respuestas.

EXPANSION: Have students write
Victoria's (brief) reply to Silvia's letter.
Suggest first to brainstorm in pairs
about several aspects of a vacation in
a big city such as Buenos Aires, using
vocabulary already known.

EXPANSION: Have students act out in
pairs or small groups some situations
that might happen while Victoria is
vacationing with Silvia's family in
Bariloche. Ask students first to
brainstorm about some possible
situations. Encourage students to be
imaginative and to use the lesson's
active vocabulary as well as the
vocabulary learned in previous
lessons.

SUGGESTIONS: Show slides or
photographs of Argentina while
discussing the cultural notes in **¿Lo
sabía Ud.?**

¡Conversemos!

Answer the following questions, basing your answers on Silvia's letter to Victoria.

1. ¿Con quiénes fue Silvia de vacaciones? ¿Se está divirtiendo?
2. ¿Cuánto tiempo hace que llegaron?
3. ¿Adónde fueron al día siguiente de llegar?
4. ¿Quiénes armaron las tiendas de campaña? ¿Dónde durmieron todos? ¿Cómo durmieron?
5. ¿Con quién fue de pesca Silvia? ¿Pescó algo?
6. Silvia no quería ir a la fiesta. ¿Por qué fue?
7. ¿A quién conoció allí?
8. ¿Qué hizo Silvia en la fiesta?
9. Según *(According to)* Silvia, ¿son caros o baratos los hoteles en Buenos Aires? (¿Cómo lo sabe usted?)

10. ¿Qué planes tiene Silvia para el año próximo?
11. ¿Adónde iban Silvia y Miguel Ángel cuando eran niños?
12. ¿Qué le dijo a Silvia su mamá?
13. ¿Qué van a hacer Silvia y Gustavo?
14. ¿Qué aprendió Silvia en este viaje?

¿Lo sabía Ud.?

■ Mar del Plata (Argentina), Viña del Mar (Chile) y Punta del Este (Uruguay) están entre *(among)* las playas más hermosas e importantes de la América del Sur. Estas ciudades son centros turísticos internacionales.

■ Mucha gente va a Chile y al sur de Argentina (Bariloche) para esquiar durante junio, julio y agosto, que son los meses de invierno en el hemisferio sur *(southern)*.

• ¿Qué ciudades de este país son centros turísticos internacionales?

• ¿Qué centros de esquí importantes hay en este país?

INTERNET

See the *¿Cómo se dice...?* Web site for activities on authentic cultural material: http://spanish.college.hmco.com/students

Vista de Mar del Plata y del océano Atlántico. Mar del Plata está a unos 400 kilómetros de Buenos Aires.

Pronunciación

STUDENT AUDIO

NOTE: To reinforce pronunciation practice, this section appears in Lecciones 10 through 18. The sentences featured as pronunciation models are taken from the lesson dialogues.

SUGGESTION: For each sentence, first model the word(s) in boldface type and have the class repeat them chorally and individually. Then have students repeat the full sentence for pronunciation practice of the target expressions in context.

In this lesson, there are some new words or phrases that may be challenging to pronounce. For further pronunciation practice of Spanish sounds, listen to your instructor and repeat the following words and phrases.

1. ¡Estaba **equivocada!**
2. Aprendí a **apreciar** la naturaleza.
3. Creí que me iba a **aburrir** y, sin embargo, me estoy **divirtiendo** mucho.
4. Monté a **caballo** y en **bicicleta.**
5. No **pesqué** nada, a pesar de que tenía una **caña de pescar** nueva.

Estructuras

1 Hace... meaning *ago*   *(Hace... como equivalente de* ago*)*

SUGGESTION: Review time expressions with **hacer** in **Lección 7** (page 176).

■ In sentences using the preterit and in some cases the imperfect, **hace** + *period of time* is the equivalent of the English *ago*. When **hace** is placed at the beginning of the sentence, the construction is as follows.

> **Hace** + *period of time* + **que**
> **Hace** + dos años   + **que** la conocí.

—¿Cuánto tiempo hace que conociste a tu novia?   *"How long ago did you meet your girlfriend?"*
—**Hace tres años que** la conocí.   *"I met her three years ago."*

—**Hace diez años que** ellos vinieron a los Estados Unidos. ¿Y tú?   *"They came to the United States ten years ago. And you?"*
—Yo llegué **hace cuatro años.**   *"I arrived four years ago."*

ATENCIÓN Note that it is also possible to say: **Yo llegué hace cuatro años.**

práctica ....

A. Say how long ago everything happened, according to the information provided.

1. Armamos la tienda de campaña a las dos. Son las cinco.
2. Ellos fueron a esquiar en agosto. Estamos en diciembre.
3. Tú montaste a caballo el lunes. Hoy es viernes.
4. Empecé a nadar a las diez. Son las diez y cuarto.
5. Yo alquilé la cabaña el quince de julio. Hoy es el treinta de julio.
6. Carlos compró el saco de dormir en 1998. Estamos en el año 200_.

B. With a partner, take turns asking each other how long ago you did each of the following things.

1. ir a la playa
2. ir al dentista
3. comprar tu coche
4. ir de compras
5. ir al teatro
6. empezar a estudiar español
7. ver a tus padres
8. ir de vacaciones
9. llamar a tu mejor amigo(-a)
10. levantarte

2 The imperfect (El imperfecto de indicativo)

There are two simple past tenses in the Spanish indicative: the preterit, which you studied in **Lecciones 7, 8,** and **9,** and the imperfect.

SUGGESTION: Ask students the following personalized questions about their childhoods that require simple affirmative or negative responses in the imperfect.

1. ¿Quería Ud. ser salvavidas?
2. ¿Hablaba Ud. mucho por teléfono con sus amigos?
3. ¿Nadaba en el lago (mar / río)?
4. ¿Sabía montar en bicicleta / a caballo?
5. ¿Pescaba/cazaba con su padre / hermano / amigo?
6. ¿Acampaba Ud. en las montañas?
7. ¿Tenía que barrer la cocina?
8. ¿Comía Ud. mucho chocolate?
9. ¿Quería beber café?
10. ¿Dormía Ud. diez horas por la noche?

A. Regular forms

■ To form the regular imperfect, add the following endings to the verb stem.

-ar *verbs*		-er *and* -ir *verbs*			
hablar		**comer**		**vivir**	
habl-	aba	com-	ía	viv-	ía
habl-	abas	com-	ías	viv-	ías
habl-	aba	com-	ía	viv-	ía
habl-	ábamos	com-	íamos	viv-	íamos
habl-	abais	com-	íais	viv-	íais
habl-	aban	com-	ían	viv-	ían

■ Note that the endings of the **-er** and **-ir** verbs are the same, and that there is a written accent on the first **í** of the endings of the **-er** and **-ir** verbs.

■ The Spanish imperfect tense is equivalent to three English forms.

Yo **vivía** en Santiago.   { *I used to live in Santiago.*
I was living in Santiago.
I lived in Santiago.

SUGGESTION: Point out that the imperfect is equivalent to the *was + -ing* construction in English.

SUGGESTION: Write the following sentence builder on the board, on an overhead transparency, or on a ditto sheet. Have students write as many sentences as they can in three minutes describing childhood memories of their families and friends.

De niño(-a),

mi padre / mi madre / mi hermano(-a) / mi mejor amigo(-a) / mi tío(-a) / mi primo(-a) / mi novio(-a)

vivir en... / pasar las vacaciones en... / mirar... en la televisión / recibir buenas (malas) notas en... / levantarse a las... / querer ser profesor(-a) (etc.) / salir con... / jugar con... / trabajar en...

■ The imperfect is used to refer to habitual or repeated actions in the past, with no reference to when they began or ended.

—¿Tú **asistías** a la universidad cuando **vivías** en Cuba?
—No, **trabajaba** cuando **vivía** en Cuba.

"Did you attend the university when you were living in Cuba?"
"No, I worked when I was living in Cuba."

■ The imperfect is also used to refer to actions, events, or conditions that the speaker views as *in the process of* happening in the past, again with no reference to when they began or ended.

—**Veníamos** para casa cuando vimos a Raúl.

We were coming home when we saw Raúl.

B. Irregular forms

■ Only three verbs are irregular in the imperfect tense: **ser, ver,** and **ir.**

ser	ver	ir
era	veía	iba
eras	veías	ibas
era	veía	iba
éramos	veíamos	íbamos
erais	veíais	ibais
eran	veían	iban

—¿**Ibas** mucho a casa de tus abuelos cuando **eras** niño?

"Did you often go to your grandparents' house when you were a child?"

—Sí, los **veía** todos los sábados.

"Yes, I used to see them every Saturday."

—¿Adónde **iban** Uds. de vacaciones cuando eran niños?

"Where did you go on vacation when you were children?"

—**Íbamos** a la playa o a las montañas.

"We used to go to the beach or to the mountains."

práctica •••

A. Ten years ago María wrote this composition about herself and her family. Rewrite her composition, using the imperfect tense.

Mi familia y yo vivimos en Buenos Aires. Mi padre trabaja para la compañía Sandoval y mi madre enseña en la universidad. Es una profesora excelente. Mis hermanos y yo asistimos a la escuela. Generalmente pasamos las vacaciones en Mar del Plata. Allí nadamos, pescamos y tomamos el sol. Como a mi padre le gusta ir a las montañas para esquiar, en invierno vamos a Bariloche. Mis abuelos viven en Rosario y no los vemos mucho, pero siempre les escribimos.

B. Now write a paragraph about your own childhood, using Exercise A as a model.

EXPANSION C: Have students complete this activity in pairs. Then have them change partners, and have each student tell his or her new partner about the childhood of the previous partner.

SUGGESTION C: Have students ask you these and other questions. After the class has had the opportunity to ask 15–20 questions, divide the class into groups of three and have students describe your childhood based on your answers. You can also use this activity as a written assignment in which students take notes as you respond and then write a paragraph that includes ten different bits of information about your childhood.

SUGGESTION: To help students acquire a feel for the difference between the tenses, narrate several paragraphs from a well-known story in English. Pause after each sentence and ask students which tense they would use and why. *Ricitos de oro y los tres ositos* (Goldilocks and the Three Bears) is a good choice.

C. Interview a classmate, using the following questions and two of your own. When you have finished, switch roles.

1. ¿Dónde vivías tú cuando eras niño(-a)?
2. ¿A qué escuela asistías?
3. ¿Te gustaba estudiar?
4. ¿Eras buen estudiante?
5. ¿Adónde iban tú y tu familia de vacaciones?
6. ¿Qué les gustaba hacer?
7. ¿Preferías pasar las vacaciones en el campo o en la ciudad?
8. ¿Te divertías mucho o te aburrías?
9. ¿Veías mucho a tus abuelos?
10. ¿Vivías cerca de tus abuelos?

D. Compare your teenage years with those of a classmate by taking turns completing the following sentences.

1. Cuando yo era adolescente...
2. Mi familia y yo siempre...
3. Mis abuelos...
4. Mi mejor amigo(-a)...
5. Frecuentemente nosotros...
6. Cuando yo tenía dieciséis años...
7. En la escuela yo...
8. Todos los fines de semana, mis amigos y yo...
9. En el verano...
10. Cuando yo quería salir con mis amigos, mis padres...

3 The preterit contrasted with the imperfect   *(El pretérito contrastado con el imperfecto)*

Once upon a time, there was a beautiful little town. *(imperfect)* In that town *lived* a lovely little girl. *(imperfect)* She *had* long, blond hair and everyone *called* her Goldilocks. *(imperfect)* One morning, she *got up* early, *washed* her face, *dressed* herself, and *went* for a walk in the forest. *(preterit)*

■ The difference between the preterit and the imperfect can be visualized in the following way.

The wavy line representing the imperfect shows an action or event taking place over a period of time in the past. There is no reference to when the action began or ended. The vertical line representing the preterit shows an action or event as completed in the past.

   In many instances, the choice between the preterit and the imperfect depends on how the speaker views the action or event. The following table summarizes some of the most important uses of both tenses.

35

SUGGESTION: Use Transparency 35 to further emphasize the use of the preterit and the imperfect. In groups of three, have students first tell the story in the present tense, then have them rewrite the story in the past using the appropriate tenses. As a class activity, have each group add one sentence until the entire story is completed.

Preterit	Imperfect
1. Reports past actions that the speaker views as finished and completed. Yo **estuve** allí el año pasado. Ayer **compré** una caña de pescar.	1. Describes past actions in the process of happening, with no reference to their beginning or end. **Iba** a la biblioteca cuando lo vi.
2. Sums up a condition or state viewed as a whole (and no longer in effect). Me **sentí** mal todo el día.	2. Refers to repeated or habitual actions or events: *used to* . . . Cuando **era** niña **iba**[1] de vacaciones a Montevideo.
	3. Describes a physical, mental, or emotional state or condition in the past. Me **sentía** muy mal.
	4. Expresses time in the past. **Eran** las ocho de la noche cuando llegaron a su casa.
	5. Is generally used in indirect discourse. Me dijo que no **sabía** apreciar la naturaleza.
	6. Describes age in the past. Cuando **tenía** veinte años, vivía en Chile.
	7. Describes or sets the stage in the past. **Hacía** frío y **llovía**.

35

SUGGESTION: Have students ask each other the following personalized questions based on the actions shown in Transparency 35.

1. **De niño(-a), ¿dónde vivías?**
2. **¿Qué juegos te gustaban?**
3. **¿Qué programas de televisión mirabas con frecuencia?**
4. **De niño(-a), ¿te perdiste** *(did you get lost)* **alguna vez? ¿Quién te encontró? ¿Se pusieron nerviosos tus padres?**
5. **¿Eras un(-a) niño(-a) bueno(-a) o travieso(-a)** *(mischievous)*?

—¿Qué **te dijo** Nora anoche?

—**Me dijo** que le **gustaba** esquiar.

—¿Qué hora **era** cuando **llegaste** a tu casa?
—**Eran** las cuatro.
—¿Por qué no te **quedaste** en el club?
—Porque no me **sentía** bien.

"What did Nora tell you last night?"
"She told me that she liked to ski."
"What time was it when you got home?"
"It was four o'clock."
"Why didn't you stay at the club?"
"Because I wasn't feeling well."

---

[1]Note that this use of the imperfect also corresponds to the English *would* used to describe a repeated action in the past: *When I was a child, I used to go to Montevideo on vacation.* = *When I was a child, I **would** go to Montevideo on vacation.*

práctica ....

A. Write the Spanish equivalent of the following sentences, paying special attention to the use of the preterit or the imperfect in each situation.

<table>
<tr><td align="center">Preterit</td><td align="center">Imperfect</td></tr>
<tr><td valign="top">

1. I *went* to the lake last year. (*Narrates an action as a completed whole.*)
2. I *was* sick all day long. (*Sums up a condition or state viewed as a whole.*)

</td><td valign="top">

1. I *was going* to the lake when I saw Mary. (*Describes an action in progress.*)
2. I always *used to be* sick. (*Describes what used to happen.*)
3. I *was* cold. They *were* very happy here. (*A physical, mental, or emotional state or condition in the past.*)
4. He said he *wanted* a sleeping bag. (*Indirect discourse.*)
5. It *was* six o'clock in the morning. (*Time in the past.*)
6. My niece *was* five years old. (*Age in the past.*)
7. My boyfriend *was* tall and handsome. (*Description in the past.*)

</td></tr>
</table>

ACTIVITY SUGGESTION: See the *IAM* for an additional in-class activity: **Entre amigos.**

B. Complete the following dialogues. Then act them out with a partner.

1. —¿Cuántos años _____ (tener) tú cuando _____ (venir) a vivir a Caracas?
   —_____ (Tener) doce años.
2. —¿Qué te _____ (decir) el instructor ayer?
   —Me _____ (decir) que yo _____ (necesitar) practicar más.
3. —¿Qué tiempo _____ (hacer) cuando Uds. _____ (salir) de casa esta mañana?
   —_____ (Hacer) frío y _____ (nevar).
4. —¿Adónde _____ (ir) Uds. de vacaciones cuando _____ (ser) niños?
   —Siempre _____ (ir) a la playa, pero un verano mis padres _____ (decidir) alquilar una cabaña en las montañas y ésas _____ (ser) nuestras mejores vacaciones.
5. —¿Qué hora _____ (ser) cuando tú _____ (llegar) a casa ayer?
   —_____ (Ser) las ocho.
   —¿_____ (Ir) a la tienda?
   —Sí, _____ (ir) con Nora. Cuando nosotras _____ (ir) a la tienda, _____ (ver) un accidente en la calle.
   —¿_____ (Morir) alguien?
   —No, por suerte no _____ (morir) nadie.

POR FIN LO QUE USTED DESEABA
COMPACT disc DIGITAL AUDIO
Música Clásica y Moderna
COD Laser
Calle 79 Nº 51B-63 L. 12

FOLLOW-UP C: After students have completed the activity, have them work in pairs, using the basic questions and responses as a guide, to role-play a reporter interviewing a famous personality (actress/actor, scientist, doctor, writer, painter, etc.).

C. This interview takes place in Buenos Aires. Play the role of a reporter interviewing a famous star.

———————————————————————————————

—Yo nací *(I was born)*[1] en Sevilla, y no te digo cuándo.

———————————————————————————————

—Yo tenía diez años cuando nos fuimos a vivir a Madrid.

———————————————————————————————

—¿Cuando era niña? Era fea y un poco gorda.

———————————————————————————————

—Sí, tenía un perro que se llamaba Chispita.

———————————————————————————————

—Cuando era niña me gustaban las actividades al aire libre. Me gustaba nadar, montar a caballo y escalar montañas.

———————————————————————————————

—Estudié en la Escuela de Arte Dramático.

———————————————————————————————

—Empecé a trabajar en televisión en 1995.

———————————————————————————————

—Vine a Buenos Aires en el año 1999.

———————————————————————————————

—Sí, el año pasado estuve en París y trabajé en un club nocturno.

———————————————————————————————

—Estuve allí por tres meses.

———————————————————————————————

—No, no pienso volver a España por ahora.

D. Interview a classmate, using the following questions and two of your own. When you have finished, switch roles.

1. ¿Cuántos años tenías cuando aprendiste a nadar?
2. ¿Adónde ibas de vacaciones?
3. ¿Te divertías durante el verano?
4. ¿Te gustaba acampar?
5. ¿Qué te gustaba hacer cuando eras niño(-a)?
6. ¿Cómo era tu primer(-a) novio(-a)?
7. ¿Qué hiciste ayer?
8. ¿A qué hora te levantaste esta mañana?
9. ¿Qué tiempo hacía cuando saliste de tu casa?
10. ¿Qué hora era cuando llegaste a la universidad?
11. ¿Tomaste una clase de inglés el año pasado?
12. ¿Quién fue tu profesor(-a)?

E. In groups of four or five, prepare 8 to 10 questions to ask your instructor about his or her life as a teenager.

———————————

[1]**Nacer** is a regular verb in the preterit.

4 Verbs that change meaning in the preterit *(Verbos que cambian de significado en el pretérito)*

SUGGESTION: Write the following incomplete sentences on the board and have students complete them in a logical manner.

1. El año pasado conocí a...
2. Cuando era niño(-a), no quería comer...
3. Ayer supe que...
4. Yo no quería estudiar porque...
5. Yo conocía a *(name)* antes de empezar las clases.
6. Yo no sabía que...

■ Some Spanish verbs change meaning when they are used in the preterit. Note the usage of the verbs in the following examples.

conocer:	conocí (preterit)	*I met*
	conocía (imperfect)	*I knew (was acquainted or familiar with)*

Anoche **conocí** a una chica muy simpática. *(met her for the first time)*
Yo no **conocía** la ciudad. *(I wasn't familiar with the city.)*

saber:	supe (preterit)	*I found out, I learned*
	sabía (imperfect)	*I knew*

Lo **supe** cuando él me lo dijo. *(I found it out.)*
Yo no **sabía** que te gustaba esquiar. *(I wasn't aware of it.)*

no querer:	no quise (preterit)	*I refused*
	no quería (imperfect)	*I didn't want*

Raúl **no quiso** ir. *(didn't want to and refused)*
Rita **no quería** ir, pero después decidió ir. *(didn't want to at the time)*

—¿Tú **conocías** al cuñado de Carmen?
—No, lo **conocí** anoche.

"Did you know Carmen's brother-in-law?"
"No, I met him last night."

—¿**Sabías** que teníamos una fiesta?
—No, lo **supe** esta mañana.

"Did you know that we were having a party?"
"No, I found (it) out this morning."

—¿Y Roberto? ¿No vino?
—No, **no quiso** venir.

"And Roberto? Didn't he come?"
"No, he refused to come."

práctica ••

SUGGESTION A: You may want to write the following questions on the board for additional practice.

1. ¿Cuándo conociste a tu mejor amigo(-a) (novio[-a])?
2. ¿De niño(-a), ¿conocías a alguien interesante? ¿A quién?
3. ¿Cuándo supiste que Santa Claus no traía los regalos?
4. De niño(-a), ¿qué cosas no querías comer?

A. Interview a classmate, using the following questions and at least two of your own.

1. ¿Conocías tú al profesor (a la profesora) antes de empezar esta clase?
2. ¿Cuándo lo (la) conociste?
3. ¿Sabías tú la nacionalidad del profesor (de la profesora)?
4. ¿Cuándo la supiste?
5. Yo no quería venir a clase hoy. ¿Y tú?
6. Tú no viniste al concierto anoche. ¿No pudiste o no quisiste?

SUGGESTION B: Have students write and act out the next episode of the soap opera. Before they begin, the class should brainstorm briefly to determine what vocabulary words are typically included in similar situations in **telenovelas.** You may write the list of words and phrases on the board to facilitate the writing task. Some suggested terms are: **el divorcio, divorciarse, el/la amante, el adulterio, marcharse de casa, la amistad, los problemas económicos, histérico(-a), rebelde, hipócrita, honesto(-a), pasivo(-a), independiente.**

B. Act out the following scene from a soap opera (**telenovela**) with a partner, providing the missing verbs.

ADRIÁN —¿Tú _____ que Rosaura estaba embarazada *(pregnant)*?

SARA —No, lo _____ anoche.

ADRIÁN —¡Qué horrible! Dicen que su esposo es un idiota. Los padres de ella no _____ ir a la boda *(wedding)*. Ese día se fueron a Europa.

SARA —Pero, ¿dónde _____ Rosaura a Lorenzo?

ADRIÁN —En una fiesta. Rosaura no _____ ir, pero Olga la llevó.

SARA —¿Olga _____ a Lorenzo?

ADRIÁN —Sí, Olga es la ex esposa de Lorenzo...

¡A ver cuánto aprendió!

¡Repase el vocabulario!

INTERNET

See the *¿Cómo se dice...?* Web site for additional grammar and vocabulary practice: http://spanish.college.hmco.com/students

Say whether the following statements are logical or not. If a statement is not logical, give one that is.

1. El caballo se hospedó en el hotel.
2. Compré un traje de baño para ir a la playa.
3. Lo pasé muy bien en México. Me divertí mucho.
4. Es muy barato; cuesta un ojo de la cara.
5. Alquilé el campo para ir de pesca.
6. Van a escalar el mar.
7. Viven en el campo porque no les gusta la ciudad.
8. Jugamos al tenis en la cabaña.
9. Ella no sabe esquiar. Yo le voy a enseñar.
10. Está en la playa tomando la nieve.
11. Viven en Nueva York porque les gusta el oeste de los Estados Unidos.
12. Voy a comprar una bicicleta para montar a caballo.
13. Papá armó la tienda de campaña.
14. Voy a poner al salvavidas en la mochila.
15. Durmió muy mal; durmió profundamente toda la noche.
16. Nunca tiene razón; siempre está equivocado.

ACTIVITY SUGGESTION: Do **¡Escucha!,** the in-class listening comprehension activity that reviews vocabulary and grammar structures introduced in the lesson. It appears in the answer key of the *IAM.*

ACTIVITY SUGGESTION: See the *IAM* for an additional in-class activity: **Palabras escondidas.**

Entrevista

ACTIVITY SUGGESTION: See the *IAM* for additional in-class activities: **Para conocernos mejor** and **Una encuesta.**

With a partner, take turns interviewing each other, using the following questions.

1. ¿Acampaste el fin de semana pasado?
2. ¿Te gustaba ir a las montañas cuando eras niño(-a)?
3. Cuando eras niño(-a), ¿preferías montar a caballo o en bicicleta?
4. ¿Quieres ir a cazar conmigo?
5. ¿Fuiste de pesca el verano pasado?

SUGGESTION: Encourage students to ask one additional question after each initial exchange. They should use a variety of interrogatives: ¿Cuándo?, ¿Dónde?, ¿Cuánto(-a, -os, -as)?, ¿Con quién?, ¿Por qué?, ¿Cómo?

S1—¿Te gustaba ir a las montañas cuando eras niño(-a)?
S2—Sí, me gustaba ir.
S1—¿Por qué?
S2—Porque me gustaba (gusta) estar al aire libre.

6. ¿Fuiste de compras el sábado pasado?
7. ¿Prefieres jugar al golf o al tenis?
8. ¿Prefieres nadar o tomar el sol?
9. ¿Prefieres vivir cerca del mar o cerca de un lago?
10. Cuando vas de vacaciones, ¿prefieres quedarte en la casa de un(-a) amigo(-a) o prefieres hospedarte en un hotel?
11. Los hoteles de tu ciudad, ¿cuestan un ojo de la cara?
12. La última vez *(The last time)* que fuiste de vacaciones, ¿cómo te fue?

Situaciones

SUGGESTION: Have several pairs of students act out their conversations for the class.

What would you say in the following situations? What might the other person say? Act out the scenes with a partner. Take turns playing each role.

1. On your vacation, you learned how to swim and ride a horse, and you caught a trout. Someone asks whether you had a good time. Say what you did.
2. A friend invites you to go camping. You don't have a tent or a sleeping bag, and you want to know what else you will need.
3. You are trying to convince a friend to go camping. Tell him or her how much fun it can be.

¿Qué pasa aquí?

In groups of three or four, look at the following photo and make up a story about the people you see. Say who they are, their professions, how long they have been on vacation, what they did yesterday, and so on.

EXPANSION: Have students role-play a conversation between Tomás and Víctor in which each describes his vacation. Each student could then write a short "letter" to another student describing his or her partner's vacation.

Para escribir

Tomás and Víctor are very good friends, but their tastes differ: Tomás likes the outdoors, while Víctor prefers city life. Using your imagination, write an account of how each of them spent his vacation last summer.

En la vida real

CD-ROM

Do the interactive exercises on the CD-ROM for additional practice.

Nuestras vacaciones

You and a classmate are going on a vacation. Make plans for the trip, including activities and things you might need to take with you. Then tell a group of classmates about your plans.

Viajes a México

EXPANSION: Have students imagine that they and another classmate are about to take part in a three-month "survival" course at one of the following locations. Each pair may take only 12 articles. Students should write their lists and include a brief justification for each article chosen.

Lugares:
**Una isla desierta en el Pacífico
El desierto de Sahara
La Patagonia (Argentina)
La selva de Brasil**

Ángela and Elena went to Ixtapa on vacation, and Alberto and Julio went to Playa Blanca on the Pacific coast of Mexico. The four went with Club Méditerranée. Read the ad below and answer the following questions.

**Conozca el nuevo y sensacional modo
de disfrutar las vacaciones
"al estilo de CLUB MEDITERRANEE" con**

**VIAJES
BOJORQUEZ**

**Dos fabulosas excursiones especiales para viajeros
sofisticados y exigentes, amantes del sol, el mar
¡y la buena vida!**

IT3AM1VB770 **CLUB MEDITERRANEE**	IT3AM1VB771 **CLUB MEDITERRANEE**
Ixtapa	**Playa Blanca**
ZIHUATANEJO	**(COSTA CAREYES)**
PLAN 1 – 4 días/3 noches	**PLAN 1 - 4 días/3 noches**
Salidas: los Jueves	Salidas: los Domingos
ADULTO MENOR	ADULTO MENOR
$ 16,300.00 $ 12,100.00	$ 19,550.00 $ 15,500.00
NOCHE ADICIONAL $ 1,640.00	NOCHE ADICIONAL $ 1,150.00
PLAN 2 - 5 días/4 noches	**PLAN 2 - 5 días/4 noches**
Salidas: los Domingos	Salidas: los Jueves
ADULTO MENOR	ADULTO MENOR
$ 20,250.00 $ 13,250.00	$ 24,650.00 $ 16,850.00
NOCHE ADICIONAL $ 1,640.00	NOCHE ADICIONAL $ 1,150.00

NOTA: Estos precios incluyen tarifa aérea especial saliendo desde México, D.F. también operamos con tarifa especial saliendo desde Guadalajara, Monterrey y otros destinos. Favor de consultar estas tarifas en cualquiera de nuestras oficinas.

**Utilice la Tarjeta American Express y disfrute los siguientes
beneficios:**

● Membresía por un año del Club Mediterranée.
● Seguro de vida contra accidentes por $ 1,000,000.00 durante el transporte aéreo.

1. ¿Cómo son las excursiones en los Viajes Bojorquez?
2. ¿Para qué tipo de viajeros son?

3. Las chicas viajaron con el plan 1 a Ixtapa. ¿Qué día salieron y cuántas noches estuvieron en Ixtapa?
4. ¿Cuánto pagaron por el viaje?
5. Las chicas usaron la tarjeta American Express para pagar el viaje. ¿Qué beneficios recibieron?
6. Los muchachos viajaron con el plan 2 y estuvieron en Playa Blanca por cinco noches. ¿Cuánto les costó el viaje?

El viaje de fin de curso

Imagine that your class is planning a field trip. One group of students would like to do outdoor activities such as camping, fishing, and swimming. Another group would prefer a visit to a large city and stay in hotels, visit museums, see films, etc. After preparing for a discussion, each group must try to convince the other to agree to its plan.

5. América central

Costa Rica   El Salvador   Guatemala

Honduras   Nicaragua   Panamá

■ Costa Rica es el país con el mayor ingreso *(income)* por persona, y con el más alto nivel de educación de Centroamérica. Es un país democrático y no tiene ejército *(army)*. A Costa Rica la llaman "la Suiza *(Switzerland)* de América" por su tradición pacifista. Uno de sus presidentes, Oscar Arias, recibió el Premio Nóbel de la Paz.

■ El Salvador es el país más pequeño de Centroamérica, pero es el más densamente poblado. Más de seis millones de habitantes viven en un área aproximadamente del tamaño del estado de Massachusetts. Nicaragua, en comparación, es cinco veces más grande que El Salvador, pero tiene una población de sólo unos 4, 8 millones de habitantes.

■ El canal de Panamá es actualmente la única vía de comunicación que conecta los dos grandes océanos. Ahorra *(It saves)* 16.000 kilómetros de travesía *(voyage)* para los barcos que ya no *(no longer)* tienen que pasar por el Cabo de Hornos.

Nicaragua se siente orgullosa *(proud)* de su poeta nacional Rubén Darío, creador y líder del modernismo, un movimiento literario que comenzó a fines del siglo XIX. En la foto aparece una de las muchas estatuas del gran poeta que hay en Managua, la capital del país.

¿Qué poetas norteamericanos puede nombrar Ud.?

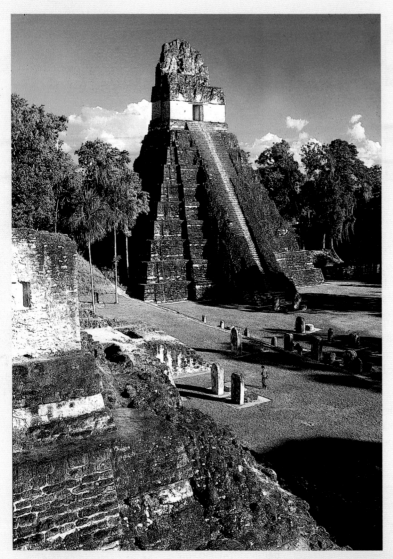

Tikal, situada en un bosque *(forest)* tropical al noroeste de Guatemala, es la ciudad más grande y más antigua de la civilización maya. En esta ciudad vivían unas 80.000 personas. Aquí se ve el Templo del Gran Jaguar, el edificio más alto y más importante de Tikal.

¿Cuáles son algunas de las ciudades más antiguas de su país?

El cultivo del banano *(banana tree)* es una de las principales fuentes *(sources)* de ingreso de los países centroamericanos. El banano se cultiva en Panamá, Costa Rica, El Salvador, Honduras, Nicaragua y Guatemala. En la foto, un agricultor verifica el tamaño de las bananas en una hacienda de El Salvador.

¿Qué frutas se cultivan en la región donde Ud. vive?

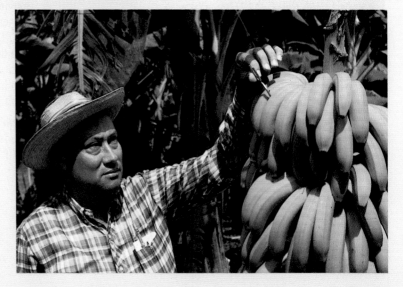

Estudiantes de la Universidad Nacional Autónoma de Honduras se dirigen a sus clases. Esta universidad, que está en Tegucigalpa, la capital de Honduras, es el centro educativo más importante del país.

¿Cuál es la universidad más importante del estado donde Ud. vive?

Guatemala es la ciudad más grande y más importante del país centroamericano del mismo nombre. La mayor parte de la ciudad es moderna, pues fue reconstruida después de una serie de terremotos *(earthquakes)* ocurridos en 1917–1918. En sus calles se mezclan las construcciones antiguas, como la Universidad de San Carlos, la Catedral y el Conservatorio Nacional de Música, y edificios modernos como la Ciudad Olímpica y el Palacio Nacional.

¿Cuáles son los edificios más antiguos de su ciudad?

Costa Rica es el país centro-americano que más se preocupa por proteger la naturaleza y la ecología. Son famosos sus parques nacionales y algunos de sus jardines, como el Jardín Botánico de Lankester, que aparece en la foto. Este jardín contiene numerosas especies de orquídeas y otras plantas tropicales.

¿Cuáles son los principales parques nacionales de su país?

La construcción del canal de Panamá por parte de los Estados Unidos duró *(lasted)* siete años y se terminó en el año 1914.

¿Puede Ud. identificar otros canales famosos?

TELEINFORME

VIDEO

CD-ROM

Do the interactive exercises on the CD-ROM for additional practice.

Preparación

NOTE: The video-related vocabulary is listed in the *Instructor's Activities Manual* for your reference. Its purpose is to facilitate students' comprehension.

NOTE: See the Instructor's Edition frontmatter for additional suggestions on implementing video in the classroom.

¿Cuánto saben Uds. ya? After reading **Panorama hispánico 5**, get together in groups of three or four students and answer the following questions.

1. ¿Cuál es la única vía *(route)* de comunicación que conecta el océano Pacífico con el océano Atlántico?
2. ¿Cómo es la educación en Costa Rica?
3. ¿Cómo llaman a Costa Rica y por qué?
4. ¿Dónde se cultiva el banano *(banana tree)*?
5. ¿Qué protegen en Costa Rica?

Comprensión

SUGGESTION: Have students read the *Panorama hispánico* segment of the textbook and do the *Preparación* activities in small groups before viewing the video segments.

SUGGESTION: Ask students what they might already know about Central America and share it with the class.

SUGGESTION: The *Comprensión* sections are organized by individual video clip to provide greater flexibility in lesson planning. Have students complete each exercise after viewing the corresponding video clip and have them compare their answers in pairs or groups.

SUGGESTION: Have students locate Panamá and Costa Rica on the map on the inside back cover of the textbook.

A. Panamá. Read the following statements. After watching the video, circle **V (Verdadero)** or **F (Falso)**, according to what you understood. If a statement is false, correct it.

V   F   1. Hay bosques lluviosos en Panamá.
V   F   2. En Panamá viven civilizaciones indígenas.
V   F   3. La ciudad de Panamá está en la costa del Atlántico.
V   F   4. La ciudad de Panamá no es una ciudad moderna.
V   F   5. La ciudad de Panamá fue el centro del imperio español en América por muchos años.
V   F   6. La ciudad de Panamá tiene muchos ejemplos de arquitectura colonial española.

B. Las carretas *(oxcarts)* costarricenses. Select the appropriate word or phrase that best completes each statement according to what you understood in the video.

1. Se usan las carretas en las (calles, fincas) de Costa Rica.
2. Las carretas están hechas *(made)* de (madera, plástico).
3. Las carretas tienen dos (ruedas, flores) grandes.
4. Lo más típico de las carretas es que usan (muchos, pocos) colores llamativos *(bright)*.

C. El Jardín Botánico de Lankester. Select the word or phrase that best completes each statement, according to what you understood.

1. La orquídea es (un pájaro, una flor) tropical.
2. En el Jardín Botánico de Lankester hay más de (80, 800) variedades de orquídeas.
3. En los jardines de Lankester hay más de (100, 150) géneros de pájaros.
4. El hombre que fundó *(founded)* el Jardín de Lankester era (costarricense, inglés, estadounidense).
5. Hoy día (la universidad, la presidencia) de Costa Rica mantiene el jardín.
6. Costa Rica tiene excelentes programas para proteger (las carretas, la naturaleza).

Ampliación

A. **Una entrevista.** You and a partner are going to conduct a series of interviews. Make a list of three questions for each of the following people:

1. a una persona de la ciudad de Panamá
2. al artesano costarricense que pinta *(paints)* las carretas
3. al administrador del Jardín Botánico de Lankester

B. **Dos culturas.** With a partner, describe a special place or typical handicraft from your area that might compare to "El Jardín Botánico de Lankester" or "las carretas costarricenses."

Haciendo diligencias

Lección 11

OBJECTIVES

Pronunciation
Pronunciation in context

Structure
The subjunctive mood • The subjunctive with verbs of volition • The subjunctive with verbs of emotion

Communication
You will learn vocabulary related to everyday activities and running errands.

Haciendo diligencias

STUDENT
AUDIO

En una casa de la calle Ponce en San Juan, Puerto Rico, vive la familia Vargas. Sergio está muy cansado hoy y quiere quedarse en la cama hasta tarde porque hoy tiene el día libre. Su mamá quiere que haga varias diligencias, de modo que el pobre muchacho tiene que levantarse en cuanto suena el despertador a las siete de la mañana.

A las nueve llega a la tintorería, que queda cerca de su casa.

SERGIO   —Vengo a recoger esta ropa. Aquí está el comprobante. *(Piensa)* Ojalá que estén listos mis pantalones.

EMPLEADA   —*(Lee)* Un abrigo de mujer y un pantalón. *(A Sergio)* Un momento, por favor. *(Al rato vuelve.)* Los pantalones son rosados, ¿verdad?

SERGIO   —¡Eran blancos cuando los traje...!

A las diez, Sergio está en el departamento de fotografía de la tienda La Francia.

SERGIO   —Hace una semana que traje un rollo de película en colores. Espero que esté listo.

EMPLEADA   —A ver... ¿Sergio Vargas...? Sí, las fotos salieron muy bien.

SERGIO   —¿Y cuánto cobran por revelar un rollo de película?

EMPLEADA   —Seis dólares, señor.

SERGIO   —Muy bien. *(Mira las fotografías.)* ¿Quién es esta señora? ¡Estas fotos no son mías!

A las once, Sergio estaciona su motocicleta frente al banco.

SERGIO   —Quiero depositar este cheque, que está a nombre de mi madre. ¿Es necesario que lo firme ella?

EMPLEADA   —Si lo va a depositar en la cuenta corriente de ella, no.

SERGIO   —Muy bien, eso es lo que quiero hacer. También quiero sacar doscientos dólares de mi cuenta de ahorros.

EMPLEADA   —Llene esta tarjeta, por favor.

SERGIO   —Necesito que me dé el saldo de mi cuenta de ahorros.

EMPLEADA   —Sólo tiene veinte dólares. Lo siento, señor Vargas, pero no tiene suficiente dinero.

Cuando Sergio sale del banco, no encuentra su motocicleta.

SUGGESTION: Refer students to **Panorama hispánico 6** and the corresponding video segment for more information about Puerto Rico.

SUGGESTION: Point out that Tuesday the thirteenth is considered unlucky in Hispanic countries versus Friday the thirteenth.

SERGIO   —*(Grita)* ¡Ay, no! ¡Alguien me robó la motocicleta!

SEÑORA   —El muchacho que se llevó su motocicleta dijo que Ud. era su hermano...

SERGIO   —¡Yo soy hijo único!

SEÑORA   —*(Piensa)* Se parecen mucho. Me sorprende que no sean hermanos.

SERGIO   —*(Mientras camina hacia la estación de policía)* ¡El próximo martes trece no salgo de casa!

Vocabulario

Cognados

el banco   bank
el cheque   check
el departamento   department, section

la motocicleta, la moto   motorcycle
suficiente   sufficient, enough

Nombres

la cama   bed
el comprobante   claim check
la cuenta   account
la cuenta corriente   checking account
la cuenta de ahorros   savings account

el despertador   alarm clock
la diligencia   errand
la estación de policía   police station
el pantalón, los pantalones   pants, trousers
el rollo de película   roll of film

la ropa[1]   clothes, clothing
el saldo   balance
la tintorería   dry cleaner

Verbos

caminar   to walk
cobrar   to charge
depositar   to deposit
esperar   to hope
estacionar, aparcar, parquear   to park

gritar   to scream
llenar   to fill out
llevarse   to take (away)
parecerse (yo me parezco)   to look like
recoger   to pick up

revelar   to develop (film)
robar   to steal
sacar   to take out, to withdraw
sonar (o:ue)   to ring
sorprender   to surprise

Adjetivos

libre   off, free
listo(-a)   ready
pobre   poor

ACTIVITY SUGGESTION: See the *IAM* for an additional in-class activity: **¿Cómo respondes?**

Otras palabras y expresiones

a ver   let's see
al rato   a while later
de modo que, de manera que   so
en cuanto, tan pronto como   as soon as
frente a   in front of

hacer diligencias   to run errands
hacia   toward
hijo(-a) único(-a)   only child
Llene...   Fill out . . .
mientras   while
ojalá   I hope, God grant

quedarse en la cama hasta tarde   to sleep late
suena el despertador   the alarm goes off
¿verdad?   right?, true?

---

[1]**Ropa** is always used in the singular.

Vocabulario adicional
En el banco

SUGGESTION: Use Transparency 36 to present the vocabulary.

en efectivo

el cajero automático

RELATED VOCABULARY: Other vocabulary words you may want to introduce at this point are: **talones** (checks/Spain); **hacer un depósito** (to make a deposit); **poner la fecha** (to date).

SERVIBANCO

la libreta de ahorros

el talonario de cheques, la chequera

la firma

a plazos on installments	Compré el coche **a plazos.**
ahorrar to save	Tienes que **ahorrar** más dinero.
al contado in cash	No voy a comprarlo a plazos; voy a comprarlo **al contado.**
fechar to date (a check, a letter, etc.)	Tiene que firmar y **fechar** el cheque.
gratis free of charge	No cuesta nada; es **gratis.**
pedir prestado(-a) to borrow	Voy a **pedirle prestados** doscientos dólares a Juan.
pedir un préstamo to apply for a loan	Voy al banco para **pedir un préstamo** de cinco mil dólares.

SUGGESTION: Write the answers to these questions on a sheet of paper, make several copies, and cut the paper into small strips with one response per slip. Divide the class into groups of three and distribute the slips of paper to each group. Students should then reconstruct the story based on the information given on the slips of paper and what they recall from the dialogues. If the questions have been assigned for homework, have students check their own work upon completion of this activity by comparing their responses with those on the slips of paper.

¡Conversemos!

Answer the following questions, basing your answers on the dialogues.

1. ¿Qué quiere hacer Sergio hoy? ¿Por qué?
2. ¿Qué pasa en cuanto suena el despertador?
3. ¿Por qué no puede quedarse en la cama hoy?
4. ¿Dónde estaban los pantalones de Sergio?
5. ¿De qué color eran los pantalones de Sergio? Y ahora, ¿de qué color son?
6. ¿A qué departamento de la tienda La Francia va Sergio?

SUGGESTION: Use Transparencies
5–6 to show the geographical location
of Puerto Rico in relation to the other
Caribbean islands and the United
States.

7. Las fotos que él quería revelar, ¿son en colores o en blanco y negro?
8. ¿Puede sacar Sergio doscientos dólares de su cuenta de ahorros? ¿Por qué o por qué no?
9. ¿Cuál es el saldo de su cuenta de ahorros?
10. ¿Por qué grita Sergio "¡Ay, no!"?
11. ¿Sergio tiene hermanos? ¿Cómo lo sabe Ud.?
12. ¿Qué dice Sergio mientras camina a la estación de policía?

¿Lo sabía Ud.?

Puerto Rico es una de las Antillas Mayores. Es un Estado Libre Asociado a los Estados Unidos, y sus lenguas oficiales son el español y el inglés. Su capital es San Juan.

Los indios llamaban a la isla de Puerto Rico "Borinquén", y hoy en día muchos de sus habitantes todavía usan el nombre "Borinquén". En vez de *(Instead of)* decir que son "puertorriqueños" dicen que son "boricuas" o "borinqueños".

Cada nación latinoamericana tiene un banco central encargado de *(in charge of)* emitir el dinero y de controlar la actividad de los bancos comerciales. En algunos países hay también sucursales *(branches)* de bancos extranjeros. El uso del cheque no es tan común en América Latina como en los Estados Unidos, pero muchos bancos tienen sus propias *(own)* tarjetas de crédito.

- ¿Cuál es el estado de este país que está formado por un grupo de islas?
- En este país, ¿qué institución está encargada de emitir el dinero?

See the *¿Cómo se dice…?* Web site for activities on authentic cultural material: http://spanish.college.hmco.com/students
INTERNET

La Puerta de San Juan, en el Viejo San Juan, parte antigua de la capital de Puerto Rico.

Pronunciación

STUDENT AUDIO

NOTE: To reinforce pronunciation practice, this section appears in Lessons 10 through 18. The sentences featured as pronunciation models are taken from the lesson dialogues.

SUGGESTION: For each sentence, first model the word(s) in boldface type and have the class repeat them chorally and individually. Then have students repeat the full sentence for pronunciation practice of the target expressions in context.

In this lesson, there are some new words or phrases that may be challenging to pronounce. For further pronunciation practice of Spanish sounds, listen to your instructor and repeat the following words and phrases.

1. Su mamá quiere que haga varias **diligencias.**
2. Sergio quiere **quedarse en la cama hasta tarde.**
3. ¿Cuánto cobran por **revelar un rollo de película?**
4. Quiero **sacar** doscientos dólares de mi **cuenta de ahorros.**
5. Cuando Sergio sale del banco, no encuentra su **motocicleta.**

Bancomer

Nuestro compromiso es servirle.

Estructuras

1 The subjunctive mood *(El modo subjuntivo)*

A. Introduction to the subjunctive

Until now, you have been using verbs in the indicative mood. The indicative is used to express factual, definite events. By contrast, the subjunctive is used to reflect the speaker's feelings or attitudes toward events, or when the speaker views events as uncertain, unreal, or hypothetical.

■ The Spanish subjunctive is most often used in subordinate or dependent clauses.

■ The subjunctive is also used in English, although not as often as in Spanish. Consider the following sentence:

> I suggest that he **arrive** tomorrow.

The expression that requires the use of the subjunctive is in the main clause, *I suggest.* The subjunctive appears in the subordinate clause, *that he **arrive** tomorrow.* The subjunctive is used because the action of arriving is not real; it is only what is *suggested* that he do.

B. Present subjunctive forms of regular verbs

■ To form the present subjunctive, add the following endings to the stem of the first-person singular of the present indicative after dropping the o.

-ar *verbs*	-er *verbs*	-ir *verbs*
habl -e	com -a	viv -a
habl -es	com -as	viv -as
habl -e	com -a	viv -a
habl -emos	com -amos	viv -amos
habl -éis	com -áis	viv -áis
habl -en	com -an	viv -an

■ Note that the endings for **-er** and **-ir** verbs are identical.

■ The following table shows how to form the first-person singular of the present subjunctive. The stem is the same for all persons.

Verb	First-person singular present indicative	Subjunctive stem	First-person singular present subjunctive
caminar	camino	camin-	camine
aprender	aprendo	aprend-	aprenda
escribir	escribo	escrib-	escriba
decir	digo	dig-	diga
hacer	hago	hag-	haga
traer	traigo	traig-	traiga
sacar	saco	sac-	saque[1]
llegar	llego	lleg-	llegue[1]
empezar	empiezo	empiez-	empiece[1]

práctica ●●

Give the present subjunctive of the following verbs.

1. *yo:* solicitar, recibir, traer, decir, caminar, comer, ver
2. *tú:* escribir, cobrar, decidir, regresar, venir, barrer, aparcar
3. *él:* gritar, hacer, mandar, salir, anotar, esperar
4. *nosotros:* cocinar, depositar, leer, poner, pagar
5. *ellos:* caminar, deber, robar, conocer, vender, salir, empezar

---

[1]Remember that in verbs ending in **-gar**, **-car**, and **-zar**, **g** changes to **gu**, **c** changes to **qu**, and **z** changes to **c** before **e**.

SUGGESTION: Before presenting the subjunctive forms, use Transparency 37 to review the present indicative. Cover up the couple at the bottom of the illustration and tell students working in groups of three to generate sentences about what the couple depicted in the transparency is planning to do and what will happen.

To introduce the concepts and structures of the subjunctive, show the complete transparency and indicate that these events are not factual or definite but refer to events that the subjects wish would occur.

Contrast several sentences generated from the first activity and place them in a context that requires the subjunctive.

Tomás espera que ellos se casen.

Note: This activity should serve only as a preview of the material to be covered in the chapter. Students should not be expected to produce sentences in the subjunctive at this point.

SUGGESTION: Write a chart on the board to contrast the forms of the **-ar**, **-er**, and **-ir** verbs in the present indicative and present subjunctive. You may indicate the change in the endings by writing them in different colored chalk.

Present indicative	Present subjunctive
habl -o	habl -e
habl -as	habl -es
habl -a	habl -e, etc.

EXPANSION: Have students practice switching from the indicative to the subjunctive by repeating the exercise quickly in groups of three. Students should give the indicative form first and then the subjunctive form.

S1—Yo solicito, yo solicite
S2—Yo recibo, yo reciba
S3—Yo traigo, yo traiga, etc.

C. Subjunctive forms of stem-changing verbs

■ Verbs that end in **-ar** and **-er** undergo the same stem changes in the present subjunctive as in the present indicative.

recomendar (e:ie)	*to recommend*	recordar (o:ue)	*to remember*
recomiende	recomendemos	recuerde	recordemos
recomiendes	recomendéis	recuerdes	recordéis
recomiende	recomienden	recuerde	recuerden

entender (e:ie)	*to understand*	devolver (o:ue)	*to return (something)*
entienda	entendamos	devuelva	devolvamos
entiendas	entendáis	devuelvas	devolváis
entienda	entiendan	devuelva	devuelvan

■ In stem-changing verbs that end in **-ir**, the unstressed **e** changes to **i** and the unstressed **o** changes to **u** in the first- and second-person plural (**nosotros** and **vosotros**) forms. The other persons follow the same pattern as the indicative.

mentir (e:ie)	*to lie*	dormir (o:ue)	*to sleep*
mienta	mintamos	duerma	durmamos
mientas	mintáis	duermas	durmáis
mienta	mientan	duerma	duerman

D. Verbs that are irregular in the subjunctive

■ The following verbs are irregular in the subjunctive.

dar	estar	saber	ser	ir
dé	esté	sepa	sea	vaya
des	estés	sepas	seas	vayas
dé	esté	sepa	sea	vaya
demos	estemos	sepamos	seamos	vayamos
deis	estéis	sepáis	seáis	vayáis
den	estén	sepan	sean	vayan

ATENCIÓN   The subjunctive of **hay** (impersonal form of **haber**) is **haya.**

práctica ···

Give the present subjunctive of the following verbs.

1. *yo:* dormir, mentir, recomendar, dar, pensar, ir
2. *tú:* volver, estar, ser, preferir, recordar, morir, ver, pedir

EXPANSION: Have students practice switching from the indicative to the subjunctive by repeating the exercise quickly in groups of three. Students should give the indicative form first and then the subjunctive form.

S1—Yo duermo, yo duerma
S2—Yo miento, yo mienta
S3—Yo recomiendo, yo recomiende

3. *él*: cerrar, saber, perder, probar, dar, servir, seguir
4. *nosotros*: sentir, ir, dar, dormir, perder, cerrar, saber, ser
5. *ellos*: estar, ser, recordar, saber, encontrar, repetir

E. Uses of the subjunctive

There are four main concepts that call for the use of the subjunctive in Spanish:

■ Volition: demands, wishes, advice, persuasion, and other attempts to impose will

Ella **quiere** que yo estacione aquí.	*She wants me to park here.*
Te **aconsejo** que no **vayas** a ese banco.	*I advise you not to go to that bank.*
Les **ruego** que no se **vayan**.	*I beg you not to leave.*

■ Emotion: pity, joy, fear, surprise, hope, and so on

Espero que **lleguen** temprano.	*I hope they arrive early.*
Siento que no **puedas** venir a clase.	*I'm sorry you can't come to class.*
Me **sorprende** que no **vayas** al concierto.	*It surprises me that you're not going to the concert.*

■ Doubt, disbelief, denial, uncertainty, and negated facts

Dudo que **paguen** la cuenta.	*I doubt they'll pay the bill.*
No creo que ella **sea** una idiota.	*I don't think she's an idiot.*
No es verdad que Antonio **sea** instructor de tenis.	*It isn't true that Antonio is a tennis instructor.*

■ Unreality, indefiniteness, and nonexistence

¿**Hay alguien** que **esté** libre hoy?	*Is there anyone who's free today?*
No hay nadie que **tenga** el comprobante.	*There's nobody that has his or her claim check.*

Bienvenido a la era del dinero electrónico

servibanca
Su dinero electronico

2 The subjunctive with verbs of volition *(El subjuntivo con verbos que indican voluntad o deseo)*

SUGGESTION: Write the following sentence builder on the board and ask students to combine the elements to form as many sentences as possible in five minutes. Encourage them to write interrogative as well as affirmative and negative statements.

Yo / Tú / Mi amigo(-a) / Mi(s) hermano(s) / La universidad / Mi profesor(-a) de...

querer / preferir / aconsejar / insistir en / sugerir

que

mi amigo(-a) / mi profesor(-a) / mi(s) padre(s) / yo / los estudiantes / nosotros(-as)

estudiar más / gastar más (menos) dinero / llegar a tiempo / viajar a... / trabajar / comprar... / dar una fiesta / venir mañana / pagar la cuenta

■ All impositions of will, as well as indirect or implied commands, require the subjunctive in subordinate clauses. The subject in the main clause must be different from the subject in the subordinate clause.

■ Note the sentence structure for this use of the subjunctive in Spanish.

Él **quiere** que yo **estudie**.	
He wants	*me to study.*
main clause	subordinate clause

—¿Quiere que le **dé** el número de mi cuenta?
"Do you want me to give you my account number?"

—Sí, y también necesito que **firme** la tarjeta.
"Yes, and I also need you to sign the card."

—Roberto quiere que tú **vayas** a la fiesta.
"Robert wants you to go to the party."

—Sí, pero yo no quiero ir.
"Yes, but I don't want to go."

ATENCIÓN   Notice that the infinitive is used after a verb of volition if there is no change of subject: **Yo no quiero *ir.***

■ Some verbs of volition are:

aconsejar	*to advise*	**querer** (e:ie)	*to want*
desear	*to want*	**recomendar** (e:ie)	*to recommend*
mandar	*to order*	**rogar** (o:ue)	*to beg, plead*
necesitar	*to need*	**sugerir** (e:ie)	*to suggest*
pedir (e:i)	*to ask for, request*		

práctica ●●●

SUGGESTION A: Have students do this exercise in pairs.

FOLLOW-UP A: Have students write a brief paragraph that explains what they or their boyfriends/girlfriends hope, wish, want, or don't want.

ACTIVITY SUGGESTION: See the *IAM* for an additional in-class activity: **Favores.**

A. Tell the following people that you want them to do something other than what they'd like to do.

> **MODELO:** Yo quiero lavarme la cabeza ahora. (más tarde)
> *Yo te sugiero que te laves la cabeza más tarde.*

1. Nosotros necesitamos comprar una motocicleta. (un coche)
2. Yo quiero probarme el vestido aquí. (tu cuarto)
3. Ella quiere abrir una cuenta corriente. (una cuenta de ahorros)
4. Ellos quieren ir al banco hoy. (mañana)
5. Esteban quiere dar una fiesta el viernes. (el sábado)
6. Mi hermano quiere ser profesor de francés. (de inglés)
7. Anita y yo queremos venir mañana. (el lunes)
8. Uds. necesitan ir al campo en bicicleta. (en auto)
9. Alicia quiere pagar la cuenta este mes. (el mes próximo)
10. Nosotros queremos hacer la sopa. (ensalada)

B. Describe what the following people want each person to do, using the present subjunctive.

Anita

MODELO: *La mamá de Anita quiere que ella estudie.*

1. Tito

2. Julia

3. Beto

4. Los estudiantes

5. Hugo

SUGGESTION C: Point out the need to include the indirect object pronoun in making recommendations with **aconsejar, recomendar,** and **sugerir.**

C. Your friends are always coming to you with their problems. Tell them what you suggest, recommend, or advise for each situation.

> MODELO: Mañana tengo un examen. ¿Qué me aconsejas que haga?
> *Te aconsejo que estudies mucho.*

1. Yo no puedo lavar mis pantalones en casa. ¿Adónde me sugieres que los lleve?
2. Un Porsche es muy caro para mí. ¿Qué coche me recomiendas que compre?
3. A mi hermano le regalaron mil dólares. ¿Qué le sugieres que haga con el dinero?
4. Mi prima no tiene suficiente dinero para ir al teatro. ¿Le aconsejas que se lo pida prestado a su papá o a su novio?
5. Alguien nos robó las maletas. ¿Adónde nos aconsejas que vayamos?
6. Tengo hambre. ¿Qué me recomiendas que coma?
7. Mi tía está enferma. ¿Qué le aconsejas que haga?
8. Los chicos ensuciaron la alfombra. ¿Qué les sugieres que hagan?
9. A mi hermana no le gusta cocinar. ¿Qué le sugieres que haga?
10. Mañana es el cumpleaños de mi padre. ¿Qué me sugieres que le regale?

D. With a classmate, look at the list of errands that must be done tomorrow. Then take turns saying what you want each other to do, and give different reasons why you can't do it.

> MODELO: Comprar la medicina para Ernesto.
> Yo quiero que tú compres la medicina para Ernesto.
> *Yo no puedo comprarla porque tengo que estudiar.*

1. Llevar los pantalones a la tintorería.
2. Llevar a revelar el rollo de película.
3. Depositar el cheque en el banco.
4. Llevar la motocicleta al taller de mecánica.
5. Comprar las bebidas para la fiesta.
6. Llevar los discos compactos a casa de Ana.
7. Alquilar un video.
8. Comprar los billetes para la excursión.
9. Recoger las entradas para el concierto.
10. Pedirle prestada la grabadora a Rosita.
11. Ir a la oficina de turismo para pedir la lista de hoteles.
12. Comprar el regalo para Eva.
13. Devolverle las maletas a Luis.

E. Discuss with a classmate things that important people in your lives (parents, relatives, friends, professors, etc.) want you to do. List at least five things, and then compare your results with the rest of the class.

F. Write two or three problems on a slip of paper. Then, form a small group with two or three classmates. Switch slips within the group and take turns offering solutions to each other's problems.

3 The subjunctive with verbs of emotion *(El subjuntivo con verbos de emoción)*

SUGGESTION: Ask students the following personalized questions about their hopes and fears.

1. ¿Cuándo esperas que tengamos un día libre?
2. ¿Cuándo te sientes triste / feliz?
3. ¿Temes que el profesor dé un examen final muy difícil?
4. ¿Sientes que tus amigos no hablen español?
5. ¿Te alegras de que tus amigos te llamen por teléfono?
6. ¿Te gusta que haya exámenes finales?

■ In Spanish, the subjunctive is always used in subordinate clauses when the verb in the main clause expresses any kind of emotion, such as fear, joy, pity, hope, pleasure, surprise, anger, regret, sorrow, likes and dislikes, and so forth.

—**Siento** que Julia no **venga** hoy. *"I'm sorry that Julia is not coming today."*

—**Espero** que **pueda** venir mañana. *"I hope she can come tomorrow."*

—Ramón no tiene dinero para comprar un coche. *"Ramón doesn't have money to buy a car."*
—Ojalá que **consiga** un préstamo. *"I hope that he obtains a loan."*

ATENCIÓN **Ojalá** is always followed by the subjunctive.

Tus envíos pueden ser cobrados en:

bancapromex **B I TAL** Woolworth

Elektra Centrales TELECOMM TELEGRAFOS hecali

■ If there is no change of subject, the infinitive is used instead of the subjunctive.

> Me alegro de estar aquí. } *I'm glad to be here.*
> (**Yo** me alegro—**yo** estoy aquí.)

■ Some verbs and expressions that express emotion are:

alegrarse (de) *to be glad*	**sorprender** *to surprise*
esperar *to hope*	**temer** *to fear*
sentir (e:ie) *to be sorry, to regret*	**es una lástima** *it's a pity*
	ojalá *I hope*

práctica ....

SUGGESTION A: Have students complete this activity in pairs, taking turns playing each role.

A. You are talking to a classmate. Say whether you are glad (**Me alegro de que...**) or sorry (**Siento que...**) about what is happening to your classmate and his or her family.

> MODELO: Estoy enferma.
> *Siento que estés enferma.*

1. Yo quiero salir, pero tengo que quedarme en casa.
2. Mi hermano y yo no nos sentimos bien.
3. Mi mamá estaba enferma, pero ahora está mejor.
4. Mi hijo es muy inteligente.
5. Mi hermana sabe cocinar muy bien.
6. No hay suficiente dinero en mi cuenta corriente.
7. Mis padres van a Buenos Aires.
8. Mis profesores me dan muchos problemas.

Now, tell your classmate about three things that are going on in your life. He or she should react appropriately.

Hablan nuestros clientes.

SUN BANK
El banco con calor humano.
A SunTrust Bank Miembro FDIC

B. Use your imagination to complete the sentence in parentheses, according to the situation described in the first sentence.

> MODELO: Mi hermano quiere depositar un cheque que está a nombre de nuestra madre. (Espero que...)
> *Espero que no tenga problemas para depositarlo.*

1. Elsa quiere sacar mil dólares de su cuenta de ahorros. (Temo que...)
2. Quiero comprar una motocicleta, pero no tengo suficiente dinero. (Es una lástima que...)
3. Vamos a ir a la tintorería para recoger mis pantalones. (Espero que...)
4. Hoy no puedo ir con Uds. porque tengo que hacer muchas diligencias. (Siento que...)
5. Ellos van a pedir un préstamo en el banco. (Ojalá que...)
6. Carlitos tiene solamente seis años y tiene cien mil dólares en el banco. (Me sorprende que...)

C. Complete the following sentences to express how you feel, using the infinitive or the subjunctive as appropriate.

FOLLOW-UP C: Use Transparency 37 and ask students in groups or pairs to generate sentences as if the man and woman were speaking directly to each other. They may do this by completing the following phrases.

1. Ojalá que (nosotros)...
2. Espero que...
3. Quiero que...

1. Yo me alegro mucho de...
2. Yo me alegro mucho de que mis amigos...
3. Yo temo no...
4. Yo temo que mi papá [mamá, hijo(-a)] no...
5. Yo siento...
6. Yo siento que el profesor (la profesora, los profesores)...
7. Yo espero...
8. Yo espero que mis padres (Ud.)...
9. Ojalá que...
10. Es una lástima que...

¡A ver cuánto aprendió!

INTERNET

See the *¿Cómo se dice...?* Web site for additional grammar and vocabulary practice: http://spanish.college. hmco.com/students

ACTIVITY SUGGESTION: Do **¡Escucha!**, the in-class listening comprehension activity that reviews vocabulary and grammar structures introduced in the lesson. It appears in the answer key of the *IAM*.

¡Repase el vocabulario!

Complete the following sentences with the appropriate words; then read them aloud.

1. Quiero comprar ____ropa____ nueva, especialmente unos pantalones.
2. ¿Cuánto __cobran__ Uds. por __revelar__ un rollo de película en colores?
3. Voy a __sacar__ mil dólares de mi cuenta de ahorros y los voy a __depositar__ en mi cuenta corriente.
4. Necesita el __comprobante__ para recoger los pantalones.
5. ¡__Pobre__ Julio! ¡Los muchachos se llevaron su motocicleta y nunca se la devolvieron!
6. A ver... No puedo verte esta semana, de __modo__ que tienes que venir la semana próxima.

ACTIVITY SUGGESTION: See the *IAM* for an additional in-class activity: **Palabras escondidas.**

7. Llegó Antonio y al _rato_ llegó Luis.
8. Anita caminó _hacia_ mí y me dio un beso.
9. ¿Lo vas a comprar al _contado_ o a plazos?
10. Tengo mi _talonario_ de cheques, pero no quiero pagar con un cheque; quiero pagar en _efectivo_
11. Si quieres asistir a la universidad, tienes que empezar a _ahorrar_ dinero.
12. Tienes tu libreta de _ahorros_ contigo, ¿verdad? ¿O la dejaste en casa?
13. Para sacar dinero, siempre uso el _cajero_ automático.
14. No me desperté porque no sonó el _despertador_
15. Mi hermano es alto y de ojos azules, como tú. Uds. se _parecen_ mucho.
16. Hoy no trabajo. Tengo el día _libre_.

Entrevista

ACTIVITY SUGGESTION: See the *IAM* for additional in-class activities: **Para conocernos mejor** and **Una encuesta.**

With a partner, interview each other by asking the following questions.

1. ¿En qué calle y en qué ciudad vives?
2. ¿Tienes hermanos o eres hijo(-a) único(-a)?
3. ¿Te pareces más a tu mamá o a tu papá?
4. ¿Te gusta levantarte temprano o quedarte en la cama hasta tarde?
5. ¿Hiciste algunas diligencias ayer? (¿Cuáles?)
6. ¿Lavas tu ropa en casa o la llevas a la tintorería?
7. ¿Estás ahorrando dinero para comprar algo especial? (¿Qué?)
8. ¿Prefieres que te regalen un coche o una motocicleta? (¿Por qué?)
9. ¿Prefieres tomar fotografías en colores o en blanco y negro?
10. La última *(last)* vez que tomaste fotos, ¿las fotos salieron bien?
11. ¿Vives cerca o lejos de la universidad?
12. ¿Trabajas los sábados o tienes los sábados libres?

Situaciones

What would you say in the following situations? What might the other person say? Act out the scenes with a partner. Take turns playing each role.

1. You are at the dry cleaner and you want to pick up your pants. You are upset because they are not ready. You want to know when they are going to be ready.
2. You are in the photo section of a large department store. Find out how much they charge to develop black-and-white and color film. Ask about the rolls of film you brought in last week for developing.
3. You are at the bank. You want to withdraw money from your savings account and deposit it in your checking account, but you're not sure what you have to do.

Para escribir

Write a short composition about the people in the photo on page 267. Describe what the employees and the customers do and want to do. Include as many banking transactions as possible.

En la vida real

CD-ROM

Do the interactive exercises on the CD-ROM for additional practice.

ACTIVITY SUGGESTION: See the *IAM* for an additional in-class activity: **El Banco de Asunción.**

Mis diligencias

Have a conversation with a classmate about the errands you have run lately, including those that did not go as planned.

Here are some words and expressions you may want to include:

mala suerte   *bad luck*
todo me fue mal   *everything went wrong (for me)*

todo el día   *all day long*
el taller de mecánica   *mechanic's shop*

¿Qué dice tu horóscopo?

SUGGESTION: After students have familiarized themselves with the format and vocabulary typically found in horoscopes, distribute current horoscopes copied from the local newspaper. In groups of three, students should tell the other members of the group what they or their families and friends should or shouldn't do, and what good or bad fortune they can expect during that day. You could also assign this activity as written homework. Students should prepare three different horoscopes for friends or family members based on the predictions in the newspaper.

Read the following horoscopes, and then compare your own horoscope with those of your classmates. Try to find a classmate for each sign of the zodiac by asking, **¿De qué signo eres?** *(What's your sign?).* Offer each other suggestions on how to fulfill your horoscopes.

CAPRICORNIO (21 de diciembre–20 de enero)

Tú eres, como siempre, ¡superpráctico! Debes recordar, sin embargo *(however),* que a veces es bueno ser impulsivo. Si recibes una invitación interesante… ¿por qué no aceptarla?

ACUARIO (21 de enero–19 de febrero)

Si quieres progresar en tus estudios o en tu profesión, no debes dejar para mañana lo que puedes hacer hoy. Alguien muy importante te está observando.

PISCIS (20 de febrero–20 de marzo)

Más que nunca, Cupido va a ser parte de tu vida *(life)* este año. Probablemente va a querer que estés preparado para cualquier cosa *(anything),* incluso una boda.

ARIES (21 de marzo–20 de abril)

¡Siempre empiezas proyectos con mucho entusiasmo pero casi nunca los terminas! Tienes que hacer lo posible por aprender a ser perseverante. Este año va a ser muy importante para ti.

TAURO (21 de abril–20 de mayo)

Buena oportunidad para mejorar *(improve)* las finanzas. Un nuevo empleo… una beca *(scholarship)*… Pero tienes que hacer tu parte y aceptar nuevas responsabilidades.

GÉMINIS

(21 de mayo–20 de junio)
¡Tienes que salir de la rutina! ¿Por qué no tomas una clase o das una fiesta? Hay muchas personas que quieren ser tus amigos... pero tú no les das la oportunidad.

CÁNCER

(21 de junio–20 de julio)
Muy pronto vas a tener que tomar una decisión muy importante. Debes pensar en todas las posibilidades antes de decidir lo que vas a hacer. Hay alguien que está esperando ansiosamente *(anxiously)* tu decisión.

LEO

(21 de julio–20 de agosto)
Pronto vas a recibir noticias *(news)* de alguien que hace mucho que no ves. También debes tratar de llamar o de escribirles a aquellas personas que son parte de tu pasado.

VIRGO

(21 de agosto–20 de septiembre)
Como siempre, estás trabajando demasiado. No debes sentirte culpable *(guilty)* si decides tomarte unas vacaciones o simplemente ir al cine o al teatro con tus amigos. Esta semana vas a tener muchas oportunidades de divertirte y debes aprovecharlas *(take advantage of them)*.

LIBRA

(21 de septiembre–20 de octubre)
Tú eres generalmente una persona muy equilibrada, pero últimamente le estás dando más importancia a tu trabajo y a tus proyectos que a tu familia. Tienes que pasar más tiempo con tu familia.

ESCORPIÓN

(21 de octubre–20 de noviembre)
Éstos son los momentos indicados para tomar decisiones importantes. Es muy posible que hagas un viaje muy largo, probablemente al extranjero *(abroad)*.

SAGITARIO

(21 de noviembre–20 de diciembre)
Hay una persona que está secretamente enamorada de *(in love with)* ti. Muy pronto vas a saber quién es. Debes aceptar las invitaciones de tus amigos porque vas a conocer a esa persona en una fiesta o en un picnic.

SUGGESTION: In order to offer oral as well as written practice, distribute "complaint" forms such as those typically found in restaurants, hotels, etc. To prepare for the activity, give each student a form with the type of establishment indicated on the top, and instruct him or her to explain the problem. Collect the forms the next day and distribute them to the group assigned to the particular establishment. These groups should then briefly answer each complaint orally or in writing.

Tenemos algunas quejas...   *(We have some complaints)*

Get ready to complain and to respond to complaints about different commercial establishments. The class will be divided into two groups owning different businesses. Group A owns a restaurant, a hotel, and a travel agency. Group B owns a bank, a beauty salon, and a maid service. Before the two groups express their complaints to each other about bad service, each group should decide on the types of concerns and problems that they'll present.

Antes de leer

A. Before you read the fable, look at the illustration. Is the milkmaid happy or sad? What is she thinking about? Why? Now make a list of situations in which the saying "Don't count your chickens before they hatch" would apply.

B. As you read the fable, find the answers to the following questions.

1. ¿Adónde va la lechera?
2. ¿Qué lleva en la cabeza?
3. ¿En qué va pensando?
4. ¿Qué es lo primero que va a comprar con el dinero que obtenga?
5. ¿En qué se van a convertir los huevos?
6. ¿Qué va a hacer con el dinero que obtenga de la venta de los pollitos?
7. ¿Qué le va a pedir a su padre que haga?
8. Cuando su padre venda el cochino, ¿qué va a comprar con el dinero de esa venta?
9. ¿Qué pasa cuando la lechera tropieza?
10. ¿Por qué pierde lo único que tenía?
11. ¿Cuál es la moraleja de la fábula?

La lechera
(Fábula de origen oriental)

Una lechera° va al mercado, llevando un cántaro° en la cabeza. Va muy contenta, pensando en el dinero que va a ganar con la venta° de la leche.

"Con el dinero que obtenga, voy a comprar un canasto° de huevos que, en el verano, se van a convertir en° pollitos que me van a rodear cantando *pío, pío*."

Entusiasmada con esta idea, la lechera piensa que, cuando venda los pollos va a tener suficiente dinero para comprar un cochino.°

"En cuanto el cochino engorde le voy a pedir a mi padre que lo lleve al mercado y que lo venda. Con el dinero que le den, voy a comprar una vaca° y un ternero.°"

Tan contenta va la lechera con estos pensamientos° que no se fija en una piedra° que hay en el camino y tropieza.° El cántaro se le cae° de la cabeza y se rompe, derramando° toda la leche. ¡Adiós leche, dinero, pollos, cochino, vaca y ternero!

¡Pobre lechera! Por estar haciendo castillos en el aire, perdió lo único que realmente tenía.

Quiero que recuerdes, lector,° esta moraleja: "No anheles° impaciente el bien futuro; mira que ni el presente está seguro".

milkmaid / jug	
sale	
basket	
se... are going to turn into	
pig	
cow	
calf	
thoughts	
stone / she trips / falls	
spilling	
reader / **No...** Don't yearn	

Díganos

Answer the following questions, based on your own thoughts and experiences.

1. ¿Hace Ud. "castillos en el aire" a veces?
2. ¿Qué animales domésticos tenía Ud. cuando era niño(-a)? ¿Perros? ¿Gatos *(cats)*? ¿Caballos? ¿Loros *(Parrots)*? ¿Conejillos de Indias *(Guinea pigs)*?
3. ¿Recuerda Ud. una circunstancia en que Ud. sufrió una desilusión *(disappointment)*?
4. ¿Qué significado tiene para Ud. la moraleja de esta fábula?

ASÍ SOMOS

  VIDEO   CD-ROM   Do the interactive exercises on the CD-ROM for additional practice.

NARRADORA —Cuando Ud. va de compras, ¿prefiere pagar con cheque, con tarjeta de crédito o en efectivo?

JUAN —Cuando voy de compras siempre pago en efectivo porque no tengo tarjeta de crédito y no tengo cheque.

NOTE: The video-related vocabulary is listed in the *Instructor's Activities Manual* for your reference. Its purpose is to facilitate students' comprehension. You may want to distribute the vocabulary to the class before viewing.

Preparación

NOTE: See the Instructor's Edition frontmatter for additional suggestions on implementing video in the classroom.

SUGGESTION: In groups, have students make a list of the activities they see people doing at the beginning of the video.

SUGGESTION: Have students brainstorm possible words and phrases related to running errands and banking.

SUGGESTION: Have students answer the *Preparación* activities before they view the video.

A. Las diligencias. Answer the following questions about who runs the errands in your family. You will hear answers to some of these questions when you watch the video. After viewing the video, compare your answers with those you hear.

1. ¿Quién hace las diligencias en su familia?
2. ¿Quién lleva la ropa a la tintorería *(dry cleaner)*?
3. ¿Quién lava la ropa?
4. ¿Quién va al banco?
5. ¿Quién lleva el carro al taller de mecánica *(mechanic's shop)*?
6. ¿Quién hace las compras?
7. ¿Quién va al correo?

B. Vamos al banco. With a partner, answer the following questions about your banking habits. You will hear answers to some of these questions when you watch the video. After viewing the video, compare your answers with those you hear.

1. ¿Cuándo va Ud. al banco?
2. ¿Usa Ud. el cajero automático frecuentemente?
3. Cuando Ud. va de compras, ¿prefiere pagar con cheque, con tarjeta de crédito o en efectivo?
4. ¿Cuántas tarjetas de crédito tiene Ud.?

Comprensión

A. Las diligencias. Select the word or phrase that best completes each statement, according to what you understood.

1. (El papá, La mamá) de Juan se ocupa de *(takes charge of)* los aspectos financieros.
2. La casa es la responsabilidad de (Olga, Ricardo).
3. (Olga, Ricardo) lleva a los niños a la escuela.
4. En la casa de Tamara (todos, la mamá y el papá) comparten *(share)* las tareas del hogar *(household chores)*.

B. El banco. Answer the following questions according to what you understood from the video.

1. ¿Qué hace Víctor en el banco?
2. ¿Va Tamara al banco con mucha frecuencia?
3. ¿Qué hace Tamara cuando va al banco?
4. ¿Con qué frecuencia deposita Gustavo dinero en el banco?

C. **¿Quién lo dijo?** Match each statement with the name of the person who said it. More than one statement may correspond with one person.

A	B
____ 1. Me permite flexibilidad en los retiros *(withdrawals)* de dinero.	a. Tamara
____ 2. No tengo tarjeta de crédito.	b. John
____ 3. El cajero automático: sí lo uso con bastante frecuencia.	c. Juan
____ 4. Lo uso solamente en emergencias.	

NOTE: Exercise D includes two interview segments (questions 4 and 5).

D. **¿Verdadero o falso?** Read the following statements. Circle **V** (**Verdadero**) or **F** (**Falso**) according to what you understood from the video. If a statement is false, correct it.

V F   1. Víctor nunca usa tarjeta de crédito.
V F   2. Víctor paga en efectivo cuando es una compra pequeña *(small)*.
V F   3. Cuando va de compras, Juan siempre paga en efectivo.
V F   4. Gustavo dice que las tarjetas de crédito no son seguras *(safe)*.
V F   5. Paola prefiere usar la tarjeta de crédito porque sus papás *(parents)* pagan la cuenta *(bill)*.
V F   6. Gustavo prefiere pagar en efectivo.
V F   7. Gustavo tiene cuatro tarjetas de crédito.
V F   8. Tamara tiene muchas tarjetas de crédito.
V F   9. Tamara dice que las tarjetas son difíciles de obtener *(to get)*.

Ampliación

A. **Mis diligencias.** Make a list of errands you need to do this week. Then in groups of three or four, compare your lists. Determine who has the most errands and who has the least errands to do.

FOLLOW-UP B: Have students compare their banking habits and decide who has the better/worse financial situation.

EXPANSION: Have students describe the banking options available to students at their school or in their town.

B. **Mis asuntos financieros.** Interview a classmate about his or her weekly expenses and banking habits. Use the following questions as a guide.

1. En una semana, ¿cuánto dinero gastas?
2. ¿Cuánto dinero necesitas para las siguientes cosas?
   - comida
   - transporte *(transportation)*
   - gastos de la casa *(household expenses)*
   - gastos personales *(personal expenses)*
3. ¿Tienes cuenta de ahorros o cuenta corriente?
4. ¿Cómo se llama tu banco?
5. ¿Dónde está tu banco?
6. ¿Usas el cajero automático con mucha frecuencia?

OBJECTIVES

Pronunciation
Pronunciation in context

Structure
The **Ud.** and **Uds.** commands • The relative pronouns **que** and **quien** • The subjunctive to express doubt, disbelief, and denial

Communication
You will learn vocabulary related to asking for directions and postal services.

Pidiendo información

STUDENT AUDIO

Julia, una chica de Honduras, llegó a Madrid hace una semana. Con sus amigos españoles visitó el Parque del Retiro, el Palacio Real y las antiguas ciudades de Segovia, Ávila y Toledo. En cada lugar compró un montón de tarjetas postales para enviárselas a sus padres y a sus amigos. Hoy decidió ir al correo para enviar las tarjetas, y recoger un paquete y un giro postal.

JULIA —*(Piensa)* Dudo que el correo esté abierto a esta hora. Creo que abren a las nueve. *(A un señor que está parado en la esquina)* Dígame, señor, ¿dónde queda la oficina de correos?

SR. GÓMEZ —Está a cinco manzanas de aquí, en la Plaza de La Cibeles.

JULIA —Es que… soy extranjera y no conozco las calles. ¿Puede decirme cómo llegar allí?

SR. GÓMEZ —¡Ah!, siga derecho por esta calle hasta llegar a la Plaza de Colón.

JULIA —¿Cuántas cuadras?

SR. GÓMEZ —Dos. Después doble a la derecha al llegar al semáforo, en la calle Alcalá.

JULIA —¿La oficina de correos está en esa calle?

SR. GÓMEZ —Sí, allí mismo. Es un edificio antiguo y está frente a la estación del metro.

En el correo, Julia habla con el empleado que está en la ventanilla de información.

JULIA —Vengo a recoger un paquete y un giro postal. Me llamo Julia Reyes.

EMPLEADO —¿Tiene un documento de identidad?

JULIA —Mi pasaporte… pero lo dejé en el hotel.

EMPLEADO —No creo que se los den sin identificación.

JULIA —Bueno, vuelvo esta tarde. ¿Dónde puedo comprar sellos?

EMPLEADO —Vaya a la ventanilla número dos, a la izquierda.

En la ventanilla número dos, Julia le pide al empleado los sellos que necesita.

JULIA —Quiero enviar estas tarjetas postales por vía aérea y una carta certificada a Honduras.

EMPLEADO —Son diez euros[1], señorita.

JULIA —¿Puede decirme cómo llegar desde aquí a El[2] Corte Inglés?

EMPLEADO —Salga por la puerta principal, cruce la Plaza de La Cibeles y camine por la Gran Vía hasta llegar a la Plaza Callao. El Corte Inglés está al lado de la plaza.

SUGGESTION: Have students act out the dialogues in pairs, then have them personalize the dialogues by changing the location and asking for directions to the post office from different places on campus. Related vocabulary items they could use are: **entrega especial** *(special delivery)*; **zona postal** *(zip code)*; **por avión** *(airmail)*; **un carnet de estudiante** *(student I.D. card/Spain)*.

SUGGESTION: Refer students to **Panorama hispánico 2** and **3** and the corresponding video segments for more information about Spain.

---

[1]The Spanish currency as of 2002.
[2]Note that **a** and **el** do not contract to form **al** since **El** is part of the store name.

En El Corte Inglés, Julia se encuentra con su amiga Pilar, con quien va a ir de compras.

JULIA —Creía que no ibas a estar aquí.

PILAR —Oye, guapa, no es cierto que los españoles siempre lleguemos tarde. A veces somos puntuales.

Las chicas suben al tercer piso, donde está el departamento de ropa para señoras.

Vocabulario

Cognados

el **documento**   document
la **estación**   station

el **palacio**   palace
el **parque**   park

puntual   punctual

Nombres

el **departamento de (ropa para) señoras (damas)**   women's department
el **documento de identidad (identificación)**   I.D.
el **edificio**   building
el (la) **español(-a)**   Spaniard
la **esquina**   corner

el (la) **extranjero(-a)**   foreigner
el **giro postal**   money order
la **manzana**[1] *(Spain)*, la **cuadra** *(Sp. Am.)*   city block
el **metro**, el **subterráneo**   subway
la **oficina de correos**, el **correo**   post office
el **paquete**   package, parcel

la **puerta principal**   main exit (door)
el **sello**, la **estampilla**, el **timbre** *(Mex.)*   stamp
el **semáforo**   traffic light
la **ventanilla**   window (of a car or booth, as in a bank or post office)

Verbos

cruzar   to cross
doblar   to turn, to bend

dudar   to doubt
encontrarse (con) (o:ue)   to meet

subir   to go up, to climb

Adjetivos

abierto(-a)   open
antiguo(-a), **viejo(-a)**[2]   old

certificado(-a)   registered, certified

parado(-a)   standing
real   royal

---

[1]In Spanish America, **manzana** is used to refer to a block of buildings, not to the distance between streets.

[2]When referring to people, use **viejo**, not **antiguo**.

Otras palabras y expresiones

a veces sometimes	**es que...** the fact is . . .	**por vía aérea** by airmail
al lado de next to	**está a... de aquí** it is . . . from here	**quien(-es)** who, whom
allí mismo right there	**frente a** across from	**sin** without
cada each	**hasta llegar** until you get	**un montón de** a pile of
derecho straight (ahead)	**No es cierto. (No es verdad.)** It's	
desde from	not true.	

Vocabulario adicional
El correo

ACTIVITY SUGGESTION: See the *IAM* for an additional in-class activity: **¿Cómo respondes?**

el casillero

arriba

el correo

bajar

el facsímil, el fax

abajo

echar una carta al correo

el buzón

el cartero

Use Transparency 38 to present the vocabulary.

La computadora

la computadora

la pantalla

Luis:
La reunión
es a las dos.

el correo
electrónico

el teclado

el ratón

la impresora

el disquete

SUGGESTION: Have students in pairs use the questions and dialogues as a guide and assume the role of Julia and her friend. In their conversation, "Julia" should tell "Pilar" about her errands in Madrid. Remind students that "Pilar" should make comments or ask questions to clarify any misunderstandings.

SUGGESTION: Bring in slides or photos of Madrid, or point to the photographs of Madrid in **Panorama hispánico 2** and **3**. Have students use the information from **¿Lo sabía Ud.?** and the dialogues, and take turns describing the visuals. To aid in the narration, you could write incomplete sentences on the board as a guide.

1. **Madrid es la capital…**
2. **Está situada…**
3. **Hay más de seis…**
4. **Tiene importancia cultural y…**

¡Conversemos!

Answer the following questions, basing your answers on the dialogues.

1. ¿Cuánto tiempo hace que Julia está en Madrid?
2. ¿Qué lugares visitó con sus amigos españoles?
3. ¿A quién le pregunta dónde queda la oficina de correos?
4. En la calle Alcalá, ¿Julia debe doblar a la izquierda o a la derecha?
5. ¿Cómo es el edificio de correos y dónde está?
6. ¿Por qué no puede Julia recoger el paquete y el giro postal?
7. ¿En qué ventanilla puede comprar sellos?
8. ¿Cómo va a enviar las tarjetas postales Julia?
9. ¿Por dónde sale Julia del correo y qué cruza?
10. ¿A qué tienda va Julia y con quién se encuentra allí?
11. ¿Qué dice Pilar de los españoles?
12. ¿En qué piso está el departamento de ropa para señoras?

¿Lo sabía Ud.?

■ Situada en la parte central de la península Ibérica, Madrid es la capital de España. Su población de más de seis millones de habitantes y su importancia cultural y económica la hacen la principal ciudad española.

Una de las calles principales de la ciudad es la Gran Vía, donde hay muchas tiendas elegantes y cafés al aire libre.

■ El correo de Madrid, o el Palacio de Comunicaciones, es un edificio monumental. Está frente a la hermosa fuente *(fountain)* de La Cibeles, que, para muchos, es el símbolo de Madrid.

■ El Palacio Real, situado frente a la Plaza de Oriente, fue la antigua residencia de los reyes de España. Está considerado uno de los mejores edificios de su tipo en Europa.

■ El metro de Madrid es un sistema de transporte muy eficiente y barato. Es el medio *(means)* de transportación que usa la mayoría de los madrileños. También hay un metro en Barcelona.

■ Segovia es un punto de atracción turístico. Entre sus muchos lugares de interés están el Alcázar, un castillo fortaleza *(fortress)*, y el famoso acueducto romano.

■ El uso del "Internet" o la "Red," como se llama en español, es cada día más popular en el mundo hispano, y muchos países tienen su propia página *(home page)*.

• ¿Qué población tiene la capital de este país?

• ¿Cuál es el "símbolo" de Nueva York?

• ¿En qué ciudades de este país hay metro?

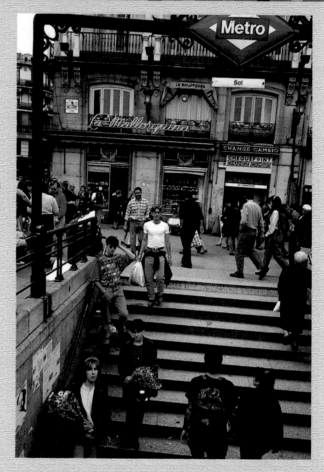

Entrada del metro en La Puerta del Sol, Madrid, España.

INTERNET

See the *¿Cómo se dice..?* Web site for activities on authentic cultural material: http://spanish.college.hmco.com/students

Pronunciación

STUDENT AUDIO

NOTE: To reinforce pronunciation practice, this section appears in Lessons 10 through 18. The sentences featured as pronunciation models are taken from the lesson dialogues.

SUGGESTION: For each sentence, first model the word(s) in boldface type and have the class repeat them chorally and individually. Then have students repeat the full sentence for pronunciation practice of the target expressions in context.

In this lesson, there are some new words or phrases that may be challenging to pronounce. For further pronunciation practice of Spanish sounds, listen to your instructor and repeat the following words and phrases.

1. Es que... soy **extranjera** y no conozco las calles.
2. Doble a la derecha al llegar al **semáforo.**
3. ¿La oficina de **correos** está en esa calle?
4. ¿Tiene un **documento de identidad**?
5. Quiero enviar estas tarjetas postales **por vía aérea.**

Estructuras

1 The Ud. and Uds. commands *(Formas del imperativo para Ud. y Uds.)*

SUGGESTION: Use TPR to introduce the command forms. Ask students to act out the following simple commands.

Abra el libro.
Vaya a la pizarra.
Hable en inglés.
Siéntese.
Tráigame su lápiz.
Lea en voz alta.
Mire hacia arriba.
Cierre el libro.
Cierre la puerta.
Levántese.
Dele el libro a (another student).
Escriba su nombre en la pizarra.
Camine.
Ponga su libro en el pupitre de...
Salga de la clase.

The command forms for **Ud.** and **Uds.**[1] are identical to the corresponding present subjunctive forms.

A. Regular forms

Endings of the Formal Commands			
		Ud.	**Uds.**
-ar verbs	cantar	cant **-e**	cant **-en**
-er verbs	beber	beb **-a**	beb **-an**
-ir verbs	vivir	viv **-a**	viv **-an**

—¿Cuándo volvemos?
—**Vuelvan** mañana y **traigan** los documentos.

"When do we return?"
"Come back tomorrow and bring the documents."

—¿Sigo derecho?
—No, no **siga** derecho. **Doble** a la izquierda.

"Do I keep going straight ahead?"
"No, don't keep going straight ahead. Turn left."

You may also write the infinitive phrases on the board and have students take turns giving each other commands.

ATENCIÓN   To give a negative **Ud./Uds.** command, place **no** in front of the verb: **No siga** derecho.

---

[1]**Tú** commands will be studied in **Lección 13.**

B. Irregular forms

■ The command forms of the following verbs are irregular.

	dar	estar	ser	ir
Ud.	dé	esté	sea	vaya
Uds.	den	estén	sean	vayan

—¿Adónde tengo que ir?   *"Where do I have to go?"*
—**Vaya** a la ventanilla número dos.   *"Go to window number two."*

—¿A qué hora tenemos que estar aquí?   *"At what time do we have to be here?"*
—**Estén** aquí a las ocho. ¡**Sean** puntuales!   *"Be here at eight. Be punctual!"*

práctica ●●

A. What commands would these people give?

1. *El profesor a los estudiantes:*

   venir a clase temprano
   abrir el libro
   ir a la pizarra
   hacer los ejercicios
   cerrar el libro
   hablar solamente español
   no hablar inglés en la clase

2. *La directora a la secretaria:*

   estar en la oficina a las ocho
   traer las cartas
   traducir los documentos
   llevar las cartas al correo
   comprar estampillas
   llamar por teléfono al Sr. Paz
   conseguir la dirección del Banco de Ponce
   no volver hasta las tres

B. María Ester, a girl from Colombia, has decided to visit a few places of interest in Madrid, but doesn't know how to get to them. Using the map below, can you help her?

EXPANSION: Using the map, give students directions to an unidentified place. Students should first write the directions as you dictate them, then trace the route on the map. At the end of the activity, have them report their final destination.

PLANO DE MADRID[1]

SUGGESTION: For additional practice in giving directions, use the map on Transparency 20.

¿Cómo voy...

1. del hotel Carlos V al Museo del Prado?
2. del Museo del Prado a la Plaza Mayor?
3. de la Plaza Mayor al Palacio Real y la Catedral?
4. de la Plaza de Oriente a la Plaza de España?
5. de la Plaza de España a la Puerta del Sol?
6. de la Puerta del Sol a Correos?

[1]This is a simplified version of an actual map of Madrid.

SUGGESTION: It would be appropriate at this time to review the direct and indirect object pronouns used together, presented in **Lección 8** (page 194).

C. Position of object pronouns with direct commands

■ In all direct *affirmative* commands, the object pronouns are placed *after* the verb and attached to it.

Ud. *form*		Uds. *form*	
Hágalo.	*Do it.*	Cómprenlo.	*Buy it.*
Dígales.	*Tell them.*	Díganle.	*Tell him/her.*
Tráiganosla.	*Bring it to us.*	Tráiganselo.	*Bring it to him/her.*
Quédese.	*Stay.*	Quédense.	*Stay.*

ATENCIÓN Note the use of the written accent, which follows the rules for accentuation. See Appendix A.

■ In all *negative* commands, the pronouns are placed *in front of the verb*.

Ud. *form*		Uds. *form*	
No **lo** haga.	*Don't do it.*	No **lo** hagan.	*Don't do it.*
No **le** hable.	*Don't speak to him/her.*	No **le** hablen.	*Don't speak to him/her.*
No **se lo** dé.	*Don't give it to him/her.*	No **se lo** den.	*Don't give it to him/her.*

■ Remember that when an indirect and a direct object pronoun are used together in the same sentence, the indirect object always precedes the direct object.

práctica ....

A. Using the direct commands, tell your younger brothers to do the following.

1. Levantarse a las siete, bañarse y vestirse.
2. Hacer unos sándwiches y ponerlos en el refrigerador.
3. Escribirle una carta a la abuela y echarla al correo.
4. Mandarle un paquete a Teresa.
5. Llamar a la Dra. Peña, pero no llamarla antes de las tres.
6. Comprarle el regalo a mamá, pero no dárselo hoy.
7. Decirle a Marta que la fiesta es mañana, pero no decírselo a Raúl.
8. No acostarse muy tarde.

SUGGESTION B: Have students role-play a waiter and a customer. If the command is negative, an affirmative command or another statement or question should follow.

S1—¿Le traigo el café?
S2—No, no me lo traiga ahora.
  Tráigamelo después del postre.

Encourage students to switch roles in order to practice initiating as well as responding to commands.

B. You are having dinner at a fancy restaurant. Tell the waiter what you want or don't want him to do.

> **MODELO:** ¿Le traigo el menú?
> *Sí, tráigamelo, por favor. (No, no me lo traiga.)*

1. ¿Le traigo la lista de vinos?
2. ¿Le sirvo la ensalada primero?
3. ¿Le pongo pimienta a la ensalada?

4. ¿Abro la botella de vino ahora?
5. ¿Le traigo una tortilla a la española?
6. ¿Le sirvo el café ahora?
7. ¿Le traigo la cuenta ahora?

C. With a partner, take turns telling a group of people what to do about the items given.

> MODELO: las estampillas
> *Cómprenlas.*

1. el paquete
2. el giro postal
3. los documentos
4. las cartas

5. el regalo
6. los pantalones
7. la cuenta corriente
8. el registro

ACTIVITY SUGGESTION: See the *IAM* for an additional in-class activity: **Las órdenes del jefe.**

D. With a partner, take turns playing the roles of a tourist who is planning a trip to an exotic location and a travel agent. The tourist should name a destination and ask whether he or she should bring along certain items. The agent should say whether each article would or would not be appropriate. List five or six items each. Follow the models.

> MODELO: —¿Debo llevar las tarjetas postales?
> —*No, no las lleve. Cómprelas allí.*
>
> —¿Debo llevar mi tienda de campaña?
> —*Sí, llévela. No hay hoteles.*

2 The relative pronouns **que** and **quien**   *(Los pronombres relativos que y quien)*

Relative pronouns are used to combine two sentences that have a common element, usually a noun or a pronoun.

A. The relative pronoun *que*

¿Dónde está **el paquete?**   Trajiste **el paquete.**

common element

¿Dónde está el paquete **que** trajiste?

R.P.

La chica se llama Rosa.   **La chica** vino esta mañana.

common element

La chica **que** vino esta mañana se llama Rosa.

R.P.

■ Note that the relative pronoun **que** not only helps to combine the two sentences in each example, but also replaces the nouns **el paquete** and **la chica** in the second sentences.

■ The relative pronoun **que** is invariable and is used for both persons and things. It is the Spanish equivalent of *that*, *which*, and *who*. Unlike its English equivalent, the Spanish **que** is never omitted.

—¿Para quién es el libro **que** compraste?
—Es para la señora **que** enseña español.

"For whom is the book that you bought?"
"It is for the woman who teaches Spanish."

SUGGESTION: Emphasize the difference between these relative pronouns and the interrogatives **qué** and **quién.** Point out the need for a written accent in indirect questions: **Quiero saber qué debo hacer.**

B. The relative pronoun *quien*

—¿La muchacha **con quien** hablabas es americana?
—No, es extranjera.

"Is the girl with whom you were talking an American?"
"No, she's a foreigner."

—¿Quiénes son esos señores?
—Son los señores **de quienes** te habló José.

"Who are those gentlemen?"
"They are the gentlemen about whom José spoke to you."

■ The relative pronoun **quien** is used only with persons.
■ The plural of **quien** is **quienes. Quien** does not change for gender.
■ **Quien** is generally used after prepositions, i.e., **con quien, de quienes.**
■ **Quien** is the Spanish equivalent of *whom* and *that.*

práctica

A. Complete the following dialogues, using **que, quien,** or **quienes.** Then act them out with a partner.

1. —¿Quién es el señor _____ trajo las cartas?
   —Es el papá de Marisa, la chica con _____ trabajo.
2. —¿Dónde están las estampillas _____ compré ayer?
   —En tu escritorio.
3. —Las chicas con _____ salimos anoche llamaron esta mañana.
   —¿Qué dijeron?
   —Que nos van a traer los libros _____ necesitamos.
4. —¿Con quién vas al museo?
   —Con María Luisa, la chica de _____ te hablé.
5. —¿Ella es la muchacha _____ trabaja contigo?
   —No, es la chica con _____ estudio.

B. Interview a classmate, using the following questions. When you have finished, switch roles.

1. ¿Cómo se llama la persona a quien más admiras?
2. ¿Cómo se llama el profesor o la profesora que enseña tu clase favorita?
3. ¿Quiénes son las personas que viven contigo?

4. ¿Cómo se llaman las personas con quienes vas a salir el sábado?
5. ¿Quién es la persona que más te quiere?
6. ¿Cuál es la comida que más te gusta?
7. ¿Cuál es el color que más te gusta?
8. ¿Dónde está el banco en el que tienes tu cuenta corriente? (¿Y tu cuenta de ahorros?)

3 The subjunctive to express doubt, disbelief, and denial
(Uso del subjuntivo para expresar duda, incredulidad y negación)

SUGGESTION: To help students remember these rules, refer to this grammar point as "the 3 D's."

A. Doubt

■ In Spanish, the subjunctive is always used in a subordinate clause when the verb of the main clause expresses doubt or uncertainty.

—Vamos al correo.	*"Let's go to the post office."*
—**Dudo** que **esté** abierto a esta hora.	*"I doubt that it's open at this time."*
—Estoy séguro de que abren a las ocho.	*"I'm sure that they open at eight."*

ATENCIÓN   When *no doubt* is expressed and the speaker is certain of the reality (**Estoy seguro[-a], No dudo**), the indicative is used: **Estoy seguro** de que **abren** a las ocho.

B. Disbelief

■ The verb **creer** is followed by the subjunctive in negative sentences, where it expresses disbelief.

—¿Uds. van a ir de compras hoy?	*"Are you going to go shopping today?"*
—No..., **no creo** que **tengamos** tiempo...	*"No..., I don't think we'll have time..."*
—Yo creo que pueden ir, si salen temprano.	*"I think you can go if you leave early."*

ATENCIÓN   **Creer** is followed by the indicative when it expresses belief or conviction: **Yo creo** que **pueden** ir.

C. Denial

■ When the main clause expresses denial of what is said in the subordinate clause, the subjunctive is used.

—¡Tú siempre llegas tarde!	*"You always arrive late!"*
—**No es verdad** que siempre **llegue** tarde. No niego que a veces llego un poco tarde, pero a veces soy puntual.	*"It's not true that I always arrive late. I don't deny that sometimes I arrive a little late, but sometimes I'm punctual."*

ATENCIÓN   When the main clause does *not* deny, but rather confirms what is said in the subordinate clause, the indicative is used: **No niego** que a veces **llego** un poco tarde.

práctica ....

A. Say whether the following statements are true or not. If a statement is false, correct it.

> MODELO: Nosotros celebramos la independencia de Chile.
> *No es verdad que nosotros celebremos la independencia de Chile; celebramos la independencia de los Estados Unidos.*

1. Texas es más grande que Maine.
2. Hace más calor en Alaska que en Arizona.
3. Buenos Aires es la capital de Chile.
4. México está al norte de los Estados Unidos.
5. El 25 de diciembre celebramos la independencia de nuestro país.
6. El presidente del país puede ser extranjero.
7. Necesitamos un documento de identidad para comprar estampillas.
8. Revelan rollos de película en el correo.
9. Echamos las cartas en el buzón.
10. Podemos comprar un giro postal en el correo.

SUGGESTION B: Have students do this exercise in pairs.

B. You and a friend are spending the weekend in a very small town. Your friend wants to know about things to do, places to go, and so on. Answer, expressing belief or disbelief, doubt or certainty.

1. ¿Tú crees que hay habitaciones libres en el hotel?
2. ¿Tú crees que un cuarto cuesta menos de cien dólares la noche?
3. ¿Tú crees que aceptan cheques de viajero en el hotel?
4. ¿Tú crees que hay un aeropuerto aquí?
5. ¿Podemos alquilar un coche?
6. Son las siete; ¿tú crees que el correo está abierto?
7. Vamos al centro. Quiero ir a una tienda elegante.
8. Tengo el pelo muy largo. Dicen que aquí hay peluquerías excelentes.
9. Quiero ir a cenar a un restaurante francés.
10. ¿Tú crees que vamos a volver aquí algún día?

C. Complete the following sentences logically, using the subjunctive or the indicative as appropriate.

1. Yo dudo que en mi cuenta de ahorros...
2. Estoy seguro(-a) de que el banco...
3. No creo que la oficina de correos...
4. Estoy seguro(-a) de que la estación del metro...
5. No es verdad que yo...
6. Yo no niego que mis padres...
7. Creo que los sellos...
8. No dudo que allí mismo...

¡A ver cuánto aprendió!

INTERNET

See the *¿Cómo se dice...?*
Web site for additional
grammar and vocabulary
practice: http://spanish.college.
hmco.com/students

¡Repase el vocabulario!

Complete the following sentences with words from the lesson vocabulary.

1. Tengo que bajar porque el departamento de señoras no está _arriba_; está _abajo_.
2. No estamos sentados; estamos _parados_
3. Hoy vamos a visitar el _parque_ del Retiro y el _palacio_ Real.
4. Dígame, ¿la _estación_ del metro está en la calle Alcalá?
5. Mis padres me van a mandar un _giro_ postal porque necesito dinero.
6. Recibí un _montón_ de tarjetas de Navidad el año pasado.
7. Le voy a decir al secretario que ponga las cartas certificadas en mi _casillero_
8. Mandé el paquete por vía _aérea_ y _certificado_
9. Está allí _mismo_, en la esquina. Va a _cruzar_ la calle.
10. Los colores del _semáforo_ son rojo, amarillo y verde.
11. Primero voy a estudiar y después voy a _encontrarme_ con Carlos en la tienda.
12. En _cada_ lugar que visitamos, compramos tarjetas.
13. La oficina está arriba. Dudo que ellos puedan _subir_ hasta el décimo piso.
14. Elsa le va a preguntar al cartero dónde queda la _oficina_ de correos.
15. Para ir al banco no debe seguir derecho. Debe _doblar_ a la izquierda.

ACTIVITY SUGGESTION: Do ¡**Escucha!**,
the in-class listening comprehension
activity that reviews vocabulary and
grammar structures introduced in the
lesson. It appears in the answer key of
the *IAM*.

ACTIVITY SUGGESTION: See the *IAM*
for an additional in-class activity:
Palabras escondidas.

Entrevista

With a partner, interview each other by asking the following questions.

1. ¿Sabes dónde queda la oficina de correos?
2. ¿Es verdad que abren el correo a las siete de la mañana?
3. ¿A cuántas cuadras de tu casa queda el correo?
4. ¿Qué queda frente a tu casa? ¿Al lado de tu casa?
5. ¿Cómo puedo ir de aquí a tu casa?
6. Para ir a la cafetería, ¿debo seguir derecho o doblar a la izquierda o a la derecha?
7. ¿Prefieres los edificios antiguos o modernos?
8. ¿Hay metro en la ciudad donde vives?
9. ¿Hay muchos extranjeros en la ciudad donde vives?
10. ¿Tienes pasaporte?
11. ¿Crees que los norteamericanos son puntuales?
12. ¿Es verdad que tú siempre llegas tarde a clase?

ACTIVITY SUGGESTION: See the *IAM*
for additional in-class activities:
Para conocernos mejor and
Una encuesta.

Situaciones

What would you say in the following situations? What might the other person say? Act out the scenes with a partner. Take turns playing each role.

1. You are in Madrid, and you want to know where the post office is located. You are a foreigner and you don't know your way around. Ask someone on the street for help.

2. A foreigner asks you for directions to a post office in your town. Explain to him or her how to get to the nearest one.

3. You are at the post office. You want to send some letters by airmail, buy some stamps, and find out how much it costs to send a registered letter to the United States. You also want to know if there is a package for you.

Para escribir

FOLLOW-UP: As a homework assignment, have students write a short letter describing a fictitious problem. Collect the letters and distribute them at random to the class. Then have each student write two or three solutions to the problem. Have selected students read aloud the letters with their respective solutions.

You are an advice columnist for a Spanish newspaper. How would you respond to the following letters? Use command forms to give your advice in writing.

1. Tengo 18 años y quiero vivir sola *(alone)* en un apartamento, pero mis padres no quieren que me vaya de la casa. ¿Qué me sugiere que haga?

Ansiosa de libertad

2. Pienso viajar a París este verano y tengo un amigo que quiere ir conmigo. Yo no quiero ofenderlo, pero no deseo ir con él porque es muy aburrido y siempre está cansado. ¿Qué puedo hacer?

Un viajero

3. Tengo un novio que es muy bueno, pero no es muy interesante. El sábado pasado fui a una fiesta y conocí a un hombre extraordinario y muy guapo que me invitó a salir. ¿Debo aceptar su invitación o no? ¿Qué me aconseja que haga?

Indecisa

4. Tenemos unos vecinos *(neighbors)* que tienen cinco hijos; los niños son terribles y lo rompen *(break)* todo. Planeamos dar una fiesta muy elegante para celebrar el fin de año y queremos invitarlos pero ellos siempre llevan a sus hijos a todas partes *(everywhere)*. ¿Cómo les pedimos que no traigan a sus hijos a la fiesta?

Entre la espada y la pared[1]

En la vida real

CD-ROM

Do the interactive exercises on the CD-ROM for additional practice.

¿Cómo voy...?

With a classmate, figure out how to give a new student the following directions:

Within the university

¿Cómo voy de la clase de español...
1. a la biblioteca?
2. al edificio de administración?
3. a la cafetería?
4. al baño?

Outside the university

¿Cómo voy de la universidad...
1. al restaurante McDonald's?
2. a la oficina de correos?
3. a la gasolinera *(gas station)*?
4. a tu casa o apartamento?

---

[1]*Between a rock and a hard place (lit., between the sword and the wall)*

Señales de tráfico   *(Traffic signs)*

You are traveling in Spain and see the following signs. What do they mean?

1. ALTO
2. UNA VÍA
3. PASO DE PEATONES
4. CEDA EL PASO
5. E

a. Yield
b. No parking
c. Stop
d. One way
e. Pedestrian crossing

Es que... Soy extranjero y no conozco las calles...

Nuestra casa es su casa

You and your roommate are going away for a couple of weeks and are letting friends from out of town stay in your apartment. With your roommate (a classmate), prepare a list of (1) recommendations of fun things to do in town, including instructions for how to get to them; (2) household chores or errands they should do in your absence.

Take this test. When you have finished, check your answers in the answer key provided for this section in Appendix E. Then use a red pen to correct any mistakes you may have made. Are you ready?

Lección 10

A. Hace... meaning *ago*

Answer the following questions, using the cues provided.

1. ¿Cuánto tiempo hace que conociste a tu mejor amigo(-a)?   (cuatro años)
2. ¿Cuánto tiempo hace que tú y tus amigos fueron a acampar?   (seis meses)
3. ¿Cuánto tiempo hace que tú y tu familia fueron a la playa?   (tres días)
4. ¿Cuánto tiempo hace que tus padres volvieron del campo?   (una semana)
5. ¿Cuánto tiempo hace que llegaste a tu casa?   (quince minutos)

B. The imperfect

Complete the following exchanges, using the imperfect of the verbs in the list.

costar (1)   vivir (3)   hospedarse (1)   ser (4)   ir (2)   ver (1)

1. —¿Qué hora _____ cuando tú llegaste a casa?
   — _____ las dos y media.
2. —¿Dónde _____ tú cuando _____ chico?
   —Yo _____ en Lima, pero todos los años mi familia y yo _____ de vacaciones a Buenos Aires.
   —¿Tú _____ a tus abuelos frecuentemente?
   —No, porque ellos _____ en Chile.
3. —¿En qué hotel _____ Julio cuando _____ a California?
   —En el Hilton.
   —¿Es verdad que _____ un ojo de la cara?
   —No, no _____ muy caro.

C. The preterit contrasted with the imperfect

Complete the following sentences, using the preterit or the imperfect of the verbs in parentheses.

1. Anoche Sergio me _____ (decir) que _____ (necesitar) una bolsa de dormir pero que tú _____ (poder) prestarle tu tienda de campaña.
2. Ayer Carlos y yo _____ (comprar) una caña de pescar. Cuando nosotros _____ (ser) niños, _____ (ir) de pesca con nuestros amigos.
3. Cuando yo _____ (tener) diez años, mi familia y yo _____ (venir) a los Estados Unidos a vivir. Nosotros _____ (hablar) inglés y español.
4. —¿Cómo te _____ (ir) anoche, en la fiesta de Margarita?
   —No muy bien. (Yo) _____ (tener) que irme a las diez porque me _____ (doler) mucho la cabeza.
5. Cuando Amalia _____ (ir) a la biblioteca, _____ (ver) un accidente en la calle Quinta. Dos personas _____ (morir).

D. Verbs that change meaning in the preterit

Answer the following questions, using the cues provided.

1. ¿Dónde conoció Beto a Marisa?   (en la universidad)
2. ¿Marisa conocía a la hermana de Beto?   (sí)
3. ¿Tú querías venir a clase hoy?   (no)
4. ¿Uds. sabían que hoy había examen?   (no)
5. David se quedó en su casa hoy. ¿No quiso venir?   (no)

E. Just words . . .

Match each question in column A with the best response in column B.

A	B
1. ¿Qué actividades al aire libre te gustan?	a. Tomo el sol.
2. ¿Fueron en coche?	b. No, alquilamos una cabaña.
3. ¿Se divirtieron en la fiesta?	c. Profundamente.
4. ¿Marcelo es chileno?	d. Sí, pero estaba equivocada.
5. ¿Acamparon?	e. No, pero Eva me convenció y fui.
6. ¿El Amazonas es un lago?	f. Sí, es de Santiago.
7. ¿Qué país está al oeste de Argentina?	g. ¡Espero que sí!
8. ¿Qué haces en la playa?	h. Me dio un abrazo.
9. ¿Tú dijiste que él planeaba trabajar toda la noche?	i. No, en bicicleta.
10. ¿Cómo dormiste?	j. Al tenis.
11. ¿Qué hizo Luis cuando te vio?	k. No, pero yo le voy a enseñar.
12. ¿Tú no querías ir a esquiar?	l. ¡No! ¡Es un río!
13. ¿El niño sabe nadar?	m. Montar a caballo y escalar montañas.
14. ¿Tus padres te van a prestar el dinero?	n. Chile.
15. ¿A qué juegan?	o. Sí, lo pasamos muy bien.

F. Culture

Answer the following questions based on the **¿Lo sabía Ud.?** section.

1. ¿Qué ciudades sudamericanas son centros turísticos internacionales?
2. ¿A dónde va mucha gente en junio, julio y agosto para esquiar?
3. ¿Cuáles son los meses de invierno en el hemisferio sur?

Lección 11

A. The subjunctive mood

Give the present subjunctive of the following verbs, according to each subject.

1. estar: nosotros
2. caminar: tú
3. sacar: yo
4. parecerse: ella
5. dar: ellos
6. saber: tú
7. recoger: nosotros
8. ser: ustedes
9. ir: usted
10. recibir: él

B. The subjunctive with verbs of volition

Complete the following exchanges, using the infinitive or the present subjunctive of the verbs in parentheses.

1. —¿Tú quieres _____ (depositar) el dinero en el banco?
   —Sí, mi esposa quiere que (yo) _____ (abrir) una cuenta de ahorros.
2. —¿Qué me aconsejas que _____ (hacer)?
   —Yo te sugiero que _____ (estar) aquí a las dos.
3. —¿Tienes que hacer diligencias?
   —Sí, mi madre quiere que _____ (ir) a la tintorería y al banco.
4. —Yo les recomiendo que _____ (pagar) a plazos.
   —No, nosotros queremos _____ (pagar) al contado.
5. —Yo te sugiero que _____ (traer) tu talonario de cheques.
   —Sí, y también necesito _____ (llenar) la tarjeta.

C. The subjunctive with verbs of emotion

Rewrite the following sentences, according to the new beginnings.

1. Ellos tienen los pantalones de Oscar.
   Me alegro de que ellos...
2. Julio estaciona el coche cerca del banco.
   Espero que Julio...
3. Tú sabes el saldo de mi cuenta corriente.
   Me sorprende que tú...
4. Ada está en la estación de policía.
   Temo que Ada...
5. Nosotros no podemos traer los comprobantes.
   Es una lástima que nosotros...
6. Ellos van al banco.
   Ojalá que ellos...

D. Just words . . .

Give the word or phrase that is equivalent to each of the following.

1. estacionar
2. moto
3. se usa para dormir
4. que no tiene hermanos
5. no levantarse temprano
6. lo que se hace con un rollo de película
7. en cuanto
8. de modo que
9. pantalones, vestidos, etc.
10. que no tiene dinero
11. escribir la fecha
12. que no cuesta nada

E. Culture

Read the following statements and circle V (Verdadero) or F (Falso), based on the ¿Lo sabía Ud.? section.

V F   1. Puerto Rico es una de las Antillas Menores.
V F   2. Las lenguas oficiales de Puerto Rico son el español y el inglés.
V F   3. La capital de Puerto Rico es San José.

V F   4. Los puertorriqueños también se llaman "boricuas".
V F   5. En Latinoamérica no existen sucursales de bancos extranjeros.
V F   6. El uso del cheque es mucho más común en América Latina que en
       los Estados Unidos.

Lección 12

A. The *Ud.* and *Uds.* commands

Complete the following sentences, using the Spanish equivalent of the words in
parentheses.

1. _____ en la oficina de correos a las ocho, señoras.   *(Be)*
2. Necesito el paquete. _____ esta tarde, señorita.   *(Bring it to me)*
3. _____ por la puerta principal, señoritas.   *(Go out)*
4. ¿Las estampillas? _____ esta tarde, señora.   *(Give them to him)*
5. _____ a la ventanilla número cuatro, señoras.   *(Go)*
6. _____ aquí, señor López.   *(Stay)*
7. Necesitamos el giro postal. _____ mañana, señorita Paz.   *(Send it to us)*
8. ¿Los libros? _____ allí mismo, señor.   *(Put them)*

B. The relative pronouns *que* and *quien*

Rewrite the following, using **que, quien,** or **quienes.**

1. Ésta es la señora. La señora vino ayer.
2. Éstos son los niños. Yo te hablé de los niños.
3. Ésa es la profesora. Nosotros compramos los libros para la profesora.

C. The subjunctive to express doubt, disbelief, and denial

Complete the following sentences, using the present subjunctive or the present
indicative of the verbs in parentheses.

1. Yo no creo que ella _____ (ser) española.
2. Dudo que el departamento de ropa para damas _____ (estar) en el
   segundo piso.
3. No es verdad que ustedes _____ (necesitar) documentos de identidad.
4. Creo que Quito _____ (estar) a cien kilómetros de aquí.
5. Estoy seguro de que ellos _____ (encontrarse) en el restaurante.
6. Es verdad que yo _____ (visitar) a mis tíos a veces.
7. No dudo que tú _____ (poder) mandar las cartas por vía aérea.
8. Yo no niego que Elena _____ (ser) la novia de mi hermano.

D. Just words . . .

Complete the following sentences using vocabulary learned in **Lección 12.**

1. Teresa vive al _____ de mi casa.
2. ¿Doblo o sigo _____?
3. Marina necesita dinero. Le voy a mandar un _____ postal.
4. ¿Vas a tomar el _____ para ir al centro?

5. La ventana está _____ . ¿Puedes cerrarla, por favor?
6. No puedes _____ la calle porque el _____ está en rojo.
7. Tenemos que _____ . El apartamento de Susana está arriba, en el segundo piso.
8. Está _____ en la esquina, leyendo.
9. ¿Es un edificio _____ o moderno?
10. El Palacio Real está a cinco _____ de aquí, _____ al parque.
11. Yo veía a mis abuelos _____ día.
12. Yo nunca llego tarde; soy muy _____ .
13. Compré un _____ de tarjetas postales.
14. Tengo que _____ una carta al correo. ¿Hay un _____ en la esquina de tu casa?
15. Escriba con _____ de molde.

E. Culture

Complete the following, based on the **¿Lo sabía Ud.?** section.

1. Madrid está situada en la parte _____ de la Península Ibérica.
2. Una de las calles principales de Madrid es la Gran _____ .
3. El Palacio de Comunicaciones está frente a la hermosa _____ de La Cibeles.
4. El Palacio Real fue la antigua residencia de los _____ de España.
5. El medio de transportación que usa la mayoría de los madrileños es el _____ .
6. En Segovia está el famoso _____ romano.

6. El caribe

Cuba

Rep. Dominicana

Puerto Rico

■ El Viejo San Juan, fundado en 1521, es uno de los barrios coloniales mejor conservados de las Américas. El barrio está casi totalmente rodeado de murallas de piedra *(stone walls)* construidas por los españoles.

■ Puerto Rico es una de las áreas más densamente pobladas del mundo. Con una extensión de unos nueve mil kilómetros cuadrados, tiene una población de cerca de *(around)* cuatro millones de habitantes.

■ La isla donde se encuentra la República Dominicana fue descubierta en 1492 durante el primer viaje de Colón al Nuevo Mundo. Colón le dio a la isla el nombre de La Española. La parte occidental *(western)* está ocupada por la República de Haití, donde se hablan francés y francés criollo *(creole)*.

■ La Habana, capital de Cuba, con más de dos millones de habitantes, es la ciudad más grande del Caribe. Antes de la revolución de Castro en 1958, era uno de los mayores centros de atracción turística del Caribe para los norteamericanos. Hoy el gobierno cubano trata de atraer a turistas de Europa y de Latinoamérica.

Puerto Rico tiene numerosas playas de arena *(sand)* blanca y fina como la Playa de las Croabas. Miles de turistas visitan estas playas todos los años, especialmente en el invierno.

¿A Ud. le gusta ir a la playa?

La sección antigua de La Habana, Cuba, se distingue por los numerosos edificios coloniales que aún conserva. "La Habana Vieja", como se conoce la parte antigua de la ciudad, fue declarada por la UNESCO *Monumento de la humanidad*, y se caracteriza por sus calles estrechas *(narrow)*, sus casas de tipo colonial y sus monumentos históricos. La Catedral de La Habana, que aparece en la foto, es uno de los edificios más característicos de la arquitectura colonial española.

¿Hay edificios de tipo colonial en la ciudad donde Ud. vive?

La fortaleza *(fortress)* del Morro está situada a la entrada de la bahía *(Bay)* de San Juan, en Puerto Rico. Los españoles la construyeron en el siglo XVI para defender la isla de los ataques de los piratas. Hoy el Morro es un monumento nacional y constituye una importante atracción turística.

¿Qué monumentos históricos se encuentran donde Ud. vive?

El béisbol es el deporte más popular en los países del Caribe. De sus equipos *(teams)* locales, como éste de Puerto Rico, han salido algunos de los mejores jugadores *(players)* de las Grandes Ligas de los Estados Unidos. El béisbol es también un deporte popular en Nicaragua, Panamá, Venezuela y México.

¿Puede Ud. nombrar algunos jugadores de béisbol hispanos de las Grandes Ligas?

La Catedral de Santa María la Menor en Santo Domingo, capital de la República Dominicana, fue la primera catedral fundada en América. Diego Colón, hijo de Cristóbal Colón, inició su construcción en 1514. La catedral se terminó de construir en 1540. Se dice que aquí están enterrados *(buried)* los restos de Cristóbal Colón.

¿En qué fecha se conmemora la llegada (arrival) *de Colón al Nuevo Mundo?*

La Universidad de La Habana, la más antigua de la isla de Cuba, fue establecida en 1728. La universidad tiene dos sedes *(campuses):* la antigua está en el centro de la ciudad, y la moderna se encuentra en las afueras *(outskirts)* de la ciudad.

¿Cuál es la universidad más antigua de su país?

El clima tropical del Caribe ofrece condiciones ideales para el cultivo de una gran variedad de frutas: el mango, la papaya, la banana y la guayaba, entre muchas otras. En la foto, un puesto de frutas en el Viejo San Juan muestra esta gran variedad.

¿Puede Ud. identificar las frutas que aparecen en la foto?

TELEINFORME

 VIDEO 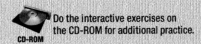 CD-ROM Do the interactive exercises on the CD-ROM for additional practice.

Preparación

NOTE: The video-related vocabulary is listed in the *Instructor's Activities Manual* for your reference. Its purpose is to facilitate students' comprehension.

NOTE: See the Instructor's Edition frontmatter for additional suggestions on implementing video in the classroom.

SUGGESTION: Have students read the *Panorama hispánico* segment of the textbook and do the *Preparación* activities in small groups before viewing the video segments.

¿Cuánto saben Uds. ya? After reading **Panorama hispánico 6**, get together in groups of three or four students and answer the following questions.

1. ¿Por qué van muchos turistas a Puerto Rico?
2. ¿Quiénes construyeron la fortaleza del Morro y para qué?
3. ¿Cuál es la ciudad más grande del Caribe?
4. ¿Cómo se llama la parte antigua de la ciudad de La Habana?
5. ¿Cuál es la universidad más antigua de Cuba y cuántas sedes *(campuses)* tiene?
6. ¿Qué nombre le dio Colón a la isla donde se encuentra la República Dominicana?
7. ¿Cuál es el deporte más popular en las islas del Caribe?
8. ¿Cuál fue la primera catedral fundada en América?

Comprensión

SUGGESTION: Ask students what they know about the history, politics, and economy of Cuba, the Dominican Republic, or Puerto Rico.

SUGGESTION: The *Comprensión* sections are organized by individual video clip to provide greater flexibility in lesson planning. Have students complete each exercise after viewing the corresponding video clip and have them compare their answers in pairs or groups.

SUGGESTION: Have students locate San Juan, La Habana, and Santo Domingo on the map on the inside back cover of the textbook.

A. San Juan, Puerto Rico. Complete the following statements with the appropriate words according to what you understood.

1. San Juan está en el _____ del país.
2. San Juan fue fundada por _____.
3. El Castillo de San Cristóbal y El Morro son dos _____ coloniales del Viejo San Juan.
4. Las _____ del Viejo San Juan son estrechas *(narrow)*.
5. Los turistas visitan las playas de Puerto Rico para jugar al _____, practicar _____ y descansar.

B. La Habana, Cuba. Select the word or phrase that best completes each statement, according to what you understood.

1. Cuba está situada en la entrada del (Mar Caribe, Golfo de México).
2. A Cuba la llaman "(el Oro, la Perla) de las Antillas".
3. Una (quinta, tercera) parte de la población cubana vive en La Habana.
4. La Catedral queda en (el Morro, La Habana Vieja).
5. Los (españoles, ingleses) construyeron fortalezas en La Habana.
6. (Muchos, Muy pocos) estudiantes toman clases en la Universidad de la Habana.

C. Santo Domingo, República Dominicana. Read the following statements. After watching the video, circle **V** (**Verdadero**) or **F** (**Falso**), according to what you understood. If a statement is false, correct it.

V F 1. La capital de la República Dominicana es Santo Domingo.
V F 2. Santo Domingo es la ciudad más antigua de las Américas.
V F 3. Diego, el hermano de Cristóbal Colón, vivió en el Alcázar de Colón.
V F 4. Cada doce de agosto celebran en Santo Domingo el Día de Colón.
V F 5. Santa María la Menor es una catedral muy antigua.

Ampliación

A. **Dos culturas.** With a partner, prepare some questions that you would like to ask a Cuban, a Puerto Rican, or a Dominican living in the U.S. about similarities and differences between life in this country and life in their homeland.

B. **Las islas del Caribe.** In small groups, discuss the similarities and differences you see between the three Caribbean islands featured in this video module. Share your observations with the class.

Se alquila un apartamento

13

OBJECTIVES

Pronunciation
Pronunciation in context

Structure
The familiar commands (**tú**) • **¿Qué?** and **¿cuál?** used with **ser** • The subjunctive to express indefiniteness and nonexistence

Communication
You will learn vocabulary related to renting an apartment, the various parts of a house, and home furnishings.

Se alquila un apartamento

STUDENT AUDIO

SUGGESTION: Refer students to **Panorama hispánico 4** and the corresponding video segments for information about Mexico.

SUGGESTION: Have students role-play the dialogue in pairs.

39

NOTE: Before they read the dialogue, have students read the cultural notes in **¿Lo sabía Ud.?** (page 322). Then ask them personalized questions based on rooms in an apartment, location, and furniture. Use Transparency 39 to introduce the new vocabulary.

1. **¿Vives en un barrio antiguo?**
2. **¿Tienes un apartamento amueblado?**
3. **¿Cuántos dormitorios hay en tu casa / apartamento?**
4. **¿Comes en el comedor o en la cocina?**
5. **¿Tienes una sala grande o pequeña?**
6. **¿Tienes muebles nuevos o viejos?**

David y su esposa Lucía son colombianos y están estudiando en la Universidad Nacional Autónoma de México. Viven en una pensión, pero quieren mudarse a un apartamento que esté más cerca de la universidad.

LUCÍA   —David, en el periódico anuncian un apartamento que está en un buen barrio[1] y tiene dos dormitorios.

DAVID   —¡A ver! Dame el periódico. *(Lee el anuncio.)*

Anuncios clasificados

Se alquila: apartamento amueblado: dos recámaras, sala, comedor, cocina y cuarto de baño. Calefacción central, aire acondicionado. Colonia 1. Para obtener más información, llame al teléfono 481-3520 de 1 a 5 de la tarde. Alquiler: $1.200.

LUCÍA   —Podemos llamar para verlo.

DAVID   —No sé… Es muy caro para nosotros, Lucía. Además, necesitamos un apartamento que tenga garaje…

Al día siguiente, en cuanto vuelven de la universidad, David y Lucía van a ver el apartamento.

LUCÍA   —¡Me encantan los muebles y las cortinas!

DAVID   —Con el sueldo que nosotros ganamos no vamos a poder pagar el alquiler.

LUCÍA   —Entonces, en vez de trabajar medio día podemos trabajar tiempo completo.

DAVID   —¡Estás loca! No hay nadie que pueda trabajar tiempo completo y al mismo tiempo estudiar en la universidad.

LUCÍA   —¡No seas tan pesimista, David!

DAVID   —No soy pesimista; soy realista. Además, vamos a necesitar dinero para comprar mantas, sábanas, fundas y utensilios de cocina.

---

[1]The word **colonia** is also used in Mexico.

LUCÍA —*(No le hace caso y va a la cocina.)* David, ven a la cocina. Mira, tiene refrigerador, microondas, lavaplatos, una cocina nueva... y un fregadero grande.

DAVID —No podemos tomar una decisión hasta ver otros apartamentos.

LUCÍA —Pero David, no vamos a encontrar ningún otro apartamento que sea tan bueno como éste.

DAVID —Tal vez no... pero no podemos pagar el alquiler de este apartamento.

LUCÍA —Oye, ¿y si ganamos la lotería?

DAVID —Hazme un favor, no digas tonterías. ¡Vámonos!

LUCÍA —*(Bromeando)* ¡Aguafiestas!

DAVID —Es que... tú te casaste con un hombre pobre, mi amor...

 # Vocabulario

Cognados

clasificado(-a) classified	**el favor** favor	**el refrigerador** refrigerator
colombiano(-a) Colombian	**el garaje** garage	**el utensilio** utensil
la decisión decision	**la lotería** lottery	

Nombres

el (la) aguafiestas spoilsport
el alquiler rent
el barrio neighborhood
la calefacción central[1] central heating
la cocina stove, kitchen
el comedor dining room
la cortina curtain
el dormitorio, la recámara bedroom
el fregadero kitchen sink

la funda pillowcase
el lavaplatos dishwasher
la manta, la frazada, la cobija blanket
el (horno de) microondas microwave (oven)
los muebles furniture
el periódico, el diario newspaper
la sábana sheet
la sala living room
el sueldo, el salario salary

Verbos

anunciar to announce
bromear to kid
casarse (con) to marry, to get married

ganar to earn, to win
mudarse to move (from one house or place to another)

Adjetivos

amueblado(-a) furnished   **mismo(-a)** same   **pobre** poor

---

[1]**poner (prender) la calefacción (el aire acondicionado)** to turn on the heat (the air conditioning)

Otras palabras y expresiones

además besides
al mismo tiempo at the same time
decir tonterías to talk nonsense
en vez de instead of

hacer caso to pay attention
medio día half a day, part time
se alquila for rent
tal vez maybe, perhaps
tiempo completo full time

tomar una decisión to make a decision
¡Vámonos! Let's go!

Vocabulario adicional
El salón de estar

SUGGESTION: Use Transparency 40 to present the vocabulary.

el jardín
el ventilador
el sillón, la butaca
el sofá

El dormitorio

la lámpara
la cómoda
la almohada
la sobrecama
la mesita de noche
el colchón

Aparatos electrodomésticos y batería de cocina   *(Home appliances and cookware)*

SUGGESTION: Use Transparency 41 to present the vocabulary.

ACTIVITY SUGGESTION: See the *IAM* for an additional in-class activity: **Muebles y aparatos electrodomésticos.**

la lavadora
la secadora
la plancha
la sartén
la cacerola
la tostadora
la cafetera
la licuadora

¡Conversemos!

Answer the following questions, basing your answers on the dialogue.

1. ¿David y Lucía estudian en su país?
2. ¿Por qué quieren mudarse?
3. Si ellos alquilan el apartamento que anuncian en el periódico, ¿van a tener que comprar muebles? ¿Por qué?
4. ¿Cómo describen el apartamento en el anuncio?
5. ¿Qué quiere Lucía que haga David?
6. ¿Cree usted que David y Lucía tienen automóvil? ¿Cómo lo sabe usted?
7. ¿Qué hacen al día siguiente en cuanto vuelven de la universidad?
8. ¿Le gustan a Lucía los muebles y las cortinas del apartamento?
9. ¿Por qué le dice David a Lucía que está loca?
10. ¿Qué tiene la cocina del apartamento?
11. ¿Qué le dice Lucía a David del apartamento?
12. ¿Por qué no quiere David alquilar el apartamento?
13. Cuando Lucía habla de ganar la lotería, ¿qué le dice David?
14. ¿Lucía se casó con un hombre que tiene mucho dinero?

¿Lo sabía Ud.?

En las grandes ciudades españolas y latinoamericanas, la mayoría de la gente vive en apartamentos, que en España se llaman "pisos." Los apartamentos se alquilan o se compran. Muchos edificios tienen oficinas o tiendas en la planta baja y apartamentos en los otros pisos.

La palabra "barrio" tiene una connotación negativa en muchos lugares de los Estados Unidos, pero en los países hispanos equivale simplemente al inglés *neighborhood*.

La Universidad Nacional Autónoma de México está situada en la parte sur de la Ciudad de México. Es la principal universidad del país, y es una de las más grandes del mundo. Unos 400.000 estudiantes asisten a la UNAM.

- En la ciudad donde usted vive, ¿la mayoría de la gente vive en casas o en apartamentos?

- ¿Le gusta a usted el barrio donde vive?

- ¿Puede usted nombrar algunas de las universidades más importantes del país?

INTERNET See the *¿Cómo se dice...?* Web site for activities on authentic cultural material: http://spanish.college.hmco.com/students

Mural del pintor mexicano David Alfaro Siqueiros en el edificio de la Administración de la Universidad de México.

Pronunciación

STUDENT AUDIO

In this lesson, there are some new words or phrases that may be challenging to pronounce. For further pronunciation practice of Spanish sounds, listen to your instructor and repeat the following words and phrases.

1. Quieren **mudarse** a un apartamento.
2. Se alquila apartamento **amueblado.**

NOTE: To reinforce pronunciation practice, this section appears in Lessons 10 through 18. The sentences featured as pronunciation models are taken from the lesson dialogues.

3. ¡Me encantan los **muebles** y las **cortinas**!
4. Tiene **refrigerador** y un **fregadero** grande.
5. **Hazme** un favor, no digas **tonterías**.

SUGGESTION: For each sentence, first model the word(s) in boldface type and have the class repeat them chorally and individually. Then have students repeat the full sentence for pronunciation practice of the target expressions in context.

1 The familiar commands (tú)   *(Las formas imperativas de tú)*

Unlike other commands in Spanish, the familiar affirmative command does not use the subjunctive.

SUGGESTION: Review the formal commands studied in **Lección 12**.

A. *Tú* commands[1]

■ The affirmative command form for **tú** has exactly the same form as the third-person singular form of the present indicative.

Verb	Present Indicative	Familiar Command (tú)[1]
hablar	él habla	**habla** (tú)
comer	él come	**come** (tú)
abrir	él abre	**abre** (tú)
cerrar	él cierra	**cierra** (tú)
volver	él vuelve	**vuelve** (tú)

—Teresa, **trae** las frazadas.
—**Espera** un momento. Estoy ocupada.

"Teresa, bring the blankets."
"Wait a moment. I'm busy."

—Me voy.
—**Vuelve** temprano y **cierra** la puerta.

"I'm leaving."
"Return early and close the door."

■ Spanish has eight irregular **tú** command forms.

decir	**di**	poner	**pon**	tener	**ten**
hacer	**haz**	salir	**sal**	venir	**ven**
ir	**ve**	ser	**sé**		

—Carlitos, **ven** aquí; **hazme** un favor. **Ve** a la casa de Rita y **dile** que la fiesta es hoy.

"Carlitos, come here. Do me a favor. Go to Rita's house and tell her the party is today."

—¿Dónde pongo el ventilador?
—**Ponlo** en la mesa.

"Where shall I put the fan?"
"Put it on the table."

SUGGESTION: Have students work in pairs and write five affirmative commands they think would be used while talking to a friend in each of the following places.

el correo   un restaurante
un hospital   un parque
una tintoreria   la playa

---

[1]The affirmative command form for **vosotros** is formed by changing the final **r** of the infinitive to **d**: hablar → **hablad**, comer → **comed**, vivir → **vivid**.

B. Negative forms

■ The negative **tú**[1] commands use the corresponding forms of the present subjunctive.

hablar   no **hables** tú
vender   no **vendas** tú
decir   no **digas** tú

—¿Voy con Julia?   *"Shall I go with Julia?"*
—No, no **vayas** con ella.   *"No, don't go with her."*

—¿Pongo las sábanas aquí?   *"Do I put the sheets here?"*
—No, no las **pongas** aquí.   *"No, don't put them here."*

ATENCIÓN   Object and reflexive pronouns are positioned with familiar commands just as they are with the formal commands.

Pon**lo** aquí.   *Put it here.*
No **lo** pongas allí.   *Don't put it there.*
Vénde**nosla**.   *Sell it to us.*
No **nos la** vendas.   *Don't sell it to us.*

práctica ....

A. Play the role of an older sibling giving instructions to a younger brother or sister, using the cues provided.

1. levantarse temprano
2. estudiar y no hablar por teléfono con sus amigos
3. hacer la tarea y no mirar televisión
4. escribirle una carta a la abuela
5. bañar al perro
6. ir al mercado *(market)* y comprar frutas
7. recoger la ropa de la tintorería
8. llamar por teléfono a Carlos y decirle que traiga los discos compactos
9. lavar el mantel y las servilletas pero no lavar las sábanas
10. limpiar su cuarto
11. poner la mesa
12. barrer la cocina pero no pasarle la aspiradora a la alfombra

EXPANSION B: After students have completed and corrected this activity, have them work in pairs asking each other for advice about similar situations. The cues should be changed to reflect the personal opinion of the individual student.

S1—No sé adónde ir esta tarde.
S2—Pues, ve al cine. Hay una nueva película de Tom Cruise.
S2—No sé con quién salir.
S1—Sal con tus amigos(-as). Te esperan en la cafetería.

B. Juana always has a hard time deciding what to do. Give her some suggestions, using the cues provided.

MODELO: No sé qué clase tomar.   (francés)
            Toma una clase de francés.

1. No sé adónde ir esta noche.   (cine)
2. No sé con quién salir.   (Mauricio)
3. No sé qué hacer mañana.   (ir de compras)

———————————

[1]The negative **vosotros** commands also use the present subjunctive: **no habléis.**

4. No sé qué comprar.   (un traje de baño)
5. No sé qué regalarle a papá.   (una cámara fotográfica)
6. No sé qué comprarle a mamá   (un vestido)
7. No sé qué hacer para comer.   (sopa y pollo)
8. No sé qué decirle a Jorge.   (que te lleve al baile)
9. No sé en qué banco poner mi dinero.   (en el Banco de América)
10. No sé qué hacer con mi pelo.   (cortártelo)

ACTIVITY SUGGESTION: See the *IAM* for an additional in-class activity: **¡Charadas!**

C. Say two commands, one affirmative and one negative, that the following people would be likely to give.

1. una madre a su hijo de quince años
2. un(-a) estudiante a su compañero(-a) de cuarto
3. una muchacha a su novio
4. una médica a una niña
5. un profesor a un estudiante

D. With a partner, play the role of roommates. Imagine that you are both telling a third roommate, who is very lazy, what to do and what not to do.

E. Lucía and David are moving into their new apartment and some friends are helping them. Based on the illustration, what does Lucía tell each person to do? Use familiar commands.

2 ¿Qué? and ¿cuál? used with ser   *(Qué y cuál usados con el verbo ser)*

■ *What* translates as **¿qué?** when it is used as the subject of the verb and it asks for a definition.

—**¿Qué** es una enchilada?   *"What is an enchilada?"*
—Es un plato mexicano.   *"It's a Mexican dish."*

■ *What* translates as **¿cuál?** when it is used as the subject of a verb and it asks for a choice. **Cuál** conveys the idea of selection from among several or many available objects, ideas, and so on.

—**¿Cuál** es su número de teléfono?   *"What is your phone number?"*
—792–4856.   *"792–4856."*

práctica ···

SUGGESTION: Have students work in pairs and ask each other to define the following terms using "¿Qué es...?"

una cómoda   un(-a) agua-
una butaca   fiestas
una cuenta   un giro postal
   corriente   una lavadora
un saco de   una trucha
   dormir

Have students share their definitions with the class.

A. Write the questions you would ask to get the following information. Use **qué** or **cuál**, as needed.

1. —_____
   —Mi apellido es Velázquez.
   —_____
   —Calle Rosales, número 420.
   —_____
   —835–2192.
2. —¿Quiere una sangría?
   —_____
   — Es una bebida que se hace con frutas y vino tinto. ¿Quiere comer una paella?
   —_____
   —Es un plato español que se prepara con arroz, pollo y mariscos.

B. With a partner, ask each other the following questions.

1. ¿Cuál es la fecha de tu cumpleaños?
2. ¿Cuál es tu color favorito?
3. ¿Cuál es la estación del año que más te gusta?

4. ¿Cuál es tu programa de televisión favorito?
5. ¿Cuál es el título de tu libro favorito?
6. ¿Cuál es la ciudad más grande de tu estado?

3   The subjunctive to express indefiniteness and nonexistence
(El subjuntivo para expresar lo indefinido y lo inexistente)

■ The subjunctive is always used when the subordinate clause refers to someone or something that is indefinite, unspecified, or nonexistent.

Necesitan **un apartamento** que **esté** cerca de la universidad.	*They need an apartment that is close to the university.*
En la oficina necesitan a **alguien** que **sepa** español.	*At the office they need someone who knows Spanish.*
Busco **un empleado** que **hable** inglés.	*I'm looking for an employee who speaks English.*
¡No hay **nadie** que **pueda** trabajar tiempo completo!	*There's nobody who can work full time!*

■ If the subordinate clause refers to existent, definite, or specific persons or things, the indicative is used instead of the subjunctive.

Viven en **un apartamento** que **está** cerca de la universidad.	*They live in an apartment that is near the university.*
En la oficina hay **alguien** que **sabe** español.	*At the office there is someone who knows Spanish.*
Busco **al empleado** que **habla** inglés.	*I'm looking for the employee who speaks English.*
Hay **alguien** que **puede** trabajar tiempo completo.	*There's someone who can work full time.*

práctica ●●

A. Indicate that there is nobody in your class to whom the circumstances below apply. Follow the model.

> MODELO: En mi clase...
> ...hay una chica que baila flamenco.
> *En mi clase no hay nadie que baile flamenco.*

En mi clase...

1. ...hay dos chicas que son de Paraguay.
2. ...hay un muchacho que conduce un Mercedes Benz.
3. ...hay un muchacho que habla francés.
4. ...hay tres estudiantes que tienen solamente quince años.
5. ...hay una chica que sabe tocar el violín.
6. ...hay dos muchachos que dan fiestas todos los sábados.
7. ...hay una chica que va a Europa todos los veranos.
8. ...hay dos muchachas que vienen a la universidad los domingos.
9. ...hay tres estudiantes que siempre están ocupados.
10. ...hay una chica que sale de su casa a las cinco de la mañana.

SUGGESTION: Write the following incomplete statements on the board. Have students complete the sentences in pairs, expressing what they need, are looking for, or want in the following situations or people.

1. Busco un apartamento que…
2. Necesito un(-a) amigo(-a) que…
3. Algún día voy a tener un coche que…
4. Quiero encontrar un restaurante que…
5. Parece que no hay nadie en la universidad que…
6. Deseo conocer a alguien que…
7. Quiero leer un libro que…

B. With a partner, play the roles of a newcomer to Mexico City and a helpful long-time resident who is able to offer solutions to all of the newcomer's needs. Follow the model.

> MODELO: una casa – tener piscina
> —*Quiero (Necesito, Busco) una casa que tenga piscina.*
> —*En mi barrio hay una casa que tiene piscina.*

1. una casa – tener tres dormitorios
2. una casa – estar cerca de la universidad
3. una casa – no costar un ojo de la cara
4. un coche – tener aire acondicionado
5. muebles – ser baratos
6. un empleo – pagar bien
7. alguien – ayudarme a mudarme
8. un restaurante – servir hamburguesas

EXPANSION C: In preparation, have students brainstorm and list on the board as many important factors as possible that should be considered before moving to another city or town. In pairs, students should ask each other questions based on the information on the board. At the end of the conversation, each student should tell his or her partner if he or she plans to move to another city and offer two or three reasons for the decision.

C. A friend of yours is planning to move to your city or town and wants some information about it. Answer his or her questions as completely as possible.

1. ¿Hay alguna casa en un buen barrio que sea barata?
2. ¿Hay alguna casa que tenga piscina?
3. ¿Hay algún apartamento que esté cerca del centro?
4. Yo necesito una secretaria. ¿Conoces a alguien que sepa hablar alemán y japonés?
5. A mí me gusta la comida argentina. ¿Hay algún restaurante que sirva comida argentina?
6. A mis padres les gusta la comida mexicana. ¿Hay algún restaurante que sirva comida mexicana?

D. Complete the following sentences logically, using the subjunctive or indicative as appropriate.

1. Necesitamos un apartamento que…
2. En mi barrio no hay ninguna casa que…
3. Alquilan un apartamento que…
4. Rosa tiene una criada (*maid*) que…
5. Busco a alguien que…
6. En esta clase no hay nadie que…
7. Mi novio(-a) necesita un empleo que…
8. ¿Hay alguien aquí que…?

E. The students want to know more about each other. The members of the class will take turns asking whether there is anybody there who speaks German, vacations in a foreign country, needs a new apartment, etc.

¡A ver cuánto aprendió!

INTERNET

¡Repase el vocabulario!

See the *¿Cómo se dice...?* Web site for additional grammar and vocabulary practice: http://spanish.college. hmco.com/students

EXPANSION: Have students work in pairs and interview each other using the same or similar questions. Encourage them to personalize each question and to respond by making minor changes where necessary.

S1—¿Es de Bogotá tu amigo?
S2—No, es mexicano.
S2—¿Dónde vas a poner el sofá?
S1—Voy a ponerlo al lado de la silla.

EXPANSION: To review vocabulary, ask students to name a room or an item on Transparency 39 while another student provides the item or room associated with it.

S1—dormitorio
S2—cama
S1—sofá
S2—sala

ACTIVITY SUGGESTION: Do ¡Escucha!, the in-class listening comprehension activity that reviews vocabulary and grammar structures introduced in the lesson. It appears in the answer key of the *IAM*.

ACTIVITY SUGGESTION: See the *IAM* for an additional in-class activity: **Palabras escondidas.**

Choose the best answer for each of the following questions.

1. ¿Es de Bogotá?
   a. Sí, es uruguayo.
   b. Sí, es chileno.
   c. Sí, es colombiano.

2. ¿Dónde vas a poner el sofá?
   a. En el comedor.
   b. En la sala.
   c. En la secadora.

3. ¿Por qué estás enojado con tu hermano?
   a. Porque no me hace caso.
   b. Porque es de estatura mediana.
   c. Porque tiene refrigerador.

4. ¿Para qué quieres la frazada?
   a. Para ponerla en la cacerola.
   b. Para ponerla en la cama.
   c. Para decir tonterías.

5. ¿Por qué no puedes alquilar ese apartamento?
   a. Porque no gano suficiente dinero.
   b. Porque se alquila.
   c. Porque tengo que pagar exceso de equipaje.

6. ¿Para dónde son las cortinas?
   a. Para aquella butaca.
   b. Para aquella ventana.
   c. Para aquel jardín.

7. ¿Por qué no te gusta Emilio?
   a. Porque es muy simpático.
   b. Porque trabaja tiempo completo.
   c. Porque es un aguafiestas.

8. ¿Qué vas a poner en la sala en vez del sofá?
   a. Un asiento de ventanilla.
   b. Una escalera.
   c. Una butaca.

9. ¿Es un apartamento amueblado?
   a. Sí, pero no tiene lavaplatos.
   b. Sí, pero no tiene tienda de campaña.
   c. Sí, pero no tiene barrio.

10. ¿Qué necesitas para el dormitorio?
    a. Una caña de pescar.
    b. Un rizador y un secador.
    c. Una cama y una mesita de noche.

11. ¿Qué aparatos electrodomésticos necesitas para la cocina?
    a. Una licuadora y una tostadora.
    b. Una lavadora y una secadora.
    c. Una butaca y una cómoda.

12. ¿Qué necesitas para freír *(fry)* el pollo?
    a. La cafetera.
    b. La sartén.
    c. La plancha.

Entrevista

ACTIVITY SUGGESTION: See the *IAM* for additional in-class activities: **Para conocernos mejor** and **Una encuesta.**

With a partner, interview each other using the following questions.

1. ¿Tu casa tiene calefacción central y aire acondicionado?
2. ¿Qué muebles tienes en tu dormitorio? ¿Y en tu sala?
3. ¿Te vas a mudar a otra ciudad?
4. ¿Prefieres alquilar un apartamento o comprar una casa? ¿Por qué?
5. ¿Prefieres una casa que tenga garaje para tres coches o una casa que tenga piscina?
6. ¿Trabajas tiempo completo o medio día?
7. ¿Dices tonterías a veces?
8. ¿Juegas a la lotería?
9. ¿Eres un(-a) aguafiestas a veces?
10. ¿Con quién te casaste? (Si eres soltero[-a], ¿con quién quieres casarte?)
11. ¿Cuál es el apellido de tu mejor amigo(-a)?
12. ¿Prefieres un amigo que sea muy inteligente o un amigo que tenga mucho dinero?

Situaciones

What would you say in the following situations? What might the other person say? Act out the scenes with a partner. Take turns playing each role.

1. You are talking to a real estate agent. You are looking for a house that is in a good neighborhood, with at least five bedrooms, air conditioning, and a three-car garage.
2. You are describing the house or apartment where you live to a friend.
3. You and your friend are going to share an apartment. Describe one you have just seen, telling him or her why you should take the apartment. Your friend doesn't think it's a good idea.

Para escribir

SUGGESTION: As a preliminary activity, have students describe their ideal homes in pairs. Provide a model by describing your own ideal house; where it would be located, what style it would be, who would live there, whether it would have a pool or a garden, etc. Point out items on Transparency 39.

Write a composition describing the house of your dreams *(sueños)*. Include the following information:

■ location

■ kind of neighborhood

■ what type of rooms you want

■ number of bedrooms and bathrooms

■ backyard (patio)

■ color scheme

■ furniture you would have in each room

■ conveniences

En la vida real

CD-ROM

Do the interactive exercises on the CD-ROM for additional practice.

Mi pareja ideal

Pair up with a classmate to write personal ads designed to help you find your ideal mate. Your description of the type of person you are looking for (use **Busco…** or **Quiero conocer a…**) should include physical characteristics, personality, age, economic status, and favorite activities. Don't forget to describe yourselves, as well.

Casas y apartamentos

SUGGESTION: Bring in actual ads from Spanish-language newspapers and have students compare and contrast what types of apartments are available, what is offered in each ad, and prices.

Imagine that you and several classmates own a real estate agency. Prepare ads for the following types of houses.

1. A very expensive house in a good neighborhood.
2. A small house in a student neighborhood.
3. Two different types of apartment for rent.

En busca de apartamento

Some friends of yours want to buy an apartment in or near Barcelona. Help them by using the information provided in the ads below to answer their questions.

VIVA EN EL CENTRO
DE BLANES
A 5 minutos de la playa

APARTAMENTOS

Con Plazas de Parking, 1 y 2 hab. Salón - Comedor – Cocina equipada – Baño completo - Acabados
ALTO STANDING. Información: FINCAS VERA.
*C. Muralla, n.° 3. BLANES. Tels.:(972) 33-53-74
y (972) 33-70-47*

Veranee todo el año en Barcelona. Vista panoramica, por encima capa polución ciudad, 135 m. sobre el nivel del mar
APARTAMENTOS
(JUNTO AL PARQUE GUINARDO)
Calle Dr. Cadevall, 1-3 Barcelona (entrada por Avda. V.de Montserrat y calle Fco. Alegre)
Gran calidad, estar-comedor, 2 ó 3 dorm., cocina, baño, calet. ind., terraza, antena colectiva, y parabólica, 70 a 90 m². A partir de ptas. 7.000.000
*Información: MANSUR, S.A. De 5.30 a 8.30 h. tarde
Tel. 257-53-45. Con financiación de Caja Postal*

CONJUNTO RESIDENCIAL DE TIANA

Con participación en Club Social, Piscina, tenis, squash, y zona ajardinada de recreo.

ALTING
Tel. 321 32 36

Vivir todo el año a 8 Km. de Barcelona.
4 dormitorios (1 suite) • cocina office • salon con chimenea • 3 baños • 1 aseo • 1 estudio
• 1 solarium y terraza • garaje 3 coches.
Acabados de calidad, 225 m² + jardin individual.

TORREDEMBARRA
Apartamentos 2 habitaciones, salón comedor, cocina, baño completo con instalación para lavadora. Situados en el centro del pueblo.
Avda. Catalunya 11.
Precio: 4.000.000 pesetas
Vd. puede ser propietario con 1 millón de pesetas más 3 milliones de hipoteca (a 15 años)
Vea apartamento de muestra y compruebe su calidad.

Información en la misma obra laborable de 10 a 14 h. y de 16.30 a 20 hs. Excepto lunes y martes

---

1. ¿Hay algún apartamento que esté cerca de la ciudad de Barcelona? ¿Cuál? ¿Cuántos dormitorios tiene? ¿Tiene piscina? ¿Cuál es el número de teléfono?
2. ¿Hay algún apartamento que quede cerca de la playa? ¿Cuál es la dirección? ¿Los apartamentos son grandes o pequeños? ¿Se puede estacionar allí?
3. ¿Hay algún apartamento que quede cerca de un parque? ¿Qué parque? ¿A qué hora se puede ver? ¿Cuánto cuesta el más barato?
4. ¿Hay algún apartamento donde se pueda poner una lavadora? ¿Cuánto tiempo hay para pagar la hipoteca *(mortgage)*? ¿Se puede ver cualquier *(any)* día de la semana? ¿Cuánto cuesta?

¡VAMOS A LEER!

Antes de leer

A. The title of this selection is "The major's calf." Taking into account that this **tradición** is about someone who constantly makes bets on everything, what do you think will happen? Is this selection going to be serious or humorous?

B. As you read the selection, find the answers to the following questions.

1. ¿A quién le escribe Juan Echerry?
2. ¿Quién es don Pedro Uriondo? ¿Cómo es?
3. ¿Qué manía tiene don Pedro Uriondo? ¿Siempre pierde las apuestas o siempre las gana?
4. ¿Qué le aconseja Juan Echerry a su amigo?
5. ¿Qué dice Domingo Echizarraga de don Pedro Uriondo?
6. ¿Cuándo sale de regreso para el Cuzco? ¿Qué lleva?
7. Según don Pedro Uriondo, ¿a qué se debía la cojera del comandante?
8. ¿Qué apuesta le hizo Uriondo a Echizarraga?
9. ¿Cuánto dinero le apostó?
10. ¿Quién ganó la apuesta? ¿Por qué?
11. ¿Cuál era la apuesta entre el capitán Uriondo y Juan Echerry?
12. ¿Cuánto dinero habían apostado?

La pantorrilla del comandante

RICARDO PALMA (PERÚ: 1833–1919)

Ricardo Palma nació en Lima y comenzó su carrera literaria escribiendo obras de teatro y poesía, pero su gloria como escritor se debe principalmente a sus "tradiciones". Este género, creado por Palma, no tiene equivalente exacto en la literatura europea.

Aunque *(Although)* es difícil definir las **tradiciones,** podemos decir que son relatos breves *(short stories)* escritos con humor e ironía, y en los cuales hay una mezcla *(blend)* de lo real y lo imaginario.

I

Fragmento de carta de Juan Echerry al segundo comandante del batallón Gerona.

Cuzco, 3 de diciembre de 1822

Mi querido amigo: Aprovecho para escribirte la oportunidad de ir el capitán don Pedro Uriondo con cartas del virrey para el general Valdés.

Uriondo es el español más simpático que madre andaluza[1] trajo al mundo, pero tiene la manía° de proponer apuestas° por todo y sobre todo, ¡y siempre las   bad habit / bets

---

[1]from Andalucía, a region in Southern Spain

gana! Hermano, te ruego que no le aceptes ninguna apuesta y que les adviertas° lo   warn
mismo a tus amigos. Uriondo se jacta° de que jamás pierde una apuesta, y dice la   se... brags
verdad. De modo que te aconsejo que abras los ojos y tengas mucho cuidado.

   Tu amigo,

Juan Echerry

II

Carta de Domingo Echizarraga a Juan Echerry.

Sama, 28 de diciembre de 1822

Mi inolvidable camarada: Te doy las gracias por haberme proporcionado la
amistad° del capitán Uriondo. El muchacho vale en oro lo que pesa° y ya es el   friendship / weighs
favorito de la oficialidad. Mañana sale de regreso para el Cuzco con cartas del
general para el virrey.

   En cuanto a sus laureles como ganador° de apuestas, digamos que van   winner
marchitos°. Dijo esta mañana que mi cojera° dependía, no del balazo° que me   withered / limp / shot
dieron, sino de un lunar° que, según él afirmaba, tenía yo en la pierna° izquierda.   mole / leg
Yo que conozco mi agujereado° cuerpo, y que sé que no tengo lunares, me empecé   full of holes
a reír. Uriondo apostó seis onzas a que me convencía de la existencia del lunar.
Aceptarle era robarle el dinero, y me negué°, pero él insistió tercamente en su   me... I refused
afirmación. Intervinieron varios oficiales, diciéndome todos:

   —¡Vamos, comandante, gánese ese dinero que le cae de las nubes!

   Me convencieron. Enseñé la pierna y todos vieron que en ella no había ningún
lunar. Uriondo se puso rojo y tuvo que confesar que estaba equivocado°. Insistió   wrong
en darme las seis onzas.

   Contra tu consejo tuve la debilidad de aceptarle una apuesta a tu amigo,
quedándome más que la ganancia de las seis onzas, la gloria de ser el primero en
vencer° al que tú considerabas invencible. ¡Que Dios te guarde de un balazo y a   defeat
mí... lo mismo!

Domingo Echizarraga

III

Carta de Juan Echerry al segundo comandante del Gerona.

Cuzco, 10 de enero de 1823

Compañero: ¡Me arruinaste!

   El capitán Uriondo había apostado° conmigo treinta onzas a que te hacía   había... had bet
enseñar la pantorrilla el día de los Inocentes.[1]

   Desde ayer hay, por culpa tuya, treinta onzas menos en el bolsillo° de tu   pocket
amigo, que te perdona° la desobediencia a su consejo.   forgives

Juan Echerry

---

[1]El día de los Inocentes se celebra el 28 de diciembre y es similar a *April Fool's Day*.

Díganos

Answer the following questions, based on your own thoughts and experiences.

1. ¿Hace usted apuestas a veces?
2. ¿Qué cosas le aconseja usted a su mejor amigo(-a)? ¿Su amigo(-a) sigue sus consejos?
3. ¿Cree usted que su mejor amigo(-a) vale en oro lo que pesa? ¿Por qué?
4. ¿Hace usted bromas *(practical jokes)* el primero de abril?
5. ¿Se pone usted rojo(-a) a veces? ¿Es usted una persona tímida?
6. ¿Perdona usted fácilmente o le es difícil perdonar?

 ASÍ SOMOS
VIDEO   CD-ROM

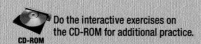 Do the interactive exercises on the CD-ROM for additional practice.

NARRADORA	—¿Cómo es su casa?
MARÍA	—Mi casa está en el centro de... del pueblo y posee dos pisos. En la parte superior *(upper level)* tiene dos habitaciones en las que dormimos mi hermano y yo, uno en cada una y una salita de estar *(small sitting room)*. En el primer piso se encuentra la cocina, el salón *(living room)* y la habitación de mis padres y un baño. Y bueno, arriba también otro baño. Y después está el bajo, que es donde está la bodega *(cellar)* y el garaje.

Preparación

NOTE: The video-related vocabulary is listed in the *Instructor's Activities Manual* for your reference. Its purpose is to facilitate students' comprehension. You may want to distribute the vocabulary to the class before viewing.

NOTE: See the Instructor's Edition frontmatter for additional suggestions on implementing video in the classroom.

SUGGESTION: Have students brainstorm a list of words and phrases to describe their homes and personalities.

A. **¿Dónde vive Ud.?** Answer the following questions about where you live. You will hear answers to some of these questions when you watch the video. After viewing the video, compare your answers with those you hear.

1. ¿Vive Ud. en una casa o en un apartamento?
2. ¿Dónde vive la mayoría *(majority)* de los estudiantes de la universidad?
3. ¿Cómo es su casa?
4. ¿Cómo es la casa de su familia?
5. ¿Cómo es la casa de sus sueños *(dream house)*?

B. **¿Cómo es su personalidad?** With a partner, answer the following questions about the different personalities of people you know. You will hear answers to some of these questions when you watch the video. After viewing the video, compare your answers with those you hear.

1. ¿Cómo es su personalidad?
2. ¿Cómo es la personalidad de su madre? ¿De su padre?

SUGGESTION: In groups, have students describe the buildings, homes, and furniture they see at the beginning of the video.

3. ¿Cómo es la personalidad de su mejor amigo(-a)?

4. ¿Cómo es la personalidad de su profesor(-a)?

Comprensión

SUGGESTION: Pause the video after each interview segment so students have time to complete the corresponding comprehension activity.

A. **¿Dónde viven?** As the people in the video describe where they live, circle **D** (**Departamento**) if they live in an apartment or **C** (**Casa**) if they live in a house, according to what you understand.

D   C   1. Alejandro

D   C   2. Leonardo

D   C   3. Otmara

D   C   4. Miriam

D   C   5. María

D   C   6. Jaime

D   C   7. Pedro

B. **¿Quién lo dijo?** Match each statement with the name of the person who said it.

A	B
_____ 1. Mi casa tiene seis habitaciones *(rooms)*, una mini-alberca *(swimming pool)* y una cochera *(garage)* para seis coches.	a. Alejandro
_____ 2. Tenemos sala-comedor pequeñita, cocinita, dos recámaras *(bedrooms)* y un baño y medio *(half bath)*.	b. Jaime c. María
_____ 3. Mi casa es un "chalet".	d. Pedro
_____ 4. Mi casa tiene cinco salas, tres comedores, una piscina y cinco garajes.	e. Yolanda f. Leonardo
_____ 5. Mi apartamento tiene dos pisos *(stories)* y un altillo *(attic)*.	
_____ 6. En el primer piso se encuentran la cocina, el salón *(living room)*, la habitación de mis padres y un baño.	

C. **Mi personalidad.** Answer the following questions, according to what you understood.

1. ¿Milka es optimista o pesimista? ¿Es idealista o realista?

2. ¿Leonardo ve lo negativo o lo positivo de la vida?

3. ¿Pedro es nervioso o muy tranquilo?

4. ¿Alejandro es una persona alegre o triste?

5. ¿Es Jaime un poco tímido o muy tímido?

6. ¿Otmara es optimista o pesimista?

7. ¿Cómo ve la vida Otmara?

EXPANSION: Show students some real estate advertisements from a Mexican newspaper after students view the *Entrevista* segment about the realtor from Guadalajara.

D. ¿Verdadero o falso? Read the following statements. Circle **V** (**Verdadero**) or **F** (**Falso**) according to what you understood from the video. If a statement is false, correct it.

V F   1. El señor Velasco Pérez es de México.

V F   2. El señor Velasco Pérez trabaja en bienes raíces *(real estate)*.

V F   3. En la oficina del señor Velasco Pérez administran propiedades *(manage properties)*.

V F   4. En la oficina hacen negocios *(do business)* sólo con mexicanos.

V F   5. La oficina está en la mejor área de Guadalajara.

V F   6. Las propiedades que venden allí son las más baratas *(the least expensive)* de la ciudad.

V F   7. Los apartamentos que venden allí son muy pequeños.

Ampliación

A. ¿Cómo es mi casa? Take turns interviewing a classmate about his or her present living situation. Then compare your living situations with each other. Use the following questions as a guide.

1. ¿Dónde vives?
2. ¿Cómo es tu casa o apartamento?
3. ¿Es grande o pequeño(-a)? ¿Cuántas habitaciones *(rooms)* hay? ¿Cuáles son?
4. ¿Cómo es tu habitación?
5. ¿Cuáles son los muebles que tienes en tu casa o en tu habitación?

SUGGESTION: Students can bring in magazine photos to illustrate their "dream house" descriptions.

B. La casa de mis sueños *(My dream house)*. With a partner, describe your dream house or apartment. Be sure to include information about the number of rooms, different types of rooms, and other important features.

Una cita

Lección
14

OBJECTIVES

Pronunciation
Pronunciation in context

Structure
The subjunctive or indicative after certain conjunctions • First-person plural commands • Constructions with **se**

Communication
You will learn vocabulary related to shopping for groceries and typical weekend activities.

Una cita

STUDENT
AUDIO

SUGGESTION: Have students role-play
the dialogue in pairs.

42&43

SUGGESTION: Use Transparencies 42
and 43 to introduce vocabulary items
related to food. To introduce additional
vocabulary, point to the transparency,
give the name of each item, and then
ask students, **¿Te gusta(n)...?** or
¿Comes... con frecuencia?

SUGGESTION: Refer students to
Panorama hispánico 1 and **9** and the
corresponding video segments for
more information about Hispanics in
the United States.

SUGGESTION: As a class activity, have
students list the errands and weekend
activities mentioned in the dialogue.
Remind them to use infinitive phrases.
When the list is complete, have students work in pairs to compare and
contrast the activities mentioned in the
dialogue with what they would buy
and do during a typical weekend.

*Oscar y Jorge, dos estudiantes cubanoamericanos que viven en Miami,
tienen una cita esta noche con dos amigas venezolanas: Elsa y Adela. Los
chicos van a preparar una cena para ellas en su apartamento. Ahora
Oscar está leyendo la guía de espectáculos para ver qué película ponen.*

CINE REX
Última semana
AMOR PROHIBIDO
con **Verónica Montiel** y **Ricardo Mirabal**

*¡Nominada como
la mejor película del año!*

**Primera función: 3 de la tarde
Última función: 9 de la noche**

OSCAR —¿Tienes ganas de ver una buena película?

JORGE —Sí, pero no vayamos a la primera función porque es muy
temprano.

OSCAR —Bueno, y cuando termine la película podemos ir a la cafetería
Versailles a tomar algo. Yo invito.

JORGE —Buena idea, pero no nos quedemos hasta muy tarde porque
mañana tenemos que trabajar.

OSCAR —No, hombre, mañana es feriado.

JORGE —Es verdad. Creo que el supermercado ya está abierto. Vamos
ahora para comprar las cosas que necesitamos para la cena.

OSCAR —Sí, el mercado se abre a las siete.

En el supermercado.

OSCAR —Necesitamos muchas cosas: mantequilla, leche, una docena de
huevos, pan, azúcar...

JORGE —¿No vamos a comprar carne?

OSCAR —Sí, compremos carne, pescado y pollo. También aceite, dos
latas de frijoles y seis de salsa de tomate.

JORGE —No, no compremos tanta salsa de tomate, a menos que quieras
comer comida italiana por el resto del mes.

OSCAR   —Tienes razón. A ver... necesitamos manzanas, uvas, naranjas, melón, toronjas y peras para la ensalada de frutas...

JORGE   —¿Dónde están las verduras? Tenemos que comprar lechuga, papas, zanahorias, cebollas y tomates.

OSCAR   —¡Caramba! Ahora que lo pienso esto va a costar una fortuna. Vamos a tener que ponernos a dieta.

JORGE   —De acuerdo. Pongámonos a dieta, con tal de que podamos comer perros calientes y hamburguesas de vez en cuando.

OSCAR   —Oye, apurémonos porque tenemos que limpiar el apartamento y preparar la cena antes de que vengan las chicas.

JORGE   —Sí, pero llamémoslas en cuanto lleguemos a casa para preguntarles si quieren ir el cine o si prefieren ir a bailar.

 # Vocabulario

Cognados

la dieta diet	**nominado(-a)** nominated	**el tomate** tomato
la docena dozen	**el resto** the rest	**venezolano(-a)** Venezuelan
el melón melon	**el supermercado** supermarket	

Nombres

el aceite oil	**el mercado** market
el azúcar sugar	**la naranja** orange
la cebolla onion	**el pan** bread
la cita date	**la papa** potato
la cosa thing	**la película** movie
el feriado, el día de fiesta holiday	**la pera** pear
la función show	**el perro caliente** hot dog
la guía de espectáculos movie guide	**la salsa** sauce
la lata, el bote *(Mex.)* can	**la toronja, el pomelo** grapefruit
la lechuga lettuce	**la verdura, el vegetal** vegetable
la mantequilla butter	**la zanahoria** carrot
la manzana apple	

Verbos

apurarse, darse prisa to hurry up   **preguntar** to ask (a question)

Adjetivos

prohibido(-a) prohibited
tanto(-a) so much
último(-a) last

Otras palabras y expresiones

a menos que   unless
ahora que lo pienso   now that I
   think about it
antes de que   before
¡caramba!   gee!
con tal (de) que   provided that

De acuerdo.   Okay.
de vez en cuando   from time to
   time
poner una película   to show a
   movie
ponerse a dieta   to go on a diet

tener ganas de   to feel like (doing
   something)
tomar algo[1]   to have something
   to drink
¡Yo invito!   My treat!

Vocabulario adicional
Cosas del supermercado

SUGGESTION: Use Transparency 44 to introduce the vocabulary.

ACTIVITY SUGGESTION: See the *IAM* for an additional in-class activity: **Palabras y más palabras.**

el apio

la piña

el vinagre

la sandía

el repollo

las fresas

el papel higiénico

el durazno, el melocotón

la margarina

---

[1]**comer algo** = to have something to eat

Las diversiones

el circo circus	Los niños querían ir al **circo** pero no tenían dinero.
la montaña rusa roller coaster	La **montaña rusa** de Disneylandia es la mejor de todas.
el parque de diversiones amusement park	Six Flags es mi **parque de diversiones** favorito.
el zoológico zoo	En ese **zoológico** hay muchos animales de África.

¡Conversemos!

SUGGESTION: Have students imagine that they are one of the characters in the dialogue and write a brief letter to a friend describing what happened during his or her date. They should use the dialogue and the discussion questions/responses as a guide. Select several students to read their letters aloud in class the next day as a review.

SUGGESTION: Bring in movie ads from Spanish newspapers and have students compare and contrast several movie titles in Spanish and in English. You may also have them compare Spanish and English names of popular television programs using T.V. schedules from the same newspapers.

Answer the following questions, basing your answers on the dialogue.

1. ¿Con quiénes tienen una cita Oscar y Jorge?
2. ¿Qué está leyendo Oscar? ¿Para qué?
3. ¿Qué película ponen hoy en el cine Rex?
4. ¿Qué dice el periódico de la película *Amor prohibido*?
5. ¿Qué le pregunta Oscar a Jorge?
6. ¿A dónde quiere ir Oscar cuando termine la película?
7. ¿A qué hora se abre el supermercado?
8. Según Oscar, ¿qué necesitan comprar?
9. ¿Cuántas latas de frijoles compran los muchachos?
10. ¿Qué frutas necesitan para la ensalada?
11. ¿Por qué dice Oscar que van a tener que ponerse a dieta?
12. ¿Por qué tienen que apurarse los muchachos?

Supermercado
ECONO-FACUNDO
Abierto todo los días de 7:30 am a 7:00 pm. Los viernes abrimos hasta las 9:00 pm y los domingos hasta las 5:00 pm.
Ext. Avenida Roosevelt Hato Rey, P.R. 00918 Tel. 756-7474

¿Lo sabía Ud.?

■ Aunque hoy en día hay un gran número de supermercados en los países hispanos, muchas personas prefieren comprar en los mercados al aire libre o en las tiendas pequeñas que generalmente se especializan en uno o dos productos. Por ejemplo, se vende **carne** en la **carnicería, frutas** en la **frutería, verduras** en la **verdulería** y **pan** en la **panadería.**

■ En España, Cuba, México y Argentina, entre otros países, la producción de películas tiene gran importancia. Algunos directores iberoamericanos famosos son Víctor Érice (España), Tomás Gutiérrez Alea (Cuba), Jaime Humberto Hermosillo (México) y Eduardo Mignogna (Argentina).

■ Las películas norteamericanas son muy populares en el mundo hispánico. Generalmente tienen subtítulos en español o están dobladas *(dubbed).* Muchos de los títulos en español son completamente diferentes a los del inglés. Por ejemplo, la película *Chicken Run* se llama **Evasión en la granja;** *Where the Heart Is* se llama **La fuerza del amor.**

• ¿Hay en su ciudad pequeñas tiendas que se especializan en dos o más productos?

• ¿Pasan películas extranjeras en los cines de su ciudad? ¿Están dobladas o tienen subtítulos?

• ¿Tiene gran importancia la producción de películas en su país?

INTERNET   See the *¿Cómo se dice...?* Web site for activities on authentic cultural material: http://spanish.college.hmco.com/students

Comprando frutas y vegetales en un mercado de aire libre.

Pronunciación

STUDENT AUDIO

In this lesson, there are some new words or phrases that may be challenging to pronounce. For further pronunciation practice of Spanish sounds, listen to your instructor and repeat the following words and phrases.

NOTE: To reinforce pronunciation practice, this section appears in Lessons 10 through 18. The sentences featured as pronunciation models are taken from the lesson dialogues.

1. Tienen una cita con dos amigas **venezolanas.**
2. Oscar está leyendo **la guía de espectáculos.**
3. **Apurémonos** porque tenemos que limpiar el apartamento.
4. **Llamémoslas** para preguntarles si quieren ir al cine.
5. Comamos **perros calientes y hamburguesas** de vez en cuando.

SUGGESTION: For each sentence, first model the word(s) in boldface type and have the class repeat them chorally and individually. Then have students repeat the full sentence for pronunciation practice of the target expressions in context.

Estructuras

1 The subjunctive or indicative after certain conjunctions
(El subjuntivo o el indicativo después de ciertas conjunciones)

SUGGESTION: Write the conjunctions on the board in the following way:

En caso de que
Sin que
Con tal que
A menos que
Para que
Antes de que

Tell students that when these expressions are used, "**nadie se ESCAPA del subjuntivo.**"

A. Conjunctions that are always followed by the subjunctive

■ Some conjunctions, by their very meaning, imply uncertainty or condition. They are, therefore, always followed by the subjunctive. Here are some of them.

en caso de que	*in case*	**a menos que**	*unless*
sin que	*without*	**para que**	*in order that*
con tal (de) que	*provided that*	**antes de que**	*before*

—Voy a ir al cine **con tal que** los chicos **vayan** conmigo.
"*I'm going to go to the movies provided the boys go with me.*"

—Llámelos **antes de que salgan.**
"*Call them before they leave.*"

—No me van a dar el préstamo **a menos que** ella **firme** la carta.
"*They're not going to give me the loan unless she signs the letter.*"

—Yo puedo firmarla **en caso de que** ella no **quiera** hacerlo.
"*I can sign it in case she doesn't want to do it.*"

—Te voy a dar dinero **para que vayas** al mercado.
"*I'm going to give you money so that you can go to the market.*"

—Voy a salir **sin que** los chicos me **vean,** porque siempre quieren ir conmigo.
"*I'm going to leave without the boys seeing me, because they always want to go with me.*"

B. Conjunctions that are followed by the subjunctive or indicative

■ The subjunctive follows certain conjunctions when the main clause refers to the future or is a command. Some of these conjunctions are:

cuando *when*	**tan pronto como, en**
hasta que *until*	**cuanto** *as soon as*

—¿Lo van a esperar?   *"Are you going to wait for him?"*
—Sí, **hasta que llegue.**   *"Yes, until he arrives."*
—**En cuanto llegue,** díganle que me   *"As soon as he arrives, tell him to*
llame.   *call me."*

■ If there is no indication of a future action, the conjunction of time is followed by the indicative.

—¿Siempre lo esperan?   *"Do you always wait for him?"*
—Sí, **hasta que llega.**   *"Yes, until he arrives."*

práctica ....

A. Complete the following dialogue between two friends who are expecting a houseguest, using **con tal que, sin que, en caso de que, a menos que, para que,** and **antes de que** and the verbs given. Then act it out with a partner adding two original lines.

—Tenemos que limpiar el apartamento _____ (llegar) él.
—Yo voy a preparar unos sándwiches _____ (tener) hambre.
—Sí, ¿y por qué no compras unos refrescos _____ (poder) tomar algo en cuanto llegue?
—Bueno, pero yo no puedo ir al supermercado _____ tú me _____ (dar) el dinero.
—Está bien. Yo te voy a dar el dinero _____ tú me lo _____ (devolver) mañana.
—Vale. Voy ahora mismo. Voy a salir _____ me _____ (ver) Paquito porque va a querer ir conmigo.
—_____
—_____

B. Compare what the people mentioned usually do to what they are going to do.

1. Todos los días yo llamo a mi amiga en cuanto llego a casa.
   Mañana,...
2. Generalmente esperamos al profesor hasta que llega.
   El próximo viernes,...
3. Todos los meses, tan pronto como recibimos el sueldo, lo depositamos en el banco.
   El mes próximo,...
4. Cuando Uds. van a verla, siempre le llevan un regalo.
   La semana próxima,...
5. Ud. se lo dice a ellos cuando los ve.
   Dígaselo a ellos...

C. Give the Spanish equivalent of the words in parentheses.

1. —Vamos a almorzar _____ . *(as soon as they arrive)*
   —Voy a preparar la ensalada _____ en seguida. *(so that we can eat)*
2. —Siempre le doy un beso a mi hijo _____ . *(when I see him)*
   —Yo no veo al mío muy frecuentemente.
3. —Tenemos que salir de la casa _____ . *(without the children seeing us)*
   —No podemos hacer eso _____ por la ventana. *(unless we leave)*
4. —Tengo que limpiar el apartamento _____ . *(before my friends arrive)*
   —¿Por qué no esperas _____ ? *(until I come back)*
   —Puedo esperarte _____ antes de las dos. *(provided that you be here)*

2   First-person plural commands   *(El imperativo de la primera persona del plural)*

■ The first-person plural of an affirmative command *(let's + verb)* may be expressed in two different ways:

■ by using the first-person plural of the present subjunctive

> **Compremos** carne y pescado.   *Let's buy meat and fish.*

■ by using the expression **vamos a** + *infinitive*

> **Vamos a comprar** carne y pescado.   *Let's buy meat and fish.*

■ The verb **ir** does not use the subjunctive for the first-person plural affirmative command.

> **Vamos** al cine.   *Let's go to the movies.*

■ For the negative command, the subjunctive is used.

> **No vayamos** al cine.   *Let's not go to the movies.*

■ In all direct affirmative commands, the object pronouns are attached to the verb. An accent must be used to maintain the original stress.

> Llamémos**lo**.   *Let's call him.*
> Escribámos**les**.   *Let's write to them.*

■ If the pronouns **nos** or **se** are attached to the verb, the final **-s** of the verb is dropped before adding the pronoun.

> Vámo**nos**.   *Let's leave.*
> Sentémo**nos** aquí.   *Let's sit here.*
> Vistámo**nos** ahora.   *Let's get dressed now.*
> Démo**selo** a los niños.   *Let's give it to the children.*
> Digámo**selo** a ella.   *Let's tell (it to) her.*

■ In direct negative commands, the object pronouns are placed in front of the verb.

> No **lo** hagamos.   *Let's not do it.*
> No **nos** vistamos ahora.   *Let's not get dressed now.*
> No **nos** vayamos todavía.   *Let's not leave yet.*

práctica ....

A. You and a classmate are going to a restaurant. Take turns asking each other what you should do and responding with first-person plural commands.

Antes de ir:

1. ¿A qué restaurante vamos?
2. ¿Hacemos reservaciones?
3. ¿Llevamos el coche o tomamos un taxi?

En el restaurante:

1. ¿Dónde nos sentamos?
2. ¿Qué pedimos para comer?
3. ¿Qué tomamos?
4. ¿Qué comemos de postre?
5. ¿Pedimos algo más?
6. ¿Cuánto le dejamos de propina al mozo?
7. ¿Adónde vamos ahora?
8. ¿Invitamos a alguien?

ACTIVITY SUGGESTION: See the *IAM* for an additional in-class activity: **Pongámonos de acuerdo.**

B. With a partner, play the roles of two friends who are planning a weekend together, but who can't agree on anything. One makes a suggestion and the other suggests something else, giving a reason for his or her refusal. Give at least eight suggestions.

MODELO: —Vamos a la playa.
—*No, no vayamos a la playa. No hace mucho sol. Vamos al campo.*

3 Constructions with **se**   *(Construcciones con se)*

SUGGESTION: Review vocabulary from the previous lessons by asking students where the following objects are found.

I—¿Dónde se compra champú?
S—Se compra en la farmacia.

1. **¿Dónde se compra un rollo de película?**
2. **¿Dónde se cambia un cheque?**
3. **¿Dónde se alquila un coche?**
4. **¿Dónde se venden pantalones?**
5. **¿Dónde se estudia español?**
6. **¿Dónde se comen mariscos?**
7. **¿Dónde se compran billetes de avión?**
8. **¿Dónde se toma el avión?**
9. **¿Dónde se toma sol?**
10. **¿Dónde se consigue un documento de identidad?**

■ In Spanish the pronoun **se** + *the third-person singular or plural form of the verb* is used as an impersonal construction. It is equivalent to the English passive voice, in which the person doing the action is not specified. It is also equivalent to English constructions that use the impersonal subjects *one, they, people,* and *you* (indefinite). The impersonal construction is widely used in Spanish.

Se habla español en Chile.   { *Spanish is spoken in Chile.*

    { *They speak Spanish in Chile.*

—¿A qué hora **se abren** los supermercados?   *"What time do the supermarkets open?"*
—**Se abren** a las nueve de la mañana.   *"They open at nine A.M."*

EXPANSION: Have students write brief advertisements, instructions, or directions for four or five places on campus. Encourage them to use commands wherever appropriate in their ads.

Joyería XYZ
Aquí se compran y se venden objetos de oro y de plata.
Vengan a visitarnos pronto.

You may want to bring in ads from magazines or newspapers and have students read and discuss the ads. You may also refer to the ads used in the text.

—**Se dice** que el tomate es una verdura.
—Sí, **se dice,** pero en realidad es una fruta.

"It's said that the tomato is a vegetable."
"Yes, it's said, but it's really a fruit."

■ The impersonal **se** is often used in ads, instructions, or directions.

FOR SALE

NO SMOKING

EXIT TO THE RIGHT

práctica ....

A. In groups of three, draw signs with the following information on them.

1. No parking
2. Exit to the left
3. Spanish spoken here
4. No littering (*to litter:* **tirar basura**)
5. No crossing
6. No swimming
7. Cars for sale

B. With a classmate, act out a scene between a tourist in Madrid and a resident of the city who responds to the tourist's questions about the city. Use constructions with **se** in your conversation.

El turista necesita saber…

1. …el horario *(schedule)* de los bancos, del correo y de las tiendas.
2. …qué idiomas habla la gente.
3. …qué y dónde comen.
4. …si venden objetos de oro y de plata.
5. …dónde alquilan coches.

¡A ver cuánto aprendió!

INTERNET

See the *¿Cómo se dice…?* Web site for additional grammar and vocabulary practice: http://spanish.college. hmco.com/students

42&43

EXPANSION: Write the following categories on the board: **Lácteos, Carnes, Pescados, Granos, Frutas, Vegetales.** Working in pairs or groups, students check the transparencies and list the items they see for each category.

ACTIVITY SUGGESTION: Do **¡Escucha!**, the in-class listening comprehension activity that reviews vocabulary and grammar structures introduced in the lesson. It appears in the answer key of the *IAM*.

ACTIVITY SUGGESTION: See the *IAM* for an additional in-class activity: **Palabras escondidas.**

45

SUGGESTION: Use Transparency 45 to introduce some of the stores listed below. As students write their grocery shopping list, tell them to include the quantity (**un kilo, 50 gramos, dos latas,** etc.) and the type of shop where each item can be purchased.

carnicería	*meats*
frutería y verdulería	*fruits and vegetables*
panadería	*bread, rolls*
lechería	*milk*
heladería	*ice cream*
pastelería	*pastry*
dulcería	*candy*

¡Repase el vocabulario!

Select the response that best answers each question.

1. ¿Vas a hacer una ensalada de frutas?
   a. Sí, necesito una lata de frijoles.
   b. Sí, necesito dos latas de salsa de tomate.
   c. Sí, necesito naranjas.

2. ¿Qué te gustó más en el parque de diversiones?
   a. El supermercado.
   b. La montaña rusa.
   c. El feriado.

3. ¿Qué película pasan hoy?
   a. Sí, las películas fueron nominadas.
   b. No sé, no tengo la guía de espectáculos.
   c. Pasan por el cine.

4. A ver… ¿qué verduras necesitamos?
   a. Agua y vinagre.
   b. Pescado y pollo.
   c. Lechuga, repollo y zanahorias.

5. ¿Vas a ponerle mantequilla al pan?
   a. No, azúcar.
   b. No, margarina.
   c. No, repollo.

6. ¿Adónde vas a llevar a los niños para que se diviertan?
   a. Al mercado.
   b. A la biblioteca.
   c. Al circo.

7. ¿No tienes una cita con Juan Carlos?
   a. Sí, pero no puedo ir porque él es famoso.
   b. Sí, pero no tengo ganas de ir.
   c. Sí, pero el supermercado no se abre hasta las diez.

8. ¿Qué vas a usar para hacer el jugo?
   a. Huevos.
   b. Toronjas.
   c. Aceite.

9. ¿Ves a tus amigos?
   a. Sí, tengo que apurarme.
   b. Sí, de vez en cuando.
   c. Sí, tengo que darme prisa.

10. Dicen que esa película es fantástica.
    a. Sí, fue nominada como la mejor.
    b. Sí, a mí tampoco me gustó.
    c. Sí, ganó la licencia para conducir.

11. Mi hermano quiere ver los elefantes.
    a. Llévalo al parque de diversiones.
    b. Llévalo al zoológico.
    c. Llévalo a la playa.

12. ¿Tienes ganas de tomar algo?
    a. Sí, pescado.
    b. Sí, carne.
    c. Sí, una copa de vino blanco.

Entrevista

ACTIVITY SUGGESTION: See the *IAM* for additional in-class activities: **Para conocernos mejor** and **Una encuesta.**

With a partner, take turns interviewing each other, using the following questions.

1. ¿Sabes a qué hora se abre y se cierra el mercado los domingos?
2. ¿Te preocupas cuando alguien viene a comer a tu casa? ¿Por qué o por qué no?
3. ¿Cuántas docenas de huevos compras para un mes?
4. ¿Qué frutas y qué verduras te gustan más? ¿Qué verdura no te gusta?
5. ¿Prefieres comer carne, pescado o pollo?
6. Los fines de semana, ¿prefieres ir al cine o a bailar?
7. Cuando vas al cine, ¿prefieres ir a la primera función o a la última?
8. ¿Te gusta ir a tomar algo cuando termina la función? ¿Adónde vas?
9. ¿Sabes qué películas están nominadas para el Óscar?
10. ¿Qué película tienes ganas de ver?
11. ¿Aceptas una cita con una persona a quien no conoces?
12. ¿Qué te gusta hacer cuando es feriado?

Situaciones

What would you say in the following situations? What would the other person say? Act out the scenes with a partner. Take turns playing each role.

1. Tell a group of friends you are going to meet them at the amusement park.
2. You and your roommate are having a party tonight, and he or she is about to go to the grocery store. Discuss the items you will need for a fruit salad.
3. Invite a friend to go see a movie with you this weekend and tell her or him it's your treat. Discuss possible movies and times, and make plans to do something afterwards.
4. Tell a friend what you are going to do as soon as you get home.

Para escribir

Write a dialogue in which you and a friend make plans for the weekend.

En la vida real

CD-ROM

Do the interactive exercises on the
CD-ROM for additional practice.

EXPANSION: Have students in pairs
write brief descriptions of several
programs that might appear in a T.V.
guide of a Spanish-speaking country.
They should include the channel, the
date and time, an introduction to the
story, and the actors.

**Miércoles, 24 de enero 20.00 h. Canal 1
Programa: Beverly Hills 90210
Título: "El problema de Donna".**

Discusión

With a classmate, discuss a movie or a T.V. show you have both seen and
summarize the plot. Say whether you liked it or not and why.

Here are some words and phrases you might want to use:

actor *actor*
actriz *actress*

Donna trabaja en una "boutique"
de ropa para señoras. Un día, una
amiga suya se lleva varios artículos
de la tienda sin pagarlos. Donna no
sabe qué hacer.

(la) película

- de acción
- de ciencia ficción
- cómica
- dramática
- de guerra *(war)*
- de horror
- de misterio
- policíaca

De la cocina a la mesa

ACTIVITY SUGGESTION: See the *IAM* for an additional in-class activity: **Tenemos huéspedes.**

You and a classmate are planning a dinner party. One of you has found a recipe (**receta**) for enchiladas, and the other, a recipe for flan. Read your recipe silently, and then tell your partner how to prepare the dish, without looking at the recipe. After your classmate does the same, read each other's recipes to see if your descriptions left out any of the steps. Here are some words you might want to use:

calentar (e:ie)   to heat up, warm up
cubrir   to cover
cucharada   spoonful
cucharadita   teaspoonful
derretir (e:i)   to melt

enfriar   to cool (down)
freír (e:í)   to fry
libra   pound
mojar   to dip
rallado(-a)   grated
revolver (o:ue)   to stir

ENCHILADAS
Ingredientes:
1 docena de tortillas de maíz
1 lata de salsa de enchilada
1/4 taza de aceite
1 libra de queso rallado
1 cebolla grande, rallada

Preparación:
Caliente la salsa en una sartén. En otra sartén caliente las tortillas en el aceite, sin freírlas. Sáquelas del aceite y mójelas en la salsa. Póngalas en un plato, y cúbralas con queso y cebolla. Enrolle las tortillas como tubos y cúbralas con el resto del queso. Póngalas en el horno a 325 grados por cinco minutos.

FLAN

Ingredientes:

Para el flan
2 tazas de leche evaporada
4 huevos
8 cucharadas de azúcar
1 cucharadita de vainilla

Para el caramelo
3 cucharadas de azúcar

Preparación: En el molde donde va a hacer el flan, ponga a derretir al fuego tres cucharadas de azúcar. Después de unos minutos el azúcar va a tener un color dorado. Mueva el molde para cubrirlo todo con el caramelo y déjelo enfriar.

Bata los huevos. Añada el azúcar, la leche y la vainilla y revuélvalo bien. Pongalo todo en el molde y cocínelo a Baño María[1] en el horno a 350 grados por una hora. (Para saber si ya está cocinado, introduzca un cuchillo en el flan y si sale limpio, ya está listo.)

Sáquelo del horno y déjelo enfriar. Póngalo en el refrigerador. Antes de servirlo, voltee el molde en un plato.

---

[1]Double boiler

7. América del sur (1)

Bolivia

Colombia

Ecuador

Perú

Venezuela

■ La cuenca *(basin)* del Amazonas, que ocupa partes de Perú, Ecuador, Colombia, Brasil y Venezuela, es la más grande del mundo. El río Amazonas tiene más de 1.000 tributarios.

■ Bolivia tiene dos capitales. Sucre es la capital histórica y sede *(seat)* del poder *(power)* judicial. La Paz es la capital administrativa y está situada a más de diez mil pies de altura. La ciudad se encuentra al pie del nevado *(snow-covered)* Illimani, que alcanza *(reaches)* una altura de más de veinte mil pies.

■ Las islas Galápagos, situadas en el océano Pacífico frente a las costas de Ecuador, se consideran una de las zonas ecológicas mejor conservadas. Las distintas especies de plantas y animales que allí se encuentran son exclusivas de las islas y no tienen similaridad con las especies del continente.

■ Caracas, la capital de Venezuela, es el lugar de nacimiento de Simón Bolívar, el Libertador de América. Bolívar luchó *(fought)* por la independencia de Colombia, Venezuela, Ecuador, Perú y Bolivia.

Este brazalete de oro, usado en ritos funerarios preincaicos, se encuentra en el Museo del Oro en Lima, Perú. En el museo existe una gran variedad de piezas precolombinas de oro y de plata con piedras preciosas. Esta colección es un ejemplo del talento artístico y de los conocimientos técnicos de las culturas indígenas que habitaban el continente antes de la llegada de Colón.

¿Cuáles son algunos museos famosos de su país? ¿Dónde están?

PANORAMA HISPÁNICO

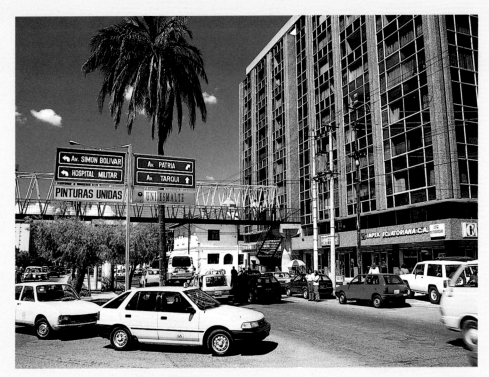

La Avenida Doce de Octubre es una de las principales de Quito, la capital de Ecuador. Esta ciudad, situada al pie del volcán Pichincha, goza de *(enjoys)* un clima primaveral todo el año por estar a una altura de 9.250 pies sobre el nivel del mar.

¿Dónde hay volcanes en su país?

En los llanos orientales *(eastern plains)* de Colombia, la ganadería *(livestock)* es la principal fuente de ingresos. Estos "llaneros" llevan una manada *(herd)* de caballos a los corrales de una hacienda en el departamento de Meta, situado al sureste de Colombia.

¿Qué región de su país es conocida por la importancia de la ganadería?

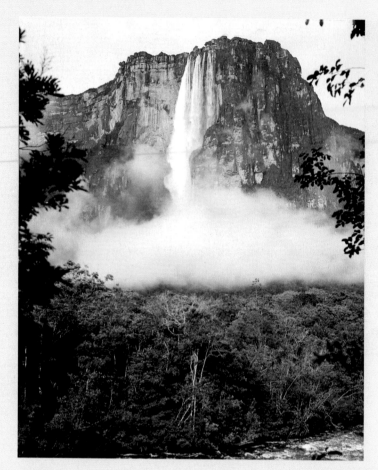

El Salto Ángel *(Angel Falls)*, localizado en el Parque Nacional de Canaima en Venezuela, es el más alto del mundo, con una altura de unos 3.200 pies. Las cataratas *(falls)* se llaman Ángel en honor al piloto norteamericano Jimmy Angel, que fue el primero en aterrizar *(land)* allí en 1937.

¿Qué cataratas de los Estados Unidos y Canadá son famosas en todo el mundo?

Entrada del metro en la estación de Sabana Grande en Caracas, Venezuela. Se comenzó a construir el metro de Caracas en los años 70.

¿Hay un metro en la ciudad donde Ud. vive?

Esta vista es de una de las típicas calles coloniales de Cartagena de Indias en la costa norte de Colombia. Durante la conquista y el período colonial, la parte antigua de la ciudad estaba completamente amurallada *(walled in)* para dar protección contra los ataques de piratas ingleses y franceses.

¿En qué ciudades de su país se ve la influencia de otras culturas?

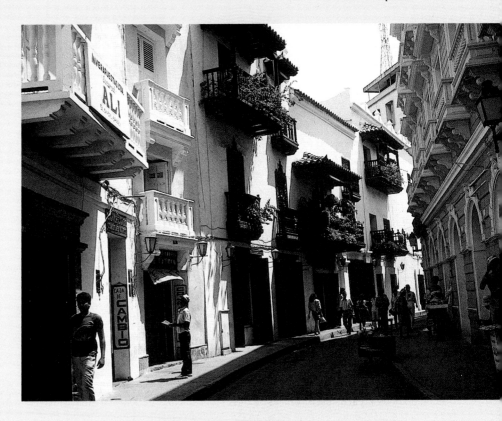

En el centro de Lima hay dos grandes plazas: la Plaza de Armas y la Plaza de San Martín. La Plaza de San Martín, que aparece en la foto, se llama así en honor a José de San Martín, considerado héroe nacional por haber liberado Perú, además de Argentina y Chile, del dominio español.

¿Cuáles son algunos lugares o monumentos norteamericanos nombrados en honor a héroes nacionales?

Las islas Galápagos deben su nombre a sus tortugas gigantes, llamadas galápagos, que pesan unos 280 kilos y viven unos 250 años. Las Galápagos se hicieron famosas por los estudios sobre la evolución de las especies que hizo en ellas el naturalista británico Charles Darwin. El gobierno ecuatoriano estableció el Parque Nacional de las Islas Galápagos en 1959.

¿Cuáles son algunos de los lugares de Norteamérica que tienen interés especial para los naturalistas?

Una manada de alpacas pace *(grazes)* en las montañas de Bolivia. La alpaca pertenece a la familia de las llamas, especie relacionada con los camellos, que habita la región de los Andes. La llama se usa principalmente como animal de transporte mientras que la lana *(wool)* de la alpaca se utiliza para hacer alfombras y diferentes artículos de ropa.

¿En qué países de Sudamérica se pueden encontrar llamas y alpacas?

TELEINFORME

VIDEO CD-ROM Do the interactive exercises on the CD-ROM for additional practice.

Preparación

NOTE: The video-related vocabulary is listed in the *Instructor's Activities Manual* for your reference. Its purpose is to facilitate students' comprehension.

NOTE: See the Instructor's Edition frontmatter for additional suggestions on implementing video in the classroom.

¿Cuánto saben Uds. ya? After reading **Panorama hispánico 7**, get together in groups of three or four students and answer the following questions.

1. ¿En qué países está la cuenca *(basin)* del río Amazonas?
2. ¿Cuál es la capital de Ecuador? ¿Y de Venezuela?
3. ¿Cuáles son las dos capitales de Bolivia?
4. ¿Cómo se llaman las cataratas *(waterfalls)* más altas del mundo?
5. ¿Quién fue José de San Martín?

Comprensión

SUGGESTION: Have students read the *Panorama hispánico* segment of the textbook and do the *Preparación* activities in small groups before viewing the video segments.

SUGGESTION: The *Comprensión* sections are organized by individual video clip to provide greater flexibility in lesson planning. Have students complete each exercise after viewing the corresponding video clip and have them compare their answers in pairs or groups.

SUGGESTION: Have students locate Bogotá, Colombia; Maracaibo, Venezuela; and Quito, Ecuador on the map on the inside back cover of the textbook.

A. Santa Fe de Bogotá, Colombia. Select the word or phrase that best completes each statement, according to what you understood.

1. El nombre completo (de la capital, del barrio histórico) de Colombia es Santa Fe de Bogotá.
2. En el barrio de la Candelaria hay muchas casas de estilo (moderno, colonial) con hermosos balcones.
3. La ciudad es una mezcla de lo antiguo y (lo tropical, lo moderno).
4. En el Museo del Oro hay (cientos, miles) de piezas de oro prehispánicas.
5. Desde *(from)* (el cerro, los rascacielos [*skyscrapers*]) de Monserrate se ve una bonita vista de Bogotá.

B. Ecoturismo en Venezuela. Read the following statements. After watching the video, circle **V** (**Verdadero**) or **F** (**Falso**), according to what you understood. If a statement is false, correct it.

V F   1. Hay variedad de regiones geográficas en Venezuela.
V F   2. Venezuela está a más de seis horas de Miami por avión.
V F   3. En los llanos *(plains)* de Maracaibo trabajan vaqueros *(cowboys)*.
V F   4. El ecoturismo no atrae a muchos turistas a Venezuela.
V F   5. El gobierno de Venezuela considera que la protección de la naturaleza es muy importante.

C. Ecuador. Select the word or phrase that best completes each statement, according to what you understood.

1. La geografía de Ecuador es muy _____.
2. Pichincha y Cayambe son dos _____ cerca de Quito.
3. El Panecillo está al pie del barrio _____ de Quito.
4. Quito fue fundada sobre las ruinas de una ciudad _____.
5. "La mitad del mundo" es un _____ que marca el lugar por donde pasa la línea que separa los hemisferios norte y sur.
6. La Plaza de los Ponchos es un famoso _____ donde los otavaleños venden su artesanía.

Ampliación

A. **¿Adónde vamos?** Divide the class into three groups: one group prefers to travel to Colombia, the second group prefers to travel to Venezuela, and the third group prefers to travel to Ecuador. Each group should list the reasons for their choice of travel destination. Share the results with the rest of the class.

B. **Dos culturas.** In pairs, discuss what you observed about ecotourism in Venezuela and what you know about ecotourism in your local area, state, or country. What are the benefits and attractions of ecotourism? Share your observations with the rest of the class.

De compras

OBJECTIVES

Pronunciation
Pronunciation in context

Structure
The past participle • The present perfect • The past perfect (pluperfect)

Communication
You will learn vocabulary related to clothing and shopping.

De compras

STUDENT
AUDIO

SUGGESTION: Before students read the dialogues, use Transparency 46 to review numbers and colors, introduce articles of clothing, and use verbs like **llevar, usar,** and **calzar.** Write seven to ten articles of clothing and approximate sizes on the transparency with a water-soluble marker. *(The young mother:* **vestido/42;** *the student:* **camisa/38, zapatos/41.)** Have the class describe what the people in the transparency are wearing.
     Then ask students to describe the clothing of several of their classmates.

SUGGESTION: Refer students to **Panorama hispánico 2** and **3** and the corresponding video segments for more information about Spain.

SUGGESTION: Have students role-play the dialogues in groups of four.

ANITA   —Esta mañana he abierto el armario y he llegado a la conclusión de que ni tú ni yo tenemos nada que ponernos. ¡Tenemos que ir de compras hoy mismo! ¡Mira este anuncio!

EL CORTE INGLÉS

Gran liquidación — viernes y sábado

Hemos rebajado toda la ropa. Aproveche estas grandes rebajas.
¡VERDADERAS GANGAS!

Blusas de seda
~~80€~~ 56€[1]

Chaquetas de cuero importadas
~~600€~~ 420€

Faldas de algodón
~~100€~~ 70€

Camisas de hilo
~~90€~~ 63€

Trajes de lana
~~1000€~~ 700€

Abierto
de 9.00 de la mañana a 9.00 de la noche

HUGO   —Gerardo me ha pedido que lo ayude... Además, yo tengo ropa...
ANITA   —¡Vieja y pasada de moda! Y ayer tú me dijiste que necesitabas cambiar las botas que habías comprado en El Corte Inglés porque son muy anchas... ¡Y tienes que comprarte zapatos!

Anita ha convencido a su esposo y ahora están en El Corte Inglés, una tienda por departamentos que está en el centro de Madrid. Hugo sube por

---

[1]Sign of the euro, the Spanish currency as of 2002.

la escalera mecánica hasta el primer piso, donde está el departamento de ropa para caballeros. Anita se queda en la planta baja, donde está el departamento de ropa para señoras. Allí se encuentra con su amiga Tere.[1]

ANITA	—¿Qué tal? Aprovechando las rebajas, ¿no? Dime Tere, ¿cuánto cuesta esa blusa de seda?
TERE	—Cincuenta y seis euros. ¿Qué talla usas?
ANITA	—Uso talla treinta y ocho.[2] Voy a probármela.
TERE	—Espera, ¿no te gusta esta falda? Combina muy bien con la blusa y es talla mediana. Pruébatela. El probador está a la izquierda.
ANITA	—*(Desde el probador)* Tere, hazme un favor. Tráeme una falda talla treinta y seis.
TERE	—Espera… Lo siento, no hay tallas más pequeñas. ¿Por qué no te pruebas este suéter?
ANITA	—No… no me gusta…

Anita compró la blusa, pero no compró la falda porque le quedaba grande y era demasiado cara. Después fue a la zapatería porque necesitaba comprar un par de sandalias rojas para combinar con un bolso rojo que Hugo le había regalado.

En el departamento de ropa para caballeros, Hugo compró dos camisetas y un chaleco. Ahora está en la zapatería.

HUGO	—Quiero cambiar estas botas.
DEPENDIENTE	—Muy bien, señor. ¿Qué número calza?
HUGO	—Calzo el cuarenta y cuatro.[3]
DEPENDIENTE	—En seguida vuelvo. *(Al rato)* Pruébese éstas.
HUGO	—Éstas son un poco estrechas. Me aprietan…
DEPENDIENTE	—*(Le prueba otro par.)* ¿Qué tal éstas?
HUGO	—Éstas me quedan bien. Me las llevo. ¿Puede envolvérmelas, por favor?

Hugo, Anita y Tere se encuentran a la salida.

ANITA	—Hugo, llévanos a comer. ¡Estamos muertas de hambre!
HUGO	—¡Yo también! Esperadme[4] aquí. Yo voy por el coche.
ANITA	—¿Has estado en el restaurante Villa Alegre alguna vez?
TERE	—Sí, es muy bueno. Vamos a ése.

Cuando Anita y Hugo llegan a su casa, ella ve las compras de su esposo.

ANITA	—¡Un chaleco y dos camisetas! ¿Esto es todo lo que has comprado? ¡Ay! ¿Qué voy a hacer yo contigo?
HUGO	—Bueno, puedes regalarme un traje para mi cumpleaños…

---

[1]nickname for Teresa
[2]equivalent to an American size 10
[3]equivalent to an American size 11
[4]Hugo is a Spaniard, so he uses the **vosotros** form here.

Vocabulario

Cognados

el centro   center
la conclusión   conclusion
importado(-a)   imported

el par   pair
la sandalia   sandal
el suéter   sweater

Nombres

el algodón   cotton
el armario, el ropero   wardrobe, closet
la blusa   blouse
la bota   boot
la camisa   shirt
la camiseta   T-shirt
el chaleco   vest
la chaqueta   jacket
la compra   purchase
el cuero   leather
el departamento de (ropa para) caballeros   men's department
el (la) dependiente(-a)   store clerk
la escalera mecánica   escalator
la falda   skirt

la ganga   bargain
el hilo, el lino   linen
la lana   wool
el número   size (of shoes)
la planta baja   ground floor
el probador   fitting room
la rebaja, la liquidación   sale
la seda   silk
la talla, la medida   size
la tienda por departamentos, el almacén   department store
el traje   suit
la zapatería   shoe department, shoe store
el zapato   shoe

Verbos

apretar (e:ie)   to be tight
aprovechar   to take advantage of
ayudar   to help, assist
calzar   to take (a certain size in shoes)

cambiar   to exchange, change
envolver (o:ue)   to wrap
llevarse   to take (buy)
rebajar   to mark down

RELATED VOCABULARY: Other vocabulary words you may want to introduce are: **el bikini; los calzoncillos** (men's undershorts); **el cinturón** (belt); **el gorro** (cap); **los vaqueros/los tejanos/bluejeans** (jeans); **el pijama** (pajamas); **seguir la moda** (follow fashion); **el sostén/sujetador** (bra); **el traje de ejercicio** (jogging suit); **las zapatillas** (slippers); **el centro comercial** (shopping mall).

Adjetivos

ancho(-a)   wide
estrecho(-a)   narrow
mediano(-a)   medium
verdadero(-a)   real

Otras palabras y expresiones

alguna vez   ever
de compras   shopping
En seguida vuelvo.   I'll be right back.
estar muerto(-a) de hambre   to be starving
¿Esto es todo lo que has comprado?   Is this all you've bought?
hacer juego, combinar   to match, go together

hoy mismo   this very day
me aprietan   they feel tight (on me)
no tener nada que ponerse   not to have anything to wear
pasado(-a) de moda   out of style
quedarle grande (chico) a uno   to be too big (small) on someone

Vocabulario adicional
Mirando vidrieras *(window shopping)*

SUGGESTION: Ask students how much each item costs.

I—¿Cuánto cuesta el camisón?
S1—Cuesta 50 euros.

ACTIVITY SUGGESTION: See the *IAM* for an additional in-class activity: **De compras.**

GRANDES REBAJAS
¡¡ TODOS LOS DEPARTAMENTOS !!

el vestido de noche
las pantimedias
la ropa interior
el camisón
el pañuelo
los calcetines
los guantes
la billetera, la cartera
la corbata

2
5 – 25
50
4
2.000
3.5
20
15
50 – 250

Diseños *(designs)*

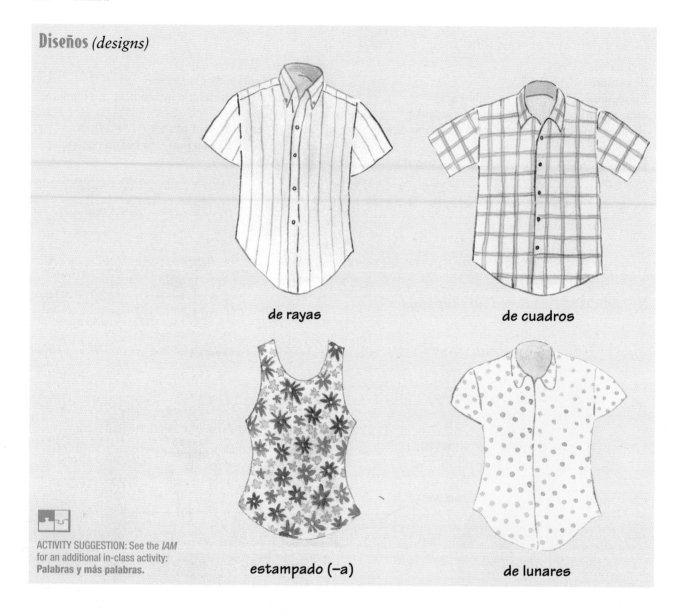

de rayas

de cuadros

estampado (–a)

de lunares

ACTIVITY SUGGESTION: See the *IAM* for an additional in-class activity: **Palabras y más palabras.**

¡Conversemos!

FOLLOW-UP: Have students imagine they are in **El Corte Inglés** and wish to try on several articles of clothing. In pairs, have them write six to eight lines of dialogue, mentioning the type of clothing, the size, and the price. Have several pairs act out their presentations the next day in class as a review.

Answer the following questions, basing your answers on the dialogues.

1. ¿Qué van a hacer Anita y Hugo hoy? ¿Por qué?
2. ¿Qué tienen el viernes y el sábado en El Corte Inglés?
3. ¿Cuántas horas va a estar abierta la tienda?
4. ¿Qué tipo de ropa para mujer aparece *(appears)* en el anuncio? ¿Y para hombre?
5. Según Anita, ¿cómo es la ropa de Hugo?
6. ¿A qué tienda van? ¿Dónde está?
7. ¿Dónde se queda Anita y con quién se encuentra allí?

8. ¿Qué se prueba Anita y dónde va para probársela?
9. ¿Por qué no compró Anita la falda?
10. ¿Qué compró Hugo y adónde fue después? ¿Qué hizo allí?
11. ¿Qué van a hacer Hugo, Anita y Tere después de encontrarse a la salida? ¿Por qué?
12. ¿Qué quiere Hugo que Anita le regale para su cumpleaños?

¿Lo sabía Ud.?

■ Lo que en los Estados Unidos es el primer piso es la planta baja en los países hispanos. Entonces el primer piso en España, por ejemplo, corresponde al segundo piso en los Estados Unidos.

■ En las ciudades hispanas hay excelentes tiendas donde se puede comprar ropa hecha *(ready-to-wear)*, pero muchas personas prefieren utilizar los servicios de un sastre *(tailor)* o de una modista *(dressmaker)*.

■ Aunque ahora hay muchos grandes almacenes, todavía existen en los países hispanos muchas tiendas pequeñas especializadas en un solo producto. Por ejemplo, se vende **perfume** en la **perfumería, joyas** *(jewelry)* en la **joyería** y **relojes** en la **relojería.**

■ Actualmente *(Nowadays)*, los dependientes de las tiendas a menudo tutean *(use the **tú** form of address)* a los clientes en España.

■ En España y en Latinoamérica, muchas personas tienen sobrenombres *(nicknames)*; por ejemplo: Teresa: **Tere;** Enrique: **Quique;** Roberto o Alberto: **Beto;** Francisco: **Paco;** María Teresa: **Marité;** Antonia: **Toña;** Dolores: **Lola;** José: **Pepe;** Luis: **Lucho;** Manuel: **Manolo.**

Una joyería elegante en la Ciudad de México.

• ¿Dónde prefiere comprar ropa la mayoría de los norteamericanos?

• En su país, ¿la mayoría de las tiendas especializadas están en centros comerciales *(malls)* o en edificios independientes?

• ¿Qué sobrenombres son comunes en su país?

INTERNET

See the *¿Cómo se dice...?* Web site for activities on authentic cultural material: http://spanish.college.hmco.com/students

Pronunciación

STUDENT AUDIO

NOTE: To reinforce pronunciation practice, this section appears in Lessons 10 through 18. The sentences featured as pronunciation models are taken from the lesson dialogues.

SUGGESTION: For each sentence, first model the word(s) in boldface type and have the class repeat them chorally and individually. Then have students repeat the full sentence for pronunciation practice of the target expressions in context.

In this lesson, there are some new words or phrases that may be challenging to pronounce. For further pronunciation practice of Spanish sounds, listen to your instructor and repeat the following words and phrases.

1. He llegado a **la conclusión** de que ni tú ni yo tenemos **nada que ponernos.**
2. Hugo sube por **la escalera mecánica** hasta el primer piso.
3. **Tráeme** una falda **talla** treinta y seis.
4. ¿Puede **envolvérmelas** por favor?
5. Puedes regalarme un **traje** para mi cumpleaños.

Estructuras

1 The past participle *(El participio pasado)*

A. Forms of the past participle

Past Participle Endings		
-ar *verbs*	**-er *verbs***	**-ir *verbs***
habl-**ado** *(spoken)*	com-**ido** *(eaten)*	decid-**ido** *(decided)*

■ The following verbs have irregular past participles.

abrir	**abierto**	*opened*
cubrir	**cubierto**	*covered*
decir	**dicho**	*said*
hacer	**hecho**	*done*
escribir	**escrito**	*written*
morir	**muerto**	*died*
poner	**puesto**	*put*
romper	**roto**	*broken*
ver	**visto**	*seen*
volver	**vuelto**	*returned* (somewhere)
devolver	**devuelto**	*returned* (something)
envolver	**envuelto**	*wrapped*

ATENCIÓN   Verbs ending in **-er** and **-ir** whose stem ends in a strong vowel require an accent mark on the **i** of the **-ido** ending.

creer	**creído**	*believed*
leer	**leído**	*read*
oír[1]	**oído**	*heard*
traer	**traído**	*brought*

práctica ....

SUGGESTION: Divide the class into groups of three. Write the verb infinitives on pieces of paper and put them in containers for each group in the class. Have each student in the group choose an infinitive and give the past participle of that verb. The other students in the group should listen and make corrections.

Supply the past participle of each of the following verbs.

1. tener	13. entrar
2. traer	14. salir
3. cerrar	15. hacer
4. decir	16. poner
5. aprovechar	17. abrir
6. apretar	18. escribir
7. cortar	19. ver
8. volver	20. aceptar
9. romper	21. devolver
10. cubrir	22. leer
11. cambiar	23. dar
12. sentir	24. sacar

SUGGESTION: Write the following dehydrated sentences on the board. Ask students to imagine that they have just entered a room in which a crime has been committed, and that they must give the police accurate information about the condition of the room and its objects.

ventana/abrir
S1—La ventana está abierta.

1. puertas / abrir
2. armarios / cerrar
3. luz / encender
4. lámpara / mesita de noche / romper
5. cama / hacer
6. almohadas / cubrir / plumas (feathers)
7. joyas / poner / cómoda
8. perro / morir
9. sobrecama / manchar (stain) / barro (mud)
10. gato / sentar / butaca

B. Past participles used as adjectives

■ In Spanish, most past participles may be used as adjectives. As such, they agree in number and gender with the nouns they modify.

La peluquería está **abierta** hoy.	*The beauty parlor is open today.*
El restaurante está **abierto** hoy.	*The restaurant is open today.*
Las peluquerías están **abiertas** hoy.	*The beauty parlors are open today.*
Le mandé dos cartas **escritas** en inglés.	*I sent him two letters written in English.*
No dejen los libros **abiertos**.	*Don't leave the books open.*

---

[1]Present tense: **oigo, oyes, oye, oímos, oís, oyen.**

práctica ··

SUGGESTION A: Have students do this activity in pairs. After completion of the exercise, each student should ask his or her partner three additional questions that require the use of the past participle.

A. You are very efficient. When a friend asks whether you did something, you say it is already done.

> MODELO: ¿Ya pusiste la mesa?
> *Sí, ya está puesta.*

1. ¿Ya cerraste la puerta?
2. ¿Ya abriste las ventanas?
3. ¿Ya hiciste la ensalada?
4. ¿Ya envolviste el regalo?
5. ¿Ya escribiste las cartas?
6. ¿Ya pagaste la cuenta?
7. ¿Ya cubriste los muebles?
8. ¿Ya lavaste la blusa?

B. Act out the following dialogues with a partner, providing the missing adjectives (past participle form) of the verbs listed.

abrir	servir
cerrar	traducir
escribir	usar
hacer	envolver
poner	

1. —¿Dónde fueron _____ las sandalias?
   —En México.
2. —Oye, ¿está _____ la puerta?
   —Sí, pero las ventanas están _____.
   —Pues ábrelas, porque hace mucho calor.
3. —¿Ya podemos comer?
   —Sí, la mesa ya está _____ y la comida está _____.
4. —¿Aquí se vende ropa _____?
   —Sí, este vestido de noche es _____.
5. —¿Esos libros están _____ en español?
   —Sí, pero también están _____ al inglés y al francés.
6. —¿Ya compraste los regalos?
   —Sí, y ya están _____.

2 The present perfect *(El pretérito perfecto)*

■ The present perfect tense is formed by using the present indicative of the auxiliary verb **haber** with the past participle of the verb that expresses the action or state. This tense is equivalent to the English present perfect *(have + past participle*, as in *I have spoken.*).

SUGGESTION: After presenting the present perfect tense, carry out several actions. Write your name on the board, open and close a window, and speak to a student, each time asking, **"¿Qué he hecho?"** Then have one or two students do things and ask them or the rest of the class what they have done.

I—¿Qué has hecho?
S1—He cerrado el libro.

SUGGESTION: Have students ask you whether you have ever done certain things (gone to Madrid, studied French, etc.).

Present indicative of haber

he	hemos
has	habéis
ha	han

Formation of the Present Perfect Tense

	hablar	tener	venir
yo	**he** hablado	**he** tenido	**he** venido
tú	**has** hablado	**has** tenido	**has** venido
Ud. / él / ella	**ha** hablado	**ha** tenido	**ha** venido
nosotros(-as)	**hemos** hablado	**hemos** tenido	**hemos** venido
vosotros(-as)	**habéis** hablado	**habéis** tenido	**habéis** venido
Uds. / ellos / ellas	**han** hablado	**han** tenido	**han** venido

SUGGESTION: Use the following activity to illustrate that past participles used as adjectives must agree in number and gender with the nouns they modify, but that when used as part of a perfect tense, they are invariable. Go around the room doing things, telling students what you have done. Then have them tell you what the result of each action is using the past participles as adjectives.

I(Open the window and say)
—He abierto la ventana.
S—Sí, la ventana está abierta.

—¿**Has pagado** más de cien dólares por una blusa alguna vez?
—No, nunca **he pagado** tanto dinero.

"Have you ever paid more than one hundred dollars for a blouse?"
"No, I've never paid that much money."

—¿**Has visto** a Teresa?
—No, no la **he visto.**

"Have you seen Teresa?"
"No, I haven't seen her."

■ Note that when the past participle is part of a perfect tense, it is invariable. The past participle only changes in form when it is used as an adjective.

Ella ha escrito la carta.
La carta está escrita.

She has written the letter.
The letter is written.

■ In the Spanish present perfect tense the auxiliary verb **haber** can never be separated from the past participle as it can in English.

Yo nunca **he estado** en Lima.

I have never been in Lima.

■ Remember that when reflexive or object pronouns are used with compound tenses, the pronouns are placed immediately before the auxiliary verb.

Le ha dado mucho dinero a su hijo.
María y José **se** han ido.

He has given a lot of money to his son.
María and José have left.

práctica ....

SUGGESTION: Have students close
their books and use Transparency 48
for this activity.

ACTIVITY SUGGESTION: See the *IAM*
for an additional in-class activity:
¿Qué has hecho...?

A. Look at the following illustrations and describe what these people have done
today, using the present perfect.

1. Tú

2. Tú y yo

3. Los chicos

4. Yo

5. Mi mamá

6. Uds.

B. With a partner, take turns asking each other what you have done lately.

>   MODELO: ir al cine / con quién
>   —¿Has ido al cine últimamente?
>   —Sí, he ido.
>   —¿Con quién?
>   —Con mi novio(-a).

1. comprar ropa / qué
2. ver alguna película / cuál
3. dar alguna fiesta / dónde
4. mandar algún mensaje electrónico / a quién
5. tomar algún examen / en qué clase
6. visitar algún lugar interesante / cuál
7. escribir alguna carta / a quién
8. poner dinero en el banco / en cuál
9. leer un libro / cuál
10. recibir algún regalo / de quién

C. With a partner, discuss five things that you or your family and friends have never done and five things you have done many times. Compare your own experiences with those of your partner.

>   MODELO: —*Yo nunca he estado en España.*
>   —*Yo tampoco he estado en España.*
>   *(Yo he estado en España dos veces.)*

3 The past perfect (pluperfect)   *(El pluscuamperfecto)*

■ The past perfect tense is formed by using the imperfect tense of the auxiliary verb **haber** with the past participle of the verb that expresses the action or state.

■ This tense is equivalent to the English past perfect *(had + past participle*, as in *I had spoken.).* Generally, the past perfect tense expresses an action that had taken place before another action in the past.

Imperfect of haber	
había	habíamos
habías	habíais
había	habían

Formation of the Past Perfect Tense			
	estudiar	**beber**	**ir**
yo	**había** estudiado	**había** bebido	**había** ido
tú	**habías** estudiado	**habías** bebido	**habías** ido
Ud.			
él	**había** estudiado	**había** bebido	**había** ido
ella			
nosotros(-as)	**habíamos** estudiado	**habíamos** bebido	**habíamos** ido
vosotros(-as)	**habíais** estudiado	**habíais** bebido	**habíais** ido
Uds.			
ellos	**habían** estudiado	**habían** bebido	**habían** ido
ellas			

—¿No hablaste con Teresa?   *"Didn't you speak with Teresa?"*
—No, cuando yo llegué, ella ya **se**   *"No, when I arrived, she had*
había ido.   *already left."*

práctica ....

A. One of your brothers is never around when there is work to be done. Say what had already been done by the time he got home last night.

> MODELO: nosotros / lavar los platos
> *Cuando él llegó, nosotros ya habíamos lavado los platos.*

1. yo / barrer la cocina
2. los chicos / pasarle la aspiradora a la alfombra
3. Roberto y yo / hacer la comida
4. Elsa / planchar la ropa
5. tú / limpiar el refrigerador
6. Carmen y Elena / bañar al perro
7. Anita / poner la mesa
8. Raúl y Carlos / comprar las bebidas
9. Mirta / lavar las sábanas
10. Raúl y yo / envolver los regalos

B. Interview a classmate, using the following questions. When you have finished, switch roles.

1. Cuando llegaste a tu casa anoche, ¿las otras personas ya habían cenado?
2. A las once de la noche, ¿ya te habías acostado?
3. Cuando te levantaste esta mañana, ¿alguien te había preparado el desayuno?
4. Cuando yo llegué a clase, ¿ya habías llegado tú?
5. Cuando llegaste a clase hoy, ¿ya habías hecho todos los ejercicios de esta lección?
6. ¿Ya habías tomado español antes de tomar esta clase?

C. Complete the following sentences logically, using the pluperfect tense.

1. Antes de venir a esta universidad, yo nunca…
2. Antes de tomar esta clase, mis compañeros y yo nunca…
3. Hasta el año pasado, mis amigos y yo siempre…
4. Hasta el semestre pasado, los estudiantes de esta clase nunca…
5. Hasta que yo cumplí dieciséis años, yo nunca…
6. Hasta el verano pasado, mi familia y yo siempre…

 ¡A ver cuánto aprendió!

INTERNET

See the *¿Cómo se dice…?* Web site for additional grammar and vocabulary practice: http://spanish.college. hmco.com/students

¡Repase el vocabulario!

Choose the correct word or phrase to complete each statement.

1. Puede probarse (la ganga, el chaleco, el armario) en el probador.
2. Mi bolso (hace juego, está muerto de hambre, va de compras) con mis sandalias.
3. Yo calzo el número siete y estos zapatos son número diez. (Me aprietan mucho. Me quedan grandes. Me quedan bien.)
4. Necesito un par de (calcetines, tallas, escaleras mecánicas).
5. Pagué solamente treinta dólares por el vestido de lino. Hoy hubo una gran (bota, liquidación, billetera) en la tienda París.
6. Estos pantalones me quedan un poco chicos, pero no los he devuelto todavía porque (me gustan mucho, son muy estrechos, no me quedan bien).
7. Hace frío. Ponte (la chaqueta, las sandalias, el pañuelo) de lana.
8. Mi ropa es vieja y está pasada de (cuero, compra, moda).
9. ¿Qué medida (usa, vuela, camina) Ud.?
10. El traje tiene que hacer juego con (la corbata, la ropa interior, el camisón).
11. Puse el dinero en (la billetera, la lana, el algodón).
12. No hay ropa en mi ropero. No tengo nada que (ponerme, bañarme, afeitarme).
13. ¿Usa Ud. talla grande, chica o (abierta, ancha, mediana)?
14. Pues yo me quedo en la (seda, taza, planta baja).
15. Compré una falda estampada y una falda (de lunares, muy sabrosa, enfadada).

SUGGESTION: Use Transparency 49 to review articles of clothing. Have students describe the articles of clothing they see, how much each item costs, and what the people are doing or going to do.

ACTIVITY SUGGESTION: Do ¡Escucha!, the in-class listening comprehension activity that reviews vocabulary and grammar structures introduced in the lesson. It appears in the answer key of the *IAM*.

ACTIVITY SUGGESTION: See the *IAM* for an additional in-class activity: **Palabras escondidas.**

Entrevista

ACTIVITY SUGGESTION: See the *IAM* for additional in-class activities: **Para conocernos mejor** and **Una encuesta.**

With a partner, interview each other by asking the following questions.

1. ¿Prefieres camisas (blusas) de rayas o de cuadros?
2. ¿Qué talla de camisa (blusa) usas?
3. ¿Qué número calzas?
4. ¿Te aprietan los zapatos que llevas puestos?
5. Cuando compras un par de zapatos, ¿te los llevas puestos?
6. ¿Dónde has comprado esa falda (chaqueta, camisa)?
7. ¿Tu camisa (blusa) y tus pantalones siempre hacen juego?
8. ¿Cuál es la tienda que más te gusta? ¿Por qué te gusta?
9. ¿Prefieres comprar cuando hay una liquidación? ¿Por qué?
10. ¿Qué ropa prefieres?
11. ¿Tienes mucha ropa o no tienes nada que ponerte?
12. ¿Prefieres usar la escalera o la escalera mecánica?

Situaciones

EXPANSION: In pairs, have students role-play a clerk and a customer who is trying to purchase an article of clothing for a relative who is very difficult to please. The student role-playing the customer should make up a shopping list with four different articles of clothing, colors, and sizes. The clerk should ask questions about the likes and dislikes of the relative and make alternative suggestions. Have several pairs act out their presentations in class the next day.

What would you say in the following situations? What would the other person say? Act out the scenes with a partner. Take turns playing each role.

1. You are shopping in a large department store. You need a pair of gloves, a white shirt, and a blue tie. You also saw a brown suit in the window that you liked, and you want to know how much it costs.
2. You are a clerk. A customer is admiring a pink blouse. Ask her what size she wears, and tell her the fitting room is on the left.
3. A clerk at a shoe store wants to sell you a pair of boots. The ones he is showing you are too expensive and too tight on you.
4. Tell your friend that you haven't eaten yet, that you are starving, and that you want to have something to eat.

Para escribir

S1—¿En qué puedo servirle, señorita?
S2—Quiero comprar una blusa roja para mi prima.
S1—¿Qué talla usa?
S2—Usa talla treinta y ocho.
S1—¿Prefiere una blusa de seda o de algodón?

Write a dialogue between yourself and a clerk at a department store. You should mention what size you wear, what colors you like, and whether or not something fits you. Describe different things you want to buy.

En la vida real

CD-ROM

Do the interactive exercises on the CD-ROM for additional practice.

Haciendo las maletas

You and a classmate are going on vacation. You are going to Hawaii in August and she or he is going to Colorado in December. Help each other select the type of clothes you will need for the trip, according to the different activities you are planning.

ACTIVITY SUGGESTION: See the *IAM* for an additional in-class activity: **¿Cómo te vistes?**

Here are some other words and phrases you may want to use in addition to the lesson vocabulary:

los bluejeans, los vaqueros   *jeans*   **de rayón**   *made of rayon*
la bufanda   *scarf*   **los pantalones cortos**   *shorts*

¡De compras!

Help a friend of yours who is shopping at El Corte Inglés in Madrid. Answer her questions, using the information provided in the ad.

Ahora en El Corte Inglés, Rebajas sobre Rebajas. Todo cuesta mucho menos.

SEÑORAS
• Vestidos lisos y estampados, en poliéster-algodón   **95€**
• Pareos estampados, en distintos dibujos y colores   **15€**

CABALLEROS
• Pantalones de sport y de vestir, lisos y fantasía, en poliéster-lana y poliéster-algodón   **59€**
• Mocasines en piel de búfalo, con piso de suela   **150€**

JÓVENES
• Para ellas, bañadores y bikinis, lisos y fantasía   **85€**
• Para ellos, bañadores, lisos y estampados   **45€**

NIÑOS
• Camisetas para niños y niñas, lisas y estampadas   **10€**
• Playeros en distintos colores, todas las tallas   **12€**

MENAJE
• Batería de cocina ocho piezas, en acero vitrificado, tres colores   **150€**

TEXTILES
• Mantelería de seis servicios estampada, acabada en festón   **35€**

MUEBLES
• Sillón cromado, con asiento y respaldo en piel   **25€**

LAS REBAJAS DE EL CORTE INGLÉS

1. ¿En qué mes son las rebajas?
2. Tengo una hija de nueve años. ¿Qué puedo comprarle?
3. Mi esposo necesita zapatos. ¿Qué tipo de zapatos venden y cuánto cuestan?
4. No tengo nada que ponerme. ¿Qué puedo comprar para mí?
5. Pensamos ir a la playa. ¿Qué puedo comprar para mí y para mis hijos?
6. Es el cumpleaños de mi padre. ¿Qué puedo regalarle? ¿Cuánto me va a costar?
7. ¿Para cuántas personas son los manteles?
8. ¿Cuánto cuesta el sillón?

La última moda

SUGGESTION: Have several students give up to four clues that describe the articles of clothing of someone in the class, and have the other members try to guess the identity of the "mystery" student.

Stage a fashion show in class. A few students will play the role of runway models, and other students will describe the clothes and shoes the models are wearing. The rest of the class will be customers and will ask the price and size of the clothes and shoes the models are wearing.

¡VAMOS A LEER!

Antes de leer

A. As you read the selection, keep in mind that the author criticizes the lack of punctuality. Think about the problems that are caused by not being punctual and how this affects other people.

B. As you read the selection, find the answers to the following questions.

1. ¿Por qué dice el autor que "después de almorzar" es algo demasiado elástico?
2. ¿Tiene el amigo del autor una hora exacta para almorzar?
3. ¿A qué hora dice el señor que va a estar en el café sin falta?
4. ¿Qué sucede al día siguiente a las ocho?
5. ¿Qué piensa el amigo del autor sobre la puntualidad?
6. ¿Por qué es una buena idea acudir puntualmente a una cita?

Julio Camba (España)(1882–1962)

Julio Camba, escritor de estilo satírico y humorístico, publicó numerosos artículos en los cuales da sus impresiones sobre la vida y la cultura de los distintos países que visitó.

El artículo que ofrecemos a continuación pertenece al libro de ensayos *La rana viajera*. Otros libros del autor son *Alemania*, *Londres*, *Aventuras de una peseta*, *Lúculo o el arte de comer*, *La ciudad automática*, *Mis páginas mejores*, y otros.

El tiempo y el espacio (Adaptado)

Tengo algo urgente que discutir con un amigo. Por supuesto el amigo dice que hoy no puede ser.

—¿Mañana...?

—Muy bien. ¿A qué hora?

—A cualquier hora. Después de almorzar, por ejemplo...

Yo digo que eso no es una hora. "Después de almorzar" es algo demasiado° vago, demasiado elástico.　　　　*too*

—¿A qué hora almuerza usted? —pregunto.

—A la hora de almorzar.

—Pero ¿qué hora es la hora de almorzar para usted? ¿El mediodía? ¿La una de la tarde? ¿Las dos...?

—Más o menos... —dice mi amigo—. Yo almuerzo de una a dos. A veces a las tres... De todos modos° a las cuatro siempre estoy libre.°　　*De... Anyway / free*

—Entonces, ¿a las cuatro?

—Sí, claro que, si llego unos minutos tarde —añade°— usted me puede　　*he adds* esperar, ¿verdad? Quien dice a las cuatro, dice a las cuatro y media. En fin, de cuatro a cinco yo estoy sin falta° en el café.　　*sin... without fail*

Yo quiero ser exacto.

—¿A las cinco?

—Muy bien. A las cinco... Es decir, de cinco a cinco y media... Uno no es un tren, ¡qué diablo°!　　*qué... what the heck*

—Pues podemos decir a las cinco y media —propongo yo. Entonces mi amigo tiene una idea brillante.

—¿Por qué no decimos a la hora del aperitivo? —sugiere.

Finalmente, decidimos reunirnos de siete a ocho. Al día siguiente son las ocho, y claro está, mi amigo no viene. Llega a las ocho y media echando el bofe° y no me　　*echando... out of breath* encuentra.

—No es justo —exclama días después al encontrarnos en la calle—. Me hace usted fijar una hora, me hace usted correr, y no me espera ni diez minutos. Yo llego a las ocho y media en punto°, y usted no está　　*en... on the dot* esperándome.

Y lo más curioso es que la indignación de mi amigo es auténtica. Para él, la puntualidad es algo completamente absurdo.

Pero —digo yo— una cita es una cosa que tiene que estar tan limitada en el tiempo como en el espacio.

De despreciar° el tiempo, podemos despreciar también el espacio. Y de　　*If we scorn* respetar el espacio, ¿por qué no considerar también el tiempo?

—Pero con esa precisión, con esa exactitud°, la vida es imposible —opina   accuracy
mi amigo.

—¿Cómo explicarle que esa exactitud y esa precisión sirven, al contrario,
para simplificar la vida? ¿Cómo convencerle de que, llegando
puntualmente a las citas uno ahorra mucho tiempo para hacer otras
cosas?

Díganos

Answer the following questions, based on your own thoughts and experiences.

1. ¿Es Ud. puntual o generalmente llega tarde?
2. Si Ud. tiene una cita y la persona llega tarde, ¿cúanto tiempo la espera?
3. Para Ud. ¿la puntualidad es importante o algo absurdo?
4. ¿Está Ud. de acuerdo con el autor o con el amigo del autor? ¿Por qué?

ASÍ SOMOS

VIDEO   CD-ROM

Do the interactive exercises on
the CD-ROM for additional practice.

NARRADORA	—¿Qué estilo *(style)* de ropa usa Ud. para ir a clase?
LEONARDO	—Normal... o sea, jeans, una camiseta, zapatos y una chaqueta de jeans también.
NARRADORA	—¿Cómo se viste Ud. cuando tiene una cita *(date)*?
LEONARDO	—Dependiendo de la cita también, pero regularmente con pantalón y camisa y a veces corbata.

Preparación

NOTE: The video-related vocabulary
is listed in the *Instructor's Activities
Manual* for your reference. Its
purpose is to facilitate students'
comprehension. You may want to
distribute the vocabulary to the class
before viewing.

NOTE: See the Instructor's Edition
frontmatter for additional suggestions
on implementing video in the
classroom.

A. ¿Cómo se viste...? Answer the following questions about the clothes you wear
to go to school. You will hear answers to some of these questions when you
watch the video. After viewing the video, compare your answers with those
you hear.

1. ¿Qué estilo *(style)* de ropa usa Ud. para ir a clase?
2. ¿Qué estilo de zapatos usa Ud. para ir a clase?
3. ¿Qué estilo de ropa usa su profesor(-a) para ir a clase?
4. ¿Cómo se viste Ud. cuando tiene una cita?
5. ¿Cómo se viste Ud. cuando está en casa?

SUGGESTION: Have students describe the clothing they see people wearing in the beginning of the video.

SUGGESTION: Bring in magazine photos for students to use when trying to determine the latest styles.

B. La ropa de moda. With a partner, answer the following questions about the latest styles of clothing. You will hear answers to some of these questions when you watch the video. After viewing the video, compare your answers with those you hear.

1. ¿Qué estilo de ropa está de moda ahora?
2. ¿Qué estilo de ropa no está de moda ahora?
3. ¿Qué estilo de ropa le gusta a Ud.?
4. ¿Qué estilo de ropa no le gusta a Ud.?
5. ¿Compra Ud. la ropa en los grandes almacenes o en las boutiques?
6. ¿Compra Ud. los zapatos en los grandes almacenes o en las boutiques?

Comprensión

SUGGESTION: Pause the video after each interview segment so students have time to complete the corresponding comprehension activity.

EXPANSION: Have students compare the styles of clothing described in the video to the styles of clothing worn by students at their school.

NOTE: You can point out the many regional differences in the vocabulary used to describe clothing in different parts of the Spanish-speaking world. For example, "jeans" are described as **vaqueros** or **pantalones de mezclilla** or simply **jeans**.

A. ¿Cómo se visten? Answer the following questions according to what you understood from the video.

1. Para ir a clase, ¿Paola usa falda o jeans?
2. ¿Leonardo usa camisas o camisetas?
3. ¿Se viste María de una manera *(manner)* informal o formal?
4. ¿Lleva Juan uniforme o ropa casual para ir a clase?
5. A Miriam, ¿le gusta más usar jeans o usar faldas?
6. ¿La mayoría *(majority)* de los estudiantes entrevistados usa ropa formal o ropa informal para ir a clase?

B. ¿Quién lo dijo? Match each statement with the name of the person who said it.

_____ 1. Utilizo *(I use)* traje *(suit)*, corbata y una buena colonia *(cologne)*.	a. Juan b. Paola
_____ 2. Utilizo los zapatos bien embolados *(polished)*.	c. Otmara
_____ 3. Me visto con saco y camisa sport.	d. Jaime
_____ 4. Uso pantalón y camisa y a veces corbata.	e. Leonardo
_____ 5. No me gusta vestirme muy sofisticado.	f. Pedro
_____ 6. Uso pantalones de tela o una falda.	
_____ 7. Casi siempre me gusta ponerme minifaldas, zapatos altos y blusas.	

C. La moda de hoy. Read the following statements. Circle **V** (**Verdadero**) or **F** (**Falso**) according to what you understood from the video. If a statement is false, correct it.

V F   1. En Bogotá usan camisas de lana *(wool)* o sacos.
V F   2. En España la gente va bien arreglada *(dressed up)* para ir a una cita o a una fiesta.
V F   3. En España está de moda ir a clase con ropa formal.
V F   4. Juan dice que los pantalones de mezclilla también se llaman "jeans".
V F   5. Alejandro dice que los jeans y las playeras están de moda.
V F   6. En el país de Otmara hace mucho frío.

D. **De compras.** Answer the following questions, according to what you understood.

1. ¿Hay muchos almacenes grandes en Nicaragua?
2. ¿Compra Juan ropa en los grandes almacenes o en las boutiques?
3. ¿Miriam prefiere comprar ropa en un almacén o en una boutique?
4. ¿En Colombia hay muchos o pocos centros comerciales?
5. ¿Cómo es la calidad de la ropa en los centros comerciales de Colombia?
6. Para una ocasión especial, ¿Otmara compra en un almacén o en una boutique?
7. ¿Otmara compra ropa de diario *(everyday)* en un almacén o en una boutique?
8. Para Alejandro, ¿es importante el precio de la ropa?

E. **Entrevista.** Read the following statements. After watching the video, circle **V** (**Verdadero**) or **F** (**Falso**), according to what you understood. If a statement is false, correct it.

V	F	1. En la tienda sólo venden jeans.
V	F	2. Venden sólo una marca *(brand)* de jeans.
V	F	3. A Jorge le gusta trabajar en la tienda.
V	F	4. A Jorge no le gusta el ambiente de la tienda.
V	F	5. Jorge hace amistad con algunos clientes.
V	F	6. Los artículos más populares son los Levi's.

Ampliación

A. **Vamos de compras.** Make a list in Spanish of the new clothes you would like to buy at the local shopping center. Then in groups of three or four, compare your lists.

B. **Mi ropa favorita.** Interview a classmate about his or her favorite clothes. Use the following questions as a guide.

1. ¿Cuál es tu ropa favorita?
2. ¿Qué ropa te gusta ponerte para salir?
3. ¿Cuál es tu ropa favorita para estar en casa?
4. ¿Qué ropa usas para ir a una fiesta?
5. ¿Cómo te vistes para ir a clase?

Take this test. When you have finished, check your answers in the answer key provided for this section in Appendix E. Then use a red pen to correct any mistakes you may have made. Are you ready?

Lección 13

A. The familiar commands (*tú*)

Give the Spanish equivalent of the words in parentheses.

1. _____ , Paco. ¿Pusiste los platos en el fregadero?   *(Tell me)*
2. _____ el trabajo y luego _____ la cocina, Ana.   *(Do / clean)*
3. _____ de mi recámara, Carlos.   *(Leave)*
4. _____ con ella y _____ las cortinas para el cuarto, Pepe.   *(Go / buy)*
5. ¿Los libros? _____ en la mesa, querida.   *(Put them)*
6. _____ conmigo.   *(Come)*
7. _____ buena y _____ las sábanas y la frazada, Anita.   *(Be / bring me)*
8. _____ paciencia. _____ unos minutos más.   *(Have / Wait for me)*
9. _____ la casa si no tiene aire acondicionado, Luis.   *(Don't buy)*
10. ¿El té? _____ todavía *(yet)*, Petrona.   *(Don't serve it.)*
11. _____ , querido.   *(Don't go away)*
12. _____ a las seis y _____ hasta las once.   *(Get up / work)*

B. *Qué* and *cuál* used with *ser*

Supply the questions that elicited the following responses, beginning with **qué** or **cuál**, as needed.

1. Mi número de teléfono es 862–4031.
2. El apellido de mi madre es Lovera.
3. Un pasaporte es un documento que necesitamos para viajar a un país extranjero.
4. Las lecciones que necesitamos son la once y la doce.
5. Su dirección es calle Universidad, número treinta.
6. La paella es un plato hecho *(made)* con pollo, arroz y mariscos.

C. The subjunctive to express indefiniteness and nonexistence

Complete the following sentences, using the present subjunctive or the present indicative of the verbs given in parentheses.

1. ¿Hay alguien aquí que _____ (saber) hablar español?
2. Vivo en una casa que _____ (tener) cinco dormitorios.
3. No conozco a nadie que _____ (ser) colombiano.
4. ¿Ud. quiere una casa que _____ (tener) piscina?
5. Necesito un empleado que _____ (trabajar) tiempo completo.
6. Aquí hay una chica que _____ (hablar) francés, pero no hay nadie que _____ (hablar) ruso.

383

D. Just words . . .

Match the questions in column A with the appropriate responses in column B. Use each response once.

A	B
1. ¿Tienes frío?	a. No, pero tiene terraza.
2. ¿Por qué es tan cara la casa?	b. No, uso el fregadero.
3. ¿Por qué necesitas un garaje tan grande?	c. No, necesito una cafetera.
	d. Porque era más cómodo.
4. ¿Cuánto va a costar el refrigerador?	e. La semana próxima.
	f. Está en un buen barrio.
5. ¿La casa tiene jardín?	g. Una cómoda y una butaca.
6. ¿Dónde lo leíste?	h. No, tiempo completo.
7. ¿Necesitas una tostadora?	i. En el periódico.
8. ¿Tienes lavaplatos?	j. Sí, pero no tenemos fundas.
9. ¿Cuándo se mudan?	k. ¡Tengo tres coches!
10. ¿Tienen dinero?	l. Póngalo en la sala.
11. ¿Por qué compraste este sofá en vez del otro?	m. Sí, pon la calefacción, por favor.
	n. Sí, ganaron la lotería.
12. ¿Vas a trabajar medio día?	o. Quinientos dólares.
13. ¿Qué muebles necesitas?	p. En el microondas.
14. ¿Dónde pongo el sofá?	
15. ¿Tienen almohadas?	
16. ¿Dónde vas a poner el pollo?	

E. Culture

Read the following statements and circle **V** (**Verdadero**) or **F** (**Falso**) based on the **¿Lo sabía Ud.?** section.

V F 1. En España llaman "pisos" a los apartamentos.

V F 2. En los países latinos muchos edificios tienen oficinas o tiendas en la planta baja.

V F 3. La palabra "barrio" tiene una connotación negativa en los países de habla hispana.

V F 4. La Universidad Nacional Autónoma de México es la menos importante del país.

V F 5. Unos 400.000 estudiantes asisten a la UNAM.

Lección 14

A. The subjunctive or indicative after certain conjunctions

Give the Spanish equivalent of the verbs in parentheses.

1. Tan pronto como Marta _____ a casa, le voy a dar las entradas. *(arrives)*

2. Voy a esperarlos hasta que _____. *(they return)*

3. Cuando ellos _____ a trabajar, siempre dejan las ventanas abiertas. *(go)*

4. Cuando lo _____, dile que somos seis. *(see)*

5. Vamos antes de que _____ la lámpara que te gusta.   *(they sell)*
6. Ella va a ir al parque con tal que tú _____ con ella.   *(go)*
7. No puedo sacar el sillón de la casa sin que ellos me _____.   *(see)*
8. En caso de que ella _____ otras frutas, yo puedo traérselas.   *(needs)*
9. No puedo comprar las verduras a menos que tú me _____ el dinero.   *(give)*
10. Voy a llamar a Raúl para que nos _____ al cine.   *(takes)*

B. First-person plural commands

Answer the following questions, using appropriate command forms and the cues provided.

1. ¿Adónde vamos?   (al supermercado)
2. ¿A qué hora vamos?   (a las dos)
3. ¿Qué compramos?   (frutas y vegetales)
4. ¿A quién le pedimos el dinero?   (a mamá)
5. ¿Adónde vamos después? ¿Al teatro?   (no, al cine)
6. ¿A qué hora volvemos a casa?   (a las siete)
7. ¿A qué hora nos acostamos esta noche?   (a las once)
8. ¿A qué hora nos levantamos mañana?   (a las seis)

C. Constructions with *se*

Form questions with the elements given, adding the necessary connectors. Follow the model.

> MODELO: a qué hora / abrir / las tiendas
> *¿A qué hora se abren las tiendas?*

1. qué idioma / hablar / Chile
2. a qué hora / cerrar / las cafeterías
3. a qué hora / abrir / el supermercado
4. dónde / vender / aceite
5. por dónde / subir / segundo piso

D. Just words . . .

Complete the following sentences, using words learned in **Lección 14.**

1. ¿Tú le pones crema y _____ al café?
2. Quiero una _____ de salsa de tomate y una de frijoles.
3. ¿Compraste mantequilla o _____? A mí me gusta el pan con mantequilla.
4. No quiero zanahorias; no me gustan las _____.
5. ¿Te vas a _____ a dieta?
6. Tengo una _____ con Rosalía. Vamos a ir al cine.
7. ¿Qué _____ ponen en el cine Rex?
8. El 4 de julio es _____; no tenemos que trabajar.
9. Voy a comprar una _____ de huevos.
10. Necesitamos papel _____ para el baño.
11. Fuimos al parque de _____ el sábado pasado.
12. A él le gustan mucho los animales. Lo voy a llevar al _____.

E. Culture

Read the following statements and circle **V** (**Verdadero**) or **F** (**Falso**) based on the **¿Lo sabía Ud.?** section.

V F   1. En los países hispanos no existen los supermercados.

V F   2. En los países hispanos muchas personas prefieren comprar en tiendas pequeñas especializadas, como carnicerías y panaderías.

V F   3. La producción de películas no tiene gran importancia en los países hispanos.

V F   4. Las películas norteamericanas no son populares en el mundo hispano.

V F   5. Las películas norteamericanas que se ven en el mundo hispano generalmente están dobladas o tienen subtítulos en español.

Lección 15

A. The past participle

Give the Spanish equivalent of the following past participles.

1. written
2. opened
3. seen
4. done
5. broken
6. gone
7. spoken
8. eaten
9. drunk
10. received

B. Past participles used as adjectives

Give the Spanish equivalent of the words in parentheses.

1. Los espejos están _____. *(broken)*
2. ¿Están _____ las puertas de la tienda? *(open)*
3. El hombre estaba _____. *(dead)*
4. El departamento de señoras está _____. *(closed)*
5. Estas sandalias fueron _____ aquí. *(made)*

C. The present perfect

Complete the sentences with the present perfect tense of the verbs in the list, as needed.

decir —to tell   usar —to use   comer
quedarse —to stay hacer —to make envolver —to wrap

1. ¿Tú nunca _____ esa falda?
2. Él me _____ los zapatos.
3. Ellos me _____ que no tienen nada que hacer.
4. Nosotros _____ demasiado.
5. Yo _____ en la planta baja.
6. ¿Uds. no _____ el trabajo todavía?

D. The past perfect (pluperfect)

Complete the following sentences with the past perfect tense of the verbs in parentheses.

1. Cuando yo llegué, la liquidación ya _____ (terminar).
2. Elsa dijo que ellos _____ (ir) al departamento de ropa para caballeros.
3. El dependiente me _____ (decir) que la cartera costaba cincuenta dólares.
4. Yo ya _____ (abrir) la puerta del probador.
5. Nosotros todavía no _____ (comprar) la camisa.
6. ¿Tú le _____ (preguntar) qué talla usaba?

E. Just words . . .

Choose the appropriate answer to each of the following questions.

1. ¿Qué número calza Ud.?
    a. Talla mediana.
    b. El treinta y seis.
    c. No tengo pantimedias.

2. ¿Quiere las botas negras y el bolso azul?
    a. No, no hacen juego.
    b. En seguida vuelvo.
    c. No, me gusta la ropa interior.

3. ¿Puedo probarme estos zapatos?
    a. Sí, pero antes tiene que ponerse calcetines.
    b. Sí, pero necesita esta corbata.
    c. Sí, pero necesita ponerse estos guantes.

4. ¿Va a llevar este par de zapatos?
    a. No, me quedan muy bien.
    b. No, están en la zapatería.
    c. No, me aprietan un poco.

5. ¿Dónde pusiste el traje?
    a. ¡En la billetera, por supuesto!
    b. ¡En el ropero, por supuesto!
    c. ¡En la rebaja, por supuesto!

6. ¿Tiene frío, señora?
    a. Sí, tráigame el pañuelo.
    b. Sí, tráigame las sandalias.
    c. Sí, tráigame la chaqueta.

7. ¿Quieres comer algo?
    a. Sí, estoy muerta de hambre.
    b. Sí, me gusta este vestido.
    c. Sí, quiero esa camisa y esa blusa.

8. ¿Cómo subieron al tercer piso?
    a. Nos encontramos en la planta baja.
    b. Por la escalera mecánica.
    c. Compramos ropa.

F. Culture

Circle the correct answer, based on the **¿Lo sabía Ud.?** section.

1. El primer piso en España corresponde (a la planta baja, al segundo piso) en los Estados Unidos.
2. En las ciudades hispanas muchas mujeres prefieren (comprar ropa hecha, utilizar los servicios de una modista).
3. En los países hispanos (existen, no existen) grandes almacenes de ropa.
4. En España los dependientes de las tiendas (a veces, nunca) tutean a los clientes.

Las carreras

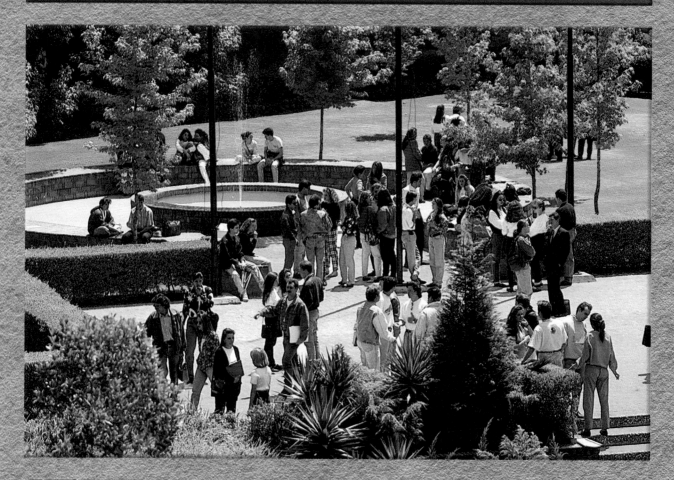

OBJECTIVES

Pronunciation
Pronunciation in context

Structure
The future • The conditional • The future perfect and the conditional perfect

Communication
You will learn vocabulary related to college activities and careers.

Las carreras

SUGGESTION: Write a list of professions and courses on the board and use Transparency 50 to introduce the vocabulary. Give the name of the professions shown or elicit them from students as you point to the different drawings. Then ask students, **¿Quiénes estudian para...?** (see Appendix F for professions not taught in **Lección 16**) and **¿Qué asignaturas estás tomando este trimestre/ semestre?**

Los Ángeles, California
24 de agosto del 2002

Estimado Sergio:

Te diré que no te he escrito antes porque no he tenido tiempo. Mañana estaré también muy ocupado porque tendré que matricularme para las clases de otoño. Pienso tomar administración de empresas, sociología y psicología. Mi consejero me ha sugerido que tome una clase de química o de física pero, como sabes, nunca me han gustado las ciencias. ¡Prefiero la literatura!

Me gustaría mucho ir a Buenos Aires en diciembre, pero tengo exámenes finales hasta el 20 y tengo que sacar buenas notas. Debo mantener un promedio de "A" porque tengo una beca.

¿Por qué no vienes tú a Los Ángeles? Podríamos ir a Disneylandia y visitar San Diego, mi ciudad favorita. Tienes que venir antes del año 2004 porque para entonces ya me habré graduado. ¡Trataré de conseguir un trabajo antes, porque la vida de estudiante es vida de pobre!

Escríbeme pronto. Un abrazo de tu amigo,

Daniel

P.D. [1] ¡Saludos a tu hermana!

SUGGESTION: Refer students to **Panorama hispánico 6** and the corresponding video segment for information about Argentina.

Buenos Aires, Argentina
15 de septiembre del 2002

Estimado Daniel:

¡Gracias por la invitación! De haber sabido que ibas a invitarme a Los Ángeles, no habría gastado tanto dinero en mi viaje a Río de Janeiro y habría ahorrado dinero para el pasaje.

Yo también estoy muy ocupado. La carrera de abogado no es fácil, y todos los profesores de la Facultad de Derecho creen que sus clases son lo único que debería importarnos.

Mi hermana Amalia (le di tus saludos) está estudiando periodismo y se pasa la vida haciendo investigación y escribiendo informes. Yo supongo que algún día será una periodista magnífica.

---

[1]Post Data: post scriptum

¿Te acuerdas de José Luis? Está estudiando ingeniería y probablemente el año próximo irá a los Estados Unidos para tomar unos cursos especiales. ¡Yo haría lo mismo! De haber seguido los consejos de su padre, ya habría terminado la carrera de médico.

¿Y tú? ¿Cuál es tu especialización? Yo pensé que tu asignatura favorita era la contabilidad...

Bueno, me voy porque Marcos me invitó a un partido de fútbol. Es en el estadio de Boca y juega nuestro equipo. ¡Chau!

Afectuosamente,

Sergio

P.D. Saludos de Amalia.

Titulaciones Oficiales

Ingenierías:
- Informática
- Industrial

Licenciaturas:
- Administración y Dirección de Empresas
- Derecho
- Periodismo
- Publicidad y Relaciones Públicas
- Comunicación Audiovisual
- Lenguas Aplicadas a la Comunicación y al Marketing
- Lenguas Aplicadas a las Actividades Empresariales
- Filología Inglesa

Vocabulario

Cognados

afectuosamente	affectionately	**la literatura**	literature
la ciencia	science	**probablemente**	probably
especial	special	**la psicología**	psychology
el estadio	stadium	**la sociología**	sociology
la física	physics		

Nombres

la administración de empresas business administration	**el curso** course, class	**la investigación** research
la asignatura, la materia (school) subject	**el equipo** team	**la nota** grade
la beca scholarship	**la especialización** major (field of study)	**el partido** game
la carrera university studies, career	**el examen final** final exam	**el periodismo** journalism
el (la) consejero(-a) advisor	**la facultad de derecho** law school	**el (la) periodista** journalist
el consejo advice	**el fútbol** soccer	**el promedio** grade point average
la contabilidad accounting	**el informe** paper, report	**la química** chemistry
	la ingeniería engineering	**el tiempo** time
		la vida life

SUGGESTION: Point out that, in contrast to the English *career,* **carrera** refers both to one's profession and to the course of studies required to attain a profession.

Verbos

gastar to spend (i.e., money)
graduarse[1] to graduate
importar to matter
mantener to maintain (conj. like **tener**)

matricularse to register
sacar to get, to receive (a grade)
suponer to suppose (conj. like **poner**)
tratar (de) to try

Adjetivo

estimado(-a) dear

Otras palabras y expresiones

como as
de haber seguido had he followed

lo único[2] the only thing
para entonces by then

pronto soon
Saludos a... Say hello to

Vocabulario adicional
Profesiones y oficios (trades)[3]

el (la) bibliotecario(-a) librarian

el (la) carpintero(-a) carpenter

el (la) cocinero(-a) cook, chef

---

[1]Present tense: **me gradúo, te gradúas, se gradúa, nos graduamos, os graduáis, se gradúan**
[2]**Lo** + *adjective* is equivalent to *the* + *adjective* + *thing*: **lo importante** = *the important thing;* **lo bueno** = *the good thing*
[3]For an extensive list of professions and trades, see Appendix F.

SUGGESTION: Use Transparency 51 to introduce vocabulary related to professions.

el (la) contador(-a)   accountant

el (la) electricista   electrician

el hombre (la mujer) de negocios
businessman (woman)

el (la) ingeniero(-a)   engineer

el (la) plomero(-a)   plumber

el (la) programador(-a)   programmer

el (la) psicólogo(-a)   psychologist

el (la) vendedor(-a)   salesperson

Para hablar de los estudios

aprobar (o:ue)	to pass (an exam or course)	**Aprobé** el examen.
entregar	to turn in, deliver	**¿Entregaste** la tarea?
el examen parcial (de mitad de curso)	midterm exam	Tengo dos **exámenes parciales.**
el horario	schedule	Tengo un buen **horario** este semestre.
el laboratorio	laboratory	Trabajo en el **laboratorio** de lenguas.
las matemáticas	mathematics	Mi profesor de **matemáticas** es el profesor Trujillo.
la matrícula	registration, tuition	Tengo que pagar la **matrícula.**
quedar suspendido(-a)	to fail (an exam or course)	Eva **quedó suspendida** en química.
el requisito	requirement	Yo he tomado todos los **requisitos** generales.
el trimestre	quarter, trimester	Este **trimestre** tengo una clase de física.

ACTIVITY SUGGESTION: See the *IAM* for an additional in-class activity: **¿Cómo respondes?**

SUGGESTION: Have students do this activity in pairs. Based on Daniel's and Sergio's letters, and the discussion questions, have students talk among themselves about their majors, what their families would like them to study, and what courses they are currently taking.

¡Conversemos!

Answer the following questions, basing your answers on the letters.

1. ¿Daniel estará ocupado mañana? ¿Qué tendrá que hacer?
2. ¿Qué asignaturas piensa tomar Daniel?

3. ¿Qué le ha sugerido su consejero? ¿Por qué no quiere él seguir su consejo?
4. ¿Adónde le gustaría ir a Daniel? ¿Podrá ir? ¿Por qué?
5. ¿Qué promedio debe mantener Daniel? ¿Por qué?
6. ¿Para qué año se habrá graduado Daniel?
7. ¿Qué habría hecho Sergio de haber sabido que Daniel lo iba a invitar a Los Ángeles?
8. Según Sergio, ¿qué creen todos los profesores de la Facultad de Derecho?
9. ¿Qué dice Sergio que Amalia será algún día?
10. ¿Adónde irá José Luis el año próximo? ¿Qué va a hacer allí?
11. De haber seguido los consejos de su padre, ¿qué carrera habría estudiado José Luis?
12. ¿Para qué van a ir Sergio y Marcos al estadio de Boca?

¿Lo sabía Ud.?

■ En la mayoría de las universidades hispanas no existe el concepto de *"major"* usado en los Estados Unidos. Los estudiantes españoles y latinoamericanos toman muy pocas clases optativas *(electives)*, ya que la mayoría comienza a especializarse a partir de su primer año en la universidad.

■ En España y en Latinoamérica, las universidades se dividen en "facultades", donde los estudiantes toman clases directamente relacionadas con su especialización (por ejemplo, la Facultad de Medicina, la Facultad de Ingeniería, la Facultad de Arquitectura, etc.). No existen requisitos generales, pues éstos se toman en la escuela secundaria.

■ En lugar de letras, el sistema de calificaciones *(grading system)* en las universidades hispanas usa números. Por lo general, se califica asignando notas de 1 a 5 en Hispanoamérica y de 1 a 10 en España. Una nota de 3 o de 6 es normalmente la nota mínima para aprobar una clase o un examen.

● ¿Cuáles son algunos de los requisitos generales que se toman en las universidades de su país?

Estudiantes de la Facultad de Derecho en Lima, Perú.

● En su país, ¿cuál es la nota mínima para aprobar una clase o un examen?

INTERNET   See the *¿Cómo se dice...?* Web site for activities on authentic cultural material: http://spanish.college.hmco.com/students

Pronunciación

STUDENT AUDIO

NOTE: To reinforce pronunciation practice, this section appears in Lessons 10 through 18. The sentences featured as pronunciation models are taken from the lesson dialogues.

In this lesson, there are some new words or phrases that may be challenging to pronounce. For further pronunciation practice of Spanish sounds, listen to your instructor and repeat the following words and phrases.

1. Pienso tomar **administración de empresas.**
2. Me ha sugerido que tome una clase de **química** o de **física.**
3. Para entonces ya **me habré graduado.**
4. **Habría ahorrado** dinero para el pasaje.
5. ¿Cuál es tu **especialización?**

SUGGESTION: For each sentence, first model the word(s) in boldface type and have the class repeat them chorally and individually. Then have students repeat the full sentence for pronunciation practice of the target expressions in context.

Estructuras

1 The future *(El futuro)*

SUGGESTION: Ask students personalized questions about what they plan to do in the future.

1. ¿Adónde irás de vacaciones? ¿Cuándo? ¿Con quién?
2. ¿Qué cursos tomarás el semestre / trimestre que viene? ¿Cuál será el más fácil / difícil?
3. ¿Comprarás un coche nuevo el año que viene? ¿De qué marca?
4. ¿Trabajarás este verano? ¿Dónde?
5. ¿Cuándo te graduarás?
6. ¿Dónde vivirás cuando termines tus estudios?
7. ¿Tomarás más clases de español?

■ Most Spanish verbs are regular in the future tense. The infinitive serves as the stem of almost all of them, and the endings are the same for all three conjugations.

The Future Tense				
Infinitive		**Stem**	**Ending**	
trabajar	yo	trabajar-	é	trabajaré
aprender	tú	aprender-	ás	aprenderás
escribir	Ud.	escribir-	á	escribirá
hablar	él	hablar-	á	hablará
decidir	ella	decidir-	á	decidirá
dar	nosotros(-as)	dar-	emos	daremos
ir	vosotros(-as)	ir-	éis	iréis
caminar	Uds.	caminar-	án	caminarán
perder	ellos	perder-	án	perderán
recibir	ellas	recibir-	án	recibirán

ATENCIÓN   Note that all the endings, except the one for the **nosotros** form, have written accents.

—¿Qué clases **tomarás** el año próximo?

—No sé. Lo **decidiré** cuando hable con mi consejero.

"What classes will you take next year?"

"I don't know. I'll decide when I talk with my advisor."

■ The English equivalent of the Spanish future is *will* or *shall* + *a verb*. As you have already learned, Spanish also uses the construction **ir a** + *infinitive* or *the present tense with a time expression* to express future action, very much like the English present tense or the expression *going to*.

Vamos a ir al estadio esta noche.
or: **Iremos** al estadio esta noche. } *We're going (We'll go) to the stadium tonight.*

Anita **toma** el examen mañana.
or: Anita **tomará** el examen mañana. } *Anita is taking (will take) the exam tomorrow.*

ATENCIÓN   The Spanish future is *not* used to express willingness, as is the English future. In Spanish this is expressed with the verb **querer.**

¿Quieres llamar a Tomás?   *Will you call Tomás?*

SUGGESTION: Ask students the following personalized questions or have them interview each other in groups of three. Remind them to use the irregular future forms of the verbs in their responses.

1. ¿Con quién vas a salir este fin de semana?
2. ¿A qué hora vas a venir a la universidad mañana?
3. ¿Qué vas a hacer después de la clase?
4. ¿Cuándo vas a poder comprar un coche?
5. ¿Cuándo vas a tener una fiesta?
6. ¿Cuánto va a valer tu coche en tres años?
7. ¿Qué van a decir tus amigos si ganas la lotería?
8. ¿Cuándo vas a saber las notas finales del semestre?

■ A small number of verbs are irregular in the future. These verbs use a modified form of the infinitive as a stem, but have the same endings as the regular verbs.

Irregular Future Stems		
Infinitive	*Modified form (Stem)*	*First-person singular*
decir	dir-	diré
hacer	har-	haré
querer	querr-	querré
saber	sabr-	sabré
poder	podr-	podré
caber	cabr-	cabré
poner	pondr-	pondré
venir	vendr-	vendré
tener	tendr-	tendré
salir	saldr-	saldré
valer[1]	valdr-	valdré

—¿Qué les **dirás** a tus padres?   *"What will you tell your parents?"*
—Les **diré** que no **podremos** venir   *"I will tell them that we won't be*
en enero y que **vendremos** en   *able to come in January and that*
febrero.   *we will come in February."*

ATENCIÓN   The future of **hay** (impersonal form of **haber**) is **habrá.**

¿Habrá una fiesta?   *Will there be a party?*

práctica ●

A. Say what the following people will do after classes are over, using the future tense.

1. Jorge / ir de vacaciones / México
2. Marta y yo / salir para Colombia / julio

---

[1]*to be worth*

SUGGESTION A: Write these incomplete statements on the board or on a transparency. Have students complete the sentences orally or in writing using two verbs in the future.

1. **El año que viene, mi familia…**
2. **Esta noche, mis amigos y yo…**
3. **El último día de clase, nosotros…**
4. **Cuando tenga mucho dinero, yo…**
5. **Este fin de semana, mi amigo(-a)…**
6. **Mañana, el profesor / la profesora…**
7. **En el año 2004, yo…**
8. **Durante las vacaciones, yo…**

ACTIVITY SUGGESTION: See the *IAM* for an additional in-class activity: **Planes para el futuro.**

3. Mis padres / venir / a visitarme / agosto
4. Ana / tener que / trabajar / verano
5. Yo / tomar / una clase / francés
6. Uds. / poner / alfombra nueva / casa
7. Tú / viajar / por Latinoamérica
8. Ud. / pasar / dos semanas / Sevilla

B. You and a friend will be attending a special program in Spain next year. Take turns answering these questions about your trip.

1. ¿A qué ciudad irán?
2. ¿Cuándo saldrán de viaje?
3. ¿Viajarán en barco o en avión?
4. ¿Cuánto tiempo estarán estudiando?
5. ¿Podrán visitar muchas ciudades?
6. ¿Qué lugares visitarán?
7. ¿Les enviarán tarjetas postales a sus amigos?
8. ¿Cuánto dinero necesitarán para el viaje?
9. ¿Se lo pedirán a sus padres?
10. ¿Cuándo volverán?

C. Now, use the questions in Exercise B as a model to ask a classmate about his or her upcoming study-travel plans.

SUGGESTION D: Have students complete this activity in groups of three. Each student should first write his or her own solution. The group should then compare solutions and select the one they believe best solves the problem. Have several groups share their lists with the class.

D. Say what the following people will do in each situation.

1. Los estudiantes tienen que escribir un informe para su clase de sociología.
2. Jorge no tiene dinero para pagar la matrícula.
3. Ud. y yo tenemos un examen mañana.
4. Antonio y Luis no saben qué clases pueden tomar.
5. Yo tengo un examen de matemáticas y no tengo calculadora.
6. Los muchachos tienen mucha hambre.

E. With a partner, write predictions about five of your classmates and what will happen to them in the future. Compare your predictions to those of other groups.

MODELO: *Dentro de cinco años, John será periodista y trabajará para el periódico* Los Angeles Times.

2   The conditional   *(El condicional)*

SUGGESTION: Have students work in pairs to practice giving excuses. One student should "invite" his or her partner to do something. The partner should then decline the invitation and offer an excuse. Remind students to switch roles.

S1—¿Quieres ir a una fiesta conmigo esta noche?
S2—Iría contigo pero tengo que estudiar.

Write the following suggested phrases on the board or on an overhead transparency.

1. **ayudarme / con las diligencias**
2. **trabajar / por mí / mañana**
3. **lavar / mi coche**
4. **prestarme / veinte dólares**
5. **ir de compras / conmigo**
6. **pagar / la cuenta**
7. **planchar / mi ropa**
8. **prepararme / la comida**
9. **limpiar / mi apartamento**
10. **revisar / mi tarea**

■ The conditional tense in Spanish is equivalent to the conditional in English, expressed by *should* or *would* + *a verb*.[1] Like the future tense, the conditional uses the infinitive as the stem and has only one set of endings for all three conjugations.

The Conditional Tense					
Infinitive		**Stem**		**Ending**	
trabajar	yo	trabajar-	ía	trabajaría	
aprender	tú	aprender-	ías	aprenderías	
escribir	Ud.	escribir-	ía	escribiría	
ir	él	ir-	ía	iría	
ser	ella	ser-	ía	sería	
dar	nosotros(-as)	dar-	íamos	daríamos	
hablar	vosotros(-as)	hablar-	íais	hablaríais	
servir	Uds.	servir-	ían	servirían	
estar	ellos	estar-	ían	estarían	
preferir	ellas	preferir-	ían	preferirían	

■ All of the conditional endings have written accents.

—Él dijo que **tomaría** esta clase.   *"He said that he would take this class."*

—Sí, y también dijo que **hablaría** con una consejera.   *"Yes, and he also said that he would speak with an advisor."*

■ The conditional is also used as the future of a past action. The future states what *will* happen; the conditional states what *would* happen.

Future	*Conditional*
(states what *will* happen)	(states what *would* happen)
Él **dice** que **estará** aquí mañana.	Él **dijo** que **estaría** aquí mañana.
He says that he will be here tomorrow.	*He said that he would be here tomorrow.*

----

[1]The conditional is never used in Spanish as an equivalent of *used to*.
    Cuando era pequeño siempre **iba a la playa**. *When I was little I would always go to the beach.*

SUGGESTION: Write the following incomplete statements on the board or on an overhead transparency. Have students complete the sentences orally or in writing using the irregular conditional verbs to tell what they, their friends, or their families would never do.

Yo / Mi(s) amigo(s) / Mi novio(-a) / Mi(s) padre(s) / El (La) profesor(-a)

nunca

decir una mentira *(lie)*... / querer visitar un país extranjero / poder conseguir un trabajo en... / tener una familia grande / venir tarde a clase / ponerle un pleito *(sue)* a un amigo / salir solo(-a) de noche

■ The verbs that have irregular stems in the future tense are also irregular in the conditional. The endings are the same as those for regular verbs.

Irregular Conditional Stems

Infinitive	*Modified form (Stem)*	*First-person singular*
decir	dir-	diría
hacer	har-	haría
querer	querr-	querría
saber	sabr-	sabría
poder	podr-	podría
caber	cabr-	cabría
poner	pondr-	pondría
venir	vendr-	vendría
tener	tendr-	tendría
salir	saldr-	saldría
valer	valdr-	valdría

—¿A qué hora te dijo que **vendría**?   *"What time did he tell you he would come?"*

—Dijo que **saldría** de casa a las dos.   *"He said he would leave home at two."*

ATENCIÓN   The conditional of **hay** (impersonal form of **haber**) is **habría.**

Dijo que **habría** un examen mañana.   *He said there would be an exam tomorrow.*

práctica ....

ACTIVITY SUGGESTION: See the *IAM* for an additional in-class activity: ¿Qué hacer...?

A. Nobody would do the things that Carlos does. With a partner, take turns saying what the following people would do instead.

> MODELO: Carlos come en la cafetería. (yo)
> *Yo no comería en la cafetería; comería en mi casa.*

Carlos...

1. se levanta a las cinco. (Uds.)
2. estudia por la mañana. (Ana y Luis)
3. viene a la universidad en ómnibus. (nosotros)
4. toma clases de alemán. (yo)
5. se baña por la noche. (Elsa)
6. se acuesta a las nueve de la noche. (Ud.)
7. va a las montañas los fines de semana. (ellos)
8. sale con Margarita. (tú)

EXPANSION B: Encourage students to expand upon each answer by providing a reason.

S1—¿Qué harías con mil dólares?
S2—Yo iría de vacaciones porque necesito descansar. ¿Qué harías tú?
S1—Yo me compraría un traje elegante porque me gusta vestirme bien.

B. Interview a classmate, using the following questions.

1. ¿Qué harías con mil dólares?
2. ¿Adónde irías de vacaciones? ¿En qué mes saldrías de vacaciones? ¿Por qué?
3. ¿Qué te gustaría hacer hoy?

4. ¿Dónde te gustaría almorzar mañana?
5. ¿Preferirías ver un partido de fútbol o un partido de fútbol americano?
6. ¿Qué asignaturas te gustaría tomar el semestre (trimestre) próximo?
7. ¿Preferirías un apartamento en la planta baja o en el séptimo piso? ¿Por qué?
8. Vamos a tener una fiesta. ¿Qué podrías traer?

SUGGESTION C: Have students complete this activity in groups of three. Each student should first write his or her own solution. The group should then compare solutions and select the one they believe best solves the problem. Have several groups share their lists with the class.

C. Describe what you would do in the following situations, using the conditional.

1. Su amigo(-a) le pide consejos sobre la carrera que debe seguir.
2. Su equipo de fútbol americano favorito juega hoy.
3. Un compañero quiere que Ud. lo ayude con su informe.
4. Sus amigos lo (la) invitan a ir al cine esta noche y Ud. tiene que trabajar mañana.
5. Una persona muy antipática lo (la) invita a salir.
6. Usted tiene que estar en la universidad a las siete de la mañana.
7. Usted tiene una beca y necesita mantener un buen promedio.
8. Ud. va a matricularse y no sabe qué asignaturas debe tomar.

D. With a partner, take turns telling each other what you would do if you won a million dollars in the lottery. Say at least five things each, and then compare your responses with those of other classmates.

3 The future perfect and the conditional perfect (El futuro perfecto y el condicional perfecto)

A. The future perfect

■ The future perfect in Spanish corresponds closely in formation and meaning to the same tense in English. The Spanish future perfect is formed with the future tense of the auxiliary verb **haber** + *the past participle* of the main verb.

Future tense of haber

habré	habremos
habrás	habréis
habrá	habrán

Formation of the Future Perfect Tense

yo	**habré terminado**	*I will have finished*
tú	**habrás vuelto**	*you will have returned*
Ud. / él / ella	**habrá comido**	*you (he, she) will have eaten*
nosotros(-as)	**habremos escrito**	*we will have written*
vosotros(-as)	**habréis dicho**	*you (fam.) will have said*
Uds. / ellos / ellas	**habrán salido**	*you (they) will have left*

■ Like its English equivalent, the future perfect is used to indicate an action that will have taken place by a certain time in the future.

—¿Tus padres estarán aquí para el dos de junio?

—Sí, para esa fecha ya **habrán vuelto** de Madrid.

"Will your parents be here by June second?"

"Yes, by that date they will have returned from Madrid."

práctica •••

A. Complete the following dialogues, using the future perfect forms of the verbs listed. Then act them out with a partner.

acostarse
cenar
limpiar
salir
terminar (2)
volver (2)

1. —Esta noche a las once voy a llamar a Quique.
   —¿Estás loco(-a)? Para esa hora él ya _____. Llámalo mañana a las siete.
   —Para esa hora ya _____ de su casa.
2. —¿Uds. _____ de México para el 4 de julio?
   —No, no _____ todavía. Vamos a estar allí hasta agosto.
3. —Tú y yo podemos salir para España el 12 de diciembre porque ya estaremos de vacaciones.
   —Bueno, tú _____ las clases para entonces, pero yo no las _____ todavía.
4. —No podemos traer a mis amigos esta noche porque la casa está muy sucia *(dirty)*.
   —No te preocupes. Para cuando Uds. vengan, las chicas ya la _____.
5. —¿Quieres cenar con nosotros hoy?
   —Gracias, pero para cuando yo vuelva, Uds. ya _____.

B. With your partner, discuss things that you will or will not have done by the following times.

1. para las once de la noche
2. para mañana a las cinco de la mañana
3. para mañana a las seis de la tarde
4. para el sábado próximo
5. para junio del año próximo
6. para el año 2008

B. The conditional perfect

■ The conditional perfect is formed with the conditional tense of the auxiliary verb **haber** + *the past participle* of the main verb.

Conditional tense of haber

habría	habríamos
habrías	habríais
habría	habrían

Formation of the Conditional Perfect Tense

yo	habría vuelto	*I would have returned*
tú	habrías comido	*you would have eaten*
Ud. / él / ella	habría salido	*you (he, she) would have left*
nosotros(-as)	habríamos estudiado	*we would have studied*
vosotros(-as)	habríais hecho	*you (fam.) would have done*
Uds. / ellos / ellas	habrían muerto	*you (they) would have died*

■ Like the English conditional perfect, the Spanish conditional perfect is used to indicate an action that would have taken place but didn't.

—Yo me matriculé ayer. *"I registered yesterday."*
—Yo me **habría** matriculado la semana pasada. *"I would have registered last week."*

práctica

SUGGESTION: Write the following infinitive phrases on the board. Then have students tell about the things they or their friends wanted to do or should have done over the weekend but for some reason did not.

Mi compañero habría limpiado el apartamento.
 ver a la familia
 leer una novela interesante
 lavar el coche
 bañar al perro
 pasar más tiempo en la biblioteca
 ir al banco para sacar dinero
 limpiar el apartamento
 ir al supermercado para hacer las compras de la semana
 lavar la ropa

A. Last summer, my family, a friend, and I took a trip to New York. Based on what I tell you about our trip, say what you and each member of your family would have done differently, if anything.

MODELO: Mi padre llevó tres maletas.
Mi padre habría llevado una maleta.

1. Nosotros fuimos a Nueva York.
2. Viajamos en tren.
3. Yo me senté en la sección de no fumar.
4. Mi mamá preparó sándwiches para el viaje.
5. Mi amigo y yo bebimos refrescos en el café del tren.
6. En Nueva York, mi amigo se quedó en casa de su abuelo.
7. Nosotros nos quedamos en un hotel.
8. Mis padres fueron a ver una comedia musical.
9. Yo fui a bailar.
10. Nosotros visitamos el Museo de Arte Moderno.
11. Mi amigo visitó la Estatua de la Libertad.
12. Estuvimos en Nueva York por dos semanas.

B. You and your family had unannounced guests last Saturday. You were not prepared! Say what you and other members of your family would have done, had you known that they were coming.

> MODELO: mi mamá
> *Mi mamá habría limpiado la casa.*

1. yo
2. mi papá
3. mi hermana y yo
4. mis hermanos
5. mis padres
6. mi mamá y yo

Summary of the Tenses of the Indicative			
Simple Tenses			
	-ar	**-er**	**-ir**
Presente	hablo	como	vivo
Pretérito	hablé	comí	viví
Imperfecto	hablaba	comía	vivía
Futuro	hablaré	comeré	viviré
Condicional	hablaría	comería	viviría
Compound Tenses			
Pretérito perfecto	he hablado	he comido	he vivido
Pretérito plus-cuamperfecto	había hablado	había comido	había vivido
Futuro perfecto	habré hablado	habré comido	habré vivido
Condicional perfecto	habría hablado	habría comido	habría vivido

¡A ver cuánto aprendió!

INTERNET

See the *¿Cómo se dice…?* Web site for additional grammar and vocabulary practice: http://spanish.college. hmco.com/students

¡Repase el vocabulario!

Complete the following sentences with the missing words; then read them aloud.

1. Como Fernando sacó una "F" en física, quedó _____ en esa asignatura.
2. Estoy tomando una clase de administración de _____.
3. Voy a _____ de no gastar mucho dinero.
4. Quiere ser abogado. Estudia en la Facultad de _____.
5. Tengo que preparar un _____ para mi clase de literatura.
6. Fue elegido *(chosen)* el mejor _____ porque vendió cien casas en un año.

EXPANSION: Use Transparencies 50 and 51 to review the vocabulary. Ask students to describe what the people in Transparency 50 will do after they graduate, where they will work, etc.

ACTIVITY SUGGESTION: Do ¡Escucha!, the in-class listening comprehension activity that reviews vocabulary and grammar structures introduced in the lesson. It appears in the answer key of the *IAM*.

7. Voy a hablar con mi _____ para que me diga qué clases debo tomar.
8. ¿Quieres jugar al _____ esta tarde?
9. Tengo que _____ un promedio alto o pierdo la beca.
10. Para Juan, lo _____ importante es el fútbol.
11. Escribe para la revista *Time*. Es _____.
12. Para ser _____ tienes que estudiar en la Facultad de Ingeniería.
13. ¿Cuál es tu _____? ¿Matemáticas o contabilidad?
14. Mañana tengo un examen de _____ de curso.
15. Mi papá es un hombre de _____.
16. El _____ de ese restaurante cocina muy bien.

ACTIVITY SUGGESTION: See the *IAM* for an additional in-class activity: **Palabras escondidas.**

Entrevista

ACTIVITY SUGGESTION: See the *IAM* for additional in-class activities: **Para conocernos mejor** and **Una encuesta.**

Use the following questions to interview a classmate.

1. ¿Estarás muy ocupado(-a) mañana? ¿Qué tendrás que hacer?
2. ¿Tendrás que matricularte pronto? ¿Qué clases piensas tomar?
3. ¿Has hablado con tu consejero(-a) últimamente?
4. ¿Cuál es tu asignatura favorita? ¿Cuál es tu especialización?
5. ¿Tú preferirías ser bibliotecario(-a), contador(-a), abogado(-a) o psicólogo(-a)? ¿O preferirías tener alguna otra profesión? ¿Cuál?
6. Al terminar este semestre, ¿ya habrás tomado todos los requisitos?
7. ¿Qué promedio mantienes en tus clases? ¿Apruebas todos los cursos?
8. ¿Tú te habrás graduado para el año 2006?
9. ¿Tú podrías venir a la universidad los domingos?
10. ¿Qué harás tú el verano próximo? ¿Adónde te gustaría viajar?
11. ¿Tratarás de tomar otras clases de español?
12. De haber sabido lo que sabes ahora acerca *(about)* del español, ¿lo habrías estudiado cuando eras niño(-a)?
13. ¿Cuándo crees tú que el profesor (la profesora) nos dará el próximo examen?
14. Para las once de la noche, ¿ya te habrás acostado?
15. Mañana a las nueve, ¿ya habrás salido de tu casa?

Situaciones

What would you say in the following situations? What might the other person say? Act out the scenes with a partner. Take turns playing each role.

1. A freshman asks you what courses to take. Find out something about his or her interests and plans, and make some appropriate course recommendations. Be sure to mention some of your school's requirements.
2. You are talking with a friend about classes you like, classes you don't like, and the reasons why.
3. You have just graduated, and one of your parents has taken you out for a celebration dinner. You haven't done everything they had hoped you would do in college, but you are pleased with your decisions. Discuss your plans for the future.

¿Qué pasa aquí?

In groups of three or four, make up a story about the people in the photo. Say who they are, what subjects they are taking, their majors, their grade point averages, when they will graduate, and so forth.

Para escribir

Write a composition about your college activities. Include the following information:

- your major
- classes you are taking this semester
- classes you took last semester
- classes you like and classes you don't like
- your extracurricular activities
- your career plans

En la vida real

CD-ROM

Do the interactive exercises on the CD-ROM for additional practice.

El primer empleo

With a classmate, play the roles of a recent college graduate who is applying for a job and a prospective employer. The interviewer wants to know about the applicant's college courses and activities and how they are relevant to the job.

Here is a list that might help you answer the interviewer's questions:

Lista de materias

Administración de empresas	Ciencias económicas	Francés	Literatura
Alemán	Ciencias políticas	Geología	Matemáticas
Álgebra	Contabilidad	Geometría	Música
Antropología	Drama	Historia	Química
Arte	Educación física	Humanidades	Relaciones públicas
Astronomía	Electrónica	Informática	Ruso
Biología	Español	*(Computer Science)*	Sociología
Cálculo	Estadística	Inglés	Telecomunicaciones
	Física		

Necesitamos trabajo...

SUGGESTION: Point out that want ads in Hispanic countries often list "job requirements" involving age, sex, marital status, or physical appearance that would be illegal in the U.S.

Some friends of yours are looking for jobs. Help them by answering their questions about the classified ads below.

1. ¿Qué empresa necesita secretario(-a)?
2. Si deseo trabajar de secretario(-a) en la compañía Optim, ¿qué idioma necesito hablar?
3. ¿En qué ciudad está el laboratorio farmacéutico?
4. ¿Qué experiencia mínima debo tener si solicito el puesto de director de servicio extranjero?
5. ¿Para solicitar qué empleos necesito mandar una foto?
6. ¿Qué edad debo tener para trabajar en la empresa financiera?
7. ¿Qué debo enviar a la empresa financiera antes del día 20 de noviembre?

IMPORTANTE LABORATORIO FARMACEUTICO NACIONAL

BUSCA

TECNICO

Capacitado para crear y dirigir una linea de productos OTC

- Se requiere persona con experiencia en este campo.
- Condiciones a convenir.

Interesados escribir adjuntando curriculum a GISPERT PUBLICIDAD, c. Balmes, 1008007-Barcelona, indicando en el sobre la Ref.° 21 210

EMPRESA FINANCIERA

PRECISA

DIRECTOR DE SERVICIO EXTRANJERO

SE REQUIERE:
⇨ Capacidad de organización y gestión.
⇨ Edad: entre 35 y 45 años.
⇨ Perfecto dominio del idioma inglés y conocimientos de otros idiomas.
⇨ Experiencia mínima de 3 años en el servicio de extranjero.
⇨ Titulado en Ciencias Económicas o Empresariales.

SE OFRECE:
⇨ Incorporación inmediata.
⇨ Remuneración a convenir, de acuerdo con la experiencia y conocimientos aportados por el candidato.
⇨ Proceso de selección con garantía de absoluta reserva en los datos aportados.

Los candidatos enviarán "curriculum vitae" antes del día 20 de noviembre, acompañado de fotografía, dirección y teléfono al Apartado 1.540 de Vigo.

(Oferta INEM nº 2.971 OR.)

Multinacional Alemana dedicada a la hidráulica, ubicada en el Vallés Occidental, precisa:

SECRETARIA/O

DPTO. COMPRAS

SE REQUIERE:
- Dominio del idioma alemán a nivel conversación.
- Experiencia Administrativa en área de Compras.
- Facilidad de trato con proveedores.
- Edad 22-37 años.

Condiciones económicas según aptitudes.
Interesadas escribir historial a:

OPTIM

OPTIM
C. Estació, n.º 9, 1.º, 1.º
08814 PALAU DE PLEGAMANS
Indicar ref. 2.475.

Argentina

Chile

Paraguay

Uruguay

- Buenos Aires, la capital de Argentina, tiene una población de alrededor de doce millones de habitantes, y su área metropolitana es una de las más extensas del mundo. Su sistema de metro, "el subterráneo", es el más antiguo de Latinoamérica.

- Uruguay es el país de habla hispana más pequeño de la América del Sur. El 45% de la población del país está concentrado en Montevideo, la capital. Muy cerca de esta ciudad está la playa de Punta del Este, de fama internacional.

- La represa *(dam)* de Itaipú, entre Brasil y Paraguay, es la represa hidroeléctrica más grande del mundo y fue construida por los gobiernos de Brasil y Paraguay.

- Paraguay es conocido por sus joyas de oro y de plata, sus objetos de madera tallada *(carved wood)* y sus encajes *(laces)* de "ñandutí". Estos encajes son hechos a mano, y para hacerlos, se utilizan más de cien diseños diferentes.

- La isla de Pascua, situada en el océano Pacífico, pertenece a Chile y es famosa por las gigantescas estatuas de piedra que se encuentran allí.

El centro de Santiago, capital de Chile, se distingue por el contraste de modernos rascacielos y edificios coloniales como la Casa Colorada, residencia del primer presidente de la República; el Palacio de la Moneda, palacio presidencial actual, y la catedral, construida en 1780.

¿Cómo se llama, en español, la residencia del presidente de los Estados Unidos?

PANORAMA HISPÁNICO

Una pareja baila el tango, el baile típico de Argentina. El tango se hizo *(became)* popular en Latinoamérica a principios del siglo XX y fue introducido en los Estados Unidos alrededor de 1912.

¿Conoce Ud. algunos otros bailes típicos latinoamericanos? ¿Cuáles?

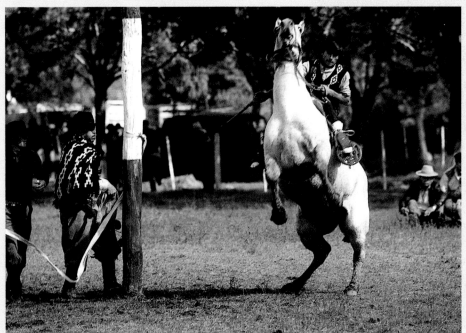

El gaucho argentino, inmortalizado en la literatura y en la música popular argentinas, es hoy día más una leyenda que un personaje real. Una de las costumbres de los gauchos que persiste es la del rodeo, como se ve en la foto.

¿En qué son similares los vaqueros norteamericanos y los gauchos argentinos?

Vista panorámica del puerto de Asunción, la capital de Paraguay. En esta ciudad se mezclan armoniosamente la arquitectura colonial y la moderna. Aquí se ve la Plaza de los Héroes y, al fondo, el río Paraguay, que sirve como vía de comunicación con el océano Atlántico.

¿Cuáles son algunos de los puertos principales de su país?

Vista del Obelisco y de la avenida Nueve de Julio, en Buenos Aires. La avenida Nueve de Julio es una de las más anchas del mundo y lleva este nombre para conmemorar la fecha de la independencia de Argentina.

¿Le gusta a Ud. la idea de vivir en una gran ciudad como Buenos Aires? ¿Por qué o por qué no?

Las cataratas *(falls)* de Iguazú, formadas por los ríos Iguazú y Paraná, están situadas en el punto de unión entre Argentina, Brasil y Paraguay. Se consideran las cataratas más anchas y caudalosas *(abundant)* del mundo, y de ahí su nombre, que en el idioma guaraní significa "agua grande".

¿Son exclusivamente de los Estados Unidos las cataratas del Niágara?

Punta del Este, en Uruguay, es uno de los centros turísticos más importantes de la América del Sur. Es, además, sede *(site)* de competencias de veleros *(sailboats)*, de carreras *(races)* de automóviles y de torneos *(tournaments)* de tenis, de golf y de polo.

¿Vive Ud. cerca de algún centro turístico importante?

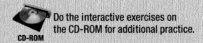

Preparación

NOTE: The video-related vocabulary is listed in the *Instructor's Activities Manual* for your reference. Its purpose is to facilitate students' comprehension.

NOTE: See the Instructor's Edition frontmatter for additional suggestions on implementing video in the classroom.

¿Cuánto saben Uds. ya? After reading **Panorama hispánico 8**, get together in groups of three or four students and answer the following questions.

1. ¿Cuál es la capital de Argentina? ¿Y de Chile?
2. ¿Cuál es la población de Buenos Aires?
3. ¿Qué monumento importante está en la avenida Nueve de Julio?
4. ¿Dónde está situada la represa *(dam)* de Itaipú?
5. ¿Qué ríos forman las cataratas *(waterfalls)* de Iguazú?
6. ¿Qué significa la palabra guaraní *Iguazú*?

Comprensión

SUGGESTION: Have students read the *Panorama hispánico* segment of the textbook and do the *Preparación* activities in small groups before viewing the video segments.

SUGGESTION: The *Comprensión* sections are organized by individual video clip to provide greater flexibility in lesson planning. Have students complete each exercise after viewing the corresponding video clip and have them compare their answers in pairs or groups.

SUGGESTION: Have students locate Buenos Aires, Asunción, el río Paraguay, and el río Paraná on the map on the inside back cover of the textbook.

A. Buenos Aires, Argentina. Complete the following statements according to what you understood.

1. Buenos Aires ha sido llamada "el _____ de Suramérica."
2. Los inmigrantes de Buenos Aires son ingleses, _____, griegos, _____, españoles y, sobre todo, _____ .
3. La Avenida Nueve de Julio es una de las avenidas más _____ del mundo.
4. Muchos _____ se establecieron en el barrio de La Boca.
5. El género musical más conocido *(famous)* de Argentina es _____ .

B. Paraguay. Read the following statements. After watching the video, circle **V (Verdadero)** or **F (Falso)**, according to what you understood. If a statement is false, correct it.

V F 1. La película *La misión* fue filmada en Paraguay.
V F 2. La capital de Paraguay es Montevideo.
V F 3. Paraguay significa "aguas que corren hacia el mar".
V F 4. El río Paraguay divide el país en cuatro regiones.
V F 5. Paraguay tiene varias salidas al mar.
V F 6. Itaipú es la planta hidroeléctrica más grande del mundo.
V F 7. Las cataratas *(waterfalls)* de Iguazú están cerca de la frontera *(border)* de Paraguay con Brasil.

C. La Patagonia. Select the word or phrase that best completes each statement, according to what you understood.

1. La Patagonia es (un país, una región).
2. La Patagonia está en el extremo (sur, norte) de Suramérica.
3. El punto más alto de los Andes mide *(measures)* (6.600, 660) metros de altura.
4. Chile y (Brasil, Argentina) son países del Cono Sur.
5. Ushuaia, cerca de la Antártida, es la (región, ciudad) más meridional *(southernmost)* del mundo.

Ampliación

A. **Otros países, otras culturas.** With a partner, discuss in Spanish what aspect of each place (Buenos Aires, Paraguay, or La Patagonia) appealed to you and why. Share your observations with the rest of the class.

B. **Dos culturas.** With a partner, make a list of counterparts you can find in your local area, city, state, or country for each of the following items.

1. Buenos Aires
2. el barrio de La Boca
3. la represa Itaipú
4. las cataratas de Iguazú
5. los Andes
6. La Patagonia

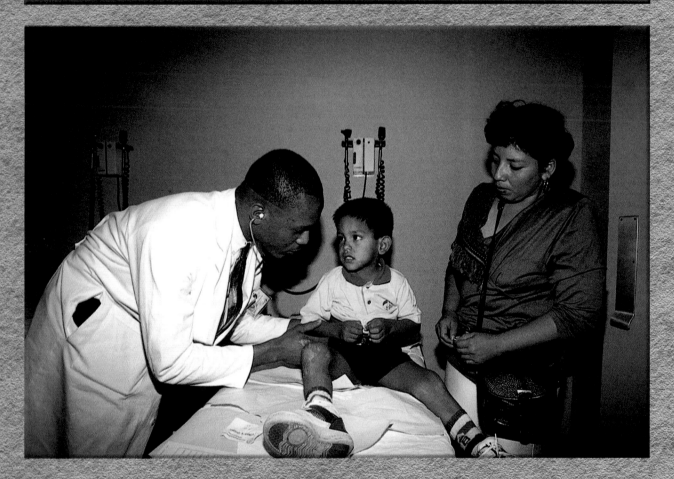

OBJECTIVES

Pronunciation
Pronunciation in context

Structure
The imperfect subjunctive • Uses of some prepositions after certain verbs • The present perfect subjunctive

Communication
You will learn vocabulary related to medical emergencies and visits to the doctor's office.

Problemas médicos

STUDENT AUDIO

SUGGESTION: Before students read the dialogues, ask them personalized questions based on body parts, illnesses, or injuries. Point to the parts of the body as you ask the questions. Write the results of this "survey" on the board and have the class decide if they are in good or bad health (**tiene buena o mala salud**).

1. **¿Te duele la pierna (el brazo, la cabeza)?**
2. **¿Te rompiste la pierna (el brazo, el pie) alguna vez?**
3. **¿Tienes dolores de cabeza con frecuencia?**
4. **¿Tienes catarro a menudo?**
5. **¿Te pusieron una inyección antitetánica el año pasado?**
6. **¿Te operaron alguna vez?**
7. **¿Eres alérgico(-a) a la penicilina?**

Mirta y su esposo se encuentran en un restaurante para almorzar. Ella no se siente muy bien hoy.

MIRTA —No sé qué me pasa. Tengo fiebre y me duele mucho la cabeza.[1] Ya tomé cuatro aspirinas.

HÉCTOR —Te dije que fueras al médico para que te hiciera un buen chequeo. Espero que ya hayas llamado al doctor Valdivia.

MIRTA —Él está de vacaciones. Teresa me sugirió que viera a la doctora Vargas. Tengo una cita para esta tarde.

Más tarde, en el consultorio de la doctora Vargas.

DOCTORA —Tiene una temperatura de ciento dos grados. ¿Cuánto tiempo hace que tiene esos dolores de cabeza?

MIRTA —Una semana. Tengo tos y me duele la garganta. ¿Cree que tengo catarro o gripe?

DOCTORA —Tiene gripe. Voy a recetarle un antibiótico. ¿Es Ud. alérgica a alguna medicina?

MIRTA —Sí. Soy alérgica a la penicilina.

DOCTORA —¿Está Ud. embarazada?

MIRTA —No, doctora.

DOCTORA —Tome estas pastillas cuatro veces al día. Empiece a tomarlas hoy mismo. Aquí tiene la receta.

En la sala de emergencia del mismo hospital. Oscar tuvo un accidente y lo trajeron al hospital en una ambulancia. Ahora está hablando con un médico.

MÉDICO —¿Qué le pasó?

OSCAR —Me atropelló un coche. Me duele mucho la pierna. Creo que me la rompí.

MÉDICO —Sí, temo que se la haya roto. Vamos a hacerle unas radiografías. Veo que también tiene una herida en el brazo. Voy a llamar a la enfermera.

Con la enfermera

ENFERMERA —El doctor me dijo que le desinfectara y le vendara la herida para evitar una infección. ¿Cuándo fue la última vez que le pusieron una inyección antitetánica?

OSCAR —Hace dos años.

La enfermera lleva a Oscar a la sala de rayos X. Oscar tiene la pierna rota y el médico se la enyesa.

MÉDICO —¿Hay alguien que pueda venir a buscarlo?

OSCAR —Sí, voy a llamar a mi compañero de cuarto, pero no creo que haya llegado a casa todavía.

---

[1]Note that definite articles, rather than possessive adjectives, are used in Spanish with parts of the body.

Vocabulario

Cognados

el accidente   accident
alérgico(-a)   allergic
la ambulancia   ambulance
el antibiótico   antibiotic

la aspirina   aspirin
la emergencia   emergency
la infección   infection
la inyección   injection, shot

la medicina   medicine
la penicilina   penicillin
la temperatura   temperature

Nombres

el brazo   arm
la cabeza   head
el catarro, resfriado, resfrío   cold
el chequeo, examen   checkup
el (la) compañero(-a) de cuarto
   roommate
el consultorio   doctor's office
el dolor   pain

— de cabeza   headache
la fiebre   fever
la garganta   throat
el grado   degree
la gripe   flu
la herida   wound
la inyección antitetánica   tetanus
   shot

la pastilla   pill
la pierna   leg
la radiografía   X-ray
la receta   prescription
la sala de emergencia   emergency
   room
la sala de rayos X   X-ray room
la tos   cough

Verbos

atropellar   to run over, hit
   someone (i.e., with a car)
buscar   to pick up, to get
desinfectar   to disinfect
doler[1] (o:ue)   to hurt, to ache
enyesar   to put in a cast

evitar   to avoid
recetar   to prescribe
romper(se), quebrar(se) (e:ie)   to
   break
vendar   to bandage

RELATED VOCABULARY: Other
vocabulary words you may want
to introduce are: **el cuerpo** *(body)*;
cuidarse *(take care of oneself)*; **el
jarabe** *(cough syrup)*; **las muletas**
(crutches); **la silla de ruedas**
(wheelchair); **la curita** *(adhesive
bandage)*; **tomarle la temperatura**
(take someone's temperature); **la
venda** *(bandage)*.

Adjetivos

embarazada   pregnant
médico(-a)   medical

52

SUGGESTION: Use Transparency 52 to
introduce the body parts. Point to parts
as you write the words on the board or
on the transparency with a water-
soluble marker.

Otras palabras y expresiones

al día   a day
hacer una radiografía   to take
   an X-ray
poner una inyección   to give an
   injection, a shot

todavía   yet
la última vez   the last time

---

[1]**Doler** has the same structure as **gustar: Me duele la cabeza.**

Vocabulario adicional
El cuerpo

1. el pelo, el cabello
2. el ojo
3. la nariz
4. los dientes
5. la lengua
6. la boca
7. la oreja
8. el oído

ACTIVITY SUGGESTION: See the *IAM* for an additional in-class activity: **¿Cómo respondes?**

9. la cabeza
10. la cara
11. el pecho
12. el estómago
13. la mano
14. la rodilla
15. el tobillo
16. el dedo del pie
17. el pie

18. el cuello
19. la espalda
20. el dedo

¡Conversemos!

FOLLOW-UP: Have students use the dialogues, questions, and responses as a guide and imagine they are medical students observing the care given to Mirta in the doctor's office and Oscar in the emergency room. They should write a brief report describing what happened to each patient.

Answer the following questions, basing your answers on the dialogues.

1. ¿Dónde se encuentran Mirta y su esposo, y por qué están allí?
2. ¿Qué problemas tiene Mirta?
3. ¿Qué espera Héctor que haya hecho Mirta?
4. ¿Qué le sugirió Teresa a Mirta?
5. ¿Por qué no le receta la doctora penicilina a Mirta?
6. ¿Cuántas veces al día tiene que tomar Mirta las pastillas?
7. ¿Qué le pasó a Oscar y dónde está ahora?
8. ¿Qué clase *(kind)* de accidente tuvo Oscar?
9. ¿Qué le dijo el médico a la enfermera?
10. ¿Cree Ud. que la enfermera le va a poner una inyección antitetánica a Oscar? ¿Por qué o por qué no?
11. ¿Adónde lleva la enfermera a Oscar y para qué?
12. ¿Qué le hace el médico a Oscar? ¿Por qué?

¿Lo sabía Ud.?

■ En la mayoría de los países de habla hispana, los hospitales son gratis *(free)* y subvencionados *(subsidized)* por el gobierno. Hay clínicas privadas para la gente de mejor posición económica que no quiere ir a un hospital público.

■ Especialmente en las grandes ciudades hispanas, la medicina está muy adelantada *(advanced)*, pero en muchos pueblos *(towns)* remotos no hay médicos ni hospitales. En ese caso, mucha gente recurre a *(turn to)* los servicios de un curandero *(healer)*. Muchas mujeres tienen sus bebés con la ayuda de una partera *(midwife)*.

■ En España y en algunos países latinoamericanos, las farmacias venden principalmente medicinas. En algunos países hispanos es posible comprar ciertas medicinas —como la penicilina —sin tener receta médica.

• En este país, ¿los hospitales son gratis?

• La mayoría de las mujeres de este país, ¿tienen su bebé en un hospital o en su casa, con la ayuda de una partera?

• ¿En este país se pueden comprar antibióticos sin receta médica?

Comprando medicinas en una farmacia de Humacao, Puerto Rico.

 INTERNET See the *¿Cómo se dice...?* Web site for activities on authentic cultural material: http://spanish.college.hmco.com/students

Pronunciación

 STUDENT AUDIO NOTE: To reinforce pronunciation practice, this section appears in Lessons 10 through 18. The sentences featured as pronunciation models are taken from the lesson dialogues.

SUGGESTION: For each sentence, first model the word(s) in boldface type and have the class repeat them chorally and individually. Then have students repeat the full sentence for pronunciation practice of the target expressions in context.

In this lesson, there are some new words or phrases that may be challenging to pronounce. For further pronunciation practice of Spanish sounds, listen to your instructor and repeat the following words and phrases.

1. ¿Es Ud. **alérgica** a alguna medicina?
2. Tuvo un accidente y lo trajeron al hospital en una **ambulancia.**
3. Veo que también tiene una **herida** en el brazo.
4. Me dijo que le **desinfectara** y le **vendara** la herida.
5. ¿Cuándo fue la última vez que le pusieron una **inyección antitetánica**?

Estructuras

1 The imperfect subjunctive   (El imperfecto de subjuntivo)

A. Forms

■ To form the imperfect subjunctive of all Spanish verbs—regular and irregular—drop the -**ron** ending of the third-person plural of the preterit and add the following endings to the stem.[1]

Imperfect Subjunctive Endings

-ra form

-ra	´-ramos
-ras	-rais
-ra	-ran

Forms of the Imperfect Subjunctive

Verb	Third-person plural preterit	Stem	First-person singular imperfect subjunctive
hablar	hablaron	habla-	hablara
aprender	aprendieron	aprendie-	aprendiera
vivir	vivieron	vivie-	viviera
dejar	dejaron	deja-	dejara
ir	fueron	fue-	fuera
saber	supieron	supie-	supiera
decir	dijeron	dije-	dijera
poner	pusieron	pusie-	pusiera
pedir	pidieron	pidie-	pidiera
estar	estuvieron	estuvie-	estuviera

ATENCIÓN   The **nosotros** form of the imperfect subjunctive always takes an accent on the vowel that precedes the **-ra** ending.

---

[1]A second form of the imperfect subjunctive ends in -se rather than -**ra: hablase, hablases, hablase, hablásemos, hablaseis, hablasen.** The two forms are interchangeable, but the -**ra** form is more commonly used.

práctica ••

Give the imperfect subjunctive forms of the following verbs.

1. yo: ganar, volver, pedir, decir, recibir
2. tú: ser, dormir, querer, dar, conocer
3. él: ir, estar, poner, conducir, servir
4. nosotros: saber, poder, regresar, conseguir, hacer
5. ellos: tener, recetar, comenzar, seguir, mentir

B. Uses

■ The imperfect subjunctive is used in a subordinate clause when the verb of the main clause is in the past and calls for the subjunctive.

—¿Qué te dijo el médico?	*"What did the doctor tell you?"*
—Me dijo que **comiera** menos.	*"He told me to eat less."*
—Yo esperaba que el profesor me **diera** una "A".	*"I was hoping that the professor would give me an A."*
—Bueno, yo te sugerí que **estudiaras** más.	*"Well, I suggested that you study more."*

■ When the verb of the main clause is in the present, but the subordinate clause refers to the past, the imperfect subjunctive is used.

—Es una lástima que no **fueras** al teatro ayer.	*"It's a pity that you didn't go to the theater yesterday."*
—No me sentía bien.	*"I wasn't feeling well."*

práctica ••

EXPANSION: Use Transparency 53 and have students describe what happened when Roberto went for a medical checkup yesterday.

A. Complete the following dialogues, using the imperfect subjunctive of the verbs given. Then act them out with a partner.

1. —¿Qué te dijo Roberto?
   —Me dijo que _____ (ir) al médico para que me _____ (hacer) un chequeo y me recomendó que _____ (ver) al Dr. Salgado.
2. —No fui al hospital porque no tenía coche.
   —¿Por qué no le pediste a alguien que te _____ (llevar)?
   —No había nadie que _____ (poder) llevarme a esa hora.
   —Pues yo te dije que me _____ (llamar) si me necesitabas.
3. —¿Fuiste al médico?
   —Sí, y me dijo que _____ (tomar) estas pastillas para el dolor de garganta y me sugirió que no _____ (hablar) mucho.
4. —¿Le dieron el trabajo a Sandra?
   —No, porque necesitaban una enfermera que _____ (saber) español.
   —Yo le dije que _____ (estudiar) español, pero no me hizo caso.

5. —Siento que tú no _____ (poder) venir a mi casa ayer.

—No me sentía bien... Yo le pedí a Ramón que te _____ (llamar) por teléfono y te _____ (decir) que yo estaba enferma.

—Pues yo esperaba que tú _____ (venir) con los niños.

B. Describe all the things your parents did and did not want you to do at college, using the cues provided and the imperfect subjunctive.

ACTIVITY SUGGESTION: See the *IAM* for an additional in-class activity: **¡Qué aguafiestas!**

Mis padres querían que yo...

1. *escribirles* todas las semanas
2. *llamarlos* por teléfono los domingos
3. *tomar* varias clases el primer semestre
4. *estudiar* mucho
5. *abrir* una cuenta corriente en el banco
6. *hacer* la tarea todos los días
7. *levantarme* temprano
8. *visitarlos* en las vacaciones

Mis padres no querían que yo...

1. *vivir* lejos de la universidad
2. *ir* a muchas fiestas
3. *comer* hamburguesas todos los días
4. *gastar* mucho
5. *pedirles* dinero extra todos los meses
6. *conducir* muy rápido
7. *olvidarme* de tomar la medicina
8. *acostarme* muy tarde

C. Compare your childhood and adolescence to those of a classmate by completing the following sentences.

1. Cuando yo era chico(-a), mis padres esperaban que yo...
2. Cuando yo era niño(-a), mi mamá no me permitía que...
3. Cuando yo estaba en la escuela primaria, mis maestros *(teachers)* querían que yo...
4. Cuando yo tenía diez años, quería que mis amigos...
5. Cuando yo estaba en la escuela secundaria, no quería que mi papá...
6. Cuando yo tenía dieciséis años, esperaba que mis padres...

2 Uses of some prepositions after certain verbs *(Usos de algunas preposiciones con ciertos verbos)*

In Spanish, some verbs are used with prepositions that have no equivalent to or are different from the ones used in English. The prepositions used most often are **a, de, con,** and **en.**

■ The preposition **a**

aprender a *to learn (how)*	**enseñar a** *to teach*
asistir a *to attend*	**invitar a** *to invite*
ayudar a *to help*	**ir a** *to go*
empezar (comenzar) a *to begin, to start*	**venir a** *to come*

—¿**Fuiste a** estudiar con Rafael?   *"Did you go to study with Rafael?"*

—Sí, **empezamos a** estudiar para el examen final.   *"Yes, we started to study for the final exam."*

—Yo quiero **aprender a** bailar bailes latinoamericanos.   *"I want to learn how to dance Latin American dances."*

—Yo te puedo **enseñar a** bailar.   *"I can teach you how to dance."*

■ The preposition **de**

acordarse de *to remember*	**enamorarse de** *to fall in love with*
alegrarse de *to be glad*	**olvidarse de** *to forget*

—No te **olvides de** llamar al médico.   *"Don't forget to call the doctor."*

—Bueno..., y tú, **acuérdate de** tomar las pastillas.   *"Okay . . . , and you, remember to take your pills."*

■ The preposition **con**

casarse con   *to marry, to get married to*
comprometerse con   *to get engaged to*
soñar (o:ue) con   *to dream about (of)*

—Teresa se **comprometió con** Antonio.   *"Teresa got engaged to Antonio."*

—Debe estar muy contenta. Siempre **soñó con** casarse **con** él.   *"She must be very happy. She always dreamed of marrying him."*

■ The preposition **en**

fijarse en   *to notice*
insistir en   *to insist on*
pensar en   *to think about*

—¿**En** que estás **pensando**?   *"What are you thinking about?"*

—Estoy **pensando en** la fiesta de Beatriz. Ella **insistió en** invitar a Pablo y él siempre causa problemas...   *"I am thinking about Beatriz's party. She insisted on inviting Pablo and he always causes problems . . ."*

práctica ....

A. Complete the following dialogues with the Spanish equivalent of the words in parentheses. Then act them out with a partner.

1. —¿_____ pedir la receta, Anita?   *(Did you remember)*
   —Sí, pero _____ dejarla en la farmacia.   *(I forgot)*

2. —¿Ángel te dijo que le dolía el estómago?
   —Sí, él _____ que lo llevara a la sala de emergencia.   *(he insisted on)*
3. —¿Dónde _____ poner inyecciones tu mamá?   *(did learn)*
   —En Cuba. Y también le _____ hacer radiografías.   *(they taught)*
4. —Luis _____ Raquel, pero ella nunca _____ él.
   (fell in love with / noticed)
   —No, ella _____ Ernesto.   *(married)*
5. —¡Hola, Luisa! _____ verte.   *(I'm glad)*
   —¡Hola! Vengo a _____ ir al cine.   *(to invite you)*
   —Ay, no puedo porque tengo que _____ la conferencia *(lecture)* de la Dra. Ruiz.   *(to attend)*

B. With a partner, take turns asking and answering questions about the people in the following situations.

1.

2.

3.

4.

5.

6.

C. With a partner discuss the following:

1. things you would like to learn to do or can teach others to do
2. what time you start to work and to study
3. what you always (never) remember to do and what you always (never) forget to do
4. what you dream about doing
5. what you insist on doing

3 The present perfect subjunctive *(El pretérito perfecto de subjuntivo)*

■ The present perfect subjunctive is formed with the present subjunctive of the auxiliary verb **haber** + *the past participle* of the main verb.

Present subjunctive of haber

haya	hayamos
hayas	hayáis
haya	hayan

Formation of the Present Perfect Subjunctive

yo	**haya cambiado**
tú	**hayas temido**
Ud. / él / ella	**haya salido**
nosotros(-as)	**hayamos hecho**
vosotros(-as)	**hayáis puesto**
Uds. / ellos / ellas	**hayan visto**

■ The present perfect subjunctive is used in the same way as the present perfect tense in English, but only in sentences that require the subjunctive in the subordinate clause. It is used to describe events that have ended prior to the time indicated in the main clause.

—Me alegro de que **hayas venido.** — *"I'm glad you have come."*
—Es una lástima que papá no **haya podido** venir conmigo. — *"It is a pity that Dad has not been able to come with me."*

—¿Hay alguien aquí que **haya estado** en Guadalajara? — *"Is there anyone here who has been in Guadalajara?"*
—No, no hay nadie que **haya viajado** a México. — *"No, there's no one who has travelled to Mexico."*

SUGGESTION: Write the following sentence builder on the board or on an overhead transparency. Have students form, orally or in writing, as many sentences as possible in three minutes, using the present perfect subjunctive.

Me alegro de que / Es posible que / No creo que / Espero que / Siento que / Ojalá que

mis amigos(-as) / el (la) profesor(-a) / tú / mi(s) padre(s) / mi novio(-a)

aprobar todos los cursos / terminar el examen de… / comprar un coche nuevo / poder obtener trabajo / no estar enfermo(-a) / tener tiempo para… / ir de vacaciones / ver… en la televisión

práctica

A. Complete the following dialogues, using the present perfect subjunctive forms of the verbs listed. Then act them out with a partner.

morir   tener   tomar   poner   decir   llevar   ir

1. —Rafael se cortó la rodilla. Espero que el médico le _____ una inyección antitetánica.
   —Yo dudo que él _____ al médico.
2. —¿Ana ha traído las pastillas?
   —No creo que ella _____ tiempo de ir a la farmacia.

3. —Ha habido un accidente en la calle Lima.
   —Ojalá que no _____ nadie.
4. —¿Tú dices que Marta está embarazada?
   —No es verdad que yo _____ eso.
5. —Yo creo que Alberto se ha roto una pierna.
   —Espero que sus hermanos lo _____ a la sala de emergencia.
6. —Mamá no cree que nosotros _____ la medicina.
   —Es que Uds. nunca hacen lo que ella les dice.

B. Express your own feelings and those of the people mentioned, using the present perfect subjunctive.

1. Yo espero que el médico...
2. Ojalá que mis padres...
3. Es una lástima que la enfermera...
4. Mis padres no creen que yo...
5. No es verdad que mis amigos...
6. Me alegro mucho de que Ud....
7. Yo siento que mi compañero de cuarto...
8. Mi profesor siente que los estudiantes...

C. With a partner, prepare two questions to ask your classmates about their life experiences and what they have done. Use the present perfect subjunctive and always begin with "¿Hay alguien aquí que...?"

¡A ver cuánto aprendió!

INTERNET

See the ¿Cómo se dice...? Web site for additional grammar and vocabulary practice: http://spanish.college. hmco.com/students

¡Repase el vocabulario!

A. Say whether the following statements are logical or not. If a statement is not logical, give one that is.

1. En serio, los muchachos vinieron a esquiar en una ambulancia.
2. Cuando tengo dolor de estómago voy al médico.
3. Si necesito una radiografía voy al aeropuerto.

ACTIVITY SUGGESTION: Do ¡**Escucha!**, the in-class listening comprehension activity that reviews vocabulary and grammar structures introduced in the lesson. It appears in the answer key of the *IAM*.

ACTIVITY SUGGESTION: See the *IAM* for an additional in-class activity: **Palabras escondidas.**

EXPANSION: Have students, working in pairs or groups, write a description of the scene in Transparency 54.

4. Me vendaron la herida.
5. Tiene fiebre. Tiene una temperatura de ciento tres grados.
6. Algunas personas son alérgicas a la penicilina.
7. Las orejas sirven para planchar.
8. La aspirina es un antibiótico.
9. La lengua está en la boca.
10. La rodilla es parte de la cara.
11. Tenemos treinta dedos.
12. Necesitamos la nariz para caminar.
13. Para hacerle una radiografía, debemos ir a la sala de rayos X.
14. Roberto está embarazado.
15. Está enferma. Debe ir al consultorio del médico.
16. Cada vez que tengo dolor de cabeza tomo dos aspirinas.
17. Lo atropelló una bolsa de dormir en el mar.
18. Fuimos de pesca a la sala de emergencia y nos divertimos mucho.

B.   Name all the parts of the body numbered below.

Entrevista

ACTIVITY SUGGESTION: See the *IAM* for additional in-class activities: **Para conocernos mejor** and **Una encuesta.**

With a partner, interview each other by asking the following questions.

1. ¿Cómo te sientes hoy?
2. ¿Te duelen los oídos? (¿la garganta?)
3. ¿Qué haces cuando te duele la cabeza?

4. Si te duele el estómago, ¿qué tomas?
5. ¿Cuándo fue la última vez que te hicieron un chequeo?
6. ¿Eres alérgico a alguna medicina? (¿A cuál?)
7. ¿Te hicieron radiografías del pecho alguna vez?
8. ¿Te han puesto una inyección antitetánica alguna vez? (¿Cuándo?)
9. ¿Qué medicina tomas cuando tienes tos?
10. ¿Has tenido un accidente alguna vez? (¿Cuándo?)
11. ¿Te has roto una pierna (un brazo) alguna vez?
12. ¿Vas al médico frecuentemente?

Situaciones

ACTIVITY SUGGESTION: See the *IAM* for an additional in-class activity: **Problemas médicos.**

What would you say in the following situations? What might the other person say? Act out the scenes with a partner. Take turns playing each role.

1. A friend wants you to go to the store with him or her. You can't go, for the following reasons: you've just taken two aspirins because you have a headache, your little brother cut his hand and you have to disinfect the wound.
2. You have had an accident and are in the emergency room, talking to the doctor. You need something for the pain.
3. You are at the doctor's office because you started having headaches three days ago. The doctor wants to know whether you are allergic to any medications.

Para escribir

Write a note to your instructor, explaining that you cannot take an exam because you are sick. Describe your symptoms.

En la vida real

CD-ROM

Do the interactive exercises on the CD-ROM for additional practice.

SUGGESTION: Have students prepare a report on the "patient's" medical history as a writing activity.

Llenando una hoja clínica

With a partner, play the role of a health care worker who is taking the history of a new patient. Refer to the list of words and phrases on pages 416–417. Be as thorough as possible in obtaining both personal information (such as date of birth, family history, childhood experiences, education, and marital status) and medical data (including illnesses, accidents, and surgeries, and how long ago the patient had them; allergies; and any general pains the patient is currently suffering) for the patient's permanent file. Write down his or her responses. When you have finished, switch roles with your partner.

Here are some words and phrases you might want to use:

la amigdalitis	*tonsilitis*	nacer	*to be born*
la apendicitis	*appendicitis*	la operación	*surgery*
el asma	*asthma*	las paperas	*mumps*
la bronquitis	*bronchitis*	la presión arterial	*blood pressure*
las enfermedades de la niñez		la pulmonía	*pneumonia*
	childhood diseases	el sarampión	*measles*
el mareo	*dizziness, dizzy spell*	la varicela	*chicken pox*

Buenos consejos

What advice from this list would you give to the people below?

Buenos consejos para conservar la salud[1]

Debe
- ✔ comer más vegetales y frutas
- ✔ dormir lo suficiente
- ✔ visitar al médico periódicamente
- ✔ hacer ejercicio
- ✔ consumir menos calorías
- ✔ aprender a relajarse
- ✔ evitar la tensión (*stress*)
- ✔ pensar positivamente
- ✔ tener una dieta balanceada
- ✔ controlar su peso (*weight*)

No debe
- ✗ fumar
- ✗ consumir mucho alcohol
- ✗ consumir mucha sal o azúcar
- ✗ usar drogas
- ✗ comer mucha grasa
- ✗ trabajar en exceso

1. El Sr. Vega toma diez cervezas todos los días.
2. La Srta. Díaz está siempre sentada, mirando la televisión.
3. Elsa come muchos dulces *(sweets)*.
4. El Dr. Álvarez trabaja catorce horas cada día.
5. La Sra. Carreras duerme sólo cuatro horas cada noche.
6. Estela se preocupa constantemente por todo.
7. Adela siempre come papas fritas, hamburguesas, mantequilla, pollo frito, etc.
8. Hace cinco años que Carlos no va a ver a su médico.
9. La dieta de Eduardo es de 5.000 calorías al día.
10. Raúl pesa *(weighs)* 300 libras *(pounds)*.
11. Raquel solamente come carne y pastas.
12. A Jorge le gustan mucho los cigarrillos.

[1]*health*

¡VAMOS A LEER!

Antes de leer

A. Reading a poem is different from reading a story or an essay. The poet often uses words in original ways to express his or her feelings. Visualizing the words or images in a poem will help you better understand the feelings or message the poet is conveying. Think about the following words from the poems you are going to read. What feelings do they convey?

arte	*art*	**carbón**	*coal*
monte	*mountains*	**pena**	*sorrow*
joya	*jewel*	**esclavo**	*slave*
diamante	*diamond*	**oscuro**	*dark*
luz	*light*	**sol**	*sun*

B. As you read the introduction to Martí, and the poems, answer the following questions.

1. ¿En que año nació *(was born)* el poeta?
2. ¿Dónde y en qué año murió?
3. ¿Cuáles son los temas principales de la poesía de Martí?
4. ¿De dónde viene el poeta y adónde va?
5. ¿Cómo se describe el poeta?
6. ¿Qué es más importante para el poeta: la amistad *(friendship)* o el amor?
7. ¿Con qué compara Martí a un amigo sincero?
8. ¿Qué dice el poeta del diamante?
9. Teniendo en cuenta la biografía de Martí, ¿por qué cree Ud. que él dice que es hijo de un pueblo esclavo?
10. ¿Cómo dice Martí que quiere salir del mundo?
11. Según el poeta, ¿cómo mueren los traidores?
12. ¿Cómo dice Martí que morirá él y por qué?

JOSÉ MARTÍ
(CUBA: 1853–1895)

José Martí dedicó su vida y su obra a la independencia de Cuba, donde murió en el campo de batalla° en 1895. Es famoso no sólo como poeta y ensayista, sino también como orador.

campo... *battlefield*

Los poemas de Martí se caracterizan por la melodía, el ritmo y el uso de frases cortas, con las que expresa ideas muy profundas. Sus temas principales son la libertad, la justicia, la independencia de su patria y la defensa de los pobres y de los oprimidos.

De *Versos sencillos*
I

Yo vengo de todas partes°,
y hacia todas partes voy:
arte soy entre las artes,
y en los montes, monte soy.

todas... *everywhere*

Si dicen que del joyero
tome la joya mejor
tomo a un amigo sincero
y pongo a un lado el amor.

Todo es hermoso y constante,
todo es música y razón,°   *reason*
y todo, como el diamante,
antes que luz es carbón.

Oculto° en mi pecho bravo   *I hide*
la pena que me lo hiere°:   *hurts*
el hijo de un pueblo° esclavo   *people*
vive por él, calla° y muere.   *is silent*

XXIII

Yo quiero salir del mundo
por la puerta natural:
en un carro° de hojas° verdes   *carriage / leaves*
a morir me han de llevar°.   **han...** *will take*

No me pongan en lo oscuro
a morir como un traidor:
¡yo soy bueno, y como bueno
moriré de cara al sol!

Díganos

Answer the following questions based on your own thoughts and experiences.

1. ¿Le gusta a Ud. la poesía?
2. ¿Quién es su poeta favorito(-a)?
3. ¿Conoce Ud. otros poetas hispanos? ¿Cuáles?
4. ¿Cuál es la "mejor joya" para Ud.?
5. Para Martí todo es hermoso y constante, ¿cree Ud. lo mismo?

ASÍ SOMOS

VIDEO

CD-ROM

Do the interactive exercises on
the CD-ROM for additional practice.

NARRADORA	—¿Cuándo fue la última vez que Ud. visitó al médico?
MIRIAM	—La última vez que fui al médico fue porque tuve una infección del estómago. Eh... Bueno, fui a la playa y no sé qué fue lo que comí, a lo mejor pescado *(fish)* o algo así y me cayó mal *(it made me sick)* y estuve muy mal, muy delicada del estómago.

Preparación

NOTE: The video-related vocabulary is listed in the *Instructor's Activities Manual* for your reference. Its purpose is to facilitate students' comprehension. You may want to distribute the vocabulary to the class before viewing.

NOTE: See the Instructor's Edition frontmatter for additional suggestions on implementing video in the classroom.

SUGGESTION: Have students brainstorm words or phrases to describe health and medical care. Point out the numerous cognates in medical terminology, such as **clínica, cardiología, dermatología, ortopedia, pediatría, psiquiatría, ultrasonido,** etc.

A. Mente sana en cuerpo sano. Answer the following questions about your healthy habits. You will hear answers to some of these questions when you watch the video. After viewing the video, compare your answers with those you hear.

1. ¿Qué hace Ud. para conservar la salud?
2. ¿Cuándo fue la última vez que Ud. visitó al médico?
3. ¿Qué tipo de comida come Ud.?
4. ¿Qué tipo de ejercicio o deporte practica Ud.?

B. La asistencia médica. With a partner, answer the following questions about the state of healthcare in your country. You will hear answers to some of these questions when you watch the video. After viewing the video, compare your answers with those you hear.

1. ¿Qué tipo de asistencia médica hay en su país?
2. ¿Qué opina Ud. de la asistencia médica en su país?
3. ¿Cómo son los médicos?
4. ¿Cómo son los hospitales?

Comprensión

SUGGESTION: Pause the video after each interview segment so students have time to complete the corresponding comprehension activity.

A. Para conservar la salud. Select the word or phrase that best completes each statement.

1. Alejandro hace mucho (ejercicio, alimentos).
2. Otmara no come (frutas, carnes rojas).
3. Juan no (consume drogas, toma mucha agua).
4. Miriam sale a (caminar, comer) en los parques.
5. El doctor Brambilla habla de (las reglas universales, los aspectos sociales) de la salud.

B. **¿Quién lo dijo?** Match each statement with the name of the person who said it.

_____ 1. Tuve hepatitis A y me hicieron exámenes médicos.
_____ 2. Tuve un examen de la vista y me pusieron lentes *(eyeglasses)*.
_____ 3. Tuve una infección del estómago.
_____ 4. Tuve amigdalitis *(tonsilitis)* y el médico me dio tratamiento *(treatment)*.

a. Miriam
b. Jaime
c. Otmara
d. Alejandro

C. **¿Verdadero o falso?** Read the following statements. Circle **V** (**Verdadero**) or **F** (**Falso**) according to what you understood from the video. If a statement is false, correct it.

V   F   1. La gente trabajadora no recibe asistencia médica en El Salvador.
V   F   2. En el país de Otmara, el Seguro Social es para la gente que trabaja.
V   F   3. En el país de Otmara, el Seguro Social no incluye las medicinas.
V   F   4. En el país de María, sólo las personas que trabajan tienen Seguridad Social.

SUGGESTION: In groups, have students compare what the people say about health and medical care in the video with their own views and health-related experiences.

D. **¿Qué opinan?** Select the word or phrase that best completes each statement.

1. Según Leonardo, los hospitales de su país son muy (buenos, malos).
2. Según Juan, la gente pobre necesita (comida, asistencia médica) en Nicaragua.
3. Según la doctora González, la preparación de los médicos en su país es (mala, buena).
4. En la clínica donde trabaja la doctora, hay carencia *(shortages)* de (médicos, medicinas).

E. **Entrevista.** Select the word or phrase that best completes each statement.

1. En la clínica de la Dra. González ofrecen (veinte, veintiún, treinta) servicios.
2. La Dra. González menciona los servicios en especialidades como (cardiología, hematología).
3. El (gabinete [*room*] de rayos equis [*X-ray*], servicio de farmacia) es importante en la evaluación de los pacientes *(patients)*.
4. En la clínica tienen un gabinete de (ultrasonido, servicio de psiquiatría).

Ampliación

A. **Para conservar mejor la salud.** Make a list in Spanish of the things you need to do to get in better shape. Assign deadlines by which to accomplish the items on your list. Then in groups of three or four, compare your lists. Determine who has the healthiest lifestyle now, and who will have the healthiest lifestyle after accomplishing their lists.

B. **Cuando fui al médico...** Interview a classmate about the last time he or she visited the doctor's office. Use the following questions as a guide.

1. ¿Cuándo fue la última vez que visitaste al médico?
2. ¿Por qué fuiste al médico?
3. ¿Fuiste a la sala de emergencia, al consultorio del médico o a una clínica?
4. ¿Qué tipo de tratamiento te dio el médico?

¡Este coche no sirve!

Lección

18

OBJECTIVES

Pronunciation
Pronunciation in context

Structure
The pluperfect subjunctive • *If* clauses • Summary of the uses of the subjunctive

Communication
You will learn vocabulary related to automobiles, including going to a service station and dealing with road emergencies.

¡Este coche no sirve!

STUDENT
AUDIO

SUGGESTION: Refer students to
Panorama hispánico 5 and the corresponding video segment for more
information about Costa Rica.

*Gloria y Julio, una pareja de recién casados, están de vacaciones en Costa
Rica. Ahora están en la carretera, camino a San José.*

GLORIA —Julio, ¡estás manejando muy rápido! La velocidad máxima
es de noventa kilómetros por hora. ¡Si te ve un policía, te
va a poner una multa!

JULIO —No te preocupes. ¿Dónde estamos? ¿Tú tienes el mapa?

GLORIA —Está en el portaguantes pero, según ese letrero, estamos a
cuarenta kilómetros de San José.

JULIO —¿Hay una gasolinera cerca? El tanque está casi vacío.

GLORIA —Es una lástima que no hayas llenado el tanque antes…

JULIO —Si me lo hubieras dicho antes, lo habría hecho.

GLORIA —¡Hablas como si yo tuviera la culpa!

JULIO —*(Bromeando)* ¿Y a quién voy a culpar? Mira, allí hay una
estación de servicio…

Julio para en la estación de servicio para comprar gasolina.

JULIO —*(Al empleado)* Llene el tanque, por favor. Además, ¿podría
revisar el aceite y las llantas?

EMPLEADO —Sí, señor.

JULIO —Ayer tuve un pinchazo y cuando fui al taller, el mecánico
me dijo que necesitaba neumáticos nuevos.

EMPLEADO —Sí, si yo fuera usted, los cambiaría… y también compraría
un acumulador nuevo.

GLORIA —¡Ay, Julio! El mecánico también te dijo que arreglaras los
frenos e instalaras una bomba de agua nueva.

JULIO —Haremos todo eso en San José, si es necesario.

GLORIA —¿No dijiste que también cambiarías el filtro del aceite y
que comprarías limpiaparabrisas nuevos?

JULIO —Si yo hubiera sabido que íbamos a tener tantos problemas,
habría comprado un coche nuevo antes de salir de viaje.

GLORIA —Sí, porque vamos a gastar una fortuna en arreglos.

JULIO —¡Y ayer el motor estaba haciendo un ruido extraño…!

SUGGESTION: Have students briefly
skim the dialogue and make a list of all
the problems Gloria and Julio have
with their car. Enlist the help of students with mechanical expertise to
decide if each of the problems
requires: **una reparación mayor /
difícil / costosa** or **una reparación
sin importancia / fácil / barata.**
    Then have students tell the class
about one or two problems they or a
friend have had with a car in the past
few months.

SUGGESTION: Have students act out
the dialogue in groups of three.

Cuando Julio trata de arrancar, el coche no funciona.

JULIO —¡Ay, no! Tendremos que llamar una grúa para remolcar el
coche hasta San José.

GLORIA —No vale la pena. Yo lo dejaría aquí.

JULIO —¡Estoy de acuerdo contigo! Si yo pudiera, compraría un
coche nuevo ahora mismo.

Vocabulario

Cognados

el filtro filter
la gasolina gasoline
el kilómetro kilometer
el mecánico mechanic

el motor motor, engine
necesario(-a) necessary
el tanque tank

Nombres

el acumulador, la batería battery
el arreglo repair
la bomba de agua water pump
el camino road
la carretera highway
la culpa blame, fault
el freno brake
la gasolinera, la estación de servicio gas (service) station
la grúa, el remolcador tow truck

el letrero sign
el limpiaparabrisas windshield wiper
la multa fine, ticket
el neumático, la llanta, la goma tire
la pareja couple (people)
el policía police officer
el portaguantes, la guantera glove compartment

los recién casados newlyweds
el ruido noise
el taller (de mecánica) repair shop
la velocidad speed

RELATED VOCABULARY: Other vocabulary words you may want to introduce are: **la bujía** *(sparkplug)*; **la camioneta** *(station wagon/van)*; **el exceso de velocidad** *(speeding)*; **los guardafangos / guardabarros** *(fenders)*; **el parachoques** *(bumper)*; **el ventilador** *(fan)*.

Verbos

arrancar to start (a car)
arreglar to repair, to fix
culpar to blame

funcionar to work, to function
instalar to install
parar to stop

remolcar to tow
revisar, chequear to check

Adjetivos

extraño(-a) strange
vacío(-a) empty

Otras palabras y expresiones

ahora mismo right now
camino a... on the way to . . .
casi almost
como si as if
estar de acuerdo to agree
no sirve it's no good

(no) vale la pena it's (not) worth the trouble
poner (dar) una multa to give a ticket (fine)
rápido fast, rapidly
salir de viaje to leave on a trip

según according to
tener la culpa to be one's fault
tener un pinchazo to have a flat tire
velocidad máxima speed limit

Vocabulario adicional
En el taller de mecánica

SUGGESTION: Use Transparency 55 to introduce the vocabulary.

Para hablar del coche

automático(-a) automatic	Yo prefiero un coche **automático.**
la autopista freeway, highway	En California hay muchas **autopistas.**
la bocina horn	Aquí está prohibido tocar la **bocina.**
la bolsa de aire air bag	Este coche tiene dos **bolsas de aire.**
el carburador carburetor	El mecánico revisó el **carburador.**
de cambios mecánicos standard shift	No sé conducir un coche **de cambios mecánicos.**
descompuesto(-a) out of order, not working	No pude usar el coche porque estaba **descompuesto.**
lleno(-a) full	El tanque está **lleno.**
la milla mile	La velocidad máxima es de 65 **millas** por hora.
la pieza de repuesto spare part	¿Se venden **piezas de repuesto** aquí?
el teléfono celular cellular phone	Tengo un **teléfono celular** en el coche.

ACTIVITY SUGGESTION: See the *IAM* for an additional in-class activity: **¿Cómo respondes?**

¡Conversemos!

Answer the following questions, basing your answers on the dialogue.

1. ¿Quiénes están en la carretera y adónde van?
2. ¿Cuál es la velocidad máxima en la carretera?
3. Julio está manejando muy rápido. ¿Qué va a pasar si un policía lo ve?

4. Según el letrero, ¿a qué distancia están Julio y Gloria de San José?
5. ¿Por qué necesitan ir a una gasolinera?
6. ¿Tiene el tanque mucha gasolina?
7. ¿Qué cosas hace el empleado de la gasolinera?
8. ¿Qué le pasó al coche de Julio ayer y qué le dijo el mecánico que necesitaba?
9. ¿Está de acuerdo el empleado con el mecánico?
10. ¿Qué otros problemas tiene el coche?
11. ¿Cree Gloria que va a costar mucho dinero arreglar el coche?
12. ¿Qué haría Julio si pudiera?

¿Lo sabía Ud.?

■ En las grandes ciudades como Madrid, Caracas, la Ciudad de México y Buenos Aires, hay muchísimos automóviles y autobuses, lo cual *(which)* está causando graves problemas de contaminación del aire *(smog)*. Sin embargo, en muchas zonas rurales de los países hispanos, particularmente en Hispanoamérica, hay muy pocos automóviles, ya que no hay carreteras, o las que existen están en muy malas condiciones.

■ En la mayoría de los países hispanos, la gasolina y los automóviles son mucho más caros que en los Estados Unidos. Por esta razón es muy popular la motocicleta, especialmente entre la gente joven.

■ En los países hispanos, se usa el sistema métrico decimal. Un kilómetro equivale a 0,6 millas; un galón equivale a 3,8 litros.

• ¿En qué ciudades de este país hay mucha contaminación del aire?

• ¿Qué medio de transporte prefiere usar la gente joven en la ciudad donde Ud. vive?

See the *¿Cómo se dice…?* Web site for activities on authentic cultural material: http://spanish.college.hmco.com/students

INTERNET

Congestión de tráfico en San José, Costa Rica.

Pronunciación

**STUDENT
AUDIO**

NOTE: To reinforce pronunciation
practice, this section appears in
Lessons 10 through 18. The sentences
featured as pronunciation models are
taken from the lesson dialogues.

SUGGESTION: For each sentence, first
model the word(s) in boldface type and have the class repeat them chorally
and individually. Then have students repeat the full sentence for pronunciation practice of the target expressions in context.

In this lesson, there are some new words or phrases that may be challenging to
pronounce. For further pronunciation practice of Spanish sounds, listen to your
instructor and repeat the following words and phrases.

1. La **velocidad máxima** es de noventa kilómetros por hora.
2. Si me lo **hubieras dicho** antes, lo **habría hecho.**
3. El **mecánico** me dijo que necesitaba **neumáticos** nuevos.
4. Dijiste que comprarías **limpiaparabrisas** nuevos.
5. Tendremos que llamar una **grúa** para **remolcar** el coche.

Estructuras

1 The pluperfect subjunctive   *(El pluscuamperfecto de subjuntivo)*

■ The pluperfect subjunctive is formed with the imperfect subjunctive of the
auxiliary verb **haber** + *the past participle* of the main verb. It is used in the
same way that the past perfect is used in English, but only in sentences in
which the main clause calls for the subjunctive.

Imperfect subjunctive of haber

hubiera	hubiéramos
hubieras	hubierais
hubiera	hubieran

Formation of the Pluperfect Subjunctive

yo	**hubiera hablado**
tú	**hubieras comido**
Ud. él ella	**hubiera vivido**
nosotros(-as)	**hubiéramos visto**
vosotros(-as)	**hubierais hecho**
Uds. ellos ellas	**hubieran vuelto**

—Yo me alegré de que ellos
hubieran vendido el coche.
—Sí, porque no servía para nada.

*"I was glad that they had sold
the car."*
"Yes, because it was no good."

—¿No había nadie que **hubiera
visto** esa película?
—Sí, Eva la había visto ya.

*"Wasn't there anybody who had
seen that movie?"*
"Yes, Eva had already seen it."

práctica

A. Say what your mother had expected everyone in the family to do by the time she got home yesterday.

MODELO: Aída / planchar la ropa
*Mamá esperaba que Aída **hubiera planchado** la ropa.*

Mamá esperaba que…

1. yo / hacer la comida
2. Quique / lavar el coche
3. nosotros / llevar a Raulito a la escuela
4. tú / escribirle a tío Carlos
5. Uds. / devolver los libros a la biblioteca
6. Eva y Luis / comprar la batería
7. Irma / poner la mesa
8. Eva y yo / pasarle la aspiradora a la alfombra
9. Daniel / llevar el coche al taller
10. Jorge y yo / cambiar las llantas

B. Say that you doubted that the following things had occurred.

MODELO: Carlos / venir muy tarde
Yo dudaba que Carlos hubiera venido muy tarde.

1. Pepe / arreglar los frenos
2. tú / salir de viaje
3. mis amigos / poder cambiar el filtro
4. el policía / ponerles una multa
5. nosotros / tener la culpa
6. el mecánico / conseguir las piezas de repuesto
7. Uds. / venir ayer
8. Irma / comprar un coche con bolsas de aire

C. With a partner, take turns deciding how the people mentioned reacted to the following. Always use the pluperfect subjunctive.

MODELO: Yo había comprado un coche nuevo. (Mis padres)
Mis padres se alegraron de (lamentaron) que yo hubiera comprado un coche nuevo.

1. Los recién casados se habían ido a Costa Rica.   (La madre del muchacho)
2. El mecánico había revisado el coche.   (Tú)
3. Ella había conducido el coche a cien millas por hora.   (El esposo de Elsa)
4. Carlos había tenido que llamar una grúa.   (Yo)

5. Nosotros habíamos decidido no arreglar el coche.   (El mécanico)
6. El policía le había puesto una multa a mi hermano.   (Mis padres)
7. Ellos habían llevado el coche al taller de mecánica.   (Nosotros)
8. Tú habías cambiado la llanta.   (Tu amigo)

2 If clauses *(Cláusulas con si)*

SUGGESTION: Write the following sentence builder on the board or on an overhead transparency. Have students tell, orally or in writing, what they or their friends would do if they followed certain careers. Remind them that they should use the imperfect subjunctive in the **si** clause and the conditional in the main clause.

Si yo fuera actriz, viajaría por todo el mundo.

Si

mi amigo(-a) / tú / mi compañe-ro(-a) de cuarto / mi novio(-a) / mi hermano(-a)

actor, actriz / cantante / médico(-a) / psicólogo(-a) / profesor(-a) / arquitecto(-a) / escritor(-a) / científico(-a) / comerciante

hacer / tener / trabajar / participar / viajar / escribir / necesitar / ganar / especializarse en / estar

■ In Spanish, the imperfect subjunctive is used in *if* clauses when a contrary-to-fact statement is made.

—Si **tuviera** dinero, compraría la batería hoy.
—Usa tu tarjeta de crédito...

"If I had money, I would buy the battery today."
"Use your credit card..."

■ Note that the imperfect subjunctive is used in the *if* clause and the conditional is used in the main clause. When a statement expresses a contrary-to-fact situation in the past, the pluperfect subjunctive is used in the *if* clause and the conditional perfect is used in the main clause.

—No pude comprar el coche.
—**Si hubieras ahorrado** tu dinero, habrías podido comprarlo.

"I wasn't able to buy the car."
"If you had saved your money, you would have been able to buy it."

■ The imperfect subjunctive is also used in *if* clauses that express an unlikely fact, or simply the Spanish equivalent of the English *if . . . were to . . .*

—Si Raúl me **invitara** a salir con él, aceptaría.
—No creo que te invite...

"If Raúl were to ask me to go out with him, I would accept."
"I don't think he'll ask you . . . "

■ The imperfect subjunctive is also used after the expression **como si** *(as if)*.

—Pepe se compró otro coche.
—Ese hombre gasta dinero **como si fuera** millonario.

"Pepe bought himself another car."
"That man spends money as if he were a millionaire."

■ When an *if* clause refers to something that is possible or likely to happen, the indicative is used.

—¿Me vas a comprar los zapatos?
—Si **tengo** dinero, te los compro.

"Are you going to buy me the shoes?"
"If I have money, I'll buy them for you."

ATENCIÓN   The present subjunctive is *never* used in an *if* clause.

National CarRental.

" CON NOSOTROS OBTENGA LOS MEJORES BENEFICIOS "

10 % DE DESCUENTO

Calle 100 No. 14 - 46   812 5610 - 812 5635

práctica

ACTIVITY SUGGESTION: See the *IAM* for an additional in-class activity: **¿Una promesa o una excusa?**

A. Interview a classmate, using the following questions.

1. Si tuvieras un pinchazo, ¿tratarías de cambiar la llanta?
2. ¿Qué harías si los frenos de tu coche no funcionaran?
3. ¿Qué haces si tu coche no arranca?
4. Si tu coche hubiera estado descompuesto, ¿cómo habrías venido a la universidad hoy?
5. Si el tanque de tu coche estuviera casi vacío, ¿a qué gasolinera irías?
6. Si no quieres que te pongan una multa, ¿a qué velocidad debes manejar en la autopista?
7. Si el arreglo de tu coche costara mil dólares, ¿podrías pagarlo?
8. ¿Qué harías si alguien te dejara una fortuna?
9. ¿Qué harías si tuvieras que comprar un coche nuevo?
10. Si tu mejor amigo(-a) quiere usar tu coche, ¿se lo prestas?

B. Say what the following people are going to do, would do, or would have done according to each situation.

> MODELO: María quiere comprar ropa, pero no tiene dinero.
> *Si María tuviera dinero compraría ropa.*

1. Yo no estudié mucho el semestre pasado y mi promedio fue de "C".
2. Teresa quiere ir al cine, pero no tiene tiempo.
3. Nosotros necesitamos comprar un coche nuevo. Es posible que tengamos suficiente dinero.
4. Juan quiere que yo le dé la dirección de Pedro, pero yo no la sé.
5. Mi madre quería que yo fuera contador, pero no me gustaban las matemáticas.
6. Tú quieres estudiar para programador(-a), pero no tienes computadora. Es posible que tus padres te regalen una.
7. Yo habría llevado a Marta al estadio, pero tuve que trabajar.
8. Nosotros habríamos hablado con el profesor, pero él no estaba en la universidad hoy.

C. With a partner, take turns asking each other what you would do or what would happen if the following were true.

> MODELO: tener mucho dinero
> —¿Qué harías tú si tuvieras mucho dinero?
> —*Si yo tuviera mucho dinero, compraría mucha ropa.*

1. necesitar dinero
2. perder tus tarjetas de crédito
3. tener más tiempo libre
4. enseñar esta clase
5. querer aprender otro idioma
6. poder viajar a cualquier país
7. dar una gran fiesta
8. estar cansado(-a)
9. no sentirse bien
10. llover a cántaros

3 Summary of the uses of the subjunctive   *(Resumen de los usos del subjuntivo)*

- Use the subjunctive . . .

  a. After verbs of volition (when there is change of subject).

     Yo quiero que **él salga.**

  b. After verbs of emotion (when there is change of subject).

     Me alegro de que **tú estés** aquí.

- Use the subjunctive . . .

  a. To express doubt, denial, and disbelief.

     Dudo que **pueda** venir.
     Niego que él **esté** aquí.
     No creo que él **vaya** con Eva.

  b. To refer to the indefinite or non-existent.

     Busco una casa que **sea** cómoda.
     No había nadie que lo **supiera.**

  c. With certain conjunctions when referring to a future action.[1]

     Lo **llamaré** cuando **llegue.**

  d. In an *if* clause, to refer to something contrary-to-fact or to something impossible or very improbable.

     Si **pudiera,** iría.
     Si el presidente me **invitara** a la Casa Blanca, yo aceptaría.

- Use the infinitive . . .

  a. After verbs of volition (when there is no change of subject).

     Yo quiero **salir.**

  b. After verbs of emotion (when there is no change of subject).

     Me alegro de **estar** aquí.

- Use the indicative . . .

  a. When there is no doubt, denial, or disbelief.

     No dudo que **puede** venir.
     No niego que él **está** aquí.
     Creo que él **va** con Eva.

  b. To refer to something specific.

     Tengo una casa que **es** cómoda.
     Había alguien que lo **sabía.**

  c. With certain conjunctions when there is no indication of future action.

     Lo **llamo** cuando **llego.**

  d. In an *if* clause, when not referring to anything that is contrary-to-fact, impossible, or very improbable.

     Si **puedo,** iré.
     Si Juan me **invita** a su casa, aceptaré.

práctica •••

SUGGESTION: Use Transparency 56 to review the use of the subjunctive vs. the infinitive and the subjunctive vs. the indicative.

A. Complete the following dialogue, using the subjunctive, indicative, or infinitive of the verbs given, and act it out with a partner.

—¿Qué vas a hacer cuando _____ (llegar) a tu casa?
—Yo quiero _____ (estudiar) para el examen, pero mi mamá quiere que yo _____ (llevar) el coche al taller de mecánica.
—No creo que _____ (valer) la pena arreglar ese coche, porque no sirve.
—Es verdad, pero dudo que nosotros _____ (poder) comprar uno nuevo.

_____

[1]The subjunctive is always used after the conjunctions **con tal que, sin que, en caso de que, a menos que, para que,** and **antes de que,** which by their very meaning imply uncertainty or condition: **Puedo salir sin que los chicos me vean, a menos que estén en la sala.**

—Yo espero _____ (poder) comprar uno el mes próximo.

—Yo conozco a una chica que _____ (querer) vender su coche. Si tú _____ (querer) verlo, podemos ir mañana a su casa.

—Si _____ (poder) iría, pero tengo que trabajar.

B. With a partner, take turns asking each other the following questions.

1. ¿A quién llamarías tú si tu coche no arrancara?
2. Tengo que arreglar mi coche. ¿A qué taller me recomiendas que lo lleve?
3. Si tú vas a comprar un coche, ¿prefieres uno que sea automático o de cambios mecánicos?
4. ¿Es cierto que tú tienes un teléfono celular en tu auto?
5. ¿Tú crees que es una buena idea aumentar *(to increase)* la velocidad máxima en la autopista?
6. ¿Esperas que tus padres te regalen un coche para tu cumpleaños?
7. ¿Tú podrías comprar una casa sin que tus padres te ayudaran?
8. ¿Es verdad que tú gastas dinero como si fueras millonario(-a)?
9. ¿Tú tratas de llegar a la clase antes de que llegue el profesor?
10. ¿Qué vas a hacer hoy tan pronto como llegues a tu casa?

C. Complete the following, according to your own thoughts and experience regarding college and family life.

1. Mis profesores quieren que yo...
2. Mis padres me aconsejan que...
3. Mi mejor amigo me sugirió que...
4. Yo habría sacado una "A" si...
5. Yo voy a llamar a mi amigo(-a) en cuanto...
6. Yo no tendría que pagar la matrícula si...
7. Yo no creo que mi profesor(-a) de español...
8. En mi clase de español no hay nadie que...
9. Yo dudo que mis amigos...
10. El verano próximo, yo espero...

¡A ver cuánto aprendió!

INTERNET

See the *¿Cómo se dice...?* Web site for additional grammar and vocabulary practice: http://spanish.college. hmco.com/students

¡Repase el vocabulario!

Circle the word or phrase that best completes each sentence.

1. Tuve un pinchazo. Tendré que cambiar (el acumulador, el neumático, la bomba de agua).
2. Voy a llevar el coche al taller porque está (sabroso, sentado, descompuesto).
3. Tendrá que llenar el tanque porque está casi (preocupado, extraño, vacío).
4. Te van a poner una multa porque estás (manejando muy rápido, mirando las luces, abriendo el maletero).

ACTIVITY SUGGESTION: Do **¡Escucha!**, the in-class listening comprehension activity that reviews vocabulary and grammar structures introduced in the lesson. It appears in the answer key of the *IAM*.

ACTIVITY SUGGESTION: See the *IAM* for an additional in-class activity: **Palabras escondidas.**

ACTIVITY SUGGESTION: See the *IAM* for additional vocabulary activities (Lessons 1–8): **Familias de palabras** and **¡Dilo rápido!**

5. No pude parar porque (los frenos no funcionaban, no tenía limpiaparabrisas, tenía las manos en el volante).
6. Iba (autopista, carretera, camino) a Quito cuando tuvimos un accidente.
7. Vino (una ambulancia, una chapa, una grúa) para remolcar el coche.
8. Los recién (cansados, casados, cazados) salieron de viaje ayer.
9. Según (ese letrero, esa ventanilla, ese gato), estamos a cien kilómetros de San José.
10. Pondré los mapas en el (arreglo, aceite, portaguantes).
11. Gasté una fortuna en el (ruido, arreglo, taller) del coche.
12. No vale la (pareja, chapa, pena) arreglar el coche.
13. Cuando él tiene problemas con el coche, siempre (gasta, para, culpa) al mecánico.
14. Ella dice que necesitamos un coche nuevo porque el nuestro no sirve, pero yo no estoy de (extraño, acuerdo, ruido).
15. Levantó (el maletero, el capó, la ventanilla) para revisar el motor.
16. Mi coche tiene (bomba, bolsas, bocina) de aire.

Entrevista

ACTIVITY SUGGESTION: See the *IAM* for additional in-class activities: **Para conocernos mejor** and **Una encuesta.**

With a partner, interview each other by asking the following questions.

1. ¿Tendrás que ir a la gasolinera mañana?
2. ¿Está lleno o vacío el tanque de tu coche?
3. ¿Necesita tu coche un acumulador nuevo?
4. ¿Cuándo piensas comprar neumáticos nuevos para tu coche?
5. ¿Tienes que cambiar el filtro de aceite de tu coche?
6. ¿Cuál es el número de la chapa de tu coche?
7. ¿Cuántas millas hay de tu casa a la universidad?
8. Generalmente ¿a qué velocidad manejas en la autopista?
9. ¿Te gustaría manejar un Mercedes Benz?
10. ¿Qué harías si tu coche no funcionara bien?

Situaciones

ACTIVITY SUGGESTION: See the *IAM* for an additional in-class activity: **El taller de mecánica.**

What would you say in the following situations? What might the other person say? Act out the scenes with a partner. Take turns playing each role.

1. You have a flat tire, and you think the brakes on your car are out of order. You want your mechanic to check them.
2. Tell a tourist that he or she can buy gasoline at the service station located at the next corner.
3. You are a police officer, and you have stopped a motorist. The car doesn't have a license plate, and the lights aren't working. Ask to see the motorist's driver's license.
4. Your car won't start, and you're going to need a tow truck. Someone passes by as you fiddle with the ignition.
5. Your friend bought a car that was a lemon, and then spent three thousand dollars to have it fixed. Say what you would have done in this situation.

¿Qué pasa aquí?

SUGGESTION: Select several students to act out their dialogues the next day in class.

ACTIVITY SUGGESTION: See the *IAM* for an additional in-class activity: **Informe de accidente.**

In groups of three or four, look at the cartoon and write a dialogue between the mechanic and the driver.

 ## Para escribir

What if **Romeo** and **Julieta** were living now? Write an account of what their circumstances would be and what they would be doing. In our story, of course, they *don't* die! Start out with: **Romeo y Julieta vivirían en...**

En la vida real

CD-ROM

Do the interactive exercises on the CD-ROM for additional practice.

¡Nos vamos!

You and a classmate are planning to drive to Mexico. Working together, make a list of everything you need to do before you leave. Make sure you include things you need to do to get the car and yourselves ready.

Comprando coche

What questions would you ask before buying a car? Carefully read the following brochure and identify the questions that would cover these topics:

1. la condición del coche (dos preguntas)
2. la garantía
3. las reparaciones (dos preguntas)
4. la inspección del estado
5. el precio de reventa *(resale)*

Cuando vaya a comprar un automóvil, ¡pregunte!

Ciertas preguntas le ahorrarán dinero.
Determine primero qué automóvil necesita y cuánto dinero puede invertir.
Consulte por lo menos con tres comerciantes de automóviles antes de decidir a cuál le comprará.

Pregunte a cada comerciante:
– ¿Qué garantía tiene el automóvil?
– Si el automóvil se descompone, ¿quién va a componerlo?
– ¿El automóvil será aprobado en la inspección del Estado?
– ¿Qué precio de reventa tendrá el automóvil cuando Ud. quiera venderlo?
– ¿Está el automóvil en perfectas condiciones?
– ¿Le dejarán probar el automóvil antes de entregárselo?
– Si el automóvil necesita ser reparado, ¿quién pagará la reparación?
Recuerde hacer estas preguntas y ahorrará mucho dinero.
Asegúrese de que el vendedor no lo engañe. Muchos vendedores tratarán de engañarlo para hacer la venta.

¡PREGUNTE EL PRECIO!
Hágale saber al vendedor que Ud. ya conoce los precios de otros competidores.
Recuerde que los vendedores a veces pueden cambiar el precio. No cierre el trato si el precio que le ofrecen no le parece correcto o justo.

RECUERDE, ES SU DINERO.

En la agencia de seguros

With a classmate, play the roles of an insurance agent and a student who wants to purchase an auto insurance policy (**un seguro de automóvil**). The agent wants to determine the overall condition of the car, whether the student is a conscientious driver, and how much the car is worth. The student is anxious to make a good impression.

Take this test. When you have finished, check your answers in the answer key provided for this section in Appendix E. Then use a red pen to correct any mistakes you have made. Are you ready?

Lección 16

A. The future

Rewrite the following sentences using the future tense.

1. Le *vamos a decir* la verdad.
2. ¿Qué *van a hacer* Uds.?
3. No *van a querer* ir.
4. Lo *voy a saber* mañana.
5. No *van a poder* venir.
6. ¿Adónde *vamos a ir*?
7. ¿Dónde lo *vas a poner*?
8. Nosotros *vamos a venir* con él.
9. *Voy a tener* que trabajar.
10. *Vamos a salir* mañana.

B. The conditional

Rewrite the following sentences to say what the people named *would* do, using the conditional tense.

1. Yo *voy* a México.
2. Nosotros les *escribimos*.
3. ¿Tú se lo *dices*?
4. Ellos *hablan* con Ana.
5. ¿Ud. lo *pone* en el banco?
6. ¿Uds. *vienen* el domingo?
7. Julio *pide* ensalada.
8. Nosotros lo *hacemos* hoy.
9. Tú no *sales* con ella.
10. Ella *no camina*; *va* en coche.

C. The future perfect

Complete the following sentences, using the future perfect of the verbs listed.

comer
terminar
escribir
volver
decir

1. Para mañana, el consejero me _____ qué clases tomar.
2. Para las cuatro de la tarde, ellos _____ a casa.
3. Para junio, yo _____ las clases.
4. Para las dos, nosotros ya _____ el postre.
5. ¿Tú _____ todas las cartas para las cinco de la tarde?

D. The conditional perfect

Complete the following, using the Spanish equivalent of the words in parentheses.

1. Yo _____ más para el examen. (would have studied)
2. Julio me _____ con el informe. (would have helped)
3. Luis y yo _____ al partido de fútbol. (would have gone)
4. Mis padres _____ la matrícula. (would have paid)
5. ¿Qué _____, Anita? (would you have done)

E. Just words . . .

Match the questions in column A with the answers in column B.

A	B
1. ¿Adónde vas?	a. Sí, porque juega nuestro equipo.
2. ¿Qué materias estás tomando?	b. El año próximo.
3. ¿Quién es tu consejero?	c. No, es plomero.
4. ¿Asiste a la Facultad de Derecho?	d. Al laboratorio.
5. ¿Qué tienes que escribir?	e. Sí, para pagar la matrícula.
6. ¿Qué nota sacaste?	f. Física, química y sociología.
7. ¿Es periodista?	g. No, quedé suspendido.
8. ¿Necesitas dinero?	h. El Dr. Peña.
9. ¿Aprobaste el examen?	i. Un informe para mi clase de biología.
10. ¿Es carpintero?	j. Sí, quiere ser abogado.
11. ¿Vamos al estadio hoy?	k. Una "B".
12. ¿Cuándo te gradúas?	l. Sí, trabaja para el *Times*.

F. Culture

Circle the correct answer, based on the **¿Lo sabía Ud.?** section.

1. En las universidades hispanas no (entrega, existe, queda) el concepto de "*major*" usado en los Estados Unidos.
2. La mayoría de los estudiantes comienzan a (matricularse, graduarse, especializarse) a partir de su primer año en la universidad.
3. En España, las universidades se dividen en (facultades, carreras, administraciones).
4. Los estudiantes toman clases relacionadas con su (consejero, equipo, especialización).
5. Una nota de (1 a 4, 3 a 6, 2 a 5) es la mínima para aprobar una clase.

Lección 17

A. The imperfect subjunctive

Rewrite the following sentences with the new beginnings.

1. Quiere que vaya con ellos.
   Quería...
2. Les digo que no se preocupen.
   Les dije...
3. Me alegro de que el doctor te vea hoy.
   Me alegré...
4. Temo que me ponga una inyección.
   Temí...
5. Necesito una enfermera que sepa español.
   Necesitaba...
6. No creo que tengan que desinfectarme la herida.
   No creí...
7. ¿Hay alguien que pueda recetar penicilina?
   ¿Había...?
8. Me alegro de que te sientas bien.
   Me alegré...
9. No es verdad que necesitemos una ambulancia.
   No era verdad...
10. No creo que esté embarazada.
    No creía...

B. Uses of some prepositions after certain verbs

Complete the following sentences, using the verbs listed and the appropriate prepositions.

| insistir | comprometerse | olvidarse |
| venir | enamorarse | soñar |

1. Yo nunca _____ traer mis libros a clase.
2. Julio y Estrella _____ casarse el año que viene.
3. El profesor _____ que todos los estudiantes hagan los ejercicios.
4. Nosotros _____ verla cinco días a la semana.
5. Adela _____ Pepe en la fiesta de anoche.
6. Yo _____ mi novia la primera vez que la vi.

C. The present perfect subjunctive

Complete these sentences with the present perfect subjunctive form of the verbs in parentheses.

1. Es una lástima que los enfermeros no _____ (encontrar) las radiografías.
2. Pedro, me alegro de que (tú) _____ (ir) a la sala de emergencias.
3. ¿Hay alguien que _____ (comprar) el antibiótico?
4. Los padres de Clara esperan que la médica _____ (enyesarle) la pierna.
5. No creo que Ud. _____ (romperse) el brazo, señor.
6. No es verdad que nosotros _____ (volver) al hospital.

D. Just words . . .

Choose the word or phrase in parentheses that best completes each of the following sentences.

1. Ella es alérgica a la (radiografía, penicilina, clase).
2. Comemos con (los oídos, los dientes, el pecho).
3. Hablamos con (la espalda, los dedos, la lengua).
4. Vemos con (los ojos, la boca, las orejas).
5. Caminamos con (las manos, el cuello, los pies).
6. Me desinfectaron (el dolor, la herida, la receta).
7. ¿Te (rompiste, atropellaste, evitaste) el brazo alguna vez?
8. Me dolía mucho (la pierna, el pelo, el consultorio).
9. Le vendé (el tobillo, el pelo, el catarro).
10. Tenía ciento tres (fiebre, gripe, grados) de temperatura.
11. ¿Cuándo fue la última vez que le (cortaron, quebraron, pusieron) una inyección antitetánica?
12. ¿Por qué tomaste aspirinas? ¿Tenías (dolor de cabeza, tos, frío)?
13. ¿Tienes Alka Seltzer? Es para (el pecho, el estómago, los dedos de los pies).
14. Va a tener un niño. Está (cansada, enferma, embarazada).
15. Raúl no se siente bien. El médico dice que tiene (pastillas, gripe, recetas).

E. Culture

Answer the following questions, based on the **¿Lo sabía Ud.?** section.

1. ¿Quién subvenciona (*subsidizes*) los hospitales en los países de habla hispana?
2. ¿Adónde va la gente que no quiere ir a un hospital público?
3. ¿Qué clase de servicios médicos hay en muchos pueblos remotos?
4. ¿Quién ayuda a algunas mujeres hispanas cuando van a tener un bebé?
5. ¿Es posible comprar ciertas (*certain*) medicinas en algunos países hispanos sin tener receta?

Lección 18

A. The pluperfect subjunctive

Give the Spanish equivalent of the words in parentheses.

1. No había nadie que _____ el accidente.   *(had seen)*
2. Yo me alegré de que ellos no _____ un pinchazo.   *(had had)*
3. Ellos no creían que nosotros _____ la gasolina.   *(had paid)*
4. Yo temía que _____ la pierna, Anita.   *(you had broken)*
5. Ellos se alegraron de que yo _____.   *(had returned)*

B. *If* clauses

Complete the following sentences, using the present indicative, the imperfect subjunctive, or the pluperfect subjunctive, as needed.

1. Si yo _____ (tener) tiempo, iré a buscarte.
2. Nosotros iríamos con ellos si _____ (poder).
3. Si ellos _____ (ir) a la biblioteca, habrían encontrado el libro.
4. Si Uds. _____ (querer) ir con nosotros, podemos llevarlos.
5. Tú habrías hablado con ella si la _____ (ver).
6. Antonio gasta dinero como si _____ (ser) rico.

C. Summary of the uses of the subjunctive

Complete the following sentences, using the verbs in parentheses in the appropriate tense of the subjunctive or the indicative.

1. Yo quería que ellos _____ una batería nueva. *(install)*
2. Espero que ellos _____ hablar con el mecánico. *(can)*
3. Dile que me _____ si quiere ir. *(call)*
4. Yo no creo que nosotros _____ ir al partido, pero creo que _____ ir al cine. *(can / can)*
5. ¿Hay alguien aquí que _____ administración de empresas? *(has taken)*
6. Voy a ayudar a mi mamá cuando _____ a casa. *(arrive)*
7. Le di dinero para que _____ pagar la multa. *(could)*
8. No es verdad que su coche no _____ bueno. *(is)*

D. Just words . . .

Complete the following sentences, using words learned in **Lección 18.**

1. ¿Cuál es la _____ máxima en la carretera?
2. Adela y Fernando son _____ casados.
3. No pude parar porque los _____ estaban descompuestos.
4. ¿Tienes tu licencia de _____?
5. Fuimos a la estación de _____.
6. Está lloviendo, y el _____ de mi coche no funciona. ¡No veo nada!
7. ¿Está lleno o _____ el tanque?
8. Voy a poner las maletas en el _____.
9. Mi coche no arranca; la grúa lo va a _____.
10. Un sinónimo de "batería" es _____.
11. Yo pongo los mapas en la _____ del coche.
12. No es mi _____ que el coche no tenga gasolina.
13. Yo no arreglaría el coche. ¡No _____ la pena!
14. Mis padres van a salir de _____ el 15 de junio.
15. No estoy de _____ contigo; no creo que debamos comprar un coche nuevo.

E. Culture

Circle the correct answer, based on the **¿Lo sabía Ud.?** section.

1. Madrid, Buenos Aires y México tienen graves problemas de (asimilación, contaminación, introducción) del aire.
2. En zonas rurales de Hispanoamérica, las carreteras están en muy (buenas, medianas, malas) condiciones.
3. La gasolina es más (cara, barata, libre) en la mayoría de los países hispanos.
4. La gente joven usa más (el camión, la motocicleta, la bicicleta).
5. Un kilómetro equivale a (0,7; 0,6; 0,5) millas.

9. Las minorías hispanas en los Estados Unidos

Estados Unidos

- Muchas de las estrellas *(stars)* de cine y de televisión en los Estados Unidos son de ascendencia hispana: Rita Moreno, Ricardo Montalbán, Charlie Sheen, Emilio Estévez, Edward James Olmos, María Conchita Alonso, Linda Ronstadt, Andy García y Rosie Pérez, entre muchos otros.

- En la ciudad de Nueva York hay más de dos millones de hispanos, la mayoría de los cuales son puertorriqueños. Otros grupos hispanos concentrados en Nueva York son los dominicanos, los centroamericanos y los cubanos.

- La minoría hispana más numerosa en los Estados Unidos es la de origen mexicano, que se concentra principalmente en los estados de Tejas, Colorado, Nuevo México, Arizona y California.

- Más de medio millón de cubanos viven en Miami, donde ejercen una gran influencia cultural y económica. Hace cuatro décadas, cuando los cubanos empezaron a llegar a Miami, la ciudad era fundamentalmente un centro turístico. Hoy Miami es un centro industrial y comercial de primer orden, y el puente que une la economía de los Estados Unidos con la de América Latina y aun la de España.

Para las muchachas latino-americanas, tiene mucha importancia la celebración de los quince años. En México la fiesta recibe el nombre de "quinceañera"; en otros países se llama la celebración de "los quince". Las familias latinas en los Estados Unidos, generalmente siguen la tradición con un baile y una comida especial.

¿Qué cumpleaños es muy importante para muchas chicas norteamericanas?

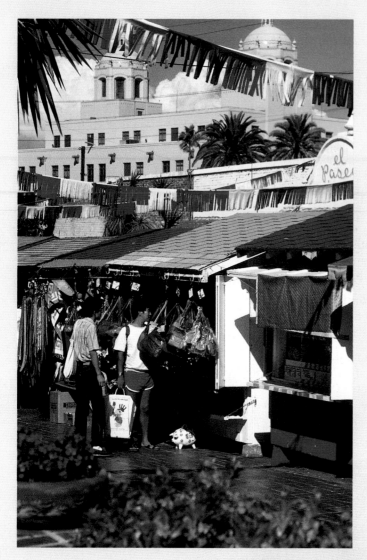

La calle Olvera, con sus aceras adoquinadas *(tiled sidewalks)*, sus piñatas, sus mariachis y sus puestos de artesanía mexicana es un trozo *(piece)* del viejo México en el corazón de Los Ángeles. Aquí se ve el edificio Ávila, construido de adobe y considerado el más antiguo de los edificios existentes en Los Ángeles.

¿Puede Ud. describir lo que ve en esta foto?

Uno de los grupos minoritarios más numerosos en la ciudad de Nueva York es el de los puertorriqueños. Aquí se ve un festival hispano en la calle 14 de Manhattan, el centro de Nueva York.

¿Cuál es el grupo minoritario más numeroso en su ciudad?

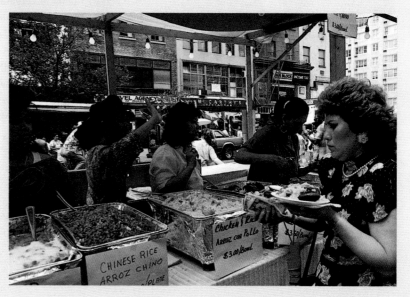

La cantante cubana Gloria Estefan es una de las más populares de los Estados Unidos. Gloria canta y compone canciones en español y en inglés. Recientemente su nombre fue añadido *(was added)* al famoso *Walk of Fame* de Hollywood.

¿Cuál es su cantante favorito?

La actriz Jennifer López, de origen puertorriqueño, se ha convertido en una de las actrices y cantantes latinas más populares. Ella interpretó el papel *(role)* de *Selena*, la trágicamente desaparecida cantante de la música *"Tex-Mex"*, en la película del mismo nombre. Jennifer López ya había participado en varias películas, entre ellas *My Family*, *U Turn*, *Money Train* y *The Cell*.

¿Cuál es su actriz favorita?

Edward James Olmos, nacido en Los Ángeles, de padres mexicanos, es uno de los actores hispanos más conocidos en los Estados Unidos. Entre sus películas están *Stand and Deliver*, *My Family* y *Selena*, donde representa el papel del padre de la famosa cantante de origen mexicano.

¿Cuál es su actor favorito?

No hay duda de que en la ciudad de San Antonio, Tejas, la cultura mexicana es la predominante. En la foto, una familia come en el restaurante mexicano "Mi tierra".

¿Cuál es su restaurante mexicano favorito?

Ileana Ros-Lehtinen, cubana de nacimiento, es una muestra del poder político de los hispanos en los Estados Unidos. Educadora de profesión, y ya con una maestría de Ciencias en Lideratura Educacional y una candidatura al doctorado, se decidió por la política. Fue Representante a la Cámara y Senadora de la Florida y, desde 1989, es Representante al Congreso de los Estados Unidos. Ileana Ros fue la primera mujer hispana elegida para esta posición.

¿Puede Ud. nombrar otros políticos hispanos? ¿Cuáles?

TELEINFORME

VIDEO

CD-ROM

Do the interactive exercises on
the CD-ROM for additional practice.

Preparación

NOTE: The video-related vocabulary is listed in the *Instructor's Activities Manual* for your reference. Its purpose is to facilitate students' comprehension.

NOTE: See the Instructor's Edition frontmatter for additional suggestions on implementing video in the classroom.

¿Cuánto saben Uds. ya? After reading **Panorama hispánico 9** get together in groups of three or four students and answer the following questions.

1. ¿En qué estados vive la mayoría de las personas de origen mexicano?
2. ¿De dónde son los hispanos que viven en Nueva York?
3. ¿Dónde vive la mayor parte de los cubanos?
4. ¿En qué ciudad está la calle Olvera?
5. ¿Qué se ve en la calle Olvera?
6. ¿Cuál es uno de los edificios *(buildings)* más antiguos de la ciudad de Los Ángeles?

Comprensión

SUGGESTION: Have students read the *Panorama hispánico* segment of the textbook and do the *Preparación* activities in small groups before viewing the video segments.

SUGGESTION: The *Comprensión* sections are organized by individual video clip to provide greater flexibility in lesson planning. Have students complete each exercise after viewing the corresponding video clip and have them compare their answers in pairs or groups.

A. La calle Olvera, Los Ángeles. Select the word or phrase that best completes each statement, according to what you understood.

1. La calle Olvera es una de las calles más _____ de Los Ángeles.
2. En el mercado mexicano venden _____ típicas.
3. El Cinco de Mayo es una _____ mexicoamericana.
4. Algunos ejemplos de la comida mexicana son _____, _____ y _____.
5. Los fines de semana hay _____, _____ y presentaciones de baile en la calle Olvera.

B. El desfile puertorriqueño de Nueva York. Read the following statements. After watching the video, circle **V** (**Verdadero**) or **F** (**Falso**), according to what you understood. If a statement is false, correct it.

V F 1. La bandera *(flag)* puertorriqueña fue creada en Puerto Rico.
V F 2. La bandera puertorriqueña ondeó por primera vez en Puerto Rico en el año 1902.
V F 3. Puerto Rico es un Estado Libre Asociado *(Commonwealth)* de los Estados Unidos.
V F 4. El desfile puertorriqueño se inició en el año 1957.
V F 5. Muy pocas personas asisten al desfile puertorriqueño.
V F 6. Algunos políticos participan en el desfile puertorriqueño de Nueva York.

Ampliación

A. Celebraciones hispanas. With a partner, discuss in Spanish what you would like to see and do if you went to a festival on Olvera Street in Los Angeles or the Puerto Rican Day celebration in New York City.

B. Dos culturas. After viewing all the video modules, what have you learned about the Hispanic world and its people that you did not know before? Discuss this in Spanish with a partner.

Appendix A Spanish Sounds

STUDENT AUDIO

Vowels

There are five distinct vowels in Spanish: **a, e, i, o,** and **u.** Each vowel has only one basic, constant sound. The pronunciation of each vowel is constant, clear, and brief. The length of the sound is practically the same whether it is produced in a stressed or unstressed syllable.[1]

While producing the sounds of the English stressed vowels that most closely resemble the Spanish ones, the speaker changes the position of the tongue, lips, and lower jaw, so that the vowel actually starts as one sound and then glides into another. In Spanish, however, the tongue, lips, and jaw keep a constant position during the production of the sound.

English: ban*a*na   **Spanish:** banana

The stress falls on the same vowel and syllable in both Spanish and English, but the English stressed *a* is longer than the Spanish stressed **a.**

English: ban*a*na   **Spanish:** banana

Note also that the English stressed *a* has a sound different from the other *a*'s in the word, while the Spanish **a** sound remains constant.

a The Spanish **a** sounds similar to the English *a* in the word *father.*

alta	casa	palma	Ana
cama	Panamá	alma	apagar

e The Spanish **e** is pronounced like the English *e* in the word *eight.*

mes	entre	este	deje
ese	encender	teme	prender

i The Spanish **i** has a sound similar to the English *ee* in the word *see.*

fin	ir	sí	sin	dividir	Trini	difícil

o The Spanish **o** is similar to the English *o* in the word *no,* but without the glide.

toco	como	poco	roto
corto	corro	solo	loco

u The Spanish **u** is pronounced like the English *oo* sound in the word *shoot* or the *ue* sound in the word *Sue.*

su	Lulú	Úrsula	cultura
un	luna	sucursal	Uruguay

Diphthongs and Triphthongs

When unstressed **i** or **u** falls next to another vowel in a syllable, it unites with that vowel to form what is called a *diphthong.* Both vowels are pronounced as one syllable. Their sounds do not change; they are only pronounced more rapidly and with a glide. For example:

traiga	Lidia	treinta	siete	oigo	adiós
Aurora	agua	bueno	antiguo	ciudad	Luis

---

[1]In a stressed syllable, the prominence of the vowel is indicated by its loudness.

A triphthong is the union of three vowels: a stressed vowel between two unstressed ones (**i** or **u**) in the same syllable. For example: Para**guay**, estu**diéis**.

NOTE: Stressed **i** and **u** do not form diphthongs with other vowels, except in the combinations **iu** and **ui**. For example: **rí-o**, sa-**bí**-ais.

In syllabication, diphthongs and triphthongs are considered a single vowel; their components cannot be separated.

Consonants

p   Spanish **p** is pronounced in a manner similar to the English *p* sound, but without the puff of air that follows after the English sound is produced.

pesca	pude	puedo	parte	papá
postre	piña	puente	Paco	

k   The Spanish **k** sound, represented by the letters **k, c** before **a, o, u** or a consonant, and **qu,** is similar to the English *k* sound, but without the puff of air.

casa	comer	cuna	clima	acción	que
quinto	queso	aunque	kiosko	kilómetro	

t   Spanish **t** is produced by touching the back of the upper front teeth with the tip of the tongue. It has no puff of air as in the English *t*.

todo	antes	corto	Guatemala	diente
resto	tonto	roto	tanque	

d   The Spanish consonant **d** has two different sounds depending on its position. At the beginning of an utterance and after **n** or **l**, the tip of the tongue presses the back of the upper front teeth.

día	doma	dice	dolor	dar
anda	Aldo	caldo	el deseo	un domicilio

In all other positions the sound of **d** is similar to the *th* sound in the English word *they*, but softer.

medida	todo	nada	nadie	medio
puedo	moda	queda	nudo	

g   The Spanish consonant **g** is similar to the English *g* sound in the word *guy* except before **e** or **i**.

goma	glotón	gallo	gloria	lago	alga
gorrión	garra	guerra	angustia	algo	Dagoberto

j   The Spanish sound **j** (or **g** before **e** and **i**) is similar to a strongly exaggerated English *h* sound.

gemir	juez	jarro	gitano	agente
juego	giro	bajo	gente	

b, v   There is no difference in sound between Spanish **b** and **v**. Both letters are pronounced alike. At the beginning of an utterance or after **m** or **n**, **b** and **v** have a sound identical to the English *b* sound in the word *boy*.

vivir	beber	vamos	barco	enviar
hambre	batea	bueno	vestido	

When pronounced between vowels, the Spanish **b** and **v** sound is produced by bringing the lips together but not closing them, so that some air may pass through.

sábado	autobús	yo voy	su barco

y, ll In most countries, Spanish **ll** and **y** have a sound similar to the English *y* sound in the word *yes*.

el llavero	trayecto	su yunta	milla
oye	el yeso	mayo	yema
un yelmo	trayectoria	llama	bella

NOTE: When it stands alone or is at the end of a word, Spanish **y** is pronounced like the vowel **i**.

rey	hoy	y	doy	buey
muy	voy	estoy	soy	

r The sound of Spanish **r** is similar to the English *dd* sound in the word *ladder*.

crema	aroma	cara	arena	aro
harina	toro	oro	eres	portero

rr Spanish **rr** and also **r** in an initial position and after **n, l,** or **s** are pronounced with a very strong trill. This trill is produced by bringing the tip of the tongue near the alveolar ridge and letting it vibrate freely while the air passes through the mouth.

rama	carro	Israel	cierra	roto
perro	alrededor	rizo	corre	Enrique

s Spanish **s** is represented in most of the Spanish world by the letters **s, z,** and **c** before **e** or **i**. The sound is very similar to the English sibilant *s* in the word *sink*.

sale	sitio	presidente	signo
salsa	seda	suma	vaso
sobrino	ciudad	cima	canción
zapato	zarza	cerveza	centro

h The letter **h** is silent in Spanish.

hoy	hora	hilo	ahora
humor	huevo	horror	almohada

ch Spanish **ch** is pronounced like the English *ch* in the word *chief*.

hecho	chico	coche	Chile
mucho	muchacho	salchicha	

f Spanish **f** is identical in sound to the English *f*.

difícil	feo	fuego	forma
fácil	fecha	foto	fueron

l Spanish **l** is similar to the English *l* in the word *let*.

dolor	lata	ángel	lago	sueldo
los	pelo	lana	general	fácil

m Spanish **m** is pronounced like the English *m* in the word *mother*.

mano	moda	mucho	muy
mismo	tampoco	multa	cómoda

n In most cases, Spanish **n** has a sound similar to the English *n*.

nada	nunca	ninguno	norte
entra	tiene	sienta	

The sound of Spanish **n** is often affected by the sounds that occur around it. When it appears before **b**, **v**, or **p**, it is pronounced like an **m**.

tan bueno	toman vino	sin poder
un pobre	comen peras	siguen bebiendo

ñ   Spanish **ñ** is similar to the English *ny* sound in the word *canyon*.

señor	otoño	ñoño	uña
leña	dueño	niños	años

x   Spanish **x** has two pronunciations depending on its position. Between vowels the sound is similar to English *ks*.

examen	exacto	boxeo	éxito
oxidar	oxígeno	existencia	

When it occurs before a consonant, Spanish **x** sounds like *s*.

expresión	explicar	extraer	excusa
expreso	exquisito	extremo	

NOTE: When **x** appears in **México** or in other words of Mexican origin, it is pronounced like the Spanish letter **j**.

Rhythm

Rhythm is the variation of sound intensity that we usually associate with music. Spanish and English each regulate these variations in speech differently, because they have different patterns of syllable length. In Spanish the length of the stressed and unstressed syllables remains almost the same, while the English stressed syllables are considerably longer than unstressed ones. Pronounce the following Spanish words, enunciating each syllable clearly.

es-tu-dian-te	bue-no	Úr-su-la
com-po-si-ción	di-fí-cil	ki-ló-me-tro
po-li-cí-a	Pa-ra-guay	

Because the length of the Spanish syllables remains constant, the greater the number of syllables in a given word or phrase, the longer the phrase will be.

Linking

In spoken Spanish, the different words in a phrase or a sentence are not pronounced as isolated elements but are combined together. This is called *linking*.

Pepe come pan. Pe-pe-co-me-pan
Tomás toma leche.   To-más-to-ma-le-che
Luis tiene la llave.   Luis-tie-ne-la-lla-ve
La mano de Roberto.   La-ma-no-de-Ro-ber-to

■ The final consonant of a word is pronounced together with the initial vowel of the following word.

Carlos anda Car-lo-san-da
un ángel   u-nán-gel
el otoño   e-lo-to-ño
unos estudios interesantes   u-no-ses-tu-dio-sin-te-re-san-tes

■ A diphthong is formed between the final vowel of a word and the initial vowel of the following word. A triphthong is formed when there is a combination of three vowels (see rules for the formation of diphthongs and triphthongs on pages 459–460).

su hermana	suher-ma-na
tu escopeta	tues-co-pe-ta
Roberto y Luis	Ro-ber-toy-Luis
negocio importante	ne-go-cioim-por-tan-te
lluvia y nieve	llu-viay-nie-ve
ardua empresa	ar-duaem-pre-sa

■ When the final vowel of a word and the initial vowel of the following word are identical, they are pronounced slightly longer than one vowel.

Ana alcanza	A-n*a*l-can-za
lo olvido	l*o*l-vi-do
tiene eso	tie-n*e*-so
Ada atiende	Ad*a*-tien-de

The same rule applies when two identical vowels appear within a word.

cr*ee*s	cr*e*s
T*ee*herán	T*e*-rán
coordinación	cor-di-na-ción

■ When the final consonant of a word and the initial consonant of the following word are the same, they are pronounced as one consonant with slightly longer than normal duration.

e*l* lado	e-*l*a-do
Carlos salta	Car-lo-*s*al-ta
tienes sed	tie-ne-*s*ed

Intonation

Intonation is the rise and fall of pitch in the delivery of a phrase or a sentence. In general, Spanish pitch tends to change less than English, giving the impression that the language is less emphatic.

As a rule, the intonation for normal statements in Spanish starts in a low tone, rises to a higher one on the first stressed syllable, maintains that tone until the last stressed syllable, and then goes back to the initial low tone, with still another drop at the very end.

Tu amigo viene mañana.	José come pan.
Ada está en casa.	Carlos toma café.

Syllable Formation in Spanish

General rules for dividing words into syllables:

Vowels

■ A vowel or a vowel combination can constitute a syllable.

   a-lum-no   a-bue-la   Eu-ro-pa

■ Diphthongs and triphthongs are considered single vowels and cannot be divided.

   bai-le   puen-te   Dia-na   es-tu-diáis   an-ti-guo

■ Two strong vowels (**a, e, o**) do not form a diphthong and are separated into two syllables.

>   em-ple-ar   vol-te-ar   lo-a

■ A written accent on a weak vowel (**i** or **u**) breaks the diphthong, separating the vowels into two syllables.

>   trí-o   dú-o   Ma-rí-a

Consonants

■ A single consonant forms a syllable with the vowel that follows it.

>   po-der   ma-no   mi-nu-to

NOTE: Spanish **ch, ll,** and **rr** are considered single consonants: **a-ma-ri-llo, co-che, pe-rro.**

■ When two consonants appear between two vowels, they are separated into two syllables.

>   al-fa-be-to   cam-pe-ón   me-ter-se   mo-les-tia

EXCEPTION: When a consonant cluster composed of **b, c, d, f, g, p,** or **t** with **l** or **r** appears between two vowels, the cluster joins the following vowel: **so-bre, o-tros, ca-ble, te-lé-gra-fo.**

■ When three consonants appear between two vowels, only the last one goes with the following vowel.

>   ins-pec-tor   trans-por-te   trans-for-mar

EXCEPTION: When there is a cluster of three consonants in the combinations described in rule 2, the first consonant joins the preceding vowel and the cluster joins the following vowel: **es-cri-bir, ex-tran-je-ro, im-plo-rar, es-tre-cho.**

Accentuation

In Spanish, all words are stressed according to specific rules. Words that do not follow the rules must have a written accent to indicate the change of stress. The basic rules for accentuation are as follows.

■ Words ending in a vowel, **n,** or **s** are stressed on the next-to-last syllable.

>   **hi**-jo   **ca**-lle   **me**-sa   fa-**mo**-sos
>   flo-**re**-cen   **pla**-ya   **ve**-ces

■ Words ending in a consonant, except **n** or **s,** are stressed on the last syllable.

>   ma-**yor**   a-**mor**   tro-pi-**cal**   na-**riz**   re-**loj**   co-rre-**dor**

■ All words that do not follow these rules must have the written accent.

>   ca-**fé**   **lá**-piz   **mú**-si-ca   sa-**lón**
>   **án**-gel   **lí**-qui-do   fran-**cés**   **Víc**-tor
>   sim-**pá**-ti-co   rin-**cón**   a-**zú**-car   de-**mó**-cra-ta
>   sa-**lió**   **dé**-bil   e-**xá**-me-nes

■ Pronouns and adverbs of interrogation and exclamation have a written accent to distinguish them from relative pronouns.

>   ¿**Qué** comes?   *What are you eating?*
>   La pera que él no comió.   *The pear that he did not eat.*

¿**Quién** está ahí?	*Who is there?*
El hombre a quien tú llamaste.	*The man whom you called.*

¿**Dónde** está él?	*Where is he?*
En el lugar donde trabaja.	*At the place where he works.*

■ Words that have the same spelling but different meanings take a written accent to differentiate one from the other.

el	*the*	él	*he, him*	te	*you*	té	*tea*
mi	*my*	mí	*me*	si	*if*	sí	*yes*
tu	*your*	tú	*you*	mas	*but*	más	*more*

Appendix B Verbs

Regular Verbs

Model -ar, -er, -ir verbs

INFINITIVE

amar *(to love)* comer *(to eat)* vivir *(to live)*

PRESENT PARTICIPLE

amando *(loving)* comiendo *(eating)* viviendo *(living)*

PAST PARTICIPLE

amado *(loved)* comido *(eaten)* vivido *(lived)*

SIMPLE TENSES

Indicative Mood

PRESENT

(I love)		*(I eat)*		*(I live)*	
amo	amamos	como	comemos	vivo	vivimos
amas	amáis	comes	coméis	vives	vivís
ama	aman	come	comen	vive	viven

IMPERFECT

(I used to love)		*(I used to eat)*		*(I used to live)*	
amaba	amábamos	comía	comíamos	vivía	vivíamos
amabas	amabais	comías	comíais	vivías	vivíais
amaba	amaban	comía	comían	vivía	vivían

PRETERIT

(I loved)		*(I ate)*		*(I lived)*	
amé	amamos	comí	comimos	viví	vivimos
amaste	amasteis	comiste	comisteis	viviste	vivisteis
amó	amaron	comió	comieron	vivió	vivieron

FUTURE

(I will love)		*(I will eat)*		*(I will live)*	
amaré	amaremos	comeré	comeremos	viviré	viviremos
amarás	amaréis	comerás	comeréis	vivirás	viviréis
amará	amarán	comerá	comerán	vivirá	vivirán

CONDITIONAL

(I would love)		*(I would eat)*		*(I would live)*	
amaría	amaríamos	comería	comeríamos	viviría	viviríamos
amarías	amaríais	comerías	comeríais	vivirías	viviríais
amaría	amarían	comería	comerían	viviría	vivirían

Subjunctive Mood

PRESENT

([that] I [may] love)		*([that] I [may] eat)*		*([that] I [may] live)*	
ame	amemos	coma	comamos	viva	vivamos
ames	améis	comas	comáis	vivas	viváis
ame	amen	coma	coman	viva	vivan

IMPERFECT (two forms: -ra, -se)

([that] I [might] love)	*([that] I [might] eat)*	*([that] I [might] live)*
amara(-ase)	comiera(-iese)	viviera(-iese)
amaras(-ases)	comieras(-ieses)	vivieras(-ieses)
amara(-ase)	comiera(-iese)	viviera(-iese)
amáramos(-ásemos)	comiéramos(-iésemos)	viviéramos(-iésemos)
amarais(-aseis)	comierais(-ieseis)	vivierais(-ieseis)
amaran(-asen)	comieran(-iesen)	vivieran(-iesen)

Imperative Mood

(love)	*(eat)*	*(live)*
ama (tú)	come (tú)	vive (tú)
ame (Ud.)	coma (Ud.)	viva (Ud.)
amemos (nosotros)	comamos (nosotros)	vivamos (nosotros)
amad (vosotros)	comed (vosotros)	vivid (vosotros)
amen (Uds.)	coman (Uds.)	vivan (Uds.)

COMPOUND TENSES

PERFECT INFINITIVE

haber amado	haber comido	haber vivido

PERFECT PARTICIPLE

habiendo amado	habiendo comido	habiendo vivido

Indicative Mood

PRESENT PERFECT

(I have loved)	*(I have eaten)*	*(I have lived)*
he amado	he comido	he vivido
has amado	has comido	has vivido
ha amado	ha comido	ha vivido
hemos amado	hemos comido	hemos vivido
habéis amado	habéis comido	habéis vivido
han amado	han comido	han vivido

PLUPERFECT

(I had loved)	*(I had eaten)*	*(I had lived)*
había amado	había comido	había vivido
habías amado	habías comido	habías vivido
había amado	había comido	había vivido
habíamos amado	habíamos comido	habíamos vivido
habíais amado	habíais comido	habíais vivido
habían amado	habían comido	habían vivido

FUTURE PERFECT

(I will have loved)	*(I will have eaten)*	*(I will have lived)*
habré amado	habré comido	habré vivido
habrás amado	habrás comido	habrás vivido
habrá amado	habrá comido	habrá vivido
habremos amado	habremos comido	habremos vivido
habréis amado	habréis comido	habréis vivido
habrán amado	habrán comido	habrán vivido

CONDITIONAL PERFECT

(I would have loved)	*(I would have eaten)*	*(I would have lived)*
habría amado	habría comido	habría vivido
habrías amado	habrías comido	habrías vivido
habría amado	habría comido	habría vivido
habríamos amado	habríamos comido	habríamos vivido
habríais amado	habríais comido	habríais vivido
habrían amado	habrían comido	habrían vivido

Subjunctive Mood

PRESENT PERFECT

([that] I [may] have loved)	*([that] I [may] have eaten)*	*([that] I [may] have lived)*
haya amado	haya comido	haya vivido
hayas amado	hayas comido	hayas vivido
haya amado	haya comido	haya vivido
hayamos amado	hayamos comido	hayamos vivido
hayáis amado	hayáis comido	hayáis vivido
hayan amado	hayan comido	hayan vivido

PLUPERFECT (two forms: -ra, -se)

([that] I [might] have loved)	*([that] I [might] have eaten)*	*([that] I [might] have lived)*
hubiera(-iese) amado	hubiera(-iese) comido	hubiera(-iese) vivido
hubieras(-ieses) amado	hubieras(-ieses) comido	hubieras(-ieses) vivido
hubiera(-iese) amado	hubiera(-iese) comido	hubiera(-iese) vivido
hubiéramos(-iésemos) amado	hubiéramos(-iésemos) comido	hubiéramos(-iésemos) vivido
hubierais(-ieseis) amado	hubierais(-ieseis) comido	hubierais(-ieseis) vivido
hubieran(-iesen) amado	hubieran(-iesen) comido	hubieran(-iesen) vivido

Stem-Changing Verbs

The -ar and -er stem-changing verbs

Stem-changing verbs are those that have a spelling change in the root of the verb. Stem-changing verbs that end in **-ar** and **-er** change the stressed vowel **e** to **ie**, and the stressed **o** to **ue**. These changes occur in all persons, except the first- and second-persons plural, of the present indicative, present subjunctive, and imperative.

Infinitive	Indicative	Imperative	Subjunctive
cerrar	cierro	——	cierre
(to close)	cierras	cierra	cierres
	cierra	cierre	cierre
	cerramos	cerremos	cerremos
	cerráis	cerrad	cerréis
	cierran	cierren	cierren
perder	pierdo	——	pierda
(to lose)	pierdes	pierde	pierdas
	pierde	pierda	pierda
	perdemos	perdamos	perdamos
	perdéis	perded	perdáis
	pierden	pierdan	pierdan
contar	cuento	——	cuente
(to count;	cuentas	cuenta	cuentes
to tell)	cuenta	cuente	cuente
	contamos	contemos	contemos
	contáis	contad	contéis
	cuentan	cuenten	cuenten
volver	vuelvo	——	vuelva
(to return)	vuelves	vuelve	vuelvas
	vuelve	vuelva	vuelva
	volvemos	volvamos	volvamos
	volvéis	volved	volváis
	vuelven	vuelvan	vuelvan

Verbs that follow the same pattern:

acordarse	*to remember*	entender	*to understand*
acostar(se)	*to go to bed*	extender	*to stretch*
almorzar	*to have lunch*	llover	*to rain*
atravesar	*to go through*	mover	*to move*
cocer	*to cook*	mostrar	*to show*
colgar	*to hang*	negar	*to deny*
comenzar	*to begin*	nevar	*to snow*
confesar	*to confess*	pensar	*to think; to plan*
costar	*to cost*	probar	*to prove; to taste*
demostrar	*to demonstrate, show*	recordar	*to remember*
		rogar	*to beg*
despertar(se)	*to wake up*	sentar(se)	*to sit down*
empezar	*to begin*	soler	*to be in the habit of*
encender	*to light; to turn on*	soñar	*to dream*
encontrar	*to find*	torcer	*to twist*

The -ir stem-changing verbs

There are two types of stem-changing verbs that end in -ir: one type changes stressed e to ie in some tenses and to i in others, and stressed o to ue or u; the second type changes stressed e to i only in all the irregular tenses.

Type I: -ir: e > ie or i / o > ue or u

These changes occur as follows.

Present Indicative: All persons except the first- and second-persons plural change e to ie and o to ue. *Preterit:* Third-person singular and plural changes e to i and o to u. *Present Subjunctive:* All persons change e to i and o to u. *Imperfect Subjunctive:* All persons change e to i and o to u. *Imperative:* All persons except the first- and second-persons plural change e to ie and o to ue; first-person plural changes e to i and o to u. *Present Participle:* This form changes e to i and o to u.

Infinitive	Indicative		Imperative	Subjunctive	
sentir *(to feel)*	**PRESENT**	**PRETERIT**		**PRESENT**	**IMPERFECT**
	siento	sentí		sienta	sintiera(-iese)
	sientes	sentiste	siente	sientas	sintieras
PRESENT PARTICIPLE *sintiendo*	siente	sintió	sienta	sienta	sintiera
	sentimos	sentimos	sintamos	sintamos	sintiéramos
	sentís	sentisteis	sentid	sintáis	sintierais
	sienten	sintieron	sientan	sientan	sintieran
dormir *(to sleep)*	duermo	dormí		duerma	durmiera(-iese)
	duermes	dormiste	duerme	duermas	durmieras
PRESENT PARTICIPLE *durmiendo*	duerme	durmió	duerma	duerma	durmiera
	dormimos	dormimos	durmamos	durmamos	durmiéramos
	dormís	dormisteis	dormid	durmáis	durmierais
	duermen	durmieron	duerman	duerman	durmieran

Other verbs that follow the same pattern:

advertir	*to warm*	herir	*to wound, hurt*
arrepentirse	*to repent*	mentir	*to lie*
consentir	*to consent; to pamper*	morir	*to die*
convertir(se)	*to turn into*	preferir	*to prefer*
discernir	*to discern*	referir	*to refer*
divertir(se)	*to amuse oneself*	sugerir	*to suggest*

Type II: -ir: e > i

The verbs in the second category are irregular in the same tenses as those of the first type. The only difference is that they have only one change: e > i in all irregular persons.

Infinitive	Indicative		Imperative	Subjunctive	
pedir *(to ask for, request)*	**PRESENT**	**PRETERIT**		**PRESENT**	**IMPERFECT**
	pido	pedí		pida	pidiera(-iese)
PRESENT PARTICIPLE	pides	pediste	pide	pidas	pidieras
	pide	pidió	pida	pida	pidiera
pidiendo	pedimos	pedimos	pidamos	pidamos	pidiéramos
	pedís	pedisteis	pedid	pidáis	pidierais
	piden	pidieron	pidan	pidan	pidieran

Verbs that follow this pattern:

concebir	*to conceive*	repetir	*to repeat*
competir	*to compete*	reñir	*to fight*
despedir(se)	*to say good-bye*	seguir	*to follow*
elegir	*to choose*	servir	*to serve*
impedir	*to prevent*	vestir(se)	*to dress*
perseguir	*to pursue*		

Orthographic-Changing Verbs

Some verbs undergo a change in the spelling of the stem in some tenses in order to maintain the sound of the final consonant. The most common ones are those with the consonants **g** and **c**. Remember that **g** and **c** in front of **e** or **i** have a soft sound, and in front of **a**, **o**, or **u** have a hard sound. In order to keep the soft sound in front of **a**, **o**, or **u**, **g** and **c** change to **j** and **z**, respectively. In order to keep the hard sound of **g** or **c** in front of **e** and **i**, **u** is added to the **g** (**gu**) and the **c** changes to **qu**. The most important verbs that are regular in all the tenses but change in spelling are the following.

1. Verbs ending in **-gar** change **g** to **gu** before **e** in the first person of the preterit and in all persons of the present subjunctive.

pagar   *to pay*
Preterit: pagué, pagaste, pagó, etc.
Pres. Subj.:   pague, pagues, pague, paguemos, paguéis, paguen
Verbs that follow the same pattern: **colgar, llegar, navegar, negar, regar, rogar, jugar.**

2. Verbs ending in **-ger** or **-gir** change **g** to **j** before **o** and **a** in the first person of the present indicative and in all the persons of the present subjunctive.

proteger   *to protect*
Pres. Ind.:   protejo, proteges, protege, etc.
Pres. Subj.:   proteja, protejas, proteja, protejamos, protejáis, protejan
Verbs that follow the same pattern: **coger, corregir, dirigir, elegir, escoger, exigir, recoger.**

3. Verbs ending in **-guar** change **gu** to **gü** before **e** in the first person of the preterit and in all persons of the present subjunctive.

averiguar   *to find out*
Preterit: averigüé, averiguaste, averiguó, etc.
Pres. Subj.:   averigüe, averigües, averigüe, averigüemos, averigüéis, averigüen
The verb **apaciguar** follows the same pattern.

4. Verbs ending in **-guir** change **gu** to **g** before **o** and **a** in the first person of the present indicative and in all persons of the present subjunctive.

conseguir   *to get*
Pres. Ind.:   consigo, consigues, consigue, etc.
Pres. Subj.:   consiga, consigas, consiga, consigamos, consigáis, consigan
Verbs that follow the same pattern: **distinguir, perseguir, proseguir, seguir.**

5. Verbs ending in **-car** change **c** to **qu** before **e** in the first person of the preterit and in all persons of the present subjunctive.

tocar   *to touch; to play (a musical instrument)*
Preterit: toqué, tocaste, tocó, etc.
Pres. Subj.:   toque, toques, toque, toquemos, toquéis, toquen
Verbs that follow the same pattern: **atacar, buscar, comunicar, explicar, indicar, pescar, sacar.**

6. Verbs ending in **-cer** or **-cir** preceded by a consonant change **c** to **z** before **o** and **a** in the first person of the present indicative and in all persons of the present subjunctive.

torcer   *to twist*
Pres. Ind.:   tuerzo, tuerces, tuerce, etc.
Pres. Subj.:   tuerza, tuerzas, tuerza, torzamos, torzáis, tuerzan
Verbs that follow the same pattern: **convencer, esparcir, vencer.**

7. Verbs ending in **-cer** or **-cir** preceded by a vowel change **c** to **zc** before **o** and **a** in the first person of the present indicative and in all persons of the present subjunctive.

conocer   *to know, be acquainted with*
Pres. Ind.:   conozco, conoces, conoce, etc.
Pres. Subj.:   conozca, conozcas, conozca, conozcamos, conozcáis, conozcan
Verbs that follow the same pattern: **agradecer, aparecer, carecer, entristecer** *(to sadden)*, **establecer, lucir, nacer, obedecer, ofrecer, padecer, parecer, pertenecer, reconocer, relucir.**

8. Verbs ending in **-zar** change **z** to **c** before **e** in the first person of the preterit and in all persons of the present subjunctive.

rezar   *to pray*
Preterit: recé, rezaste, rezó, etc.
Pres. Subj.:   rece, reces, rece, recemos, recéis, recen
Verbs that follow the same pattern: **abrazar, alcanzar, almorzar, comenzar, cruzar, empezar, forzar, gozar.**

9. Verbs ending in **-eer** change the unstressed **i** to **y** between vowels in the third-persons singular and plural of the preterit, in all persons of the imperfect subjunctive, and in the present participle.

creer   *to believe*
Pres. Part: creyendo
Preterit: creí, creíste, creyó, creímos, creísteis, creyeron
Imp. Subj.:   creyera(-ese), creyeras, creyera, creyéramos, creyerais, creyeran
Past Part.:   creído
Verbs that follow the same pattern: **leer, poseer.**

10. Verbs ending in **-uir** change the unstressed **i** to **y** between vowels (except **-quir**, which has the silent **u**) in the following tenses and persons.

huir   *to escape, flee*
Pres. Part.:   huyendo
Pres. Ind.:   huyo, huyes, huye, huimos, huís, huyen
Preterit: huí, huiste, huyó, huimos, huisteis, huyeron
Imperative: huye, huya, huyamos, huid, huyan

Pres. Subj.: huya, huyas, huya, huyamos, huyáis, huyan
Imp. Subj.: huyera(-ese), huyeras, huyera, huyéramos, huyerais, huyeran
Verbs that follow the same pattern: **atribuir, concluir, constituir, construir, contribuir, destituir, destruir, disminuir, distribuir, excluir, incluir, influir, instruir, restituir, sustituir.**

11. Verbs ending in **-eír** lose the **e** in the third-person singular and plural of the preterit, in all persons of the imperfect subjunctive, and in the present participle.

    reír   *to laugh*
    Pres Ind.: río, ríes, ríe, reímos, reís, ríen
    Preterit: reí, reíste, rio, reímos, reísteis, rieron
    Pres. Subj.: ría, rías, ría, riamos, riáis, rían
    Imp. Subj.: riera(-ese), rieras, riera, riéramos, rierais, rieran
    Pres. Part.: riendo
    Verbs that follow the same pattern: **freír, sonreír.**

12. Verbs ending in **-iar** add a written accent to the **i**, except in the first- and second-persons plural of the present indicative and subjunctive.

    fiar(se)   *to trust*
    Pres. Ind.: (me) fío, (te) fías, (se) fía, (nos) fiamos, (os) fiáis, (se) fían
    Pres. Subj.: (me) fíe, (te) fíes, (se) fíe, (nos) fiemos, (os) fiéis, (se) fíen
    Verbs that follow the same pattern: **ampliar, criar, desviar, enfriar, enviar, guiar, telegrafiar, vaciar, variar.**

13. Verbs ending in **-uar** (except **-guar**) add a written accent to the **u**, except in the first- and second-persons plural of the present indicative and subjunctive.

    actuar   *to act*
    Pres. Ind.: actúo, actúas, actúa, actuamos, actuáis, actúan
    Pres. Subj.: actúe, actúes, actúe, actuemos, actuéis, actúen
    Verbs that follow the same pattern: **acentuar, continuar, efectuar, exceptuar, graduar, habituar, insinuar, situar.**

14. Verbs ending in **-ñir** lose the **i** of the diphthongs **ie** and **ió** in the third-person singular and plural of the preterit and all persons of the imperfect subjunctive. They also change the **e** of the stem to **i** in the same persons in the present indicative and present subjunctive.

    teñir   *to dye*
    Pres. Ind.: tiño, tiñes, tiñe, teñimos, teñís, tiñen
    Preterit: teñí, teñiste, tiñó, teñimos, teñisteis, tiñeron
    Pres. Subj.: tiña, tiñas, tiña, tiñamos, tiñáis, tiñan
    Imp. Subj.: tiñera(-ese), tiñeras, tiñera, tiñéramos, tiñerais, tiñeran
    Verbs that follow the same pattern: **ceñir, constreñir, desteñir, estreñir, reñir.**

Some Common Irregular Verbs

Only those tenses with irregular forms are given below.

adquirir   *to acquire*
Pres. Ind.: adquiero, adquieres, adquiere, adquirimos, adquirís, adquieren
Pres. Subj.: adquiera, adquieras, adquiera, adquiramos, adquiráis, adquieran
Imperative: adquiere, adquiera, adquiramos, adquirid, adquieran

andar   *to walk*
Preterit: anduve, anduviste, anduvo, anduvimos, anduvisteis, anduvieron
Imp. Subj.: anduviera (anduviese), anduvieras, anduviera, anduviéramos, anduvierais, anduvieran

avergonzarse   *to be ashamed, to be embarrassed*

Pres. Ind.:   me avergüenzo, te avergüenzas, se avergüenza, nos avergonzamos, os avergonzáis, se avergüenzan

Pres. Subj: me avergüence, te avergüences, se avergüence, nos avergoncemos, os avergoncéis, se avergüencen

Imperative: avergüénzate, avergüéncese, avergoncémonos, avergonzaos, avergüéncense

caber   *to fit, to have enough room*

Pres. Ind.:   quepo, cabes, cabe cabemos, cabéis, caben

Preterit: cupe, cupiste, cupo, cupimos, cupisteis, cupieron

Future: cabré, cabrás, cabrá, cabremos, cabréis, cabrán

Conditional: cabría, cabrías, cabría, cabríamos, cabríais, cabrían

Imperative: cabe, quepa, quepamos, cabed, quepan

Pres. Subj.:   quepa, quepas, quepa, quepamos, quepáis, quepan

Imp. Subj.:   cupiera (cupiese), cupieras, cupiera, cupiéramos, cupierais, cupieran

caer   *to fall*

Pres. Ind.:   caigo, caes, cae, caemos, caéis, caen

Preterit: caí, caíste, cayó, caímos, caísteis, cayeron

Imperative: cae, caiga, caigamos, caed, caigan

Pres. Subj.:   caiga, caigas, caiga, caigamos, caigáis, caigan

Imp. Subj.:   cayera (cayese), cayeras, cayera, cayéramos, cayerais, cayeran

Past Part.:   caído

conducir   *to guide, to drive*

Pres. Ind.:   conduzco, conduces, conduce, conducimos, conducís, conducen

Preterit: conduje, condujiste, condujo, condujimos, condujisteis, condujeron

Imperative: conduce, conduzca, conduzcamos, conducid, conduzcan

Pres. Subj.:   conduzca, conduzcas, conduzca, conduzcamos, conduzcáis, conduzcan

Imp. Subj.:   condujera (condujese), condujeras, condujera, condujéramos, condujerais, condujeran

(All verbs ending in -**ducir** follow this pattern.)

convenir   *to agree (see* **venir***)*

dar   *to give*

Pres. Ind.:   doy, das, da, damos, dais, dan

Preterit: di, diste, dio, dimos, disteis, dieron

Imperative: da, dé, demos, dad, den

Pres. Subj.:   dé, des, dé, demos, deis, den

Imp. Subj.:   diera (diese), dieras, diera, diéramos, dierais, dieran

decir   *to say, tell*

Pres. Ind.:   digo, dices, dice, decimos, decís, dicen

Preterit: dije, dijiste, dijo, dijimos, dijisteis, dijeron

Future: diré, dirás, dirá, diremos, diréis, dirán

Conditional: diría, dirías, diría, diríamos, diríais, dirían

Imperative: di, diga, digamos, decid, digan

Pres. Subj.:   diga, digas, diga, digamos, digáis, digan

Imp. Subj.:   dijera (dijese), dijeras, dijera, dijéramos, dijerais, dijeran

Pres. Part.:   diciendo

Past Part.:   dicho

detener   *to stop; to hold; to arrest (see* **tener***)*

entretener   *to entertain, amuse (see* **tener***)*

errar   *to err; to miss*

Pres. Ind.:   yerro, yerras, yerra, erramos, erráis, yerran

Imperative: yerra, yerre, erremos, errad, yerren

Pres. Subj.:   yerre, yerres, yerre, erremos, erréis, yerren

estar   *to be*
Pres. Ind.:   estoy, estás, está, estamos, estáis, están
Preterit: estuve, estuviste, estuvo, estuvimos, estuvisteis, estuvieron
Imperative: está, esté, estemos, estad, estén
Pres. Subj.:   esté, estés, esté, estemos, estéis, estén
Imp. Subj.:   estuviera (estuviese), estuvieras, estuviera, estuviéramos, estuvierais, estuvieran

haber   *to have*
Pres. Ind.:   he, has, ha, hemos, habéis, han
Preterit: hube, hubiste, hubo, hubimos, hubisteis, hubieron
Future: habré, habrás, habrá, habremos, habréis, habrán
Conditional: habría, habrías, habría, habríamos, habríais, habrían
Pres. Subj.:   haya, hayas, haya, hayamos, hayáis, hayan
Imp. Subj.:   hubiera (hubiese), hubieras, hubiera, hubiéramos, hubierais, hubieran

hacer   *to do, to make*
Pres. Ind.:   hago, haces, hace, hacemos, hacéis, hacen
Preterit: hice, hiciste, hizo, hicimos, hicisteis, hicieron
Future: haré, harás, hará, haremos, haréis, harán
Imperative: haz, haga, hagamos, haced, hagan
Pres. Subj.:   haga, hagas, haga, hagamos, hagáis, hagan
Imp. Subj.:   hiciera (hiciese), hicieras, hiciera, hiciéramos, hicierais, hicieran
Past Part.:   hecho

imponer   *to impose; to depose (see* **poner***)*

ir   *to go*
Pres. Ind.:   voy, vas, va, vamos, vais, van
Imp. Ind.:   iba, ibas, iba, íbamos, ibais, iban
Preterit: fui, fuiste, fue, fuimos, fuisteis, fueron
Imperative: ve, vaya, vayamos, id, vayan
Pres. Subj.:   vaya, vayas, vaya, vayamos, vayáis, vayan
Imp. Subj.:   fuera (fuese), fueras, fuera, fuéramos, fuerais, fueran

jugar   *to play*
Pres. Ind.:   juego, juegas, juega, jugamos, jugáis, juegan
Imperative: juega, juegue, juguemos, jugad, jueguen
Pres. Subj.:   juegue, juegues, juegue, juguemos, juguéis, jueguen

obtener   *to obtain (see* **tener***)*

oír   *to hear*
Pres. Ind.:   oigo, oyes, oye, oímos, oís, oyen
Preterit: oí, oíste, oyó, oímos, oísteis, oyeron
Imperative: oye, oiga, oigamos, oíd, oigan
Pres. Subj.:   oiga, oigas, oiga, oigamos, oigáis, oigan
Imp. Subj.:   oyera (oyese), oyeras, oyera, oyéramos, oyerais, oyeran
Pres. Part.:   oyendo
Past Part.:   oído

oler   *to smell*
Pres. Ind.:   huelo, hueles, huele, olemos, oléis, huelen
Imperative: huele, huela, olamos, oled, huelan
Pres. Subj.:   huela, huelas, huela, olamos, oláis, huelan

poder   *to be able to*
Preterit: pude, pudiste, pudo, pudimos, pudisteis, pudieron
Future: podré, podrás, podrá, podremos, podréis, podrán

Conditional: podría, podrías, podría, podríamos, podríais, podrían
Imperative: puede, pueda, podamos, poded, puedan
Pres. Subj.: pueda, puedas, pueda, podamos, podáis, puedan
Imp. Subj.: pudiera (pudiese), pudieras, pudiera, pudiéramos, pudierais, pudieran
Pres. Part.: pudiendo

poner   *to place, put*
Pres. Ind.: pongo, pones, pone, ponemos, ponéis, ponen
Preterit: puse, pusiste, puso, pusimos, pusisteis, pusieron
Future: pondré, pondrás, pondrá, pondremos, pondréis, pondrán
Conditional: pondría, pondrías, pondría, pondríamos, pondríais, pondrían
Imperative: pon, ponga, pongamos, poned, pongan
Pres. Subj.: ponga, pongas, ponga, pongamos, pongáis, pongan
Imp. Subj.: pusiera (pusiese), pusieras, pusiera, pusiéramos, pusierais, pusieran
Past Part.: puesto

querer   *to want, wish; to like, love*
Preterit: quise, quisiste, quiso, quisimos, quisisteis, quisieron
Future: querré, querrás, querrá, querremos, querréis, querrán
Conditional: querría, querrías, querría, querríamos, querríais, querrían
Imp. Subj.: quisiera (quisiese), quisieras, quisiera, quisiéramos, quisierais, quisieran

resolver   *to decide on, to solve*
Past Part.: resuelto

saber   *to know*
Pres. Ind.: sé, sabes, sabe, sabemos, sabéis, saben
Preterit: supe, supiste, supo, supimos, supisteis, supieron
Future: sabré, sabrás, sabrá, sabremos, sabréis, sabrán
Conditional: sabría, sabrías, sabría, sabríamos, sabríais, sabrían
Imperative: sabe, sepa, sepamos, sabed, sepan
Pres. Subj.: sepa, sepas, sepa, sepamos, sepáis, sepan
Imp. Subj.: supiera (supiese), supieras, supiera, supiéramos, supierais, supieran

salir   *to leave; to go out*
Pres. Ind.: salgo, sales, sale, salimos, salís, salen
Future: saldré, saldrás, saldrá, saldremos, saldréis, saldrán
Conditional: saldría, saldrías, saldría, saldríamos, saldríais, saldrían
Imperative: sal, salga, salgamos, salid, salgan
Pres. Subj.: salga, salgas, salga, salgamos, salgáis, salgan

ser   *to be*
Pres. Ind.: soy, eres, es, somos, sois, son
Imp. Ind.: era, eras, era, éramos, erais, eran
Preterit: fui, fuiste, fue, fuimos, fuisteis, fueron
Imperative: sé, sea, seamos, sed, sean
Pres. Subj.: sea, seas, sea, seamos, seáis, sean
Imp. Subj.: fuera (fuese), fueras, fuera, fuéramos, fuerais, fueran

suponer   *to assume, to suppose (see* **poner***)*

tener   *to have*
Pres. Ind.: tengo, tienes, tiene, tenemos, tenéis, tienen
Preterit: tuve, tuviste, tuvo, tuvimos, tuvisteis, tuvieron
Future: tendré, tendrás, tendrá, tendremos, tendréis, tendrán
Conditional: tendría, tendrías, tendría, tendríamos, tendríais, tendrían
Imperative: ten, tenga, tengamos, tened, tengan
Pres. Subj.: tenga, tengas, tenga, tengamos, tengáis, tengan
Imp. Subj.: tuviera (tuviese), tuvieras, tuviera, tuviéramos, tuvierais, tuvieran

traducir   *to translate (see* **conducir***)*

traer   *to bring*

Pres. Ind.:   traigo, traes, trae, traemos, traéis, traen
Preterit: traje, trajiste, trajo, trajimos, trajisteis, trajeron
Imperative: trae, traiga, traigamos, traed, traigan
Pres. Subj.:   traiga, traigas, traiga, traigamos, traigáis, traigan
Imp. Subj.:   trajera (trajese), trajeras, trajera, trajéramos, trajerais, trajeran
Pres. Part.:   trayendo
Past Part.:   traído

valer   *to be worth*

Pres. Ind.:   valgo, vales, vale, valemos, valéis, valen
Future: valdré, valdrás, valdrá, valdremos, valdréis, valdrán
Conditional: valdría, valdrías, valdría, valdríamos, valdríais, valdrían
Imperative: vale, valga, valgamos, valed, valgan
Pres. Sub.:   valga, valgas, valga, valgamos, valgáis, valgan

venir   *to come*

Pres. Ind.:   vengo, vienes, viene, venimos, venís, vienen
Preterit: vine, viniste, vino, vinimos, vinisteis, vinieron
Future: vendré, vendrás, vendrá, vendremos, vendréis, vendrán
Conditional: vendría, vendrías, vendría, vendríamos, vendríais, vendrían
Imperative: ven, venga, vengamos, venid, vengan
Pres. Subj.:   venga, vengas, venga, vengamos, vengáis, vengan
Imp. Subj.:   viniera (viniese), vinieras, viniera, viniéramos, vinierais, vinieran
Pres. Part.:   viniendo

ver   *to see*

Pres. Ind.:   veo, ves, ve, vemos, veis, ven
Imp. Ind.:   veía, veías, veía, veíamos, veíais, veían
Preterit: vi, viste, vio, vimos, visteis, vieron
Imperative: ve, vea, veamos, ved, vean
Pres. Subj.:   vea, veas, vea, veamos, veáis, vean
Imp. Subj.:   viera (viese), vieras, viera, viéramos, vierais, vieran
Past Part.:   visto

volver   *to return*

Past Part.:   vuelto

Appendix C Glossary of Grammatical Terms

adjective: A word that is used to describe a noun: *tall* girl, *difficult* lesson.

adverb: A word that modifies a verb, an adjective, or another adverb. It answers the questions "How?" "When?" "Where?": She walked *slowly*. She'll be here *tomorrow*. She is *here*.

agreement: A term applied to changes in form that nouns cause in the words that surround them. In Spanish, verb forms agree with their subjects in person and number (**yo** habl**o**, **él** habl**a**, etc.). Spanish adjectives agree in gender and number with the noun they describe. Thus, a feminine plural noun requires a feminine plural ending in the adjective that describes it (cas**as** amarill**as**) and a masculine singular noun requires a masculine singular ending in the adjective (libro negr**o**).

auxiliary verb: A verb that helps in the conjugation of another verb: I *have* finished. He *was* called. She *will* go. He *would* eat.

command form: The form of the verb used to give an order or a direction: *Go! Come* back! *Turn* to the right!

conjugation: The process by which the forms of the verb are presented in their different moods and tenses: I *am*, you *are*, he *is*, she *was*, we *were*, etc.

contraction: The combination of two or more words into one: *isn't, don't, can't*.

definite article: A word used before a noun indicating a definite person or thing: *the* woman, *the* money.

demonstrative: A word that refers to a definite person or object: *this, that, these, those*.

diphthong: A combination of two vowels forming one syllable. In Spanish, a diphthong is composed of one *strong* vowel (**a, e, o**) and one *weak* vowel (**u, i**) or two weak vowels: **ei, ua, ui.**

exclamation: A word used to express emotion: *How* strong! *What* beauty!

gender: A distinction of nouns, pronouns, and adjectives, based on whether they are masculine or feminine.

indefinite article: A word used before a noun that refers to an indefinite person or object: *a* child, *an* apple.

infinitive: The form of the verb generally preceded in English by the word *to* and showing no subject or number: *to do, to bring*.

interrogative: A word used in asking a question: *Who? What? Where?*

main clause: A group of words that includes a subject and a verb and by itself has complete meaning: *They saw me. I go now.*

noun: A word that names a person, place, or thing: *Ann, London, pencil*.

number: Refers to singular and plural: *chair, chairs*.

object: Generally a noun or a pronoun that is the receiver of the verb's action. A direct object answers the question *"What?"* or *"Whom?"*: We know *her*. Take *it*. An indirect object answers the question *"To whom?"* or *"To what?"*: Give *John* the money. Nouns and pronouns can also be objects of prepositions: The letter is *from Rick*. I'm thinking *about you*.

past participle: Past forms of a verb: *gone, worked, written*.

person: The form of the pronoun and of the verb that shows the person referred to: *I* (first-person singular), *you* (second-person singular), *she* (third-person singular), and so on.

possessive: A word that denotes ownership or possession: This is *our* house. The book isn't *mine*.

preposition: A word that introduces a noun or pronoun and indicates its function in the sentence: They were *with* us. She is *from* Nevada.

present participle: A verb form in English that ends in *-ing: eating, sleeping, working*. In Spanish, this form cannot be used as a noun or after a preposition.

pronoun: A word that is used to replace a noun: *she, them, us*, and so on. A **subject pronoun** refers to the person or thing spoken of: *They* work. An **object pro-**

noun receives the action of the verb: They arrested *us* (direct object pronoun). She spoke to *him* (indirect object pronoun). A pronoun can also be the object of a preposition: The children stayed with *us*.

reflexive pronoun: A pronoun that refers back to the subject: *myself, yourself, himself, herself, itself, ourselves,* and so on.

subject: The person, place, or thing spoken of: *Robert* works. *Our car* is new.

subordinate clause: A clause that has no complete meaning by itself but depends on a main clause: They knew *that I was here.*

tense: The group of forms in a verb that show the time in which the action of the verb takes place: *I go* (present indicative), *I'm going* (present progressive), *I went* (past), *I was going* (past progressive), *I will go* (future), *I would go* (conditional), *I have gone* (present perfect), *I had gone* (past perfect), *that I may go* (present subjunctive), and so on.

verb: A word that expresses an action or a state: We *sleep*. The baby *is* sick.

Appendix D English Translations of Opening Passages

Lección 1

NICE TO MEET YOU!

Good morning! My name is Juan Carlos Mirabal and I am from California. I'm a student at the University of California. And you? Where are you from?

Good afternoon! My name is Laura Estévez and I am from Arizona. What is your name? Are you a student? I'm a teacher.

Hello! My name is Maria Luisa Vargas Peña and I am from New Mexico. I'm a secretary. And my name is Marcos Fuentes and I'm from Texas. I'm a systems analyst. Are you students?

How is it going? My name is Marisa Barrios and I am Mexican. I'm a dentist. Are you American?

Good evening! My name is Rafael Hernández and I am from Texas. I'm a pilot. How are you (all)? Fine?

My name is Beatriz López and I am from Puerto Rico. I am a Spanish teacher. How are you? What's new?

See you later!
See you tomorrow!
See you Monday!
Good-Bye!
Bye!

Lección 2

THE FIRST DAY OF CLASSES

MISS A. *(At the door)* Excuse me. Good morning, professor.
PROF. Good morning. Come in and have a seat, please.
MISS A. Thank you very much.
PROF. Miss Alba, (this is) Dr. Díaz.
MISS A. It's a pleasure, Dr. Díaz.
DR. D. The pleasure is mine, Miss Alba.
MISS A. Excuse me, professor, what time is it?
PROF. It's eleven thirty.

MISS A. At what time is the class today?
PROF. It's at three in the afternoon.

L. What's your address, Mario?
M. Ninety-eight Magnolia Street.
L. Oh, I also need Pedro's address. He is Rocío's friend, isn't he?
M. Yes. The address is one hundred seventy-five Olmos Avenue.
R. Mario, how many students are there in the class?
M. There are forty students.

S. Professor, how do you say "*de nada*" in English?
PROF. You say, "You're welcome."
S. What does "to return" mean?
PROF. It means "*regresar.*"

L. Do you work, Daniel?
D. Yes, I work at a hospital. And you?
L. I don't work; I only study.
D. How many classes are you taking?
L. I'm taking five classes. Listen, are you taking French this semester?
D. No, because I already speak French. I'm taking a German class with Dr. Smith.
L. I don't speak French, but I speak a little Italian and Portuguese.

Lección 3

ON THE PHONE

Raquel, Pedro, Marisa, and Carmen are university students who live in Los Angeles, and are very good friends. Raquel wants to be a doctor, Pedro wants to be a lawyer, and Marisa and Carmen want to be teachers. Pedro is dark, tall, and very charming. The girls are intelligent and pretty. Raquel wishes to speak with Pedro.

M. Yes?
R. Hello. Is Pedro there?
M. No, he's not. I'm sorry.
R. What time is he coming back?
M. At nine o'clock at night.
R. Then I will call later.
M. Very well. Good-bye.

Carmen speaks with her friend Marisa.

M. Hello.

C. Hello. Is Marisa there?

M. Yes, speaking . . . Carmen?

C. Yes. How's it going, Marisa?

M. Very well, thank you. What's new?

C. Nothing. Listen! Where do we eat tomorrow? In the cafeteria?

M. No, tomorrow I have to write a report and I must read several articles in the library.

C. I also have to study for an exam.

M. Then we shall see each other on Tuesday.

Pedro speaks with Raquel.

RO. Hello.

P. Hello. Is Raquel there?

RO. Yes. Who is speaking?

P. Pedro Morales.

RO. One moment, please.

RA. *(To Rosa)* Who is it?

RO. It's your friend Pedro.

RA. Hi, Pedro. How's it going?

P. Fine, and you?

RA. So-so.

P. Why? Love problems?

RA. No, financial problems. I need money!

P. So do I! Listen, are you working at the hospital tonight?

RA. No, today I am not working at night. On Mondays my boyfriend and I study at the library.

P. Are you coming to my house tomorrow?

RA. No, because tomorrow I have to go to another hospital to apply for work.

RO. *(To Raquel)* Listen. What is your friend Pedro like? Is he handsome?

RA. Yes, and very intelligent, but . . . he has a girlfriend.

Lección 4

```
          AN INVITATION
You are invited to a ___New Year's Eve___ party
At the home (address) of __Adela Benavente__
Street: _18 de Julio_ Number: ___923___
City: __Montevideo__
The party starts at ___9:00 P.M.___
```

BEFORE THE PARTY

A. Many of my classmates are going to come to my party. Are you going to bring your cousin?

H. Yes, and I'm also going to bring some compact discs and the *empanadas* that my Mom is going to prepare.

A. And we are going to prepare chicken, hors-d'oeuvres, and potato salad. Everything is going to be delicious!

H. Oh, Adela, I'm hungry now!

A. Do you want a sandwich? And, if you're thirsty, there's soda pop, beer, and mineral water.

H. Yes, I want a sandwich and a soda pop . . . No . . . I prefer a glass of water. Listen, what time does the dance start at the club?

A. At eleven. Are you going to call Julio and Teresa?

H. Yes, because they plan to go to the club with us. Today is Teresa's birthday.

A. Oh, yea? How old is she?

H. I think she turns twenty today. She's giving a party on Saturday and we are invited.

Adela and her friends have a very good time at the party. They all dance, talk, eat, and drink. Afterwards, they go to the Yacht Club to celebrate the arrival of the new year. Julio is not going because he's sick.

At the Yacht Club

H. The band is great. Shall we dance, Adela?

A. Not now, Humberto. I'm a little tired and I'm very hot. Why don't we go to the terrace?

H. Good idea. I'm going to take the drinks. Do you want champagne, cider, or (a) cocktail?

A. To toast, a glass of champagne, please. Afterwards, sangria . . .

J. Don't you have grapes? In Spain we always eat twelve grapes at midnight on the 31st of December.

A. No, Javier. We don't have grapes. It's twelve o'clock!

E. Happy new year! Happy new year!

Lección 5

PLANS FOR A WEEKEND

Carol, a student from the United States, is in Spain. She attends the University of Salamanca and lives in a boarding house near the Plaza Mayor. She wants to learn to speak Spanish perfectly, and that is why she never misses the opportunity to practice the language. Now she is talking with two Spanish friends at a sidewalk cafe. They are eating sandwiches and drinking coffee.

- L. Hey, Carol, can you go with us to Madrid this weekend?
- CL. No, I can't . . . I have to write a lot of letters: to my grandmother, to my uncle, to my brother . . .
- L. You miss your family very much, don't you?
- CL. Yes, . . . especially my older brother.
- CN. What is your brother like? Blond? Dark?
- CL. He's blond, slim, and medium height. He is studying medicine.
- CN. Very interesting! When is he coming to Spain? In the summer?
- CL. No, he's going to travel to Mexico with his wife and two daughters.
- CN. Bah! He's married . . . What a pity! Don't you have another brother?
- CL. No, I'm sorry. I have here a photograph of my nieces.
- CN. *(She looks at the photo.)* These are your nieces? They're very pretty!
- CL. They start attending school on September fifteenth.
- L. Listen! Why don't you come to Madrid with us? It's more interesting than writing letters . . .
- CL. Are you going by car?
- L. No, we prefer to go by bus. It's as comfortable as the car, it doesn't cost much, and we don't have to drive.
- CL. Good idea! I never drive in Madrid. And where do you plan to go?
- CN. To the Prado Museum. They have there some of the most famous paintings in the world.
- L. It's very interesting! And Madrid has some very good restaurants! We always have lunch at Casa Botín; as far as I'm concerned it's the best of all.

- CL. Okay. Let's go to Madrid! . . . If it doesn't rain! Because if it rains, I will not go.
- CN. No, dear, it isn't going to rain.
- CL. When do we return?
- L. Saturday night or Sunday.
- CL. Oh, Luis, Marisol's party is tomorrow. Where is it?
- L. It's at her house. Do you want to go with me?
- CL. Yes, we (will) go with you.
- L. Great! Be ready at nine.

Lección 6

A TRIP TO PERU

Teresa, a Mexican teacher, is going to spend her vacation in Peru. She has just arrived in Lima, where she's planning to spend a few days before going to Machu Picchu to visit the famous Incan ruins. Teresa shows her passport and then goes through customs. In the airport, Teresa sees gold and silver objects, and buys some for her family.

Teresa goes to the tourist office in order to get information.

- T. Good morning, sir. I don't know Lima. Do you have a list of hotels and boarding houses?
- E. Yes, Miss. Here it is.

Teresa reads an ad about Hotel Bolívar.

Hotel Bolívar

The best hotel in Lima, located downtown and near many places of interest, is the favorite of thousands of tourists who visit our beautiful capital. We have ample rooms overlooking the street and interior ones. All the rooms have private bathrooms, air conditioning, and television. The hotel has two restaurants that offer international meals and room service. We accept credit cards and traveler's checks. To make reservations, call 285-3946.

- T. I wish to go to the Hotel Bolívar. Where can I find a taxi?
- E. Go to the second door on the right. There is also a bus that takes you downtown.

At the Hotel Bolívar, Teresa asks for a room.

T. I need a single room with a private bathroom, please.

E. We have one overlooking the street that costs 208 soles per day. There's also another interior one on the second floor for 130 new soles.

T. They are rather expensive. Don't you have any cheaper rooms?

E. No, there isn't any. There are few vacant rooms now.

T. I prefer the interior room. What is the exchange rate?

E. I don't know . . . I am going to find out. Please sign here.

Teresa signs the register.

T. I want to have dinner in my room. Until what time do they serve dinner?

E. They serve it until eleven.

T. Can someone take my suitcases to the room, please?

E. Yes, the bellhop will come to take them right away. Here's the key.

Since it is warm, Teresa decides to go to the swimming pool.

Lección 7

SPEAKING OF VACATIONS

Teresa arrived yesterday from her trip to Peru, and now she is talking on the phone with her friend Silvia. The girls have been talking for a half hour, and Teresa is telling her about her trip.

T. I liked the capital very much, but I liked Machu Picchu better.

S. And you didn't send me a postcard!

T. I bought you two, but I didn't send them. Listen, I have to return (to you) the suitcase and the carry-on bag that you lent me.

S. There is no hurry. Did you take a lot of luggage?

T. Yes, I took three suitcases. I paid excess baggage fees.

S. How much did the plane ticket cost you? Did you travel first class?

T. Are you crazy? I traveled in tourist class. It cost me three thousand five

hundred pesos! Round-trip, of course . . .

S. How was the flight?

T. A little long . . . And since the plane left two hours behind schedule, we arrived very late.

S. Did anything interesting happen to you in Lima?

T. Well . . . at the travel agency where I bought the ticket to Machu Picchu, I met a very charming young man.

S. Did he travel with you? You have to tell me everything that happened.

T. Yes, I traveled with him by plane to Cuzco, where we had lunch together. Then we talked during the entire train ride to Machu Picchu.

S. I don't know why your vacations are always great and my vacations are so boring.

T. Then next time we have to travel together.

S. Okay, but only if we go by train or by boat. I don't like to travel by plane.

T. Okay, we'll travel by train. Listen, this Saturday, I'm going to the movies with Cecilia. Do you want to go with us?

S. Who is Cecilia?

T. She is the girl that I introduced to you at the library last month.

S. Oh, that one . . . I remember now. Yes, let's go together.

T. Do you want to go have lunch with me now?

S. No, thanks, I already had lunch.

T. Okay, then I'll see you tomorrow.

Lección 8

AT A CUBAN RESTAURANT

Today is December first. It's Lidia and Jorge Torres's wedding anniversary and to celebrate it they are going to dinner at one of the best restaurants in Miami. Now they arrive at the El Caribe Restaurant.

L. What a surprise! This is a very elegant restaurant!

J. And the food is excellent.

W. This way, please. Here is the menu.

L. Thanks. *(She reads the menu.)*

FOR DINNER

(All dishes are served with the soup of the day and salad.)

Fish and shellfish

Lobster	$18.00	Trout	$11.50
Salmon	$14.50	Shrimp	$11.00

Meat

Meatballs	$ 6.00	Stuffed turkey	$10.00
Steak	$12.00	Fried chicken	$ 8.50
Lamb	$13.00	Chicken & rice	$ 6.00
Roast pork	$17.00		

J. Why don't you order a tenderloin steak? They prepare some delicious steaks here. Or lobster?

L. No, last night I went to dinner at the Ruiz's, and they served lobster.

W. I recommend to you the specialty of the house: roast pork and rice with black beans. For dessert, ice cream, caramel custard, or ice cream cake.

J. I want roast pork and rice with black beans. And you?

L. I want soup, shrimp, and rice.

J. To drink, bring us a vermouth and then a half bottle of red wine.

W. Very well, sir. *(He writes down the order.)*

Before eating dinner, Lidia and Jorge drink vermouth and talk.

L. Did your parents go to the party that Eva gave yesterday?

J. Yes. It was at the Los Violines Club.

L. Did they give her the gift (that) they bought for her in Mexico?

J. The bracelet? Yes, they gave it to her. She loved it.

L. Did they show it to you before they gave it to her?

J. Yes, they showed it to me when I went for them the day before yesterday in the afternoon.

L. They got it at a very good price in a very elegant store.

After eating, Lidia and Jorge drink coffee. Jorge asks for the bill, pays it, leaves the waiter a good tip and they leave. They have tickets to see a comedy and, since it is raining cats and dogs, and the theater is far, they take a taxi.

J. Happy anniversary, my love. *(He gives her a kiss.)*

L. *(She hugs him.)* Happy anniversary, dear.

Lección 9

A VERY BUSY DAY

Although today is Saturday, Mirta and Isabel got up early to finish cleaning the apartment. Tonight, the two girls are invited to a concert at the House of Paraguayan Culture. Isabel is a little tired because last night she went to bed late.

M. Why did you come (home) so late last night? Where were you?

I. At the store. I had to buy a present for Eva because tomorrow is her birthday. Well, shall we start cleaning?

M. Yes, I'm going to sweep the kitchen and I'm going to vacuum the rug.

I. Then I'm going to clean the bathroom. Later I'm going to cook and iron my red dress. I'm going to wear it tonight.

M. I don't know what to wear.

I. Why don't you wear your blue dress? It's very pretty.

M. No, I tried it on yesterday and it doesn't fit. Oh! Where's the dustpan?

I. On the terrace. Oh! I need to bathe the dog, shower, and get dressed . . . and I have an appointment at the hairdresser's at three!

M. I want to wash my hair and I didn't remember to buy shampoo. May I use yours?

I. Yes, it's in the medicine cabinet.

M. Thanks. I couldn't go to the pharmacy yesterday.

When she arrived at the beauty parlor, Isabel asked the hairdresser for a magazine and sat down to wait for her turn.

I. *(To the hairdresser)* I want a haircut, shampoo, and set.

P. You have very straight hair. Don't you want a perm?

I. No, when I want curls, I use the curling iron. Oh, my hair is very long!

P. Short hair is in style now. *(He cuts her hair and, when he finishes, Isabel looks at herself in the mirror.)*

I. Very good! Now I want to make an appointment for my friend for next week.

P. Wednesday, February first, at nine-thirty? Generally, there are fewer people in the morning.

I. That's fine. My friend's name is Mirta Ortega.

Isabel leaves her purse on the counter. The hairdresser calls her.

P. Miss! Is this purse yours?

I. Yes, it's mine. Thank you.

Lección 10

SILVIA'S VACATION

Córdoba, Argentina
February 12, 2002

Dear Victoria,

I was wrong! I thought I wasn't going to like going on vacation with my parents and that I was going to be bored; however, I am having a very good time.

We arrived in Cordoba one week ago. The day after we arrived, we went camping near Río de los Sauces. My Dad and my brother pitched the tents and we all slept soundly in our sleeping bags. I did everything! I swam, I went fishing with Miguel Ángel (I didn't catch anything, in spite of the fact that I had a new fishing rod), I rode on horseback, and I rode a bike.

Last night a few Chilean friends gave a party. I didn't want to go, but my Dad convinced me and I went. There I met Gustavo, a young man from Santiago. I danced with him all night.

And how did it go for you in Buenos Aires? Did you go shopping? Did you stay at your aunt and uncle's home? I hope so, because hotels in Buenos Aires cost an arm and a leg. I stayed in one three months ago and it cost me a fortune . . .

Next year you have to come with us. Seriously! We plan to go to Bariloche and rent a cabin. Miguel Ángel says he's going to teach you how to ski (when we were children we used to go to Bariloche every year and he learned to ski very well).

Okay, I'm leaving, because Mom told me that Gustavo was waiting for me. We're going to plan another party!

A hug,
Silvia

P.S. On this trip I learned to appreciate nature, the country, and . . . Chilean young men!

Lección 11

RUNNING ERRANDS

In a house on Ponce Street in San Juan, Puerto Rico, lives the Vargas family. Sergio is very tired today and wants to sleep late because today he has the day off. His mother wants him to run several errands, so the poor boy has to get up as soon as the alarm goes off at seven in the morning.

At nine, he arrives at the dry cleaner's that is (located) near his house.

S. I'm here to pick up my clothes. Here's the claim check. *(Thinking)* I hope my trousers are ready.

E. *(Reads)* A woman's overcoat and a pair of trousers. *(To Sergio)* One moment, please. *(She comes back a while later.)* The pants are pink, right?

S. They were white when I brought them in . . . !

At ten, Sergio is in the photo section of the La Francia store.

S. I brought in a roll of color film a week ago. I hope it's ready.

E. Let's see . . . Sergio Vargas . . . ? Yes, the pictures came out very well.

S. And how much do you charge to develop a roll of film?

E. Six dollars, sir.

S. Very well. *(He looks at the photographs.)* But who is this lady? These pictures aren't mine!

At eleven, Sergio parks his motorcycle in front of the bank.

S. I want to deposit this check, which is in my mother's name. Is it necessary for her to sign it?

C. If you're going to deposit it in her checking account, no.

S. Very well, that's what I want to do. I also want to withdraw two hundred dollars from my savings account.

C. Fill out this card, please.

S. I need you to give me the balance of my savings account.

C. You only have twenty dollars. I'm sorry, Mr. Vargas, but you don't have enough money.

When Sergio leaves the bank, he doesn't find his motorcycle.

S. *(Screaming)* Oh no! Somebody stole my motorcycle!

L. The young man who took (away) your motorcycle said he was your brother . . .

S. I'm an only child!

L. *(Thinking)* They look a lot like each other. I'm surprised they're not brothers.

S. *(As he walks to the police station)* Next Tuesday the thirteenth I'm not leaving the house!

Lección 12

ASKING FOR INFORMATION

Julia, a girl from Honduras, arrived in Madrid a week ago. With her Spanish friends she visited the Parque del Retiro, the Palacio Real, and the old cities of Segovia, Avila, and Toledo. At each place, she bought a pile of postcards to send to her parents and friends. Today she decided to go to the post office to send the postcards and to pick up a package and a money order.

J. *(Thinking)* I doubt that the post office is open at this hour. I think it opens at nine. *(To a gentleman who is standing on the corner)* Tell me, sir, where is the post office located?

MR. G. It's five blocks from here, at the Plaza de La Cibeles.

J. The fact is . . . I'm a foreigner, and I don't know the streets. Can you tell me how to get there?

MR. G. Oh! Continue straight ahead on this street until you get to the Plaza de Colón.

J. How many blocks?

MR. G. Two. Then turn right when you get to the traffic light, on Alcalá Street.

J. Is the post office on that street?

MR. G. Yes, right there. It's an old building, and it's across from the subway station.

At the post office, Julia speaks with the employee who is at the information window.

J. I'm here to pick up a package and a money order. My name is Julia Reyes.

E. Do you have an I.D.?

J. My passport . . . but I left it at the hotel.

E. I don't think they'll give it to you without identification.

J. Fine, I'll come back this afternoon. Where can I buy stamps?

E. Go to window number two, to the left.

At window number two, Julia asks the employee for the stamps she needs.

J. I want to send these postcards by air mail and a registered letter to Honduras.

E. It's ten euros, miss.

J. Can you tell me how to get from here to El Corte Inglés?

E. Go out through the main door, cross the Plaza de La Cibeles and walk along the Gran Vía until you get to the Plaza Callao. El Corte Inglés is next to the plaza.

At El Corte Inglés, Julia meets her friend Pilar, with whom she is going to go shopping.

J. I thought you wouldn't be here.

P. Listen, girl, it's not true that Spaniards always arrive late. Sometimes we're punctual.

The girls go up to the third floor, where the ladies' department is.

Lección 13

APARTMENT FOR RENT

David and his wife, Lucía, are Colombian and they are studying at the Universidad Nacional Autónoma de México. They live in a boarding house, but they want to move to an apartment which is closer to the university.

L. David, in the newspaper they are advertising an apartment that's in a good neighborhood and has two bedrooms.

D. Let's see! Give me the newspaper. *(He reads the ad.)*

Classified Ads

For rent: furnished apartment: two bedrooms, living room, dining room, kitchen, and bathroom. Central heating, air conditioning. Colonia 1. For information, call 481-3520 from 1 to 5 in the afternoon. Rent: $1,200.

L. We can call to go see it.
D. I don't know . . . It's very expensive for us, Lucía. Besides, we need an apartment that has a garage . . .

On the following day, as soon as they return from the university, David and Lucía go see the apartment.

L. I love the furniture and the curtains!
D. With the salary we're earning, we're not going to be able to pay the rent.
L. Then, instead of working part time we can work full time.
D. You're crazy! There's nobody who can work full time and at the same time study at the university.
L. Don't be so pessimistic, David!
D. I'm not pessimistic; I'm realistic. Besides, we're going to need money to buy blankets, sheets, pillowcases, and kitchen utensils.
L. *(She doesn't pay attention to him and goes to the kitchen.)* David, come to the kitchen. Look, it has a refrigerator, a microwave oven, a dishwasher, a new stove . . . and a big sink.
D. We cannot make a decision until we see other apartments.
L. But David, we're not going to find any apartment that's as good as this one.
D. Perhaps not . . . but we can't pay the rent for this apartment.
L. Listen, and if we win the lottery?
D. Do me a favor. Don't talk nonsense. Let's go!
L. *(Kidding)* Spoilsport!
D. The fact is . . . you married a poor man, my love . . .

Lección 14

A DATE

Oscar and Jorge, two Cuban American students who live in Miami, have a date

tonight with two Venezuelan friends: Elsa and Adela. The boys are going to fix dinner for them in their apartment. Now Oscar is reading the movie guide to see what movie is being shown.

REX Cinema
Last week

Forbidden Love

With Verónica Montiel and Ricardo Mirabal. Nominated as the best movie of the year!

First show: 3:00 P.M.
Last show: 9:00 P.M.

O. Do you feel like seeing a good movie?
J. Yes, but let's not go to the first show because it's too early.
O. Okay, and when the movie ends, we can go to the Versailles cafeteria to have something to drink. My treat.
J. Good idea. But let's not stay too late because tomorrow we have to work.
O. No, man, tomorrow is a holiday.
J. That's true. I think the supermarket is (already) open. Let's go now to buy the things we need for the dinner.
O. Yes, the market opens at seven.

At the supermarket.

O. We need many things: butter, milk, a dozen eggs, bread, sugar . . .
J. Aren't we going to buy meat?
O. Yes, let's buy meat, fish, and chicken. Also oil, two cans of beans, and six (cans) of tomato sauce.
J. No, let's not buy so much tomato sauce, unless you want to eat Italian food for the rest of the month.
O. You're right. Let's see . . . we need apples, grapes, oranges, melon, grapefruit, and pears for the fruit salad . . .
J. Where are the vegetables? We have to buy lettuce, potatoes, carrots, onions, and tomatoes.
O. Gee! Now that I think about it, this is going to cost a fortune. We'll have to go on a diet.

J. OK. Let's go on a diet, provided that we can eat hot dogs and hamburgers from time to time.

O. Listen, let's hurry up because we have to clean the apartment and prepare dinner before the girls arrive.

J. Yes, but let's call them as soon as we get home to ask them if they want to go to the movies or if they prefer to go dancing.

Lección 15

SHOPPING

A. This morning I have opened the closet and I have come to the conclusion that neither you nor I have anything to wear. We have to go shopping today. Look at this advertisement!

El Corte Inglés

Grand sale—Friday and Saturday
We have lowered our prices on all of our clothes. Take advantage of these great reductions.

REAL BARGAINS
Silk blouses—Cotton shirts—Imported leather jackets—Linen shirts—Wool suits
Open from 9 A.M. to 9 P.M.

H. Gerardo has asked me to help him . . . Besides, I have clothes . . .

A. Old and out of style! And yesterday you told me that you needed to exchange the boots that you had bought in El Corte Inglés because they were too wide . . . And you have to buy shoes!

Anita has convinced her husband and they are now in the Corte Inglés, a department store that is in downtown Madrid. Hugo takes the escalator up to the first floor, where the men's clothing department is. Anita stays on the ground floor, where the women's clothing department is. There she meets her friend Tere.

A. How's it going? Taking advantage of the sales, right? Tell me, Tere, how much does that silk blouse cost?

T. Fifty-six euros. What size do you wear?

A. I wear size thirty-eight. I'm going to try it on.

T. Wait, don't you like this skirt? It goes very well with the blouse, and it's a medium. Try it on. The fitting room is to the left.

A. *(From the fitting room)* Tere, do me a favor. Bring me a size thirty-six skirt.

T. Wait . . . I'm sorry, there are no smaller sizes. Why don't you try on this sweater?

A. No . . . I don't like it . . .

Anita bought the blouse, but she did not buy the skirt because it was too big on her and it was too expensive. Afterwards, she went to the shoe department because she needed to buy a pair of red sandals to match a red purse Hugo had given her.

In the men's clothing department, Hugo bought two T-shirts and a vest. Now he is in the shoe department.

H. I wish to exchange these boots.

C. Very well, sir. What size do you take?

H. I take size forty-four.

C. I'll be right back. *(A little while later)* Try these.

H. These are a little narrow. They are tight . . .

C. *(He tries on another pair.)* How are these?

H. These fit well. I'll take them. Can you wrap them up, please?

Hugo, Anita, and Tere meet at the exit.

A. Hugo, take us out to eat. We are starving!

H. I am too! Wait for me here. I'll go get the car.

A. Have you ever been to the Villa Alegre Restaurant?

T. Yes, it is very good. Let's go to that one.

When Anita and Hugo arrive at their home, she sees her husband's purchases.

A. A vest and two T-shirts! Is that all that you have bought? Ah! What am I going to do with you?

H. Well, you can give me a suit for my birthday . . .

Lección 16

CAREERS

Los Angeles, California
August 24, 2002

Dear Sergio,

I want you to know that I haven't written to you before because I haven't had time. Tomorrow I will be very busy also because I will have to register for the fall classes. I plan to take business administration, sociology, and psychology. My advisor has suggested that I take chemistry or physics but, as you know, I have never liked science. I prefer literature!

I would very much like to go to Buenos Aires in December, but I have final exams until the twentieth and I have to get good grades. I must maintain an "A" average because I have a scholarship.

Why don't you come to Los Angeles? We could go to Disneyland and visit San Diego, my favorite city. You have to come before the year 2004 because by then I will have graduated. I will try to get a job before then, because the life of a student is a poor person's life!

Write soon. A hug from your friend,

Daniel

P.S. Say hi to your sister!

Buenos Aires, Argentina
September 15, 2002

Dear Daniel,

Thank you for the invitation! Had I known that you were going to invite me to Los Angeles, I wouldn't have spent so much money on my trip to Rio de Janeiro and I would have saved money for the ticket.

I'm very busy too. Studying to be a lawyer is not easy, and all the professors in law school think that their classes are the only thing that should matter to us.

My sister Amalia (I said hi to her for you) is studying journalism and spends her whole life doing research and writing reports. I suppose that some day she will be a great journalist.

Do you remember José Luis? He's studying engineering and probably next year he'll go to the United States to take some special courses. I would do the same thing! Had he followed his father's advice, he would have finished medical school.

And you? What's your major? I thought your favorite subject was accounting . . . Well, I'm leaving because Marcos invited me to a soccer game. It's at the Boca Stadium and our team is playing. Bye!

Affectionately,
Sergio

P.S. Amalia says hi.

Lección 17

MEDICAL PROBLEMS

Mirta and her husband are in a restaurant to have lunch. She doesn't feel very well today.

M. I don't know what's wrong. I have a fever and my head hurts a lot. I already took four aspirins.

H. I told you to go to the doctor so he could give you a good check up. I hope you have (already) called Dr. Valdivia.

M. He's on vacation. Teresa suggested that I see Dr. Vargas. I have an appointment for this afternoon.

Later in Dr. Vargas' office.

DR. You have a temperature of 102 degrees. How long have you had those headaches?

M. A week. I have a cough and my throat aches. Do you think I have a cold or the flu?

DR. Yes, you have the flu. I am going to prescribe an antibiotic for you. Are you allergic to any medication?

M. Yes. I am allergic to penicillin.

DR. Are you pregnant?

M. No, doctor.

DR. Take these pills four times a day. Start taking them this very day. Here is the prescription.

In the emergency room of the same hospital. Oscar had an accident and they brought him to the hospital in an ambulance. Now he is talking with the doctor.

M. What happened to you?

O. A car hit me. My leg hurts a lot. I think I broke it.

M. Yes, I'm afraid you may have broken it. We are going to take some X-rays. I see you also have a wound on your arm. I am going to call the nurse.

With the nurse

N. The doctor told me to disinfect and bandage your wound in order to avoid an infection. When was the last time you had (they gave you) a tetanus shot?

O. Two years ago.

The nurse takes Oscar to the X-ray room. Oscar's leg is broken and the doctor puts it in a cast.

M. Is there anybody who can come pick you up?

O. Yes, I'm going to call my roommate, but I don't think he's arrived home yet.

Lección 18

THIS CAR IS NO GOOD!

Gloria and Julio, a newlywed couple, are on vacation in Costa Rica. Now they're on the highway, on the way to San José.

G. Julio, you're driving very fast! The speed limit is ninety kilometers per hour. If a police officer sees you, he's going to give you a ticket!

J. Don't worry. Where are we? Do you have the map?

G. It's in the glove compartment but, according to that sign, we are forty kilometers from San José.

J. Is there a gas station nearby? The tank is almost empty.

G. It's a pity that you didn't fill the tank before . . .

J. If you had told me (it) before, I would have done it.

G. You talk as if it were my fault!

J. *(Kidding)* And who am I going to blame? Look, there's a service station . . .

Julio stops at the service station to buy gasoline.

J. *(To the attendant)* Fill the tank, please. Also, could you check the oil and the tires?

A. Yes, sir.

J. Yesterday I had a flat, and when I went to the repair shop, the mechanic told me that I needed new tires.

A. Yes, if I were you, I would change them . . . and I would also buy a new battery.

G. Ah, Julio! The mechanic also told you to fix the brakes and install a new water pump.

J. We'll do all that in San José, if it's necessary.

G. Didn't you also say that you'd change the oil filter and that you'd buy new windshield wipers?

J. If I had known that we were going to have so many problems, I would have bought a new car before leaving on this trip.

G. Yes, because we're going to spend a fortune on repairs.

J. And yesterday, the motor was making a strange noise . . . !

When Julio tries to start (it), the car doesn't work.

J. Oh, no! We'll have to call a tow truck to tow the car to San José.

G. It's not worth it. I would leave it here.

J. I agree with you! If I could, I would buy a new car right now.

Appendix E Answer Key to the Self-Tests

Self-Test Lecciones 1–3

Lección 1

A. 1. be-a-erre-i-o-ese
2. a-ce-o-ese-te-a 3. de-i-a-zeta
4. efe-e-erre-e-i griega-ere-a
5. ge-u-e-ve-a-ere-a
6. hache-e-ene-a-o
7. jota-i-eme-e-ene-e-zeta
8. ele-e-igriega-ve-a

B. 1. once 2. diecisiete (diez y siete)
3. treinta 4. veinte 5. quince
6. trece 7. veintiocho (veinte y
ocho) 8. diecinueve (diez y nueve)
9. doce 10. catorce

C. 1. verde 2. anaranjado
3. amarillo 4. rosado 5. negro
6. morado 7. café (marrón)
8. rojo, blanco y azul

D. 1. domingo 2. miércoles
3. viernes 4. martes 5. sábado
6. jueves

E. 1. noviembre 2. marzo 3. julio
4. enero 5. mayo 6. septiembre
7. otoño 8. primavera

F. son / somos / eres / soy / es / es / son

G. 1. g 2. j 3. l 4. a 5. c 6. i
7. e 8. k 9. b 10. d 11. h
12. f

H. 1. María. 2. Sí. José María.

Lección 2

A. 1. la 2. la 3. los 4. el 5. los
6. los 7. el 8. las 9. la 10. el

B. 1. unas 2. unos 3. una 4. unos
5. una 6. un 7. unos 8. un

C. 1. treinta y ocho 2. cien
3. noventa y uno 4. ochenta y cinco
5. setenta y dos 6. cincuenta y siete
7. cuarenta y seis 8. sesenta y tres

D. 1. La clase de español es a las diez y
media de la mañana. 2. La clase de
inglés es a la una y cuarto de la tarde.
3. La clase de literatura es a las nueve
menos veinte de la noche.

E. 1. trabajas / trabajo / regresas
2. estudian / no estudiamos / toman
3. necesitan / necesita / necesita
4. Deseas / llamo 5. Hablan
ustedes / no hablamos

F. 1. los estudiantes de la señorita Vega
2. el profesor de Amanda 3. los
amigos de Paco

G. 1. avenida 2. dirección 3. dice
4. quiere 5. asiento 6. alemán /
francés 7. Cuántos 8. permiso
9. solamente 10. poco

H. 1. las seis de la tarde 2. el inglés

Lección 3

A. 1. la 2. la 3. los 4. la 5. la
6. las 7. el 8. las 9. los
10. la

B. 1. mi bolígrafo / mis libros 2. La
casa de él / la casa de ella 3. Nuestra
profesora 4. Nuestros amigos
5. tus lápices 6. El profesor de ellos
/ el profesor de ustedes

C. 1. ciento noventa y cinco
2. doscientos ochenta y seis
3. trescientos setenta y uno
4. cuatrocientos sesenta
5. quinientos cincuenta y tres
6. seiscientos cuarenta y cuatro
7. setecientos treinta y dos
8. ochocientos veintisiete
9. novecientos dieciocho
10. mil quinientos trece

D. 1. La chica es alta. 2. El escritorio
es pequeño. 3. Las chicas son
norteamericanas. 4. Es una mujer
muy simpática. 5. Necesito las
plumas rojas.

E. 1. aprendemos   2. comes   3. creo
4. leen   5. bebe   6. debe
7. venden   8. abro   9. reciben
10. escribimos

F. 1. m   2. f   3. i   4. k   5. b
6. o   7. a   8. d   9. h   10. c
11. n   12. e   13. g   14. l   15. j

G. 1. ¿Bueno?   2. Sí, son equivalentes.

Self-Test Lecciones 4-6

Lección 4

A. 1. Yo llevo a mi prima a la universidad.   2. Nosotros llevamos los refrescos a la fiesta.   3. Ellos invitan a Julio y a su novia.
4. Nosotros tenemos cuatro primos.

B. 1. al señor Estrada   2. del club
3. de la terraza   4. a las chicas (a las muchachas)   5. del señor Soto

C. 1. Mis compañeros de clase tienen prisa.   2. Yo no tengo hambre, pero tengo mucha sed.   3. ¿Tienes (Tiene Ud.) calor? ¡Yo tengo frío!   4. Mis amigos tienen sueño.   5. (Nosotros) no tenemos miedo.   6. (Ud.) tiene razón, Srta. Peña. Mary tiene treinta años.

D. 1. voy   2. damos   3. está   4. está
5. van   6. dan   7. estoy   8. van
9. estás   10. doy

E. 1. Yo no voy a hablar con mi mamá hoy.   2. Mis hijos van a estudiar en España.   3. Mi amiga va a leer el libro.   4. Uds. van a traer los discos compactos.   5. Tú vas a bailar en la fiesta.   6. Nosotros vamos a brindar con sidra.

F. 1. quiere (piensa)   2. entendemos (empezamos, comenzamos)   3. pierde
4. Cierras   5. empiezan (comienzan)
6. empezamos (comenzamos)
7. pienso (quiero)   8. preferimos (queremos, pensamos)

G. 1. Invitamos   2. comemos   3. sidra
4. magnífica   5. nuevo   6. cocteles
7. brindamos   8. discos compactos

H. 1. no existe   2. santo   3. no existe
4. ¡Salud!

Lección 5

A. 1. Alfredo es el estudiante más inteligente de la clase.   2. La Lección 2 es menos interesante que la Lección 7.   3. Mi novia es más bonita que tu novia.   4. Roberto es el más guapo de la familia.   5. El profesor tiene menos de veinte estudiantes.   6. Ana es tan alta como Roberto.

B. 1. más grande   2. mejor   3. mejor / peor   4. mayor   5. más pequeño

C. 1. cuesta   2. pueden   3. Recuerda
4. cuento   5. almorzamos
6. vuelves

D. 1. está diciendo   2. estoy hablando
3. estamos leyendo   4. estás comiendo   5. está durmiendo
6. están pidiendo

E. 1. Elsa es la mamá de Marta.
2. El Club Náutico está en la calle Siete.   3. ¡Mmmm! el pollo está delicioso.   4. Roberto es de México y ahora está en California.   5. La cerveza está fría.   6. El escritorio es de metal.   7. Hoy es lunes y mañana es martes.   8. Elvira es médica.   9. La fiesta es en casa de Alicia.   10. La orquesta es magnífica.   11. Ellos están cansados.   12. Laura es mexicana.

F. 1. mí   2. ti   3. ellos   4. nosotros
5. conmigo   6. contigo

G. 1. nieto   2. las pinturas   3. cartas
4. almorzar   5. echas de menos
6. ¡Qué lástima!   7. conducen su auto   8. fotos   9. viajar
10. mediana

H. 1. V   2. F   3. F   4. V   5. V

Lección 6

A. 1. En el restaurante México sirven la cena a las nueve.   2. Ella pide una habitación con vista a la calle.
3. (Nosotros) seguimos al botones a la habitación.   4. ¿Consiguen Uds. reservaciones en diciembre?   5. (Yo) digo que él debe firmar el registro ahora.

B. 1. Ellos van a querer algo.   2. Hay alguien en el baño.   3. Tengo algunos objetos de oro y de plata.   4. Ellos siempre pasan por la aduana.   5. Yo también ceno a las nueve.   6. Siempre tiene las listas de los hoteles. 7. Puedes ir o a la derecha o a la izquierda.   8. Ellos siempre quieren algo también.

C. 1. conduzco   2. sé   3. quepo 4. salgo   5. traduzco   6. veo 7. hago   8. pongo   9. conozco 10. traigo

D. 1. sé   2. conoce / sabe 3. conoce / sabe   4. saben

E. 1. comprarlo   2. te llamo   3. la sirven   4. los tiene   5. me lleva 6. las necesito   7. los aceptan 8. llevarlo   9. las tengo 10. llamarla

F. 1. Llueve   2. Hace mucho frío 3. calor   4. nieva   5. hace mucho sol   6. lluvia

G. 1. b   2. a   3. b   4. c   5. b 6. a   7. c   8. a   9. a   10. b 11. c   12. c

H. 1. Perú   2. 25%   3. dólar 4. fácil

Self-Test Lecciones 7-9

Lección 7

A. 1. estas tarjetas postales y aquéllas 2. esa maleta y ésta   3. estas agencias de viajes y aquéllas   4. este avión y aquél   5. este barco y ése 6. estas cartas y ésas

B. 1. Ella les trae la lista.   2. Yo te voy a preparar (voy a prepararte) un sándwich.   3. Él le trae el equipaje. 4. Ana me va a comprar (va a comprarme) las tarjetas postales. 5. El agente de viajes nos trae los pasajes.   6. Les traen los cheques de viajeros.

C. 1. No me gusta esa agencia de viajes. 2. A él le gusta el asiento de pasillo. 3. ¿Le (Te) gusta este bolso de mano? 4. No nos gusta viajar por avión. 5. ¿Les gusta (a ellos) su hotel?

D. 1. Hace dos días que yo no duermo. 2. Hace un mes que tú no me llamas. 3. Hace media hora que nosotros estamos aquí.   4. Hace un año que ellos viven en España.   5. Hace doce horas que mi hija no come.

E. 1. Ayer Luisa y yo compramos los billetes.   2. La semana pasada yo viajé.   3. Ayer ella me presentó a sus padres.   4. ¿No pagaron Uds. los pasajes ayer?   5. Al mediodía ellos abrieron las ventanas.   6. El lunes nosotros comimos en la cafetería. 7. ¿Empezaste a estudiar esta mañana? 8. Ayer yo le presté las maletas.

F. 1. viajes   2. Buen viaje   3. turista 4. ida   5. retraso   6. devolver 7. próxima   8. salida   9. mano 10. juntas   11. exceso   12. barco

G. 1. Cuzco está situada a más de diez mil pies de altura.   2. Es la antigua capital del imperio de los incas. 3. Es un gran centro turístico y artístico.   4. Se conoce como "la ciudad perdida de los incas".   5. Se extendió desde el sur de Colombia hasta el norte de Chile y Argentina.

Lección 8

A. 1. Se lo van a mandar (Van a mandárselo) mañana.   2. Elsa me las va a comprar (va a comprármelas). 3. Luis nos las va a traducir (va a traducírnoslas).   4. Se (Te) lo voy a traer (voy a traérselo / traértelo) esta tarde.   5. La profesora me la va a dar (va a dármela).

B. 1. Nosotros fuimos al restaurante y comimos pavo asado.   2. Él no fue mi profesor el año pasado.   3. ¿Tú le diste la botella, querido?   4. ¿Quién pidió el bistec? ¿Fue Ud., señorita? 5. Nosotras no le dimos el flan a Pedro.

6. Yo fui al teatro.   7. Yo no le di la cuenta.   8. ¿Fuiste tú al restaurante anoche?   9. Ellos fueron a la fiesta la semana pasada. 10. ¿Raúl y Eva fueron mis estudiantes el año pasado?   11. Yo te di la propina.   12. Ellos nos dieron una torta helada.

C. 1. ¿Durmieron ellos en el hotel el jueves?   2. Los chicos siguieron a sus padres a la tienda.   3. Nosotros sêrvimos / pedimos sándwiches de jamón y queso.   4. Ella me mintió. No tiene viente años; tiene diez y siete. 5. ¿No consiguió Ud. el dinero para ir de vacaciones?   6. ¿Qué le pidieron los niños a Santa Claus?   7. El hombre murió en un accidente. 8. Ella me repitió la pregunta.

D. para / para / por / para / por / Por / para / para / por / para / por / por / por / para

E. 1. tercer   2. quinto   3. cuarto 4. décimo   5. octavo   6. primer

F. 1. s   2. i   3. a   4. m   5. q   6. t 7. o   8. d   9. g   10. h   11. c 12. f   13. b   14. r   15. e   16. k 17. n   18. j   19. l   20. p

G. l. latinoamericanos   2. cubanos 3. después   4. sobremesa   5. 10%

Lección 9

A. 1. Tú te vistes muy bien.   2. Ellos se afeitan todos los días.   3. Ellos se acuestan a las once.   4. ¿Ud. no se preocupa por sus hijos?   5. Yo me pongo el vestido.   6. Juan se sienta aquí.   7. Tú te lavas la cabeza todos los días.   8. Yo no me corté el pelo. 9. Yo no me acordé de eso.   10. Uds. se fueron.   11. ¿Cómo te llamas (tú)? 12. Daniel no se despertó hasta las diez.

B. 1. ¿Tú te quitas el suéter?   2. El barbero me corta el pelo.   3. La peluquera me lava la cabeza.   4. Uds. no se lavan las manos.   5. Nosotros preferimos el té.   6. Las madres se preocupan por sus hijos.   7. La comunicación es lo más importante.

C. 1. El mío   2. las suyas   3. las nuestras   4. las tuyas   5. los nuestros   6. El suyo

D. 1. tuvieron   2. estuvieron 3. traduje   4. pude   5. pusiste 6. hubo   7. hizo   8. vino   9. no dijeron   10. trajo

E. 1. especialmente   2. frecuentemente 3. lenta y claramente 4. recientemente   5. Generalmente 6. Desafortunadamente

F. 1. escoba   2. lavado / peinado 3. moda   4. aspiradora   5. cocinar 6. champú   7. lacio   8. revista 9. peine   10. máquina (crema) / afeitar   11. regalo

G. 1. F   2. V   3. F   4. F   5. V

Self-Test Lecciones 10-12

Lección 10

A. 1. Hace cuatro años que conocí a mi mejor amigo(-a).   2. Hace seis meses que mis amigos y yo fuimos a acampar. 3. Hace tres días que mi familia y yo fuimos a la playa.   4. Hace una semana que mis padres volvieron del campo.   5. Hace quince minutos que llegué a mi casa.

B. 1. era / Eran   2. vivías / eras / vivía / íbamos / veías / vivían   3. se hospedaba / iba / costaba / era

C. 1. dijo / necesitaba / podías 2. compramos / éramos / íbamos 3. tenía / vinimos / hablábamos 4. fue / Tuve / dolía   5. iba / vio murieron

D. 1. Beto conoció a Marisa en la universidad.   2. Sí, Marisa conocía a la hermana de Beto.   3. No, yo no quería venir a clase hoy.   4. No, nosotros no sabíamos que hoy había examen.   5. No, no quiso venir.

E. 1. m   2. i   3. o   4. f   5. b   6. l 7. n   8. a   9. d   10. c   11. h 12. e   13. k   14. g   15. j

F. 1. Punta del Este, Mar del Plata y Viña del Mar.   2. A Chile y a Bariloche.
3. Junio, julio y agosto.

Lección 11

A. 1. estemos   2. camines   3. saque
4. se parezca   5. den   6. sepas
7. recojamos   8. sean   9. vaya
10. reciba

B. 1. depositar / abra   2. haga / estés
3. vaya   4. paguen / pagar
5. traigas / llenar

C. 1. Me alegro de que ellos tengan los pantalones de Oscar.   2. Espero que Julio estacione el coche cerca del banco.   3. Me sorprende que tú sepas el saldo de mi cuenta corriente.
4. Temo que Ada esté en la estación de policía.   5. Es una lástima que nosotros no podamos traer los comprobantes.   6. Ojalá que ellos vayan al banco.

D. 1. aparcar, parquear   2. motocicleta
3. cama   4. hijo(-a) único(-a)
5. quedarse en la cama hasta tarde
6. revelar   7. tan pronto como
8. de manera que   9. ropa
10. pobre   11. fechar   12. gratis

E. 1. F   2. V   3. F   4. V   5. F
6. F

Lección 12

A. 1. Estén   2. Tráigamelo   3. Salgan
4. Déselas   5. Vayan   6. Quédese
7. Mándenoslo   8. Póngalos

B. 1. Ésta es la señora que vino ayer.
2. Éstos son los niños de quienes te hablé.   3. Ésa es la profesora para quien nosotros compramos los libros.

C. 1. sea   2. esté   3. necesiten
4. está   5. se encuentran   6. visito
7. puedes   8. es

D. 1. lado   2. derecho   3. giro
4. metro (subterráneo)   5. abierta
6. cruzar / semáforo   7. subir
8. parado(-a)   9. antiguo
10. cuadras (manzanas) / frente

11. cada   12. puntual   13. montón
14. echar / buzón   15. letra

E. 1. central   2. Vía   3. fuente
4. reyes   5. metro   6. acueducto

Self-Test Lecciones 13-15

Lección 13

A. 1. Dime   2. Haz / limpia   3. Sal
4. Ve / compra   5. Ponlos   6. Ven
7. Sé / tráeme   8. Ten / Espérame
9. No compres   10. No lo sirvas
11. No te vayas   12. Levántate / trabaja

B. 1. ¿Cuál es su (tu) número de teléfono?   2. ¿Cuál es el apellido de su (tu) madre?   3. ¿Qué es un pasaporte?   4. ¿Cuáles son las lecciones que Uds. necesitan?
5. ¿Cuál es su (tu) dirección?
6. ¿Qué es la paella?

C. 1. sepa   2. tiene   3. sea   4. tenga
5. trabaje   6. habla / hable

D. 1. m   2. f   3. k   4. o   5. a   6. i
7. c   8. b   9. e   10. n   11. d
12. h   13. g   14. l   15. j   16. p

E. 1. V   2. V   3. F   4. F   5. V

Lección 14

A. 1. llegue   2. vuelvan (regresen)
3. van   4. veas   5. vendan
6. vayas   7. vean   8. necesite
9. des   10. lleve

B. 1. Vamos al supermercado.
2. Vamos a las dos.   3. Compremos frutas y vegetales.   4. Pidámoselo a mamá.   5. No, no vayamos al teatro. Vamos al cine.   6. Volvamos a las siete.   7. Acostémonos a las once.
8. Levantémonos a las seis.

C. 1. ¿Qué idioma se habla en Chile?
2. ¿A qué hora se cierran las cafeterías?   3. ¿A qué hora se abre el supermercado?   4. ¿Dónde se vende aceite?   5. ¿Por dónde se sube al segundo piso?

D. 1. azúcar   2. lata   3. margarina
4. verduras   5. poner   6. cita
7. película   8. feriado   9. docena
10. higiénico   11. diversiones
12. zoológico

E. 1. F   2. V   3. F   4. F   5. V

Lección 15

A. 1. escrito   2. abierto   3. visto
4. hecho   5. roto   6. ido
7. hablado   8. comido   9. bebido
(tomado)   10. recibido

B. 1. rotos   2. abiertas   3. muerto
4. cerrado   5. hechas

C. 1. has usado   2. ha envuelto
3. han dicho   4. hemos comido
5. me he quedado   6. han hecho

D. 1. había terminado   2. habían ido
3. había dicho   4. había abierto
5. habíamos comprado   6. habías
preguntado

E. 1. b   2. a   3. a   4. c   5. b   6. c
7. a   8. b

F. 1. al segundo piso   2. utilizar los
servicios de una modista   3. existen
4. a veces

Self-Test Lecciones 16–18

Lección 16

A. 1. Le diremos la verdad.   2. ¿Qué
harán Uds.?   3. No querrán ir.
4. Lo sabré mañana.   5. No podrán
venir.   6. ¿Adónde iremos?
7. ¿Dónde lo pondrás?   8. Nosotros
vendremos con él.   9. Tendré que
trabajar.   10. Saldremos mañana.

B. 1. Yo iría a México.   2. Nosotros les
escribiríamos.   3. ¿Tú se lo dirías?
4. Ellos hablarían con Ana.   5. ¿Ud.
lo pondría en el banco?   6. ¿Uds.
vendrían el domingo?   7. Julio
pediría ensalada.   8. Nosotros lo
haríamos hoy.   9. Tú no saldrías con
ella.   10. Ella no caminaría; iría en
coche.

C. 1. habrá dicho   2. habrán vuelto
3. habré terminado   4. habremos
comido   5. habrás escrito

D. 1. Yo habría estudiado y habría
aprobado el examen.   2. Julio me
habría ayudado con el informe.
3. Luis y yo habríamos ido al partido.
4. Mis padres habrían pagado la
matrícula.   5. ¿Qué habrías hecho tú,
Anita?

E. 1. d   2. f   3. h   4. j   5. i   6. k
7. l   8. e   9. g   10. c   11. a
12. b

F. 1. existe   2. especializarse
3. facultades   4. especialización
5. 3 ó 6

Lección 17

A. 1. Quería que fuera con ellos.   2. Les
dije que no se preocuparan.   3. Me
alegré de que el doctor te viera hoy.
4. Temí que me pusiera una inyección.
5. Necesitaba una enfermera que
supiera español.   6. No creí que
tuvieran que desinfectarme la herida.
7. ¿Había alguien que pudiera escribir
una receta para penicilina?   8. Me
alegré de que te sintieras bien.   9. No
era verdad que necesitáramos una
ambulancia.   10. No creí que
estuviera embarazada.

B. 1. me olvido de   2. sueñan con
3. insiste en   4. venimos a   5. se
comprometió con   6. me enamoré de

C. 1. hayan encontrado   2. hayas ido
3. haya comprado   4. le haya
enyesado   5. se haya roto

D. 1. penicilina   2. los dientes   3. la
lengua   4. los ojos   5. los pies
6. la herida   7. rompiste   8. la
pierna   9. el tobillo   10. grados
11. pusieron   12. dolor de cabeza
13. el estómago   14. embarazada
15. gripe

E. 1. El gobierno subvenciona los
hospitales.   2. Van a las clínicas
privadas.   3. En muchos pueblos
remotos, la gente va a un curandero.

4. Las ayuda una partera.   5. Sí, se pueden comprar medicinas como la penicilina sin receta médica.

Lección 18

A. 1. hubiera visto   2. hubieran tenido   3. hubiéramos pagado   4. te hubieras roto (quebrado)   5. hubiera vuelto

B. 1. tengo   2. pudiéramos   3. hubieran ido   4. quieren   5. hubieras visto   6. fuera

C. 1. instalaran   2. puedan   3. llame   4. podamos / podemos   5. haya tomado   6. llegue   7. pudiera   8. sea

D. 1. velocidad   2. recién   3. frenos   4. conducir   5. servicio   6. limpia-parabrisas   7. vacío   8. maletero   9. remolcar   10. acumulador   11. guantera   12. culpa   13. vale   14. viaje   15. acuerdo

E. 1. contaminación   2. malas   3. cara   4. motocicleta   5. 0,6

Appendix F Professions and Trades

accountant **contador(-a)**
actor **actor**
actress **actriz**
administrator **administrador(-a)**
agent **agente**
architect **arquitecto(-a)**
artisan **artesano(-a)**
artist **artista**
baker **panadero(-a)**
bank officer **empleado(-a) bancario(-a)**
bank teller **cajero(-a)**
banker **banquero(-a)**
barber **barbero(-a)**
bartender **barman, cantinero(-a)**
bill collector **cobrador(-a)**
bookkeeper **tenedor(-a) de libros**
brickmason (bricklayer) **albañil**
butcher **carnicero(-a)**
buyer **comprador(-a)**
camera operator **camarógrafo(-a)**
carpenter **carpintero(-a)**
cashier **cajero(-a)**
chiropractor **quiropráctico(-a)**
clerk **dependiente(-a)** *(store)*, **oficinista** *(office)*
computer operator **computista**
construction worker **obrero(-a) de la construcción**
constructor **constructor(-a)**
contractor **contratista**
cook **cocinero(-a)**
copilot **copiloto(-a)**
counselor **consejero(-a)**
dancer **bailarín(-ina)**
decorator **decorador(-a)**
dental hygienist **higienista dental**
dentist **dentista**
designer **diseñador(-a)**
detective **detective**
dietician **especialista en dietética**
diplomat **diplomático(-a)**
director **director(-a)**
dockworker **obrero(-a) portuario(-a)**
doctor **doctor(-a), médico(-a)**
draftsman **dibujante**
dressmaker **modista**
driver **conductor(-a)**
economist **economista**

editor **editor(-a)**
electrician **electricista**
engineer **ingeniero(-a)**
engineering technician **ingeniero(-a) técnico(-a)**
eye doctor **oculista**
farmer **agricultor(-a)**
fashion designer **diseñador(-a) de alta costura**
fire fighter **bombero(-a)**
fisherman **pescador(-a)**
flight attendant **auxiliar de vuelo**
foreman **capataz, encargado(-a)**
funeral director **empresario(-a) de pompas fúnebres**
garbage collector **basurero(-a)**
gardener **jardinero(-a)**
guard **guardia**
guide **guía**
hairdresser **peluquero(-a)**
home economist **economista doméstico(-a)**
housekeeper **mayordomo, ama de llaves**
inspector **inspector(-a)**
instructor **instructor(-a)**
insurance agent **agente de seguros**
interior designer **diseñador(-a) de interiores**
interpreter **intérprete**
investigator **investigador(-a)**
janitor **conserje**
jeweler **joyero(-a)**
journalist **periodista**
judge **juez(-a)**
lawyer **abogado(-a)**
librarian **bibliotecario(-a)**
machinist **maquinista**
maid **criada**
mail carrier **cartero(-a)**
manager **gerente**
mechanic **mecánico(-a)**
midwife **comadrón(-ona), partero(-a)**
miner **minero(-a)**
model **modelo**
musician **músico(-a)**
nurse **enfermero(-a)**
optician **óptico(-a)**
optometrist **optometrista**

painter **pintor(-a)**
paramedic **paramédico(-a)**
pharmacist **farmacéutico(-a)**
photographer **fotógrafo(-a)**
physical therapist **terapista físico(-a)**
physician **médico(-a)**
pilot **piloto** *(masc., fem.)*, **aviador(-a)**
plumber **plomero(-a)**
police officer **policía**
printer **impresor(-a)**
psychologist **psicólogo(-a)**
public relations agent **agente de relaciones públicas**
real estate agent **agente de bienes raíces**
receptionist **recepcionista**
reporter **reportero(-a), periodista**
sailor **marinero(-a)**
sales representative **vendedor(-a)**
scientist **científico(-a)**
secretary **secretario(-a)**
security guard **guardia**
social worker **trabajador(-a) social**
sociologist **sociólogo(-a)**
soldier **soldado, militar**
stenographer **estenógrafo(-a)**
stockbroker **bolsista**
student **estudiante**
supervisor **supervisor(-a)**
surgeon **cirujano(-a)**
systems analyst **analista de sistemas**
tailor **sastre**
taxi driver **chofer de taxi, taxista**
teacher **maestro(-a)** *(elem. school)*, **profesor(-a)** *(high school and college)*
technician **técnico(-a)**
telephone operator **telefonista**
television and radio announcer **locutor(-a)**
television and radio technician **técnico(-a) de radio y televisión**
teller **cajero(-a)**
therapist **terapista**
travel agent **agente de viajes**
truck driver **camionero(-a)**
typist **mecanógrafo(-a), dactilógrafo(-a)**

undertaker   **director(-a) de pompas fúnebres**
veterinarian   **veterinario(-a)**

waiter   **mozo, camarero**
waitress   **camarera**
watchmaker   **relojero(-a)**

worker   **obrero(-a)**
writer   **escritor(-a)**

Vocabulary

The Spanish-English vocabulary contains all active and passive vocabulary that appears in the student text. Active vocabulary includes words and expressions that appear in the vocabulary lists that follow the dialogues and in charts and word lists that are part of the grammar explanations. Passive vocabulary consists of words and expressions that are given an English gloss in photo captions, the **Panorama hispánico** and **¿Lo sabía Ud.?** sections, readings, exercises, activities, and authentic documents.

The English-Spanish Vocabulary contains only those words and expressions that are considered active.

The following abbreviations are used in the vocabularies:

abbr.	abbreviation	*form.*	formal	*pl.*	plural
adj.	adjective	*i.o.*	indirect object	*prep.*	preposition
adv.	adverb	*inf.*	infinitive	*pron.*	pronoun
aux.	auxiliary	*lang.*	language	*p.p.*	past participle
d.o.	direct object	*m.*	masculine noun	*sing.*	singular
f.	feminine noun	*Mex.*	Mexico	*Sp.*	Spain
fam.	familiar	*obj.*	object	*Sp. Am.*	Spanish America

SPANISH–ENGLISH

A

a   at, to, 3; toward
_____ **casa**   home
¿_____ **cómo está el cambio de moneda?**   What is the exchange rate?, 6
_____ **la derecha**   to the right, 6
_____ **la(s)…**   at (*hour*), 2
_____ **menos que**   unless, 14
_____ **menudo**   often
_____ **pesar de (que)**   in spite of, despite, 10
_____ **plazos**   in installments, 11
¿_____ **qué hora?**   At what time?, 2
_____ **sus órdenes**   at your service
_____ **(en) todas partes**   everywhere
_____ **veces**   sometimes, 12
_____ **ver**   let's see, 11
downstairs, 12

abierto(-a) (*p.p.* of **abrir** *and adj.*)   open(ed), 12
abogado(-a) (*m., f.*)   lawyer, 3
abrazar   to hug, 8
abrazo (*m.*)   hug, 10
abrigo (*m.*)   overcoat, 11; coat
abril   April, 1
abrir   to open, 3
abuela (*f.*)   grandmother, 5
abuelo (*m.*)   grandfather, 5
aburrido(-a)   bored, 4; boring, 7
aburrirse   to be bored, 10
acabado(-a)   finished
acabar   to finish
_____ **de**   to have just, 6
acampar   to camp, 10
accidente (*m.*)   accident, 17
acción (*f.*)   action
aceite (*m.*)   oil, 14
aceptar   to accept, 6
acera (*f.*)   sidewalk
aclamar   to applaud
aconsejar   to advise, 11
acordarse (o:ue) (de)   to remember, 9
acostar (o:ue)   to put to bed, 9
   acostarse   to go to bed, 9
actividad (*f.*)   activity, 10
actor (*m.*)   actor

actriz (*f.*)   actress
actualmente   nowadays
actuar   to perform
acumulador (*m.*)   battery, 18
adelantado(-a)   advanced
además   besides, 13
adicional   additional
adiós   good-bye, 1
adjetivo (*m.*)   adjective
administración de empresas (*f.*)   business administration, 16
adónde   where? (*destination*), 4
adoquinado(-a)   tiled
aduana (*f.*)   customs, 6
advertir (e:ie)   to warn
aeropuerto (*m.*)   airport, 6
afectuosamente   affectionately, 16
afeitar(se)   to shave, 9
afueras (*f. pl.*)   outskirts
agencia de viajes (*f.*)   travel agency, 7
agente (*m., f.*)   agent
   _____ **de viajes** (*m., f.*)   travel agent, 7
agosto   August, 1
agua (*f.*)   water, 4
   _____ **caliente** (*f.*)   hot water
   _____ **mineral** (*f.*)   mineral water, 4

aguafiestas (*m., f.*)　spoilsport, 13
agujereado(-a)　full of holes
ah　oh, 2
ahora　now, 4
　　_____ **mismo**　right now, 18
　　_____ **que lo pienso**　now that
　　I think about it, 14
ahorrar　to save, 11
ahorros (*m. pl.*)　savings, 11
aire acondicionado (*m.*)　air
　conditioning, 6
al (*m. sing.*) (*contraction*)　to the, 4
　　_____ **aire libre**　outdoor, 10
　　_____ **contado**　in cash, 11
　　_____ **día**　a day, 17
　　_____ **día siguiente**　the
　　following day, 10
　　_____ **extranjero**　abroad
　　_____ **lado de**　next to, 12
　　_____ **medio día**　at noon, 4
　　_____ **mismo tiempo**　at the
　　same time, 13
　　_____ **rato**　a while later, 11
albóndiga (*f.*)　meatball, 8
alcanzar　to achieve, to reach
aldea (*f.*)　small town
alegrarse (de)　to be glad, 11
alegre　merry
alemán (*m.*)　German (*lang.*), 2
alérgico(-a)　allergic, 17
alfabetizar　to alphabetize
alfabeto (*m.*)　alphabet
alfombra (*f.*)　carpet, rug, 9
algo　something, anything, 6
algodón (*m.*)　cotton, 15
alguien　someone, somebody,
　anyone, 6
alguno(-a), algún　any, some, 6
　　alguna vez　ever, 15
algunos(-as)　some, 5
allí　there, 4
　　_____ **mismo**　right there, 12
almacén (*m.*)　department store, 15
almohada (*f.*)　pillow, 13
almorzar (o:ue)　to have lunch, 5
almuerzo (*m.*)　lunch, 6
alojamiento (*m.*)　lodging, 6
alquilar　to rent, 10
　　se alquila　for rent, 13
alquiler (*m.*)　rent, 13
alrededor de　around
alto　stop (*sign*)
alto(-a)　tall, 3
alumno(-a) (*m., f.*)　student, 2
amarillo(-a)　yellow, 1

ambos(-as)　both
ambulancia (*f.*)　ambulance, 17
amigdalitis (*f.*)　tonsilitis
amigo(-a) (*m., f.*)　friend, 2
amistad (*f.*)　friendship
amor (*m.*)　love, 8
　　mi _____　my love, my
　　darling, 8
amplio(-a)　ample, 6
amueblado(-a)　furnished, 13
amurallado(-a)　walled in
analista de sistemas (*m., f.*)　systems
　analyst, 1
anaranjado(-a)　orange, 1
ancho(-a)　wide, 15
anhelar　to yearn for
aniversario (*m.*)　anniversary, 8
　　_____ **de bodas**　wedding
　　anniversary, 8
anoche　last night, 8
anotar　to write down, 8
ansiosamente　anxiously
anteayer　the day before yesterday,
　8
antes (de)　before, 4
　　_____ **de que**　before, 14
antibiótico (*m.*)　antibiotic, 17
antiguo(-a)　old, 12
antipático(-a)　unpleasant, 3
anunciar　to announce, 13
anuncio (*m.*)　ad, 6
añadir　to add
año (*m.*)　year, 3
aparato electrodoméstico (*m.*)　home
　appliance, 13
aparcar　to park, 11
aparecer　to appear
apartamento (*m.*)　apartment, 9
apellido (*m.*)　surname, 3; last name
apenas　hardly
apendicitis (*f.*)　appendicitis
apio (*m.*)　celery, 14
apostar (o:ue)　to bet
apreciar　to appreciate, 10
aprender (a)　to learn, 3
apretar (e:ie)　to be tight, 15
　　me aprietan　they feel tight
　　(on me), 15
aprobar (o:ue)　to pass (*an exam or
　course*), 16
aprovechar　to take advantage of, 15
apuesta (*f.*)　bet
apurarse　to hurry (up), 14
apuro (*m.*): **No hay apuro.**　There's
　no hurry., 7

aquel(los), aquella(s) (*adj.*)　that,
　those (*distant*), 7
aquél(los), aquélla(s) (*pron.*)　that
　one, those (*distant*), 7
aquello (*neuter pron.*)　that, 7
aquí　here, 5
　　_____ **la tiene.**　Here it is.
　　(Here you have it.), 6
árbol (*m.*)　tree
　　_____ **de Navidad**　Christmas
　　tree, 4
　　_____ **genealógico** (*m.*)
　　family tree
arena (*f.*)　sand
Argentina　Argentina, 10
argentino(-a)　Argentinian, 16
armar　to pitch (a tent), 10
armario (*m.*)　closet, wardrobe, 15
arrancar　to start (*car*), 18
arreglar　to fix, to repair, 18
arreglo (*m.*)　repair, 18
arriba　upstairs, 12
arroz (*m.*)　rice, 8
　　_____ **con leche** (*m.*)　rice
　　pudding, 8
　　_____ **con pollo** (*m.*)　chicken
　　with rice, 8
arte (*f.*)　art
artículo (*m.*)　article, 3
asado(-a)　roasted, 8
ascensor (*m.*)　elevator, 6
asiento (*m.*)　seat
　　_____ **de pasillo** (*m.*)　aisle
　　seat, 7
　　_____ **de ventanilla** (*m.*)
　　window seat, 7
　　Tome _____.　Have a seat., 2
asignatura (*f.*)　(*school*) subject, 16
asistir (a)　to attend, 5
asma (*f.*)　asthma
aspiradora (*f.*)　vacuum cleaner, 9
aspirina (*f.*)　aspirin, 17
aterrizar　to land (*plane*)
atraso (*m.*)　delay, 7
　　tener... de _____　to be . . .
　　behind schedule, 7
atropellar　to run over, 17
aumentar　to gain
aún　still
aunque　although, 9
auto (*m.*)　car, 5
autobús (*m.*)　bus, 5
automático(-a)　automatic, 18
automóvil (*m.*)　car, 5
autopista (*f.*)　freeway, highway, 18

auxiliar de vuelo (*m., f.*)   flight attendant, 1
avenida (*f.*)   avenue, 2
avergonzado(-a)   ashamed
averiguar   to find out, 6
avión (*m.*)   plane, 7
ayer   yesterday, 7
ayudar (a)   to help, to assist, 15
azafata (*f.*)   female flight attendant, 7
azúcar (*m.*)   sugar, 14
azul   blue, 1

B

¡Bah!   Bah!, 5
bailar   to dance, 4
¿Bailamos?   Shall we dance?, 4
baile (*m.*)   dance, 4
bajar   to descend, to go down, 12
bajo(-a) (*adj.*)   short, 3
balazo (*m.*)   shot
baloncesto (*m.*)   basketball
banano (*m.*)   banana tree
banco (*m.*)   bank, 11
bañadera (*f.*)   bathtub, 6
bañar(se)   to bathe (oneself), 9
baño (*m.*)   bathroom, 6
_____ **María** (*m.*)   double boiler
barato(-a)   cheap, inexpensive, 6
barbería (*f.*)   barber shop, 9
barbero(-a) (*m., f.*)   barber, 9
barco (*m.*)   boat, ship, 7
barrer   to sweep, 9
barrio (*m.*)   neighborhood, 13
barro (*m.*)   clay, mud
básquetbol (*m.*)   basketball
bastante   enough
batería (*f.*)   battery, 18
_____ **de cocina** (*f.*)   cookware, 13
beber   to drink, 3
bebida (*f.*)   drink, beverage, 4
beca (*f.*)   scholarship, 16
béisbol (*m.*)   baseball
belleza (*f.*)   beauty
beso (*m.*)   kiss, 8
biblioteca (*f.*)   library, 3
bibliotecario(-a) (*m., f.*)   librarian, 16
bicicleta (*f.*)   bicycle, 10
montar en _____   to ride a bicycle, 10
bien   well, fine, 1; okay, 7
bikini (*m.*)   bikini, 15

billete (*m.*)   ticket, 7
_____ **de ida** (*m.*)   one-way ticket, 7
_____ **de ida y vuelta** (*m.*)   round-trip ticket, 7
_____ **de primera clase** (*m.*)   first-class ticket, 7
billetera (*f.*)   wallet, 15
biología (*f.*)   biology
bisabuela (*f.*)   great-grandmother, 4
bisabuelo (*m.*)   great-grandfather, 4
bistec (*m.*)   steak, 8
blanco(-a)   white, 1
bluejeans (*m. pl.*)   jeans, 15
blusa (*f.*)   blouse, 15
boca (*f.*)   mouth, 17
bocina (*f.*)   horn, 18
boda (*f.*)   wedding
boleto (*m.*)   ticket (*for a show*), 8
bolígrafo (*m.*)   pen, 2
bolsa (*f.*) (*Mex.*)   purse, handbag, 9
_____ **de aire** (*f.*)   air bag, 18
_____ **de dormir** (*f.*)   sleeping bag, 10
bolsillo (*m.*)   pocket
bolso (*m.*)   purse, handbag, 9
_____ **de mano** (*m.*)   carry-on bag, 7
bomba de agua (*f.*)   water pump, 18
bonito(-a)   pretty, 3
borrador (*m.*)   eraser, 2
bosque (*m.*)   forest
bota (*f.*)   boot, 15
bote (*m.*) (*Mex.*)   can, 14
botella (*f.*)   bottle, 8
botiquín (*m.*)   medicine cabinet, 9
botones (*m.*)   bellhop, 6
brazo (*m.*)   arm, 17
brindar   to toast, 4
brindis (*m.*)   toast (*wine*), 4
broma (*f.*)   practical joke
bromear   to joke, to kid, 13
bronquitis (*f.*)   bronchitis
bueno(-a), buen   good, 3; hello (*phone*), 3; fine, okay, 7; well, 8
¡Buen viaje!   Have a nice trip!, 7
buenas noches   good evening, good night, 1
buenas tardes   good afternoon, 1
buenos días   good morning, 1
bufanda (*f.*)   scarf
bujía (*f.*)   sparkplug, 18

burlarse de   to make fun of
buscar   to pick up, to get, 17; to look for
butaca (*f.*)   armchair, 13
buzón (*m.*)   mailbox, 12

C

caballeros (*m. sing.*)   gentlemen, 6
caballo (*m.*)   horse, 10
montar a _____   to ride a horse, 10
cabaña (*f.*)   cabin, 10
cabello (*m.*)   hair, 17
caber   to fit, 6
cabeza (*f.*)   head, 17
dolor de _____ (*m.*)   headache, 17
cacerola (*f.*)   saucepan, 13
cada (*invariable adj.*)   each, 12
caer(se)   to fall
café (*m.*)   brown, 1; coffee, 5
_____ **al aire libre** (*m.*)   sidewalk cafe, 5
cafetera (*f.*)   coffee maker, 13
cafetería (*f.*)   cafeteria, 3
cajero automático (*m.*)   automatic teller, 11
cajuela (*f.*)   trunk (*car*), 18
calcetín (*m.*)   sock, 15
calefacción (*f.*)   heater
_____ **central** (*f.*)   central heating, 13
calentar (e:ie)   to heat up, to warm up
cálido(-a)   hot, warm
caliente   hot, 7
calificativo(-a)   descriptive
callar   be silent
calle (*f.*)   street, 2
calor (*m.*)   heat, 4
calzar   to take (*a certain size in shoes*), 15
calzoncillos (*m. pl.*)   men's undershorts, 15
cama (*f.*)   bed, 11
cámara (fotográfica) (*f.*)   camera, 6
_____ **de video** (*f.*)   video camera, 6
camarero(-a) (*m., f.*)   waiter, waitress, 8
camarones (*m. pl.*)   shrimp, 8
cambiar   to change, to exchange, 15

cambio (*m.*)   exchange

_____ **de moneda**   exchange rate, 6

cambios mecánicos (*m. pl.*)   standard shift, 18

caminar   to walk, 11

camino (*m.*)   road, 18

_____ **a**   on the way to, 18

camioneta (*f.*)   station wagon, van, 18

camisa (*f.*)   shirt, 15

camiseta (*f.*)   T-shirt, 15

camisón (*m.*)   nightgown, 15

campo (*m.*)   country, 10

_____ **de batalla** (*m.*)   battlefield

canasto (*m.*)   basket

cancelación (*f.*)   cancellation, 6

cancelar   to cancel, 6

canción (*f.*)   song

cansado(-a)   tired, 4

cantar   to sing, 4

cántaros:

llover a _____   to rain cats and dogs, 8

caña de pescar (*f.*)   fishing rod, 10

capital (*f.*)   capital (*city*), 6

capó (*m.*)   hood, 18

cara (*f.*)   face, 17

¡caramba!   gee!, 14

carbón (*m.*)   coal

carburador (*m.*)   carburetor, 18

cárcel (*f.*)   jail

carne (*f.*)   meat, 8

carnicería (*f.*)   meat market

caro(-a)   expensive, 6

carpintero(-a) (*m., f.*)   carpenter, 16

carrera (*f.*)   university studies, career, 16; race

carretera (*f.*)   highway, 18

carro (*m.*)   car, 5; carriage

carroza (*f.*)   float

carta (*f.*)   letter, 5; menu, 8

cartera (*f.*)   handbag, 9; wallet, 15

cartero (*m.*)   mailman, 12

casa (*f.*)   house, home, 3

casado(-a)   married, 3

casarse (con)   to get married (to), 13; to marry, 17

casete (*m.*)   cassette, tape, 4

casi   almost, 18

casillero (*m.*)   mailbox, 12

castaño   brown (*hair, eyes*), 3

catarata (*f.*)   waterfall

catarro (*m.*)   cold, 17

catorce   fourteen, 1

caudaloso(-a)   abundant

cebolla (*f.*)   onion, 14

ceda el paso   yield (*sign*)

celebrar   to celebrate, 4

cena (*f.*)   dinner, supper, 6

cenar   to have dinner, supper, 6

centro (*m.*)   downtown (*area*), 6; center, 15

_____ **comercial**   shopping mall, 15

cepillo (*m.*)   brush, 9

cerca (de)   close to, near, 5; around

cereal (*m.*)   cereal

cero   zero, 1

cerrar (e:ie)   to close, 4

certidumbre (*f.*)   certainty

certificado(-a)   certified, registered 12

cerveza (*f.*)   beer, 4

cesto de papeles (*m.*)   wastebasket, 2

chaleco (*m.*)   vest, 15

champán (*m.*)   champagne, 4

champú (*m.*)   shampoo, 9

chapa (*f.*)   license plate, 18

chaqueta (*f.*)   jacket, 15

charlar   to talk, chat, 4

chau   bye, 1

cheque (*m.*)   check, 11

_____ **de viajero** (*m.*)   traveler's check, 6

chequear   to check, 18

chequeo (*m.*)   checkup, examination, 17

chequera (*f.*)   checkbook, 11

chica (*f.*)   girl, young woman, 3

chico (*m.*)   boy, young man, 3

Chile   Chile, 10

chileno(-a)   Chilean, 10

chino(-a)   Chinese

chocolate (*m.*)   chocolate, 8

_____ **caliente** (*m.*)   hot chocolate, 8

chorizo (*m.*)   sausage

cien, ciento   one hundred, 2

ciencia (*f.*)   science, 16

_____ **ficción**   science fiction

cierto   true

No es _____.   It's not true., 12

cinco   five, 1

cincuenta   fifty, 2

cine (*m.*)   movie theater, movies, 7

cinta (*f.*)   cassette, tape, 4

cinturón (*m.*)   belt, 15

circo (*m.*)   circus, 14

cita (*f.*)   appointment, 9; date, 14

ciudad (*f.*)   city, 3

claro(-a)   light; clear

claro   of course, 7

clase (*f.*)   class, 2; kind

_____ **de alemán** (*f.*)   German class, 2

_____ **optativa** (*f.*)   elective

_____ **turista** (*f.*)   tourist class, 7

primera _____   first class, 7

clasificado(-a)   classified, 13

clima (*m.*)   climate

club (*m.*)   club, 4

cobija (*f.*)   blanket, 13

cobrar   to charge, 11

coche (*m.*)   car, automobile, 5

cochino (*m.*)   pig

cocina (*f.*)   kitchen, 9; stove, 13; cuisine

cocinar   to cook, 9

cocinero(-a) (*m., f.*)   cook, chef, 16

coctel (*m.*)   cocktail, 4

cognado (*m.*)   cognate

cojera (*f.*)   limp

colchón (*m.*)   mattress, 13

colombiano(-a)   Colombian, 13

Colón: Cristóbal Colón   Christopher Columbus

color (*m.*)   color, 1

combinar   to match, to go together, 15

comedia (*f.*)   comedy, 8

comedor (*m.*)   dining room, 13

comenzar (e:ie) (a)   to begin, to start, 4

comer   to eat, 3

_____ **algo**   to have something to eat, 14

cómico(-a)   funny

comida (*f.*)   food, 6; meal, 8

cuarto y _____   room and board

como   since, 7; as, 16

_____ **si**   as if, 18

cómo   how?, 1; what?

¿_____ **es...?**   What is . . . like?, 3

¿_____ **está usted?**   How are you? (*form.*), 1

¿_____ **estás?**   How are you? (*fam.*), 1

_____ **están ustedes**   How are you?, 1

¿_____ **se dice...?**   How do you say . . . ?, 2

¿_____ se llama usted? What's your name? (*form.*), 1

¿_____ te llamas tú? What's your name? (*fam.*), 1

¿_____ te va? How is it going (for you) (*fam.*)?, 1

¿_____ te fue? How did it go for you?, 10

cómoda (*f.*) bureau, chest of drawers, 13

cómodo(-a) comfortable, 5

compañero(-a) de clase (*m., f.*) classmate, 4

compañero(-a) de cuarto (*m., f.*) roommate, 17

compañía (*f.*) company, 3

comparativo(-a) comparative

compra (*f.*) purchase, 15

comprar to buy, 6

comprobante (*m.*) claim check, 11

comprometerse con to get engaged to, 17

computador(-a) (*m., f.*) computer, 12

con with, 2

_____ ella habla this is she (*speaking*), 3

_____ permiso. Excuse me., 2

_____ tal (de) que provided that, 14

_____ vista a overlooking, 6

concierto (*m.*) concert, 9

conclusión (*f.*) conclusion, 15

concordancia (*f.*) agreement

condicional conditional

conducir to drive (*Sp.*), 5; to conduct, 6

conferencia (*f.*) lecture

confirmar to confirm, 6

conmigo with me, 5

conocer to know, to be acquainted, 6; to meet, 7

conocido(-a) known

conseguir (e:i) to get, to obtain, 6

consejero(-a) (*m., f.*) advisor, 16

consejo (*m.*) advice, 16

consulado (*m.*) consulate, 6

consultorio (*m.*) doctor's office, 17

contabilidad (*f.*) accounting, 16

contador(-a) (*m., f.*) accountant, 16

contaminación del aire (*f.*) smog

contar (o:ue) to count, 5; to tell, 7

contento(-a) happy, 4

contestar to answer

contigo (*inf. sing.*) with you, 5

convencer to convince, 10

conversación (*f.*) conversation

conversar to talk, to chat, 4

conversemos let's talk

convertirse (e:ie) en to turn into

copa (*f.*) glass, goblet, 4

corbata (*f.*) tie, 15

cordero (*m.*) lamb, 8

correo (*m.*) mail, 12; post office, 12

_____ **electrónico** (*m.*) E-mail, 12

cortar(se) to cut (oneself), 9

cortarse el pelo to get a haircut, 9

corte (*m.*) haircut, cut, 9

cortesía (*f.*) courtesy

cortina (*f.*) curtain, 13

corto(-a) short, 9

cosa (*f.*) thing, 14

costar (o:ue) to cost, 5

_____ **un ojo de la cara** to cost an arm and a leg, 10

crecimiento (*m.*) growth

creer to believe, think, 3

creído (*p.p. of* **creer**) believed, 15

crema (*f.*) cream, 8

_____ **de afeitar** (*f.*) shaving cream, 9

criollo(-a) creole

cruzar to cross, 12

cuaderno (*m.*) notebook, 2

cuadra (*f.*) (*Sp. Am.*) city block, 12

cuadro (*m.*) picture, painting, 5

_____ **de cuadros** plaid, 15

cuál what?, which?, 2

¿_____ es tu (su) dirección? What's your address?, 2

¿_____ es tu (su) número de teléfono? What is your telephone number?

cualquier(a) any; anybody

cuando when, 5

cuándo when?, 2

cuánto(-a) how much?, 4

¿_____ tiempo hace que...? How long . . . ?, 7

cuántos(-as) how many?, 2

cuarenta forty, 2

cuarto (*m.*) quarter, 2; room, 6

_____ **de baño** (*m.*) bathroom, 6

_____ **y comida** room and board

menos _____ quarter of/to (*time*), 2

y _____ quarter after/past (*time*), 2

cuarto(-a) fourth, 8

cuatro four, 1

cuatrocientos four hundred, 3

cubano(-a) Cuban, 8

cubierto(-a) (*p.p. of* **cubrir** *and adj.*) covered, 15

cubiertos (*m. pl.*) place settings, 8

cubrir to cover

cucaracha (*f.*) cockroach

cuchara (*f.*) spoon, 8

cucharada (*f.*) spoonful

cucharadita (*f.*) teaspoonful

cucharita (*f.*) teaspoon, 8

cuchillo (*m.*) knife, 8

cuello (*m.*) neck, 17

cuenca (*f.*) (river) basin

cuenta (*f.*) bill, 8; account, 11

_____ **corriente** (*f.*) checking account, 11

_____ **de ahorros** (*f.*) savings account, 11

cuero (*m.*) leather, 15

cuerpo (*m.*) body, 17

cuidarse to take care of oneself, 17

culpa (*f.*) blame, fault, 18

culpable guilty

culpar to blame, 18

cultura (*f.*) culture, 9

cumpleaños (*m.*) birthday, 4

cumplir... años to turn _____ (*age*), 4

cuñada (*f.*) sister-in-law, 5

cuñado (*m.*) brother-in-law, 5

curandero (*m.*) healer

curita (*f.*) adhesive bandage, 17

curso (*m.*) course, class, 16

D

damas ladies, 6

dar to give, 4

_____ **una multa** to give a ticket (*fine*), 18

darse por vencido(-a) to give up

darse prisa to hurry (*up*), 14

datos (*m. pl.*) data, 3

de from, 1; of, 3; about, 7

_____ **acuerdo** okay, I agree, 14

_____ **compras** shopping, 10
_____ **cuadros** plaid, 15
_____ **estatura mediana** of medium height, 5
_____ **haber sabido** had I known, 17
_____ **haber seguido** had he followed, 16
_____ **la mañana** A.M., 2
_____ **la tarde** P.M., 2
_____ **manera que** so, 11
_____ **modo que** so, 11
_____ **nada** you're welcome, 2
¿_____ **parte de quién?** Who is speaking?, 3
_____ **postre** for dessert, 8
_____ **quién(es)** whose?, 4
_____ **todo** everything, 10
_____ **vez en cuando** from time to time, 14
_____ **viaje** traveling
_____ **vuelta** back
deber (+ _infinitive_) must, to have to, should, 3
deberse a to be due to
decidir to decide, 3
décimo(-a) tenth, 8
decir (e:i) to say, to tell, 6
_____ **tonterías** to talk nonsense, 13
decisión (_f._) decision, 13
dedo (_m._) finger, 17
_____ **del pie** (_m._) toe, 17
dejar to leave (_behind_), 8
del (_m. sing._) (_contraction_) of the, from the, 4
delante de in front of
delgado(-a) thin, slender, 3
delicioso (-a) delicious, 4
demasiado(-a)(s) too; too much, too many
demostrativo(-a) demonstrative
dentista (_m., f._) dentist, 1
departamento (_m._) department, section, 11; apartment
_____ **de (ropa para) caballeros** (_m._) men's department, 15
_____ **de (ropa para) señoras (damas)** (_m._) women's department, 12
dependiente(-a) (_m., f._) store clerk, 15
deporte (_m._) sport
depositar to deposit, 11
derecho (_m., adv._) straight ahead, 12

derecho(-a) (_adj._) right
a la derecha to the right, 6
derramar to spill
derretir (e:i) to melt
desafiar to challenge
desafortunadamente unfortunately
desafortunado(-a) unfortunate
desayuno (_m._) breakfast, 6
descomponerse to break down
descompuesto(-a) (_p.p. of_ **descomponer** _and adj._) out of order, not working, 18
desde from, 12
desear to want, 11
desierto (_m._) desert, 10
desilusión (_f._) disappointment
desinfectar to disinfect, 17
despedida (_f._) farewell
despertador (_m._) alarm clock, 11
despertarse (e:ie) to wake up, 9
despreciar to scorn
después afterwards, 4; then, 7
_____ **de** after, 8
desvestirse (e:i) to get undressed, 9
detenerse to stop
determinado(-a) definite
devolver (o:ue) to return (_something_), 7
devuelto(-a) (_p.p. of_ **devolver** _and adj._) returned, 15
día (_m._) day, 2
_____ **de fiesta** (_m._) holiday, 14
_____ **de la semana** day of the week
¿**Qué** _____ **es hoy?** What day is today?, 1
diamante (_m._) diamond
diario (_m._) newspaper, 13
diciembre December, 1
dicho(-a) (_p.p. of_ **decir** _and adj._) said, told, 15
diecinueve nineteen, 1
dieciocho eighteen, 1
dieciséis sixteen, 1
diecisiete seventeen, 1
diente (_m._) tooth, 17
dieta (_f._) diet, 14
diez ten, 1
difícil difficult, 4
¡dígame! hello! (_phone_), 3
díganos tell us
diligencia (_f._) errand, 11
hacer _____**s** to run errands, 11

dinero (_m._) money, 3
Dios (_m._) God
dirección (_f._) address, 2
disco (_m._) record
_____ **compacto** (_m._) compact disc (CD), 4
discoteca (_f._) disco
diseño (_m._) design, 15
disfrutar to enjoy
divertido(-a) entertaining
divertirse (e:ie) to have a good time, to enjoy oneself, 10
divorciado(-a) divorced, 3
doblar to turn, to bend, 12; to dub
doce twelve, 1
docena (_f._) dozen, 14
doctor(-a) (_m., f._) doctor, 1
documento (_m._) document, 12
_____ **de identidad (identificación)** (_m._) I.D., 12
doler (o:ue) to ache, to hurt, 17
dolor (_m._) pain, 17
_____ **de cabeza** (_m._) headache, 17
domicilio (_m._) address, 2
domingo (_m._) Sunday, 1
dónde where?, 1
dormir (o:ue) to sleep, 5
dormirse to fall asleep, 9
dormitorio (_m._) bedroom, 13
dos two, 1
doscientos two hundred, 3
dramático(-a) dramatic
ducha (_f._) shower, 6
ducharse to take a shower, 9
dudar to doubt, 12
dulces (_m. pl._) sweets
durante during, 7
durar to last
durazno (_m._) peach, 14

E

echar to throw
_____ **de menos** to miss, 5
_____ **el bofe** to be out of breath
_____ **una carta al correo** to mail a letter, 12
edad (_f._) age, 3
edificio (_m._) building, 12
educación (_f._) education, 3
efectivo (_m._) cash, 11
en _____ in cash, 11

ejército (*m.*)   army

el   the (*m. sing.*), 1

él   he, 1; him, 5

electricista (*m., f.*)   electrician, 16

elegante   elegant, 8

elevador (*m.*)   elevator, 6

ella   she, 1; her, 5

ellas (*f. pl.*)   they, 1; them, 5

ellos (*m. pl.*)   they, 1; them, 5

embajada (*f.*)   embassy, 6

embarazada   pregnant, 17

emergencia (*f.*)   emergency, 17

empezar (e:ie) (a)   to begin, to start, 4

empleado(-a) (*m., f.*)   clerk, 6; employee

empleo (*m.*)   job, 3

en   in, at, 2; on, 3

    _____ caso de que   in case, 14

    _____ cuanto   as soon as, 11

    _____ efectivo   in cash, 11

    _____ inglés   in English, 2

    _____ punto   on the dot

    _____ seguida   right away, 6

    _____ seguida vuelvo   I'll be right back, 15

    _____ serio   seriously, 10

    _____ vez de   instead of, 13

enamorado(-a)   in love

enamorarse de   to fall in love with, 17

encaje (*m.*)   lace

encantado(-a)   charmed, it's a pleasure

encantador(-a)   charming

encantar   to love, to like very much, 8

encargado(-a) de   in charge of

encima de   above, on top of

encontrar (o:ue)   to find, 5

encontrarse (con)   to meet, 12

encuentro (*m.*)   encounter

enero   January, 1

enfadado(-a)   angry, 4

enfermedad (*f.*)   disease, sickness

    _____ de la niñez   childhood disease

enfermero(-a)   (*m., f.*)   nurse, 1

enfermo(-a)   sick, 4

enfriar   to cool down

enojado(-a)   angry, 4

ensalada (*f.*)   salad, 4

    _____ de papas (*f.*)   potato salad, 4

enseñanza (*f.*)   teaching

enseñar (a)   to show, 6; to teach, 10

ensuciar(se)   to get (oneself) dirty, 9

entender (e:ie)   to understand, 4

enterrado(-a)   buried

entonces   then, in that case, 3

entrada (*f.*)   entrance, 7; ticket (*for a show*), 8

entre   between, among

    _____ la espada y la pared   between a rock and a hard place

entregar   to deliver, to turn in, 16

entremeses (*m. pl.*)   hors d'oeuvres, 4

entrevista (*f.*)   interview

entrevistar   to interview

enviar   to send, 3

envolver (o:ue)   to wrap, 15

envuelto(-a) (*p.p. of* envolver *and adj.*)   wrapped, 15

enyesar   to put in a cast, 17

equipaje (*m.*)   luggage, 7

equipo (*m.*)   team, 16

    _____ estereofónico (*m.*)   stereo system, 4

equivocado(-a)   wrong, 4

es que...   the fact is . . . , 12

escalar   to climb, 10

escalera (*f.*)   stairs, 6

    _____ mecánica (*f.*)   escalator, 15

esclavo(-a) (*m., f.*)   slave

escoba (*f.*)   broom, 9

escribir   to write, 3

escrito(-a) (*p.p. of* escribir *and adj.*)   written, 15

escritorio (*m.*)   desk, 2

escuchar   to listen to

escuela (*f.*)   school, 5

    _____ secundaria (*f.*)   high school

ese(-os), esa(s) (*adj.*)   that, those, (*nearby*), 7

ése(-os), ésa(s) (*pron.*)   that one, those (*nearby*), 7

eso (*neuter pron.*)   that, 7

    a _____ de   at about, 14

Esopo   Aesop

espalda (*f.*)   back, 17

España   Spain, 4

español (*m.*)   Spanish (*lang.*), 1

español(-a) (*m., f.*)   Spaniard, 12

especial   special, 16

especialidad (*f.*)   specialty, 8

especialización (*f.*)   major (*field of study*), 16

especialmente   especially, 5

especie (*f.*)   sort

espejo (*m.*)   mirror, 9

esperar   to wait (for), 9; to hope, 11

    —Espero que sí.   I hope so., 10

esposa (*f.*)   wife, 3

esposo (*m.*)   husband, 3

esquiar   to ski, 10

esquina (*f.*)   corner, 12

estación (*f.*)   season, 1; station, 12

    _____ de policía (*f.*)   police station, 11

    _____ de servicio (*f.*)   gas (*service*) station, 18

estacionar   to park, 11

estadio (*m.*)   stadium, 16

estado (*m.*)   state

    _____ civil (*m.*)   marital status, 3

Estados Unidos (*m. pl.*)   United States, 5

estampado(-a)   print (fabric), 15

estampilla (*f.*)   stamp, 12

estar   to be, 4

    _____ a... de aquí   to be . . . from here, 12

    _____ de acuerdo   to agree, 18

    _____ de moda   to be in style, 9

    _____ de vuelta   to be back

    _____ equivocado(-a)   to be wrong, 4

    _____ invitado(-a)   to be invited, 9

    _____ listo(-a)   to be ready, 5

    _____ muerto(-a) de hambre   to be starving, 15

    ¿Está... (*name*)?   Is... (*name*) there?, 3

estatura (*f.*)   height, 5

este   east, 10

este(-os), esta(s) (*adj.*)   this, 5; these, 7

este semestre (*m.*)   this semester, 2

éste(-os) ésta(s) (*pron.*)   this one; these, 7

estilo (*m.*)   style

estimado(-a)   dear, 16

esto (*neuter pron.*)   this, 7

estómago (*m.*)   stomach, 17

estrecho(-a)   narrow, 15

estrella (*f.*)   star

estudiante (*m., f.*)   student, 1

estudiar to study, 2
evitar to avoid, 17
exactitud (*f.*) accuracy
examen (*m.*) exam, 3; checkup, 17
_____ **final** (*m.*) final exam, 16
_____ **parcial (de mitad de curso)** (*m.*) midterm exam, 16
excelente excellent, 8
exceso (*m.*) excess, 7
_____ **de equipaje** (*m.*) excess baggage, 7
_____ **de velocidad** (*m.*) speeding, 18
excursión (*f.*) tour, 6; excursion, 10
experiencia (*f.*) experience, 3
expresión (*f.*) expression, 1
extranjero(-a) foreigner, 12; (*adj.*) foreign
al extranjero abroad
extrañar to miss, 5
extraño(-a) strange, 18

F

fácil easy, 4
fácilmente easily, 10
facsímil (*m.*) fax (*letter*), 12
facultad (*f.*) college, school
_____ **de derecho** (*f.*) law school, 16
falda (*f.*) skirt, 15
familia (*f.*) family, 5
famoso(-a) famous, 5
farmacia (*f.*) pharmacy, drugstore, 9
favor (*m.*) favor, 13
favorito(-a) favorite, 6
fax (*m.*) fax (*letter*), 12
febrero February, 1
fecha (*f.*) date, 3
_____ **de nacimiento** (*f.*) date of birth, 3
fechar to date (*check or letter*), 11
feliz happy, 4
femenino(-a) feminine, 3
feo(-a) ugly, 3
feria (*f.*) fair
feriado (*m.*) holiday, 14
fiebre (*f.*) fever, 17
fiesta (*f.*) party, 4
_____ **de fin de año** (*f.*) New Year's Eve party, 14
fijarse en to notice, 17

filete (*m.*) tenderloin steak, 8
filtro (*m.*) filter, 18
fin (*m.*) end
_____ **de año** (*m.*) New Year's Eve, 4
_____ **de semana** (*m.*) weekend, 5
firma (*f.*) signature, 11
firmar to sign, 6
Firme aquí. Sign here., 6
física (*f.*) physics, 16
flan (*m.*) caramel custard, 8
formal (*f.*) formal
fortaleza (*f.*) fortress
fortuna (*f.*) fortune, 10
foto (*f.*) photograph, 5
fotografía (*f.*) photograph, 5
francés (*m.*) French (*lang.*), 2
frazada (*f.*) blanket, 13
frecuente frequent
frecuentemente frequently
fregadero (*m.*) kitchen sink, 13
freír (e:i) to fry
freno (*m.*) brake, 18
frente a in front of, 11; across from, 12
fresa (*f.*) strawberry, 14
frijoles (*m. pl.*) beans, 8
frito(-a) fried, 8
fruta (*f.*) fruit, 8
fuente (*f.*) fountain; source
fumar to smoke
función (*f.*) show, 14
funcionar to work, to function, 18
funda (*f.*) pillowcase, 13
fútbol (*m.*) soccer, 16
_____ **americano** (*m.*) football
futuro (*m.*) future

G

gamba (*f.*) shrimp (*Sp.*), 8
ganadería (*f.*) cattle raising; livestock
ganador(-a) (*m., f.*) winner
ganar to earn, 13; to win, 13
ganas: tener _____ **de** to feel like, 14
ganga (*f.*) bargain, 15
garaje (*m.*) garage, 13
garganta (*f.*) throat, 17
gasolina (*f.*) gasoline, 18
gasolinera (*f.*) gas (*service*) station, 18
gastar to spend (*money*), 16

gato (*m.*) car jack, 18
general general
generalmente generally, 9
género (*m.*) gender
gente (*f.*) people
geográfico(-a) geographical
giro postal (*m.*) money order, 12
gobierno (*m.*) government
goma (*f.*) tire, 18
_____ **de borrar** eraser, 2
gordo(-a) fat
gorro (*m.*) cap, 15
gozar (de) to enjoy
gracias thank you, thanks
—Muchas _____ Thank you very much, 2
grado (*m.*) degree, 17
graduarse to graduate, 16
grande big, 4
gratis free (*of charge*), 11
gripe (*f.*) flu, 17
gris gray, 1
gritar to scream, 11
grúa (*f.*) tow truck, 18
guante (*m.*) glove, 15
guantera (*f.*) glove compartment, 18
guapo(-a) handsome, 3
guardafangos (guardabarros) (*m.*) fender, 18
guerra (*f.*) war
guía de espectáculos (*f.*) movie guide, 14
guía telefónica (*f.*) telephone book
gustar to like, to be pleasing to, 7
gusto (*m.*) pleasure
El _____ **es mío.** The pleasure is mine., 2
Mucho _____. How do you do? Nice (*pleased*) to meet you., 2

H

haber (*aux.*) to have, 15
habitación (*f.*) room, 6
_____ **doble** (*f.*) double room, 6
habla: de _____ **hispana** Spanish-speaking
hablado(-a) spoken
hablar to speak, to talk, 2
hacer to do, to make, 6
_____ **buen tiempo** to be good weather, 6
_____ **calor** to be hot, 6

_____ **caso** to pay attention, 13

_____ **diligencias** to run errands, 11

_____ **frío** to be cold, 6

_____ **juego** to match, to go together, 15

_____ **las maletas** to pack

_____ **mal tiempo** to be bad weather, 6

_____ **sol** to be sunny, 6

_____ **un depósito** make a deposit, 11

_____ **una radiografía** to take an x-ray, 17

_____ **viento** to be windy, 6

hace + *time* ago, 11

hace + *time* + que + *verb* (*present*) to have been doing something for a length of time, 7

hace + *time* + que + *verb* (*preterit/imperfect*) to have done something in the past (ago), 10

hacerse to become

hacia toward, 11

hambre (*f.*) hunger, 4

tener _____ to be hungry, 4

harto(-a) de fed up

hamburguesa (*f.*) hamburger, 8

hasta until, 6; up to

_____ **la vista** until I see you again, 1

_____ **llegar** until you get, 12

_____ **luego** see you later, 1

_____ **mañana** see you tomorrow, 1

_____ **pronto.** See you later., 1

_____ **que** until, 14

hay there is, there are, 2

_____ **niebla** it's foggy, 6

hecho(-a) (*p.p. of* **hacer** *and adj.*) done, made, 15

helado (*m.*) ice cream, 8

helado(-a) iced, ice cold, 8

torta helada (*f.*) ice cream cake, 8

herida (*f.*) wound, 17

herir (e:ie) to hurt

hermana (*f.*) sister, 5

hermanastra (*f.*) stepsister, 5

hermanastro (*m.*) stepbrother, 5

hermano (*m.*) brother, 5

hermoso(-a) beautiful, 6

hierba (*f.*) herb; grass

hija (*f.*) daughter, 5

hijastra (*f.*) stepdaughter, 5

hijastro (*m.*) stepson, 5

hijo (*m.*) son, 5

hijo(-a) único(-a) (*m., f.*) only child, 11

hijos (*m. pl.*) children, 3

hilo (*m.*) linen, 15

hipoteca (*f.*) mortgage

hoja (*f.*) leaf

_____ **de papel** (*f.*) sheet of paper, 2

hola hello, 1

hombre (*m.*) man

_____ **de negocios** (*m.*) businessman, 16

hora (*f.*) time, 2; hour, 7

¿A qué _____**...?** (At) what time . . . ?, 2

¿Qué _____ **es?** What time is it?, 2

horario (*m.*) schedule, 16

horno de microondas (*m.*) microwave oven, 13

horror (*m.*) horror

hospedarse en to stay (*at a hotel*), 10

hospital (*m.*) hospital, 2

hotel (*m.*) hotel, 6

hoy today, 2

_____ **mismo** this very day, 15

hubo There was, were, 9

huevo (*m.*) egg, 8

I

ida (*f.*): **de** _____ one-way (*ticket*), 7

de _____ **y vuelta** round-trip, 7

ido (*p.p. of* **ir**) gone, 15

idea (*f.*) idea, 4

identidad (*f.*) identity, 3

idioma (*m.*) language

iglesia (*f.*) church

imperativo (*m.*) command

imperfecto (*m.*) imperfect

imperio (*m.*) empire

impermeable (*m.*) raincoat

importado(-a) imported, 15

importante important, 16

importar to matter, 16

incómodo(-a) uncomfortable

incredulidad (*f.*) disbelief

indeterminado(-a) indefinite

indicativo(-a) indicative

infección (*f.*) infection, 17

información (*f.*) information, 6

informática (*f.*) computer science

informe (*m.*) report, 3; paper, 16

ingeniería (*f.*) engineering, 16

ingeniero(-a) (*m., f.*) engineer, 16

inglés (*m.*) English (*lang.*), 2

en _____ in English, 2

ingreso(s) (*m. pl.*) income

inodoro (*m.*) toilet, 6

insistir en to insist on, 17

instalar to install, 18

institución (*f.*) institution, 3

inteligente intelligent, 3

interés (*m.*) interest, 6

interesante interesting, 5

interior interior, 6

internacional international, 6

interrogativo(-a) interrogative

investigación (*f.*) research, 16

invierno (*m.*) winter, 1

invitación (*f.*) invitation, 4

invitado(-a) invited, 4

invitar (a) to invite, 4

¡Yo invito! My treat!, 14

inyección (*f.*) injection, shot, 17

_____ **antitetánica** (*f.*) tetanus shot, 17

poner una _____ to give a shot, an injection, 17

ir (a) to go, 4

ir a + *infinitive* to be going (to) + *infinitive*, 4

_____ **de compras** to go shopping, 10

_____ **de pesca** to go fishing, 10

_____ **de vacaciones** to go on vacation, 10

_____ **mal** to go wrong

irse to go away, to leave, 9

italiano (*m.*) Italian (*lang.*), 2

izquierdo(-a) left

a la izquierda to (on, at) the left, 6

J

jabón (*m.*) soap, 6

jactarse (de) to brag (about)

jamás never, 6

jamón (*m.*) ham, 8

japonés(-esa) Japanese

jarabe (*m.*)   cough syrup, 17
jardín (*m.*)   garden, 13
joven (*m., f.*)   young
joyas (*f. pl.*)   jewels, jewelry
joyería (*f.*)   jewelry store
jueves (*m.*)   Thursday, 1
juez (*m.*)   judge
jugador(-a) (*m., f.*)   player
jugar (*u:ue*)   to play (*game, sport*)
    _____ **al golf**   to play golf, 10
    _____ **al tenis**   to play tennis, 10
jugo (*m.*)   juice, 8
julio   July, 1
junio   June, 1
junto a   next to, 10
juntos(-as)   together, 7

K

kilómetro (*m.*)   kilometer, 18

L

la (*f. sing.*)   the, 1; (*pron.*) her, it, you (*form.*), 6
laboratorio (*m.*)   laboratory, 16
    _____ **de lenguas** (*m.*) language lab
labrador(-a) (*m., f.*)   farmer
lacio(-a)   straight (*hair*), 9
ladrón(-ona) (*m., f.*)   robber
lago (*m.*)   lake, 10
lámpara (*f.*)   lamp, 13
lana (*f.*)   wool, 15
langosta (*f.*)   lobster, 8
lápiz (*m.*)   pencil, 2
largo(-a)   long, 7
las (*f. pl.*)   the, 1; (*pron.*) them, you (*form.*), 6
lástima (*f.*)   pity, shame
    es una _____   it's a pity, 11
    ¡Qué _____!   What a pity!, 5
lata (*f.*)   can, 14
latinoamericano(-a)   Latin American
lavabo (*m.*)   sink, 6
lavado (*m.*)   shampoo, wash, 9
lavadora (*f.*)   washing machine, 13
lavaplatos (*m.*)   dishwasher, 13
lavar(se)   to wash (oneself), 9
    _____ **la cabeza**   to wash one's hair, 9
le   (to, for) her, (to, for) him, (to, for) you (*form.*), 7
leche (*f.*)   milk, 8

lechera (*f.*)   milkmaid
lechón (*m.*)   pork, 8
lechuga (*f.*)   lettuce, 14
lector(-a) (*m., f.*)   reader
leer   to read, 3
leído (*p.p. of* **leer**)   read, 15
lejos (*adv.*)   far, 8
lengua (*f.*)   tongue, 17; language
lentamente   slowly
lento(-a)   slow
les   (to, for) them, (to, for) you, (*form. pl.*), 7
letrero (*m.*)   sign, 18
levantar   to lift, to raise, 9
    levantarse   to get up, 9
libertad (*f.*)   liberty
libra (*f.*)   pound
libre   vacant, 6; off, free, 11
libreta de ahorros (*f.*)   savings passbook, 11
libro (*m.*)   book, 2
licencia de conducir (*f.*)   driver's license, 3
licuadora (*f.*)   blender, 13
liebre (*f.*)   hare
limpiaparabrisas (*m.*)   windshield wiper, 18
limpiar(se)   to clean (oneself), 9
limpio(-a)   clean
lindo(-a)   pretty, 3
lino (*m.*)   linen, 15
liquidación (*f.*)   sale, 15
lista (*f.*)   list, 6; menu, 8
    _____ **de espera** (*f.*)   waiting list, 6
listo(-a)   ready, 11
literatura (*f.*)   literature, 16
llamar   to call, 2
    llamarse   to be called, 9
        ¿Cómo se llama usted? What is your name? (*form.*), 1
        ¿Cómo te llamas?   What's your name? (*fam.*), 1
        Me llamo…   My name is . . . , 1
llano (*m.*)   plain
llanta (*f.*)   tire, 18
llanura (*f.*)   plain
llave (*f.*)   key, 6
llegada (*f.*)   arrival, 4
llegar   to arrive, 6
    _____ **tarde**   to be late, 7
    _____ **temprano**   to be early
llenar   to fill, to fill out, 11

lleno(-a)   full, 18
llevar   to take (*someone or something someplace*), 4; to wear, to use, 15
    llevarse   to take (away), 11; to buy, to take, 15
llover (*o:ue*)   to rain, 5
    _____ **a cántaros**   to rain cats and dogs, to pour, 8
lloviznar   to drizzle, 6
lluvia (*f.*)   rain, 6
lo   him, it, you (*form.*), 6
    _____ **cual**   which
    _____ **siento**   I'm sorry, 3
    _____ **único**   the only thing, 16
loco(-a)   crazy, 7
Londres   London
los (*m. pl.*)   the, 1; (*pron.*) them, you (*form.*), 6
lotería (*f.*)   lottery, 13
luchar   to fight
luego   afterwards, then, 6
lugar (*m.*)   place, 6
    _____ **de nacimiento** (*m.*) place of birth, 3
    _____ **donde trabaja** (*m.*) place of employment, 3
lumbre (*f.*)   fire
lunar (*m.*)   mole
    de lunares   polka dot, 15
lunes (*m.*)   Monday, 1
luz (*f.*)   light, 2; headlight, 18

M

madera (*f.*)   wood
madrastra (*f.*)   stepmother, 5
madre (*f.*)   mother, 4
maestro(-a) (*m., f.*)   teacher (*elementary school*), 1
magnífico(-a)   great, 4
maleta (*f.*)   suitcase, 6
maletero (*m.*)   (*car*) trunk, 18
maletín (*m.*)   briefcase
malo(-a)   bad, 4
mamá   mom, 4
manada (*f.*)   herd
manchar   to stain
mandar   to send, 7; to order, 11
manejar   to drive, 5
manía (*f.*)   bad habit
mano (*f.*)   hand, 17
manta (*f.*)   blanket, 13

mantecado (*m.*)   ice cream (*Mex.*, *Puerto Rico*), 8

mantel (*m.*)   tablecloth, 8

mantener (*conj. like* **tener**)   to maintain, 16

mantequilla (*f.*)   butter, 14

manzana (*f.*)   apple, 14; (*Sp.*) city block, 12; block (*of buildings*), (*Sp. Am.*), 12

mañana (*f.*)   morning, 2; (*adv.*) tomorrow, 3

de la _____   A.M., 2

mapa (*m.*)   map, 2

máquina de afeitar (*f.*)   razor, 9

mar (*m.*)   sea, 10

_____ **Mediterráneo**   Mediterranean Sea, 10

marcador (*m.*)   felt-tip marker, 2

marchito(-a)   faded, withered

mareo (*m.*)   dizziness, dizzy spell

margarina (*f.*)   margarine, 14

mariscos (*m. pl.*)   shellfish, 8

marrón   brown, 1

martes (*m.*)   Tuesday, 1

marzo   March, 1

más   more, 5

el (la) _____... **de**   the most ... in, 5

_____ **de**   more than, 5

_____ **o menos**   so-so, more or less, 3

_____... **que**   more ... than, 5

_____ **tarde**   later, 3

masculino   male, 3

matemáticas (*f. pl.*)   mathematics, 16

materia (*f.*)   (*school*) subject, 16

matrícula (*f.*)   registration, tuition, 16

matricularse   to register, 16

mayo   May, 1

mayor   older, 5; bigger, 5

el (la) _____   the oldest, 5

me   me, 6; (to, for) me, 7; (to) myself, 9

_____ **llamo...**   My name is ..., 1

mecánico (*m.*)   mechanic, 18

mediano(-a)   medium, 15

medianoche (*f.*)   midnight, 4

medicina (*f.*)   medicine, 5

médico(-a) (*m., f.*)   doctor, 1; (*adj.*) medical, 17

medida (*f.*)   size, 15

medio (*m.*)   means

medio(-a)   half, 8

media hermana (*f.*)   half sister, 5

media hora   half an hour, 7

medio ambiente (*m.*)   environment

medio día   half a day; part-time, 13

medio hermano (*m.*)   half brother, 5

y media   half-past (*telling time*), 2

mediodía (*m.*)   noon, 4

al _____   at noon, 4

mejor   best; better, 5

el (la) _____   the best, 5

mejorar   to improve

melocotón (*m.*)   peach, 14

melón (*m.*)   melon, 14

menor   younger, 5

el (la) _____   youngest, 5

menos   less, 5

a _____ **que**   unless, 14

el (la) _____... **de**   the least ... in, 5

_____ **de +** *number*   less than + *number*, 5

_____... **que**   less ... than, 5

mentir (e:ie)   to lie, 8

menú (*m.*)   menu, 8

menudo: a _____   often

mermelada (*f.*)   jam

mercado (*m.*)   market, 14

mes (*m.*)   month, 1

mesa (*f.*)   table, 4

mesita de noche (*f.*)   nightstand, 13

metro (*m.*)   subway, 12

mexicano(-a)   Mexican, 1

mezcla (*f.*)   mix, mixture, blend

mi (*sing.*)   my, 3

_____ **amor**   my love, my darling, 8

_____ **dirección es...**   my address is ..., 2

mí (*obj. of prep.*)   me, 5

microondas   microwave, 13

miedo (*m.*)   fear, 4

mientras   while, 11

_____ **tanto**   meanwhile

miércoles (*m.*)   Wednesday, 1

mil   one thousand, 3

milla (*f.*)   mile, 18

mío(s), mía(s) (*pron.*)   mine, 9

mirar   to look at, 5; to watch (*T.V.*), 3

_____ **vidrieras**   to window shop, 15

mis (*pl.*)   my, 3

mismo(-a)   same, 13

al mismo tiempo   at the same time, 13

misterio (*m.*)   mystery

mochila (*f.*)   backpack, 10

moda (*f.*)   fashion

modista (*f.*)   dressmaker

modo (*m.*)   way

de _____ **que**   so, 11

de todos modos   anyway

mojar   to dip

molino de viento (*m.*)   windmill

momento (*m.*)   moment, 3

moneda (*f.*)   currency

montaña (*f.*)   mountain, 10

_____ **rusa** (*f.*)   roller coaster, 14

montar   to mount, to ride, 10

_____ **a caballo**   to ride a horse, 10

_____ **en bicicleta**   to ride a bicycle, 10

monte (*m.*)   mountains

montón (*m.*): **un montón de**   a pile of, 12

morado(-a)   purple, 1

moreno(-a)   dark, brunette, 3

morir (o:ue)   to die, 5

moro(-a)   Moorish, Moor

mostrador (*m.*)   counter, 9

mostrar (o:ue)   to show, 6

moto (*f.*)   motorcycle, 11

motocicleta (*f.*)   motorcycle, 11

motor (*m.*)   motor, 18

mozo (*m.*)   waiter, 8

muchacha (*f.*)   girl, young woman, 3

muchacho (*m.*)   boy, young man, 3

mucho(-a)   much, a lot (of), 4

Muchas gracias.   Thank you very much., 2

Mucho gusto.   How do you do? Nice to meet you., 1; Pleased to meet you, 2

no mucho   not much

muchos(-as)   many, 4

mudarse   to move (*from one house to another*), 13

muebles (*m. pl.*)   furniture, 13

muerto(-a) (*p.p. of* **morir** *and adj.*)   dead, 15

mujer (*f.*)   woman

_____ **de negocios** (*f.*)
   businesswoman, 16

muleta (*f.*)   crutch, 17

multa (*f.*)   fine, ticket, 18

mundo (*m.*)   world, 5

muralla (*f.*)   wall

museo (*m.*)   museum, 5

muy   very, 1

_____ **bien**   very well, 1

N

nacer   to be born

nacimiento (*m.*)   birth, 3

nacionalidad (*f.*)   nationality, 3

nada   nothing, 3; not anything, 6

nadar   to swim, 10

nadie   nobody, no one, not anyone,
   6

naranja (*f.*)   orange, 14

nariz (*f.*)   nose, 17

naturaleza (*f.*)   nature, 10

Navidad (*f.*)   Christmas, 4

necesario(-a)   necessary, 18

necesitar   to need, 2

negación (*f.*)   denial

negar (e:ie)   to deny, 12

negarse   to refuse

negativo(-a)   negative

negro(-a)   black, 1

nervioso(-a)   nervous, 4

neumático (*m.*)   tire, 18

nevado(-a)   snow-covered

nevar (e:ie)   to snow, 6

ni   nor, 6

_____ **... ni...**   neither . . .
   nor . . . , 6

niebla (*f.*)   fog, 6

nieta (*f.*)   granddaughter, 5

nieto (*m.*)   grandson, 5

nieve (*f.*)   snow, 10

ninguno(-a), ningún   no, none, not
   any, 6

niñez (*f.*)   childhood

niño(-a) (*m., f.*)   child, 10

no   no, not, 1

_____ **está**   he or she is not
   here, 3

_____ **mucho**   not much

_____ **muy bien**   not very
   well, 1

noche (*f.*)   evening, night, 3

esta _____   tonight, 3

nombrar   to name

nombre (*m.*)   (*first*) name, 3; noun

nominado(-a)   nominated, 14

noroeste   northwest

norte   north, 10

norteamericano(-a)   North
   American, 1

nos   us, 6; (to, for) us, 7; (to, for)
   ourselves, 9

_____ **vemos.**   See you., 1

nosotros(-as)   we, 1; us, 5

nota (*f.*)   grade, 16

notar   to note

noticias (*f. pl.*)   news

novecientos   nine hundred, 3

noveno(-a)   ninth, 8

noventa   ninety, 2

novia (*f.*)   girlfriend, fiancée, bride,
   3

noviembre   November, 1

novio (*m.*)   boyfriend, fiancé, groom,
   3

nuera (*f.*)   daughter-in-law, 5

nuestro(-a)   our, 3; (*pron.*) ours, 9

nuestro(-as)   our (*pl.*), 3

nueve   nine, 1

nuevo(-a)   new, 4

número (*m.*)   number, 2; size (*of
   shoes*), 15

nunca   never, 5

O

o   or, 3

_____**... o...**   either . . .
   or . . . , 6

objeto (*m.*)   object, 6

occidental   western

océano (*m.*)   ocean, 10

_____ **Atlántico**   Atlantic
   Ocean, 10

_____ **Pacífico**   Pacific Ocean,
   10

octavo(-a)   eighth, 8

octubre   October, 1

ocupación (*f.*)   occupation, 3

ocupado(-a)   busy, 4

ochenta   eighty, 2

ocho   eight, 1

ochocientos   eight hundred, 3

ocultar   to hide

oeste   west, 10

oficina (*f.*)   office, 6

_____ **de correos** (*f.*)   post
   office, 12

oficio (*m.*)   trade, 16

ofrecer   to offer, 6

oído (*m.*)   (*p.p. of* **oír**) heard, 15; ear
   (*inner*), 17

oír   to hear, 15

ojalá   I hope, God grant, 11

ojo (*m.*)   eye, 17

olvidar(se) (de)   to forget, 9

once   eleven, 1

operación (*f.*)   surgery

oportunidad (*f.*)   opportunity, 5

optativo(-a)   elective

optimista (*invariable adj.*)
   optimistic, 3

oración (*f.*)   sentence

orden (*f.*)   order

oreja (*f.*)   ear, 17

orgullo (*m.*)   pride

orgulloso(-a)   proud

oriental   eastern

oro (*m.*)   gold, 6

orquesta (*f.*)   orchestra, band, 4

os   you (*fam. pl.*), 6; (to, for) you, 7;
   (to) yourselves, 9

oscuro(-a)   dark

otoño (*m.*)   autumn, fall, 1

otro(-a)   another, other, 3

otra vez   again

oveja (*f.*)   sheep

oye   listen, 2

P

pacer   to graze

padrastro (*m.*)   stepfather, 5

padre (*m.*)   father, 5

padres (*m., pl.*)   parents, 5

pagar   to pay, 7

_____ **por adelantado**   to pay
   in advance, 6

país (*m.*)   country, 10

País Vasco (*m.*)   Basque Country

palabra (*f.*)   word

palacio (*m.*)   palace, 12

palita (*f.*)   dustpan, 9

pan (*m.*)   bread, 14

panqueque (*m.*)   pancake

pantalla (*f.*)   screen, 12

pantalón (*m.*)   pants, trousers, 11

pantalones (*m. pl.*)   pants,
   trousers, 11

pantalones cortos   shorts

pantimedias (*f. pl.*)   pantyhose, 15

pantorrilla (*f.*)   calf (*of leg*)

pañuelo (*m.*)   handkerchief, 15

papa (*f.*)   potato, 8
    —s **fritas** (*f. pl.*)   French
      fries, 8
papá   dad, 5
papel (*m.*)   paper, 2; role
    — **higiénico** (*m.*)   toilet
      tissue, 14
paperas (*f. pl.*)   mumps
paquete (*m.*)   package, parcel, 12
par (*m.*)   pair, 15
para   for, 3; to, in order to, 4; by, 8
    — **entonces**   by then, 16
    — **que**   in order that, 14
parabrisas (*m.*)   windshield, 18
parachoques (*m.*)   bumper, 18
parado(-a)   standing, 12
paraguas (*m.*)   umbrella
paraguayo(-a)   Paraguayan, 9
parar   to stop, 18
parecerse (a)   to look like, 11
pared (*f.*)   wall, 2
pareja (*f.*)   couple, 18
parque (*m.*)   park, 12
    — **de diversiones** (*m.*)
      amusement park, 14
parquear   to park, 11
parte (*f.*): **a (de) todas** —s
  everywhere
partera (*f.*)   midwife
partido (*m.*)   game, 16
pasado(-a)   last, 7
    — **de moda**   out of style,
      15
pasaje (*m.*)   ticket, 7
    — **de ida** (*m.*)   one-way
      ticket, 7
    — **de ida y vuelta** (*m.*)
      round-trip ticket, 7
    — **de primera clase** (*m.*)
      first-class ticket, 7
pasaporte (*m.*)   passport, 6
pasar   to pass; to spend (*time*), 6; to
  happen, 7
    — **la aspiradora**   to
      vacuum, 9
    — **por**   to go by,
      through, 6
pasarlo bien   to have a good time, 4
Pase.   Come in., 2
pasillo (*m.*)   aisle, 7
paso (*m.*)   step
    — **de peatones**   pedestrian
      crosswalk
pastilla (*f.*)   pill, 17
pavo (*m.*)   turkey, 8

paz (*f.*)   peace
pecho (*m.*)   chest, 17
pedido (*m.*)   order, 8
pedir (e:i)   to ask for, to request, 6; to
  order, 8
    — **prestado**   to borrow,
      11
    — **turno (cita)**   to make
      an appointment, 9
    — **un préstamo**   to apply
      for a loan, 11
peinado (*m.*)   hairstyle, hairdo, 9
peinarse   to comb or style one's hair,
  9
peine (*m.*)   comb, 9
película (*f.*)   film (*for camera*), 11;
  movie, 14
pelirrojo(-a)   red-headed, 3
pelo (*m.*)   hair, 9
peluquería (*f.*)   beauty parlor, 9
peluquero(-a)   hairdresser,
  beautician, 9
pena (*f.*)   sorrow
penicilina (*f.*)   penicillin, 17
pensamiento (*m.*)   thought
pensar (e:ie)   to think, 4; (+*inf.*) to
  plan, 4
    — **en**   to think about, 17
pensión (*f.*)   boarding house, 5
peor   worse, 5
    el (la) —   the worst, 5
pequeño(-a)   small, little, 4
pera (*f.*)   pear, 14
perder (e:ie)   to lose, 4
Perdón. (*m.*)   Pardon me., 2
perdonar   to forgive
perfectamente   perfectly, 5
perfecto(-a)   perfect
perfume (*m.*)   perfume
perfumería (*f.*)   perfume shop
periódico (*m.*)   newspaper, 13
periodismo (*m.*)   journalism, 16
periodista (*m., f.*)   journalist, 16
permanente (*m., f.*)   permanent
  (wave), 9
permiso (*m.*)   Excuse me., 2
pero   but, 4
perro(-a) (*m., f.*)   dog, 9
    — **caliente** (*m.*)   hot dog,
      14
personaje (*m.*)   character
personal   personal, 3
pesar   to weigh
pesca (*f.*)   fishing, 10
    ir de —   to go fishing, 10

pescado (*m.*)   fish, 8
pescar   to fish, to catch (*a fish*), 10
peseta   monetary unit (*Sp.*)
pesimista (*m., f.*)   pessimistic, 3
peso (*m.*)   weight; monetary unit
  (*Mex.*)
pesquero(-a)   fishing
picnic (*m.*)   picnic
pie (*m.*)   foot, 17
piedra (*f.*)   stone
piel (*f.*)   leather
pierna (*f.*)   leg, 17
pieza de repuesto (*f.*)   spare part, 18
pijama (*m.*)   pajamas, 15
piloto (*m., f.*)   pilot, 1
pimienta (*f.*)   pepper, 8
pinchazo (*m.*)   flat tire, 18
pintura (*f.*)   painting, picture, 5
piña (*f.*)   pineapple, 14
piscina (*f.*)   swimming pool, 6
piso (*m.*)   floor, 6; (*Sp.*) apartment
pizarra (*f.*)   chalkboard, 2
placa (*f.*)   license plate, 18
plan (*m.*)   plan, 5
plancha (*f.*)   iron, 13
planchar   to iron, 9
planear   to plan, 10
planta baja (*f.*)   ground floor, 15
plata (*f.*)   silver, 6
platillo (*m.*)   saucer, 8
plato (*m.*)   dish, 8; plate, 8
playa (*f.*)   beach, 10
plaza (*f.*)   town square, 5
plazo: a —s   in installments, 11
plomero(-a) (*m., f.*)   plumber, 16
pluma (*f.*)   pen, 2; feather
    — **estilográfica** (*f.*)
      fountain pen, 2
pluscuamperfecto (*m.*)   pluperfect
población (*f.*)   population
pobre   poor (*unfortunate*), 11; poor,
  13
poco(-a)   little (*quantity*), 2
    un poco + *adjective*   a little +
      adjective, 4
pocos(-as)   few, 6
poder (o:ue)   to be able to, can, 5;
  (*m.*) power
poema (*m.*)   poem
policía (*m.*)   police officer, 18; (*f.*)
  police
policíaco(-a) (*adj.*)   detective
pollo (*m.*)   chicken, 4
    — **frito** (*m.*)   fried chicken
pomelo (*m.*)   grapefruit, 14

ponche (*m.*) punch, 4
poner to put, to place, 6; to turn on (*heat, air conditioning*), 13
   _____ la fecha to date (check, letter), 11
   _____ la mesa to set the table, 8
   _____ una inyección to give an injection, shot, 17
   _____ un multa to give a ticket (*fine*), 18
   _____ una película to show a movie, 14
  ponerse to put on, 9
   _____ a dieta to go on a diet, 14
  no tener nada que _____ not to have anything to put on, 15
por along, 8; around, 8; because of, 8; by, 8; during, 8; for, 6; in, 8; in exchange for, 8; in search of, 8; on account of, 8; on behalf of, 8; per, 6; through, 8
   _____ aquí this way, 8
   _____ ejemplo for example
   _____ eso that is why, 5
   _____ favor please, 2
   _____ la mañana (tarde) in the morning (*afternoon*), 2
   ¿_____ qué? why?, 3
   _____ supuesto of course, 7
   _____ teléfono by phone; on the phone, 3
   _____ vía aérea by airmail, 12
porque because, 2
portaguantes (*m. sing.*) glove compartment, 18
Portugal Portugal
portugués (*m.*) Portuguese (*lang.*), 2
posibilidad (*f.*) possibility
posición (*f.*) position
postre (*m.*) dessert, 8
  de _____ for dessert, 8
practicar to practice, 5
precio (*m.*) price, 8
preferir (e:ie) to prefer, 4
pregunta (*f.*) question
preguntar to ask (*a question*), 14
preocupado(-a) worried, 4
preocuparse (por) to worry (about), 9
preparar to prepare, 4
presentación (*f.*) introduction
presentar to introduce, 7

presente present
presión (*f.*): _____ arterial blood pressure
préstamo (*m.*) loan
  pedir un _____ to apply for a loan, 11
prestar to lend, 7
primavera (*f.*) spring, 1
primero(-a), primer first, 8
  primer día de clases first day of classes, 2
primo(-a) (*m., f.*) cousin, 4
prisa (*f.*) hurry
  darse _____ to hurry (up), 14
  No hay _____. There's no hurry., 7
  tener _____ to be in a hurry, 4
privado(-a) private, 6
probablemente, probably, 16
probador (*m.*) fitting room, 15
probar (o:ue) to try, 9; to taste, 9
  probarse to try on, 9
problema (*m.*) problem
  _____ financiero (*m.*) money problem, 3
  _____ sentimental (*m.*) love problem, 3
profesión (*f.*) profession, 3
profesor(-a) (*m., f.*) professor, teacher, instructor, 1
  _____ de español Spanish teacher, 1
profundamente soundly, 10
programa (*m.*) program
programador(-a) (*m., f.*) programmer, 1
prohibido(-a) prohibited, 14
promedio (*m.*) grade point average, 16
pronto soon, 16
propina (*f.*) tip, 8
propio(-a)(s) own
  propia página (*f.*) home page
próximo(-a) next, 7
psicología (*f.*) psychology, 16
psicólogo(-a) (*m., f.*) psychologist, 16
pueblo (*m.*) town, people, nation
puerta (*f.*) door, 2; gate
  _____ de salida (*f.*) airline departure gate, 7
  _____ principal (*f.*) main exit (*door*), 12

pues then, 7
puesto(-a) (*p.p. of* poner *and adj.*) set, placed, put, 15
pulmonía (*f.*) pneumonia
pulsera (*f.*) bracelet, 8
puntual punctual, 12
pupitre (*m.*) desk, 2

Q

que (*rel. pron.*) that, 3; who, 3; which, 6; (*conj.*) than, 5
qué what?, 2
  ¿A _____ hora? (At) what time?, 2
  _____ diablo what the heck
  ¿_____ hay (de nuevo)? What's up (new)?, 1
  ¿_____ hora es? What time is it?, 2
  ¡_____ horrible! How horrible!, 10
  ¡_____ lástima! What a pity!, 5
  ¡_____ pena! What a pity!, 5
  ¿_____ quiere decir… ? What does . . . mean?, 2
  ¡_____ sorpresa! What a surprise!, 8
  ¿_____ tal? How's it going? (*fam.*), 1; How was (is) . . . ?, 7
  ¿_____ tiempo hace? What's the weather like?, 6
quebrar(se) (e:ie) to break, 17
quedar to be located, 8; to fit, 9
  _____le grande (chico) a uno to be too big (small) on someone, 15
  _____ suspendido(-a) to fail (*exam or course*), 16
  quedarse to remain, to stay, 10
  _____ en la cama hasta tarde to sleep late, 11
  _____ sentado to remain seated
queja (*f.*) complaint
querer (e:ie) to want, to wish, 4; to love, 4
  no quise I refused, 10
querido(-a) dear, darling, 8
queso (*m.*) cheese, 8
quien(es) who, whom, that, 12

quién who?, 3
  ¿de _____? whose?, 4
  ¿_____ es? Who is it?, 3
  ¿_____ habla? Who is speaking?, 3
  ¿De parte de _____? Who is speaking?, 3
quiere decir... it means . . . , 2
química (*f.*) chemistry, 16
quince fifteen, 1
quinientos five hundred, 3
quinto(-a) fifth, 8
quitar to take away, 9
  quitarse to take off, 9

R

radiografía (*f.*) X-ray, 17
rallado(-a) grated
rápidamente rapidly
rápido (*adv.*) fast, rapidly, 18
raqueta (*f.*) racket, 10
raro(-a) rare
ratón (*m.*) mouse, 12
raya (*f.*) stripe, 15
rayón (*m.*) rayon
razón (*f.*) reason
  tener _____ to be right, 4
real royal, 12; real
realista realistic, 3
rebaja (*f.*) sale, 15
rebajar to mark down, 15
recámara (*f.*) (*Mex.*) bedroom, 13
recepción (*f.*) registration, 6
recepcionista (*m., f.*) receptionist, 1
receta (*f.*) prescription, 17; recipe
recetar to prescribe, 17
recibir to receive, 3
recién casados (*m. pl.*) newlyweds, 18
reciente recent
recientemente recently
recogedor (*m.*) dustpan, 9
recoger to pick up, 11
recomendar (e:ie) to recommend, 8
recordar (o:ue) to remember, 5
recurrir a to turn to
refresco (*m.*) soft drink, soda pop, 4
refrigerador (*m.*) refrigerator, 13
regalar to give (*as a gift*), 9
regalo (*m.*) gift, 8
registro (*m.*) register, 6
regla (*f.*) ruler, 2
regresar to return, 2
relato breve (*m.*) short story

reloj (*m.*) clock, 2
relojería (*f.*) watch store
relleno(-a) stuffed, 8
remolcador (*m.*) tow truck, 18
remolcar to tow, 18
repetir (e:i) to repeat, 8
repollo (*m.*) cabbage, 14
represa (*f.*) dam
reproductor de discos (*m.*) CD player, 4
requisito (*m.*) requirement, 16
reserva (*f.*) reservation, 6
reservación (*f.*) reservation, 6
resfriado (*m.*) cold, 17
resfrío (*m.*) cold, 17
residencia universitaria (*f.*) dorm
respuesta (*f.*) answer
resta (*f.*) subtraction
restaurante (*m.*) restaurant, 5
resto (*m.*) the rest, 14
retraso (*m.*) delay, 7
  tener... de _____ to be . . . behind schedule, 7
revelar to develop (*film*), 11
reventa (*f.*) resale
revisar to check, 18
revista (*f.*) magazine, 9
revolver (o:ue) to mix
rey (*m.*) king
rezar to pray
rico(-a) tasty, delicious, 8; rich
rifle (*m.*) rifle, 10
río (*m.*) river, 10
rizador (*m.*) curling iron, 9
rizo (*m.*) curl, 9
robar to steal, 11
rodilla (*f.*) knee, 17
rogar (o:ue) to beg, to plead, 11
rojo(-a) red, 1
rollo de película (*m.*) roll of film, 11
románico(-a) Romanesque
romper(se) to break, 17
ropa (*f.*) clothes, clothing, 11
  _____ hecha (*f.*) ready-to-wear clothes
  _____ interior (*f.*) underwear, 15
ropero (*m.*) closet, wardrobe, 15
rosado(-a) pink, 1
roto(-a) (*p.p. of* **romper** *and adj.*) broken, 15
rubio(-a) blond, 3
ruido (*m.*) noise, 18
ruinas (*f. pl.*) ruins, 6

S

sábado (*m.*) Saturday, 1
sábana (*f.*) sheet, 13
saber to know, 6; to find out, 10
saborear to taste
sabroso(-a) tasty, delicious, 8
sacapuntas (*m.*) pencil sharpener, 2
sacar to take out, to withdraw, 11; to get, to receive (*a grade*), 16
saco de dormir (*m.*) sleeping bag, 10
sal (*f.*) salt, 8
sala (*f.*) living room, 13
  _____ de emergencia (*f.*) emergency room, 17
  _____ de rayos X (equis) (*f.*) X-ray room, 17
salario (*m.*) salary, 13
saldo (*m.*) balance, 11
salida (*f.*) exit, 7; departure, 7
salir to leave, to go out, 6
  _____ de viaje to leave on a trip, 18
salmón (*m.*) salmon, 8
salón (*m.*) room
  _____ de belleza (*m.*) beauty parlor, 9
  _____ de estar (*m.*) family room, 13
salsa (*f.*) sauce, 14
Salto Ángel Angel Falls
salud (*f.*) health
  ¡Salud! cheers!
saludo (*m.*) greeting
  _____s a... Say hello to . . . , 16
salvavidas (*m., f.*) lifeguard, 10
sandalia (*f.*) sandal, 15
sandía (*f.*) watermelon, 14
sándwich (*m.*) sandwich, 4
sangría (*f.*) sangría, 4
sarampión (*m.*) measles
sartén (*f.*) skillet, 13
sastre (*m.*) tailor
sauce (*m.*) (*weeping*) willow, 10
se (to) himself, (to) herself, (to) yourself (*form.*), (to) yourselves, (to) themselves, 9
  _____ dice... You say . . . , One says . . . , 2
  _____ prohíbe fumar. No smoking.
  _____ sale por la derecha exit to the right
  _____ vende for sale

secador (*m.*)   blow dryer, 9
secadora (*f.*)   dryer, 13
sección (*f.*)   section
_____ de (no) fumar (*f.*)   (no) smoking section, 7
secretario(-a) (*m., f.*)   secretary, 1
sed (*f.*)   thirst, 4
tener _____   to be thirsty, 4
seda (*f.*)   silk, 15
sede (*f.*)   headquarters; campus; seat
seguir (e:i)   to follow, 6; to continue, 6
_____ la moda   to follow fashion, 15
según   according to, 18
segundo(-a)   second, 6
segundo nombre (*m.*)   middle name
seguro (*m.*)   insurance
_____ de automóvil (*m.*)   auto insurance
_____ social (*m.*)   social security, 3
seis   six, 1
seiscientos   six hundred, 3
sello (*m.*)   stamp, 12
semáforo (*m.*)   traffic light, 12
semana (*f.*)   week, 9
Semana Santa   Holy Week
sencillo(-a)   single, 6; simple, 6
sentarse (e:ie)   to sit (down), 9
sentir(se) (e:ie)   to feel, 9; to be sorry, to regret, 11
lo siento   I'm sorry
señal (*f.*)   sign
señor (*abbr.* Sr.)   Mr., sir, gentleman, 1
señora (*abbr.* Sra.)   Mrs. madam, lady, 1
señorita (*abbr.* Srta.)   Miss, young lady, 1
septiembre   September, 1
séptimo(-a)   seventh, 8
ser   to be, 1
servicio de habitación (cuarto) (*m.*)   room service, 6
servicios (*m. pl.*)   restrooms, 6
servilleta (*f.*)   napkin, 8
servir (e:i)   to serve, 6
no sirve   it's no good, 18
sesenta   sixty, 2
setecientos   seven hundred, 3
setenta   seventy, 2
sexo (*m.*)   sex, 3
sexto(-a)   sixth, 8

si   if, 5
sí   yes, 2
sidra (*f.*)   cider, 4
siempre   always, 4
siesta (*f.*)   nap
siete   seven, 1
silla (*f.*)   chair, 2
_____ de ruedas (*f.*)   wheelchair, 17
sillón (*m.*)   armchair, 13
simpático(-a)   nice, charming, 3
sin   without, 12
_____ embargo   however, nevertheless, 10
_____ falta   without fail
_____ que   without, 14
sino   but
_____ que   but rather
sistema (*m.*)   system
_____ de calificaciones (*m.*)   grading system
situado(-a)   located, 6
sobre   about, 6; over
sobrecama (*f.*)   bedspread, 13
sobrenombre (*m.*)   nickname
sobrina (*f.*)   niece, 5
sobrino (*m.*)   nephew, 5
sociología (*f.*)   sociology, 16
sofá (*m.*)   couch, sofa, 13
sol (*m.*)   sun
solamente   only, 2
solicitar   to apply for, 3
solicitud (*f.*)   application, 3
_____ de trabajo (*f.*)   job application, 3
solo(-a)   alone
sólo   only, 7
soltar (o:ue)   to turn loose
soltero(-a)   single, 3
sollozar   to weep
sombrero (*m.*)   hat
son las...   it's . . . (*time*), 2
sonar (o:ue)   to ring, 11; to go off, 11
soñar (o:ue) con   to dream about (of), 17
sopa (*f.*)   soup, 8
_____ del día (*f.*)   soup of the day, 8
sorprender   to surprise, 11
sorpresa (*f.*)   surprise, 8
sostén (*m.*)   bra, 15
su   his, her, its, your (*form.*), their, 3
subir   to climb, to go up, 12
subterráneo (*m.*)   subway, 12
subvencionado(-a)   subsidized

sucio(-a)   dirty
sucursal (*f.*)   branch (*office*)
suegra (*f.*)   mother-in-law, 5
suegro (*m.*)   father-in-law, 5
sueldo (*m.*)   salary, 13
sueño (*m.*)   dream
tener _____   to be sleepy, 4
suerte (*f.*)   luck
suéter (*m.*)   sweater, 15
suficiente   enough, sufficient, 11
sugerir (e:ie)   to suggest, 11
Suiza   Switzerland
sujetador (*m.*)   bra
suma (*f.*)   addition
supermercado (*m.*)   supermarket, 14
suponer (*conj. like* poner)   to suppose, 16
sur   south, 10; southern
suspendido(-a): quedar _____   to fail (*exam or course*), 16
sus   his, her, its, your (*form.*), 3
suyo(s), suya(s) (*pron.*)   his, hers, theirs, yours, 9

T

tablero de anuncios (*m.*)   bulletin board, 2
tal vez   maybe, perhaps, 13
talla (*f.*)   size, 15
tallado(-a)   carved
taller (de mecánica) (*m.*)   repair shop, mechanic's shop, 18
talonario de cheques (*m.*)   checkbook, 11
talones (*m. pl.*)   checks (*Sp.*)
tamaño (*m.*)   size
también   also, too, 2
tampoco   neither, not either, 6
tan   as, so, 5
_____... como...   as . . . as . . . , 5
_____ pronto como   as soon as, 11
tanque (*m.*)   tank, 18
tanto(-a)   as much, 5; so much, 14
_____ como   as much as, 5
tantos(-as)   as many, 5
_____ como   as many as, 5
tarde (*f.*)   afternoon, 2; (*adv.*) late, 7
de la _____   P.M., 2
llegar _____   to be late, 7
más _____   later, 2
por la _____   in the afternoon, 2

tarjeta (*f.*) card, 7
    ———— **de crédito** (*f.*) credit card, 6
    ———— **de embarque** (*f.*) boarding pass, 7
    ———— **de turista** (*f.*) tourist card, 6
    ———— **postal** (*f.*) postcard, 7
taxi (*m.*) taxi, 6
taza (*f.*) cup, 8
te (*pron.*) you (*fam.*), 6; (to, for) you, 7; (to) yourself, 9
té (*m.*) tea
teatro (*m.*) theater, 8
teclado (*m.*) keyboard, 12
tejanos (*m. pl.*) jeans, 15
teléfono (*m.*) telephone, 3
    ———— **celular** (*m.*) cellular phone, 18
telegrama (*m.*) telegram
televisor (*m.*) television set, 6
tema (*m.*) subject, theme, 2; topic
temer to fear, 11
temperatura (*f.*) temperature, 17
temprano early, 9
tenedor (*m.*) fork, 8
tener to have, 3
    no ———— **nada que ponerse** not to have anything to put on, 15
    no ———— **razón** to be wrong, 4
    ————**... años (de edad)** to be ... years old, 4
    ———— **calor** to be hot, 4
    ———— **correspondencia** to correspond
    ———— **cuidado** to be careful, 4
    ———— **éxito** to be successful, 4
    ———— **frío** to be cold, 4
    ———— **ganas (de)** to feel like (*doing something*), 14
    ———— **hambre** to be hungry, 4
    ———— **la culpa** to be one's fault, 18
    ———— **lugar** to take place
    ———— **miedo** to be afraid, 4
    ———— **prisa** to be in a hurry, 4
    ———— **que** to have to, 3
    ———— **razón** to be right, 4
    ———— **sed** to be thirsty, 4

    ———— **sueño** to be sleepy, 4
    ———— **suerte** to be lucky, 4
    ————**... de retraso (atraso)** to be ... behind schedule, 7
    ———— **un pinchazo** to have a flat tire, 18
tercero(-a), tercer third, 8
terminar to finish, 9
ternero (*m.*) calf
terraza (*f.*) terrace, 4
terremoto (*m.*) earthquake
ti you (*fam. sing.*), 5
tía (*f.*) aunt, 5
tiempo (*m.*) weather, 6; time, 16
    ———— **completo** full-time, 13
tienda (*f.*) store, 8
    ———— **de campaña** (*f.*) tent, 10
    ———— **por departamentos** (*f.*) department store, 15
tierra (*f.*) earth, land
timbre (*m.*) (*Mex.*) stamp, 12
tinto red (*wine*), 8
tintorería (*f.*) dry cleaner's, 11
tío (*m.*) uncle, 5
tirar basura to litter
título (*m.*) title
tiza (*f.*) chalk, 2
toalla (*f.*) towel, 6
tobillo (*m.*) ankle, 17
tocar to play (*music, an instrument*)
tocino (*m.*) bacon
todavía yet, 17
todo(-a) all, 7
    toda la noche all night long, 10
    todo el día all day long
    todo el viaje the whole trip, 7
todo everything, 4
    ———— **lo que pasó** everything that happened, 7
todos(-as) everybody, 4
tomar to take, 2; to drink, 8
    ———— **algo** to have something to drink, 14
    ———— **el sol** to sunbathe, 10
    ———— **la temperatura a alguien** take someone's temperature, 17
    ———— **una decisión** to make a decision, 13
    Tome asiento. Have a seat., 2
tomate (*m.*) tomato, 14
tonterías (*f.*): **decir** ———— to talk nonsense, 13
torneo (*m.*) tournament

toro (*m.*) bull
toronja (*f.*) grapefruit, 14
torta (*f.*) cake, 8
    ———— **helada** (*f.*) ice cream cake, 8
tortilla a la española (*f.*) omelette, 8
tortilla mexicana (*f.*) Mexican tortilla, 8
tortuga (*f.*) tortoise
tos (*f.*) cough, 17
tostadora (*f.*) toaster, 13
trabajador(-a) hard-working
trabajar to work, 2
trabajo (*m.*) job, work, 3
traducir to translate, 6
traer to bring, 4
tráfico (*m.*) traffic
trágico(-a) tragic
traído brought (*p.p. of* **traer**)
traje (*m.*) suit, 15
    ———— **de baño** (*m.*) bathing suit, 10
    ———— **de ejercicio** (*m.*) jogging suit, 15
traslado (*m.*) transportation
tratar to treat
    ———— **(de)** to try (to), 16
travesía (*f.*) voyage
trece thirteen, 1
treinta thirty, 1
tren (*m.*) train, 7
tres three, 1
trescientos three hundred, 3
trimestre (*m.*) quarter, 16
triste sad, 4
tropezar (e:ie) to trip
trozo (*m.*) piece
trucha (*f.*) trout, 8
tu your (*fam. sing.*), 3
tú you (*fam. sing.*), 1
turismo (*m.*) tourism, 6
turista (*m., f.*) tourist, 6
turno (*m.*) turn, 9
    pedir ———— to make an appointment, 9
tus your (*fam. pl.*), 3
tutear to use the **tú** form
tuyo(s), tuya(s) (*pron.*) yours (*fam. sing.*), 9

U

últimamente lately, 9
último(-a) last, 14
    última vez the last time, 17

un(a)   a, an, one, 2
   un momento   one moment, 3
   un poco + *adj.*   a little + *adj.* 4
   un poco de   a little, 2
   una vía   one way
único(-a)   only, 11
   lo único   the only thing, 16
universidad (*f.*)   university, 1
universitario(-a)   (*adj.*) university, 3
uno (*m.*)   one, 1
unos(-as)   a few, some, 2; about
usar   to wear, to use, 9
   se usa   it is used
usted (Ud.)   you (*form., sing.*), 1; (*obj. of prep.*), 5
ustedes (Uds.)   you (*form. pl.*), 1; (*obj. of prep.*), 5
utensilio (*m.*)   utensil, 13
útil   useful
uva (*f.*)   grape, 4

V

vaca (*f.*)   cow
vacaciones (*f. pl.*)   vacation, 6
vacío(-a)   empty, 18
vale   okay (*Sp.*), 5
valer   to be worth
   (no) vale la pena   it's (not) worth the trouble, 18
valija (*f.*)   suitcase, 6
¡vámonos!   let's go, 13
¡vamos!   let's go!, 5
vaqueros (*m. pl.*)   bluejeans
varicela (*f.*)   chickenpox
varios(-as)   several, 3
vasija (*f.*)   pot
vaso (*m.*)   glass, 4
vaya a   go to, 6
veces: a _____   at times, sometimes, 12
vecino(-a) (*m., f.*)   neighbor
vegetal (*m.*)   vegetable, 14
veinte   twenty, 1
veinticinco   twenty-five, 1
veinticuatro   twenty-four, 1
veintidós   twenty-two, 1
veintinueve   twenty-nine, 1
veintiocho   twenty-eight, 1
veintiséis   twenty-six, 1
veintisiete   twenty-seven, 1
veintitrés   twenty-three, 1
veintiuno   twenty-one, 1
vela (*f.*)   candle

velero (*m.*)   sailboat
velocidad (*f.*)   speed, 18
   _____ **máxima** (*f.*)   speed limit, 18
vencer   to beat, defeat
venda (*f.*)   bandage, 17
vendar   to bandage, 17
vendedor(-a) (*m., f.*)   salesperson, 16
vender   to sell, 3
venezolano(-a)   Venezuelan, 14
venir (a)   to come, 3
venta (*f.*)   sale
ventana (*f.*)   window, 2
ventanilla (*f.*)   window (*of a vehicle or booth*), 12
ventilador (*m.*)   fan, 18
ver   to see, 6
   a _____   let's see, 11
verano (*m.*)   summer, 1
verbo (*m.*)   verb
verdad (*f.*)   truth
   ¿verdad?   right?, true?, 11
   No es _____.   It's not true., 12
verdadero(-a)   real, 15
verde   green, 1
verdura (*f.*)   vegetable, 14
vermut (*m.*)   vermouth, 8
vestido (*m.*)   dress, 9
   _____ **de noche** (*m.*)   evening gown, 15
vestirse (e:i)   to get dressed, 9
vez (*f.*)   time (occasion), 7
   a veces   at times, 12
   alguna _____   ever, 15
   de _____ **en cuando**   from time to time, 14
   en _____ **de**   instead of, 13
   otra _____   again
   próxima _____   next time, 7
   tal _____   maybe, 13
vía (*f.*)   street, way
   por _____ **aérea**   airmail, 12
viajar   to travel, 5
viaje (*m.*)   trip, 6
   de _____   traveling
   salir de _____   to leave on a trip, 18
viajero(-a) (*m., f.*)   traveler, 7
vida (*f.*)   life, 16
viejo(-a)   old, 12
viento (*m.*)   wind, 6
   hacer _____   to be windy, 6
viernes (*m.*)   Friday, 1
vinagre (*m.*)   vinegar, 14

vino (*m.*)   wine, 4
   _____ **tinto** (*m.*)   red wine, 8
visitar   to visit, 6
vista (*f.*)   view
   con _____ **a**   overlooking, 6
   hasta la _____   until I see you again, I'll see you later, 1
visto(-a) (*p.p. of* **ver** *and adj.*)   seen, 15
viudo(-a)   widowed, 3
vivir   to live, 3
vocabulario (*m.*)   vocabulary
volante (*m.*)   steering wheel, 18
volar (o:ue)   to fly, 5
volver (o:ue)   to return, 5
vosotros(-as)   (*subject pron.*) you (*fam. pl.*), 1; (*object of preposition*), you (*fam. pl.*), 5
vuelo (*m.*)   flight, 7
vuelto(-a)   (*p.p. of* **volver** *and adj.*) returned, 15
vuestro(-a)   your (*fam. sing.*), 3; (*pron.*) yours (*fam. pl.*), 9
vuestros(-a)   your (*fam. pl.*), 3

Y

y   and, 1; past, after (*time*), 2
ya   already, 2; now, 7
   _____ **no**   no longer
yerno (*m.*)   son-in-law, 5
yo   I, 1
yogur (*m.*)   yogurt

Z

zanahoria (*f.*)   carrot, 14
zapatería (*f.*)   shoe department, shoe store, 15
zapatillas (*f. pl.*)   slippers, 15
zapato (*m.*)   shoe, 15
zona postal (*f.*)   zip code, 3
zoológico (*m.*)   zoo, 14
zorro(-a) (*m., f.*)   fox

ENGLISH–SPANISH

A

a, an   un(a), 2
   a little   un poco de, 2
about   sobre, 6; de, 7; acerca de; unos(-as)

abundant   caudaloso(-a)

accept   aceptar, 6

accident   accidente (*m.*), 17

accommodation   alojamiento (*m.*), 6

according to   según, 18

account   cuenta (*f.*), 11

       checking _____   cuenta corriente (*f.*), 11

       on _____ **of**   por, 8

       savings _____   cuenta de ahorros (*f.*), 11

accountant   contador(-a) (*m., f.*), 16

accounting   contabilidad (*f.*), 16

accuracy   exactitud (*f.*)

ache   doler (o:ue), 17

across from   frente a, 12

action   acción (*f.*)

activity   actividad (*f.*), 10

actor   actor (*m.*)

actress   actriz (*f.*)

ad   anuncio (*m.*), 6

add   añadir

addition   suma (*f.*)

additional   adicional

address   dirección (*f.*), 2; domicilio (*m.*), 2

adjective   adjetivo (*m.*)

advanced   adelantado(-a)

advice   consejo (*m.*), 16

advise   aconsejar, 11

advisor   consejero(-a) (*m., f.*), 16

Aesop   Esopo

affectionately   afectuosamente, 16

afraid: to be _____   tener miedo, 4

after   (*time*) y, 2; después (de), 8

afternoon   tarde (*f.*), 2

       good _____   buenas tardes, 1

       in the _____   de (por) la tarde, 2

afterwards   después, 4; luego, 6

again   otra vez

age   edad (*f.*), 3

ago: . . . ago   hace + *time*, 10

agree   estar de acuerdo, 18

agreement   concordancia (*f.*)

air   aire (*m.*)

       _____ **bag**   bolsa de aire (*f.*), 18

       _____ **conditioning**   aire acondicionado (*m.*), 6

airmail   por vía aérea, 12

airport   aeropuerto (*m.*), 6

aisle seat   asiento de pasillo (*m.*), 7

alarm clock   despertador (*m.*), 11

all   todo(-a), 7; (*pron.*) todo, 7

       _____ **day long**   todo el día

       _____ **night long**   toda la noche, 10

allergic   alérgico(-a), 17

almost   casi, 18

alone   solo(-a)

along   por, 8

alphabet   alfabeto (*m.*)

alphabetize   alfabetizar

already   ya, 2

also   también, 2

although   aunque, 9

always   siempre, 4

A.M.   de la mañana, 2

ambulance   ambulancia (*f.*), 17

among   entre

ample   amplio(-a), 6

amusement park   parque de diversiones (*m.*), 14

and   y, 1

angry   enfadado(-a), enojado(-a), 4

ankle   tobillo (*m.*), 17

anniversary   aniversario (*m.*), 8

announce   anunciar, 13

another   otro(-a), 3

answer   respuesta (*f.*); contestar

antibiotic   antibiótico (*m.*), 17

anxiously   ansiosamente

any   alguno(-a), algún, 6; cualquier

       not _____   ninguno(-a), ningún, 6

anyone   alguien, 6

anything   algo, 6

       not _____   nada, 6

anyway   de todos modos

apartment   apartamento (*m.*), 9; departamento (*m.*); piso (*m.*) (*Sp.*)

appear   aparecer

appendicitis   apendicitis (*f.*)

applaud   aclamar

apple   manzana (*f.*), 14

application   solicitud (*f.*), 3

apply (for)   solicitar, 3

       _____ **for a loan**   pedir (e:i) un préstamo, 11

appointment   cita (*f.*); turno (*m.*), 9

       to make an _____   pedir (e:i) turno, cita, 9

appreciate   apreciar, 10

April   abril, 1

Argentina   Argentina, 10

Argentinian   argentino(-a), 16

arm   brazo (*m.*), 17

armchair   butaca (*f.*); sillón (*m.*), 13

army   ejército (*m.*)

around   por, 8; alrededor de, cerca de

arrival   llegada (*f.*), 4

arrive   llegar, 6

art   arte (*f.*)

article   artículo (*m.*), 3

as   como, 16

       _____ . . . _____   tan... como, 5

       _____ **if**   como si, 18

       _____ **many**   tantos(-as), 5

       _____ **many** . . .   tantos(-as)... como, 5

       _____ **much**   tanto, 5

       _____ **much** _____   tanto como, 5

       _____ **soon** _____   en cuanto, 11; tan pronto como, 11

ashamed   avergonzado(-a)

ask   preguntar, 6

       _____ **(for)**   pedir (e:i), 6

asleep: to fall _____   dormirse (o:ue), 9

aspirin   aspirina (*f.*), 17

assist   ayudar (a), 15

asthma   asma (*m.*)

at   a, 3; en, 2

       _____ **noon**   al mediodía, 4

       _____ **what time . . . ?**   ¿a qué hora... ?, 2

       at + *time*   a la (las) + *time*, 2

Atlantic Ocean   océano Atlántico, 10

attend   asistir (a), 5

attention: to pay _____   hacer caso, 13

August   agosto, 1

aunt   tía (*f.*), 5

auto insurance policy   seguro de automóvil (*m.*)

automatic   automático(-a), 18

       _____ **teller**   cajero automático (*m.*), 11

automobile   automóvil (*m.*), auto (*m.*), carro (*m.*); coche (*m.*), 5

autumn   otoño (*m.*), 1

avenue   avenida (*f.*), 2

average   promedio (*m.*), 16

avoid   evitar, 17

B

back   espalda (*f.*), 17; de vuelta

backpack   mochila (*f.*), 10

bacon   tocino (*m.*)

bad   malo(-a), 4
Bah!   ¡Bah!, 5
balance   (*bank*) saldo (*m.*), 11
banana tree   banano (*m.*)
band   orquesta (*f.*), 4
bandage   vendar, 17; venda (*f.*), 17; (adhesive) curita (*f.*), 17
bank   banco (*m.*), 11
barber   barbero(-a), (*m., f.*), 9
_____ **shop**   barbería (*f.*), 9
bargain   ganga (*f.*), 15
baseball   béisbol (*m.*)
basin   cuenca (*f.*)
basket   canasto (*m.*)
basketball   basquetbol (*m.*), baloncesto (*m.*)
Basque Country   País Vasco (*m.*)
bathe (oneself)   bañar(se), 9
bathing suit   traje de baño (*m.*), 10
bathroom   baño (*m.*), 6; cuarto de baño (*m.*), 6
bathtub   bañadera (*f.*), 6
battery   acumulador (*m.*), batería (*f.*), 18
battlefield   campo de batalla (*m.*)
be   ser, 1; estar, 4
_____ **able to**   poder (o:ue), 5
_____ **acquainted with**   conocer, 6
_____ **afraid**   tener miedo (de), 4
_____ **bad weather**   hacer mal tiempo, 6
_____ **. . . behind schedule**   tener... de atraso (retraso), 7
_____ **bored**   aburrirse, 10
_____ **born**   nacer
_____ **called**   llamarse, 9
_____ **careful**   tener cuidado, 4
_____ **cold**   (*weather*) tener frío, 4; hacer frío, 6
_____ **due to**   debido a
_____ **early**   llegar temprano
_____ **. . . from here**   estar a... de aquí, 12
_____ **glad**   alegrarse (de), 11
_____ **going to** + *inf.*   ir a + *inf.*, 4
_____ **good weather**   hacer buen tiempo, 6
_____ **hot**   (*weather*) hacer calor, 6; tener calor, 4
_____ **hungry**   tener hambre, 4

_____ **in a hurry**   tener prisa, 4
_____ **invited**   estar invitado(-a), 9
_____ **late**   llegar tarde, 7
_____ **located**   quedar, 8
_____ **lucky**   tener suerte, 4
_____ **named**   llamarse, 9
_____ **pleasing to**   gustar, 7
_____ **ready**   estar listo(-a), 5
_____ **right**   tener razón, 4
_____ **right back**   volver en seguida, 15
_____ **scared**   tener miedo, 4
_____ **silent**   callar
_____ **sleepy**   tener sueño, 4
_____ **sorry**   sentir (e:ie), 11
_____ **starving**   estar muerto(-a) de hambre, 15
_____ **successful**   tener éxito, 4
_____ **sunny**   hacer sol, 6
_____ **thirsty**   tener sed, 4
_____ **tight**   apretar (e:ie), 15
_____ **too big (small) on someone**   quedarle grande (chico) a uno, 15
_____ **windy**   hacer viento, 6
_____ **worth the trouble**   valer la pena, 18
_____ **wrong**   estar equivocado(-a), no tener razón, 4
_____ **. . . years old**   tener... años, 4
beach   playa (*f.*), 10
beans   frijoles (*m. pl.*), 8
beautician   peluquero(-a) (*m., f.*), 9
beautiful   hermoso(-a), 6
beauty   belleza (*f.*)
_____ **parlor**   peluquería (*f.*), 9; salón de belleza (*m.*), 9
because   porque, 2
_____ **of**   por, 8
become   hacerse
bed   cama (*f.*), 11
to go to _____   acostarse (o:ue), 9
to put to _____   acostar (o:ue), 9
bedroom   dormitorio (*m.*); recámara (*f.*) (*Mex.*), 13
bedspread   sobrecama (*f.*), 13
beer   cerveza (*f.*), 4
before   antes (de), 4; antes de que, 14

beg   rogar (o:ue), 11
begin   comenzar (e:ie) (a); 4; empezar (e:ie) (a), 4
behalf: on _____ **of**   por, 8
believe   creer, 3
believed   creído (*p.p. of* **creer**), 15
bellhop   botones (*m.*), 6
belt   cinturón (*m.*), 15
bend   doblar, 12
besides   además, 13
best   el (la) mejor, 5
bet   apuesta (*f.*); apostar (o:ue)
better   mejor, 5
beverage   bebida (*f.*), 4
bicycle   bicicleta (*f.*), 10
big   grande, 4
to be too _____   quedar grande, 15
bigger   mayor, 5
bill   cuenta (*f.*), 8
biology   biología (*f.*)
birth   nacimiento (*m.*), 3
birthday   cumpleaños (*m.*), 4
black   negro(-a), 1
blame   culpa (*f.*), 18; culpar, 18
blanket   cobija (*f.*), frazada (*f.*), manta (*f.*), 13
blend   mezcla (*f.*)
blender   licuadora (*f.*), 13
block   (*city*) cuadra (*f.*) (*Sp. Am.*), manzana (*f.*) (*Sp.*), 12
_____ (*of buildings*)   manzana (*f.*) (*Sp. Am.*), 12
blond   rubio(-a), 3
blood pressure   presión arterial (*f.*)
blouse   blusa (*f.*), 15
blow dryer   secador (*m.*), 9
blue   azul, 1
boarding house   pensión (*f.*), 5
boarding pass   tarjeta de embarque (*f.*), 7
boat   barco (*m.*), 7
body   cuerpo (*m.*), 17
book   libro (*m.*), 2
boot   bota (*f.*), 15
bored   aburrido(-a), 4
to be _____   aburrirse, 10
boring   aburrido(-a), 7
borrow   pedir (e:i) prestado, 11
both   ambos(-as)
bottle   botella (*f.*), 8
boy   chico (*m.*), muchacho (*m.*), 3
boyfriend   novio (*m.*), 3
bra   sostén (*m.*), sujetador (*m.*), 15
bracelet   pulsera (*f.*), 8

brake freno (*m.*), 18
branch (*office*) sucursal (*f.*)
bread pan (*m.*), 14
break romper(se), quebrar(se) (e:ie), 17
breakfast desayuno (*m.*), 6
bride novia (*f.*), 3
briefcase maletín (*m.*), 2
bring traer, 4
broken roto(-a), 15
bronchitis bronquitis (*f.*)
broom escoba (*f.*), 9
brother hermano (*m.*), 5
brother-in-law cuñado (*m.*), 5
brown marrón, café, 1; (*hair, eyes*) castaño, 3
brought traído (*p.p. of* **traer**)
brunette morena, 3
brush cepillo (*m.*), 9
building edificio (*m.*), 12
bull toro (*m.*)
bulletin board tablero de anuncios (*m.*), 2
bumper parachoques (*m.*), 18
bureau cómoda (*f.*), 13
buried enterrado(-a)
bus autobús (*m.*), ómnibus (*m.*), 5
business administration administración de empresas (*f.*), 16
businessman (woman) hombre (mujer) de negocios (*m., f.*), 16
busy ocupado(-a), 4
but pero, 4; sino, 14
butter mantequilla (*f.*), 14
buy comprar, 6; llevarse, 15
by para, 8; por, 8
    _____ **then** para entonces, 16
    to go _____ pasar (por), 6
bye chau, 1

C

cabbage repollo (*m.*), 14
cabin cabaña (*f.*), 10
cafe café (*m.*), 5
cafeteria cafetería (*f.*), 3
cake torta (*f.*), 8
calf ternero (*m.*), (*of leg*) pantorilla (*f.*)
call llamar, 2
called: to be _____ llamarse, 9
camera cámara fotográfica (*f.*), 6
    video _____ cámara de video (*f.*), 6

camp acampar, 10
campus sede (*f.*)
can poder (o:ue), 5; bote (*m.*) (*Mex.*), lata (*f.*), 14
cancel cancelar, 6
cancellation cancelación (*f.*), 6
candle vela (*f.*)
cap gorro (*m.*), 15
capital capital (*city*) (*f.*), 6
car auto (*m.*), automóvil (*m.*), carro (*m.*), coche (*m.*), 5
caramel custard flan (*m.*), 8
carburetor carburador (*m.*), 18
card tarjeta (*f.*), 7
career carrera (*f.*), 16
carpet alfombra (*f.*), 9
carpenter carpintero(-a), (*m., f.*), 16
carriage carro (*m.*)
carrot zanahoria (*f.*), 14
carry-on bag bolso de mano (*m.*), 7
carved tallado(-a)
case caso (*m.*), 14
    in _____ en caso de que, 14
cash efectivo (*m.*), 11
    in _____ al contado, en efectivo, 11
cassette casete (*m.*), cinta (*f.*), 4
catch a fish pescar, 10
celebrate celebrar, 4
celery apio (*m.*), 14
cellular phone teléfono celular (*m.*), 18
center centro (*m.*), 15
central heating calefacción central (*f.*), 13
cereal cereal (*m.*)
certainty certidumbre (*f.*)
certified certificado(-a), 12
chair silla (*f.*), 2
chalk tiza (*f.*), 2
chalkboard pizarra (*f.*), 2
challenge desafiar
champagne champán (*m.*), 4
change cambiar, 15
character personaje (*m.*)
charge cobrar, 11
    in _____ **of** encargado(-a) de
charmed encantado(-a)
charming simpático(-a), 3; encantador(-a)
chat conversar, charlar, 4
cheap barato(-a), 6
check cheque (*m.*), talón, (*m.*) 11; chequear, revisar, 18

checkbook talonario de cheques (*m.*), chequera (*f.*), 11
checking account cuenta corriente (*f.*), 11
checkup examen (*m.*), chequeo (*m.*), 17
Cheers! ¡Salud!
cheese queso (*m.*), 8
chef cocinero(-a), (*m., f.*), 16
chemistry química (*f.*), 16
chest pecho (*m.*), 17
    _____ **of drawers** cómoda (*f.*), 13
chicken pollo (*m.*), 4
    _____ **and rice** arroz con pollo (*m.*), 8
    _____ **pox** varicela (*f.*)
child niño(-a), 10
    only _____ hijo(-a) único(-a), 11
childhood niñez (*f.*)
children hijos (*m. pl.*), 3
Chile Chile, 10
Chilean chileno(-a), 10
Chinese chino(-a)
chocolate chocolate (*m.*), 8
    hot _____ chocolate caliente (*m.*), 8
Christmas Navidad (*f.*), 4
    _____ **tree** árbol de Navidad (*m.*), 4
church iglesia (*f.*)
cider sidra (*f.*), 4
circus circo (*m.*), 14
city ciudad (*f.*), 3
claim check comprobante (*m.*), 11
class clase (*f.*), 2; curso (*m.*), 16
classified clasificado(-a), 13
classmate compañero(-a) de clase (*m., f.*), 4
clay barro (*m.*)
clean (oneself) limpiar(se), 9; (*adj.*) limpio(-a)
clerk empleado(-a) (*m., f.*), 6
climate clima (*m.*)
climb escalar, 10, subir, 12
clock reloj (*m.*), 2
close cerrar (e:ie), 4
    _____ **to** (*prep.*) cerca de, 5
closet amario (*m.*), ropero (*m.*), 15
clothes ropa (*f.*), 11
clothing ropa (*f.*), 11
club club (*m.*), 4
coal carbón (*m.*)
coat abrigo (*m.*)

cockroach   cucaracha (*f.*)
cocktail   coctel (*m.*), 4
coffee   café (*m.*), 5
_____ maker   cafetera (*f.*), 13
cognate   cognado (*m.*)
cold   catarro (*m.*), resfriado (*m.*), resfrío (*m.*), 17
to be _____ (*weather*) hacer frío, 6; tener frío, 4
color   color (*m.*), 1
Colombian   colombiano(-a), 13
Columbus   Colón (*m.*)
comb   peine (*m.*), 9
_____ (one's hair)   peinar(se), 9
come   venir (a), 3
_____ in!   ¡pase!, 2
comedy   comedia (*f.*), 8
comfortable   cómodo(-a), 5
command   imperativo (*m.*)
compact disc   disco compacto (*m.*), 4
_____ player   reproductor de discos (*m.*), 4
company   compañía (*f.*), 3
comparative   comparativo(-a)
complaint   queja (*f.*)
computer   computador(-a), (*m., f.*), 12
_____ science   informática (*f.*)
concert   concierto (*m.*), 9
conclusion   conclusión (*f.*)
conditional   condicional (*m.*)
conduct   conducir, 6
confirm   confirmar, 6
consulate   consulado (*m.*), 6
continue   seguir (e:i), 6
conversation   conversación (*f.*), 2
convince   convencer, 10
cook   cocinar, 9; cocinero(-a) (*m., f.*), 16
cookware   batería de cocina (*f.*), 13
cool (down)   enfriar
corner   (*street*) esquina (*f.*), 12
correspond   tener correspondencia
cost   costar (o:ue), 5
_____ an arm and a leg   costar un ojo de la cara, 10
cotton   algodón (*m.*), 15
couch   sofá (*m.*), 13
cough   tos (*f.*), 17
_____ syrup   jarabe (*m.*), 17

count   contar (o:ue), 5
counter   mostrador (*m.*), 9
country   campo (*m.*), 10; país (*m.*), 10
couple   pareja (*f.*), 18
course   curso (*m.*), 16
of _____!   ¡claro!, por supuesto, 7
courtesy   cortesía (*f.*)
cousin   primo(-a) (*m., f.*), 4
covered   cubierto(-a), 15
cover   cubrir
cow   vaca (*f.*)
crazy   loco(-a), 7
cream   crema (*f.*), 8
credit card   tarjeta de crédito (*f.*), 6
creole   criollo(-a)
cross   cruzar, 12
crutch   muleta (*f.*), 17
Cuban   cubano(-a), 8
culture   cultura (*f.*), 9
cup   taza (*f.*), 8
curl   rizo (*m.*), 9
curling iron   rizador (*m.*), 9
currency   moneda (*f.*)
curtain   cortina (*f.*), 13
customs   aduana (*f.*), 6
cut   corte (*m.*), 9
_____ (oneself)   cortar(se) (9)

D

dad   papá (*m.*), 5
dam   represa (f.)
dance   baile (*m.*), 4; bailar, 4
dark   moreno(-a), 3; oscuro(-a)
darling   (mi) amor (*m.*), 8; (*adj.*) querido(-a), 8
data   datos (*m.*), 3
date   fecha (*f.*), 3; (*check or letter*) fechar, poner la fecha, 11; cita (*f.*), 14
What's the _____ today?   ¿Qué fecha es hoy?, 1
daughter   hija (*f.*), 5
_____-in-law   nuera (*f.*), 5
day   día (*m.*), 2
a _____   al día, 17
_____ before yesterday   anteayer, 8
What _____ is today?   ¿Qué día es hoy?, 1
days of the week   días de la semana (*m. pl.*)
dear   querido(-a), 8; estimado(-a), 16

December   diciembre
decide   decidir, 3
decision   decisión (*f.*), 13
to make a _____   tomar una decisión, 13
defeat   vencer
definite   determinado(-a)
degree   grado (*m.*), 17
delay   atraso (*m.*), retraso (*m.*), 7
delicious   delicioso(-a), 4; rico(-a), sabroso(-a), 8
deliver   entregar, 16
demonstrative   demonstrativo(-a)
denial   negación (*f.*)
dentist   dentista (*m., f.*), 1
deny   negar (e:ie), 12
department   departamento (*m.*), 11
_____ store   almacén (*m.*), tienda por departamentos (*f.*), 15
departure gate   puerta de salida (*f.*), 7
deposit   depositar, 11
descend   bajar, 12
describe   describir
descriptive   calificativo(-a)
desert   desierto (*m.*), 10
design   diseño (*m.*), 15
desk   escritorio (*m.*), 2; pupitre (*m.*), 2
despite   a pesar de (que), 10
dessert   postre (*m.*), 8
for _____   de postre, 8
detective   (*adj.*) policíaco(-a)
develop   (*film*) revelar, 11
diamond   diamante (*m.*)
die   morir (o:ue), 5
died   muerto(-a), 15
diet   dieta (*f.*), 14
to go on a _____   ponerse a dieta, 14
difficult   difícil, 4
dining room   comedor (*m.*), 13
dinner   cena (*f.*), 6
to have _____   cenar, 6
dip   mojar
dirty   sucio(-a)
to get (oneself) _____   ensuciar(se), 9
disappointment   desilusión (*f.*)
disbelief   incredulidad (*f.*)
disco   discoteca (*f.*)
disease   enfermedad (*f.*)
dish   plato (*m.*), 8
dishwasher   lavaplatos (*m.*), 13

disinfect desinfectar, 17
divorced divorciado(-a), 3
dizziness (dizzy spell) mareo (*m.*)
do hacer, 6
doctor doctor(-a) (*m., f.*), 1; médico(-a), (*m., f.*), 1
_____'s **office** consultorio (*m.*), 17
document documento (*m.*), 12
dog perro(-a), 9
dollar dólar (*m.*)
done hecho(-a), 15
door puerta (*f.*), 2
dorm residencia universitaria (*f.*)
dot: on the _____ en punto
double: _____ **room** habitación doble (*f.*), 6
doubt dudar, 12
downstairs abajo, 12
downtown (*area*) centro (*m.*), 6
dozen docena (*f.*), 14
dramatic dramático(-a)
dream about (of) soñar (o:ue) con, 17
dress vestido (*m.*), 9
dressed: to get _____ vestirse (e:i), 9
dressmaker modista (*f.*)
drink beber, 3; tomar, 8; bebida (*f.*), 4
drive conducir, manejar, 5
driver's license licencia de conducir (*f.*), 3
drizzle lloviznar, 6
dry cleaner's tintorería (*f.*), 11
dryer secadora (*f.*), 13
drugstore farmacia (*f.*), 9
dubbed doblado(-a)
during durante, 7; por, 8
dustpan palita (*f.*), recogedor (*m.*), 9

E

each cada, 12
ear (*inner*), oído (*m.*), 17; (*external*) oreja (*f.*), 17
early temprano, 9
to be _____ llegar temprano, 7
earn ganar, 13
earthquake terremoto (*m.*)
easily fácilmente, 10
east este, 10
eastern oriental
easy fácil, 4
eat comer, 3

education educación (*f.*), 3
egg huevo (*m.*), 8
eight ocho, 1
_____ **hundred** ochocientos, 3
eighteen dieciocho, 1
eighth octavo(-a), 8
eighty ochenta, 2
either . . . or o... o, 6
not _____ tampoco, 6
elective clase optativa (*f.*)
electrician electricista (*m., f.*), 16
elegant elegante, 8
elevator ascensor (*m.*), elevador (*m.*), 6
eleven once, 1
E-mail correo electrónico (*m.*), 12
embassy embajada (*f.*), 6
emergency emergencia (*f.*), 17
_____ **room** sala de emergencia (*f.*), 17
empty vacío(-a), 18
encounter encuentro (*m.*)
engaged: to get _____ **to** comprometerse con, 17
engine motor (*m.*), 18
engineer ingeniero(-a) (*m., f.*), 16
engineering ingeniería (*f.*), 16
English (*lang.*) inglés (*m.*), 2; (*nationality*) inglés(-a), 3
enjoy disfrutar, gozar de
_____ **oneself** divertirse (e:ie), 10
enough suficiente, 11; bastante
entertaining divertido(-a)
entrance entrada (*f.*), 7
eraser borrador (*m.*), 2; goma de borrar, 2
errand diligencia (*f.*), 11
to run _____s hacer diligencias, 11
escalator escalera mecánica (*f.*), 15
especially especialmente, 5
evening noche (*f.*), 3
_____ **gown** vestido de noche (*m.*), 15
ever alguna vez, 15
everybody todos(-as), 4
everything todo, 4; de todo, 10
_____ **that happened** todo lo que pasó, 7
everywhere a (de) todas partes
exam examen (*m.*), 3; (*checkup*) examen (*m.*), 17
excellent excelente, 8

excess baggage exceso de equipaje (*m.*), 7
exchange cambiar, 15
in _____ **for** por, 8
_____ **rate** cambio de moneda, 6
excuse me (con) permiso, 2
exit salida (*f.*), 7
main _____ puerta principal (*f.*), 12
expensive caro(-a), 6
experience experiencia (*f.*), 3
expression expresión (*f.*)
eye ojo (*m.*), 17

F

face cara (*f.*), 17
fact: the _____ **is . . .** es que... , 12
fail (*course or exam*) quedar suspendido(-a), 16
fair feria (*f.*)
fall otoño (*m.*), 1; caer
_____ **asleep** dormirse (o:ue), 9
_____ **in love with** enamorarse de, 17
family familia (*f.*), 5
_____ **room** salón de estar (*m.*), 13
_____ **tree** árbol genealógico (*m.*)
famous famoso(-a), 5
fan ventilador (*m.*), 18
farewell despedida (*f.*)
farmer labrador(-a) (*m., f.*)
fashion moda (*f.*), 15
fast (*adv.*) rápido, 18
fat gordo(-a), 3
father padre (*m.*), 5
father-in-law suegro (*m.*), 5
fault culpa (*f.*), 18
to be one's _____ tener la culpa, 18
favor favor (*m.*), 13
favorite favorito(-a), 6
fax facsímil (*m.*), fax (*m.*), 12
fear miedo (*m.*), 4; temer, 11
feather pluma (*f.*)
February febrero, 1
fed up harto(-a)
feel sentir(se) (e:ie), 9
_____ **like** (*doing something*) tener ganas de, 14
feminine femenino(-a), 3

fender guardafangos (*m.*), guardabarros (*m.*), 18
fever fiebre (*f.*), 17
few pocos(-as), 6; unos(-as), 1
fiancé novio (*m.*), 3
fiancée novia (*f.*), 3
fifteen quince, 1
fifth quinto(-a), 8
fifty cincuenta, 2
fight luchar
fill llenar, 3
_____ **out** llenar, 11
film (*for camera*) película (*f.*), 11
filter filtro (*m.*), 18
final exam examen final (*m.*), 16
finally por fin, 10
financial problems problemas económicos (*m. pl.*), 3
find encontrar (o:ue), 5
_____ **out** averiguar, 6; saber, 10
fine (*adv.*), bien, 1; bueno, 7; multa (*f.*), 18
finger dedo (*m.*), 17
finish terminar, 9
finished acabado(-a)
fire lumbre (*f.*)
first primero(-a), primer, 8
_____ **class** primera clase, 7
_____ **day of classes** primer día de clases, 2
fish pescado (*m.*), 8; pescar, 10
fishing pesca (*f.*), 10; pesquero(-a)
to go _____ ir de pesca, 10
fishing rod caña de pescar (*f.*), 10
fit caber, 6; quedar, 9
fitting room probador (*m.*), 15
five cinco, 1
_____ **hundred** quinientos, 3
fix arreglar, 18
flat tire: have a _____ tener un pinchazo (*m.*), 18
flight vuelo (*m.*), 7
_____ **attendant** auxiliar de vuelo (*m.*), 1; azafata (*f.*), 7
float carroza (*f.*)
floor piso (*m.*), 6
flu gripe (*f.*), 17
fly volar (o:ue), 5
fog niebla (*f.*), 6
foggy: it's _____ hay niebla, 6
follow seguir (e:i), 6
food comida (*f.*), 6
foot pie (*m.*), 17
football fútbol americano (*m.*)

for para, 3; por, 6
foreign extranjero(-a)
foreigner extranjero(-a), 12
forest bosque (*m.*)
forget olvidar(se) (de), 9
forgive perdonar
fork tenedor (*m.*), 8
form forma (*f.*)
fortress fortaleza (*f.*)
fortune fortuna (*f.*), 10
forty cuarenta, 2
fountain fuente (*f.*)
_____ **pen** pluma estilográfica (*f.*), 2
four cuatro, 1
_____ **hundred** cuatrocientos, 3
fourteen catorce, 1
fourth cuarto(-a), 8
fox zorro(-a) (*m., f.*)
free (*of charge*) gratis; libre, 11
freedom libertad (*f.*)
freeway autopista (*f.*), 18
French (*lang.*) francés (*m.*), 2
_____ **fries** papas fritas (*f. pl.*), 8
frequent frecuente
Friday viernes (*m.*), 1
fried frito(-a), 8
friend amigo(-a), (*m., f.*)
friendship amistad (*f.*)
from de, 1; desde, 12
_____ **the** (*contraction*) del, 4
front: in _____ **of** frente a, 11; delante de
fruit fruta (*f.*), 8
fry freír (e:i)
full lleno(-a), 18
_____ **-time** tiempo completo, 13
function funcionar, 18
funny cómico(-a)
furnished amueblado(-a), 13
furniture muebles (*m. pl.*), 13
future futuro (*m.*)

G

gain aumentar
game partido (*m.*), 16
garage garaje (*m.*), 13
garden jardín (*m.*), 13
gas station gasolinera (*f.*), estación de servicio (*f.*), 18
gasoline gasolina (*f.*), 18

gate puerta (*f.*), 7
gee! ¡caramba!, 14
gender género (*m.*)
generally generalmente, 9
gentleman señor (*m.*), 1
geographical geográfico(-a)
German (*lang.*) alemán (*m.*), 2
_____ **class** clase de alemán (*f.*), 2
get conseguir (e:i), 6; (*grade*) sacar, 16; buscar, 17
_____ **a haircut** cortarse el pelo, 9
_____ **dirty** ensuciar(se), 9
_____ **dressed** vestirse (e:i), 9
_____ **engaged to** comprometerse con, 17
_____ **married** casarse con, 13
_____ **undressed** desvestirse (e:i), 9
_____ **up** levantarse, 9
gift regalo (*m.*), 8
girl chica (*f.*), muchacha (*f.*), 3
girlfriend novia (*f.*), 3
give dar, 4; (*as a gift*) regalar, 9
_____ **a ticket** (**fine**) poner (dar) una multa, 18
_____ **an injection** poner una inyección, 17
glass vaso (*m.*), 4; copa (*f.*), 4
glove guante (*m.*), 15
_____ **compartment** guantera (*f.*), portaguantes (*m.*), 18
go ir (a), 4
_____ **away** irse, 9
_____ **by** pasar por, 6
_____ **camping** acampar, 10
_____ **down** bajar, 12
_____ **fishing** ir de pesca, 10
_____ **off** (*alarm*) sonar (o:ue), 11
_____ **on a diet** ponerse a dieta, 14
_____ **on vacation** ir de vacaciones, 10
_____ **out** salir, 6
_____ **shopping** ir de compras, 10
_____ **through** pasar por, 6
_____ **to** vaya a, 6
_____ **to bed** acostarse (o:ue), 9
_____ **together** hacer juego, combinar, 15

_____ **up** subir, 12

_____ **wrong** ir mal

I'm leaving me voy, 3

to be going (to) + *infinitive* ir a + *infinitive*, 4

goblet copa (*f.*), 4

God grant ojalá, 11

gold oro (*m.*), 6

gone ido, 15

good bueno(-a), buen, 3

_____ **afternoon** buenas tardes, 1

_____ **evening** buenas noches, 1

_____ **morning** buenos días, 1

_____ **night** buenas noches, 1

it's no _____ no sirve, 18

good-bye adiós, 1

grade nota (*f.*), 16

_____ **point average** promedio (*m.*), 16

grading system sistema de calificaciones (*m.*)

graduate graduar(se), 16

granddaughter nieta (*f.*), 5

grandfather abuelo (*m.*), 5

grandmother abuela (*f.*), 5

grandson nieto (*m.*), 5

grape uva (*f.*), 4

grapefruit toronja (*f.*), pomelo (*m.*), 14

grass hierba (*f.*)

grated rallado(-a)

gray gris, 1

graze pacer

great magnífico(-a), 4

great-grandfather (mother) bisabuelo(-a) (*m.*, *f.*), 4

green verde, 1

greeting saludo (*m.*)

groom novio (*m.*), 3

ground floor planta baja (*f.*), 15

growth crecimiento (*m.*)

guilty culpable

H

habit: bad _____ manía (*f.*)

hair pelo (*m.*), 9; cabello (*m.*), 17

to comb one's _____ peinarse, 9

to wash one's _____ lavarse la cabeza, 9

haircut corte (*m.*), 9

to get a _____ cortarse el pelo, 9

hairdo peinado (*m.*), 9

hairdresser peluquero(-a) (*m.*, *f.*), 9

hairstyle peinado (*m.*), 9

half medio(-a), 8

_____ **an hour** media hora, 7

_____ **brother** medio hermano, 5

_____ **past** y media (*time*), 2

_____ **sister** media hermana, 5

ham jamón (*m.*), 8

hamburger hamburguesa (*f.*), 8

hand mano (*f.*), 17

handbag bolsa (*f.*), bolso (*m.*), cartera (*f.*), 9

handkerchief pañuelo (*m.*), 15

handsome guapo(-a), 3

happen pasar, 7

happy contento(-a), 4; feliz, 4

hardly apenas

hare liebre (*f.*)

hat sombrero (*m.*)

hate odiar, 10

have tener, 3; haber (*aux.*), 15

_____ **a good time** pasarlo bien, 4; divertirse (e:ie), 10

_____ **a nice trip** buen viaje, 7

_____ **a seat.** Tome asiento., 2

to _____ **been doing something for a length of time** hace + *time* + que + *verb* (*present*), 7

_____ **dinner** cenar, 6

to _____ **done something in the past** hace + *time* + que + *verb* (*preterit/imperfect*), 10

_____ **just . . .** acabar de..., 6

_____ **lunch** almorzar (o:ue), 5

_____ **something to eat** comer algo, 14

_____ **something to drink** tomar algo, 14

_____ **supper** cenar, 6

_____ **to** deber, 3; tener que, 3

he él, 1

head cabeza (*f.*), 17

headache dolor de cabeza (*m.*), 17

headlight luz (*f.*), 18

healer curandero(-a) (*m.*, *f.*)

health salud (*f.*)

hear oír, 15

heard oído (*p.p. of* oír), 15

heat calor (*m.*), 4; calentar (e:ie)

heater calefacción (*f.*)

height estatura (*f.*), 5

hello hola, 1; (*on the phone*) bueno, 3; (*on the phone*) dígame, 3

say _____ **to . . .** saludos a..., 16

help ayudar (a), 15

her su, 3; ella, 5; la, 6; le, 7

herd manada (*f.*)

here aquí, 5

_____ **it is.** Aquí la (lo) tiene., 6

hers suyo(-a)(s), 9

herself se, 9

hide ocultar

high school escuela secundaria (*f.*)

highway autopista (*f.*), carretera (*f.*), 18

him él, 5; lo, 6; le, 7

himself se, 9

his su, 3; suyo(-a)(s), 9

hit (*with a car*) atropellar, 17

holiday feriado (*m.*), día de fiesta (*m.*), 14

Holy Week Semana Santa (*f.*)

home casa (*f.*), 3; a casa

_____ **appliance** aparato electrodoméstico (*m.*), 13

_____ **page** propia página (*f.*)

hood capó (*m.*), 18

hope esperar, 11

I _____ **. . .** ojalá..., 11

I _____ **so.** Espero que sí., 10

horn bocina (*f.*), 18

horror horror (*m.*)

hors d'oeuvres entremeses (*m. pl.*), 4

horse caballo (*m.*), 10

hospital hospital (*m.*), 2

hot caliente

to be _____ (*weather*) tener calor, 4; hacer calor, 6

_____ **chocolate** chocolate caliente (*m.*), 8

_____ **dog** perro caliente (*m.*), 14

hotel hotel (*m.*), 6

hour hora (*f.*), 7

house casa (*f.*), 3

how cómo, 1

    _____ **are you?** ¿Cómo está Ud.? (*form. sing.*), ¿Cómo están ustedes? (*form. pl.*), ¿Cómo estás? (*fam.*), 1

    _____ **did it go for you?** ¿Cómo te fue?, 10

    _____ **do you do?** Mucho gusto, 1

    _____ **do you say . . . ?** ¿Cómo se dice...?, 2

    _____ **is it going (for you)?** ¿Cómo te va?

    _____ **long . . . ?** ¿cuánto tiempo hace que...?

    _____ **many** cuántos(-as), 2

    _____ **much** cuánto(-a), 4

    _____**'s it going?** ¿Qué tal?, 1

    _____ **was (is) . . . ?** ¿Qué tal...?, 7

however sin embargo, 10
hug abrazar, 8; abrazo (*m.*), 10
hundred cien, ciento, 2
hungry: to be _____ tener hambre, 4
hurry (up) apurarse, darse prisa, 14

    to be in a _____ tener prisa, 4

    There's no _____. No hay apuro (prisa)., 7

hurt doler (o:ue), 17; herir (e:ie)
husband esposo (*m.*), 3

I

I yo, 1

    _____ **have to go.** Tengo que ir., 3

ice cream helado (*m.*), mantecado (*m.*) (*Mex., Puerto Rico*), 8

    _____ **cake** torta helada (*f.*), 8

iced (ice cold) helado(-a), 8
idea idea (*f.*), 4
identification identificación, 3

    _____ **card** documento de identidad (*de identificación*) (*m.*), 12

if si, 5
I'm sorry lo siento, 3
imperfect imperfecto(-a)
important importante, 16
imported importado(-a), 15
improve mejorar

in en, 2

    _____ **case** en caso de que, 14

    _____ **English** en inglés, 2

    _____ **exchange for** por, 8

    _____ **front of** frente a, 11

    _____ **order that** para que, 14

    _____ **order to** a, 3; para, 4

    _____ **search of** en busca de, 8

    _____ **spite of** a pesar de (que), 10

    _____ **that case** entonces, 3

    _____ **the afternoon** de la tarde, 2; por la tarde, 2

    _____ **the morning** de la mañana, 2; por la mañana, 2

income ingresos (*m. pl.*)
indefinite indeterminado(-a)
indicative indicativo(-a)
inexpensive barato(-a), 6
infection infección (*f.*), 17
information información (*f.*), 6
injection inyección (*f.*), 17

    to give an _____ poner una inyección, 17

insist on insistir en, 17
install instalar, 18
installments plazos (*m. pl.*), 11

    in (on) _____ a plazos, 11

instead of en vez de, 13
institution institución (*f.*), 3
instructor profesor(-a) (*m., f.*), 1
insurance seguro (*m.*)
intelligent inteligente, 3
interest interés (*m.*), 6
interesting interesante, 5
interior interior, 6
international internacional, 6
interrogative interrogativo(-a)
interview entrevista (*f.*); entrevistar
introduce presentar, 7
introduction presentación (*f.*)
invitation invitación (*f.*), 4
invite invitar (a), 4
invited invitado(-a), 4
iron planchar, 9; plancha (*f.*), 13
Is... (*name*) there? ¿Está... (*name*)?, 3
it la, 6; lo, 6

    _____ **means** quiere decir, 2

Italian (*lang.*) italiano (*m.*), 2
it's... (*time*) son las..., 2
its su, 3

J

jack gato (*m.*), 18
jacket chaqueta (*f.*), 15
jail cárcel (*f.*)
jam mermelada (*f.*)
January enero, 1
Japanese japonés(-a)
jeans vaqueros (*m. pl.*); tejanos (*m. pl.*), bluejeans (*m. pl.*), 15
jewel joya (*f.*)
jewelry joyas (*f. pl.*)

    _____ **store** joyería (*f.*)

job empleo (*m.*), trabajo (*m.*), 3

    _____ **application** solicitud de trabajo (*f.*), 3

jogging suit traje de ejercicio (*m.*), 15
joke bromear, 13

    practical _____ broma (*f.*)

journalism periodismo (*m.*), 16
journalist periodista (*m., f.*), 16
journey viaje (*m.*), 6
judge juez (*m., f.*)
jug cántaro (*m.*)
juice jugo (*m.*), 8
July julio, 1
June junio, 1

K

key llave (*f.*), 6
keyboard teclado (*m.*), 12
kid: to _____ (*joke*) bromear, 13
kilometer kilómetro (*m.*), 18
kind clase (*f.*)
king rey (*m.*)
kiss beso (*m.*), 8
kitchen cocina (*f.*), 9

    _____ **sink** fregadero (*m.*), 13

knee rodilla (*f.*), 17
knife cuchillo (*m.*), 8
know conocer, 6; saber, 6
knowledge conocimiento (*m.*), 3
known conocido(-a)

L

laboratory laboratorio (*m.*), 16
lace encaje (*m.*)
ladies damas, 6
lady señora (*f.*), 1
lake lago (*m.*), 10
lamb cordero (*m.*), 8
lamp lámpara (*f.*), 13

land (*plane*) aterrizar
language idioma (*m.*); lengua (*f.*)
large grande, 5
last pasado(-a), 7; último(-a), 14; durar
    _____ **month** el mes pasado (*m.*), 7
    _____ **name** apellido (*m.*)
    _____ **night** anoche, 8
    _____ **time** última vez (*f.*), 17
late tarde, 7
    to be _____ llegar tarde, 7
lately últimamente, 9
later más tarde, 3
    (I'll) see you _____ hasta luego, 1; hasta la vista, 1
Latin American latinoamericano(-a)
law school facultad de derecho (*f.*), 16
lawyer abogado(-a) (*m., f.*), 3
leaf hoja (*f.*)
learn aprender (a), 3
least el (la) menos, 5
leather cuero (*m.*)
leave salir, 5; (behind) dejar, 8; irse, 9
    _____ **on a trip** salir de viaje, 18
lecture conferencia (*f.*)
left izquierdo(-a)
    to the _____ a la izquierda, 6
leg pierna (*f.*), 17
lend prestar, 7
letter carta (*f.*), 5
less menos, 5
    _____ **. . . than** menos... que, 5
    _____ **than** + *number* menos de + *number*, 5
    more or _____ más o menos, 3
let's go vamos, 5; vámonos, 13
let's see a ver, 11
let's talk conversemos
letter carta (*f.*), 5
lettuce lechuga (*f.*), 14
liberty libertad (*f.*)
librarian bibliotecario(-a) (*m., f.*), 16
library biblioteca (*f.*), 3
license licencia de conducir (*f.*), 3
    _____ **plate** chapa (*f.*), placa (*f.*) (*Mex.*), 18

lie mentir (e:ie), 8
life vida (*f.*), 16
lifeguard salvavidas (*m., f.*), 10
lift levantar, 9
light luz (*f.*), 2; (*adj.*) claro(-a)
like gustar, 7
limp cojera (*f.*)
linen hilo (*m.*), lino (*m.*), 15
list lista (*f.*), 6
listen oye, 2; escuchar
literature literatura (*f.*), 16
litter tirar hasura
little pequeño(-a), 5
    a _____ un poco de, 2
    a _____ + *adjective* un poco + *adjective*, 4
live vivir, 3
livestock ganadería (*f.*)
living room sala (*f.*), 13
loan préstamo (*m.*), 11
lobster langosta (*f.*), 8
located situado(-a), 6
    to be _____ quedar, 8
London Londres
long largo(-a), 7
look (at) mirar, 5
    _____ **for** buscar
    _____ **like** parecerse (a), 11
lose perder (e:ie), 4
lot (of) mucho(-a), 4
lottery lotería (*f.*), 13
love querer (e:ie), 4; encantar, 8; love (*m.*), 8
    _____ **problems** problemas sentimentales (*m. pl.*), 3
    in _____ enamorado(-a)
luck suerte (*f.*)
luggage equipaje (*m.*), 7
lunch almuerzo (*m.*), 6
    to have _____ almorzar (o:ue), 5

M

madam señora (*f.*), 1
made hecho(-a), 15
magazine revista (*f.*), 9
mail correo (*m.*), 12
    _____ **a letter** echar una carta al correo, 12
mailbox buzón (*m.*), 12; casillero (*m.*), 12
mailman cartero (*m.*), 12
main principal, 12
maintain mantener, 16

major especialización (*f.*), 16
make hacer, 6
    _____ **a decision** tomar una decisión, 13
    _____ **a deposit** hacer un depósito, 11
    _____ **an appointment** pedir (e:i) turno, cita, 9
    _____ **fun of** burlarse de
male masculino(-a)
mall centro comercial (*m.*)
man hombre (*m.*)
many muchos(-as), 4
    as _____ tantos(-as), 5
map mapa (*m.*), 2
March marzo, 1
margarine margarina (*f.*), 14
marital status estado civil (*m.*), 3
mark down rebajar, 15
marker marcador (*m.*), 2
market mercado (*m.*), 14
married casado(-a), 3
marry casarse (con), 17
match combinar, hacer juego, 15
mathematics matemáticas (*f. pl.*), 16
matter importar, 16
mattress colchón (*m.*), 13
May mayo, 1
maybe tal vez, 13
me mí, 5; me (*d.o.*), 6; me (*i.o.*), 7
meal comida (*f.*), 8
mean: What does . . . _____**?** ¿Qué quiere decir...?, 2
    It _____**s . . .** Quiere decir..., 2
means medio (*m.*)
meanwhile mientras tanto
measles sarampión (*m.*)
meat carne (*f.*), 8
meatball albóndiga (*f.*), 8
mechanic mecánico (*m.*), 18
    _____ **'s shop** taller de mecánica (*m.*)
medical médico(-a), 17
medicine medicina (*f.*), 5
    _____ **cabinet** botiquín (*m.*), 9
Mediterranean Sea mar Mediterráneo, 10
medium mediano(-a), 15
meet conocer, 7; encontrarse (o:ue) (con), 12
melon melón (*m.*), 14
melt derretir (e:i)

men   hombres (*m. pl.*)

    _____ **'s department**   departamento de (ropa para) caballeros (*m.*), 15

    _____ **'s room**   caballeros, 6

    _____ **'s undershorts**   bikini (*m.*), calzoncillos (*m. pl.*), 15

menu   menú (*m.*), lista (*f.*), carta (*f.*), 8

merry   alegre

Mexican   mexicano(-a), 1

microwave (oven)   (horno de) microondas (*m.*), 13

middle name   segundo nombre (*m.*)

midnight   medianoche (*f.*), 4

    at _____   a la medianoche, 4

midterm exam   examen de mitad de curso (*m.*), examen parcial (*m.*), 16

midwife   partera (*f.*)

mile   milla (*f.*), 18

milk   leche (*f.*), 8

milkmaid   lechera (*f.*)

mine   mío(-a), míos(-as), 9

mineral water   agua mineral (*f.*), 4

mirror   espejo (*m.*), 9

miss   echar de menos, 5; extrañar, 5

Miss   señorita, Srta. (*f.*), 1

mix   revolver (o:ue)

modern   moderno(-a), 6

mole   lunar (*m.*)

mom   mamá (*f.*), 4

Monday   lunes (*m.*), 1

money   dinero (*m.*), 3

    _____ **order**   giro postal (*m.*), 12

month   mes (*m.*), 1

    last _____   mes pasado, 7

Moor   moro(-a) (*m., f.*)

more   más, 5

    _____ **or less**   más o menos, 3

    _____ **. . . than**   más... que, 5

    _____ **than** + *number*   más de + *number*, 5

morning   mañana (*f.*), 2

mortgage   hipoteca (*f.*)

most   el (la) más, 5

mother   madre (*f.*), 4

mother-in-law   suegra (*f.*), 5

motor   motor (*m.*), 18

motorcycle   motocicleta (*f.*), moto (*f.*), 11

mountain   montaña (*f.*), 10; monte (*m.*)

mouse   ratón (*m.*), 12

mouth   boca (*f.*), 17

move (*from one house to another*)   mudarse, 13

movie   película (*f.*), 14

    _____ **guide**   guía de espectáculos (*f.*), 14

    _____ **theater**   cine (*m.*), 7

movies   cine (*m.*), 7

Mr.   señor (*m.*), Sr., 1

Mrs.   señora (*f.*), Sra., 1

much   mucho(-a), 4

mumps   paperas (*f. pl.*)

mud   barro (*m.*)

museum   museo (*m.*), 5

must   deber, 3

my   mi(s), 3

    _____ **address is . . .**   Mi dirección es..., 2

    _____ **name is . . .**   Me llamo..., 1

myself   me, 9

mystery   misterio (*m.*)

N

name   nombre (*m.*), 3; nombrar

    My _____ **is . . .**   Me llamo..., 1

    first _____   nombre (*m.*), 3

    What's your _____?   ¿Cómo se llama Ud.? (*form.*), 1; ¿Cómo te llamas? (*fam.*), 1

nap   siesta (*f.*)

napkin   servilleta (*f.*), 8

narrow   estrecho(-a), 15

nation   nación (*f.*); pueblo (*m.*)

nationality   nacionalidad (*f.*), 3

nature   naturaleza (*f.*), 10

near   cerca de, 5; junto a, 10

necessary   necesario(-a), 18

neck   cuello (*m.*), 7

need   necesitar, 2

negative   negativo(-a)

neighbor   vecino(-a) (*m., f.*)

neighborhood   barrio (*m.*), 13

neither   tampoco, 6

    _____ **. . . nor**   ni... ni, 6

nephew   sobrino (*m.*), 5

nervous   nervioso(-a), 4

never   nunca, 5; jamás, 6

nevertheless   sin embargo, 10

new   nuevo(-a), 4

New Year's Eve party   fiesta de fin de año (*f.*), 4

newlyweds   recién casados (*m. pl.*), 18

news   noticias (*f. pl*)

newspaper   diario (*m.*), periódico (*m.*), 13

next   próximo(-a), 7

    _____ **day**   al día siguiente, 10

    _____ **time**   la próxima vez, 7

    _____ **to**   al lado de, 12; junto a, 10

nice   simpático(-a), 3

    _____ **to meet you**   Mucho gusto, 1

nickname   sobrenombre (*m.*)

niece   sobrina (*f.*), 5

night   noche (*f.*), 3

nightgown   camisón (*m.*), 15

nightstand   mesita de noche (*f.*), 13

nine   nueve, 1

    _____ **hundred**   novecientos, 3

nineteen   diecinueve, 1

ninety   noventa, 2

ninth   noveno(-a), 8

no   no, 1; ningún, ninguna, 6

    _____ **one**   nadie, 6

    _____ **longer**   ya no

nobody   nadie, 6

noise   ruido (*m.*), 18

nominated   nominado(-a), 14

none   ninguno(-a), ningún, 6

nonsense: to talk _____   decir tonterías, 13

noon   mediodía (*m.*), 4

    at _____   al mediodía, 4

nor   ni, 6

    neither . . . _____ **. . .**   ni... ni..., 6

north   norte (*m.*), 10

North American   norteamericano(-a), 1

northwest   noroeste (*m.*)

nose   nariz (*f.*), 17

not   no, 1

    _____ **any**   ninguno(-a), 6

    _____ **much**   no mucho

note   notar

notebook   cuaderno (*m.*), 2

nothing   nada, 3

notice   fijarse en, 17

noun   nombre (*m.*)

November   noviembre, 1

now   ahora, 4

    _____ **that I think about it**   ahora que lo pienso, 14

nowadays   actualmente
number   número (*m.*), 2
nurse   enfermero(-a) (*m., f.*), 1

O

object   objeto (*m.*), 6
obtain   conseguir (e:i), 6
occupation   ocupación (*f.*), 3
ocean   océano (*m.*), 10
October   octubre, 1
of   de, 3;
_____ **course!**   ¡claro!, ¡por supuesto!, 7
off   libre, 11
offer   ofrecer, 6
office   oficina (*f.*), 6
often   a menudo
oh   ah, 2
oil   aceite (*m.*), 14
okay   vale (*Sp.*), 5; bien, 7; bueno, 7; de acuerdo, 14
old   antiguo(-a), 12; viejo(-a), 12
to be . . . years _____   tener... años, 4
older   mayor, 5
oldest   el (la) mayor, 5
omelette   tortilla (*f.*), 8
on   en, 3
_____ **account of**   por, 8
_____ **behalf of**   por, 8
_____ **the phone**   por teléfono, 3
_____ **the way to**   camino a, 18
top (of)   encima de
one   uno, 1
_____ **hundred**   cien, 2; ciento, 2
_____ **moment**   un momento, 3
_____ **says**   se dice, 2
_____ **thousand**   mil, 3
_____ **way**   una vía
_____ **-way (ticket)**   de ida, 7
onion   cebolla (*f.*), 14
only   solamente, 2; sólo, 7; único(-a), 11
_____ **child**   hijo(-a) único(-a), 11
_____ **thing**   lo único, 16
open   abrir, 3
open(ed)   abierto(-a), 12, 15
opportunity   oportunidad (*f.*), 5

optimist(ic)   optimista (*m., f.*), 3
or   o, 3
orange   anaranjado(-a), 1; naranja (*f.*), 14
orchestra   orquesta (*f.*), 4
order   pedir (e:i), 8; mandar, 11; pedido (*m.*), 8; orden
other   otro(-a), 3
our   nuestro(-a)(-os)(-as), 3
ours   nuestro(-a)(s), 9
ourselves   nos, 9
out of breath   echando el bofe
out of order   descompuesto(-a), 18
outdoor   al aire libre, 10
outskirts   afueras (*f. pl.*)
overlooking   con vista a, 6
own   propio(-a)

P

Pacific Ocean   océano Pacífico (*m.*), 10
pack   hacer las maletas
package   paquete (*m.*), 12
page   página (*f.*)
pain   dolor (*m.*), 17
painting   cuadro (*m.*), pintura (*f.*), 5
pair   par (*m.*), 15
palace   palacio (*m.*), 12
pancake   panqueque (*m.*)
pants   pantalón (*m.*), pantalones (*m. pl.*), 11
pantyhose   pantimedias (*f. pl.*), 15
paper   papel (*m.*), 2; (*report*) informe (*m.*), 16
Paraguayan   paraguayo(-a), 9
parcel   paquete (*m.*), 12
Pardon me.   Perdón (*m.*), 2
parents   padres (*m. pl.*), 5
park   aparcar, estacionar, parquear, 11; parque (*m.*), 12
part-time   medio día, 13
party   fiesta (*f.*), 4
pass (*an exam or course*)   aprobar (o:ue), 16
_____ **through**   pasar por, 6
passbook   libreta de ahorros (*f.*), 11
passport   pasaporte (*m.*), 6
past (*time*)   y, 2
pay   pagar, 7
_____ **attention**   hacer caso, 13
_____ **in advance**   pagar por adelantado, 6

peach   durazno (*m.*), melocotón (*m.*), 14
pear   pera (*f.*), 14
pedestrian crosswalk   paso de peatones (*m.*)
pen   pluma (*f.*), 2; bolígrafo (*m.*), 2
pencil   lápiz (*m.*), 2
_____ **sharpener**   sacapuntas (*m.*), 2
penicillin   penicilina (*f.*), 17
people   gente (*f.*), 9; pueblo (*m.*)
pepper   pimienta (*f.*), 8
per   por, 6
perfectly   perfectamente, 5
perform   actuar
perfume   perfume (*m.*)
_____ **store**   perfumería (*f.*)
perhaps   tal vez, 13
permanent wave   permanente (*m., f.*), 9
personal   personal, 3
pessimist(ic)   pesimista (*m., f.*), 3
pharmacy   farmacia (*f.*), 9
phone   teléfono (*m.*), 3
_____ **book**   guía telefónica (*f.*)
photo(graph)   fotografía (*f.*), foto (*f.*), 5
physics   física (*f.*), 16
pick up   recoger, 11; buscar, 17
picnic   picnic (*m.*)
picture   cuadro (*m.*), pintura (*f.*), 5
piece   trozo (*m.*)
pig   cochino (*m.*)
pile: a _____ **of**   un montón de (*m.*), 12
pill   pastilla (*f.*), 17
pillow   almohada (*f.*), 13
pillowcase   funda (*f.*), 13
pilot   piloto (*m., f.*), 1
pineapple   piña (*f.*), 14
pink   rosado(-a), 1
pitch (a tent)   armar, 10
pity: it's a _____   es una lástima, 11
What a _____ **!**   ¡Qué lástima!, 5
place   lugar (*m.*), 6; poner, 6
_____ **of birth**   lugar de nacimiento (*m.*), 3
_____ **of employment**   lugar donde trabaja (*m.*), 3
_____ **setting**   cubiertos (*m. pl.*), 8
placed   puesto(-a), 15
plaid   de cuadros, 15

plain llanura (*f.*), llano (*m.*)

plan plan (*m.*), 5; pensar (e:ie) (+ *inf.*), 4; planear, 10

plane avión (*m.*), 7

plate plato (*m.*), 8

play tocar; jugar (u:ue)

    _____ **golf** jugar (u:ue) al golf (*m.*), 10;

    _____ **tennis** jugar (u:ue) al tenis (*m.*), 10

player jugador(-a) (*m., f.*)

plead rogar (o:ue), 11

please por favor, 2

pleased: _____ to meet you. Mucho gusto., 2

pleasure: The _____ is mine. El gusto es mío., 2

plumber plomero(-a) (*m., f.*), 16

pluperfect pluscuamperfecto

P.M. de la tarde, 2

pneumonia pulmonía (*f.*)

pocket bolsillo (*m.*)

poem poema (*m.*), 2

police policía (*f.*)

    _____ **officer** policía (*m.*), 18

    _____ **station** estación de policía (*f.*), 11

polka dot de lunares, 15

pool piscina (*f.*), 6

poor pobre (*unfortunate*), 11; pobre, 13

pork lechón (*m.*), 8

Portugal Portugal

Portuguese (*lang.*) portugués (*m.*), 2

position posición (*f.*)

post office correo (*m.*), oficina de correos (*f.*), 12

postcard tarjeta postal (*f.*), 7

pot vasija (*f.*)

potato papa (*f.*), 8; patata (*f.*) (*Sp.*), 8

    _____ **salad** ensalada de papas (*f.*), 4

pound libra (*f.*)

pour down raining llover (o:ue) a cántaros, 8

power poder (*m.*)

practice practicar, 5

pray rezar

prefer preferir (e:ie), 4

pregnant embarazada, 17

prepare preparar, 4

prescribe recetar, 17

prescription receta (*f.*), 17

present regalo (*m.*), 8; presente

pretty bonito(-a), lindo(-a), 3

price precio (*m.*), 8

pride orgullo (*m.*)

print (*fabric*) estampado(-a), 15

private privado(-a), 6

probably probablemente, 16

problem problema (*m.*)

profession profesión (*f.*), 3

professor profesor(-a) (*m., f.*), 1

program programa (*m.*)

programmer programador(-a), (*m., f.*), 1

prohibited prohibido(-a), 14

proud orgulloso(-a)

provided that con tal (de) que, 14

psychologist psicólogo(-a) (*m., f.*), 16

psychology psicología (*f.*), 16

punch ponche (*m.*), 4

punctual puntual, 12

purchase compra (*f.*), 15

purple morado(-a), 1

purse bolsa (*f.*) (*Mex.*), bolso (*m.*), cartera (*f.*), 9

put poner, 6; puesto(-a), 15

    _____ **in a cast** enyesar, 17

    _____ **on** ponerse, 9

    _____ **to bed** acostar (o:ue), 9

Q

quarter trimestre (*m.*), 16

    _____ **after/past** …y cuarto (*time*), 2

    _____ **of/to** … menos cuarto (*time*), 2

question pregunta (*f.*)

R

race carrera (*f.*)

racket raqueta (*f.*), 10

rain lluvia (*f.*), 8; llover (o:ue), 5

    _____ **cats and dogs** llover a cántaros, 8

raincoat impermeable (*m.*)

raise levantar, 9

rapidly rápido, 18

rare raro(-a)

rayon rayón (*m.*)

razor máquina de afeitar (*f.*), 9

reach alcanzar

read leer, 3; leído (*p.p. of* **leer**)

reader lector(-a) (*m., f.*)

ready listo(-a), 11

    ready-to-wear clothes ropa hecha (*f.*)

real verdadero(-a), 15; real

realist(ic) realista (*m., f.*), 3

reason razón (*f.*)

receive recibir, 3; (*grade*) sacar, 16

recent reciente

recently recientemente

receptionist recepcionista (*m., f.*), 1

recommend recomendar (e:ie), 8

red rojo(-a), 1; (*wine*) tinto, 8

red-headed pelirrojo(-a), 3

refrigerator refrigerador (*m.*), 13

refuse no querer (e:ie) (*preterit*), 10; negarse(a)

register registro (*m.*), 6; matricularse, 16

registered certificado(-a), 12

registration recepción (*f.*), 6; matrícula (*f.*), 16

regret sentir (e:ie), 11

remain quedarse, 10

    _____ **seated** quedar(-se) sentado(-a)

remember recordar (o:ue), 5; acordarse (o:ue) (de), 9

rent alquiler (*m.*), 13; alquilar, 10

    for _____ se alquila, 13

repair arreglo (*m.*), 18; arreglar, 18

    _____ **shop** taller (de mecánica) (*m.*), 18

repeat repetir (e:i), 8

report informe (*m.*), 3

request pedir (e:i), 6

requirement requisito (*m.*), 16

resale reventa (*f.*)

research investigación (*f.*), 16

reservation reserva (*f.*), reservación (*f.*), 6

rest resto (*m.*), 14

restaurant restaurante (*m.*), 5

restroom servicio (*m.*), W.C. (*m.*), 6

return regresar, 2; volver (o:ue), 5; (*something*) devolver (o:ue), 7

returned devuelto(-a), 15; vuelto(-a), 15

rice arroz (*m.*), 8

    _____ **pudding** arroz con leche (*m.*), 8

ride (*a bicycle*) montar en bicicleta, 10; (*a horse*) montar a caballo, 10

rifle rifle (*m.*), 10
right: to the _____ a la derecha, 6
_____? ¿verdad?, 11
_____ **away** en seguida, 6
_____ **now** ahora mismo, 18
_____ **there** allí mismo, 12
to be _____ tener razón, 4
ring (*phone*) sonar (o:ue), 11
river río (*m.*), 10
road camino (*m.*), 18
roasted asado(-a), 8
role papel (*m.*)
roll of film rollo de película (*m.*), 11
roller coaster montaña rusa (*f.*), 14
Romanesque románico(-a)
room cuarto (*m.*), 6; habitación (*f.*), 6
_____ **and board** cuarto y comida
_____ **service** servicio de habitación (cuarto) (*m.*), 6
roommate compañero(-a) de cuarto (*m.*, *f.*), 17
round-trip de ida y vuelta, 7
royal real, 12
rug alfombra (*f.*), 9
ruins ruinas (*f. pl.*), 6
ruler regla (*f.*), 2
run errands hacer diligencias, 11
run over atropellar, 17

S

sad triste, 4
said dicho(-a), 15
sailboat velero (*m.*)
salad ensalada (*f.*), 4
salary salario (*m.*), sueldo (*m.*), 13
sale liquidación (*f.*), rebaja (*f.*), 15; venta (*f.*)
for _____ se vende
salesperson vendedor(-a) (*m.*, *f.*), 16
salmon salmón (*m.*), 8
salon salón (*m.*), 9
_____ **de belleza** (*m.*) beauty parlor, salon, 9
salt sal (*f.*), 8
same mismo(-a), 13
sand arena (*f.*)
sandal sandalia (*f.*), 15
sandwich sándwich (*m.*), 4
sangría sangría (*f.*), 4
Saturday sábado (*m.*), 1
sauce salsa (*f.*), 14

saucepan cacerola (*f.*), 13
saucer platillo (*m.*), 8
sausage chorizo (*m.*)
save ahorrar, 11
savings ahorros (*m. pl.*), 11
_____ **account** cuenta de ahorros (*f.*), 11
_____ **passbook** libreta de ahorros (*f.*), 11
say decir (e:i), 6
scarf bufanda (*f.*)
schedule horario (*m.*), 16
scholarship beca (*f.*), 16
school escuela (*f.*), 5
science ciencia (*f.*), 16
_____ **fiction** ciencia ficción (*f.*)
scorn despreciar
scream gritar, 11
screen pantalla (*f.*), 12
sea mar (*m.*), 10
season estación (*f.*), 1
seat asiento (*m.*), 7; sede (*f.*)
second segundo(-a), 6
secretary secretario(-a) (*m.*, *f.*), 1
section departamento (*m.*), 11
(no) smoking _____ sección de (no) fumar (*f.*), 7
see ver, 6
let's _____ ... a ver..., 11
(I'll) _____ **you later** hasta luego, 1; hasta la vista, 1
_____ **you soon.** Hasta pronto.
_____ **you tomorrow** hasta mañana, 1
_____ **you.** Nos vemos., 1
seen visto(-a), 15
sell vender, 3
send enviar, mandar, 7
sentence oración (*f.*)
September septiembre, 1
seriously en serio, 10
serve servir (e:i), 6
service station gasolinera (*f.*), estación de servicio (*f.*), 18
set the table poner la mesa, 8
seven siete, 1
_____ **hundred** setecientos, 3
seventeen diecisiete, 1
seventh séptimo(-a), 8
seventy setenta, 2
several varios(-as), 3
sex sexo (*m.*), 3
Shall we dance? ¿Bailamos?, 4

shame: it's a _____ es una lástima, 11
What a _____! ¡Qué lástima!, 5
shampoo champú (*m.*), 9; lavado (*m.*), 9
shave afeitar(se), 9
shaving cream crema de afeitar (*f.*), 9
she ella, 1
sheep ovejas (*f. pl.*)
sheet sábana (*f.*), 13
_____ **of paper** hoja de papel (*f.*), 2
shellfish mariscos (*m. pl.*), 8
ship barco (*m.*), 7
shirt camisa (*f.*), 15
shoe zapato (*m.*), 15
_____ **department (store)** zapatería (*f.*), 15
shopping de compras, 10
_____ **mall** centro comercial, 15
to go _____ ir de compras, 10
short bajo(-a), 3; corto(-a), 9
_____ **story** relato breve (*m.*)
shorts pantalones cortos (*m. pl.*)
shot inyección (*f.*), 17; balazo (*m.*)
to give a _____ poner una inyección, 17
should deber, 3
show enseñar (a), 6; mostrar (o:ue), 6; función (*f.*), 14
_____ **a movie** poner una película, 14
shower ducha (*f.*), 6
to take a _____ ducharse, 9
shrimp camarones (*m. pl.*), gambas (*f. pl.*) (*Sp.*), 8
sick enfermo(-a), 4
sidewalk cafe café al aire libre (*m.*), 5
sign firmar, 6; letrero (*m.*), 18; señal (*f.*)
_____ **here.** Firme aquí., 6
signature firma (*f.*), 11
silk seda (*f.*), 15
silver plata (*f.*), 6
simple sencillo(-a), 6
since como, 7
sing cantar, 4
single soltero(-a), 3; sencillo(-a), 6

sink lavabo (*m.*), 6; (*kitchen*) fregadero (*m.*), 13
sir señor, 1
sister hermana (*f.*), 5
sister-in-law cuñada (*f.*), 5
sit down sentarse (e:ie), 9
six seis, 1
    _____ **hundred** seiscientos, 3
sixteen dieciséis, 1
sixth sexto(-a), 8
sixty sesenta, 2
size medida (*f.*), talla (*f.*), 15; (*of shoes*) número (*m.*), 15; tamaño (*m.*)
ski esquiar, 10
skillet sartén (*f.*), 13
skirt falda (*f.*), 15
slave esclavo(-a) (*m., f.*)
sleep dormir (o:ue), 5
    _____ **late** quedarse en la cama hasta tarde, 11
sleeping bag saco de dormir (*m.*), bolsa de dormir (*f.*), 10
sleepy: to be _____ tener sueño, 4
slender delgado(-a), 3
slippers zapatillas (*f., pl.*), 15
small pequeño(-a), 4
    to be too _____ (on someone) quedar(le) chico(-a) (a uno), 15
smog contaminación del aire (*f.*)
smoking: (no) smoking section sección de (no) fumar (*f.*), 7
snow nevar (e:ie), 6; nieve (*f.*), 10
    _____ **covered** nevado(-a)
so tan, 5; de manera que, 11; de modo que, 11
    _____ **much** tanto, 14
so-so más o menos, 3
soap jabón (*m.*), 6
soccer fútbol (*m.*), 16
social security seguro social (*m.*), 3
sociology sociología (*f.*), 16
sock calcetín (*m.*), 15
soda pop refresco (*m.*), 4
sofa sofá (*m.*), 13
soft drink refresco (*m.*), 4
some unos(-as), 2; algunos(-as), 5; alguno(-a), algún, 6
somebody alguien, 6
someone alguien, 6
something algo, 6
sometimes a veces, 12
son hijo (*m.*), 5
son-in-law yerno (*m.*), 5

song canción (*f.*)
soon pronto, 16
    as _____ **as** en cuanto, 11; tan pronto como, 11
sorrow pena (*f.*)
sorry: to be _____ sentir (e:ie), 11
sort especie (*f.*)
soundly profundamente, 10
soup sopa (*f.*), 8
    _____ **of the day** sopa del día (*f.*), 8
source fuente (*f.*)
south (southern) sur (*m.*), 10
Spain España, 4
Spaniard español(-a) (*m., f.*), 12
Spanish (*lang.*) español (*m.*), 1
    _____-**speaking** de habla hispana
    _____ **teacher** profesor(-a) de español (*m., f.*), 1
spare part pieza de repuesto (*f.*), 18
sparkplug bujía (*f.*), 18
speak hablar, 2
special especial, 16
specialty especialidad (*f.*), 8
speed velocidad (*f.*), 18
    _____ **limit** velocidad máxima (*f.*), 18
speeding exceso de velocidad (*m.*), 18
spend (*time*) pasar, 6; (*money*) gastar, 16
spill derramar
spoilsport aguafiestas (*m., f.*), 13
spoken hablado(-a)
spoon cuchara (*f.*), 8
spoonful cucharada (*f.*)
sport deporte (*m.*), 16
spring primavera (*f.*), 1
stadium estadio (*m.*), 16
stain manchar
stairs escalera (*f.*), 6
stamp estampilla (*f.*), sello (*m.*), timbre (*m.*) (*Mex.*), 12
standard shift de cambios mecánicos, 18
standing parado(-a), 12
star estrella (*f.*)
start comenzar (e:ie), empezar (e:ie), 4; arrancar (*car*), 18
starving: to be _____ estar muerto(-a) de hambre, 15
station estación (*f.*), 12
    _____ **wagon** camioneta, 18

stay quedarse, 10; hospedarse (en) (*at a hotel*), 10
steak bistec (*m.*), 8
steal robar, 11
steering wheel volante (*m.*), 18
stepbrother hermanastro (*m.*), 5
stepdaughter hijastra (*f.*), 5
stepfather padrastro (*m.*), 5
stepmother madrastra (*f.*), 5
stepsister hermanastra (*f.*), 5
stepson hijastro (*m.*), 5
stereo system equipo estereofónico (*m.*), 4
still todavía, 17; aún
stomach estómago (*m.*), 17
stone piedra (*f.*)
stop parar, 18; (*moving*) detenerse; (*sign*) alto
store tienda (*f.*), 8
store clerk dependiente(-a) (*m., f.*), 15
stove cocina (*f.*), 13
straight (hair) lacio(-a), 9
    _____ **(ahead)** derecho, 12
strange extraño(-a), 18
strawberry fresa (*f.*), 14
street calle (*f.*), 2
    _____ **corner** esquina (*f.*), 12
striped a rayas, 15
student estudiante (*m., f.*), 1; alumno(-a) (*m., f.*), 2
study estudiar, 2
stuffed relleno(-a), 8
style moda, 15
    be in _____ estar de moda, 9
    out of _____ pasado(-a) de moda, 15
subject asignatura (*f.*), materia (*f.*), 16; tema (*m.*)
subsidized subvencionado(-a)
subtraction resta (*f.*)
subway metro (*m.*), subterráneo (*m.*), 12
sufficient suficiente, 11
sugar azúcar (*m.*), 14
suggest sugerir (e:ie), 11
suit traje (*m.*), 15
suitcase maleta (*f.*); valija (*f.*), 6
summer verano (*m.*), 1
sun sol (*m.*)
sunbathe tomar el sol, 10
Sunday domingo (*m.*), 1
sunny: to be _____ hacer sol, 6
supermarket supermercado (*m.*), 14

supper   cena (f.), 6
      to have _____   cenar, 6
suppose   suponer, 16
surgery   operación (f.)
surname   apellido (m.), 3
surprise   sorpresa (f.), 8; sorprender, 11
sweater   suéter (m.), 15
sweep   barrer, 9
sweets   dulces (m. pl.)
swim   nadar, 10
swimming pool   piscina (f.), 6
Switzerland   Suiza
system   sistema (m.)
      systems analyst   analista de sistemas (m., f.), 1

T

T-shirt   camiseta (f.), 15
table   mesa (f.), 4
tablecloth   mantel (m.), 8
tailor   sastre (m.)
take   tomar, 2; (_someone or something someplace_) llevar, 4; (_buy_) llevarse, 15
      _____ **a shower**   ducharse, 9
      _____ **advantage of**   aprovechar, 15
      _____ **an X-ray**   hacer una radiografía, 17
      _____ **away**   quitar, 9; llevarse, 11
      _____ **care of oneself**   cuidarse, 17
      _____ **off**   quitarse, 9
      _____ **out**   sacar, 11
      _____ **place**   tener lugar
      _____ **size . . .**   (_in shoes_) calzar, 15
      _____ **someone's temperature**   tomarle la temperatura a alguien, 17
talk   conversar, charlar, 4; hablar
tall   alto(-a), 3
tank   tanque (m.), 18
tape   casete (m.), cinta (f.), 4
taste   probar (o:ue), 9; saborear
tasty   sabroso(-a), rico(-a), 8
taxi   taxi (m.), 6
tea   té (m.), 8
teach   enseñar (a), 10
teacher   profesor(a) (m., f.), 1; (_elementary school_) maestro(-a) (m., f.), 1

team   equipo (m.), 16
teaspoon   cucharita (f.), 8
teaspoonful   cucharadita (f.)
teeth   dientes (m. pl.), 17
telegram   telegrama (m.)
telephone   teléfono (m.), 3
television   (_set_) televisor (m.), 6; televisión (f.)
tell   decir (e:i), 6; contar (o:ue), 7
      _____ **us**   díganos
temperature   temperatura (f.), 17
ten   diez, 1
tenderloin steak   filete (m.), 8
tent   tienda de campaña (f.), 10
tenth   décimo(-a), 8
terrace   terraza (f.), 4
tetanus shot   inyección antitetánica (f.), 17
than   que, 5
thank you   gracias
      _____ **very much**   muchas gracias, 2
that   (_adj._) que, 3; aquel(la), 7; (_adj._) ese, 7; (_adj._) esa, 7; (_neuter pron._) aquello, 7; (_neuter pron._) eso, 7
      _____ **one**   aquél(la),7; ése, 7; ésa, 7
the   el, 1; la, 1; las, 1; los, 1
theater   teatro (m.), 8
their   su(s), 3
theirs   suyo(-a)(s), 9
them   ellas, ellos, 5; las, 6; les, 7; los, 6
theme   tema (m.)
themselves   se, 9
then   entonces, 3; luego, 6; después, 7; pues, 7
there   allí, 4
      _____ **are, is**   hay, 2
      _____ **was, were**   hubo, 9
these   (_adj._) estos(-as), 7; (_pron._) éstos(-as), 7
they   ellos 1; ellas, 1
thin   delgado(-a), 3
thing   cosa (f.), 14
think   creer, 3; pensar (e:ie), 4
      _____ **about**   pensar en, 17
third   tercero(-a), tercer, 8
thirsty: to be _____   tener sed, 4
thirteen   trece, 1
thirty   treinta, 1
this   (_adj._) este, 5; (_adj._) esta, 7; (_neuter pron._), esto, 7
      _____ **is she (speaking)**   con ella habla, 3

      _____ **one**   (_pron._) éste(-a), 7
      _____ **semester**   este semestre (m.), 2
those   (_adj._) aquellos(-as), 7; (_pron._) aquéllos(-as), 7; (_adj._) esos(-as), 7; (_pron._) ésos(-as), 7
thought   pensamiento (m.)
thousand   mil, 3
three   tres, 1
      _____ **hundred**   trescientos, 3
throat   garganta (f.), 17
through   por, 8
Thursday   jueves (m.), 1
ticket   (_for plane, train, bus_) billete (m.) (_Sp._), pasaje (m.), 7; (_for a show_) boleto (m.), entrada (f.), 8; (_fine_) multa (f.), 18
      first-class _____   billete (pasaje) de primera clase (m.), 7
      to give a _____   poner (dar) una multa, 18
      one-way _____   billete (pasaje) de ida (m.), 7
      round-trip _____   billete (pasaje) de ida y vuelta (m.), 7
tie   corbata (f.), 15
tight: to be _____   apretar (e:ie), 15
      they feel _____ **(on me)**   me aprietan, 15
tiled sidewalk   acera adoquinada (f.)
till   menos (_telling time_), 2
time   hora (f.), 2; vez (_occasion_) (f.), 7; tiempo (m.), 16
      at the same _____   al mismo tiempo, 13
      from _____ **to** _____   de vez en cuando, 14
      have a good _____   divertirse, (e:ie), 10
      What _____ **is it?**   ¿Qué hora es?, 2
tip   propina (f.), 8
tire   goma (f.), llanta (f.), neumático (m.), 18
tired   cansado(-a), 4
to   a, 3; para, 3
      _____ **the**   al (m. sing.) (_contraction_), 3
toast   (_wine_) brindar, 4; brindis (m.), 4
toaster   tostadora (f.), 13
today   hoy, 2
toe   dedo del pie (m.), 17

together   juntos(-as), 7
toilet   inodoro (*m.*), 6
toilet tissue   papel higiénico (*m.*), 14
told   dicho(-a), 15
tomato   tomate (*m.*), 14
tomorrow   mañana, 3
tongue   lengua (*f.*), 17
tonight   esta noche, 3
tonsilitis   amigdalitis (*f.*)
too   también, 2; demasiado
tooth   diente (*m.*), 17
topic   tema (*m.*)
tortoise   tortuga (*f.*)
tour   excursión (*f.*), 6
tourism   turismo (*m.*), 6
tourist   turista (*m., f.*), 6
   _____ card   tarjeta de turista (*f.*), 6
   _____ class   clase turista (*f.*), 7
tournament   torneo (*m.*)
tow   remolcar, 18
   _____ truck   grúa (*f.*), remolcador (*m.*), 18
toward   hacia, 11
towel   toalla (*f.*), 6
town   aldea (*f.*), pueblo (*m.*)
town square   plaza (*f.*), 5
trade   oficio (*m.*), 16
traffic   tráfico (*m.*)
   _____ light   semáforo (*m.*), 12
tragic   trágico(-a)
train   tren (*m.*), 7
translate   traducir, 6
transportation   traslado (*m.*)
travel   viajar, 5
   _____ agency   agencia de viajes (*f.*), 7
   _____ agent   agente de viajes (*m., f.*), 7
traveler   viajero(-a) (*m., f.*), 7
traveler's check   cheque de viajeros (*m.*), 6
traveling   de viaje
treat   tratar
   My _____!   ¡Yo invito!, 14
trimester   trimestre (*m.*), 16
trip   viaje (*m.*), 6; tropezar (e:ie)
trousers   pantalón (*m.*), pantalones, (*m. pl.*), 11
trout   trucha (*f.*), 8
true   cierto, verdad, 12
   It's not _____.   No es cierto (verdad)., 12
   true?   ¿verdad?, 11

trunk   (*car*) cajuela (*f.*), maletero (*m.*), 18
truth   verdad (*f.*)
try   probar (o:ue), 9; tratar (de), 16
   _____ on   probarse (o:ue), 9
Tuesday   martes (*m.*), 1
tuition   matrícula (*f.*), 16
turkey   pavo (*m.*), 8
turn   turno (*m.*), 9; doblar, 12
   ... years old   cumplir ...años, 4
   _____ in   entregar, 16
   _____ into   convertirse (e:ie) en
   _____ loose   soltar (o:ue)
   _____ on (*air conditioning heat*)   poner
   _____ to   recurrir a
T.V. set   televisor (*m.*), 6
twelve   doce, 1
twenty   veinte, 1
   _____-one   veintiuno, 1
   _____-two   veintidós, 1
   _____-three   veintitrés, 1
   _____-four   veinticuatro, 1
   _____-five   veinticinco, 1
   _____-six   veintiséis, 1
   _____-seven   veintisiete, 1
   _____-eight   veintiocho, 1
   _____-nine   veintinueve, 1
two   dos, 1
   _____ hundred   doscientos, 3

U

ugly   feo(-a), 3
umbrella   paraguas (*m. sing.*)
uncle   tío (*m.*), 5
uncomfortable   incómodo(-a)
understand   entender (e:ie), 4
underwear   ropa interior (*f.*), 15
undress, get undressed   desvestir(se) (e:i), 9
unfortunate   desafortunado(-a)
unfortunately   desafortunadamente, 10
United States   Estados Unidos (*m. pl.*), 5
university   universidad (*f.*), 1; (*adj.*) universitario(-a), 3
   _____ studies   carrera (*f.*), 16
unless   a menos que, 14
unpleasant   antipático(-a), 3

until   hasta, 6; hasta que, 14
   _____ I see you again   hasta la vista, 1
   _____ you get   hasta llegar, 12
up to   hasta
upstairs   arriba, 12
us   nosotros(-as), 6; nos, 6, 7
useful   útil
utensil   utensilio (*m.*), 13

V

vacant   libre, 6
vacation   vacaciones (*f. pl.*), 6
   to go on _____   ir de vacaciones, 10
vacuum   pasar la aspiradora, 9
   _____ cleaner   aspiradora (*f.*), 9
van   camioneta (*f.*), 18
vegetable   verdura (*f.*), vegetal (*m.*), 14
Venezuelan   venezolano(-a), 14
verb   verbo (*m.*)
vermouth   vermut (*m.*), 8
very   muy, 1
   (not) _____ well   (no) muy bien, 1
   This _____ day   hoy mismo, 15
vest   chaleco (*m.*), 15
video camera   cámara de video (*f.*), 6
vinegar   vinagre (*m.*), 14
visit   visitar, 6
vocabulary   vocabulario (*m.*)
voyage   travesía (*f.*)

W

wait (for)   esperar, 9
waiter   camarero (*m.*), mozo (*m.*), 8
waiting list   lista de espera (*f.*), 6
waitress   camarera (*f.*), 8
wake up   despertarse (e:ie), 9
walk   caminar, 11
wall   pared (*f.*), 2; muralla (*f.*)
walled   amurallado(-a)
wallet   billetera (*f.*), cartera (*f.*), 15
want   querer (e:ie), 4; desear, 11
war   guerra (*f.*)
wardrobe   armario (*m.*), ropero (*m.*), 15

warm cálido(-a)

warn advertir (e:ie)

wash lavar(se), 9; lavado (*m.*)

    _____ one's hair lavarse la cabeza, 9

washing machine lavadora (*f.*), 13

wastebasket cesto de papeles (*m.*), 2

watch mirar, 3

    _____ store relojería (*f.*)

water agua (*f.*), 4

    _____ pump bomba de agua (*f.*), 18

waterfall catarata (*f.*)

watermelon sandía (*f.*), 14

we nosotros(-as), 1

wear usar, 9; llevar, 15

    not to have anything to _____ no tener nada que ponerse, 15

weather tiempo (*m.*), 6

    to be good (bad) _____ hacer buen (mal) tiempo, 6

    What's the weather like? ¿Qué tiempo hace?, 6

wedding boda (*f.*)

    _____ anniversary aniversario de bodas (*m.*), 8

Wednesday miércoles (*m.*), 1

week semana (*f.*), 9

weekend fin de semana (*m.*), 5

weigh pesar

welcome: you're _____ de nada, 2

well bien, 1; bueno, 9; pues, 10

    not very _____ no muy bien, 1

    very _____ muy bien, 1

west oeste (*m.*), 10

western occidental

what cuál, 2; qué, 2

    _____ a pity! ¡Qué pena!, ¡Qué lastima!, 5

    _____ does . . . mean? ¿Qué quiere decir...?, 2

    _____ is . . . like? ¿Cómo es...?

    _____ is the exchange rate? ¿A cómo está el cambio de moneda?, 6

    _____ is your address? ¿Cuál es tu dirección?, 2

    _____ is your name? ¿Cómo se llama Ud.? (*form.*), 1; ¿Cómo te llamas tú? (*fam.*), 1

    _____ is your phone number? ¿Cuál es tu número de teléfono?

    _____ the heck qué diablo

    _____ time is it? ¿Qué hora es?, 2

    _____'s up (new)? ¿Qué hay (de nuevo)?, 1

wheelchair silla de ruedas (*f.*), 17

when cuándo, 2; cuando, 5

where dónde, 1; adónde, 4

    _____ are you from? ¿De dónde eres?, 1

which cuál, 2; (*rel. pron.*) que, 6; lo cual

while (*conj.*) mientras, 11

    a _____ later al rato, 11

white blanco(-a), 1

who (*rel. pron.*) que, 3; quién, 3; quien(es), 12

    _____ is it? ¿Quién es?, 3

    _____ is speaking? ¿De parte de quién?, ¿Quién habla?, 3

whole: the whole trip todo el viaje, 7

whom quien, quienes, 12

whose de quién, 4

why por qué, 3

wide ancho(-a), 15

widowed viudo(-a), 3

wife esposa (*f.*), 3

willow sauce (*m.*), 10

win ganar, 13

windmill molino de viento (*m.*)

window ventana (*f.*), 2; (*of a vehicle or booth*) ventanilla (*f.*), 12

    _____ seat asiento de ventanilla (*m.*), 7

    to _____ shop mirar vidrieras, 15

windshield parabrisas (*m.*), 18

    _____ wiper limpiaparabrisas (*m.*), 18

windy: to be _____ hacer viento, 6

wine vino (*m.*), 4

    red _____ vino tinto (*m.*), 8

    white _____ vino blanco (*m.*), 8

winner ganador(-a) (*m., f.*)

winter invierno (*m.*), 1

wish querer (e:ie), 4

with con, 2

    _____ me conmigo, 5

    _____ you (*fam. sing.*) contigo, 5

withdraw sacar, 11

withered marchito(-a)

without sin, 12; sin que, 14

    _____ fail sin falta

woman mujer (*f.*)

women's department departamento de (ropa para) señoras (damas), 12

wood madera (*f.*)

wool lana (*f.*)

word palabra (*f.*)

work trabajar, 2; trabajo (*m.*), 3; funcionar, 18

world mundo (*m.*), 5

worried preocupado(-a), 4

worry (about) preocuparse (por), 9

worse peor, 5

worst el (la) peor, 5

worth: it's (not) _____ the trouble (no) vale la pena, 18

wound herida (*f.*), 17

wrap envolver (o:ue), 15

wrapped envuelto(-a), 15

write escribir, 3

    _____ down anotar, 8

written escrito(-a), 15

wrong: to be _____ estar equivocado(-a), no tener razón, 4

    to go _____ ir mal

X

X-ray radiografía (*f.*), 17

    _____ room sala de rayos X (*f.*), 17

Y

year año (*m.*), 3

    to be . . . _____s old tener... años, 4

yearn for anhelar

yellow amarillo(-a), 1

yes sí, 2

yesterday ayer, 7

yet todavía, 17

yield ceda el paso

yogurt yogur (*m.*)

you (*subj.*) tú (*fam.*), usted (Ud.) (*form.*); ustedes, vosotros(-as), 1; (*d.o. pron.*) la(s), lo(s), os, te, 6;

(*i.o. pron.*) le(s), os, te, 7; (*obj. of prep.*) ti, usted(es), vosotros(-as), 5

_____'re welcome   de nada, 2

_____ say   se dice, 2

with _____   contigo (*fam.*)

young   joven (*m., f.*)

_____ man   chico (*m.*), muchacho (*m.*), 3

_____ lady   señorita (*f.*), 1

_____ woman   chica (*f.*), muchacha (*f.*), 3

younger   menor, 5

youngest   el (la) menor, 5

your   su(s), tu(s), vuestro(-a)(-os)(-as), 3

yours   suyo(-a)(s), tuyo(-a)(s), vuestro(-a)(s), 9

yourself   se, te, 9

yourselves   os, se, 9

Z

zero   cero, 1

zip code   zona postal (*f.*), 3

zoo   zoológico (*m.*), 14

Index

Photo Credits

Chapter 1: page 1: © Jeff Greenberg/PhotoEdit; page 2TL: © Beryl Goldberg; page 2CR: © Robert Frerck/Odyssey/Chicago; page 2BL: © Bob Daemmrich/The Image Works; page 3TR: © Richard Hutchings/PhotoEdit; page 3CL: © Robert Fried; page 3CR: © Bob Daemmrich/The Image Works; page 3BL: © David Young-Wolff/PhotoEdit; page 7: © Myrleen Cate/ PhotoEdit; page 10: © Beryl Goldberg; page 19: © Michael Newman/PhotoEdit; **Chapter 2:** page 23: © Ulrike Welsch; page 45: © Robert Frerck/Odyssey/Chicago; page 46TR: © Bonnie Kamin/PhotoEdit; page 46CL: © Ulrike Welsch; page 46BR: © Tony Freeman/PhotoEdit; page 47T: © Beryl Goldberg; page 47B: © Beryl Goldberg; page 48L: © Ulrike Welsch; page 48R: © Bob Krist/Leo de Wys; **Chapter 3:** page 51: © Myrleen Cate/PhotoEdit; page 56: © Robert Frerck/Odyssey/Chicago; **Chapter 4:** page 79: © B. Bachmann/The Image Works; page 84: © Robert Frerck/Odyssey/Chicago; page 97: © David Young-Wolff/PhotoEdit; page 100: © Jon Hicks/Leo de Wys; page 101T: © Mark Antman/The Image Works; page 101BL: © Mark Antman/The Image Works; page 101BR: © Mark Antman/The Image Works; page 102T: © Mark Antman/The Image Works; page 102B: © Jose Fusta Raga/Leo de Wys; page 103TL: © Mark Antman/The Image Works; page 103TR: © Robert Frerck/Odyssey/Chicago; page 103B: © Robert Frerck/Odyssey/Chicago; **Chapter 5:** page 106: © Rogers/ Monkmeyer Press; page 110: © Beryl Goldberg; page 127: © Wesley Bocxe/The Image Works; **Chapter 6:** page 130: © Bachmann/PhotoEdit; page 135: © Beryl Goldberg; page 158: © Robert Frerck/Odyssey/Chicago; page 159T: Liaison Agency; page 159B: © Noboru Komine/Photo Researchers; page 160TL: © Robert Frerck/Odyssey/Chicago; page 160TR: © Viccari/Liaison Agency; page 160B: © Peter Menzel; page 161T: © Mark Antman/The Image Works; page 161B: © Mark Antman/The Image Works; **Chapter 7:** page 164: © George Holton/Photo Researchers; page 168: © Robert Frerck/Odyssey/ Chicago; page 181: © Beryl Goldberg; **Chapter 8:** page 187: © Ulrike Welsch; page 192: © David Frazier; page 206: © Beryl Goldberg; page 207T: © Jeff Greenberg/PhotoEdit; page 207B: © Robert Frerck/Odyssey/Chicago; page 208T: © Robert Frerck/Odyssey/Chicago; page 208B: © Porterfield-Chickering/Photo Researchers; page 209T: © Peter Menzel; page 209B: © Robert Frerck/Odyssey/Chicago; page 210T: © Spencer Grant/Stock Boston; page 210B: © MacDuff Everton/The Image Works; **Chapter 9:** page 213: © David Young-Wolff/ PhotoEdit; page 217: © Paul Griffin/Stock Boston; **Chapter 10:** page 243: © Ulrike Welsch; page 248: © George Gerster/Comstock; page 258: © B. Bachmann/The Image Works; page 261: © Byron Augustin/DDB Stock Photo; page 262T: © Robert Frerck/Odyssey /Chicago; page 262B: © Chip & Rosa Maria Peterson; page 263T: © Bob Daemmrich; page 263B: © Robert Frerck/Odyssey/Chicago; page 264T: © Francis Lepine/Earth Scenes; page 264B: © Robert Frerck/Odyssey/Chicago; **Chapter 11:** page 267: © Chip & Rosa Maria Peterson; page 271: © Robert Frerck/Odyssey/Chicago; **Chapter 12:** page 289: © Cameramann/The Image Works; page 294: © Beryl Goldberg; page 311: © Chip & Rosa Maria Peterson; page 312T: © Ulrike Welsch; page 312B: © Robert Frerck/Odyssey/Chicago; page 313T: © Peter Menzel; page 313B: © Stuart Cohen/Comstock; page 314T: © Paul Conklin/PhotoEdit; page 314B: © Robert Frerck/Odyssey/Chicago; **Chapter 13:** page 317: © Beryl Goldberg; page 322: © Robert Frerck/Odyssey/Chicago; **Chapter 14:** page 339: © Robert Frerck/Odyssey/Chicago; page 344: © Robert Frerck/Odyssey/Chicago; page 354: © Robert Frerck/Odyssey/Chicago; page 355T: © Robert Fried; page 355B: © Victor Englebert; page 356T: © Karl Weidman/Photo Researchers; page 356B: © Mark Antman/The Image Works; page 357T: © Greenberg/Monkmeyer Press; page 357B: © Robert Frerck/Odyssey/Chicago; page 358T: © Anna E. Zuckerman/PhotoEdit; page 358B: © Ulrike Welsch; **Chapter 15:** page 361: © Robert Frerck/Odyssey/Chicago; page 367: © Peter Menzel; **Chapter 16:** page 389: © Robert Frerck/Odyssey/ Chicago; page 395: © Ulrike Welsch; page 406: © Paul Conklin/PhotoEdit; page 408: © Robert Frerck/Odyssey/Chicago; page 409T: © Ken Haas/Leo de Wys; page 409B: © Robert Frerck/

Odyssey/Chicago; page 410T: © Peter Menzel; page 410B: © Owen Franken/Stock Boston; page 411T: © W. Hille/Leo de Wys; page 411B: © Daniel Rivademar/Odyssey/Chicago; **Chapter 17:** page 414: © Ulrike Welsch; page 418: © Katherine McGlynn/The Image Works; **Chapter 18:** page 433: © Ulrike Welsch; page 437: © Ulrike Welsch; page 453: © Bob Daemmrich; page 454T: © Stuart Cohen/Comstock; page 454B: © Beryl Goldberg; page 455T: © Carolyn Gangi/Liaison Agency; page 455M: © Photofest; page 455B: © Frederic de LaFosse/Sygma; page 456T: © Bob Daemmrich; page 456B: © Susan Greenwood/Liaison Agency

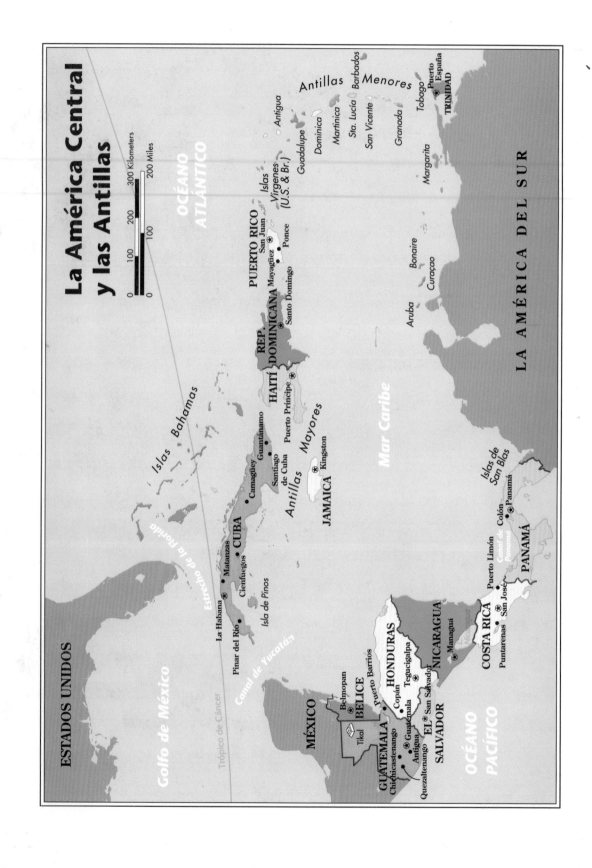

La América Central y las Antillas

ESTADOS UNIDOS

Golfo de México

Trópico de Cáncer

OCÉANO ATLÁNTICO

0   100   200   300 Kilometers
0   100   200 Miles

Islas Bahamas

Estrecho de la Florida

La Habana
Pinar del Río
Matanzas
Cienfuegos
Isla de Pinos
CUBA
Camagüey
Santiago de Cuba
Guantánamo

Antillas Mayores

JAMAICA
Kingston

HAITÍ
Puerto Príncipe
REP. DOMINICANA
Santo Domingo
Mayagüez
PUERTO RICO
San Juan
Ponce

Islas Vírgenes
(U.S. & Br.)

Antigua
Guadalupe
Dominica
Martinica
Sta. Lucía
San Vicente
Barbados
Granada
Tobago
Puerto España
TRINIDAD

Antillas Menores

Mar Caribe

Margarita
Bonaire
Curaçao
Aruba

MÉXICO

Canal de Yucatán

Belmopan
BELICE
Tikal
Puerto Barrios
Copán
HONDURAS
Tegucigalpa
Chichicastenango
Antigua
Quezaltenango
Guatemala
EL SALVADOR
San Salvador
GUATEMALA
Managua
NICARAGUA

OCÉANO PACÍFICO

COSTA RICA
Puntarenas
Puerto Limón
San José
Colón
Canal de Panamá
PANAMÁ
Panamá
Islas de San Blas

LA AMÉRICA DEL SUR